Todd

This apparently is the "flip side" of the Beatles. I'm glad they influenced the world with music and not "the love they made."

Dad
5-17-83

THE LOVE
YOU MAKE

THE LOVE YOU MAKE

AN INSIDER'S STORY OF

The Beatles

BY
PETER BROWN
& STEVEN GAINES

McGRAW-HILL BOOK COMPANY

New York • St. Louis • San Francisco • Toronto • Mexico

1 2 3 4 5 6 7 8 9 DOCDOC 8 7 6 5 4 3

ISBN 0-07-008159-X

LIBRARY OF CONGRESS CATALOGING IN PUBLICATION DATA

Brown, Peter.
The love you make.
1. Beatles. 2. Rock musicians—England—Biography.
I. Gaines, Steven S. II. Title.
ML421.B4B76 1983   784.5'4'00922 [B]   82-21645
ISBN 0-07-008159-X

Book design by Roberta Rezk

And in the end,
The love you take,
Is equal to the love,
You make.

—The last lyric
in the last song
on the last Beatles' album

Contents

Introduction

*P*ETER BROWN first introduced me to John Lennon in autumn of 1974. At the time I was "Top of the Pop" columnist for the *New York Sunday News,* and Peter was president of the Robert Stigwood Organization, which was producing a show called *Sergeant Pepper's Lonely Hearts Club Band on Broadway.* Peter was associated with the Beatles from their beginnings in Liverpool until 1970, when he joined the Robert Stigwood Organization. His positions with the Beatles included a directorship of NEMS, their management company; member of the board of directors of Beatles and Co., their partnership company; and chief operating officer of Apple Corp., their famed and ill-fated financial empire. The best man at John and Yoko Ono's wedding, he was also a close and trusted personal friend. As a favor to Peter, John Lennon agreed to lend his support to *Sergeant Pepper's Lonely Hearts Club Band on Broadway* by attending a press conference at the Beacon Theater and giving a few select interviews. I was one of the lucky journalists.

After my interview with terse and intimidating John Lennon, Peter and I rode downtown to the East Village in his chauffeur-driven Mercedes to watch a rehearsal of the show in progress. On the way down I tried to extract a few anecdotes from Peter about his Beatles days, but he was reticent. He explained that no one who was closely associated with the Beatles ever gave interviews about them. Over the years a code of silence had grown among the Beatles immediate clan that was strong as any secret society, like a Liverpool Mafia. Peter said that Brian Epstein, the Beatles famous manager, even made his employees sign a confidentiality pledge never to give interviews or talk about their work. "That's a pity," I remember telling him as I got out of his car. "You could write a fascinating book. If you ever decide to do it, call me."

By 1979 Peter Brown was producing movies in Los Angeles and was by then besieged with offers for projects about the Beatles. There were various plays and musicals, book and script offers, and positions as "special advisor" on films and documentaries. There were several offers for TV specials and requests to be interviewed on talk shows. Except for a rare and guarded interview with legitimate journalists, Peter refused all these requests. Over the years he read each of the multitude of books, watched the movies and TV shows, and listened to the experts expounding on what had happened. A few were vaguely accurate, most were grossly incorrect. Even Philip Norman's formidably documented *Shout!*, told only the public story but not the real reasons why it all happened as it did. That was partly because of the silence code, and partly because there were only a handful of people left alive who could tell the real story if they chose to: those people were John; Paul; George; Ringo; the "fifth Beatle," road manager Neil Aspinall; and Peter Brown himself.

I was therefore delighted when in October of 1979 Peter asked me to write this book with him. We agreed it was not to be a tedious documentary, or the definitive Beatles' biography that included a reference to each and every personal appearance, nor a musical analysis, but a dramatic insider's look at the saga of the Beatles' lives.* Over the next three years Peter Brown led me on an odyssey through England and the United States, unlocking doors, making introductions, arranging and assisting in interviews, and making available to me personal files and documents and diaries never before seen by the public. Under Peter's auspices I not only became privy to the Beatles' secrets but was slowly accepted into their inner circle. Cynthia Lennon, in particular, became a close friend and confidante, as did Neil Aspinall, who spent long hours with me in revealing conversation. I hope I have served them both well in these pages.

Peter Brown and I would like to thank the many people who sacrificed their time and privacy to add to the truth. John Lennon gave us his blessings. Yoko Ono was gracious and helpful during the long preparation of this book, including many hours of direct interviews. John's tragic death—halfway through the writing—only strengthened her conviction to help, which included giving Peter the use of her Palm Beach estate while we were writing the book. Paul and Linda McCartney also gave wholeheartedly of their time and trust. Paul invited us into his home and spent several days with us in Sussex and in London cooperating on the most sensitive material. George Harrison, perhaps the most private Beatle of all, invited us to his Friar Park estate at Henley on the Thames

---

* *A Day in the Life, The Beatles Day by Day* is a fascinating volume listing a daily calendar in the lives of the Beatles, including illness, travel, appearances, and personal details. For an excellent, song-by-song musical analysis, the reader is directed to Nicholas Schaffner's *Beatles Forever*.

for a rare and open interview. Our gratitude also to Ringo Starr, for his long and candid interview.

We would also like to thank for their first-time-ever taped interviews, Neil Aspinall, the Beatles aide-de-camp and closest friend; Maureen Starkey, Ringo's first wife; Pattie Harrison Clapton, George's first wife; and Alexis "Magic Alex" Mardas, who gave us nearly seven hours of his never-before-told experiences with the Beatles and the Maharishi.

Special thanks to Cynthia Lennon, who trusted us with the story of her heart as well as her marriage, and to Queenie Epstein, who painfully relived Brian's life for us as a gesture of her love for Peter Brown.

Peter Brown and I would also like to thank the following people, many of whom patiently agreed to three or four interviews: Derek Taylor, Allen Klein, Clive Epstein, Nat Weiss, Rex Makin, Hunter Davies, Robert Frazer, Geoffrey Ellis, Vic Lewis, Jenny Boyd Fleetwood, Allan Williams, Bob Wooler, Roman O'Rahilly, Ray Connolly, Martin Polden, Harry Pinsker, Stella Shamoo Dana, Ken Partridge, David Shaw, Ron Kass, Cilla Black, Bobby Willis, Robert Stigwood, Vyvienne Moynihan, Bruce Omrod, Terry Doran, David Puttnam, Alistair Taylor, John Eastman, Sir Joseph Lockwood, Martin Wesson, Barbara Bennett, John Lyndon, Victor Spinetti, Tony King, May Pang, Laurie McCaffrey, Arma Andon, Tony Bramwell, Dick James, Wendy Hanson, Lionel Bart, Tommy Nutter, John Dunbar, Leonard Richenberg, Al Aronowitz, David Nutter, Dan Richter, and Mick Jagger.

My personal thanks to Leslie Meredith, Nancy Rosenthal, David Hollander, and Marvin Olshan.

Finally, I would like to thank my agent, John Hawkins, for his selfless effort and guidance; Joseph Olshan for his astute editorial suggestions and unflagging support; and my wise and savvy editor, Gladys Justin Carr, who kept the spirit of this book and the author alive through many arduous times.

—Steven Gaines
Wainscott, New York, 1982

Chapter One

I was able to observe the whirlpool
of events without drowning . . .

—*Cynthia Lennon Bassanini Twist*

1.

*I*T TOOK HER breath away, catching them like that. Oh, she had been expecting it, almost hoping it would happen for years now; but still, when Cynthia Lennon returned home from a two-week vacation in Greece on a warm, sunny afternoon in May of 1968 and found her husband and the petite Japanese artist named Yoko Ono having breakfast in their bathrobes, she was struck mute. She tried to say something witty and self-possessed, but when she opened her mouth to speak she realized she couldn't even breathe. It wasn't that she was so surprised it was Yoko Ono, only that the moment was so casual, so cruel.

It was nearly four o'clock in the afternoon when Cynthia Lennon and her traveling companions had arrived at Kenwood, the £70,000 mock-Tudor mansion that John had purchased four years before in Weybridge, the "stockbrokers" suburb some forty minutes west of London. Cynthia had been on a short holiday with Jenny Boyd, whose sister Pattie was married to George Harrison, and one of John's best cronies, the "electronics wizard" called Magic Alex. When the three of them arrived in a taxi from the airport, the front gates were unlatched, the porch lights were on, and there was no need for Cynthia to use her magnetically coded identification card to open the front door.

Inside the high-beamed entrance foyer, the drapes were drawn and the lights off. Cynthia and her friends paused for a moment to listen. The house was oddly quiet. There was no sign of Julian, her five-year-old son; or of Mrs. Jarlett, their loyal housekeeper; or of John himself. Cynthia went to the foot of the broad, mahogany staircase that led up to the bedroom and studio levels and called out, "Hello? Where are you? Is anybody home?" But there was only silence. Shrugging her shoulders at Jenny and Magic Alex, she turned to the left and went down four steps into a vast, beamed rectangular living room. It was not the living room of a reigning pop star but the lounge of a tasteful yet prissy stockbroker. The floors were covered in thick black wool carpeting, set off by two eighteen-foot lime green sofas and two matching club chairs. The sofas faced each other across a coffee table cut from a thick slab of Italian marble, polished like a giant slice of glazed cheesecake. The open hearth, carved of oak and marble, was tall enough for a man to stand in. Around the perimeter of the room the rich oak wainscotting had been sinfully covered in an extravagant silk yellow and lime check pattern that matched the drapes on the French windows overlooking the garden. Everywhere, on every shelf and table, were little antique *chachka*. These had been purchased by Cynthia's mother, Lillian Powell, who lived nearby and often stayed with her daughter and son-in-law. John disliked his mother-in-law so much he would give her £100 every day and send her off on afternoon antique-hunting trips to get rid of her.

Still, for all the careful attention, the room looked as cold as a furniture showroom; since it had been decorated, Cynthia and John had never entertained in it much less sat in it. Instead, they spent most of their time at the back of the house in a small, cozy sunroom, which is where she went to look for him next. The sunroom was a bright, pretty room, with large windows that overlooked tiers of landscaped brick terraces leading down to a swimming pool. The pool itself had a giant green mosaic eye inlaid in the bottom that stared back aqueously at the house. The sunroom was a clutter of furniture and pop-star artifacts. Across one wall was a white shelving and cabinet unit, which contained a jumble of stereo equipment, magazines, and books on spiritualism and art. Across one of the cabinet doors John had stuck an advertising sticker that said "Milk Is Good." On the top shelf was a set of black light boxes, twinkling silently, while on a table in the corner a green lava lamp slowly undulated.

On the walls were displayed framed posters and caricatures of John, mostly promotional pieces for the two books and one play he had written, but pointedly no gold records. There was also a curved wicker sofa with brown cushions. This impractical sofa was much too short for John to stretch out on comfortably, but it was upon this sofa that he usually could be found, curled up with a book or magazine. But not today.

"John? Are you here?" Cynthia called from the empty sunroom. She thought she heard something in the kitchen, like a muffled laugh. Apprehensively, she went through a large, paneled oak door to see what it was.

John, in his dressing gown, stood facing her, holding a steaming cup of tea in his left hand and a lighted Lark cigarette in his right. Yoko Ono was sitting at the kitchen table, her back to the door. She didn't bother to turn around, but Cynthia recognized her by the voluminous columns of black hair that fell to her shoulders. The white, modern, multileveled kitchen was strewn with dirty dishes and half-eaten meals, as if the housekeeper hadn't been let in for days. The shades were drawn, the lights dim.

"Oh, hi," John said laconically, breaking the silence. He calmly took a sip of tea as Cynthia looked searchingly into his eyes. He looked very stoned, as if he had been up tripping all night and hadn't been to bed at all. His long, lanky frame was covered in a layer of puffy fat, the results of drug edema and high living. His hair was stringy and matted and he looked generally unwashed. Behind his wire-frame National Health issue spectacles his irises were tiny specks of carbon, his eyelids droopy shutters. There was a long, motionless pause.

Finally, Yoko turned in her chair to face Cynthia, or rather to confront her. There was no trace of an embarrassed smile, no glimmer of apology or explanation. Inscrutable was truly her perfect description. Cynthia looked at her. What an unlikely victor she was for John's affections. She was a grim, unsmiling woman, with a pale, oval face. At thirty-six she was eight years older than John and more than a little out of shape. Not what you'd call a sex symbol. To top it off, she was presently married and had a six-year-old daughter. Looking at her sitting there, it suddenly dawned on Cynthia that not only was Yoko in a bathrobe, it was *her* bathrobe. "Oh, hi," Yoko said, cool, unruffled.

An excruciating silence followed as a sardonic smile slowly crossed John's face. He seemed prepared to wait for Cynthia to speak first, so she decided to act the only way she knew how, the way she had acted through all the years of unexpected madness with the Beatles—as if nothing out of the ordinary was happening. In a surreal moment, she heard herself reciting the little speech she had prepared when she was on the plane with her traveling companions, who now stood speechless behind her in the doorway of the kitchen. "We were all thinking of going out for dinner tonight," Cynthia said softly. "We had breakfast in Greece and lunch in Rome, and we thought it would be lovely to all have dinner in London. Are you coming?"

Even as the words left her mouth she regretted saying them. John stared hard at her. For a moment she was terrified of him, of his saber-sharp tongue that slashed out at her so easily. She prayed he wouldn't humiliate her any further in front of Yoko. He only murmured, "No thanks."

With that she turned and ran from the kitchen. She went from room to room in the house, gathering things to pack, useless things, mementos of a marriage that had never really worked, a photograph she would never want to see again, an invitation to a party she would want to forget. While Jenny and Magic Alex waited for her in the front hall, she raced up the main staircase to the second floor and down the hall to the master bedroom, a room nearly half the size of a tennis court, with floor-to-ceiling, wall-to-wall closets, his and her dressing rooms, and a bed eight feet wide on which she had waited countless nights for him to come home, only to fall asleep alone. On the way down the hall, she spotted Yoko Ono's tattered slippers placed neatly outside the door to the guest room, and for the first of many times that day Cynthia burst into tears.

Well, she told herself, at least they hadn't used her own bed.

* * *

2.

IN HER HEART, although she could hardly admit it to herself, she knew the marriage had been doomed from the start. From the day they had met, John had struggled with demons and monsters of his own, and there was little she could do to exorcise them. Fame and fortune had turned out to be only ironies in his life. His mother and father had failed him, Paul had failed him, the Maharishi had failed him, and somehow, long ago, she had failed him. She watched as the jet-set leeches came to feed on his energy and money and sapped him dry. She stood by while, during the last few years, he kept himself afloat in a stormy sea of drugs. At twenty-eight he was virtually a drug addict; with very brief exceptions he had been high and drunk almost every day of his life since she had met him. At Kenwood, on a shelf in the sunroom, sat a white, pharmaceutical mortar and pestle with which he mixed any combination of speed, barbiturates, and psychedelics. Whenever he felt himself coming down from his mind-bending heights, he would lick a finger, take a swipe at the ingredients in the mortar, and suck the bitter film into his mouth. On some of his acid binges he would trip for weeks on end, until all the color had washed out of his vision and he was seeing things in black and white. "As far as I was concerned," Cynthia wrote, "the rot began to set in the moment cannabis and LSD seeped its unhealthy way into our lives." But it wasn't the acid and the pot that finally took John from her; it was another woman.

The fact that this seemingly wacky Japanese woman turned out to be the one was a stunning revelation to Cynthia. For as long as she could remember there was always some woman after him, or his wallet or his fame. The women ran the gamut from archetypical sleazy groupies to movie stars and writers. Only a few weeks before, John had confessed to dozens of infidelities committed during the eight years of their marriage, none of which she had suspected. He claimed in his list of conquests the American folk singer Joan Baez, the English actress Eleanor Bron, the *Evening Standard* journalist Maureen Cleave, and American pop singer Jackie De Shannon, along with what he estimated at three hundred other girls in towns and cities around the world. Yet it seemed that none of them had been capable of capturing his attention. Until Yoko.

Yoko Ono was different, so it seemed. Yoko Ono had something that all the others did not: perseverance that bordered on obsession. It was a mixture of guts and gall that went beyond *chutzpah* into the range of something spooky. By now everyone in the household was a little wary of her. After meeting John at an art exhibit she had been unshakeable. Cynthia always thought that John's first mistake was supporting Yoko's art and giving her money; that would only keep her coming round for more. In the beginning she showed up at the Apple business offices and demanded to see him. When she was told that John rarely went to the office she came on to the Beatles' loyal friend and road manager, Neil Aspinall. And when Neil rejected her, she managed to collar Ringo Starr, but Ringo couldn't understand a word the cryptic poet/artist was going on about and soon fled. The security guards at the Abbey Road EMI recording studios, where the boys recorded their albums, used to joke that she was part of the fence, and once she threatened to chain herself to the gates in an attempt to get in to see John. Then came a long-distance assault on Kenwood. It began with a barrage of phone calls, and then, when John's telephone number was changed three or four times, Yoko sent dozens of letters. The letters first insisted, then demanded, John's support for her art projects. Cynthia intercepted many of the letters and began to save them when they turned dark and despairing, in case Yoko ever followed through on the threats to kill herself. She had already tried to do herself in once in Japan, and the letters sounded sincere. According to Cynthia, Yoko wrote: "I can't carry on. You're my last hope. If you don't support me, that's it, I'll kill myself."

Very much alive, Yoko began to appear at Kenwood in person, waiting in the driveway of the house for John to come and go. She stood there from early in the morning until late at night, no matter what the weather, wearing the same scruffy black sweater and beat-up shoes, so intense and scowling that the housekeeper, Dorothy Jarlett, was afraid to go near her. One day Cynthia's mother took pity on the forlorn figure and let her into the house to make a phone call and have a glass of water. But Yoko only used the occasion to leave her ring behind, which gave her a pretense to return the next day and demand to be let inside. One morning a package arrived from Yoko which Cynthia and her mother opened; it contained a Kotex box in which Yoko had buried a broken china cup painted blood red. John had a laugh about it, but Cynthia and Lillian Powell didn't find it one bit funny.

Eventually, Yoko's dogged pursuit of John became so blatant that it developed into something of a private joke between the married couple. Yoko's *grande atrocité* occurred one night when she turned up at a Transcendental Meditation lecture John and Cynthia were attending in London. When it was over she followed them out of the lecture hall and into the back seat of John's psyche-delically hand-painted Rolls-Royce limousine and sat herself down between them. Cynthia and John exchanged embarrassed smiles over her head until the chauffeur dropped her off at Park Row, where she was living with her husband. By the time Yoko got out of the car, Cynthia had become thoroughly disheartened by the woman's apparent ability to entertain John with her crazy schemes. "Maybe Yoko's the one for you?" she asked John apprehensively.

John laughed that short, nasty laugh of his. "Her? She's daft. She's not the one for me. She's amusing is all. I don't fancy *her.*"

Yet there she was, six months later, sipping tea in the kitchen of Kenwood, looking very much like she was the lady of the house. While Jenny and Magic Alex waited with the taxi, Cynthia packed whatever she could into a single bag and rushed downstairs to the driveway and loaded her suitcase in the trunk of the taxi with the rest of her vacation luggage. Jenny and Magic Alex piled into the back seat with her, sitting on either side. They had offered to put her up for a few days at the flat they platonically shared in Victoria, so that Cynthia could have a few days to sort things out. The three of them sat in silence as the taxi moved down Kenwood's long, paved drive for what Cynthia imagined would be the last time. At the front gate she lighted a cigarette and then covered her eyes with a fluttering hand, weeping silently as she smoked.

Again and again she wondered to herself that John could be so cruel to her, and yet she could still be in love with him and willing to forgive him. Anybody else would have given up long ago. But that was the promise that Cynthia had made from the beginning, to always be there, no matter what, to never desert him no matter how bad he was to her. She knew this was a self-defeating and masochistic promise, yet there was no way to force herself to break it. She believed that she and John were destined to be together through life by a higher force, and that they would always be together, into death and after, for eternity. She still believes it to this day.

But that night, after finding him with Yoko, there was little faith left. She sat up with Magic Alex most of the night, drinking wine and talking at a candlelit table in his apartment. She had never trusted Magic Alex before, but she desperately needed someone to talk to this night, and she poured her heart out to him. Many bottles of wine were finished by dawn, when she crawled into bed with Alex and made love to John's best friend. Symbolically, it was a way of ending her relationship with John forever. Cynthia says that Alex practiced black magic and that he hypnotized her into doing it; probably, she was just drunk.

3.

*A*LTERNATING BETWEEN LOVE and hate was always what it was like with John from the very start. It scared Cynthia just to be around him when she first got to know him at Liverpool Art College. She was nineteen years old, he was eighteen and a freshman, and in just one year everybody in the school knew what a rotten egg he was. In art school in 1958 when everybody wanted to look "bohemian" and emulate the American "Beatniks," with black turtleneck sweaters and duffle jackets, John Lennon played the hood, a tough and incorrigible Teddy Boy, the current British brand of juvenile delinquent. Cynthia watched him from the corner of her eye as he breezed through the back door of lettering class on Thursday afternoons in his long tweed overcoat, battered guitar slung over his back, myopically scowling at the world from behind thick, black-framed eyeglasses. He was tall and long-legged in a clumsy sort of way, and his unwashed drainpipe trousers were so tight that he had to snake each ankle into them to get dressed in the morning. He wore his hair in a greasy, molded wave above his forehead in lame imitation of Elvis Presley, his idol. He had a quick and witty, but very, very mean, tongue. He could lay someone to waste with a few of his barbs, and no one, teachers and students alike, was safe from his lethal wit. Unfortunately for Cynthia, he sat directly behind her during lettering class, and there was no escape. He did no schoolwork, and every other word out of his mouth was "fuck." He wasted his time drawing cartoons of deformed babies and cripples, his fingers calloused from the guitar and stained from nicotine. The only time he ever spoke civilly to Cynthia was when he borrowed her ruler and pens, which he never returned and for which she was too frightened to ask. More often than not he had liquor or beer on his breath, and although he chain smoked cigarettes, they were rarely his own, and it seemed his constant mission to bum one.

Cynthia Powell neither smoked nor drank. She was a proper girl with beautiful pale skin, blond hair, and limpid blue eyes, a girl so innocent she did not even listen to dirty jokes. She had been brought up in Hoylake, a comparatively posh Liverpool suburb across the Mersey, in a terraced house by the sea. She and her two older brothers had a strict but warm and protective upbringing. She developed into a sweet and demure teenager with a kind smile and soft voice. She dressed in prim coordinated skirt and sweater outfits and had dated the same boy every weekend for three years without ever venturing past the necking-on-the-doorstep stage. When he temporarily broke up with her for another girl, she spent six months pining for him until she got him back by walking her dog past his house late at night, staring wistfully at his windows. Her father died of cancer when she was seventeen, and the following year she entered Liverpool Art College.

She kept John Lennon at arm's length with great apprehension for the first six months she knew him. She probably never would have bothered to get to know him any better if it hadn't been for his guitar. One day, in the noisy basement dining hall of the art college, Cynthia had just finished a bag lunch that her mother had made for her when she noticed a small knot of students forming around the edge of the stage on the far side of the cafeteria. She went over with her girlfriends to see what was happening and found John sitting on the stage apron, playing his guitar and singing. He was singing "Ain't She Sweet," and he looked positively beatific. His glasses were off, and she could see his eyes for the first time. He relaxed as he sang, and all the anger and malice in his face were gone. His voice was lovely but most peculiar, a kind of nasal croon with a distinctly Liverpudlian accent called "scouse." Some indefinable quality made it sound not so much sweet as poignant. Unable to tear herself away, Cynthia stood there in the enlarging crowd, listening to song after song, transfixed by the John Lennon emerging from underneath the tough shell.

She didn't admit to herself that her feelings for him had changed drastically until one morning several weeks later when Cynthia was sitting several rows behind him in the school auditorium and noticed Helen Anderson put her hand on John's head and affectionately begin to stroke his hair. Cynthia was so crazed with jealousy she almost jumped out of her seat. She sat through the rest of the auditorium period near tears, not even certain why. Was she losing her mind? Certainly she couldn't have fallen for this lout, this vulgar brute, without even realizing it. But when, this time after lettering class, John again took out his guitar and began to play, she knew as she watched him sing that she was in love with him.

"Lettering class became my fix," she later wrote in her autobiography. Now she couldn't sit close enough to him or find enough reasons to run into him "accidentally" in the hallway. "I was spending miserable, agonizing hours wandering the drafty college corridors just in the hope of a glimpse." It was only their mutual myopia that finally broke the ice. On one of those Thursday afternoons in lettering class, the students were paired off and told to give each other eye tests. Cynthia situated herself so she would become John's partner. To Cynthia's great delight, the results of the test proved that, without their glasses, they were each almost as blind as the other. John confessed how terribly self-conscious he was about his glasses and that sometimes he even refused to wear them in the cinema. By the end of the class they were friendly enough to nod hello to each other in the hallway.

When Cynthia heard through the grapevine that John's big crush of the moment was Brigitte Bardot, she began to alter her appearance to please him. Her hair took on a brassy highlight and puffed up into a new, bouffant bubble. She traded in her demure sweater sets and calf-length skirts for tight black velvet trousers and revealing sweaters. At Woolworths she bought a pair of false eyelashes and fishnet stockings. By the end of a few months she even surprised herself with how tarted up she looked, sometimes so much so that the drunks on the bus going home at night would mistake her for a "toddie" and proposition her with money. Still, John paid little or no attention to her until an end-of-term Christmas party. Cynthia arrived at the party early, hoping John would be there. She put her glasses in her pocketbook and stood at the side of the room, squinting to make him out in the crowd. John didn't arrive until the party was almost over. He made his way slowly around the room, talking to all the girls, joking with his friends. Cynthia hoped he would come toward her.

By the time John reached her she was limp from anticipation. Then he shocked her by asking her to dance. To her own surprise, she acted cool and calm with him on the dance floor. She seemed almost aloof. When John casually suggested they might go to a party together, Cynthia blurted out, "I'm awfully sorry, I'm engaged to this fellow in Hoylake." She couldn't believe she had said it. She could have kicked herself on the spot.

John's face fell. "I didn't ask you to marry me!" he snapped and walked away, leaving her on the dance floor.

Later that day, however, John had recovered enough to ask Cynthia to join him and his friends at the local student pub, Ye Cracke, on a street adjacent to the school. Cynthia took her best girlfriend, Phyllis McKenzie, along with her for "protection." The tiny pub was swollen with rowdy students celebrating the end of semester, and caught up in the good spirits, Cynthia found herself buying John and the boys a few rounds of beer. Soon she was a little tipsy herself and laughing and talking, and John was teasing Cynthia about how proper she was. "No dirty words and no dirty jokes in front of Miss Powell, if you please," he admonished them with mock sternness. "Didn't you know Miss Powell was a nun, then?" It was at that moment, in the pub, that she realized she would be hopelessly in love with him for the rest of her life.

Later that afternoon in the one-room flat of a friend of John's from art college, after a meal of fish and chips eaten from a greasy newspaper, she made love with John for the first time, on a dirty mattress thrown on the floor among paint tins and drying canvases. This flat on Gambier Terrace, where John stayed on and off, became their refuge. From that day on she met him there whenever there was an opportunity. Even when the electricity was cut off for nonpayment and there was no hot water or heat, she would spend the night with him there, curled up in blankets for warmth. They would emerge at dawn in the gray morning light as dirty as two chimney sweeps. Then Cynthia would rush home to Hoylake to take a bath, explaining to her suspicious mother that she had spent the night at a girlfriend's house, before changing her clothes and rushing off to Liverpool and John again.

She quickly learned that it was no easy chore to be in love with John Lennon. He was an angry young man with a temperament that often bordered on the nasty. He was irrationally jealous of any man Cynthia as much as looked at but wouldn't think twice about flirting with another girl right in front of her. Once, when he went so far as to kiss a girl in a pub, Cynthia burst into tears and stormed off. He was full of unreasonable rage, and Cynthia was never certain what would set him off. His temper often turned violent, and she got used to being belted around, but no more than a good swift punch in the arm or having her arm twisted behind her back. Her friends warned her, "You must be out of your mind; he's a nut case; you'll get nothing but trouble from that one; you're really asking for it, aren't you?" Cynthia was told that his former girlfriend, Thelma Pickles, had been pleased to get rid of him, she was so afraid of him. But Cynthia said she saw beyond all that anger. She saw into the hurt, helpless little boy underneath the rageful pose. John needed her. He needed her more than anybody had ever needed her in her life. And if she could just make him believe that she would stick with him, through all the bad as well as the good, she could soothe his troubled spirit. So that was her promise, not to desert him as everyone else in his life had deserted him. "I wanted desperately to see him at peace with himself and the world, for his sake and mine."

*   *   *

4.

*L*IVERPOOL IN 1958 was not exactly a fairy tale setting for a romance. It was a grim, gray city with a beleaguered population. Once one of the four busiest port cities in the world with a large influx of Welsh, Irish, and Chinese immigrants, its six hundred acres of deep docks made it a major World War II supply line across the North Atlantic and thus a prime target for Hitler's bombs. Nightly, a veritable firestorm was unleashed on the city by the Luftwaffe, turning it from a bustling, prosperous terminal into a cratered shell of sandstone from which no phoenix ever rose. The ports were so damaged it was joked that a man could walk across the river Mersey on the hulls of sunken ships. The Lancashire Cotton Mills and the Cotton Exchange, the city's industrial lifeblood, were all but closed during the war and never revived.

The city was named after the Liver (live-ah) bird, once the symbol of King John, an eagle with a fleur-de-lis in its beak. But when the city was reconstructed by Prince Rupert in 1644, it was thought the Liver bird was a cormorant holding a piece of seaweed. Thus, the humble seagull holding a drooping shred of sea grass became the city's emblem. A giant Liver bird sculpture sits atop the Royal Liver Insurance building, which faces the Mersey. According to legend, if the bird falls, so does Liverpool, so it is carefully guy wired to the building. Amazingly, the sculpture was one of the few things left standing after the air raids of World War II.

John Winston Lennon was born during one of those massive air raids on October 9, 1940, in a maternity home on Oxford Street. He was the issue of a long, only half-serious romance. His mother, Julia Stanley, had met his father, Fred Lennon, twelve years before in Sefton Park, one of Liverpool's few oases of green. It was a spring day, and Fred was a dapper sixteen-year-old who had only that week been discharged from the orphanage he grew up in. He was wearing a bowler he had just purchased to impress the girls. When Julia ran into him strolling through the park, she said, "You look silly."

"You look lovely," Fred responded, smiling, and sailed his hat off into the lake.

Julia's parents and four sisters all vehemently disapproved of Fred Lennon, but Julia thought the two of them made a good pair. The third youngest, she was a headstrong, fun-loving girl, with high cheekbones and dark devilish eyes. She loved being naughty and slightly outrageous and having a night out on the town. Fred considered himself a real smoothy and played love songs for her on his banjo at the pub. Julia thought he had the "perfect profile." Marriage, however, was over a decade in coming, largely because of Freddie's career as a steward on ocean liners and Julia's family's disapproval. One day in December of 1938, as a kind of a prank to rankle Julia's family, they posted banns at the registry office and got married. They spent the night in a movie theater in celebration, after which Julia went home to her house and Fred to his.

Two years later when John was born, Fred was off at sea. And it was off at sea he stayed. Each month Julia's only contact with him was a visit to the shipyard office to pick up the support payments he was sending for her and infant John. The payments stopped when John was eighteen months old. After a time Julia wrote Fred off, never expecting to hear from him again. She heard a rumor he had jumped ship; no one knew what had happened to him.

Little John was five years old before his father turned up, his pockets bulging with cash, boasting of an extraordinary adventure. Freddie claimed that he hadn't deserted ship at all but instead had gotten drunk during a stopover in New York and hadn't made it back to his ship in time. He was arrested and marched off to a jail cell on Ellis Island, where he was eventually remanded to a Liberty Ship heading for North Africa. His fortunes hadn't proved much better on the Liberty Ship either, where he was accused of stealing a bottle of liquor from the hold. When the ship finally docked in Africa, Freddie was thrown in jail for three months. Finally allowed to go free, he had made his long journey home, becoming involved in various wartime rackets, mainly selling black-market stockings, and he had made a killing. He reappeared in Liverpool full of easy money for his wife and child.

Julia wasn't impressed at all with his black-market money and she was hardly waiting for him. In fact, she wanted a divorce. For some time she had been involved with another man whom she wanted to marry. Fred, taken aback, said he would consider it but first asked to take his young son for a few days' holiday to the seaside resort of Blackpool, so he could get to know him. Freddie said a friend of his had rented a small cottage, and they would stay there. Although Julia disapproved of the idea, she felt she couldn't refuse Fred a visit with his own son, and she let John go off with his father.

Fred Lennon had no intention of ever returning with John. Fred's buddy in Blackpool was already making arrangements for the three of them to emigrate to New Zealand, which Fred had been told was a postwar boom town and the right place for a smart man to start his life over again. Fred was prepared to board the next freighter with John and leave England for good. Unexpectedly, Julia appeared at the door, demanding the child back.

"I'm used to John myself now," he told her, "and I'm going to take him with me."

"No you won't," Julia said firmly. "Where is he?"

Much to Julia's surprise, Freddie smiled warmly and came over to where she stood. "I can tell you still really love me," he said to her. "Why don't you come with us? We could start again."

Julia said the idea was preposterous. Freddie was always a dreamer, and he was dreaming now. All she wanted was her son back. Fred insisted that he had just as much right to the boy as she did, and then all hell broke loose, with Julia challenging Fred to just try and take him. In the end they decided to let little John decide whom he wanted to stay with, the way they did in the movies. Freddie called to him, and he came running into the living room. He was pleased and excited to see his mother there.

"Are you coming back, Mummy?" he begged, "Are you?"

"No she's not," his father told him. "I'm going to New Zealand, and your momma's going back to Liverpool. Now, who do you want to go with? Your momma or with me?"

The child's face darkened. He looked at Julia, paused, then looked at his father and said, "You."

Freddie beamed proudly. Julia took a step toward her son. "Are you sure, now?" she asked the little boy.

John looked up at her, then at his father, and nodded.

Julia kissed her son good-bye and went out the door as John clung to his father's knee. She was halfway down the street before she heard the little boy's screams. "Mummy! Mummy! I've changed my mind!" He came scurrying out of the house and up the street after her.

That was the last time Fred Lennon heard of or saw his son until he was told John had become something called a Beatle.

5.

*I*T WASN'T really Julia who wanted John back; it was her older sister Mimi Smith. It was Mimi who insisted she take the trip to Blackpool to get the little boy, and Mimi who would take him in and raise him as her own. Married but childless, Mimi fell in love with the baby from the moment she saw him in the maternity home on Oxford Street. She oohed and aahed over him so much that it even made Julia jealous. "Fine thing," she harrumphed. "All I've done is have him." But motherhood had not dulled Julia's appetite for the nightlife, and soon after Fred first disappeared, Mimi started caring for the little boy, feeding him, burping him, and diapering him like he was her own.

Mary Elizabeth Smith and her husband George, who owned a local dairy, would become as close to a real mother and father as John would ever know. They lived in a small, spotlessly clean, semidetached house at 251 Menlove Avenue. It was not a poor suburb, as it was often portrayed, but a rather nice, middle-class area called Woolton. "Mendips," as they grandly nicknamed the plain house, had bay windows, a pretty garden with carefully kept flower beds, and several bedrooms, which were at times rented out to students for extra income. Mimi was a thin but strong woman with dark hair and a warm, rarely seen smile that showed her perfect white teeth. She loved John dearly, but she also believed that sparing the rod spoiled the child and was as tough with him as she tried to be fair. She allowed him to attend the picture show at the cinema only twice a year, and John's weekly allowance was a frugal five shillings a week until he was fourteen. On Sundays Mimi saw to it that he went to church school for Bible lessons and to sing in the choir. He was confirmed when he was fifteen. If John was ever indulged as a child it was by his kindly Uncle George, whom John turned to for an extra shilling or permission to see the latest Walt Disney movie at the downtown cinema. His favorite treat, however, was going to the carnival held each summer at the Strawberry Fields Salvation Army's girls' hostel, which was just around the corner from Mendips.

The golden-haired little boy looked like Julia's side of the family, and many people mistook John for Mimi's own son. They were never corrected. Mimi found such great shame in Julia and Fred's circumstance that she never could bring herself to discuss it with the little boy. When John asked about his real parents, Mimi would tell him that they had fallen out of love and that his father was too heartbroken to face coming back. John soon forgot about Fred. "It was like he was dead," he said. But not Julia. Julia remained a living specter in John's life. She would unexpectedly appear at Mendips, demanding warmth and affection from him. Then she would just as suddenly disappear, not to be heard from for months. These visits were like a tornado descending into John's life, and he was caught in an emotional maelstrom. Finding it impossible to turn his emotions on and off, he soon cut off all feelings for her. During the longer periods of Julia's absence, John would lull himself into a feeling of security with Mimi and George, only to have Julia appear out of the blue to haunt him again.

Once she arrived at the house on Menlove Avenue in a black coat with the collar turned up around her face, which was bruised and bleeding. She pretended to the little boy that she had been in an accident on the way over to Mendips, but John knew it wasn't true. He guessed that she had been beaten up, and he hid in the garden so he wouldn't have to look at her. By the time he was old enough to be immersed in school and friends, Julia stopped coming by altogether. He once asked Mimi where she went, where she lived, but Mimi would only say, "A long, long way away."

At the Dovedale Primary School he proved himself a precocious student, a quick study, easily bored. He also had a most peculiar, almost mean, sense of humor. While he was never interested in schoolwork, he spent hours at his desk drawing satirical cartoons about his teachers and classmates, along with poems and short stories filled with puns. Mimi encouraged him to read and supplied him with an assortment of books from the local library, including *Wind in the Willows,* which he relived many times in his head after he read it. He especially loved to read poetry and Lewis Carroll's nonsense poem, "Jabberwocky," from *Through the Looking Glass* became his favorite. The rascally twelve-year-old protagonist of the *Just William* children's books became his hero.

Yet for all the good Christian upbringing and love and warmth he got at Mendips, John had an angry and rebellious streak. Perhaps it was something he inherited from his mother and father, who were in their own ways very much the same, or perhaps it was just the buried hurt of being abandoned by them. He developed a quick and corrosive wit and would take on any challenger, either verbally or physically. He loved, in particular, to verbally lacerate a helpless victim, the more helpless the better. With his neighborhood chums Ivan Vaughan, Nigel Whalley, and Pete Shotton, John indulged in increasingly dangerous schoolboy pranks. With John as their ringleader, he and the other boys pilfered candy and toys from local shops. As he got older he stole to order and began a brisk business in black-market cigarettes. A favorite feat of daring was to climb a tree and dangle a foot in the path of an oncoming bus and snatch it away just in the nick of time.

By the ripe old age of twelve, when he started at Quarry Bank School, a small, strict grammar school not far from Mendips, he was already a well-known neighborhood ringleader and street terrorist. His mischief ran from simple insubordination to getting caught with an obscene poem, "the sort you read to give yourself a hard-on," he explained. As he got into his teens he went from bad to worse. A new trick was to torture luckless neighborhood girls by grabbing their panties and pulling them down around their ankles. Once, when John and Pete Shotton were called into the office of the deputy head of the school to be disciplined over one of their many transgressions, John urinated down his pants leg so that it ran all over the office floor. The deputy head was quite astonished to find a yellow puddle on the other side of the desk when the boys left. John went home to Mendips with a wet inseam that day, but the joke was well worth it for the notoriety it gave him with his classmates. By his third year at Quarry Bank, he had been demoted to the bottom of his stream. A teacher wrote on his report, "He's just wasting other pupils' time."

Mimi couldn't understand it. Although she ruled Mendips with an iron hand, she couldn't get a grip on John. She ranted and railed at him and threatened him with all sorts of punishments, but it did not seem to have any effect on the boy. What disturbed her the most was his petty pilfering, and when he stole so much money from her purse that she was finally forced to take notice that he was stealing from her on a regular basis, she beat him. Yet nothing seemed to make him stop.

One Monday in June of 1953, John returned to Mendips from a vacation at an aunt's house to find Mimi sobbing at the kitchen table as she diced carrots. "Mimi, what's the matter?" John asked, wide-eyed.

"Your Uncle George died," she told him. George had been taken to the hospital the day before for what they suspected was cirrhosis of the liver and had died unexpectedly of a brain hemorrhage. John was dazed; another parent gone in a flash. As the house quickly began to fill with Mimi and George's relatives, the impact of it hit him. Embarrassed to show public grief, John hid upstairs in his bedroom, where he was shortly joined by his cousin Leila. The two of them sat on the bed and began to laugh. They went on like that, laughing for hours and hours, stiffling the noise when any adult came to the door. John felt horribly guilty about the laughter, but he didn't seem to be able to cry. He was only thirteen and he was getting used to losing people.

Or so he thought.

6.

A FEW MONTHS after Uncle George's death, Julia suddenly reappeared at Mendips. But this time she wasn't the woman in the black coat with the bleeding face he remembered at all. This was a young, attractive, spirited woman with a sense of humor astonishingly like his. Indeed, Julia was practically as naughty as John. It turned out that she hadn't been living far, far away at all, as Mimi said, but only a few miles away at Spring Wood. She was living with a waiter John nicknamed "Twitchy" because of a facial tic. Julia had had two daughters with Twitchy, but she was still legally married to Fred.

The more John got to know Julia, the better he liked her. In fact, it would not be inaccurate to say that John fell in love with Julia. She turned out to be much more of a chum than a mother. He raved about her to all his friends and couldn't wait for her to turn up at Mendips. Together they inspired each other to new heights of mischief. Julia would do anything to impress John and his pals, it seemed. Once, to give the boys a laugh, she walked down the street with her panties tied around her head like a scarf. Another time she had John and Pete Shotton in hysterics by wearing a pair of eyeglass frames without any lenses in them. She would stop to ask the time from a stranger on the street and nonchalantly scratch her eyebrow through the frame, convulsing the boys. When the fashion rage was brightly colored shirts for men—and Mimi had forbidden John to wear one—Julia bought one for him.

Julia's influence on him also showed at school. He grew more violent and contemptuous of authority, and the calls to Mimi from the school masters came almost every day now. Frequent canings seemed to have no effect on him. He was thin but tall and strong, and his strength was fueled by a ferocious temper. One day an argument with a school master erupted into a fistfight. John so easily overpowered the teacher in front of the other students that the man never reported the incident to the school authorities. Eventually John was suspended from school for a week, which was considered to be the harshest and most shameful punishment short of expelling him. Yet when he returned to school the following Monday, nothing changed. At sixteen he failed all his O levels, the examination everyone in his age group took to determine whether they would continue their education, and by his final year he was last in his class of twenty.

His academic career seemed finished until in his fifth and final year Mimi managed to wrangle a half-hearted letter of recommendation from Mr. Pobjoy, the headmaster, who wrote that John was "not beyond redemption and could possibly turn out to be a fairly responsible adult who might go far." Pobjoy even arranged for an interview for John at the Liverpool Art College. Drawing seemed to be the only subject John was interested in, although

Mr. Pobjoy didn't intend to inform the admissions board at the art college that John had failed his art final by drawing a grotesque hunchback with bleeding warts to illustrate the theme of "travel." Much to John's chagrin, Mimi insisted on accompanying him to the art college for his interview, lest he get lost on his own and never arrive. To her great relief, John was accepted for the fall of 1957, and Julia came by to Mendips to celebrate his future as an artist with them.

7.

*B*UT BY THAT SUMMER it had become clear that John wasn't interested in his education, or in art, or in his future at all. John's only interest seemed to be for the American craze called "rock and roll," a derivative form of black rhythm and blues with a prominent drum beat. In England there was no such thing as rock and roll music on the radio. Indeed, there was no commercial radio in the sense that Americans knew it. While in America there were thousands of competitive radio stations, free to play whatever they pleased, in England the British Broadcasting Corporation controlled the three existing radio stations and their contents. The Home station was regional and featured news, current affairs, and plays, with few musical interludes. The Light station played middle-of-the-road music, which was necessarily diversified because of the write-in request programs, like "Family Favorites." However, the musician's union carefully clocked the amount of "needle time," or prerecorded music, that was allowed on each program, so that live musicians were hired to play old standards. The third station, Classical, featured only serious talk shows and classical music.

For John Lennon in Liverpool there were only two ways to hear rock and roll. One was from records that the young men who worked on the shipping lines would bring back from America with them; the other was Radio Luxembourg, a privately owned commercial radio station with a signal strong enough to reach most of central Europe and Great Britain. Each night at eight o'clock there would be "English service," during which the English record companies would buy blocks of air time to showcase their product. John would listen to English service every night on a cheap wireless in his bedroom, galvanized by the faint, crackling sounds of rock and roll.

Then, three important musical incidents seemed to happen all in a row. First was a fad that gripped England in 1956 called "skiffle." A form of the American washboard and tin-can band, anyone with a metal washboard or old chest could play skiffle. The song that started it all, the "Rock Island Line," sung in a high-pitched wail by a young man named Lonnie Donegan, became a teenage anthem. Next came a movie about American juvenile delinquents called *Blackboard Jungle*. Not only did the movie romanticize teen rebellion in general, but the title song, "Rock Around the Clock," was unlike anything ever heard before in Great Britain. Sung by a plump and balding middle-aged man named Bill Haley, there was a driving wildness to the music that John found almost narcotic. Finally, came the musical and physical embodiment of rock and roll, the first rock star. He was not a father figure like Bill Haley but a teenager, the essence of young lust and rebellion fused with the new music. His song was called "Heartbreak Hotel," and his name was Elvis Presley.

Elvis. Elvis. Elvis. *Elvis!* It was all anybody heard at Mendips or at Julia and Twitchy's flat. Elvis' hair, his clothing, his swagger, and, most of all, his guitar. Mimi couldn't bear it after a few weeks. "Elvis Presley's all very well, John, but I don't want him for breakfast, dinner *and* tea."

John wanted a guitar more than anything he had ever wanted before in his life. Surprisingly, it wasn't Julia who broke down and bought it for him, it was Mimi who marched him to a music shop in Whitechapel and bought him his first guitar for £17. Once he got it in his hands, he wouldn't put it down. A small, Spanish model with cheap wire strings, he played it continuously until his fingers bled. Julia taught him some banjo chords she had learned from Fred, and he started with those. He sat on the bed all day, and when Mimi tried to shoo him into the sunlight, he'd go out to the sunporch and lean up against the brick wall practicing his guitar for so long that Mimi thought he'd rub part of the brick away with his behind. She watched him waste hour after hour, day after day with the damned thing and regretted having bought it for him. "The guitar's all very well, John," she warned him, "but you'll never make a living out of it."

John's first group was called the Quarrymen, after his high school. In it were his neighborhood chums Pete Shotton, Nigel Whalley, and Ivan Vaughan, along with various other schoolboys who came in and out. The Quarrymen, although they sported calling cards that announced "Open for Engagements," as if they expected to be paid, were happy to play wherever there was an audience to listen to them. They appeared in numerous competitions that were being held throughout the city and at high-school dances. They played on the backs of flatbed trucks at street fairs and at church dances and fetes. It was to one of those church fetes on a hot Saturday afternoon, on July 6, 1957, at St. Peter's Parish Church in Woolton, that Ivan Vaughan invited a school friend named Paul McCartney. Young McCartney—he was just fourteen at the time—didn't come because he was interested in hearing the Quarrymen; he came because Ivan Vaughan had convinced him that the fete would be a great place to pick up girls.

James Paul McCartney was already picking up girls at this age. He had been interested in girls, he once said proudly, for as long as he could remember. At fifteen he had already lost his baby fat and had developed into a pretty, doe-eyed, self-styled sex symbol. At fifteen, when he lost his virginity with a trusting young lady from school, he told everybody about it the next day and scandalized the poor girl. Girls were his major concern and that was what he was thinking about that day in 1956 as he rode his bicycle to the large field at the top of the church road, where the fete was already underway. He was dressed in a wide-lapeled white sports coat that came down to mid-thigh and black drainpipe trousers. A greasy pompadour was combed into a formidable wave above his forehead.

The fete had started with a parade through the streets, after which there was a carnival with makeshift stalls selling homemade cakes and kidney pies, a demonstration by a team of trained police dogs from the Liverpool police force, and entertainment by a local band called the Quarrymen. Paul watched and listened to Ivan Vaughan's childhood chums play from a distance.

Later in the afternoon, in the coolness of the church hall, Paul borrowed a guitar from one of the boys and started showing off with it. In the ranks of his immediate audience, Paul was clearly a virtuoso. The boys were particularly impressed, not only because he played so well, but because he knew how to tune a guitar, a talent that so far none of them had been able to master. Just by listening to the radio, he was able to learn all the chords and lyrics of the most popular songs, including "Twenty Flight Rock," a new favorite that was too complicated for the others to figure out. He also sang precisely on key, in a sweet, easy voice, able to hit high notes as effortlessly as a choir boy. As he played "Twenty Flight Rock" for them, his fingers flying through the difficult guitar sequence, he became aware of a drunken old man leaning over him, breathing beery breath on him. When Paul looked up into the man's face, he realized it wasn't an old man at all, but a boy not much more than sixteen. Somebody said, "This is John."

He's drunk, Paul thought, but only said, "Hi."

John was grudgingly impressed with Paul's guitar expertise but was too proud to admit it. While he watched Paul he thought, "He's half as good as me." Paul, magnanimous as always, offered to write out all the words to "Twenty Flight Rock" and to Gene Vincent's "Be Bop a Lula" so that John could learn them. A few days later Paul was riding his bicycle home across the Allerton golf course when he ran into Pete Shotton. "Hey," Shotton called after him. "They say they'd quite like to have you in the band if you'd like to join."

8.

*T*HERE WAS SOME PRECEDENT in the McCartney household for Paul's musical ability as well as his amorous preoccupations. Paul's father, James McCartney, was a swinging bachelor and musician himself until he got married at thirty-nine. Although Jim supported himself during the day as a salesman at the Cotton Exchange before the war, at nights and on weekends he was the leader of a popular Liverpool swing band called the Jim Mac Jazz Band. He gave it up only because his false teeth interfered with his trumpet playing. In 1941 Jim married Mary Patricia Mohin, a good Irish Catholic girl who was a trained nurse and midwife. She was thirty-two when she married James and immediately became pregnant with her first child. Jim, exempt from the service because of a hearing problem, went to work at an aircraft engine factory when the war closed the Cotton Exchange. His evenings were spent on "fire watch" during the nightly bombings, and that's where he was on the night of June 18, 1942, when James Paul McCartney was born at the Walton General Hospital. Mary, who had once been the head nurse of the maternity ward, was given a private room and VIP treatment. When Jim was ushered into the room to see his newborn son for the first time, the baby was red and bloody and screaming, and Jim thought he was "like a horrible piece of red meat." When Jim got home from the hospital that night he cried for the first time in years. He soon got over it, however, and a second son, Michael, was born in 1944. After the war Jim left his engine factory job for a position with the Corporation Cleansing Department as an inspector, which meant he followed the dustmen around in the streets to make sure they were cleaning up properly.

At first they lived in Anfield in a furnished room, then in a council house in Knowsley Estate, Wallasey, and then moved to Speke, six miles from Liverpool center, to another council house that was rent-free in return for Mary's midwife chores at the local housing development medical facility. It was from this house on Ardwick Road that Paul started Stockton Wood Road primary school and then with his younger brother Michael went to Joseph Williams Primary School. Finally, when Paul was thirteen they moved again, this time to a slightly better neighborhood in Allerton, at 20 Forthlin Road. Just across the golf course, a little over a mile away, lived Mimi Smith and her nephew John Lennon.

Paul was a good student, well-behaved, and an unabashed apple polisher. He learned early the value of good public relations and began to develop a canny sense of diplomacy. When it was to his benefit, he was easily insincere. In 1953 he was accepted at the Liverpool Institute, the city's best free high school. Founded in 1825 as a mechanics institute, it now shared the same blackened sandstone building with the Liverpool Art College.

The summer of 1955 Paul and Michael went to Boy Scout camp, where it rained nearly all week. Mary and Jim, concerned that the boys would be wet in their tents, drove to visit them with dry clothes and a ground sheet. On the way home in the car Mary was in such terrible pain she had to lie down. For several months she had felt a small lump in her breast but had avoided seeing the doctor, thinking it was only a symptom of menopause, but this night the pain was unbearable. Later that evening, as Olive Johnson, a close friend of Jim's from work, helped put her to bed, Mary whispered, "I don't want to leave the boys *just* yet." A few weeks later she was operated on for breast cancer at the old city Northern Hospital, but it was much too late. Hours after the operation she was dead.

Upon hearing of his mother's death, the first thing Paul said was, "What are we going to do without her money?" The boys cried themselves to sleep that night. For months after, Paul prayed that somehow God would change his mind and send his mother back.

He adjusted, at least on the surface, extremely well. Within a few months of his mother's death, the skiffle craze started, and Paul was able to bury some of the pain of the loss in what soon became an obsession for him. As it had for so many Liverpool boys, Lonnie Donegan's Liverpool appearance sparked Paul's desire for a guitar. Jim McCartney somehow found the money to purchase one for £15. Like John, once Paul had it in his hands he couldn't put it down. At first he found the instrument almost impossible to play. Then he made a startling discovery; although he was right-handed in most everything else, he played the guitar better with his left hand. He took the guitar back to the store, had it restrung, and began to pick out tunes almost by instinct. Elvis and the Everly Brothers became his idols, and he learned to play all their songs and mimic their styles. His Little Richard imitation was hysterically perfect, and one summer at Butlin's Holiday Camp he talked his brother Michael into entering the amateur talent contest with him. They didn't win, but Paul discovered how much he liked playing for an audience and the sound of applause. It wasn't long after that he met John Lennon.

* * *

9.

PAUL AND JOHN formed a close camaraderie, unusual for boys that age. The two-year age difference, which at first seemed insurmountable to them, melted away in their mutual interests and similarities, although on the surface the two boys couldn't have been more different. Baby-faced Paul was self-righteous, conscientious, and deferential to his elders. John defied authority, was hedonistic, amoral, and enjoyed his role as the outspoken iconoclast.

It was to their mutual delight that Paul's Liverpool Institute and John's Art College were in adjoining buildings. Now it was easy for John to find an accomplice in playing hookey from school, and the two of them spent long afternoons together at Paul's house on Forthlin Road, practicing songs, teaching each other chords, and raiding the pantry for jam "butties." Sometimes they'd play standing in the tub in the tiled bathroom to get a better echo. Their voices complemented each other perfectly, with Paul's sweet, round tones softening the edges of John's strained nasality. The harmony they produced, an intertwining that seemed to melt into a third, unheard voice, was lovely. An affectionate songwriting competition developed between them, one they would use to fuel their creative spirit for years to come. One day Paul played for John a song of his own composition, and John improvised one on the spot so as not to be topped. Although they composed together for only the first year or two, they wrote over 100 songs that first year.* John found that it was easy for him to compose the beginning melody for a song, but he got stuck for a transition and a break. Paul had a special facility for writing the "middle eight" bars. Paul's mellow, pretty melodies in turn complemented John's strident rock riffs. On those first afternoons in Paul's living room, it seemed like the pieces of a vast puzzle were falling into place, completing a picture that neither of them had been able to see clearly before.

As soon as Paul became a member of the Quarrymen he had a lot to say about their music. Characteristically, he started to

* These songs were lost years later when Jane Asher threw them out during a spring cleaning of Paul's London house.

tell the other band members how to play and when. What's more, he wanted to play lead guitar, which a bespectacled boy named Eric Griffiths was playing at the time. Paul badgered Griffiths until he quit, then moved into his spot. Even Pete Shotton, one of John's oldest and most loyal mates, felt a bit put out at John's constant acquiescence to Paul's demands. When Shotton saw the writing on the wall was writ by Paul's hand, he good-naturedly left the group, as did Ivan Vaughan. They were replaced with other, ever-changing musicians who played around the Lennon-McCartney core.

As far as John's Aunt Mimi was concerned, Paul McCartney was fuel to the fires that would burn John in hell. Paul's sweet persona and feckless public relations didn't fool her. It was plain to see how Paul wasted John's time with the guitar, and any boy who would dress like a Ted, with skintight pants and those awful, pastel-colored shirts, couldn't be worth his salt. Paul would come to the front door of Mendips on his bicycle, asking for John. "Hello, Mimi. Can I come in?"

"No, you certainly cannot," Mimi would say.

By the following summer of 1958, at the end of John's first year at art school, the fighting with Mimi at Mendips became onerous. Since she had paid for his first year of school out of her savings, until he could qualify for a government loan, she felt more justified than ever in having a say in how he dressed, whom he saw, and where he went. The Quarrymen were viewed with absolute and total disapproval. When Mimi's nagging became too much for him, John would simply escape to Julia's house in Spring Wood. Julia's became a refuge for him. She loved the Quarrymen and even knew the words to their songs. John began to leave his Teddy Boy outfits at Julia's, so Mimi wouldn't see them, and then stop at Julia's house to change clothes on the way to school every morning. If John and Mimi had an especially bad row, he would storm out the door and stay overnight at Julia's, sleeping on the sofa. This hurt Mimi so much—and made her so angry—that she once gave away the household pet, a little dog named Sally that John adored, saying that with John gone there'd be no one around Mendips to walk it.

Although Mimi felt Julia was giving shelter to the enemy by letting John hide out there, the two sisters remained close, and Julia became a frequent visitor to the house on Menlove Avenue.

On hot summer afternoons she often came by for tea in the garden and stayed past dinner, telling jokes and chatting with the neighbors. One evening John was watching TV with Twitchy at Spring Wood, while Julia and Mimi had dinner at Mendips. Julia left for the bus stop just about twilight. John's chum, Nigel Whalley, was at that moment on his way to Mendips to see if John was about. He met Julia on the street, and she had a few jokes and a laugh for him before she turned off to get the bus. She was just about 200 yards from the front gate of Mimi's house when the quiet of the summer night was split by the terrible sound of screeching brakes and a heavy thump. Nigel Whalley turned at the gate of Mendips just in time to see Julia's body rise up into the air above the hedges and come down on the other side. By the time Mimi got over to the tram tracks, Julia was dead.

10.

*T*HE CAR HAD BEEN DRIVEN by an off-duty policeman, and Mimi saw to it that he went to trial. Nigel Whalley was called as a witness, but the testimony of a young boy didn't seem to impress the judge very much and the driver was acquitted. This infuriated Mimi, who stood in the spectators' dock screaming and cursing at the man, threatening to beat him up with her cane. John watched in silence, knowing that it was no use. All the screaming and threatening in the world wouldn't bring Julia back. She had abandoned him for a final time.

A few months before the accident, John had asked Paul, "How can you sit there and act normal with your mother dead? If anything like that happened to me, I'd go off me head."

True to his word, John did go off his head. He seemed to blame everyone for his mother's death and was intent on revenge. There were no limits to his anger and grief. When he went back to art college six weeks later, he was meaner than ever. Fellow students remember seeing him sitting in the solitude of a rear stairwell, staring out the window and crying. He kept himself in a pain-killing stupor of alcohol and, more often than not, spent the whole day a little drunk. He began to see tragedy, deformity, and ugliness everywhere. He derived special pleasure from ridiculing street beggars and cripples. His typical behavior would be to walk up to a hapless paraplegic he encountered on the street and make cruel jokes about his useless limbs. "Where's ya legs go, mate? Run away with your wife?" His favorite targets were old people, and he seemed determined to give some senior citizen a heart attack by fright. He was rageful enough to beat up anyone who dared to challenge his aggression, and except for his band, everyone began to shy away from him. Certainly no girl in her right mind would go out with him. One girl named Thelma Pickles lasted the longest, but that relationship ended with her screaming at him in Ye Cracke, "Don't take it out on me just because your mother's dead!"

And then, in 1958, he met Cynthia Powell, who was going to save him.

Chapter Two

*. . . and I know that someday, somehow,
John and I will always be together.*
—*Cynthia Lennon Twist, 1982*

1.

*C*YNTHIA POWELL dedicated herself to John with the passion of a religious zealot. A man more sure of himself would have found the attention suffocating, but John enjoyed every minute of it. Every moment Cynthia could steal away from her schoolwork and her home she spent with him. She even met him in the few minutes between classes in art college, so she could spend a moment necking behind the lockers in the basement. She paid for his cigarettes and coffee and never tired of sitting on a hard bench with him at his favorite hangout, the Jacaranda, holding his hand under a formica table, staring into his eyes for hours as he told her the story of his life.

The Jacaranda, or the "Jac" as it was called, had become a favorite meeting spot of the city's multiplying beat groups. Once a narrow watch-repair shop on Slater Street in the bohemian district, the Jac was just on the edge of the city's bustling Chinatown. The Jac was a "sitting room" with benches around the walls and narrow tables where one could dawdle over a single cup of coffee for hours without being disturbed. Its location and laissez-faire policy brought a fascinating cross section of students, artists, beat groups, West Indians, whites, blacks, Chinese, and those coming back and forth from the public subsidy office just down the street. The Jac was owned by a short, loquacious gentleman, with more than a touch of northern charm, named Allan Williams. This self-styled entrepreneur had sold everything in his time, from electric typewriters to books door to door. Williams had become a favorite of the boys when he converted his basement into a small club. At night, on a rough brick dance floor in the basement, Williams featured—improbably—an authentic West Indian steel band. The city's many beat groups would sit at small tables and drink coffee spiked with their own liquor, listening to the steel band until dawn.

It was at the Jac that Cynthia got to know most of John's friends. Her favorite was another art student, a small, pale, ethereal young man named Stu Sutcliffe. Cynthia already knew of the nineteen-year-old artist from school, where he was widely regarded as the most talented and promising student. The girls all considered him devastatingly attractive, and it was always noted that he was a dead ringer for James Dean, particularly because of his moody, romantic scowl and his dark clip-on sunglasses. Stu was one of the few students who even lived like a real artist, in a cramped, paint-splattered studio in a house on Gambier Terrace near the art school. It was an authentic artist's garret, right down to the filth and poverty. Stu was so poor that during the winter he would have to burn his furniture to keep warm, and the ashes from the fireplace had crept out into the middle of the room, where they remained for months. John moved into this flat with Stu for awhile and slept in a silk-lined coffin, which he filched from a garbage dump. He and Stu would spend long nights, drinking beer and talking. Stu was one of the few people his own age John found intellectually stimulating. While John's friendship with Paul was special in its own way, it was only one of music and good times. With Stu, John felt a deep spiritual bond. He admired Stu, not just for his talent and creativity, but for the passion and love he had for his art.

Stu's reputation as a promising young artist was already spreading, and in 1959, when the biennial John Moore Art Exhibit was held at Liverpool's prestigious Walker Art Gallery, Stu entered one of his paintings in the competition. John Moore, a wealthy Liverpudlian art collector, personally bought Stu's painting for £65—at the time an unheard-of sum for a student's work. The sale of the painting became the talk of the art college and Stu a kind of minor celebrity. John immediately saw the perfect use for the £65. His band needed a new bass player. It didn't matter to him that Stu had no idea how to play an instrument and even less desire to join a rock group, John would show him what to do. John was so enthusiastic about the idea that eventually Stu broke down and spent the entire £65 on a bass guitar. Whether the other band members liked it or not, Stu Sutcliffe was suddenly in the group.

The friend of John's that Cynthia liked the least was a pesty little kid named George Harrison. At the age of fifteen George was nearly five years Cynthia's junior and as amusing to her as a bratty kid brother. Slight and pale, he had his fair share of adolescent pimples. More private than actually shy, it was obvious that George idolized John and did everything he could to emulate him. George was a "flash" dresser, with the longest hair of any kid around. Dressed in his pointy "winkle-picker" shoes, pink shirt with pointy collar, and canary yellow waistcoat, George tagged after John and Cynthia wherever they went. A little too young to be seriously dating, he had no idea that the young couple might have wanted to be alone, particularly on dates. But George was always lurking around in the background, trying to get John's attention, and on more than one occasion he sat on the other side of John when they went to the cinema. On the few times John and Cynthia thought they had eluded George for a while, he would suddenly round the corner ahead of them, signaling his arrival with the piercing whistle that was his trademark. The day Cynthia had her appendix removed, she waited in her hospital bed all afternoon for a visit from John, who turned up ten minutes before visiting hours were over. He wasn't there a moment when George appeared, bounding up the aisle of the ward like a puppy dog. Cynthia was so upset at seeing him she burst into tears. George, for his part, was slightly more generous in his appraisal of Cynthia than she of him. "I think she's great, John," he confided one day. "But there's one thing wrong. She's got teeth like a horse."

If Paul McCartney was a bane to Mimi, then George Harrison was anathema. John tried to smooth the way for George by telling Mimi what a great guy he was before she ever met him, but once Mimi got a look at his pink shirt, she threw him out the door. Worst of all for Mimi, George's mother, Louise Harrison, was actually encouraging the boys with their band, giving them a place to practice and food when they were hungry. It made Mimi furious.

George Harrison was the only Beatle whose childhood was not marred by divorce or death. Born on February 25, 1943, he was the youngest in a family of three sons and a daughter. His father, Harold, was a thin, quiet man who was a city bus driver. His mother was a contented housewife and the neighborhood mom all the kids knew. Her reputation was as a jovial, outgoing woman who supported and encouraged her children. The family lived for eighteen years in the same, simple, terraced house on Arnold Grove, Wavertree, before moving to a small council house on Upton's Green in Speke. George was a bright, independent child, who used to pick up the sausage for dinner at the local butcher by himself when he was only two-and-a-half years old. Like John, he went to the Dovedale Primary School, just across Penny Lane from where they lived.

George first became friendly with Paul McCartney not long after the family moved to Speke. Each morning the two boys would see each other at the corner bus stop and board the same bus headed for the Liverpool Institute, where George had started that year. One morning Paul found himself a few pennies short for his bus fare, and Louise Harrison gave them to him plus some extra for the ride home. Although George was a year behind Paul in school, the two boys found plenty to talk about on the bus: skiffle, rock and roll and guitars.

By the time George was fourteen, he was already a certifiable guitar fanatic. Like Paul, Lonnie Donegan had sparked his interest in the guitar, and Louise Harrison began to find George's pockets full of scraps of paper with guitars drawn on them, the way other boys drew jet planes. His first guitar was a used one, bought from another boy at school and financed by his mother for £3. His next was a deluxe model, which he helped pay for by doing chores for the butcher on Saturdays. Louise was a constant source of encouragement to him, telling him that he could master his playing whenever he got discouraged. Upon his meeting with John Lennon, this had not quite happened. George's playing at the time was far below the standards of the boys in the band, then called Johnny and the Moondogs. Paul introduced George to the band in the winter of 1959 in a basement teen club best remembered for its bare red lightbulbs, called, appropriately, The Morgue. George played for them his best number, an eight-note bass tune called "Ranchee," but nobody was very impressed. He tagged along after them anyway, hoping that one day he would be asked to play with them. He went to all their shows, where he stood in the back with his guitar. A few times when one of the regular guitarists failed to show up, George was allowed to sit in with the band, and on rare occasions he even got to do his own, breath-holding solo. Eventually, before anybody really noticed what was happening, he became a member of the group. Besides, Louise Harrison gave them shelter and food.

John, Paul, George, Stu, and Cynthia would meet almost every day at the Jac or in the school cafeteria. Cynthia would sit on a bench nearby and listen while the boys played. They didn't seem much different from the other kids in the busy school, and nobody took special notice of them.

2.

*T*HE PREVIOUS SPRING Elvis Presley had been inducted into the United States Armed Forces and throughout the world an army of young boys dreamed of taking his place. Hundreds of rock groups were being formed all over England, and in Liverpool every neighborhood seemed to have one. There was no lack of places to play, either. Every church hall, ballroom, town hall, and skating rink where a stage could be erected and admission charged was holding a weekend dance. There were so many groups in Liverpool that a student at the Liverpool Art College named Bill Harry—who coincidentally introduced Stu Sutcliffe to John Lennon—began taking notes on who was in what group and where they were playing and eventually started his own music paper, the *Mersey Beat.* Some groups didn't last more than a week or two, others came to prominence in their neighborhoods and developed loyal followings, and then went on to fight for citywide acceptance. Johnny and the Moondogs was not one of these.

The most famous Liverpool band was Rory Storm and the Hurricanes. Rory was a tall, athletic boy with beautifully coiffed blond hair. Dashingly handsome, he had a pronounced stutter when he spoke but not when he sang rock and roll. He was considered the most dramatic and flamboyant of all the lead singers, and the highlight of his act often included his shimmying acrobatically up the fluted columns that held up the balconies and prosceniums. Next in popularity was Cass and the Casanovas, noted for their loud drummer with a silver-glitter drum kit. Following them was Derry and the Seniors, who specialized in rhythm and blues and had a black singer. Then came Gordon Bell and the Bobby Bell Rockers, Faron and the Flamingos, the Swinging Blue Jeans, Lee Curtis and the All Stars, and on and on and on. Some groups were fortunate enough to land steady jobs at local auditoriums. Other groups had to scramble each week for employment. As the Jacaranda became the vortex of the late-night band scene, Allan Williams got to know the whole spectrum of groups as they passed through the doors. It struck him that there was a potential gold mine somewhere in that plethora of what was being called "pop" music, and he started a booking business. As a sort of a clearing house for groups, he got them jobs at £10 a night. From this, Williams was paid £1 and £1 went to the local bouncer. Johnny and the Moondogs quickly agreed to his services.

Williams had made the acquaintance of a well-known London manager and promoter named Larry Parnes. The mere mention of Larry Parnes' name summoned up visions of stardom for the multitude of Liverpool groups. Parnes was famous for discovering Tommy Steele, one of Britain's major teen singing stars, whom he had found singing in a coffee bar on Old Compton Road in London. Since Tommy Steele, Parnes had "discovered" a whole stable of young men, christening each with a distinctive name: Marty Wilde, Dickie Pride, Billy Fury, and Johnny Gentle.

While none of Parnes' other acts reached the level of stardom of Tommy Steele, they all had recording contracts and worked regularly on a profitable touring circuit of dance halls in small towns around the countryside. Williams had assured Parnes that Liverpool was an untapped lode for pop groups, all of them tailor-made to go on tour with his name acts, eager and reasonably priced. Within a few weeks Williams had won an audition for an assortment of the better known Liverpool groups to go on tour with Billy Fury, among them his personal favorites, Johnny and the Moondogs. For the audition, against the advice of their friends, the band changed their name to the Silver Beatles. The word "beetles" had been suggested by Stu Sutcliffe in response to Buddy Holly's group, the Crickets. John, who couldn't resist a pun, suggested "beatles," as a play on beat music. The "silver" was added to give the name some flash.

Temporarily bereft of a drummer—drummers seemed to come and go every few weeks—they asked Johnny Hutch, the drummer of Cass and the Casanovas, to play for them at their audition with Parnes. Along with a dozen other groups, they set up in the basement of a new club Allan Williams was opening on Seel Street called the Blue Angel and waited their turn. They gave a nervous but spirited performance, save for Johnny Hutch, who intentionally looked very bored and superior. Parnes also couldn't help but notice that Stu Sutcliffe, the little guy with the big bass guitar, had no idea how to play his instrument. Parnes wanted the Silver Beatles—but minus Stu. John wouldn't hear of this, which infuriated Paul, but nevertheless he insisted they turn Parnes down if it meant leaving Stu behind. Cass and the Casanovas got the spot. Miraculously, a week later Parnes offered them another booking, although it was a booking that no professional London band would take. They were offered a two-week tour of Scotland, as the backup group for Johnny Gentle. The Silver Beatles were to be paid the grand fee of £18 a week, including on-the-road expenses for the five of them. John had a lettering exam due that week and gave it to Cynthia to copy for him. While he was away, she sat on a wooden crate in Stu's flat under a sixty-watt bulb and wrote it for him, cheating for the first time in her life. George Harrison, who had already left school at the age of sixteen, was working part-time as an apprentice electrician at Blackler's Department Store and simply took a holiday to go to Scotland.

The tour of Scotland turned out to be less of an exhilarating experience than the boys had anticipated. Desperate to find a drummer for the tour, they hired twenty-five-year-old Tommy Moore, who worked on a forklift at the Garston Bottle Works. Moore's musical experience had been limited to playing in big dance bands. Johnny Gentle, a hulking man who had been a merchant seaman before he was discovered by Parnes, didn't much care for the Silver Beatles or their music. The tour turned out to be a depressing series of one-night stands in decrepit dance halls in backwater towns. Promoters called Larry Parnes to complain about the Silver Beatles' playing, and the Silver Beatles called to complain about their cold-water lodgings. They lived on a bowl of soup a day, and Tommy Moore couldn't stand John Lennon. One night the van they were riding in was in a collision, and Tommy Moore was hit on the head with a suitcase. He lost his two front teeth and was taken to a hospital to have his face stitched up. John laughed when he saw him on stage at the show that night. Moore quit when they got back to Liverpool.

In Liverpool Allan Williams opened up a strip club on Upper Parliament Street called the New Cabaret Artists Club with a West Indian bar man called Lord Woodbine because he smoked Woodbine cigarettes. When the Silver Beatles returned to Liverpool, Williams gave them work at the New Cabaret Artists Club backing a stripper named Shirley for a few weeks. On weekends Williams also booked them in town halls all over the city, often in the poorest and roughest sections of town. Some of these jobs turned out to be more trouble than they were worth. The most notoriously violent venues were in the town halls in Bootle, Garston, and Litherland, where the audiences were frequently composed of large gangs of Teddy Boys and their girlfriends, called "Judies." The boys in these gangs, which had names like "Bath Hall Bloods," the "Tigers," and the "Tanks," were bona fide thugs, not pretenders like the Silver Beatles. These Teds were armed with chains and knives and wore notorious steel-tipped boots with which they could stomp their prey into unconsciousness. Often a good fight was the last event on their dance cards, and the dirtier the brawl the better. At a dance in Neston, a small town across the water in the Wirral, the town hall turned into a battlefield as the Silver Beatles watched a sixteen-year-old boy stomped to death in front of them. The Teds were also an impossible audience to please. If the band was bad, the Teds had it in for them; if the band was good and managed to raise the least bit of admiration from a Judie, they were in for it anyway. The boys were constantly abused and threatened by these audiences, and even John's shenanigans and Paul's baby-faced charm did not abate the cries for blood.

Usually, the most petrified member of the entourage was Cynthia Powell, the only girl to tag along. In the rough neighborhoods Cynthia would try to pass herself off as another Judie who had never seen the Silver Beatles before, lest the Teds beat her up with the rest of them. Cynthia's Hoylake accent was her biggest giveaway, and she practiced perfecting her "scouse."

Fortunately for Cynthia, she was not with them one night in the summer of 1959 when the band was ambushed by a gang of Teds in the parking lot of Litherland Town Hall. The bigger boys in the band managed to get away, but Stu Sutcliffe, the smallest and most frail, was easily caught. He was thrown to the ground and savagely kicked in the head until he was nearly unconscious. He would have been killed on the spot if it hadn't been for John, who ran back into the melee to pull his friend off the ground and drag him to safety. When John deposited Stu on the doorstep of his mother's house that night, he was still bleeding profusely from his head wounds. Hours later, when the bleeding would not seem to stop, Stu's mother, Millie, insisted on calling the doctor. But Stu wouldn't hear of it. "Mother, if you touch that phone I go out of this house, and you'll never see me again."

3.

*T*HAT SAME SUMMER it appeared a terrible calamity had befallen the Jacaranda. The Royal Caribbean Band with their forty-gallon sawed-off steel drums that had so electrified the atmosphere every night had disappeared. Allan Williams learned they had skipped town for a higher-paying job in Hamburg, West Germany. It seemed that Hamburg's bustling St. Pauli district, with its hundreds of bars, dance halls, and nightclubs, had become a hungry market for foreign entertainment. The club owners were paying top salaries, and so great was the demand for acts that they were even pleased to book an attraction as esoteric as a West Indian steel band. Williams, surmising he might combine the overflow of Liverpool rock groups with the great thirst of Hamburg, set out for the famous city of decadence himself, armed with a tape of Liverpool groups made on a tape recorder that John had stolen from the art college and for the theft of which Stu was subsequently blamed.

Williams was not disappointed with what he found in Hamburg.

The St. Pauli district was a neon-lined nocturnal world of seedy, carnivallike clubs, doorway hookers, transvestites, and porn and weapons shops. All this served as a colorful backdrop for raging gang wars among the numerous drug and gun runners. The crowning touch, however, was the brothel district, the Herberstrasse, a fenced-in city-within-a-city that did a bustling business with a surfeit of customers from the nearby prosperous ports and American army bases.

It was in a basement club on the Grosse Freiheit called the Kaiserkeller that Allan Williams made the acquaintance of Bruno Koschmider. Koschmider was a memorable-looking man, a short, dwarflike fellow with a large head, putty nose, and a shank of carefully waved blond hair. Koschmider had once been a magician and a circus clown before opening several prosperous businesses in the Reeperbahn. As Reeperbahn business necessitated, Koschmider was suspicious and tough. Williams excitedly explained to Koschmider through an interpreter that Liverpool was a great, untapped well of entertainment and the perfect source for a club like Koschmider's. The Liverpool "beat sound" would go over big in Hamburg, Williams said, and to prove it he produced a tape recording that had been made before he left Liverpool. The tape turned out to be only electronic static and hum.

Williams returned to Liverpool without any bookings but full of inspiration. He kept pitching Liverpool groups to tour promoters and made frequent trips to London. It was on one of these trips, several months later, that he ran into Koschmider again. Koschmider was in London scouting for bands to play his clubs, and within a few minutes Williams had convinced him to sign what he promised was Liverpool's finest musical product—Derry and the Seniors.

Back in Liverpool, amidst much local envy, Derry and the Seniors were shipped to Hamburg for what seemed like the big time. When word returned to Liverpool that their engagement was proving successful, a pleased Koschmider wrote to Williams asking for yet another group to come to Hamburg, and this time it was the Silver Beatles' turn. In the flush of getting a booking in the romantic city of Hamburg and leaving Great Britain for the first time, the band dropped the Silver and became, simply, the Beatles.

The one small problem about the Beatles going off to Hamburg was that they still had no permanent drummer. In desperation more than desire, they asked Pete Best to join them. The Beatles had known Pete Best for years; George Harrison had once introduced him to Paul and John, but it was only recently that he had become a drummer—and not a very good one at that. Pete was nineteen, a dark, handsome, and mysteriously quiet young man whose mother, Mona, ran the Casbah Club. The Casbah was a popular teen club in the residential section of West Derby that Mona Best had opened as a place for Pete's friends to congregate. It was a crude basement club with wooden benches and a dragon painted on the ceiling. When the Beatles first heard through the grapevine that the Casbah was opening and might be a good place to play, they turned up there en masse, along with Cynthia, to nose around. They liked what they saw so much they stayed to help clean up the place, and it was Cynthia who painted the distinctive spiderwebs on the walls.

It was at the Casbah that they made a new friend who was to become an integral part of the group, as important as any of the members. His name was Neil Aspinall, and he was a tall, handsome young man who lived with the Best family as a boarder. Neil had a rakish sense of humor and a direct, no-nonsense northern kind of charm. He was eighteen years old and had just graduated from the Liverpool Institute. He was training to be an accountant, but as his interest in the bands that played the Casbah increased, his attention to his studies lagged. By the following spring Neil was helping the Beatles load their equipment and was driving them to all their jobs in his battered red and white van with a leaky radiator. He wasn't called the "road manager" until many years later, when the word was invented, but he was much more than that. He became a friend, aid, and protector. In his own unique way, by the force of his personality, he affected the course of the Beatles as deeply as any of the primary four.

As they had hoped, the Casbah became one of the band's regular jobs, until the boys had a falling out with Mona Best. It seemed one of their ever-changing band members hadn't shown up one night, and Mrs. Best had docked his fifteen shilling salary from their pay. The Beatles stormed out of the club and later heard that Pete had taken up the drums and formed a group with the errant guitarist. But the hard feelings between the Best family and the Beatles were short-lived, especially in light of the fact that Pete had recently purchased a shiny new set of professional-looking drums. He had left school and was running the Casbah full time when Paul McCartney rang him up and asked if he'd like to audition with them at the Jacaranda. Later that night they celebrated his inclusion as the drummer of the Beatles.

4.

*F*OR CYNTHIA POWELL the trip to Hamburg was anything but a reason to celebrate. Certainly, she believed, the pleasures of the Reeperbahn would make her seem provincial and inadequate. She was already learning to stave off the flirtatious Liverpool girls who were after John; what with Hamburg's reputation for loose women, she was sure their relationship wouldn't endure the separation. She wept bitterly as she kissed John good-bye on the morning of his departure, then dolefully returned to her mother's house in Hoylake, where Lillian Powell was delighted to have her truant daughter home again. Cynthia tried to make the best of it, reassuring herself that they were scheduled to be gone only six weeks. In the end, it turned out they stayed for over five months.

A compulsive doodler and letter writer, John's missives arrived almost daily. The envelope would be covered with kisses and verses of love like, "Postman, postman, don't be slow/I'm in love with Cynthia so go man go." Inside there would be twenty- and thirty-page handwritten epic accounts of his adventures, complete with cartoon drawings. The Beatles had set off from the Jacaranda in a dilapidated cream and green minibus along with Allan Williams, his wife Beryl, his brother-in-law Barry Chang, and his West Indian friend, Lord Woodbine. In the band's suitcases were new costumes of black crewneck sweaters and short houndstooth jackets for which Allan Williams had advanced them £15 each. The trip was long and the van broke down. At a stop in Arnhem, Holland, John shoplifted a harmonica and added it to their act.

The letters describing Hamburg made it sound as if John wouldn't need any help from his vivid imagination to improve upon the bizarre reality. They were playing not in the Kaiserkeller but in a dreary little dive called the Indra Club, with a neon sign in the shape of an elephant outside the front door. The Indra's tiny stage usually featured strippers and sex shows, and the regular customers—a cross section of the Reeperbahn's underbelly, including gun-toting gangsters, drug pushers, and transvestites—weren't very happy to find a group of oddly dressed English boys on the stage instead of nude female mud wrestlers. The Beatles were expected to entertain from seven in the evening until two or three in the morning, sometimes seven nights a week. The club's owner, Bruno Koschmider, was obligated to give them a place to live and put them up in the basement of a cinema he also owned called the Bambi Kino. The boys were given three dirty little cubby holes at the front of the theater just behind the screen. The cinema alternated porn films with gangster movies, and it wasn't unusual for the boys to be awakened in the early afternoon by the sounds of fevered panting. The rooms were literally shit holes, and it wasn't unusual to find human excrement under a newspaper, if one was brave enough to lift one. Only at Allan Williams' insistence were they given clean blankets and bedding. No towels were provided, however, and the only toilet was the public one at the rear of the theater.

Five months went by with the boys hardly taking more than a sponge bath. Their meals consisted of a bowl of cornflakes and milk when they arose in the afternoon and an occasional dinner at the Seaman's Mission, where the English manager had taken pity of them and was feeding them at cut-rate seamans' prices.

At the Indra their dressing room was also the mens' toilets, and the attendant, an old lady in ankle socks named Rosa, was happy to sell them a prodigious supply of the German-made diet pills called Preludin she kept in a candy jar. Except for Pete Best, who seemed to disassociate himself from all their wildness, the Beatles quickly found they needed the "Prellys" to keep them going through the long nights of nonstop playing. The Prellys made them thirsty, which in turn made them drink more beer, which in turn was free and plentiful from the barmaids when Koschmider wasn't looking. Also, it became quite common for customers to send drinks up to the stage to get them drunk, shouting *"Trinken! Trinken!"* The audiences came to be entertained, not to watch the Beatles stand around and play, so when Koschmider yelled *"mach shau!"* at them, "make show" they did. Their nervous systems electrified by the cheap amphetamines, their inhibitions demolished by the beer and booze, they were capable of anything on stage. John, in particular, would bring down the house with his speed-induced imitation of cripples and goblins. He would jump, crawl, and scream, sometimes taunting the audience with, "Bloody fuckin' Nazis! *Sieg Heil!*" The audiences, usually at least as drunk or high as John was, only laughed and cheered and egged him on to be still more outrageous. John was so out of control one night that when a customer over-enthusiastically approached the stage, John kicked him in the head twice, then grabbed a steak knife from a table and threw it at the man.

The Beatles' (save for Pete Best who did not indulge in such things) favorite part of the St. Pauli district was the incredible fenced-in red-light district. Considering how young they were— John and Stu were twenty, Paul was eighteen, and George only seventeen—the Herberstrasse was like a sexual Disneyland. Here, all hours of the day and night, waited prostitutes of every size, shape, and description, sitting in the parlor window of house after house facing the narrow street, reading, arguing, gossiping with tradesmen. This is not to say that the boys had to pay for their sex very often; cute, young, and randy, they had any number of women available to them for free, from the barmaids to the customers. More than once they had a "knee trembler" with some sweet young thing in a doorway only to discover her the next day sitting in the window of a house in the Herberstrasse. Screwed, blewed, and tattooed, stoned any time of the day or night, the boys became a walking laboratory of venereal diseases. During his short stay in Hamburg, Allan Williams became the self-appointed "Little Pox Doctor." The boys would come to him at the Gretle and Alfons, a small bar where they would spend their off-hours, and ask him to step into the back room for a spot examination. "I looked for swellings in the groin, a discharge from the end, and asked about pain on urinating, all the things I'd read about." He also taught them a witch doctor's method of diagnosis by holding their urine up to the light in a beer glass. The public-health facilities in Hamburg were free and very accommodating, and the boys were cured, stricken, cured, and stricken at an alarming rate. As soon as they got a shot of penicillin, they were drinking and whoring again. It was only when they returned to Liverpool for good that a venereologist managed to clean them up.

Koschmider extended the Beatles' engagement, and, after dispatching an exhausted and dissipated Derry and the Seniors back to Liverpool, he moved the Beatles to his big club, the Kaiserkeller. The Kaiserkeller was enormous compared to the Indra, with an incongruous nautical decor of portholes and fishnet. The Kaiserkeller was also much rougher than the Indra, and the club had its own highly efficient squad of bouncers. This small army, frequently called into service in the violent club, was headed by an ex-boxer named Horst Fascher who allegedly had spent time in jail for killing a sailor with his fists in a street brawl. Fortunately, Fascher took the Liverpool boys to his heart, particularly the crazy one, John, and as Kaiserkeller employees they were put under his special protection. With Fascher acting as Godfather, they felt invulnerable, and their provocative behavior increased accordingly. One night, smashed on Prellys and beer, they tried to roll an English sailor who got drunk at the bar, but they only had the heart to hit him once or twice before giving up. When Rory Storm and the Hurricanes were also booked into the Kaiserkeller, a contest ensued as to who could stomp a hole first in the rotting Kaiserkeller stage. Rory won and was feted with a case of cheap champagne at a local spot called Willy's cafe. When Koschmider heard about the contest that had pounded a hole in his stage, he dispatched a contingent of thugs to rough up the two bands. The Liverpool groups joined forces and, armed with chairs and table legs, managed to emerge from Willy's with no broken bones. By the next day's performance a truce had been called, and life went on as usual.

Summer quickly turned into autumn, and the boys' engagement was extended yet again. In Liverpool, Cynthia waited patiently. John's letters now talked about a beautiful girl named Astrid Kirchner and her roommate, Klaus Voorman. As the story unfolded, bit by bit, Astrid and Klaus seemed to be having a tremendous effect on the boys. Klaus, a Berlin-born doctor's son, was an art student in Hamburg. One night after an argument with Astrid, he had stumbled into the Kaiserkeller. He was astonished to find the Beatles with their funny-looking checkered jackets and wavy pompadours. He was particularly taken by Stu Sutcliffe, hiding behind those mysterious clip-on dark glasses, moodily playing his bass guitar. Two nights later, Klaus asked Astrid to come with him to see them and then the next night and the next, and soon Astrid was hooked on them herself.

Astrid was an exotically pretty girl with a blond pixie haircut and large, dark, sad eyes. She had met Klaus while studying art at a private academy called the Meister Schule. When she met the boys she was a photographic assistant, and Klaus was living in a room on the top floor of her mother's house. Astrid was enchanted with these peculiar English boys, and despite the language barrier, she managed to strike up a friendship with them. The boys, in return, were delighted to meet some local people their own age. Astrid photographed them frequently and brought along other German art students to the club. These students, of a vogue called "exis," after the existentialists, were a pale, intense, ascetic bunch. Like Astrid, they dressed in thick black leather trench coats and leather trousers and seemed to the boys to be half poets, half spys. It wasn't long before the Beatles started wearing leather trousers and tunics, some that Astrid designed and made for them herself.

John seemed so in awe of Astrid that Cynthia was certain this was the fraulein who would steal his heart away. But only two months after her name first appeared in John's letters, he wrote that Astrid had become engaged—to Stu! Although they hardly knew twenty-five words to say to each other, they had chipped in and bought engagement rings. Stu intended to live in Germany with her after they were married. Quite a change had come over Stu, too. Astrid was now making all his clothes, including a collarless sports jacket similar to the ones Pierre Cardin had popularized in Paris. Astrid had also talked Stu into combing his hair forward over his forehead and cutting it in bowl-shaped bangs. One by one, except for Pete Best, the other boys soon followed suit, and the Beatle haircut was born.

As their fifth month in Hamburg approached, Cynthia wondered if the boys would ever come home. From the way it sounded in John's letters, they might have stayed right through the next year—if they hadn't been thrown out by the police. The trouble began when a new club, the Top Ten, opened on the site of the old Hippodrome Club, and its owner, Peter Eckhorn, started luring employees away from the other Reeperbahn clubs. The Kaiserkeller's famed bouncer, Horst Fascher, had already defected with some of his best men, as had Rosa, the lady in the washroom who sold the Beatles Prellys. The Beatles would have gone to the Top Ten, too, if Koschmider hadn't pointed out a clause in their contracts forbidding them to take employment within thirty weeks and twenty-five miles of their employment at the Kaiserkeller. In fact, Koschmider let it be known that if the boys played at the Top Ten Club, it wouldn't be safe for them to *walk* within twenty-five miles of the Kaiserkeller. Nevertheless, by early December, as their contracts with Koschmider ran out, the boys moved into accommodations provided by Peter Eckhorn and were seen on the stage of the Top Ten Club. Word quickly filtered back to Koschmider.

The following day the boys were dragged out of bed by several very unpleasant policemen from the Reeperbahn station house who were searching for George Harrison. Someone—no doubt Bruno Koschmider—had tipped them off that George Harrison was not yet eighteen and therefore forbidden by law to be in any club on the Reeperbahn past curfew. Besides which, he had no working papers. In fact, the police discovered that none of the band members had legal permission to be working. George was ordered to pack and leave the country within twenty-four hours. Stu and Astrid took him to the train station in her car that night. In an unusual show of emotion for him, he choked back tears when he hugged them tightly on the train platform, this great adventure ending for him. Then he got on the train with his guitar under his arm and a bag of apples and biscuits that Astrid had fixed for him, and he went sorrowfully off to Liverpool.

A few days later Paul and Pete Best went back to the Bambi Kino where they had left behind a few of their meager belongings. They had expected Koschmider to have thrown their things out, but everything was just where they left it behind the cinema screen. Not smart enough to let well enough alone, an unfortunate bit of mischief occurred on the way out of the theater. Paul unfurled a two-pfenning prophylactic and lit it with a match. The dry drapes hanging on the walls of the theater quickly began to smolder, and Paul and Pete hightailed it out of the theater without stopping to mention it might burn down. The fire was discovered and put out before much damage was done, but the suspicious origin was investigated by authorities who found some rather incriminating evidence; on the ceiling of the room where the fire started, written in carbon with the flame of a candle, was the name, "The Beatles."

The next morning the police were back, this time with arson detectives who escorted Pete and Paul down to the Reeperbahn police station where they were held and interrogated for several hours on suspicion of trying to burn down the Bambi Kino. Thanks to an undeserved kindness on Koschmider's part, no charges were pressed, but the boys were ordered out of the country, *mit* haste. Paul and Pete found themselves on the next flight to England, without Pete's drums or most of their luggage.

John and Stu were now the only ones left, and there wasn't much reason for them to remain in Hamburg. John returned home the cheapest way—by train—defeated and depressed, looking forward to Cynthia and a warm bath and even Aunt Mimi. Stu, who had a touch of tonsillitis and a fever, was sent home by plane, his airfare scraped together by his concerned fiancée. He was expected to return to Hamburg in a few months to marry her.

John arrived home in the middle of the night and had to throw stones at Mimi's bedroom window to wake her. When she answered the door, John just pushed right past her and said, "Pay the taxi, Mimi."

"Where's your hundred pounds a week John?" she shouted at him.

John had promised her a large savings at the end of the Hamburg trip. He turned and sighed, exhausted. "Just like you, Mimi," he said, "to go on about one hundred pounds a week when you know I'm tired."

5.

*T*HE FIVE YOUNG MEN who returned to Liverpool that Christmas were so discouraged they didn't even bother to speak to each other for weeks after they returned home. Paul took a job working on a delivery truck for £7 a week to earn some extra money for Christmas, and John stayed in bed all day and slept, trying to escape the grim reality of being home in Mendips again. He was brought food and other sustenance by Cynthia. It was only by accident that they eventually discovered they were all in Liverpool and arranged to meet up again at the Casbah.

It was a few nights before Christmas that they set up their instruments at the Casbah and played together for the first time since coming home. The audience in the Casbah was thunderstruck; a remarkable transformation had occurred in Hamburg. Those long, nightly hours of playing had paid off in the most unexpected way: professionalism. Although they were still unorganized and casual on stage, they were no longer the amateur band that had left Liverpool five months before. They were now a slick entertainment act, full of confidence and stage presence. In particular, they were visually like no other group in town; their clothing was now an unaccountable mixture of leather pants, cowboy boots, and denim jackets; their hairstyles featured feminine bangs combed over their foreheads.

"It was Hamburg that had done it," John said. ". . . it was only back in Liverpool that we realized the difference and saw what was happening." What was happening was an instant snowballing of popularity as word spread about the new, improved Beatles back from Hamburg. Within a month they were recommended for a job as the lunchtime band at the Cavern Club on Matthew Street, which had just made a policy switch from jazz to beat groups. This was considered a plum job, although the surroundings left something to be desired. The Cavern was exactly what it sounded like, a slimy, subterranean cavern beneath a converted warehouse in the downtown business district. Eighteen steps below street level, it had three low-arched chambers. Because there was no ventilation, it was like descending into a sewer. The air was as fetid as a sweaty gymnasium, and the walls literally ran slick with condensation. No matter to the Beatles—at twenty-five shillings a day each they were ecstatic to be there; a steady lunchtime gig in a crowded club was exactly what the boys needed to build a following. In January of 1961 they began to play some evenings at the Cavern, as well as at lunchtime, and soon they were considered the house band.

It became Cynthia Powell's lunchtime routine to leave art school and go to the Cavern to hear John and the boys play. Occasionally some member or another of one of the boys' families would also stop by at lunchtime to see them. Jim McCartney was no stranger to the Cavern, and Louise Harrison made herself a frequent and welcomed visitor, cheering the boys on with the rest of the kids, although she was horrified at how awful the club was. Mrs. Harrison was sitting there with crowds of kids around her one day when John's Aunt Mimi turned up. Mimi had come not so much to cheer as to check up on where John was spending all his time. She had stormed past the owner, Ray McFall, refusing to pay admission, saying she had "come for John Lennon." She was aghast at what she found. Hundreds of kids screaming in that foul air, singing and dancing. She would have pulled John out of there by the ear if it hadn't been for the large crowd by the stage.

Louise Harrison, happy to see Mimi there, called over to her, "Aren't they great?"

"I'm glad someone thinks so," Mimi shouted back. "You thing. We'd all have had lovely peaceful lives but for you encouraging them."

6.

B Y THEN all pretense of attending school was over, and music was a full-time occupation. The band had been back in Liverpool only a few months when George Harrison turned eighteen, and they set off for another stint on the Reeperbahn. Allan Williams fixed it with the authorities by writing a letter on their behalf to the German Tribunal and managed to arrange for legitimate visas. Peter Eckhorn at the Top Ten Club was offering them £40 a week, twice as much as they had earned at the Kaiserkeller. John promised Cynthia that this time it would only be a short trip and softened the pain of parting by inviting her to join him in Hamburg during Easter vacation from art school.

Cynthia was joined on the journey to Hamburg by Dorothy Rohne, a pert, blond girl with a pixie haircut from the art college, whom Paul had been dating in Liverpool. Paul was "serious" about

Dot, who worked part-time in a pharmacy, and he even contemplated marriage. The girls were sent off at the Lime Street station by Paul's father and Cynthia's mother. They were fortified for the trip with cheese butties and a thermos of tea, but they literally starved during the two-day ride. There was no restaurant car on the train, and the girls were afraid to get off at the food stops, lest they misunderstand the stopover time alloted for them to eat and find themselves stranded in some foreign city. They arrived at the Hamburg station one morning just after sunrise, exhausted and hungry.

John and Paul were waiting for them, leaping and bounding about the station like a couple of lunatics stuffed full of speed. They had been up playing into the early morning hours and were by then too full of Prellys to go to sleep, so they had been up all night. Cynthia had never seen either one of them like that, chattering on a mile a minute, skipping down the early morning deserted streets. The boys assured the girls that everyone in Hamburg, save for Pete Best, was taking Prellys. "It's the only way to survive," John assured her, and by the end of the two-week visit Cynthia was on them too.

It had been arranged for Cynthia to officially stay at Astrid's parents' house in the suburbs, since the attic rooms the boys shared over the Top Ten Club weren't considered appropriate accommodations for a young English lady. Paul's girlfriend Dot was staying with Rosa, the washroom lady, on her houseboat. To Cynthia's great relief, Astrid turned out to be not only a warm and gracious host but a good friend to Cynthia as well. She loaned Cynthia her clothes, changed her hairstyle, and showed her how to put on makeup. Cynthia was fascinated by Astrid's exotic tastes. Her room at her parents' house was painted all in black, with silver tin foil accessories, and on the bed was a black velvet bedspread with black satin sheets. Concealed spotlights illuminated the stark room in an effect far ahead of its time. Every night after dinner, Cynthia and Astrid would spend hours getting dressed and primping in front of the mirror in Astrid's room before setting out for the Top Ten Club to watch the boys perform. The girls sat stageside for hours, oblivious to the fights and screaming and mayhem around them, waiting for the boys to take their "powsa" or break. On some nights Cynthia would brave the attic room to sleep with John. They slept in the bottom bunk of a double-decker, the smell of dirty laundry heavy in the air, and made love while George Harrison snored blissfully away in the bed a few feet above them.

Cynthia thought Astrid's relationship with Stu Sutcliffe quite peculiar, although the rest of the Liverpool contingent didn't find it as fascinating as she did. Stu and Astrid were so inseparable that Cynthia began to think of them as twins. They even started to look alike. They had the same haircut, they wore the same black leather outfits—both with an occasional bare midriff—and they even ordered the same food in restaurants. It was clear that Stu had no intention of ever leaving Hamburg without her and that his days with the band were numbered. It was a good thing, too. The closer Stu got to Astrid, the more the other boys seemed to dislike him. An enormous antipathy had developed between Stu and the others. From the start Stu had always been John's friend, but now passive tolerance had turned into malignant disapproval. Paul in particular found a lot to be critical of in Stu. He picked on the way he played, the way he dressed, even the way he said things. Everyone was on edge a lot, partly as a side effect of the constant diet of amphetamines, and tempers were short. But now, even John, Stu's perpetual champion, seemed to be taking his bad temper out on Stu with the rest of them. One night on stage at the Top Ten the boys were goading Stu unmercifully, until Paul finally went too far and said something nasty about Astrid. In front of a packed house, Stu tore off his guitar and jumped on Paul. Paul, much bigger and stronger, easily brought Stu to the ground and gave him a good walloping before the others pulled him off.

Stu also suffered from frequent terrible headaches, which sometimes manifested themselves in irrational fits of jealousy over Astrid, who if anything, was inordinately loyal. Sometimes his headaches were so painful he would bang his head against the wall in frustration. With all this it was decided that Stu would officially leave the Beatles at the end of their engagement at the Top Ten. He was going to marry Astrid and stay in Hamburg with her, where he would get a grant from the Hamburg City Council and study art at the state art college.

Stu, however, graciously took it upon himself to do a last dirty deed for the boys, since he wouldn't be with them any longer to take the blame. He wrote to Allan Williams in Liverpool, telling him that the Beatles no longer felt he was responsible for their employment in Hamburg, since they had met Peter Eckhorn on their own and acquired the job themselves. Therefore, they would be withholding his 10 percent of their salary. The only contract Williams had with them had been lost in a fire, and he was legally helpless to force them to pay. Williams went on to become their long-term detractor. He spoke out against them for years to come, and when they became successful, he wrote a bitter book called *The Man Who Gave the Beatles Away,* describing their Hamburg days in detail. It must be of some comfort to him that a portion of his income is still derived by speaking at Beatle conventions, recounting his personal adventures with them.

7.

*W*HEN CYNTHIA returned to Liverpool after her Easter trip, her mother had surprising news for her; she was leaving England to live with Cynthia's married cousins in Canada, where she would work as a nanny to their children. The house in Hoylake was being rented out to strangers, and Cynthia needed to find her own place to live. Her only alternative was to move in with an aging aunt who lived on the far side of Liverpool. Then she got what she thought was a brilliant idea; John's Aunt Mimi was already boarding students at Mendips for a little extra income and there was still room for one more. It didn't seem very hard to convince Mimi to let her move in. Cynthia even found a job on Saturdays working at the Woolworths in the nearby shopping district, Penny Lane. Once she had moved into her room at Mendips, she tried to help Mimi out with the household chores, hoping to fit in like a daughter. Then, when John came home in July, Cynthia plotted, she would already be living with him under the same roof. Could marriage be far away?

Not many days went by before Cynthia discovered that living in the same house with Mimi Smith was far from the perfect arrangement. Mimi was a stickler for having the house run exactly the way she wanted it run and what's more she was impossibly possessive of John. Mimi acted as if they were rivals for John's affections and made it more than clear that Cynthia Powell was nothing but a stranger to her, just another boarder. The atmosphere in the house turned so sour that Cynthia moved out in less than a month and found herself living with her Aunt Tess on the far side of town. Undaunted, she had another plan; she would find her own flat near the Art College, and John would move in with her when he came home. She searched for weeks before she found one she could afford. It wasn't what she dreamed of as a love nest. It was a squalid, one-room flat, with pipes that ran rusty water, only a single bar of electric fire in the fireplace, and windows that rattled all winter. But it was hers; it was her first real place on her own. Remembering Astrid's ingeniously decorated room in her parent's house, Cynthia was inspired to make the flat as wonderful as possible for John's homecoming. She bought a scrub brush and a pail, disinfectants, white paint, and pink lightbulbs. When John finally returned that summer, he found her in the clean but barren flat, sleeping on a lumpy mattress with only one set of sheets. As she hoped, he moved in with her. The Beatles resumed playing at the Cavern Club, and things seemed to go blissfully for a while.

It was one night in autumn of 1961 that John came home to her room terribly excited. "Our struggling days are over," he announced. The son of a rich Jewish merchant had stumbled into the Cavern Club, and he wanted to manage them. He was *loaded*, this guy. He was going to get them a recording contract. He knew Elvis Presley's manager, Colonel Tom Parker, and he said that the Beatles were going to be bigger than Elvis. *Bigger* than Elvis! For a while it was all Cynthia heard about, this new manager. John was possessed, the way he went overboard about things. This man seemed to consume so much of John's thoughts that Cynthia was resentful at the mention of his name. For a week it was all she heard. Brian Epstein this, Brian Epstein that.

Chapter Three

*Even if there were something
to be ashamed of, if it were
true and it were known and it
were published, I would not
complain. I am extremely
fond of the truth . . .*

—Brian Epstein
A Cellarful of Noise

1.

WHEN I, PETER BROWN, first laid eyes on Brian Epstein, he was no stranger in a strange land; he was an anomaly, a puzzlement to his family and a bizarre and hideous joke to himself. In the predominantly Irish-Welsh city of Liverpool, where the Nazi's nightly bombing hardly seemed to temper the ingrained anti-Semitism, Brian Epstein was not only from one of the city's most visible Jewish families, but he also kept a secret so dark and unheard of that for most of his life there wasn't a single person with whom he could discuss it: he was homosexual. Now, while such things were more commonplace in the larger, more sophisticated cities in the world, in the grim, hard-working northern city of Liverpool, as the eldest son of a devout Jewish family, Brian Epstein thought himself a freak. Unable to find anyone like himself, degraded by what he saw as a long series of social and academic failures, filled with a gnawing sense of disappointment and defeat, Brian sought physical satisfaction in the saddest of ways.

One night, when he was twenty-five years old, he set out in his shiny new cream and maroon Hillman California automobile for a public lavatory he frequented in the Liverpool suburb of West Derby. Sitting behind the wheel of his beautiful automobile, Brian Epstein did not look like a young man who would know of such places. He was a handsome but slight young man with a patrician air about him. His wavy brown hair was kept perfectly trimmed and combed. He was usually dressed in a hand-tailored suit, Turnbull and Asser shirt, and a silk foulard about his neck. His imperious manner and elegant dress made him seem older than he really was, a callow twenty-five. As he had done many times before, he parked his automobile down the street from the circular concrete public loo, shut off the engine and waited, drumming his fingers on the steering wheel impatiently. He waited for a long time until a man appeared walking down the street. He was burly and older than Brian, dressed like a longshoreman. The man stopped for a moment outside the loo and then went inside. Brian locked his car securely and followed him in.

This time when Brian solicited the man at the dank urinal, he did not retire to the shadows of an unoccupied booth with him. Instead, Brian was severely and mercilessly beaten and left lying on the floor of the loo. His money, watch, and wallet were stolen.

Brian ran sobbing to his car and drove frantically to his family's large, imposing home at 9 Queens Drive, Childwall, terrified at what he was going to tell his parents. Brian turned first to his mother, Queenie Epstein. Brian had long ago learned that he could confide and confess anything to his mother, and she would not only love and forgive him but persevere to find a solution. A tall, attractive woman of keen intelligence and indomitable spirit, there seemed nothing beyond her power to make things right for him. But this time the problem was beyond even Queenie's ken. He had just finished telling her a slightly edited version of the incident when the phone rang in the lounge; it was Brian's assailant from the public lavatory. The man had recognized Brian's name as that of the son of a prominent family and suggested that his silence about the encounter was worth more than the watch or the wallet. In return for keeping his mouth shut about Brian's proclivities, the man wanted money.

Queenie Epstein immediately rang up the family solicitor, Rex Makin. Makin was a small, spindly man with crooked teeth and a prosthetic ear, who had been living just next door to them for many years. Cynical and dour, Makin had handled certain legal chores for the Epstein family before: "Washing their dirty laundry," as he put it. Queenie and Brian went to see him right away, and Brian shamefully told Makin his story. The solicitor was not the least bit surprised. He had already helped Brian out of trouble in similar circumstances in London. Anyway, Makin had always thought the Epstein family a little strange. "Hadn't the grandmother thrown herself off the roof?" Makin asked. Makin insisted that the only solution was for Brian to go to the police and report the incident.

Now mortified beyond his wildest dreams, Brian repeated his pitiful story for the Liverpool police detectives, who avoided looking him in the eye as the tale progressed to its inevitable end. The detectives asked him to cooperate in setting a trap for the blackmailer. Brian was told to return home and wait for his antagonist's phone call. He was to agree to pay the man whatever sum he wanted and to arrange a rendezvous with him as soon as possible.

Late the next night in the deserted Whitechapel business district of downtown Liverpool, Brian stood trembling in the shadows of a shuttered shop. A few minutes after the appointed time, the man from the loo appeared across the street and approached Brian. As soon as he demanded the money, Brian gave a prearranged signal to the detectives who emerged from their hiding places and arrested the man.

The ensuing court trial nearly destroyed Brian. It was of small consolation to him that he was referred to only as "Mister X" during the proceedings, an English judicial tradition to protect the identity of blackmail victims. With the help of Brian's testimony, the blackmailer, who turned out to be a married dockworker with a criminal record and a predisposition to "fag-bashing," was convicted of blackmail and sentenced to prison. As they led him from the courthouse, he swore vengeance on Brian when he was released. Brian, near physical and emotional collapse, was ordered to see a psychiatrist by the court, but Brian knew it was of no use. No one could figure out who or what he was, least of all himself.

* * *

2.

*B*RIAN EPSTEIN was the great pride of the union of two wealthy Jewish business families. His mother, Malka Hyman, was the pretty and vivacious daughter of the rich and social Midlands family that owned the famous Sheffield Cabinet Ltd., a mass producer of middle-priced dining and bedroom sets. Educated at a Catholic boarding school, the Yiddish name Malka—literally Queen—was anglicized to Queenie. Despite her parochial education, she remained a devout Jew and like a good Jewish girl, when she was eighteen years old, she married a prominent Jewish bachelor from the north—a man eleven years her senior. Harry Epstein was also from a wealthy family in the furniture business. His grandfather, Isaac Epstein, was a Polish immigrant who opened his first furniture store in Liverpool at the turn of the century. Due to the easy credit terms, many struggling Liverpool families had a chair or sofa or piano that was at least partly still owned by I. Epstein and Sons. By the early 1930s, when Harry and Queenie were married, the stores had expanded to a larger building on Walton Road and incorporated the North End Music Store, which sold sheet music and instruments. As Queenie's dowry the couple were presented with an imposing five-bedroom house in Childwall, the best suburb of Liverpool, on a broad, tree-lined boulevard called Queens Drive.

It was into this grand house, with thick carpets and attentive servants, warm fires, and a sense of superiority, that Brian Epstein was born on September 19, 1934. From the start Queenie had eyes for no other. Although she would love her second child, Clive, born twenty-one months later, he never held for her the same fascination as Brian. In Brian's tastefully decorated nursery, with his nanny and his expensive toys, no outside harm, not even the German blitz, seemed to be able to intrude. When the bombings started, he was whisked off to another beautiful house in the relative safety of Southport. He developed into a spoiled, moody, anxious child, his mother's little darling and the incarnation of Little Lord Fauntleroy. His taste for elegance and grand style emerged early, and even as a little child he loved dressing up and going to expensive restaurants. He soon learned that if something was less than perfect, Queenie could make it so with the wave of her hand. When Brian was six, Queenie discovered that he had a slight squint in one eye and took him to the hospital to have it surgically corrected, although it was during one of the heaviest bombing periods in Liverpool. A friend of Queenie's asked, "The bombs are falling, what are you worried about a squint for?" But Queenie said she couldn't stand it. It made Brian less than perfect, and she saw it every time she looked at him. In the hospital Queenie sat by his bedside all night, hovering over him protectively as bombs fell all over the city. When the hospital refused to provide a bed for her, she slept sitting up in a hard-backed chair placed at Brian's side.

At the age of ten he was expelled from the Liverpool College, an exclusive private school, for drawing obscene pictures. Queenie defended her artistic son by claiming he was only drawing the frontispiece of a dance program, but she was asked that he be removed anyway. Secretly, she was happy to have him leave; she was positive that Brian was being expelled because he was Jewish. She suspected that the school had to keep their quota down. Indeed, Queenie saw symptoms of anti-Semitism everywhere. It was a common excuse when things did not go well with the outside world. She instilled this paranoia in Brian, and it became the leitmotif of his life; whenever Brian felt different because of his homosexuality, he equated it with anti-Semitism, and reacted violently to both.

A string of schools and unhappy departures followed, until Brian had attended seven schools in all by the time he was fifteen. It wasn't until he was enrolled in Wrekin, a school in Shropshire, that he took a liking to dramatics and seemed happy for a time. But it was also from Wrekin that Harry and Queenie received a letter from him that said, "I know you may not be very pleased with this, but I have decided to leave school to become a dress designer."

"You can't imagine," Queenie said, "the effect a letter like that had on Harry. He was so upset." Queenie, nevertheless, stood staunchly by her son and insisted that Harry make inquiries into the possibility of an apprenticeship for Brian with a top Parisian designer. The venture quickly proved beyond the Epsteins' influence, however. Harry, exasperated, gave Brian an ultimatum that Queenie was happy for him to accept: Brian was coming home, where he belonged, to work in the family furniture store on Walton Road.

For Brian it was a fate worse than death. At sixteen he was a thin, insolent, pink-cheeked young man who saw himself condemned to life as a furniture salesman for £5 a week. He hated everything about the shop, the old-fashioned, sturdy furniture and the dowdy, credit customers on Walton Road to whom he had to be pleasant and charming. Worst of all he had to put up with the *zaydeh*, Isaac Epstein, his grandfather, who still arrived to open the store every morning at six. Epstein had built the store by his sweat and blood, and he wasn't about to let any grandchild—especially one who wanted to become a dress designer—tell him how to run his business. One morning Epstein arrived at the store to find that Brian had placed all the furniture in the windows with their backs showing, because it was "fashionable," and Brian soon found himself working at the Times Furniture Company, where his father secured him a job safely away from his grandfather. He wasn't fated to be there long in any event. On December 9, 1952, he received notice to report for the national service.

The army tried to incorporate Brian, but he seemed to only irritate it, like sand turning to a pearl in an oyster. After basic training in Aldershot, Queenie and Harry made some calls and arranged for him to be stationed in London at the smart Albany Barracks on Regents Park. This also located Brian close to Queenie's sister, his Aunt Freda, who lived in London. Brian would report to Aunt Freda's for dinner every Monday night and on Tuesday morning Queenie would call for a complete report on his progress. On Friday nights, Queenie happily arranged for Brian to have Sabbath dinner at his grandmother's London home. He was once confined to barracks for impersonating an officer, but it wasn't an intentional offense. He returned to the barracks one night in his cousin's grand car, dressed so elegantly in his handmade suit and bowler hat that he was saluted by all the guards. When it was discovered it was Epstein—the only private not to make officer candidate training—he was brought up on charges. No matter; in less than ten months the army made a major discovery about Brian that precluded his further service as far as they were concerned. Brian phoned Queenie to say he was being discharged for medical reasons. Queenie, worried about his health, rang up the officer in charge and demanded to know on what grounds her son was being discharged. The officer replied evasively, "Psychiatric grounds."

"But what is exactly wrong?" Queenie insisted.

The officer's voice lowered somberly, "Oh, the poor, unfortunate man . . ."

The final irrevocable truth that Brian was homosexual shattered Queenie.

In her mind there was no use denying whose fault it was; it was hers, and she would pay dearly for it all the days of her life. Harry, who was less prepared to be understanding, let alone share the blame, drew closer to his younger son, Clive, who was successfully serving in the army. Queenie made a proclamation: from then on, whatever Brian wanted was his. They would move mountains to make him happy, to help him find his niche.

On his return from the service they opened for Brian his own branch of the family store in Hoylake, where he was allowed to sell modern furniture from London and display it with the backs to the window. Lo and behold, much to the credit of Brian's ingenious marketing devices and good taste, the store became an overnight success. Within a year profits were approaching those of the Walton Street store. The Epsteins breathed a sigh of relief and were just settling into a sense of security with him when Brian suddenly announced he had another farfetched scheme; he wanted to act. He had always loved the theater, and recently he had made friends with some of the players at the Liverpool Playhouse, which was a noted repertory theater. One Saturday night after a performance, in a bar frequented by the actors, Brian Bedford, then a young star, had casually encouraged Brian to go to acting school. That was all the suggestion he needed. In just weeks Brian quit the Hoylake store and auditioned for the Royal Academy of Dramatic Arts in London, perhaps the most selective of all British acting schools. Brian surprised even himself when he was accepted. Queenie and Harry saw Brian off at the train station with heavy hearts.

Brian was a dedicated acting student with some talent, but his teachers found him irrationally emotional. There were times when he was doing a scene that he would get so carried away he would break down into uncontrollable sobs. Although on the whole he seemed to blend in easily with the other students, he found that he did not like the world of acting, let alone other actors. After spending a fortnight in Stratford with the Royal Shakespeare Company, he became completely disenchanted with the profession. "They were really frightful," he wrote later in his autobiography, "and I believe that nowhere could one discover such phoney relationships nor witness hypocrisy practised on so grand a scale, almost as art."

Nevertheless, Brian stuck with RADA for three terms, and might have even gone back for a fourth, if he hadn't run into a little embarrassing trouble. He had been observed by a policeman in a public park, who had followed him into a public loo where he was arrested for "importuning." When Brian called to break the news to Queenie, she was stunned that anything this horrible had touched their lives. Rex Makin was dispatched to London at once, and the solicitor quickly and quietly settled the legal problem and sent Brian home. Brian spent a few weeks in Liverpool but insisted on returning to London to attend another semester at RADA. On the Sunday night before his departure, at a family dinner at the Adelphi Hotel, one of Brian's favorite spots, Queenie begged him to stay home in Liverpool, and on the verge of tears Brian finally relented.

His decision to rejoin the family business happened just when Harry was expanding the stores again. With Clive home from the service, he was opening another division of NEMS in the city center on Great Charlotte Street. Brian even arranged for singing star Anne Shelton to appear at the grand opening. Clive was in charge of the appliance department, as he had requested, because of the booming new business in TV sets. Brian was to run the small record department on one side of the first floor. Brian loved music and had already worked part-time in a record store in London when he was attending RADA. He took to this new challenge with unexpected gusto. The record industry was also expanding at a giant rate due to the invention of new record players and improved recordings. The sudden skiffle and beat music craze had created a large, new buying audience in teenagers. Since promotion and display were his forte, and he had an uncanny knack of picking hit songs, he felt he had found his niche, for a time. He invented his own inventory system using different colored strings and folders to keep the store well stocked, and he kept immaculate records. He prided himself on having the most extensive stock in the North, and slowly, but steadily, the record department began to branch out. It went from two to four to ten employees by the end of the first year and had pushed Clive's TV sets into a small part of the building before taking over two complete floors. To his parents enormous pleasure and not a small amount of pride, the record division turned into a substantial portion of NEMS income.

Brian's personal life still remained bleak. He had few friends and none that Queenie really approved of. I was actually a friend of his older brother, Clive, and had heard much about Brian from him. We were introduced at the birthday party of a mutual friend, where Clive and Brian arrived in black dinner jackets after attending their parents' twenty-fifth wedding anniversary at the Adelphi Hotel. Brian had a standout personality; it was obvious that he was very special from the start. Yet despite all his social aplomb and convivial conversation, I remember thinking that if one scratched the surface one would find a very unhappy man. When Brian heard that I was the manager of the record department of the Lewis department store just across the street from the Great Charlotte Street NEMS store, Brian became intent on hiring me away. He would visit me almost every day in the Lewis record department, trying to lure me across the street to NEMS, while keeping a careful eye on my merchandising techniques. Finally, he offered me a much higher salary plus a handsome commission to boot if I took the job. My parents, who were middle-class Roman Catholics who lived in Cheshire across the Mersey, thought my going to work for the Epstein family a disastrous move. I had completed my service in the Royal Air Force and a management training program at Lewis'; my corporate future seemed assured. Here I was giving up a solid job in order to toil for small Jewish shopkeepers.

I was almost immediately brought for an audience with Queenie and Harry. Although Harry was distant, and I had to lie to him about my age because he didn't think twenty-two was old enough to be a store manager, Queenie and I liked each other instantly. She was imperious yet warm, a special combination of Jewish mother and monied Englishwoman. She was very well read and just as well spoken. In turn, I could see she was favorably impressed with my own good manners and seemed most delighted that what she mistook for a West End accent belied my childhood in Bebington. My first week as manager of the NEMS record shop I became something of a hero with the family. I spotted a young shoplifter putting a record under his jacket and chased him out the door and down the street, where I collared him and dragged him back to the store by the scruff of his neck. "I just apprehended this man," I announced coolly to the assembled employees. When Queenie later heard the story she nearly applauded, and soon I became a trusted personal friend of the family as well as an employee.

Brian was a great pleasure but also a great puzzle. He was frequently depressed and unhappy and often drank too much. He began to have minor car accidents, which upset Queenie enormously. His mercurial temper was as unpredictable as it was sometimes vile. His temper tantrums were infantile at best. One moment he'd be sweet and charming, as no one else could be, and the next moment some little thing would set him off into a red-faced, screaming fit that made people run for cover. Worse was Brian's icy, acid coldness when something personally offended him. There was nothing as horrifying as Brian's silence.

One night after work we went to have a few drinks at the local pub, and Brian told me his big secret. He told me the story of the man he solicited in the men's room and the subsequent blackmail attempt. He was very disturbed about all this because he said that soon the man was going to be let out of jail. He was obviously petrified that the man would make good his threats for retribution and come after him. I told Brian I thought it was unlikely and not to worry, but the man's release began to haunt him. "What if?" he kept saying. "What if?"

Queenie saw all the warning signs of Brian's disintegration and decided to send him away on an extended holiday until he got his perspective back. This vacation coincided with the time Brian's blackmailer was going to be let out of jail. In early autumn of 1961, Brian went by himself to the south of Spain for six weeks. When he returned to Liverpool that October he seemed like a man on a precipice, waiting for something to happen, terrified, fascinated, alone.

*　*　*

3.

*I*T WAS NOT long after, on October 28, that a young lad named Raymond Jones, dressed in a leather jacket and tight jeans, walked into the Whitechapel branch of NEMS about three o'clock in the afternoon. Brian liked the look of the boy, and instead of letting a salesperson help, he approached the boy himself.

"There's a record I want," Jones said. "It's called 'My Bonnie,' and it was made in Germany. Have you got it?"

"Who's it by?" Brian asked.

"You won't have heard of them," Jones replied. "It's by a group called the Beatles."

A little research by Brian soon uncovered that this was a single recorded in Hamburg by Tony Sheridan, who had befriended the Beatles on their second Reeperbahn trip. Sheridan had a brief burst of popularity in England as a rock star, appearing on the only TV pop-music show of the time, "Oh Boy." He had recently fallen on hard times and wound up a Bruno Koschmider employee at the Kaiserkeller. In Hamburg he recorded a single for the Polydor label, "My Bonnie Lies Over the Ocean," backed with "When the Saints Go Marching In." The Beatles were asked to play backup as the "The Beat Brothers" and were paid £25 each for the session. Brian also learned that the "Beat Brothers" played just around the corner every day at lunchtime at the Cavern Club. Since the Cavern was only 200 yards away from the front door of NEMS, and as he had never been there, he decided to go over and take a look himself.

On November 8, with his usual style, Brian phoned ahead to request a VIP admission to the club, not so much to save the shilling admission but because he was afraid of being turned away at the door for lack of a leather jacket and tight jeans. Dressed in a suit and tie, he gingerly descended the eighteen greasy stone steps down into the Cavern Club. Beneath the street level an incredible scene unfolded before him. The three arched brick tunnels that comprised the club was a subterranean pit of writhing teenagers. At least 200 youngsters were crowded into the narrow passageways, dancing, shouting, wolfing down a soup and sandwich lunch served out of the Cavern kitchen, while they listened to the rock and roll being performed on the stage.

There in the center tunnel on a raised platform was a sight that galvanized him. It was in the most specific way a personification of his secret sexual desires. On stage were four young men dressed in leather pants and jackets. They played good time rock and roll and joked with each other with macho camaraderie. Brian stood in the shadows at the rear of the club, transfixed, until their forty-five-minute set was over. He fell first for the handsome, moody drummer, then for the boyishly pretty guitarist, then finally for the tall, skinny one who bobbed and squatted as he recklessly strummed the chords, nearly tearing his pants. Then, in a mixture of pleasure and embarrassment, he heard the mellifluous voice of the disc jockey, Bob Wooler, announce that Brian Epstein was in the club. He said that the owner of NEMS, the city's largest record store, had dropped by for a visit. The news was greeted with a mixture of applause and catcalls, and Brian self-consciously sank further into the shadows. He managed to pluck up his courage enough to push his way through the rowdy crowd to the bandroom, a tiny cell behind the stage where he tried to introduce himself to the band members. He said hello first to George Harrison, who sarcastically asked, "What brings Mr. Epstein here?" But Brian himself didn't know.

Back at the record shop all Brian could talk about were the Beatles. He ranted and raved about them to anyone who would listen. They were wonderful, he said, just wonderful. The music was the best he ever heard of any beat group, loud and crazy and driving, and they were so much fun to watch, there was some infectiously happy feeling about them. Within a few days he started popping back down into the Cavern Club to watch them. Sometimes he went alone, sometimes with an employee of the Whitechapel Street store named Alistair Taylor, who was surprised one day to hear himself introduced as Brian's "personal assistant" in an effort to impress the band. For to impress them seemed to be the only way to get their attention.

After their initial meeting, it became clear that Brian and the Beatles had nothing whatsoever in common, and the boys would only pay cursory attention to him as the owner of the big record shop. He was six years older than the eldest of them, a vast difference to them at the time, and they came from opposite ends of the social and economic scale. He spoke differently, looked differently, and had different interests. But he could impress them with his position as the Epstein scion, and with his shiny new Ford Zodiac automobile, and by ordering a mind-boggling 200 copies of the song "My Bonnie" by Tony Sheridan and the Beat Brothers and plastering their name across the window of his record store in letters a foot high. Yet one question remained unanswered: What on earth did he want with them? In the deep core of his soul, only Brian knew the answer. He wanted John.

Harry and Queenie knew nothing of Brian's new infatuation. They were away on a trip to London when Brian first discovered the Beatles and returned home to find him more agitated and excited then they had seen him in years. He sat them down on a sofa in the living room and put a record on the phonograph. Out came a terrible, incomprehensible sound. Then came the shocking news; Brian wanted to manage this noise, a rock group called the Beatles. Harry was furious with him for weeks. Just when he thought Brian had settled down with the record store, he was off on another farfetched scheme that would take him away from NEMS, and just when the store was so successful too! Brian promised it wouldn't take much time away from NEMS, but no one really believed him. Queenie sighed with resignation and gave it her blessings, with reservations. She knew best it was no good arguing with him. When Brian got an idea into his head, there was no stopping him.

Brian next went to Rex Makin for legal advice. Makin, who thought he was enured by now to Brian's wild schemes, found his proposal to manage the Beatles preposterous. What did Brian know about managing a beat group? It was ridiculous, he proclaimed, and the Epstein boy was hopeless.

4.

*B*RIAN WASN'T hopeless; Brian was obsessed. It wasn't that he wouldn't be dissuaded by what others saw as so futile a pursuit, it was that he couldn't be dissuaded. His fascination for the Beatles, part sexual, part showman, had transformed itself into a near-religious experience for him. Something seemed to come over him when he just mentioned their names. When Brian went to see Allan Williams to check up on them, Williams noticed that Brian not only blushed, he sweated when he talked about them. "He was hypnotized," Williams said. He warned Brian that the Beatles were thieves who had ripped him off for £15 per week commission. "My honest opinion, Brian, is this; don't touch them with a fucking bargepole." But Williams' badmouthing had no effect at all.

Brian arranged his first formal meeting with them on December 3, 1961. They were asked to come to the Whitechapel NEMS at four-thirty with Bob Wooler as their adviser. Brian had fantasized the meeting in his head for hours, like a well-rehearsed play. He imagined the four young men would be ushered through the store into the lift and up to his modern office on the third floor by his "personal assistant," Alistair Taylor. They would find Brian sitting behind his immaculate desk looking important and in control, the picture of a smart businessman. After his assistant served coffee and tea, Brian would announce his desire to manage them. Then they would discuss a contract. Brian was prepared to promise them a recording contract from a London record company. He didn't think it would prove a very difficult task, considering the importance of the large retail record business NEMS did with the record labels. He expected the boys to be so impressed that they would agree to sign management contracts immediately.

But four-thirty came and went, and there were no Beatles. It was a Wednesday and early closing, and all the employees went home and left Brian in the store alone. After a time it got dark out, and Brian stood in the shadows of the large appliances, peering anxiously out the window. Finally, after an hour, when Brian had decided he was being stood up, John arrived with Bob Wooler. They had obviously come by way of several pubs and were quite happy. Pete Best and George didn't arrive until even later, and Paul was still missing. Brian, trying to contain his temper, asked George to phone Paul's home and find out what was wrong. It turned out that Paul went home after their lunchtime Cavern gig and was still cleaning up. "He's having a bath," George informed Brian candidly.

Brian flushed. "This is disgraceful," he proclaimed angrily. "He's very late."

"And very clean," George added.

It soon turned out that the recalcitrant but hygienic Paul McCartney was only one of the many impediments to implementing Brian's fantasies. Paul was, from the start, the most skeptical and questioning of Brian, a situation that only deepened as the years passed. Paul was very competitive by nature and keenly aware of any edge John might be gaining over him in the group. It wasn't hard to notice that Brian stammered and averted his eyes when he spoke to John, and this worried and irked Paul, especially because he always considered himself the attractive one.

Paul's father was equally suspicious of the "Jew boy" who wanted, it turned out, 25 percent of the boys' hard-earned wages. Brian cleverly requested a personal audience with Jim McCartney. He found that selling himself and his dreams for the Beatles was far easier than selling some of the furniture in the Walton Street store. The senior McCartney's reservations soon melted in the face of Brian's warmth and persuasiveness.

The hardest nut to crack, however, was Aunt Mimi. There was nobody as tough as Mimi. She had heard all about young Mr. Epstein with his fancy suits and his expensive car and his money and passing fancies, and she didn't mind letting Brian know about it either.

"It's all right for you if this group turns out to be just a flash in the pan. It won't matter," she told him when he went to visit her at Mendips. "It's just a hobby for you. If it's all over in six months it won't matter to you, but what happens to them?"

Brian shook his head. "It's all right, Mrs. Smith," he assured her passionately. "I promise you, John will never suffer. He's, the only important one. The others don't matter, but I'll always take care of John."

Six weeks later, at a table at the Casbah Club, Brian and the Beatles signed a formal agreement that Brian had written himself with the aid of a sample contract he had purchased through the mails. Rex Makin had proved too contrary to help make up the contracts for him, so Brian simply mailed away for a standard one. In fact, the contract wasn't really valid; Paul and George were both under twenty-one and needed a guardian's signature to make it legal. And in all the excitement of signing this oddly marriagelike document, Brian forgot to sign his own name.

Once Brian took up with the Beatles, everyone at the store noticed a drastic change in him. At night his elegant suits would disappear into the closet and out would come newly purchased black turtleneck sweaters and a black leather jacket that was an imitation of the boys' clothes. Brian couldn't have looked more inappropriate in these outfits, for his elegance and polish showed right through the teenage disguise. For a while he even tried combing his hair forward like the Beatles, until he realized they were laughing at him behind his back. He began to pick them up in his car and drive them to jobs, allegedly in charge, but really just tagging along with them, fascinated by their world.

On one of these nights he learned from where the boys got their seemingly boundless energy. Their amphetamine habits had not ended with their Hamburg days, and, save for Pete Best, all the boys were ingesting powerful pharmaceutical diet pills they bought on the black market. Desperate to be accepted as one of the boys, Brian started taking them, too. Queenie couldn't help but notice when he arrived home late at night that his eyes were bulging and glassy and that he couldn't stop chomping on his tongue or licking his lips.

However the Beatles might have changed Brian's appearance and nocturnal habits, they didn't affect him in spirit. Within weeks of their contract signing they began to receive typed memos from him about their stage act, written in a brisk, businesslike tone, much like the memos received by the employees of the NEMS record stores. While it was understood that Brian would have no say over the boys' music, he insisted that they refashion their stage image. Brian was, after all, best at showmanship, and the boys were hardly professional looking. What might be entertaining to a crowd of hooligans on Matthew Street would certainly turn off the large audiences Brian had in mind. Brian insisted, for starters, that they neither eat nor drink on stage, although he didn't seem to be able to stop them from smoking. There was to be no further horseplay, either, no affectionate arm punching or inside jokes and mumbled dialogue. From now on they would know exactly what songs they were going to play and in what order, before they went on the stage.

Brian even insisted, much to John Lennon's revulsion, that they forsake their leather and cowboy boots in order to wear identical suits. Although this was a brilliant stroke on Brian's part, developing a striking visual image that was to become a trademark for them, John hated the idea and tried to convince the group not to do it, telling them it was selling out. Suits and ties were the antithesis of the Beatles' public identity. Surprisingly, Brian found an ally in Paul. Paul, as it turned out, had a good sense of showmanship himself, and furthermore, in his very bourgeois way, he cared about what people thought. Most of all he understood appearances and public relations. With Paul's encouragement the group gave in, and Brian ordered them gray lounge suits with velvet collars from a Liverpool tailor. Now, as far as he was concerned, they were all ready to record.

5.

*E*ARLY IN BRIAN'S explorations to secure them a recording contract, he wrote a letter to a record reviewer on the *Liverpool Evening Echo* named Tony Barrow, asking him to mention the Beatles in his column, since, according to Brian and the *Mersey Beat* music paper polls, they were the most popular group in Liverpool. Barrow wrote back saying he couldn't mention them because they had not recorded in England; however he did recommend Brian to someone at Decca's Artists and Repertoire department. At Decca, the mention of NEMS, the largest record retailer in the North, got Brian instant attention of a sort; a young assistant named Mike Smith was sent to Liverpool to hear the group play. Smith was impressed enough with their performance to offer them an audition in Decca's West Hampstead studio.

The boys were ecstatic at the news and confident that fame and fortune were the next easy step. The audition was scheduled for New Year's Day of 1962, and early on a snowy New Year's Eve, they piled into the back of Neil Aspinall's van and set off to London. Neil had never driven to London before, and he got lost in the heavy snowstorm. The boys huddled together for warmth in the back of the frigid van for ten hours before they arrived at the hotel Brian had booked for them, the Royal on Woburn Place, at a cost of twenty-seven shillings a night for bed and breakfast. The boys spent New Year's Eve wandering around the freezing streets, taking in the sights, dreaming of the audition the next day and of what 1962 might bring. They couldn't have imagined.

Brian, in the meanwhile, traveled to London on the train in a first-class coach and spent a warm New Year's Eve at his Aunt Freda's. He met up with the boys the next day at the Hampstead studios. The band was exhilarated and frightened. They felt alien in the still, clinical environment of the studio. They sang fourteen songs in sixty minutes for several anonymous men in the control booth on the other side of a glass window. Their voices cracked from nerves, and they sang most of their numbers slightly off tune. All their playing was frightened and stiff, with Pete Best the worst, mechanical and plodding at the drums. The stark, foreign quality of the studio took away all the energy and personal excitement of their performances. To make matters their very worst, only three of the fourteen songs they sang were original McCartney-Lennon compositions. Brian insisted on this. He said he knew the record market best and that Decca wanted to hear cover versions of established hit songs. The Beatles sang songs like "The Sheik of Araby," "Red Sails in the Sunset," "Till There Was You," and ended with a raveup on "Besame Mucho."

Brian returned to Liverpool later that day confident that it was just a matter of time before they were offered a recording contract. He was outraged to learn that Decca had turned them down cold. When he sheepishly told the Beatles the news they were furious with him, convinced that Brian had blown their one big chance by insisting they play standards. Brian, desperate to recover face, set out the next day for London to see Dick Rowe, Decca's head of A&R. Rowe wouldn't see him, however, and he ended up with Beecher Stevens, the general manager of wholesale sales. Brian demanded that Decca reconsider their decision, threatening Stevens by withholding all orders from NEMS for Decca products. Then, changing tack, he even personally offered to purchase 3,000 copies of any single Decca recorded with the Beatles, but no was no.

This first defeat brought home a stunning reality to Brian: managing a rock group would not be an easy task; he better get used to not getting his way; the Decca rejection was likely to be the first of many. In the next few short months he made hundreds of phone calls, wrote volumes of correspondence, and paid dozens of personal visits, only to wind up at the same dead end. Each week brought another polite rejection from another important record company. Decca, Pye, Phillips, Columbia, and HMV all said no. John half joked that they'd wind up recording on the Woolworth label, but Brian didn't think that was funny. Each rejection was like another pin in another balloon. All the while there was a Greek chorus waiting behind him, led by Rex Makin, intoning his failure at this, his latest caprice. At times he felt so disgusted he considered giving up the Beatles and going back to RADA.

Yet each time he began to falter, each time he was willing to concede defeat, his resolve was renewed by John Lennon. He was dazzled by John, by his looks, by his wit, even by his cruelty. In John's presence Brian was giddy and lightheaded. When John spoke, Brian looked away, not daring to gaze directly into his eyes lest his lovesick look expose what he thought was his secret. John was sardonically amused at the power he had over Brian and didn't hesitate to use it to be manipulative or mean. This, in turn, fueled Brian's masochism and made him desire John even more. Late at night, drunk and high on amphetamines, Brian would break down into tears about something John had said to him. Cynthia remembers Brian stamping his feet and scowling when John disagreed with him, which was frequently. Another passion might have burned itself out, but the eternal hope that one day Brian might consummate the relationship kept this one smoldering.

Brian thought his biggest impediment to seducing John was where to do it. Brian still lived at home with his parents. That spring, without letting anyone know, he rented a "secret" flat on Faulkner Street and furnished it modestly. This was to be the lair into which he would lure John, but whenever John stopped by he was always encumbered by another member of the band. Brian began to think that it was being in Liverpool that made John seem inhibited and indisposed to the possibility. He decided that if he could just get John out of town alone he would succumb to his advances. Brian made a standing offer to John to take him to Copenhagen for the weekend. This Copenhagen offer became common knowledge around the Cavern, and eventually people started teasing John about it. Yet, somehow it was still Brian's fantasy that no one knew he was homosexual, let alone that he was in love with John. After the first few months everybody had some little piece of gossip about him. Neil Aspinall's sister had heard something about him through a friend, and she soon told Neil and Neil told John. The very next night, high on pills, John blurted out that Neil accused Brian of being "queer." Brian indignantly stormed outside to where Neil was unloading equipment. "Why did you tell them I'm queer?" Brian demanded. "It's a lie!"

Neil, who was known for cutting through the bullshit, northern style, was not cowed. "You are queer," he told Brian, continuing to unload.

Brian almost swallowed his tongue with anger. "I am not!" he raged.

"Are too!"

The issue was never settled to Brian's liking, but he managed to convince himself there was at least some doubt. There wasn't. Years later Paul admitted, "We were more confused by it than turned off. We really didn't know what it meant to be 'gay' at the time."

Naturally, it did not please Brian to discover that he had a rival for John's attention. From the moment he heard about Cynthia Powell, Brian was prepared and eager to dislike her, but upon meeting her backstage at a show his antagonistic feelings disappeared. She turned out to be magnanimous and sweet and very unthreatening. He could even see why John liked her so much. And as far as competition went, Brian realized that Cynthia's hold on John was even more tenuous than his own.

6.

*O*N APRIL 13 the Beatles were scheduled to return to Hamburg for an appearance at the Star Club, the Reeperbahn's latest and largest nightclub. Brian, to impress Liverpool fans, grandly billed the seven-week German stint as a "European tour" and in a show of style paid for the boys to go by plane. Queenie and Harry, continually exasperated at his largesse, were positive he would never see the plane fare back from the promised profits. Now they were even less happy to learn that Brian was to accompany the Beatles to Hamburg.

On April 10, the day of their departure, two telegrams arrived from Astrid Kirchner in Hamburg. Stu had been ill; Stu had died. Stu had died in her arms in an ambulance on the way to the hospital. For many of his friends in Liverpool the news was of small surprise. On his occasional trips back home to visit his family, it was obvious something was terribly wrong with him, but nobody could figure out what it was. The previous Christmas he was so pale and thin he was virtually transparent, like a holograph. His headaches had become paralytic, his behavior was erratic, and he was seeing double. He had all the symptoms of a brain tumor, yet specialists in both Hamburg and Liverpool could find nothing wrong with him.

It wasn't until two years after his death that a probable cause was discovered. Stu's mother, Millie, donated his body to scientific research. In examining the exposed skull and brain, pathologists discovered a small tumor previously invisible on the X-rays. It was caused by a small traumatic depression in the skull, probably the result of a good, hard kick to the head by a Teddy Boy's steel-tipped shoe.

An emotional scene ensued at the Hamburg airport. Paul, John, and Pete flew out first and were waiting at the airport with Astrid the next day when Brian, George, and Millie Sutcliffe's plane landed. Brian, who had not known Stu Sutcliffe, tried to lend his support and comfort. He noticed, as did Mrs. Sutcliffe, that John Lennon was the only dry-eyed member of their group, dispassionate as only he could be. Astrid believed that John only pretended to be heartless, and she found strength in his clinical attitude. "You can't behave as a widow," he told her. "Make up your mind, you either live or you die. You can't be in the middle." Later, when they got back to Liverpool, he asked Mrs. Sutcliffe for the long scarf Stu had worn in art class.

The grief and shock of Stu's death sent them full tilt into the neon netherworld of the Reeperbahn. The Star Club was an excellent setting for an emotional purge. Built on the site of an old cinema, it was by far the biggest place they had ever played. The club alternated music with sex shows and lady mud wrestlers; often as many as 18,000 patrons would pass through its doors on a single evening and from the stage the place looked like a writhing snakepit. The Beatles, who were now booked as headliners, were joined on the bill by two other Liverpool groups, The Big Three and Kingsize Taylor and the Dominoes.

On this trip John managed to surpass his previous craziness. One night he walked on stage naked with a toilet seat around his neck to the cheers of the audience. His sleeping quarters were across the street from the club next to a hapless Catholic church, which became the target for countless assaults. On Sunday mornings, still awake from Prellys taken the night before, he would hang a water-filled condom outside the window of his room to taunt the Catholics on their way to mass, or he would construct an effigy of Jesus with an inflated condom for a penis. One morning he urinated off the rooftop onto the heads of three passing nuns.

Brian did not find the city of Hamburg with its whores and thugs as enchanting as the Beatles obviously did. He couldn't fathom the boys constant preoccupation with prostitutes, considering the rate they contracted venereal diseases. One of the first things he planned to do when he got back was to ask Rex Makin to recommend a urologist so the Beatles could get proper treatment when they returned home. Brian made it clear that he was to see to *every* aspect of their welfare.

After just a week he fled back to Liverpool and concerned himself with their recording career. In the six weeks more they were gone he was determined to explore every remaining possible avenue to secure the boys a contract. Despite a large backlog of work waiting for him in Whitechapel, his commutation to London from Liverpool was almost weekly now. Much to Harry's distress he was spending only half his time in the store. It was on one of those frequent London trips he decided to have the Beatles' demonstration tape transferred to a disc so it could be heard more easily. The EMI-owned record shop on Oxford Street provided such a service, and the engineer there recommended that Brian take the newly made disc to someone at EMI's publishing company. Founded in 1931, EMI was a large British corporation famous for the manufacture of televisions and electronic equipment. In 1954 the company had been revitalized by Sir Joseph Lockwood, who had acquired several record companies and their presses under EMI ownership. EMI's premier labels were Columbia and HMV, both of which had already rejected the Beatles;

but EMI had also acquired a small German company in the prewar years called Parlophone. Parlophone became EMI's stepchild, known mostly for its comedy records and novelty albums. The man at EMI's publishing company liked the disc, however, and recommended it to an associate, the head of A&R at Parlophone records, George Martin. Brian set up an appointment for the next day.

The gentleman who greeted Brian at his office the following afternoon was unlike any of the record company executives Brian had previously met. He was tall, handsome, and elegant, with a quiet authoritative way about him that Brian admired. His air of breeding gave no hint of his poor North London background, where he grew up the son of a carpenter. He studied piano and oboe at the London School of Music, and his first job was at the BBC where he was a news reader and where he cultivated his clipped, upper-class accent. He had joined EMI in 1950 as an assistant and became head of the Parlophone label when Sir Joseph Lockwood took over in 1954, making him, at the age of twenty-nine, the youngest head of a label, young, but not as young as the twenty-seven-year-old manager who walked through the door of his office. What Brian didn't know that day was there was gossip in the record industry that Parlophone was about to be closed by EMI and Martin was in danger of losing his eleven hundred pounds a year job. Brian liked Martin immediately, and Martin was equally impressed with Brian, who was a far cry from the type of managers he was accustomed to in the record business.

In Hamburg, the Beatles received a telegram that would become a talisman to Brian, who subsequently carried it with him in his briefcase as they traveled around the world: CONGRATU-LATIONS BOYS, EMI REQUESTS RECORDING SESSION. PLEASE REHEARSE NEW MATERIAL. Unfortunately, Brian's enthusiasm caused them to believe this was a preliminary step to recording an album. In fact, this was only another audition. Brian made arrangements for the session as soon as they arrived home from Germany, and in early June the boys set out again for London in a friend's van.

The EMI studios were in a prepossessing mansion house on Abbey Road, a residential tree-lined street in St. John's Wood. The Beatles instantly developed a rapport with George Martin, whom they found to be part schoolmaster, part collaborator. The various electronic magic tricks that Martin could perform in the control room, although relatively simple in retrospect, made him seem like the Wizard of Oz behind his control panel. John was impressed in particular that Martin had recorded with Peter Sellers and Spike Milligan in the "Goon Show" series. Martin put them through a thorough, professional audition. He listened to each musician play separately, then had them run through each of their songs together. As usual, Brian had prepared a list of songs for them to play, still convinced that standard tunes would be the most appealing. Martin disagreed. He thought "Besame Mucho" and "Red Sails in the Sunset" were banal, but he was even less impressed with their original compositions. The Beatles cheerfully informed him they had already decided to record one of their own songs for their first single, one called "Love Me Do," which they had written in the back of a van on the way to a job. Martin hated the lyrics, "Love, love me do, you know I love you," as dumb as a nickel greeting card. He was particularly critical of Pete Best's heavy, uninventive drumming. The loud drum beat around which many of the songs were built might have worked in the noisy Star Club but not in a recording studio. When the audition was over the most George Martin would say was "maybe"—and then only if they got rid of Pete Best. Perhaps they could keep Pete Best for live performances, but if they wanted a recording contract, they'd have to use a session drummer in the studio.

In John, Paul, and George's minds, Pete Best was already doomed as he sat next to them in the van on the way back to Liverpool.

7.

*T*HAT SUMMER George Martin finally offered the Beatles a formal recording contract to record on the Parlophone label under his direction. For the first of many times, Brian would demonstrate that for all his panache and urban affectations, he was still only a twenty-seven-year-old furniture salesman from a provincial city. Brian negotiated—or rather gracefully accepted—a substandard contract, even for an unknown group. Under the terms, Parolophone was indebted to record only four sides, or two double-sided singles, in a one-year period. The royalty rate was a laughable one penny for each single sold, both sides, and the increments would only be a farthing each side—an amount that came to about one-half of a penny. It was just about the lowest possible offer a record company could make them, without being accused of usury. Considering how many times they had been turned down, Brian felt lucky at that.

But if Brian was weak at making deals, he was, however, strong at administration, and on August 16 he took on the task of firing Pete Best as the Beatles' drummer. Pete had intentionally not been told about George Martin's offer of a contract, because Brian and the boys didn't want him involved, yet all along Brian was reluctant to fire him. He felt that Pete was an important member of the group as far as the loyal Liverpool audience was concerned and a visual, if not musical asset. Also, in many ways the Best family was inextricably involved with the group. Mona Best had done a great amount of booking and management chores for several months between Allan Williams' demise and Brian's arrival. She continued, blindly, to call the Beatles "Pete's group," and she was not an easy woman to scorn. Even worse, Neil Aspinall, who lived with the Best family as a boarder, had become an indispensable aid to the band. If losing Pete Best meant losing Neil Aspinall, they were all in a lot of trouble.

But it had to be done. That day in August Neil drove Pete to the Whitechapel NEMS. Pete, dressed in a tee shirt and jeans, made his way through the aisles of television sets and refrigerators to the lift. Upstairs in his office, Brian was waiting for him behind his desk, his face an icy mask. Brian said, "The boys want you out of the group. They don't think you're a good enough drummer.

Pete was astonished. "It's taken them two years to find out I'm not a good enough drummer?" he exploded. Numb with shock, he went downstairs to where Neil was waiting for him in the van. Neil pledged allegiance to Pete, and the two of them went directly to the nearest pub and got good and drunk. Neil insisted that if the Beatles didn't want Pete, he wouldn't have anything to do with them either. But that night at their engagement at the River Park Ballroom in Chester, Neil showed up to do his job as usual. A few days later Brian tried to diplomatically console Pete Best by offering to build another group around him, but it was of no use, Pete was disgusted with them. His place in history was already reserved as the most luckless of all might-have-beens. In the next twenty-four months, the Beatles would gross $40 million. Pete Best became a baker, earning £8 a week, and married a girl named Kathy who worked at the biscuit counter in Woolworths.

8.

*A*LONG WITH the Beatles' popularity came the girls Cynthia Powell called "the submissive dollie birds." When the word was later coined, these girls would be called groupies, and their specialty was to sexually ensnare rock musicians. At the time these girls were a totally new phenomenon to Cynthia, and she watched with great apprehension as these dollie birds became fixtures in the Beatles' daily lives. They seemed to follow the band everywhere, whether it was lurking outside the changing room at the Cavern Club or "just happening" to be passing by one of the boy's houses. They flirted and cooed and brought the boys presents and in every way posed a threat to Cynthia's survival.

Cynthia had already witnessed firsthand the dangers of the dollie birds. Dorothy Rohne, Paul's girl for several years, had been given her walking papers. Dot had moved into a bedsitter flat just next to Cynthia's. One night the girls were sitting around in their bathrobes and curlers, smoking cigarettes and drinking tea, when Paul arrived pounding on Dorothy's door. He insisted on having a private talk with her in her room. They emerged a few minutes later with Dot in tears and Paul on the run. Paul had told her that with so many girls available to him he didn't want to be tied down to just one steady anymore. Dot soon moved out of her bedsitter and disappeared from the scene, never to be heard from again. For all Cynthia knew, the same fate awaited her.

That summer of 1962 was a bad one for Cynthia. Her mother was away in Canada, and John was working and traveling constantly. She was completely broke and much to her embarrassment had to apply for public assistance. Being "on the dole" depressed her even further and her one-room flat was so hot and stuffy she sometimes felt she would suffocate. She felt trapped, with no way out, no salvation ahead.

By August she was pregnant.

She had never, she said, used birth control during her two-and-a-half-year sexual relationship with John. "Ignorance," she claimed, "was bliss." And if that was so, then Cynthia had been blissfully lucky for a long time. When she started getting sick every morning, she went to her girlfriend Phyllis' doctor who examined her and frostily confirmed she was pregnant. The next night, after a drink to shore up her confidence, she told John, weeping silent tears. John was quiet for a moment, then, stoically, he said he would do the only thing any good northern man would do if he got his girl pregnant; he said he would marry her.

As fate would have it, Lillian Powell was due back in Liverpool for a visit from Canada. But Cynthia couldn't bring herself to tell her mother she was pregnant until the very last day of her trip, when she confessed it in an emotional scene at her brother's house in Wirral. Lillian Powell was disappointed but eventually understanding when Cynthia told her John was willing to marry her. However, Mrs. Powell refused to postpone her return to Canada to attend the wedding and set sail two days before the event was scheduled. Cynthia saw her mother off at the pier with eyes so puffy from crying she couldn't even see to whom she was waving.

John absolutely dreaded breaking the news to Aunt Mimi. He saved it for the night before the wedding. He went to Mendips alone and told her he was getting married because Cynthia was pregnant. Mimi groaned as if she were mortally wounded. "You're too young!" Mimi cried. He was nearly twenty-two. Mimi couldn't have been more cantankerous. She refused to give them her blessing or come to the wedding. When John told Brian of his predicament, Brian knew of no other way than to respond gallantly and graciously, although he was temporarily pleased that John's Aunt Mimi had stopped speaking to them.

On a rainy and gray August twenty-fourth, Cynthia Powell

and John Winston Lennon were married by a magistrate in a short civil ceremony, much of which could not be heard because of the rat-tat-tat of a jackhammer digging up the pavement outside the window of the magistrate's office. Cynthia wore her best clothing, a purple and black two-piece checkered suit with a frilly shirt that Astrid had sent her from Hamburg as a hand-me-down. Cynthia's brother Tony gave the bride away, and her sister-in-law, Margery, was her bridesmaid. Paul and George also attended, stuffed into constraining suits with white shirts and ties, looking on sad-eyed and somber. In a sweet irony, Brian was John's best man.

After the ceremony the wedding party dashed through the streets in the pouring rain to a local lunchtime joint called Reece's Cafe. Brian had chosen this spot for the wedding meal because he thought no one would recognize them there. There were no seats, and the wedding party had to wait on line twenty minutes for a table. Soup and chicken were served, and Brian toasted the young marrieds with a glass of water. He also paid the check, noting to himself that the wedding reception had only cost him fifteen shillings per person. As a final gesture of largesse, he gave Cynthia and John the permanent use of his "secret" flat on Faulkner Street. With John married, what use was it to him now anyway?

There was only one condition: Brian felt strongly that John's marriage and impending fatherhood would have a disastrous effect on the Beatles image and ruin their chances for success. A pregnant wife would cause a scandal with female fans. How would it look for Cynthia to be seen waiting for him backstage with her big belly or walking around with him in the street? If Cynthia was to be John's wife, she was to be a secret wife. She was to be totally anonymous. The marriage was never to be talked about, much less admitted to. Cynthia was baffled and more than a little hurt by this request, but she didn't know or understand much about rock groups or image or fancy managers. She knew only that she loved John and was having his child, so she agreed to the terms. She was put in the house on Faulkner Street and hidden away. She waited there, patiently, for her husband to come home.

It turned out that she didn't see John very much during her pregnancy anyway. The group was by now always out on tour or camped in cheap London hotels. Occasionally, John would show up at Faulkner Street to pick up his clean shirts and drop off the dirty ones. On one of these rare visits, Cynthia convinced John that it was time for a truce between him and Mimi and that it would be nice for her to have Mimi's support during her pregnancy. One afternoon they arrived at Mendips unannounced and rang the bell. When Mimi opened the door and found them standing there, a big smile cracked her dour face, and she threw her arms around John and invited them in. That night she cooked them a big meal, and Mimi was so happy to have John back in the fold that she asked Cynthia to move back into Mendips for a second time, so that she could help care for her until the baby was born. Once again, Cynthia moved back into Mimi's domain, but still keeping to Brian's dictum, she tried to pretend she was not John's wife at all but an unmarried pregnant student just boarding in.

Chapter Four

*What's a scruff like me doing
with all this lot?*

—*Ringo Starr*

1.

THE SACKING of Pete Best caused a local storm that included protests by loyal fans who slept on the doorstep of Pete's mother's house and girls who picketed NEMS and the Cavern Club with placards saying, "Pete is Best" and "Pete Forever." There were even pushing and shoving matches at the Cavern when the Beatles turned up, and Brian helped dramatize the event by insisting the owner of the Cavern Club provide a bodyguard to protect him from irate fans. But the worst wrath of all came from Mona Best herself, who attributed Pete's firing to the jealousy of the three other members of the group. She was justifiably angry at the way Pete was fired, particularly in light of the contract George Martin had offered them. Brian's most pressing problem, however, wasn't Pete Best, but that the group was in desperate need of a replacement drummer. George Martin had already scheduled a recording session for them in early September, only weeks away. Naturally, they would have preferred to hire the best drummer possible, but any drummer would do as long as he was good enough to record.

At the age of twenty-two, when he was asked to join the Beatles, Ringo Starr was an unlikely candidate to sign on as a character player in the greatest bit part ever written. He was short, skinny, and unassuming, with a homely countenance and sad blue eyes. Up until this point, his life had been a gothic horror story of misfortune.

He was born Richard Starkey, Jr., on July 7, 1940, the son of bakery workers Elsie Gleave and Richard Starkey, Sr. He was brought up in the great, gray section of Liverpool called the Dingle, a dockside slum of tenements known as the Cast Iron Shore. Richard Sr. deserted when Ritchie was only three years old, and the child was to see his father only three more times in the rest of his life. Although Starkey Sr. sent thirty shillings a week support payments in the beginning, after a few months the money stopped coming, and Elsie was unable to pay the rent on the flat in which they lived. She took a job as a barmaid to support herself, and the little boy was left alone most of the evening.

At the age of six, only a year after starting St. Silas's Junior School, Ritchie developed what was thought to be a simple stomachache. But when the pain lasted through the night he was finally taken to the hospital in an ambulance. It was too late; his appendix had already burst and peritonitis had set in. He remained in a coma for ten weeks, and with various complications, including falling out of his hospital bed on his seventh birthday, he spent a solid year in the hospital. By the time he was back in school he was so far behind the other children he couldn't read or write, and what little he learned from that point on was taught to him by a sympathetic neighborhood girl.

The year in the hospital had left him sickly and weak but miraculously did not destroy his spirit. He was a happy, satisfied child, and when his mother met and married a Liverpool corporation house painter named Harry Greaves, Ritchie took the man to his heart. Greaves was the closest thing he ever knew to a father. For a time life seemed placid enough. Then, at the age of thirteen, a cold developed into pleurisy and weakened his lungs. One rainy morning a big black car came to fetch him in the Dingle and took him away to the Heswall Children's Hospital, a huge, gray children's sanitorium in the Wirral. There he was put to bed, where he remained for the next two years. He never went back to school. When he got out of the hospital, still only partially recovered, he was fifteen years old and fit only for a job as a messenger. When he finally secured a job at British Railways, he was fired after six weeks for failing the medical exam. Out of pity, Harry Greaves found him a job as a joiner's apprentice at a local engineering firm.

It was 1956 and the beginning of the skiffle craze. Ritchie

had played the drums in a hospital ward band, and skiffle was a logical next step for him. Like so many other youngsters in Liverpool, he formed a group with a friend, another apprentice joiner named Eddie Clayton, and they hit the same neighborhood circuit as the Quarrymen. Skiffle died out, but Ritchie's percussion only got better. By 1959 he was drumming professionally, now with the biggest of all the Liverpool groups, Rory Storm and the Hurricanes. It was during Rory Storm's popularity that Ritchie became "Ringo," because he wore so many rings on his fingers, and "Starr" instead of Starkey, so that his drum solo could be announced as "Starr Time."

The Beatles knew Ringo well, not only from the Liverpool circuit but from Hamburg, where they had spent months observing him with Rory Storm. He was fun-loving and uncomplicated and got along well with everyone in the group—much better than Pete Best had. In recent months Rory Storm's popularity had been on the wane, and the Hurricanes were stuck playing a grueling summer booking at Butlin's Holiday Camp. It was at Butlin's that George Harrison finally reached him by phone to tell him that he was wanted to fill the open drumming spot with the Beatles. He would be on salary at first, £25 a week, during a probationary period. Then if things worked out he would be made a full-fledged member. He immediately cut his hair like one of them.

2.

*I*T WAS QUITE a surprise to George Martin when on September 12, 1962, the Beatles arrived at the studio with Ringo Starr. Not only had Brian not told him that Pete Best had been fired, but Martin had already hired his own drummer for the recording, a respected session drummer named Andy White. Martin asked to audition Ringo and, after hearing him play, decided to go right ahead and use Andy White on the drums, much to Ringo's mortification. Ringo was handed a tambourine and told when to use it. Later in the session, because George Martin thought he looked so miserable, he allowed Ringo to record on a few of the drum tracks.* Only two songs were recorded that first day, in any event. Between the time of their audition and the recording session, George Martin had relented and decided to allow them to record two of their own songs, both, as it turned out, Paul McCartney compositions. The side chosen for the A side was called "Love Me Do," the one with the banal lyrics that Paul had written when he was sixteen. It was greatly enhanced by a catchy harmonica riff played by John on the harmonica he had shoplifted in Arnhem. The B side was another simple love song called "P.S. I Love You," with lyrics only slightly more sophisticated but which George Martin arranged to feature what was to become the Beatles' trademark harmonies.

Again, the Beatles were very lucky; their alchemy with George Martin synthesized real gold. Although Martin's role in the production of their records changed over the years, he was always their primary conduit, the intermediary who transposed their inarticulate ideas into music. None of the Beatles could read or write music, although Paul was later to teach himself. They had no knowledge or command of any instruments except those they already played, and they knew nothing whatsoever about how records were made or the capabilities of the recording studio; albeit, the recording studio was prehistoric in terms of the capabilities available today. The Beatles first songs were recorded on four-track recorders in monaural, compared with the sixteen- and thirty-two-track overdubbings of later years. In any event, Martin was to become the interpretive vessel through which they were presented to the world.

When "Love Me Do" was released on October 4, 1962, Brian expected the record company to offer publicity and support. He got none at all. When George Martin first announced the impending release of a record by the Beatles at a meeting of EMI executives, the other executives laughed, thinking it was a joke perpetrated by Spike Milligan whom Martin also produced. Besides, at the moment in England only American acts like Bobby Vee and Del Shannon were making it. In America the craze called the Twist was sweeping the nation, and that's what was expected

---

* Ringo says that Andy White is on the single but that he can hear himself on the album cut.

to be big in England. It was generally agreed in the music business that guitar groups were finished and "Love Me Do" was released and forgotten.

Putting a record out on the market without any support is akin to not feeding a newborn child. Brian organized a fierce assault to nourish his baby. He unblinkingly ordered 10,000 copies of "Love Me Do" for NEMS, a magic number he thought would automatically land it a place on the British charts. Then he mustered his forces and started a letter-writing campaign to Radio Luxembourg and the BBC. All of the Beatles relatives and their friends were enlisted to write letters requesting the Beatles' new song. NEMS employees wrote, as did their families. After every personal appearance the Beatles' fans were urged to write or phone radio stations and demand "Love Me Do" to be played. Queenie enlisted herself to walk all over Liverpool, from store to store, asking if they had "Love Me Do" by the Beatles. When she and Harry went off to Majorca on vacation, she wrote letters to the radio stations saying she was a housewife on holiday who wanted to hear the song when she returned home. In the interim Brian began to organize and promote his own concerts, all of which headlined the Beatles. NEMS quickly became one of the busiest concert promoters in the North. One day, when a friend ran into Paul McCartney on the street in Liverpool, Paul confessed that he hadn't had anything to eat all day. "Somebody," Paul joked, "had to pay for those ten thousand records Brian bought."

After hundreds of requests, Radio Luxembourg played it. The BBC followed with one or two playings and then, like a tiny spark that at a single moment kindles into flames, "Love Me Do" appeared at forty-nine on the *New Record Mirror* charts. When it climbed to number twenty-one on the *Melody Maker* charts, the entire northern city of Liverpool was talking about the Beatles. By mid-December, "Love Me Do" had managed to battle its way up to number seventeen on the hit parade. They were dazzled. "Could anything be more important than this?" Brian asked proudly.

That February George Martin rushed the Beatles back into the EMI studios to record a follow-up song, this one called "Please Please Me," another upbeat love song that John had written years before, sitting on the pink eyelette of Aunt Mimi's bed. George Martin was so delighted with the recording session that when it was done he announced over the intercom from the control booth, "Gentlemen, you have just recorded your first number one." In the meantime, Brian kept them working the road, this time opening the bill for Helen Shapiro, the teenage singing star now riding the downward crest of her popularity. It was a second-rate tour, but it took them up the backbone of England, introducing them to the hinterlands in an almost methodical fashion. They spent the rest of the icy winter piled in the back of Neil Aspinall's van, the snowy towns and cities melting into a white blur: Wakefield, Carlisle, Peterborough, Mansfield, Coventry, Taunton, Gloucester, Romford, Exeter, Lewisham, Croydon, and Sheffield. Each week Brian called them on the road to tell them the progress of "Please Please Me" on the record charts. Slowly, as they worked their way around the country, the song began to gnaw its way up the charts like a mole burrowing up from under a tremendous weight. It appeared in *Melody Maker* first at an impressive number forty-seven, then the next week at thirty-nine, and then made a breathtaking jump to twenty-one. Its fourth week it was number nine, and, finally, on March 2, 1963, the Beatles had their first number-one hit.

Now a recording pattern began to develop. The week that "Please Please Me" hit number one the Beatles rushed back into the studios at Abbey Road and in one fifty-three-hour recording session laid down the contents of an entire album, fourteen songs' worth entitled *Please Please Me*, to cash in on the success of the single. The album was in the record stores within six weeks, as was another new single, "From Me to You." A likable, send-my-love-in-a-letter, upbeat love song, they had written it on a bus on the Helen Shapiro tour, traveling between York and Shrewsbury. Walking home late at night, sitting on the backstairs, or locked away in the loo for some privacy, they seemed to be able to turn out these hit songs effortlessly, without even touching the backlog of dozens of songs they had written over the years. Within two weeks of its release, "From Me to You" was number one on the charts. It would stay there, too, selling over 500,000 copies before it was replaced by yet another Beatles song, their fourth and watershed single.

* * *

3.

"*COULD ANYTHING* be more important than this?" Brian was heard to ask time and time again, knowing that now there always seemed to be something more important, some feat to top the previous dizzying success his boys had achieved. Brian walked around NEMS beaming like a child proud of blowing the perfect soap bubble. He turned to Queenie, to Harry, to his brother Clive, to me (Peter Brown), even to Rex Makin, and basked in the satisfaction of his success. Suddenly, we were all treating him just a little differently, even Queenie. Brian was no longer just a charming eccentric, he was a genius, and he was indulged even more.

It seemed to Brian that once he had secured a recording contract for the Beatles it wasn't very hard at all to turn them into chart-topping stars. He decided that if he could do it with one group, why not another, and another? It never crossed his mind at the start that the Beatles were completely unique or that the chemistry that existed between him and the group could not be duplicated. He figured, Svengali to one, Svengali to all, and set out to sign an enormous catalog of music acts. He asked me to completely take over the day-to-day affairs of the Whitechapel and Great Charlotte Street stores, and he turned to band management full-time, including promoting his own concerts. NEMS Enterprises was now incorporated as a talent management and booking company.

Brian's next "discovery" was announced in early 1963. It was a boyishly cute, one-time delivery boy named Gerry Marsden who had been knocking around Liverpool since 1958 in a group called the Pacemakers. Brian ordered for Gerry and his band members distinctive handmade suits from the same tailor who made the Beatles' clothes, observed Gerry's performances, and sent him typed memos about his stage deportment. He arranged a contract for him with EMI's prestigious Columbia Label, much to the chagrin of the Beatles, who were stuck on Parlophone. Gerry and the Pacemakers' first record was a song that had earlier been recommended for the Beatles to record called "How Do You Do It?" George Martin produced, and the record was released in March. Within a month it was number one on the charts, where it remained until the end of April when it was replaced with a new Beatle tune called "From Me to You."

By now we were all astonished. Brian *had* done it a second time and had made it look easy at that. We hadn't had a chance to catch our breath when Brian announced he was signing a *third* group, Billy Kramer and the Coasters. Brian had a crush on the lead singer, whose real name was Billy Ashton, and bought the band's contract from a small-time Liverpool manager. He changed the name of the group to Billy J. Kramer and the Dakotas, ordered them new suits, sent memos on showmanship, and supplied them with a Lennon-McCartney composition, one of the many extras they seemed to have floating around, called "Do You Want to Know a Secret?" It was a line John remembered that Jiminy Cricket asks Pinocchio. Less than a month after its release on the Parlophone label, Billy J. Kramer and the Dakota's "Do You Want to Know a Secret?" was number two on the charts, just behind the Beatles.

Then came the Big Three, a Cavern group who played at the Star Club with the Beatles, then the Four Jays, whose name Brian changed to the Fourmost. Then a local, freckle-faced lad named Tommy Quigly, who was rechristened Tommy Quickly. They were all given suits and songs and recording contracts. There was even a female star under Brian's management, an ex-clerk-typist named Cilla White. Cilla was what they called a "Cavern screamer," a girl with a zesty, full voice. However there was some quality about the warm, funny, round-faced girl that sparked Brian's interest. He changed her name to Cilla Black, because it was more "her," got her a new haircut of short pixie bangs, redid her makeup, and restyled her clothes. Most importantly, he gave her a Lennon-McCartney tune, one Paul had written while walking home late at night across the Allerton golf course called "Love of the Love," which instantly placed her on the record charts. Billy J. Kramer scored again with another Lennon-McCartney tune called "Bad to Me," followed by Gerry Marsden's number-one smash "I Like It." Then Billy J. Kramer came through yet again with "From a Window," followed by Cilla Black with "It's for You."

The music business was all abuzz about this thing called the "Mersey sound," for want of a better description for Brian's and the Beatles' self-generated monopolizing of the charts. That spring and summer Liverpool became the focus of a massive talent hunt. Every record company that had rejected the Beatles now sent A&R men to Liverpool. These talent scouts descended on the clubs and dance halls like hungry wolves, signing up every band with a scouse accent. Contracts went to the Searchers, Faron and the Flamingoes, Earl Preston and the TT's, the Merseybeats, the Undertakers, and the Chants. Even Rory Storm and the Hurricanes, famous now for their ex-drummer Ringo Starr, were given a recording contract with an obscure label. Some of these groups recorded singles, others never made it any further than signing a contract. One or two of them had hits because of the airplay afforded them because they were Liverpool groups, but most of them eventually returned to Liverpool on that long train ride home from London, wondering what made Brian Epstein and the Beatles so different.

For Brian, success had fulfilled many cravings save one; Brian was still in love with John Lennon. He was the light of Brian's life and in some small way the impetus for almost everything Brian did for the Beatles. As far as Cynthia was concerned, Brian hadn't seen her in months, nor had anyone else. She was in her ninth month of pregnancy by then and safely tucked out of the way. Anyway, between touring and London recording sessions John had hardly been in Liverpool. In May they were signed up to do yet another tour, and in between Brian felt that the Beatles needed a little vacation. Paul, George, and Ringo went off to Tenerife in the Canary Islands for some sun.

Brian had other ideas for John.

4.

*C*YNTHIA LIVED in solitude in a room at Aunt Mimi's house and watched her husband's success with a mixture of awe and silent pride—awe because nobody expected his success to be *this* big, and silent pride because she was unable to tell anyone she even knew John Lennon, let alone that she was married to him. He was gone so much it hardly seemed to matter, and although everyone said the money must be pouring in, she never saw any of it.

Her husband had been on the road for weeks when Cynthia went into labor one Saturday in April while shopping on Penny Lane. Late that night, dressed in her nightie and slippers, curlers still in her hair, she boarded an ambulance in front of Mendips and went to Sefton General Hospital. She spent two days alone in a long and difficult labor. A son was born Monday morning, April 8. He was named Julian, after his grandmother who had been pronounced dead in the same hospital five years before. Cynthia held the little boy in her arms and marveled at how much he looked like his daddy. John called her at the hospital that night, but it was a full week until he was able to come and visit.

At Sefton General Hospital it was not known that Cynthia was John Lennon's wife. Brian saw to it that a private room had been secured for Cynthia "Powell" at a cost of twenty-seven shillings a day, so that if John did arrive at the hospital to see the child, there would be a modicum of privacy. However, the only private room had a large glass window, with one side adjoining a public ward. John eventually appeared on the last day of Cynthia's confinement, dressed in a serious attempt at a disguise in a hat, fake moustache, and dark glasses. Cynthia laughed when she saw him. John was ecstatic at the sight of Julian, and his hands trembled as he took the tiny boy in his arms. "He's bloody marvelous, isn't he Cyn?" he said.

Out in the hallway Cynthia heard one of the other new mother's say, "It's 'im! It's one of them, the Beatles!" Soon there were a dozen people staring in the window, patients and nurses alike, ruining the moment for both of them. John gave Julian back to her and said he better go before he attracted too much attention and made them suspicious about his connection to the baby, although he had a few things to tell her. First, he wanted to make Brian the baby's godfather. Second, he was leaving on holiday as soon as this tour was over. He was going away with Brian— just the two of them. The other Beatles were going to the Canary Islands. This meant John wouldn't see Cynthia for several weeks, long after she had returned home from the hospital.

Cynthia lay back in the hospital bed, her head spinning. How could John go off and leave her and Julian like that, she demanded, and with Brian Epstein no less? John flared up at her. "Being selfish again, aren't you?" he said. "I've been workin' my bloody ass off on one-night stands for months now. Those people starin' from the other side of the glass are bloody everywhere, hauntin' me. I *deserve* a vacation. And anyway, Brian wants me to go, and I owe it to the poor guy. Who else does he have to go away with?"

Brian and John went to Barcelona at the end of April 1963. It was a city that Brian had explored on his 1959 solo trip to Spain. He had since become a great fan of the bullfights and considered himself something of an aficionado. He took great pleasure in introducing John to the pageantry and excitement. They spent the days shopping and taking side trips. At night they toured the nightclubs. Later in the week they rented a car and drove down the coast to the glistening white town of Sitges on the Costa Brava. Each night they would sit in the candlelit cafés and watch the couples stroll by in the moonlight. Over many bottles of wine they talked candidly about Brian's personal life. It was a great relief for Brian to finally be able to talk honestly with John. He told John that for a man who valued honesty as dearly as he did, it was a terrible burden for him to live his life a lie.

"If you had a choice, Eppy," John said, "if you could press a button and be hetero, would you do it?"

Brian thought for a moment. "Strangely, no," he said.

A little later a peculiar game developed. John would point out some passing man to Brian, and Brian would explain to him what it was about the fellow that he found attractive or unattractive. "I was rather enjoying the experience," John said, "thinking like a writer all the time: *I am experiencing this.*" And still later, back in their hotel suite, drunk and sleepy from the sweet Spanish wine, Brian and John undressed in silence. "It's okay, Eppy," John said, and lay down on his bed. Brian would have liked to have hugged him, but he was afraid. Instead, John lay there, tentative and still, and Brian fulfilled the fantasies he was so sure would bring him contentment, only to awake the next morning as hollow as before.

*　*　*

5.

*I*T WASN'T LONG before word spread among the Beatles' families and close friends that John and Brian had gone off to Spain together. The trip became the number one topic of conversation and conjecture around NEMS and the Cavern Club. The most puzzling question was, "What could have gotten into John to agree to such a trip? He knew that Brian had been trying to 'set him up' for years." The person most confused by this question was Cynthia Lennon. John's explanation, that he owed Brian the pleasure of his company, didn't make much sense to her in retrospect. What was even more peculiar, she realized, was that she and John's infant son lived in total secrecy at his Aunt Mimi's house, unable to admit to anyone that she was married. Some acquaintances took it for granted that Julian was an illegitimate child, and Cynthia never corrected them. John's newfound fame made the situation even more delicate. Mendips had recently become an object of fascination for the growing legion of local fans. Going to visit the house where Beatle John was raised became a pilgrimage, and more often than not there were two or three girls waiting at the gate with a camera. Mimi found that if she left the back door to the house open, her teacups would be stolen as souvenirs.

The fans with their cameras kept Cynthia a virtual prisoner in the house. Her only break was a daily trip to the greengrocer. She would slip out the rear door and wheel Julian surreptitiously through the streets in his grand Silver Cross carriage, a gift from Brian. Occasionally, a girl waiting at the front gates of Mendips would spot her and ask if she knew John Lennon. Cynthia would say, "Who? John who?" and keep walking. Once, startled that a girl asked her point blank if she was married to John, Cynthia snapped, "My name's McKenzie!" and rushed away.

In a sense, John never really returned to Mendips after Julian was born, except for a few overnight visits. John was usually on the road or staying in a London hotel, and for the next six months it seemed as if they weren't really married at all. Cynthia didn't even have Julian christened for six months, waiting for John to be home to attend the ceremony, and then went ahead and did it without him anyway. On the rare occasions he came to Mendips, he would play with Julian for only a few minutes before he got disgusted with his crying, and if Cynthia had to change a diaper, John would bolt for the door, and that would be the end of the visit.

To make matters worse, the jealousy and thinly veiled dislike between Cynthia and Aunt Mimi was exacerbated by the baby. Now it wasn't only John they quarreled over, it was the raising of Julian. In some ways Mimi saw Julian as belonging as much to *her* as to Cynthia, and having reared John, she had a lot of opinions about his son. The baby turned out to be what Cynthia called "a crier." In fact, he howled ferociously every hour of the day and night, and there didn't seem to be anything Cynthia could do to make him stop. Of course, Mimi blamed every second of the child's unhappiness on Cynthia's mishandling of him. Sometimes Cynthia would get so exasperated with the howling she would just push the baby out to the farthest corner of the walled-in garden and let him cry his heart out—much to Mimi's grating dismay. Yet when it came to her baby, Cynthia was a formidable opponent, and in her own quiet way she began to defy Aunt Mimi at every turn.

To add a lighted match to this combustible brew, Lillian Powell, encouraged by Cynthia's letters and clippings describing John's success, decided to return to Liverpool and move into Mendips with her. It was decided that Lillian Powell's arrival was the perfect excuse for Cynthia and the baby to move out of Aunt Mimi's without offending Mimi or John. Unfortunately, there was nowhere for Cynthia and her mother to move; the family house in Hoylake was still rented to tenants for several more months. Ideally, they would have stayed on at Mendips, but the three women and one crying child wouldn't have lasted a fortnight. Very quickly Cynthia and her mother found themselves living in a seedy bedsitter for which they paid £5 a week. It never dawned on her that John was earning hundreds of thousands of pounds at the time and could have afforded better accommodations for his wife and child. Cynthia never thought of asking him for more money—and he never offered any.

One of the few times Cynthia saw John that spring was at Paul McCartney's twenty-first birthday party. Paul's family house on Forthlin Road also had recently been put under surveillance by Beatles fans, and in order to avoid them the party was being held at Paul's Auntie Gin's house across the Mersey in Birkenhead. More than just a birthday celebration for Paul, the afternoon garden affair had turned into a wild celebration of the Beatles' success. It was a spirited, happy occasion, where old friends were reunited, and all the NEMS groups entertained for each other. Cynthia was ecstatic at being brought as John's date and was having the best time she had in months. As the hours passed, the guests got drunker and the celebrating more frenzied and rowdy. Suddenly, at the other end of the garden from where Cynthia was sitting, there was a great commotion. John, in a mad rage and obviously very drunk, was pummeling Bob Wooler, the Cavern disc jockey who had been so instrumental in the Beatles' earlier bookings. It took three men to pull John off, but not before he managed to break three of Wooler's ribs and send him to the hospital.

This fistfight brought the party to a sudden halt. Cynthia, trembling and on the brink of tears, approached John timidly; if he was in a bad mood, she knew he would consider her a handy punching bag.

"I broke his bloody ribs for him," John told her, wiping his lips with the back of his hand.

"What did he do?" Cynthia asked.

"He called me bloody queer," John said. "He said that Brian and I were queer."

Bob Wooler sued John Lennon for damages, and the incident threatened to mushroom into an impending scandal. Brian was very anxious not to publicize his vacation to Spain with John or John's fistfight at Paul's party. He had Rex Makin settle the suit quietly out of court for £200, quite a generous sum of money in Liverpool in those days. It was not the end of the conjecture about Brian and John, either, and Cynthia, in her £5 bedsitter, sat and wondered herself.

* * *

6.

*W*HILE JOHN LENNON'S marriage had no romance, Paul McCartney's life was filled with it. Since
Paul had become famous in Liverpool, he had been having a
romance a night. Generally acclaimed to be the "cutest" member
of the group, he also was the most available. His already healthy
ego exploded as though it had been detonated by twenty tons
of TNT. Of the four Beatles it was Paul who never tired of having
his photo taken, and Paul who volunteered to do interviews. It
was Paul who wooed the girls with sly smiles and encouraged
them to run after his car, shouting at them from the rear window,
"Run, girls, run!" It was Paul who devised various disguises of
hats and fake moustaches and took them on tour with him so
he could wander about the crowds of girls waiting outside the
stage entrances and eavesdrop on what they were saying about
him.

After having dumped his childhood sweetheart, Dot Rohne,
Paul took up with Rory Storm's sister, Iris Caldwell, for a short
time. Like Rory, she was tall and blond and effervescent, but
the relationship soon palled with the availability of so many dollie-
birds after Paul's tail.* Paul indulged himself like a starving man
at a feast yet somehow never managed to fulfill his appetite. Such
were the spoils of fame. Yet for Paul, no matter how many girls
he duly dated and bedded, there seemed to be something missing
in each of them. They were not "nice" girls, not the kind of
girl he could take home to his mother, Mary, if she were alive.
For although every northern man likes his whores, in the center
of his predominantly Irish-Catholic, middle-class heart, what he
wants most is a nice girl to settle down with and raise his children.

On May 9, 1963, shortly after Paul returned from his vacation
in the Canary Islands with George and Ringo, he met such a
girl. She was only seventeen years old, as pure as she was beautiful.
Her name was Jane Asher, and she was a titian-haired, green-
eyed gem. Already an accomplished actress, she had made her
film debut at the age of five as a deaf mute in *Mandy*. After numer-

---

* Iris Caldwell later married British pop star Alvin Stardust.

ous stage roles in the West End, she became the youngest actress to play the part of Wendy in *Peter Pan* on the English stage and subsequently starred as the ingenue in the Walt Disney film production of *The Prince and the Pauper*. At the time Paul met her at a concert of pop groups at the Royal Albert Hall, she was a frequent panalist on the TV show "Juke Box Jury," and Paul had seen her several times. She was at the concert as the celebrity teen reporter for the BBC radio program "Radio Times," and they were introduced in between acts when the Beatles were asked to pose for a photograph with her.

Later, after the show, she joined the group at the Royal Court Hotel on Sloane Square for sandwiches and coffee. After, they went to the flat of a *New Musical Express* journalist off the Kings Road. Although they all fancied Jane more or less, and George Harrison monopolized most of the conversation, it was moon-eyed Paul at whom she smiled the most. When it became obvious later in the evening that Paul was swooning over her, the others left on the pretext of getting dinner to give Paul some time alone with her. Much to their surprise, when they returned to the flat two hours later, Paul and Jane were still sitting in the same place, engrossed in a conversation about, of all things, favorite foods. Paul had never made a move toward her.

It would be accurate to say that Paul fell in love with the whole idea of Jane Asher as much as the girl herself. She was a girl of breeding and innocence, a girl heretofore unavailable to a Liverpool lad the likes of Paul McCartney. She was, first of all, a bona fide virgin. Born on April 5, 1946, she still lived with her family in a grand, five-story town house on Wimpole Street in London. Her father was Dr. Richard Asher, a respected psychiatrist and consultant in blood and mental diseases at the Central Middlesex Hospital. Her mother, Margaret, was a professional musician and a one-time professor of music at the London School of Music, where, coincidentally, she taught oboe to George Martin. Jane's younger brother Peter was a Cambridge graduate and a promising musician and songwriter. He would shortly form a singing duo, Peter and Gordon, and with a McCartney composition called "World Without Love," he would hit the top of the record charts alongside the Beatles. Jane also had a younger sister, Clare, as pretty as she.

From the start, there was no doubt in Paul's mind that this

was the perfect tableau into which he wanted to step. The Ashers as a clan were unlike any family he had ever met in Liverpool. Paul was invited to join in frank, often exciting family discussions around the dinner table, and it wasn't uncommon to spend an evening at home with them just talking. Dr. Asher, Paul found to his delight, was a brilliant storyteller, and Paul looked forward to spending time with him. A bit intimidated by this group at first, Paul started to read for knowledge for the first time in his life. Jane supplied direction with books and tickets to the ballet and theater. He soaked it up like a sponge, gratefully, happily, settling into this new life with Jane. "I don't want to sound like Jonathan Miller going on," he told the *Evening Standard* in an interview, "but I'm trying to crowd everything in. I vaguely mind anyone knowing anything I don't know. I'm trying to cram everything in, all the things that I've missed. People are saying things and painting things and writing things and composing things that are great, and I want to know . . ." He took to quoting poetry in conversation, often incorrectly, but no one bothered to correct him. They could see he was a young man in love.

Eventually Paul and Jane's romance was discovered by the press when a photographer took a photo of them as they left the Prince of Wales Theater after seeing Neil Simon's *Never Too Late*. The question that followed them around for the next five years was, "Will they get married?" It was asked almost everywhere they went. "Just say I smiled when you asked me that," Paul told a reporter enigmatically. Years later Paul himself couldn't quite believe that he had courted her for such a long time without bedding her, but he did. At the end of each evening he either went back to a hotel room or caught the last flight out of Heathrow for Liverpool. One night, when he missed his flight, Mrs. Asher graciously offered the guest room to Paul, just a flight of stairs away from where Jane slept. It was, after all, foolish of him to rent hotel rooms in London all the time. Paul moved in with his clothing and guitar and stayed for two years, with all the blessings the household offered.

Love also found Ringo Starr. Ringo was the most bewildered of all with the Beatles' sudden success. Although outgoing, he was shy and suspicious of strangers. He never considered himself especially attractive and now fast city women were throwing themselves at his feet. Although he loved women as well as the next northern man, he didn't feel comfortable on the nightly round of conquests, pulling a bird at a nightclub. Most of his free time was still spent in Liverpool, where he stayed at his mother's little house in the Dingle. For a long time, while he was in the Rory Storm group, he had gone out with a girl named Geraldine. He had even asked her to marry him and gave her an engagement ring, but she returned it after the engagement was broken off, and Elsie Greaves still has the ring to this day. While he was dating Geraldine he had noticed a small, chirpy girl named Maureen Cox, who went out with Rory Storm's guitarist Johnny "Guitar." But Maureen was somebody else's girl at the time, and he didn't even speak to her until three weeks after he joined the Beatles. She was an assistant hairdresser at a second-floor beauty salon near the Cotton Exchange called Ashley Du Pre's. He noticed her standing in a crowd of girls in front of the Cavern Club one lunchtime as he drove up in his new car, a used blue and cream Ford Zodiac, not unlike Brian Epstein's car. Maureen remembers the moment vividly and to this day remembers the car's license plate number, NWM 466. Ringo parked the car out front and on his way into the club he smiled shyly at her. He asked if she was coming to the show the next night, and Maureen said she was. She had big, dark, sad eyes, and she was barely sixteen years old. Ringo asked if she wanted to go out after the show, and Maureen said that would be difficult; the show didn't end until after eleven P.M. and she had a standing rule with her parents to be on the front doorstep of their house by ten minutes to midnight.

Therefore it was arranged that their first date be in the afternoon. Ringo made plans to pick her up at the beauty parlor when her shift was over. Maureen was so nervous that morning the other girls sent her out to do some shopping to keep her mind off the forthcoming date. Ringo arrived while she was gone and self-consciously took a seat in the reception area, while the ladies waiting to get their bouffants combed cooed and giggled over him. When Maureen returned to Ashley Du Pre's and began to climb the flight of steps up to the second floor, she immediately spotted Ringo's black, ankle-high boots through the glass door to the salon. "Oh my God," she whispered to herself as she went up the steps, "this is really going to happen . . ."

The first date went extremely well. The two discovered they were a perfect match for each other. He was simple and uneducated, she was a sweet, giggly thing with not much to say, as mousey as he was homely. She had been educated for the previous five years at a convent school, which she left to become a manicurist's assistant. She had been a fan of the Beatles even from her Rory Storm days, and just looking into Ringo's eyes gave her palpitations. That first date they kept busy; they went to the park, then to hear singer Frank Ifield, then to the cinema for a double feature, then to the Pink Parrot, a popular bar, for drinks, and finally to Allan Williams' Blue Angel club for a last dance. Exhausted from the full day of activity, Ringo returned Maureen to her parents' house at exactly ten minutes to midnight. She saw him exclusively after that, and at least to Maureen's knowledge he saw no other girl. The affair, she had to admit, had its drawbacks. Ringo was often out of town, and when he was in Liverpool the Beatles show didn't end until very late. For the first six months of their relationship they never spent more than an hour together at night.

The other girls in the Beatles' loyal coterie of fans at the Cavern saw Maureen as an interloper, but she was tenacious and cunning as far as her "Ritchie" was concerned. As for the relationship progressing past the dating stage into something more serious, Maureen didn't even entertain such notions. Marrying a Beatle was a Liverpool taboo. Part of their attraction was their availability. Still, she had hope; perhaps one day when she was seventeen or eighteen things would change. Once, when she heard a rumor that John Lennon was secretly married, she asked Ringo about it. "If he is," Ringo said, "we don't want to talk about it."

Chapter Five

1.

*D*ESPITE THE ENORMOUS recording success, despite the sold-out concerts and growing popularity with the public, the mainstream, "Fleet Street" London press continued to ignore the Beatles. What little press they received was on the entertainment pages about a band from the North country that had made good. Although they were drawing record-breaking, hysterical crowds in small cities all over the North, in London they had appeared only at a few minor pop concerts and teen TV music shows. While Brian was trying to bring them into the mainstream London bookings, with exposure that would be commensurate with their recording popularity, he always seemed to come up against a brick wall. In Brian's mind, at least, it was all part of a conspiracy by three brothers.

The brothers were Lew and Leslie Grade and Bernard Delfont. As Brian saw it, the Grades practically had a cartel on the English entertainment business that crisscrossed to form a web which entrapped him and his boys. Lew Grade, later to become Lord Grade, owned the huge Associated Television Corporation, Britain's largest independent producer of TV programs. Lew Grade also personally produced the United Kingdom's most popular TV variety show, "Sunday Night at the Palladium," on which an appearance was crucial for an act to gain national attention. Brother Leslie Grade headed the largest show business agency in the country, which represented personalities such as Laurence Olivier and also packaged films, stage shows, and TV programs. The third brother, Bernard, owned several prestigious theaters, was a major force behind the West End theater business, and by appointment to the Queen booked the most prestigious of all live shows, the Royal Command Performance. The fact that the three brothers had anglicized their name from Winogradsky and that Bernard had chosen a name as pretentious as "Delfont" was a topic of much discussion in Brian's office, where his Jewish heritage was both a matter of pride and a sore point. Something about the brothers' success irked Brian, and it irked him even more when they chose to ignore the Beatles.

The problem began when at the first sign of the Beatles' success, Leslie Grade's agency had approached Brian to sign the Beatles to the Grade agency for representation and booking. Since it was a large, powerful agency that could help the Beatles the most, this seemed like a reasonable move. But for these services the Grade Agency would receive 10 percent of the Beatles' very considerable income from live performances. Brian, who had been acting as both manager and booking agent for the boys, would then be expected to reduce his commission to only 15 percent. What's more, Brian was now busily promoting his own concerts all over the north of England, using lesser known NEMS-managed acts to open the bill for the Beatles. In this way he made money as manager of all the groups, as booking agent and as promoter. His income—much of it in cash—was enormous. With the Grades "muscling in," as Brian put it, all that would stop. Even though it might have been beneficial for the Beatles to make some sort of a deal with them, Brian ruled it out of the question—so out of the question that he didn't even tell the Beatles about it.

Yet by turning the Grades down it appeared that Brian had caused himself a major problem; the three brothers were blackballing him from mainstream entertainment. Whether or not this was a reality, it was very much the truth for Brian, and one that he perceived as a major stumbling block for the boys' progress. Still, he would not give in. He was confident that the boys would become so big on their own that the Grades would be forced into dropping their demands.

Brian finally had his way in September of 1963, when the Beatles had the number-one single, the number-one album, and the best-selling extended play record in the British Isles. Orders for

the single called "She Loves You" had been coming in since June, when they didn't even have a title, and by the time the lyrics were written, in a hotel room three nights before it was recorded, over half a million copies were already presold to record stores. In "She Loves You" George Martin had been able to incorporate in magic proportions all the ingredients of the three previous singles into one ineluctably attractive song. It had easy, "sad-glad" rhymes and lyrics sung in those distinctive harmonies, every chorus tagged with a sly, infectious musical hook, a simple "yeah, yeah, yeah" that became not only the Beatles' trademark but an international euphemism for rock music. "She Loves You" didn't climb the charts, it exploded with a fury into the number-one position, selling faster and harder than any single ever released, and became the largest-selling single in the history of Great Britain, not to be outsold until fifteen years later by, ironically but not surprisingly, a Paul McCartney tune called "Mull of Kintyre."*
At this point Lew Grade could do nothing in the face of the tens of thousands of requests to see them on "Sunday Night at the Palladium," and an invitation was extended for them to appear on October 13. Brian, not willing to let well enough alone, insisted the Beatles top the bill, and had his way, too.

An audience of fifteen million saw them that night, a staggering number at the time and the largest of their career so far. The day of the performance Argyle Street, where the Palladium was located, was filled with fans waiting for their arrival, while inside the theater a stack of presents piled up in their dressing room. It was only a matter of hours before the press and TV newsmen heard what was happening on Argyle Street and were sent to cover the event. The newspaper reports the next day varied from estimates of 500 fans to thousands waiting in the street, chasing after their limousine as it pulled up to the stage door. One photographer, Dezo Hoffman, who had been covering the Beatles for several weeks, claims that only eight girls were in the street in front of the Palladium. He says the photographs were cropped so they would look like more and that the press reports were a clever ruse instigated by Brian. Whatever actually happened that night, the Beatles were irrefutably front-page headlines the next

---

* Even more ironic, "Mull of Kintyre" was McCartney's only unmitigated flop record in America and one of the many reasons he left Capitol Records in the seventies.

day for the first of countless times. Now even the man-on-the-street, who didn't listen to rock and roll, was beginning to hear about something called, improbably, unforgettably, "the Beatles."

Three days later the Beatles made further headlines when Bernard Delfont announced, with Brian's and the Beatles' permission, that the Beatles would also be on the bill at the Royal Command Variety Performance the first week of November at which Princess Margaret and the Queen Mother would be in attendance. In the intervening weeks the elite of the Fleet Street press bore down on them as they continued to tour, and the population at large learned more about the peculiar phenomenon that followed the Beatles wherever they appeared; the audiences cheered, wept, screamed, and sometimes even tore their clothing in what sociologists explained as "the focus of a form of mass hysteria." The main story, however, was hair. Nobody could get over the Beatles haircut.

On November 5, the night of the Royal Command Performance, 500 policemen cordoned off the Prince of Wales Theater. It was uncertain who was the bigger draw or the more difficult to protect, the Beatles or the Royal Family. After a very boring show consisting of a trio of zither players, barnyard animal puppets, and Marlene Dietrich, the boys were announced to an uproar in the audience. John's ad lib, "Will the people in the cheaper seats clap your hands, the rest of you can just rattle your jewelry," brought the house down.* The following day the newspaper headlines were again unanimous about the Beatles. The *Daily Express* story, "Beatles Rock Royals," was not uncommon. The *Express* put a photograph of the Beatles on the front page five times that week, they were such a good story. But it was the *Daily Mirror* that summed it up best in a single headline, just one word, a word the whole world would soon hear: BEATLEMANIA!

* Earlier in the evening, discussing possible "ad libs" during the concert, John had threatened to tell the royal audience to "rattle their fucking jewelry."

* * *

2.

THE DAY AFTER the Royal Command Performance Brian carefully packed all the newspaper
headlines and press reports about his clients into his suitcase
and boarded a plane for New York. Across the Atlantic, America
beckoned to him like some glittering Shangri-la, a land of prosperity and glamour, a country he wanted desperately to claim for
the Beatles. Even though Prime Minister Harold Macmillan had
told the British, "You never had it so good," Great Britain seemed
dull in comparison to what was happening in the United States.
Unemployment was relatively low, salaries high, gas was cheap
and tail fins big and flashy. Most homes had TV, some of them
color. New York had become the center of jet-set society, leaving
Paris a haughty second. The leaders of the New Elegance, Jack
and Jackie Kennedy, were so much like royalty their kingdom
was referred to as Camelot. America also had California, with a
musical phenomenon that was totally endemic to its shores, "surf-
ing music," introduced by a new group called the Beach Boys.
It spoke of a way of life of sun and surf and souped-up cars
that no Englishman could possibly understand. In America there
was a smug, chauvinistic superiority, and it was quite clear that
nothing was either wanted or needed from Great Britain. Not
even the Beatles.

Brian Epstein was bent on proving otherwise, but all along
it had been an uphill fight. The EMI-owned record company in
America, Capitol Records, was routinely alerted at the first signs
of chart activity on "Love Me Do" but didn't show any interest
in releasing the song in the United States. When the Beatles second single, "Please Please Me" became number one, George Martin personally recommended the single to a Capitol Records executive in New York. Martin received a polite note in return saying,
"They won't do anything in this market." Now free to take the
single to another record company in the U.S., Brian subsequently
pitched "Please Please Me" all over the American market, but
nobody "heard" the Beatles happening in America. It was beach
music they wanted. Finally, Brian managed to sign the single to
a small record label in Chicago called Vee Jay, whose claim to

fame was that it had once been the label on which the Four Seasons recorded. True to the predictions of the bigger record companies, "Please Please Me" died on the vine with sales of only a few hundred copies. The next single, "She Loves You," an immediate number-one hit in England, was also turned down by all the major record companies and was signed to an even less well known label than Vee Jay, this one called Swan. "She Loves You" also vanished the moment it was released.

Thus the elegant Englishman with the clippings under his arm was determined to make a beachhead in America. The trip would be short but crucial. He would have to convince a major record company to take them on, and he would have to book the right venue to present them to the American public. The only glimpse of them had been on a few seconds' worth of footage on Jack Paar's NBC series, "Prime Time." Television was, naturally, the right way to present them to a country as vast as America. The Beatles appearance on "Sunday Night at the Palladium" had proved the power of television to Brian when record sales quadrupled the next day. In America, Brian set his sites on the "Ed Sullivan Show," the top-rated entertainment TV show in 1963.

Not surprisingly, Ed Sullivan was willing to negotiate for an appearance by the Beatles on his show. Sullivan was a keen-eyed showman and impresario. He knew the potential of giving the Beatles their first American exposure, even if as a curiosity. Sullivan remembered, first of all, their return to England from their Swedish concert the previous autumn. Sullivan—along with Prime Minister Edward Heath—was at Heathrow and had his trip interrupted by their tumultuous arrival. He was impressed that this "gimmick" was not only still around but had a string of number-one hits in their homeland. His London sources were full of Beatles' exploits, and the time seemed ripe to book them.

A meeting was arranged in Brian's hotel suite with Sullivan's son-in-law, Bob Precht, who produced the show. Precht explained diplomatically that Sullivan would be interested in signing them for one appearance but only as a sort of a novelty item. Brian was astonished; he intended for them to headline. Indeed, Brian would have it no other way. They wanted to appear on the Sullivan show because he was the best, but they were the best too, he explained. The deal that Brian and Precht finally struck was rather extraordinary. The Beatles would headline not one, but two shows on consecutive Sundays, February 9 and 16, 1964. For each show they would receive, in toto, $3,500. Even with Sullivan paying the airfares—which were arranged as a promotional consideration on the show—the $7,000 fee wouldn't cover expenses. Brian, in effect, had signed them to headline but had to float the trip to the tune of some $50,000.

Now, with a signed contract from Ed Sullivan in his pocket, Brian went to Capitol records. At a meeting with the director of eastern operations, Brown Meggs, Brian played their newest single, "I Want to Hold Your Hand," which, he said, had been produced specifically with the "American sound" in mind so that it would appeal to the U.S. market. Brian insisted that coupled with their appearance on the Ed Sullivan show, the new song could break as big in America as it had in England. But Meggs was not as positive, and reluctantly, he agreed to release "I Want to Hold Your Hand" on a limited basis in January of 1964, a month before their appearance on the Ed Sullivan show. Brian couldn't have been happier with the timing.

Brian returned home to England a satisfied man that mid-November of 1963. It was just a week before Lee Harvey Oswald would lay America wide open to his boys. For the first of many times, the American dream was shattered by an assassin's bullet. In a country that seemed so invulnerable to harm, everything was lost in a single moment. December and January in America would be months of grim mourning. The funeral dirges that played relentlessly on American radio stations faded into the soft yet still-sad Christmas carols of the season. By January the nation wanted desperately to hear something happy, to find a diversion, some distraction from the morbid tragedy that had intruded into our lives. America needed a tonic. Little would anyone have expected it to be a pop group.

* * *

3.

B *ACK IN LIVERPOOL* the money started pouring into NEMS with a ferocity that was at first stupefying. What was originally thought to be hundreds of thousands of pounds in grosses was turning out to be millions. *Millions!* The Beatles' families couldn't even understand what that meant at first, not in Woolton or the Dingle or the NEMS stores, which I (Peter Brown) was then managing for the family. It was estimated that the first year the Beatles would sell £6 million worth of albums in the United Kingdom, skyrocketing EMI's profits that year by 80 percent. Even with the Beatles' miniscule royalty rates, all of them would be rich men in a year, particularly John and Paul, who were making many times more than George and Ringo on their songwriting royalties.

Yet as the boys became paper millionaires, a new, equally extraordinary problem presented itself to them; they were in a 94 percent tax bracket. Quite simply, 94 percent of the Beatles' earnings were owed to the British Inland Revenue Service. The mathematics were disheartening; they took home only 6 percent of every pound, after which Brian took his 25 percent cut.

It became quite clear to Brian that if he and the boys were going to grab any money at all in what might be just a few fleeting moments of great prosperity, he had better grab it in cash, and cash meant touring. Thus Brian kept them out on the road in a series of one-night stands, often in grinding five-week stretches at a time, without a night off. Brian found that most promoters were so anxious to book the Beatles—a guaranteed sell-out show— that £1,000 in cash in a brown paper bag passed discreetly in the manager's office on the night of the performance was not too much to be expected. Brian was no stranger to this system of "brown paper bag" money. As early as the Beatles' last trip to Hamburg, Horst Fascher reportedly gave Brian 1,000 marks under the table for the Beatles to appear at his club. This brown paper bag money was later distributed to the Beatles after Brian had removed his customary 25 percent cut, a fact revealed here for the first time. In later years, when they were on world tours, Brian would often deposit the cash in local banks and return for it on subsequent trips. In the beginning, Brian obliquely explained to the boys where the money was coming from. Characteristically, they forgot about it. It was never mentioned by any of them again in all the years to come, although the practice was continued up until they stopped touring for good.

Brian seemed to figure that a few hundred thousand pounds under the table was justified because of the millions they were already paying the government through legitimate means, particularly when overseas money started coming into Great Britain. The accounting firm for NEMS, Bryce-Hamner, knew nothing about the brown paper bag money. They were a conservative, rather uninventive company that had a few show business clients, but none of the financial magnitude of the Beatles. Yet Brian decided to turn the Beatles' finances over to them, under the personal consultation of one of the firm's senior partners in their London office, a Dr. Walter Strach. Strach was a tall, imposingly grave man in a black waistcoat, who was given the urgent task of finding a legitimate tax shelter for the income. In the meanwhile, the best advice was to spend some of it. They were certainly entitled.

All this time they still lived in Liverpool at their family homes, and it was generally decided that it was high time the whole organization was moved to London where the action was. Brian moved first to smooth the way for the Beatles. Brian had already been renting a two-room office in London, and now he took a lease on a large suite of rooms in a building on Argyle Street, just next to the Palladium Theater. He made a very cheery announcement about this at NEMS and then individually invited all his key staff to move to London with him. Many did, including the telephone operator, Laurie McCaffrey, and secretary, Barbara Bennett. I remained in Liverpool to run the family NEMS stores.

In London Brian found himself a spacious, two-bedroom penthouse in Wadham House, a modern building on Williams Mews in Knightsbridge. Brian decorated the flat himself with dramatic wall-to-wall white carpet and heavy black leather furniture. The west wall of the flat was a series of floor-to-ceiling sliding glass panels leading to a small terrace that overlooked the tiled rooftops of the town houses across the way. A black manservant named Lonnie was hired to cook Brian's meals and pack his bags for his constant traveling. A red Rolls-Royce was ordered from a

Park Lane dealership, customized with a vanity case in the armrest in which Brian could keep a monogrammed brush and mirror to make sure his hair wasn't mussed on arrivals. When the red Rolls arrived, Brian hired a young Cockney lad he fancied named Reg to drive it for him.

Paul needed no London accommodations; he simply moved in full-time with the Ashers at Wimpole Street. George and Ringo roomed together in a small flat on Green Street. It wasn't long before their fans discovered the address of the Green Street flat, and the boys were forced to move out. In a mixed blessing, Brian found them the duplicate flat to his two floors below him in Wadham House. The building was chosen for convenience and security, but Brian was always worried that one night George or Ringo would stop upstairs to borrow a cup of sugar and notice that Brian often invited only boys to his parties. Aware that Brian felt this way, Ringo and George would arrive at Brian's door unexpectedly, just to tease him. The sudden presence of two Beatles in Brian's flat would often bring all activity to a complete halt.

John's move to London was more perplexing than the rest; what to do about Cynthia and the baby? They had recently moved out of the £5 bedsitter and back to her mother's house in Hoylake. John hoped that if she were out of sight, she would be out of mind, but with the Fleet Street press now fascinated by the minutiae of the Beatles' personal lives, it was soon ferreted out that he was married. John vigorously denied this rumor when approached in interviews, and a carload of Fleet Street reporters set out to prove him a liar. It wasn't hard to ascertain Lillian Powell's Hoylake address from some ne'er-do-well, and a veritable division of reporters and photographers descended on Trinity Place. Half a dozen of them actually slept in a car in front of the house, waiting for Cynthia to emerge. She waited nearly a week before she ventured outside, when she wheeled Julian to the greengrocer in his carriage. She was secretly photographed by hidden photographers with telephoto lenses. Inside the grocery store two reporters approached her and demanded to know if she was John Lennon's wife. Terrified that she would be blamed for spoiling John's ruse, Cynthia insisted she was her own twin sister and that the photographs were worthless. The compassionate grocer tried to back up this ridiculous story, but it was transparently a lie. The next morning Cynthia peeked at the newspapers with dread. There on the front pages of several national papers were photographs of her pushing Julian in his Silver Cross pram.

John was furious. He viewed the revelation of his marriage as a terrible personal embarrassment. "Walking about married," he said. "It was like walking about with odd socks on, your fly open." Mostly, John was just worried that the girls would stop chasing him. They didn't.

It was Brian, curiously, who prevailed on John not to be too hard on Cynthia. Since the secret was out, they might as well make the best of it. A married Beatle with an adorable baby son was wholesome enough for their image—as long as none of the newspapers pointed out that Cynthia was obviously pregnant before John married her. It was a fairly easy computation to make, but one never addressed by the press when discussing John's marriage or Julian.* It was the beginning of an extraordinary period of tolerance and discretion by Fleet Street, heretofore accorded only to members of the Royal Family. In a sense, the editorial wisdom was that the Beatles' popularity was too good a story in itself to besmirch. This philosophy kept them safe from scandal for many years to come.

It was decided that John should take Cynthia and the baby with him when he moved to London. They took a trip to Paris together first, their only real honeymoon, and when John went to London the next time he brought Cynthia with him to look for an apartment. The first people she met in London were the Beatles' official photographer of the moment, Bob Freeman, and his wife. A top London fashion photographer, Freeman had shot the distinctive album cover for their second LP, the one with half their faces in dark shadows. He was now in the profitable position of supplying most of the fan photos of the Beatles for the *Beatles Monthly Fan Club Magazine,* which had a circulation of over 100,000. At Cynthia's first meeting with the Freemans it was mentioned that a maisonette directly above their flat was becoming available. Since Cynthia knew no one in London, the proximity of the photographer and his wife just downstairs seemed

* Years later, when Cynthia Twist wrote about her marriage in her heavily self-censored autobiography, *A Twist of Lennon,* she changed the date of her marriage to 1962. This inaccuracy has been noted many times in Beatles biographies. Recently, Cynthia confessed it was an inadvertent mistake; she has a mental block against admitting Julian was conceived out of wedlock and often still confuses the dates.

important to her, and John rented the flat sight unseen. Cynthia was less happy about moving to London after she saw their new place. It was the top floor of a sixth-floor walk-up on Emperor's Gate, just off the Cromwell Road. The gloomy flat was in a run-down Georgian building situated just across the street from a large student hostel. The view from the apartment windows was of dingy rooftops and the West London Airlines Terminal.

Cynthia tried to make the best of it and began to decorate and clean, but it was only a few weeks before John's new address leaked out, and the building was besieged by fans, particularly the girls who lived in the student hostel across the street. Cynthia was accosted daily on the front steps of the building or faced with the constant indignity of signs hung out of the hostel windows, welcoming her husband home or bidding him good-bye in the morning. She began to resent the fans, and her isolation in the big city increased. One night shortly after they had moved in, on one of the many nights that John was away on the road, the airlines terminal building burned down. Cynthia stood at the window, holding Julian in her arms, watching as the rooftops around her were consumed by flames. Both she and the baby were crying hysterically. None of it was happening the way she had planned, but at least she was a secret no more.

A 1963 shot of four of the most famous grins in history.
(*Beat Publications, Ltd.*)

John, his knee socks at his ankles, knees black with dirt, pauses for a photograph with Aunt Mimi and Uncle George outside of Mendips, circa 1948. (*Globe Photos*)

Aunt Mimi in 1964 with her favorite cat, "Suky." (*Pictorial Parade*)

A rare photograph of thirteen-year-old George Harrison in the front room of his Liverpool home, trying to master a guitar that's almost as big as he is. (*Beat Publications, Ltd.*)

George in familiar guitarist's stance. (*Beat Publications, Ltd.*)

The young and not-so-innocent newly declared superstars in 1964, with every hair combed and blown-dry in place. (*Beat Publications, Ltd.*)

Brian and Queenie Epstein
dressed up for a family wedding.
(*Mrs. Queenie Epstein*)

Brian's official publicity photo,
with his signature across the
collar of his Turnbull and Asser
shirt. Brian was so popular with
the fans that tens of thousands of
photographs were distributed.
(*Mrs. Queenie Epstein*)

Brian, George, George Martin, John, and Sir Joseph
Lockwood. Ringo and Paul flank Sir Joe's secretary.
(*Sir Joseph Lockwood*)

Movie-star-handsome George Martin, the Beatles'
record producer, and music publisher Dick James,
their kindly "uncle." (*Beat Publications, Ltd.*)

Brian with that amused and adoring look on his face as he chats with Paul and George in their dressing room before a show in Blackpool.
(*Beat Publications, Ltd.*)

his photo, taken in Liverpool the summer of 1963,
aptures some of Brian Epstein's musical stable.
rom left: John, Paul, George, Billy J. Kramer
idden behind George), Tony Mansfield, Neil
spinall, and Mike Maxfield.
Beat Publications, Ltd.)

In this 1968 photo, Paul rehearses with Cilla Black on the song "Step Inside, Love," which he wrote as the theme music for his BBC TV series.
(*Pictorial Parade*)

The quartet in a posed photograph. (*Beat Publications, Ltd.*)

One of the earliest candid photos of Paul and Ringo in existence. Note the collarless jackets, pegged pants, and pointy black boots. (*Beat Publications, Ltd.*)

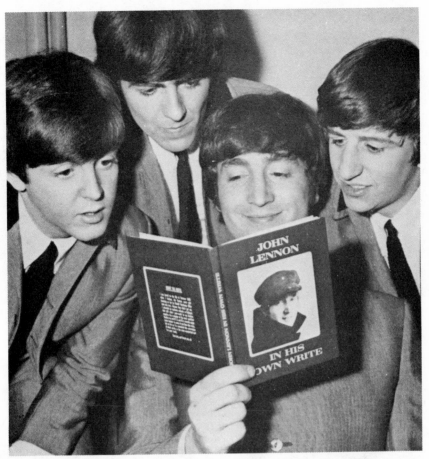

All the boys together around John's book, *In His Own Write*.
(*Beat Publications, Ltd.*)

John and Paul at
work and at play
in the early days
(1963). (*Beat
Publications, Ltd.*)

Greeting cheering crowds in Australia. Whenever the Beatles appeared on a balcony, they couldn't resist giving Hitler-type salutes. (*Beat Publications, Ltd.*)

George, Paul, John, and Jimmy Nichol (who stood in for a sick Ringo at the beginning of their spring 1964 world tour) being interviewed by a Dutch reporter. (*Beat Publications, Ltd.*)

Brian beams proudly as the boys are introduced to Ed Sullivan at a rehearsal for their first appearance on his show in 1964. (*Beat Publications, Ltd.*)

A disheveled Ringo, still in his pajama top, reaches for the milk for his cereal during a communal breakfast in a hotel suite on the Beatles' first American tour. (*Camera Press, Ltd.*)

Mounted police are used to help quell rioting as the Beatles arrive at Buckingham Palace in John Lennon's Rolls-Royce to receive their MBE's. (*Pictorial Parade*)

The Beatles films, clockwise:
escaping fans in *A Hard Day's
Night;* in Indian regalia for
Magical Mystery Tour; the
Austrian skiing sequence from
Help!; pitching in some publicity
for *Yellow Submarine,* the Beatles
only "franchised" project.

The inner circle, Paul, John, Neil, Mal, Ringo, and George, in the studios, 1967. (*Beat Publications, Ltd.*)

Ringo and John in a recording session on Salisbury Plain during the filming of "Help!" in 1965. (*Beat Publications, Ltd.*)

Brian, thirty-one, outside the Saville Theater, which he had just leased. He told reporters "A student at the Royal Academy of Dramatic Art eight years ago, I promised myself that one day I would run a West End theater . . . Paul McCartney and John Lennon are to write a musical soon, and I would be interested in [producing] that." (*Beat Publications, Ltd.*)

Rehearsing for the special *Hello Goodbye* film, shot on stage at the Saville Theater. The finished film was never shown in the U.K. due to the mining ban. (*Beat Publications, Ltd.*)

Ringo and the new Mrs. Starr pose at their wedding
for a photograph with Brian. (*Beat Publications, Ltd.*)

Ringo
and Ewa Aulin
at their
first meeting. (*Beat
Publications, Ltd.*)

Chapter Six

*America is at our feet! Could anything
be more important than this?*

—*Brian Epstein in a phone
call to Peter Brown*

1.

*W*HEN THE BEATLES exploded in America, the force of the blast nearly knocked them over. "I Want to Hold Your Hand," released on December 26, had leaped onto the *Billboard* record charts at number forty-five by January 18, a feat that made the recalcitrant executives at Capitol Records sit up and take notice. It was assumed that the few minutes of film on Jack Paar's show had sparked minimum interest. Yet a week later "I Want to Hold Your Hand" leaped to the number three spot, and the following week it was number one. The Beatles, who were performing a three-week stint at the Olympia Theater in Paris, to bad reviews, received the news in a telegram. They were informed that within five days the song had sold 1.5 million copies. Even in a country like America, where a hit record was expected to peak at 200,000 in sales, the figures were enormously out of proportion. If sales continued, "I Want to Hold Your Hand" would sell two million copies in another month. A companion album, *Meet the Beatles*, was rushed into American record stores as fast as it could be pressed, and overnight it became the fastest selling LP in American recording history.

It was early on the morning of February 7, 1964, that Brian and the Beatles and a small entourage of aides set out for America to appear on the Ed Sullivan show and at a double-header concert at Carnegie Hall that had been subsequently booked for Lincoln's Birthday, a federal holiday. The entourage consisted of a newly hired press representative, Tony Barrow, who wrote the "Disker" column in the *Liverpool Echo;* Neil Aspinall, who had become as important as any member of the group; Dezo Hoffman, the official photographer; and a road manager and bodyguard named Mal Evans. Evans was a kindly but menacing-looking young man. Mal had been a telephone repairman in Liverpool when he met Neil and the boys at the Cavern Club, where he sometimes worked as a part-time bouncer. One night the previous winter, when Neil Aspinall had come down with the flu and was unable to drive the boys to London for a radio interview, Evans substituted for him and since had slowly been incorporated into the inner circle. Although Evans never reached the "brotherhood" level of Neil Aspinall, he became an omnipresent member of their day-to-day lives for the rest of the time the Beatles were together.

There was another, unexpected member of the entourage: Mrs. John Lennon. In an invitation that absolutely amazed her, Cynthia had been asked to accompany John in her official capacity as wife. Cynthia was terribly pleased yet somehow afraid that the invitation had been instigated by a recent odd incident. She didn't quite understand the connection, but she decided she didn't want to examine it too closely. One evening while John was away and Cynthia was home alone with Julian, there was a loud banging on the door of the Emperor's Gate flat. It was an unexpected visit from a young couple she and John saw socially. They had apparently been arguing, and the wife was sobbing. Her husband pushed her into the flat, where she landed on the floor. "Tell her!" he shouted at his wife. "Tell her!" But the woman only sobbed and said nothing. Later, when John returned home and Cynthia asked him about the incident, he responded only with an icy stare. The next thing she knew she was being whisked out of London on her way to America.

At Heathrow Airport, dressed in a mushroom-style cap with a matching three-quarter length coat and a dark miniskirt, she was ushered into the VIP lounge along with the Beatles. A farewell press conference had been arranged to bid farewell to these national heroes, and Cynthia sank self-consciously into the crowded audience as John assumed his place with the other boys. The Beatles had perfected their droll, schoolboy wisecracks into a surprisingly charming banter they kept up with reporters at press conferences, and they had become pros at delivering one-liners.

But the press conference had only just begun when a cameraman unexpectedly called out, "Come on, Cynthia, love, let's have one of you. Come sit over in the light."

Cynthia froze where she was, certain that Brian and John did not want her to come forward. She peered nearsightedly in John's direction at the front of the room.

"Hey John, is it okay if we take a couple of shots of the missus?" another photographer asked. "How about you and Cynthia together?"

The goading from the reporters and photographers kept up until John shrugged uncomfortably and motioned Cynthia over. They sat next to each other on chairs, awkwardly balanced, as the photographers descended, strobe lights flaring. As far as she remembered, this was the first official time they were photographed as husband and wife. She had finally stepped out of the shadows and into the limelight with him, yet somehow the moment felt less wonderful than she expected. In time, she would learn to hate it.

The entourage was met on the plane by several English journalists assigned to cover their trip, including the *Evening Standard*'s Maureen Cleave, who had written the original, quintessential newspaper piece describing them; Phil Spector, the American record producer who had met them on the London scene; the singing group the Ronettes, one of whom George had been dating; and some doting Capitol Records executives. The plane also contained several desperate businessmen who had booked themselves on the flight in order to have Brian Epstein captive. They had been unsuccessfully pursuing Brian for weeks with business propositions. All the same, they never got to him. All their notes sent via the stewardesses were politely denied, and most of them caught the next flight back to England.

Mal Evans and Neil Aspinall kept busy on the nine-hour flight counterfeiting Beatles' signatures on the thousands of photographs they intended to pass out to the fans at the New York airport. Mal and Neil were becoming quite adept at forging the Beatles' handwriting, but it would have taken ten men working a month to sign enough photographs for the crowd waiting at Kennedy Airport. New York had been whipped into a Beatle frenzy by Capitol Records. When "I Want to Hold Your Hand" blew off the top of the charts, Capitol splurged an unheard-of $50,000 on an advertising blitz the likes of which had never before been attempted. *The Beatles are coming!* was the cry, and they smothered the city with it in radio promos, on posters and bumper stickers and buttons. The print journalists were eating it up, with sarcastic articles about their hair and music. Capitol also came up with the clever gimmick of prerecording just the answer portions of carefully scripted interviews with the Beatles and sending thousands of these answer tapes to radio stations all around the country, each with a list of questions. This gave every community in the U.S.A. a personalized effect, as if the Beatles were coming *to your hometown.* The New York radio stations were having a field day cashing in on live, moment-to-moment coverage. WMCA, the nation's biggest and most influential local rock station, gave breathless bulletins of their progress across the Atlantic: "It is now eight-seventeen, Beatle-time, and the four Mop Tops are now eleven-hundred miles off-shore . . ."

By the time the Beatles' plane touched down in New York and taxied to the arrivals building, the spectacle that was waiting for them was slightly incomprehensible. Never had there been an airport reception like this, save for Lindbergh. The International Arrivals Building was literally swarming with fans, like bees on a hive, fans screaming, waving banners, hanging from railings on the observation deck, pressed flat against the tinted windows of the terminal by a pack five-deep behind them. When the plane door was opened, the screaming of the fans was louder than the sound of the jet engines. For the first time the size of the crowd was slightly more disquieting than complimentary.

A cordon of New York policemen hustled the Beatles inside the terminal to the customs area. Although they did not have to wait in line, the unimpressed New York customs agents thoroughly searched each and every suitcase. In the large outer lounge a noisy crowd of over 200 American journalists waited for them, including a documentary film crew making a movie of their trip for English TV that dogged their every move. Unlike the Fleet Street press, which had been nothing but adoring once they took notice of them, the American press was out to nail the Beatles. The sudden hype from Capitol Records, coupled with the dubiousness of the lasting quality of such songs as "I Want to Hold Your Hand," reeked of a gimmick. At best, the New York press thought the Beatles would be a passing fad, and if they could make fools of them at the press conference, they would.

The conference started with the Beatles assuming positions at a table in front of individual microphones. Brian hung back, nervously stroking his chin. When the room did not at once quiet down for the press conference to begin, John Lennon himself started the proceedings with a big, scouse, *"Shaaaaarup!"*

"How do you like this welcome?" a reporter asked.

"So this is America," Ringo said, looking around. "They all seem out of their minds."

"Are you going to get a haircut?" they were asked, which brought much laughter from the crowd.

"We had one yesterday," John said cheerfully.

"Are you part of a social rebellion against the older generation?"

"It's a dirty lie."

"What about the campaign in Detroit to stamp out the Beatles?"

"We've got a campaign of our own to stamp out Detroit," Paul said.

"What do you do when you're cooped up in your rooms between shows?"

George: "We ice skate."

"Do you guys hope to take anything home with you?"

"Rockefeller Center."

By now the press were having a good time with them. "What do you think of Beethoven?" they were asked.

"I love him," Ringo said, "especially his poems."

"Was your family in show business?" John was asked.

John smiled slyly, "Well, me dad used to say me mother was a great performer."

At this point the Beatles recognized Murray the K, the fast-talking, slightly abrasive American disc jockey, who was dressed in a loud sportsjacket and porkpie hat. Murray had worked his way up to the front of the room and was trying to get the Beatles' attention. George snidely told Murray, "I love your hat."

Murray whipped the hat off his head and handed it to George. "Here, you can have it."

A technician from CBS hollered, "Tell Murray the K to stop the crap." Ringo looked at Murray and said, "Cut the crap out, the guy says."

When it was clear that the boys had charmed the most cynical reporter, Brian brought the press conference to a halt, and the

Beatles were ushered from the terminal into a waiting fleet of limousines. They were escorted by four New York City police cars plus two motorcycle cops, all with sirens wailing, to the Plaza Hotel. The Plaza, which had innocently booked the rooms not knowing who or what the Beatles were, was now an armed camp. Police barricades crisscrossed the Fifth Avenue entrance of the hotel, holding back a throng of fans ten feet deep on the Grand Army Plaza, some of whom had been waiting since dawn in the freezing February weather. As the day wore on the crowd grew larger still, until traffic on Fifth Avenue had to be diverted. All the business in the hotel was disrupted, including the switchboard, which was swamped with calls for the Beatles. The hotel security had to be doubled for the length of their stay, and guests who were dining in the gracious Palm Court restaurant had to be asked to remove their Beatle wigs.

The Beatles, unable to leave the hotel because of the overwhelming crowds, were ensconced on the twelfth floor in ten interconnecting rooms. Although they were too high up to hear the screaming of the crowd below, just venturing near enough to the windows to be seen caused a visible wave of frenzied emotion on Fifth Avenue. They spent the day watching American television, which offered extensive news footage of their arrival and press conference. They also chatted amiably and freely with scores of disc jockeys who had managed to fast-talk their way through the bewildered operators at the Plaza switchboard. The phone calls were taped or broadcast live on stations around the country, and the Beatles blithely and ignorantly gave away thousands of dollars' worth of free promotion. When Brian found out about it, he stormed into their suite and ordered them off the phone. They spent the rest of the afternoon amusing themselves by taunting the crowds in the street below until a police sergeant appeared at the door demanding they keep away from the windows. When Neil Aspinall told them this, the windows became a major plaything, much to the frustration of the New York police below.

While most visitors were kept out of the Beatles' rooms, Murray the K had managed to be escorted upstairs by one of the Ronettes. The Beatles had met the Ronettes on the London social circuit that previous fall, and George Harrison had had a brief affair with Mary. After the Ronettes brought Murray the K upstairs, he was impossible to remove. He was soon overriding Brian's instructions and started broadcasting live over the phone from the Beatles' rooms. Yet he was so powerful on New York radio that no one dared ask him to leave, and he was allowed to fasten himself onto the entourage like a barnacle. Much to Brian's great annoyance, Murray the K soon pronounced himself the "Fifth Beatle," and the name stuck for all time.*

The first night in town, George Harrison came down with the flu, accompanied by a high fever and inflamed throat. The hotel doctor confined him to his room. George's sister Louise, who had married an American and emigrated to St. Louis several years before, flew to New York to nurse her twenty-year-old brother.

On Sunday, the day of the actual broadcast, the entire nation was kept abreast of George Harrison's progress with the flu. As the day wore on news bulletins emanating from the Beatles twelfth-floor encampment said that George was indeed improving and that he would be well enough to join the group on the program that evening. In truth, George Harrison was seriously ill and running a high fever. However, it was generally agreed between Brian and the rest of the boys that short of death it would be folly for George to miss their premier performance in America. Even Ed Sullivan said that if George was too sick to appear on his show, he'd put on a Beatle wig and join them himself. A doctor was summoned to the suite to shoot George full of medicines and, according to Neil, a whopping dose of amphetamines, which the other boys were already gulping down orally. George was loaded into a limousine and driven to the Sullivan studio, where a guitar was stuck in his hands. It is much to his credit that he managed to give a lively performance that evening.

Ed Sullivan was having one of the most difficult weeks in the history of his program. For a man who had presented entire marching contingents from the Soviet Union in full costume, followed by the Mormon Tabernacle Choir on the same stage moments later, hosting the four-man group was a nightmare. Sullivan was a great exploiter but an even greater cynic. He thought he had seen just about everything the week he introduced Elvis on his show, but it was nothing compared to the Beatles. The press hadn't let them alone all week; his rehearsals were disrupted and the schedules wrecked. Like the Plaza Hotel, the theater had been

---

* The real "fifth Beatle" was without doubt Neil Aspinall.

turned into an armed camp. Sullivan had received 50,000 requests for tickets for a theater that seated a little over 700. Several thousand of the requests were from VIP's in the entertainment business or government, and turning them down was a giant diplomatic headache. Just before the show, Brian searched out Sullivan backstage and in his finest West End accent informed him, "I would like to know the exact wording of your introduction."

Sullivan gave Brian a sidelong glance. "I would like you to get lost," he told him.

Considering the auspiciousness of the event, the actual introduction was superb. In his inimitable, deadpan delivery of a mortician, interrupted by the periodic screams of the audience at just the mention of the Beatles' name, Sullivan first read a congratulatory telegram sent to them from Elvis Presley wishing them luck.* The Beatles, who were in their places behind the curtain at the time, were thrilled. Then, shouting over the screams from the audience—screams that did not abate for the entire five minutes the Beatles were on the air—Sullivan intoned, "America, judge for yourself."

Seventy-three million Americans watched the Ed Sullivan show that snowy, cold February night. Families throughout the country, kept in by the inclement weather, gathered around their sets curious to see for the first time this thing called the Beatles. In New York, it is said, not one hubcap was stolen from an automobile, not one major crime was committed by a teenager. Even Billy Graham broke with tradition by watching TV on the Sabbath.

2.

*T*HE BEATLES WERE overnight the most talked about phenomenon in America. By the following morning the demand for information about the Beatles was so great that Brian had to hold another press conference in the ballroom of the Plaza Hotel. More than 250 newspapers, TV and

---

* The Beatles discovered many years later that Elvis never sent the telegram or even knew about it. It was sent, instead, by Colonel Tom Parker.

radio stations, and wire services were represented, including the BBC, the three major American networks, *Time* magazine, and Dr. Joyce Brothers, the syndicated psychologist who was there to determine the psychological ramifications of the Beatles. For those who enjoyed the Beatles' performance at the airport when they landed, this second conference topped it by lasting so long that the Beatles were served a roast chicken lunch while it went on.

The following day a blizzard grounded all planes, and Brian had to arrange to transport his precious cargo by rail to Washington, D.C., where they were to perform that evening at the Washington Coliseum. Three thousand youngsters were waiting for them in the snow at the station, while another 7,000 turned up outside of the coliseum. At the Shoreham Hotel, where they stayed, the management tried to clear the entire seventh floor for them, but one family refused to vacate their room. Shortly before the Beatles' arrival, the management pretended there was a power failure and shut off the lights, water, and heat on that floor until the guests moved out.

At the concert several new problems were becoming apparent to them. George had capriciously mentioned in an interview that he liked jelly beans, and now the group was pelted with so many of them on stage it was like playing in a stinging hailstorm. Jellybeans, peppered with flashbulbs that exploded on impact, began to nearly blind them. Worse, the puny amplifiers the Beatles played through couldn't carry their sound through the coliseum. Although they would eventually be equipped with the best stadium amplification possible, the necessary hardware just didn't exist in 1964. Even worse, there was probably no amplification short of dropping a bomb that could be heard over the screaming. From the moment the Beatles were introduced to the moment they went off, they only heard one long scream of the crowd.

After the Washington concert they were invited to a party at the British embassy, and Brian decided they would go. When they arrived it turned out that they had been invited to a rather stuffy embassy party. They immediately felt conspicuous and out of place in their Beatle haircuts and gray suits among the black ties and evening gowns. David Ormsby-Gore, the British Ambassador, later to be Lord Harlech, met them in the foyer. "Hello John," he said, extending his hand.

"I'm not John," John said. "I'm Charlie. That's John."

"Hello John," Ambassador Ormsby-Gore said to George.

"I'm not John," George said, pointing to Ringo, "I'm Frank, that's John."

The rest of the party crowd converged on the boys demanding they sign autographs. One of the guests, watching John sign, remarked sotto voce, "Look, he can actually write!" Brian and the others froze, expecting John to haul off and punch the man. Instead, he shoved the pens and paper back and refused to sign. One official of the Foreign Office stuck a piece of paper under his nose and said, "You'll sign this and like it!" Ringo shrugged amiably and said to John, "Come on and let's get it over with." He managed to get him to sign a few, but Ringo himself eventually lost his temper when a woman in an evening gown produced a pair of cuticle scissors from her evening bag and before he could stop her, snipped off a lock of his hair as a souvenir for her daughter. Brian whisked the boys out of the embassy in a huff. On the way back to the hotel he promised them that they would never be humiliated like that again. He invoked a solemn rule: no diplomat, no royalty, no president would ever have the Beatles at their beck and call for their amusement. From that night on it was firm NEMS policy that the Beatles simply did not attend official government functions.

When a report of the incident at the embassy appeared in the English press it raised a great cry of indignation. Public sentiment was one of great pride in the Beatles, and to be so rudely treated by Englishmen in a foreign country was considered an outrage. The Foreign Secretary, R. A. Butler, was asked by a member of Parliament to confirm whether the incident had actually happened. Brian, who didn't want it to attract more attention than it already had, cleverly wrote a saccharine thank-you note to Ambassador Ormsby-Gore and his wife, expressing gratitude for the Beatles' evening at the embassy. A copy of the note was offered to the Foreign Secretary as evidence that the Beatles themselves had a wonderful time, and the incident was squelched.

The evening of the Beatles' double Carnegie Hall performance was especially festive in New York, since it was also Lincoln's birthday and a school and bank holiday. The sold-out show was another triumph, attended by the usual celebrities and VIPs. After the second show Brian left the theater with concert promoter Sid Bernstein and walked through the snowy Manhattan streets to where Madison Square Garden then stood on Eighth Avenue and Fifty-second Street. Bernstein told Brian he had no doubt that the Beatles could sell it out. He was so anxious for Brian to try, he offered to donate $5,000 to the British Cancer Fund if Brian allowed him to book and promote the show. But Brian preferred to wait. He told Bernstein that his boys would fill bigger halls than Madison Square Garden. Bernstein reminded him that there hardly were bigger halls than Madison Square Garden.

"Then we'll book football stadiums," Brian promised. "We'll fill the largest arenas in the world."

3.

*O*N *FEBRUARY 22* Brian and the Beatles left for England from America, a scant fifteen days after they had left. The Beatles were now the entertainment rage on *both* sides of the Atlantic. Europe and Japan could not be far behind. In terms of statistics, they were clearly bigger than the biggest, Mr. Presley. The day after they left the United States, they became the cover story of *Newsweek* magazine. It was pointed out that the Beatles were barely out of their teens—John was the oldest at twenty-four—and that their twenty-eight-year-old manager, who had been the manager of a record store eighteen months previously, was one of the most admired businessmen in the entertainment industry and at least as famous as his wards.

But what did that mean to the troubled young man who sat in the first-class section of a BOAC jet on the way home, a double Cognac in his right hand, his stomach filled with prickly burrs of anxiety? Brian was most unhappy at the way things were turning out, things the Beatles weren't even aware of. First, he had begun to depend heavily on amphetamine pills to keep his energy up, which made his temper short. Although the Beatles themselves were taking just as many pills as Brian during the U.S. trip, it didn't seem to affect them as badly. He had a temper tantrum with the press agent, Tony Barrow, and had almost fired him, and he had shouted at each of the Beatles at one point or another.

And he was beside himself over business mistakes—one that could cost them millions of dollars, as much as $50 million.

Soon after the Beatles appeared on "Sunday Night at the Palladium," Brian's office was besieged with offers for merchandise licensing and personal endorsements. Within a few weeks he received offers to manufacture Beatle embossed belts, balls, balloons, bedspreads, beanies, buttons, cookies, candies, cards, pencil sharpeners, towels, toothbrushes, aprons, record holders, scrapbooks, TV trays, all manner of clothing, and, of course, a Beatle wig. Brian knew nothing about personal endorsements, as few people did in 1963. What he did know was that he didn't want the Beatles to look cheap or as if they were cashing in on their popularity. He decided that the Beatles would refuse *all* offers for personal endorsements, no matter how much money was offered, but that licensing agreements could be made as long as the product was of the finest quality. Brian would have no Beatles guitars with cheap plastic strings falling apart just a week after purchase and no Beatles lunch boxes that would rust with the first leaky tuna sandwich. Beatle merchandise would be costly but first quality.

In the beginning Brian's office handled the merchandising requests, deciding which would be honored and which denied, but Brian soon became bored with perusing dolls and rubber boots and began to look around for someone to take care of the matter for him. He made some inquiries around London for a solicitor. Brian wanted an attorney who would be a confidant as well as a legal advisor, and he was always referred to the firm of one David Jacobs. Of course, Brian had already heard of David Jacobs, the flamboyant celebrity attorney whose exploits were carefully covered by the Fleet Street press. Jacobs' clients included Diana Dors, Judy Garland, and Laurence Harvey, and he was frequently photographed, not at his desk, but in expensive restaurants or getting out of a limousine on the arm of some international movie star. He was perhaps best known for the large money award he won against the *Daily Mirror* on behalf of American pianist Lee Liberace. A *Mirror* journalist had written that when Liberace entered the room, he was not sure if a man or woman had arrived.

This was certainly a most appropriate case for Mr. Jacobs, who stood over six feet two inches tall and was heavily made up, at all times, in bright orange stage makeup. His hair was combed back in a dramatic wave and dyed an unnatural jet black color, like shoe polish had been painted on it. His makeup was sometimes so thick that it caked in the summer when it was humid. It was joked that David Jacobs often mesmerized judge and jury not only with his legal expertise but because of his dazzling court performances in full makeup.

David Jacobs adored the young Brian Epstein and took him under his wing. The two men were similar in many coincidental ways. Their families were both in the furniture business, both were born and bred of money, and both had doting Jewish mothers. Both were homosexual. David Jacobs became Brian's chief solicitor. From then on all legal decisions and contracts would be made with David Jacobs' advice, and it was Jacobs' law office that took over the task of sorting out the merchandising offers. Jacobs assigned the chore to a young lawyer in his office, but the task soon overran the space as the waiting room began to fill with Beatles combs and cereal bowls. Jacobs finally advised Brian to set up a completely separate company for the merchandising end, from which Brian and the Beatles would simply take a percentage of the profits, while they did the work. Jacobs said he knew of someone who would "take the merchandising business off their hands," which is exactly what he did.

His name was Nicky Byrne, and Jacobs knew him primarily through social circles. He admired Byrne because he gave wonderful parties, and Jacobs, who loved parties, considered himself an expert.* At one fabled gala a grand piano and pianist were pushed out the front door and down the streets. Byrne's ex-wife, Kiki, was a well-known London skiwear designer who ran a chic boutique in Chelsea. Byrne had once been a partner in a club called the Candor Club, so he knew all about show business, Jacobs contended. Byrne agreed to take on the job of merchandising and formed a partnership with five friends, none of whom Brian or Jacobs knew. His other partners were all in their twenties, and one of them was allowed to buy a 20 percent share in the business for only £1000. The business was incorporated under

---

* Jacobs gave notorious, elaborate theme parties on weekends at his Brighton mansion, which would begin in the afternoon and continue through the next day. Luminaries like Sophie Tucker would often entertain, and once a guest expired in the bedroom in the service of a young male courtesan. Jacobs simply locked the bedroom door and didn't mention it until the party was over.

the name Stramsact in Great Britain, and Seltaeb—Beatles spelled backward—in America.

Byrne had his own solicitors make up the agreement between Seltaeb, Stramsact, and NEMS. David Jacobs had Brian's power of attorney in the matter and was prepared to sign the contracts in his absence. The one point still unnegotiated in the contracts was simple: the percentages to each of the parties. Now Brian and Jacobs knew there was a lot of money to be made in merchandising, but no one knew exactly how much. A little bit of research would have turned up the fact that Elvis Presley-licensed soft goods had grossed over $20 million in 1957 alone. If Nicky Byrne got 10 or 15 percent of the Beatles licensing, he and his partners could be very, very rich.

David Jacobs casually asked Nicky Byrne what percentage he wanted. Byrne glibly suggested 90 percent for himself, expecting Jacobs to start bargaining. Jacobs nodded. "Well," he said, "10 percent is better than nothing," and he signed the contracts.

Brian had never studied the finalized agreements, nor thought about the terms until he had a meeting with Nicky Byrne in New York. Byrne had recently moved to America to run the company there. Byrne looked rather prosperous in his long coat with a luxurious astrakhan collar to help him brave the New York winter. He was also full of himself. He claimed that he had helped fill the New York airport for the Beatles' arrival by bribing the crowd to show up with promises of dollar bills and free tee shirts. Brian dismissed this; he had already learned that everyone was taking credit for the Beatles' success, from Bob Wooler to Sid Bernstein. Then Nicky presented him with a check, collected funds for merchandising, for $9,700. Brian was delighted. It was an unexpected $9,700 and after all, he had agreed to three appearances on the Ed Sullivan show for what had averaged out to be $2,400 an appearance. This would help offset some of the losses.

"How much of this do I owe you?" Brian asked Nicky Byrne, smiling.

"Nothing, Brian. That's your 10 percent," Byrne said.

Brian still didn't quite understand, except that he was to keep the entire $9,700. "That's marvelous, Nicky. How do you do it?"

Nicky explained that he had already collected over $100,000 and that after expenses there was $97,000, of which Nicky was keeping eighty-eight grand. And that was only the beginning,

Nicky jovially told him. Nicky had already been offered half a million dollars for his share of Seltaeb by the Columbia Pictures Corporation, with Ferrari automobiles thrown in for all the partners, according to Nicky. He disclosed that they were all living quite comfortably at the Drake Hotel on Park Avenue and that they had offices on the best block of Fifth Avenue. Nicky was allegedly employing the services of two limousines on twenty-four-hour call and had hired a private helicopter to ferry businessmen to and from the airport.

When it dawned on Brian what had happened, it started to make him physically ill. He couldn't think of it without wanting to vomit. As each revelation was made, he got angrier and angrier. One of the first deals that Byrne had made was with the Reliant Shirt Corporation for the privilege of manufacturing Beatles tee shirts for which they would pay $100,000. Brian at first thought this sum was ridiculously inflated, until he learned that in only three days the Reliant company had sold more than one million tee shirts, and the money had been earned back three times over. REMCO, one of the largest and best-known toy manufacturers in America, had bought the licensing to manufacture dolls. They had produced 100,000 dolls already and had orders for half a million more. The Beatles wig was such a popular item that the Lowell Toy Corporation couldn't produce them fast enough, although their factories were manufacturing them at a rate of over 35,000 a day. The *Wall Street Journal,* in an analysis of the Beatles' business impact, estimated that by the end of the first year of their success more than fifty million dollars worth of Beatles products would be purchased in America, and that was surely only the beginning if they managed to sustain their popularity.

It took a long, long time for the magnitude of it to sink in. Nicky Byrne's personal income alone, Brian estimated, could add up to five million dollars. Brian was sick. *They had given it away!* An incomprehensible sum signed away for nothing! He wondered what the Beatles would say when they found out. He decided it was best they know nothing about it, for the time being, and plotted to keep it from them. The task of getting it back began to gnaw at him. It was his first major failure, and for all the good success, he felt a fool.

Chapter Seven

The Sixties were not so much a decade, an era, an epoch, as a very long happening.

—*Peter Evans,*
Goodbye Baby & Amen

1.

I T HAD A TOUCH of the naughty nineties of Paris, the decadence of prewar Berlin. It had a sprinkling of the glamour of Hollywood in the forties and the sexual passions and peccadilloes of la dolce vita in the fifties. It was like an F. Scott Fitzgerald novel rewritten by Ian Fleming. Like all good dramas, it had a beginning, a middle, and an end. It was the single most important creative period in modern history, irrevocably changing all that followed it in fashion, music, and mores. Yet it wasn't until 1967, when it was nearly halfway over, that *Time* magazine gave it a name, "Swinging London."

Peter Evans, in his wickedly snide commentary on the era called *Goodbye Baby & Amen,* suggests that Swinging London started at precisely 11:03 A.M. on the morning of March 22, 1963, when John Dennis Profumo, the Minister of War, rose in the House of Commons to lie about his association with call girl Christine Keeler. "There was no impropriety whatsoever," he said in his famous speech. "I shall not hesitate to issue writs for libel and slander if scandalous allegations are made or repeated outside the house." On June 4 Profumo issued a statement saying he had lied to his colleagues and was resigning as both Minister of War and as a member of Parliament. Three days after Profumo resigned, Dr. Stephen Ward was arrested for "living off the improper immoral earnings" of Keeler and Mandy Rice-Davies. The ensuing trial, with testimony of orgies in high places and two-way mirrors, destroyed the government. On August 3, Stephen Ward took an overdose of Nembutal and died. On October 2 Harold Macmillan resigned as Prime Minister from a hospital bed at King Edward VII Hospital, where he was confined for a prostate operation. Anything Goes, Swinging London was then formally inaugurated the following week by the Beatles' appearance on "Sunday Night at the London Palladium."

For all its creativity and real excitement, Swinging London was something of a joke, a capricious prank on the old guard. The leaders of this revolution were the so-called new aristocracy, who came from the working classes. In fact, it was so important to have a modest background in Swinging London that socially active, born aristocrats shed their titles in order to be accepted, and one up-and-coming rock star, Mick Jagger, pretended to be from the tough East End, when in fact he was rather well off. David Bailey, the handsome, blond photographer who epitomized the era, was the son of a tailor. Terrance Donovan, another popular photographer, was the son of a lorry driver. The most popular new actors, Michael Caine and Terence Stamp, spoke with Cockney accents and were the sons, respectively, of a fish porter and a tugboat captain.

There was a general aversion to anything faintly conventional. Indeed, even the professions that were venerated had changed. For the first time in modern history, being a male hairdresser was an esteemed and envied position. At Christmas of 1965, David Bailey immortalized the Swinging London set in a published collection of oversized photographs. The cast of characters included, generically, two actors (Caine and Stamp); eight pop singers (John and Paul and Jagger included); one pop artist; one interior decorator; four photographers; two managers of pop groups (including Brian Epstein); one hairdresser (Vidal Sassoon); two photographers' designers; one ballet dancer (Rudolf Nureyev); three models; one film producer; one dress designer; one milliner; one discotheque manager (Brian Morris of the Ad Lib); one creative advertising man; plus the murderous underworld twins, the Kray Brothers.

The fashion and cosmetics business dubbed what was happening a "youthquake," and it was certainly in fashion and grooming that the changes were most apparent. A young designer named Mary Quant had single-handedly revolutionized the look in women's clothing with what she called the miniskirt, unleashing upon the world an unobstructed view of legs of all sizes, shapes, and attractiveness. A narrow side street named Carnaby Street was now the center of fashion excitement, spewing out new designers from its many shops every week. Long hair for men, a trend directly attributable to the Beatles, was de rigueur. To be considered attractive one needed to be very thin, very pale, very bored, and exclusively British. Candy-striped shirts were in vogue for a time, as was driving an E-Jag, but no trend seemed to last more than a few weeks. Two new, eye-boggling geometric art forms, called Pop Art and Op Art, assaulted the eye from the walls of every smart gallery in Mayfair.

Sex, too, was very different, as were morals. Sex was "free," talked about frequently in public, indulged in only slightly less frequently, and all without the shame or messy guilt of the fifties. Kenneth Tynan said "fuck" on television, and homosexuality was legalized among consenting adults. Everything was very casual but had an edge of the outrageous to it. When David Bailey dumped model Jean Shrimpton to marry Catherine Deneuve, he wore a sweater and she smoked at the ceremony. Best man Mick Jagger wore jeans. "David Bailey makes love daily" became the nursery rhyme of the Chelsea set. Stores were no longer shops but "boutiques," and the esteemed form of comedy was satire; the targets were pomposity and tradition.

There were new words too, like pow! and Zap! and gear and grotty. Everybody smoked, cigarettes by the packfuls, then marijuana. Eventually LSD came along and crystalized it all. As the Swinging Sixties progressed, the drugs got harder—heroin was chic—and a lot of people were arrested or died. It was thought to be a compliment to be called "decadent," and the suicide rate was peaking. It was more of a sparkler than a full fireworks show, but it was a beautiful bright burst. When the Beatles returned to London that winter, this was the Swinging London they came to lead, as easily as monarchs returning to their ancestral seats of power.

* * *

2.

*O*N MARCH 2, less than two weeks after their return from America, the Beatles began work on their first feature film, tentatively entitled *Beatlemania*. Brian had arranged this deal six months before, when the idea was as dangerous as it was glamourous. Music exploitation films of the fifties and sixties were inevitably cheap-looking and moronically scripted, usually of the *Beach Blanket Bingo* genre. But Elvis had made movies, and successful ones, too, so Brian decided the Beatles would make one. Anyway, Brian's showman's mentality couldn't resist the lure of the silver screen, with his boys thirty feet high. Now *that* was Brian's idea of show biz.

At the time the Beatles had made the deal, at the beginning of their success, they had been in a vastly different bargaining position than they were just a few months later on the first day of production. The previous October Brian had been approached by an American film producer named Walter Shenson who had the financial blessings of United Artists in asking the Beatles to appear in their own movie. Brian happily agreed to a meeting with Shenson and Bud Orenstein, the United Artists executive in Great Britain. Although Brian didn't realize it at the time, U.A. was less interested in making the movie than they were in releasing the soundtrack album; even if the movie was a flop, United Artists would almost certainly make a profit from record sales.*

Shenson and Orenstein told Brian they were prepared to budget the film at $300,000, a low budget for a feature film but about average for a music exploitation film. They offered the boys a £25,000 fee for appearing in the movie, plus a percentage of the profits. Insofar as the percentage, they were prepared to be more generous. Between themselves they had agreed to offer Brian as high as a 25 percent cut. Brian thought about the percentage for a moment, then said, "I wouldn't accept anything less than 7.5 percent." To make a poor business deal even worse, Brian agreed to a three-picture deal, in which all rights to the movies would revert back to Walter Shenson in fifteen years. After

---

* Neither EMI or Capitol thought to cover movie soundtracks in their contracts with the Beatles at the time.

all, Brian thought, the Beatles were a pop group, and what pop group would still be popular after fifteen years?

Seven months later, when the Beatles assembled to make the movie, they were international stars and could have demanded to renegotiate their contracts. But Brian, ever the gentleman, had given his word, and financial matters proceeded as planned.

Brian and Shenson chose a young British director of TV commercials named Richard Lester to direct the film. Lester was best known for his *The Running, Jumping and Standing Still Film* he made with Spike Milligan, and he promised to bring a fresh visual sense to the movie. It was Brian's idea to hire Alun Owens, a writer of TV dramas and a fellow Liverpudlian, best known for his British TV film called *No Trains to Lime Street*. Owens was touted as having a special ear for Liverpool dialogue and was sent out to spend a few days on the road with the Beatles to pick up a sense of their personalities. The script turned out to be arguably the best cinematic representation of Swinging London, along with *Blow-Up* and *Alfie*. Owens had adeptly characterized each Beatle in cartoon strokes in the script; John was the sardonically funny one, Paul the adorable Lothario, George the handsome romantic, and Ringo the lonely, lovable runt of the litter. By virtue of Lester's jump-cutting, op-art direction, the Beatles were turned into modern-day, swinging Marx Brothers. It was another uncanny example of how the most potentially disastrous experiment could coalesce artistically into moments of great genius for them. The accolades the film received in the press when it opened the following summer reached a level of hysteria. American film critic Andrew Sarris later dubbed *A Hard Day's Night*, "The *Citizen Kane* of juke-box movies." *Newsweek* magazine summed it up when they announced, "The legitimacy of the Beatles phenomenon is inescapable."

As shooting for *A Hard Day's Night* started in earnest, the Beatles found the pace of the six-week shooting schedule to be a snail's crawl compared to the frantic pace of their lives over the last six months. Despite the fact that the Beatles were on-screen for virtually the entire length of the movie, they spent many hours just sitting around their dressing trailers, smoking and talking, and idle hands find the Devil's work. Eventually an 8-mm projector was moved into one of their dressing trailers, and they were entertained by a caseload of porno movies. Boys being boys, the young girls on the set being used as extras were discreetly lured into the trailers for quickies between takes.

One of the girls who wouldn't visit in the dressing trailer was nineteen-year-old Pattie Boyd. George Harrison picked her out on the first day of shooting. A one-time Mary Quant model, Pattie had worked with Lester once before in a Smith's Crisps commercial. She was pretty and blond with a round face and big, blue button eyes, the essence of a Swinging London sex kitten in her pale makeup, fun-fur short jacket, and Quant mini that showed miles and miles of gorgeous legs. Pattie had a genuinely warm and kittenish personality, which could make the most milquestoast man feel virile.

Pattie remembers George staring at her the first day of shooting at the Waterloo train station but didn't think much of the twenty-one-year-old pop star. After the day's shooting ended, Pattie asked each of the Beatles—save for John who frightened her with his sarcasm—to sign autographs for her younger sisters, Jenny and Paula. "George signed his name and put two kisses under it for my sisters," Pattie says. "Then he signed one for me and put seven kisses."

The next day he followed Pattie around the set but was turned down flat on an offer for a visit to the dressing trailer. When he was also turned down for a respectable date, he was a little annoyed. "I explained that I had a steady boyfriend of two years and that I had an old-fashioned view of romance," Patti said. "That meant fidelity." But George wouldn't give up. Whenever his mind would stray, it would stray right to Pattie. On the third day he nearly begged her to go out with him, he was so attracted to her, and Pattie broke down and accepted a dinner invitation. "I was loyal, not stupid," she says.

By the end of their first week of dating, Pattie had already introduced him to her mother and sisters. At the end of a month he took her to see a magnificent country bungalow he was considering buying in the toney suburb of Esher. He said he didn't want to be living there alone. It was a long, low, one-story bungalow on a private development owned by the National Trust, situated on a thickly wooded estate. Two long wings were separated by a spacious, rectangular courtyard, which had a heated swimming pool. Semicircular floor-to-ceiling windows projected out from the living room onto a landscaped backyard. As Pattie and

George wandered hand in hand through the rambling, unfurnished house, Pattie giggled dreamily when George asked her for her decorating ideas. By the end of the fourth week George bought the house for them to live in together, and their relationship was official.

George took some getting used to for Pattie. She was accustomed to the polished young men in the fast-moving, trendy set she traveled in that included model Jean Shrimpton and David Bailey. As far as polish went, George had none. He was virtually uneducated, graciousness was not his strong point, and he fluctuated between being an ill-mannered, know-it-all Liverpool lout to a sex-crazed teenager. George's personality problems were an intricate web of monomania and self-doubt. He was an overnight sensation and yet was still treated like a kid and a third-rate citizen by John and Paul. Pattie noticed, as did everyone, that none of George's compositions ever appeared on a Beatles album.

George expected Pattie to tend to his ego, his sex, and his meals. He expected her to learn to be the perfect northern woman; servile, dedicated, available. Pattie decided that if their relationship was ever to work out, he would have to learn that she was no northern woman and never would be. In the interim, he adored and worshipped her and pointed out her resemblance to Brigitte Bardot to anyone who would listen.

Brian was still maintaining that publicly acknowledging any of the single Beatles' relationships with any one girl would be disastrous for the image, although this was now probably more a function of his misogyny than public relations. Brian requested that if George continued to see this young lady, that he do so in secret. This was a lot harder to do than when John first married Cynthia, simply because now the Beatles were routinely photographed wherever they went. It was decided that in order to get to know each other better without any attendant publicity, George and Pattie should take a secret vacation in West Ireland at Easter time, with John and Cynthia chaperoning them.

The arrangements were made in cloak-and-dagger secrecy. Under assumed names the men and women flew from Manchester airport to Heathrow on separate planes, the two Beatles well disguised with hats, false moustaches, and mufflers. Then the two couples flew to Dromoland airport in the far reaches of Ireland in a private six-seater plane, and from there they went by private car to the Dromoland Castle Hotel, a staid and secluded resort where there would be no suspicious fans—or probably anybody under the age of sixty.

The vacation got off to a wonderful start. Cynthia and Pattie were delighted with each other's friendship. Women in the Beatles' entourage were rare, and there was a lot about living with a Beatle that Cynthia could teach Pattie. Cynthia found her congenial and ready to laugh, and Pattie even managed to tone down some of George's adolescent edge, although George never for a minute stopped saying how much Pattie looked like Brigitte Bardot. The first morning in Ireland it was pouring rain, but that made very little difference to the two couples, who intended to spend most of the day lounging in bed anyway. It was barely ten o'clock when the manager woke them up. He was sorry to inform them that somehow word had leaked that they were staying at the hotel. Early that morning a contingent of twenty journalists and photographers had begun arriving at the hotel. The reporters were asking the name of the young girl George had spent the night with, and the photographers were sneaking around the lobby, determined to get a picture of her.

Up in their rooms the four trapped young people became just as determined not to let this happen. They knew from personal experience that such a seamy-sounding story would find its way onto the wire services in fifteen minutes. Together they devised a complicated plan to escape.

Two hours later John and George checked out of the hotel in full view of the reporters. They were besieged with questions about the two women they stayed with. Was John with Cynthia? And what was the name of George's friend? John and George casually insisted there weren't any girls at all. They said they were vacationing alone to get away from it all. They rushed outside into the pouring rain and into a car waiting to take them to the airport. As the car pulled away from the front of the hotel, John and George looked out the rear window, hoping that the press corps would follow them. Instead, almost the entire contingent stayed behind, certain that the two girls had remained up in the rooms.

Upstairs, Cynthia and Pattie were already disguised in maids' uniforms with white frilly aprons and caps, courtesy of the management of the Dromoland Hotel. They pushed a large wicker basket of dirty laundry through the corridors down to the hotel's laundry room where baskets of laundry were emptied. Pattie and Cynthia climbed in, and the baskets were wheeled onto a loading platform under the watchful eyes of reporters, put in the back of a laundry truck, and driven off. The driver, who had been hired by John and George, got carried away with the drama of his mission, and once out of sight of the hotel, he screeched away on two wheels like a getaway car fleeing a robbery. He never gave the girls a chance to get out of the baskets and drove them to the airport as they rolled around in the back pleading for help. "Cynthia, we'll suffocate! We'll die in here! Shout, Cyn, shout!" When the laundry truck arrived at the airport, the boys were waiting to get them, none too happy that they smelled of dirty sheets.

They rode back on the plane, satisfied they had avoided the photographers in Ireland, only to find another contingent waiting for them at Heathrow. By the next day pictures and stories about Pattie and George filled the front pages, and their relationship became public.

3.

*A*S THAT SPRING passed, Brian learned to no longer ask, "Can anything be more important than this?" because there always was something. As the days grew warmer, the hysterical accolades and media attention only increased, and the unprecedented sales figures became more commonplace. "Can't Buy Me Love," their latest single, was number one in Great Britain and the United States, as well as in twenty other countries around the world. In the month of April the Beatles had an astonishing five songs in a row topping the American charts, and it seemed as if nothing else was being played on the radio.

Already, their fame had transcended their craft; they became the single most popular entertainment story in the world and learned to live their lives in a goldfish bowl. The first concentrated dose of fame in London was a little hard to take. It wasn't the limousines or the glamourous nights spent table-hopping at the Ad Lib with Mick and Chrissie Shrimpton and Verushka that were hard to get used to, but the omnipresent photographers, the reporters, and sycophants who hung on their every word, who analyzed their every nuance and gesture in the next day's editions. While the Beatles were a little put out at being spied on constantly, they read all the newspaper accounts of their activities voraciously—Paul in particular didn't miss a thing—and further took on the characteristics the reporters assigned to them. They became caricatures of themselves, partly because it was the only way to hide whatever privacy was left, and partly because it was expected of them.

John wore his new mantle of fame most uneasily. While Paul and George could bask in the adulation, and Ringo seemed only happily bewildered, John felt slightly betrayed by it all. Here he was, the rebel, the iconoclast, who had become a plaster icon himself. John was being singled out as the great intellect, because of his wit and easy verbal facility in press conferences and interviews. Suddenly, all the wise-ass, mean-tempered humor he had exhibited as a youth that had gotten him into so much trouble was being interpreted as wit. It became, in a way, more difficult to insult people who didn't know him, because he sounded so pithy and bright.

That March a slim edition of his doodlings and puns was published in England under a title suggested by Paul McCartney, *John Lennon in His Own Write*. In it were the same sophomoric punning jokes and cartoons that once had gotten him into so much hot water at Quarry Bank High School, but which now rushed the book to the top of the nation's best-seller lists. The *Times Literary Supplement* said it was "worth the attention of anyone who fears for the impoverishment of the English language." It went on to say that John's writings and drawings were reminiscent of "Klee, Thurber, the Goons . . . and very noticeably, late Joyce." The book became such a sensation that John was to be honored with a Foyles Literary Lunch on the occasion of Shakespeare's four hundredth birthday.

It seemed like such a giggle to the Beatles and their girls that a celebration was held at the Ad Lib club. But what was planned as a small party ended up as a long drunken bash that didn't wind up until five in the morning. John and Cynthia had only a few hours sleep and were so hung over and bleary eyed at the awards luncheon at the Dorchester Hotel ballroom that they could hardly keep their heads up straight. When a reporter shoved a microphone in John's face and asked, "Do you make conscious use of the onomatopoeia?" John snapped back from behind dark glasses, "Automatic pier? I don't know what you're going on about, son."

After a queasy lunch, during which Cynthia watched in awe as John drowned his hangover in white wine, he was asked to make a speech. Now nearly as drunk as the night before, he stumbled to the microphone, mumbled, "Thank you very much. It's been a pleasure," and went back to his seat.

There was a shocked stillness in the room. "What did he say?" a lone voice finally asked aloud.

Another guest suggested, "He said, 'You've got a lucky face.' "

News of this witticism, this Lennonesque gem, raced through the room as the cream of the literati repeated it from table to table: "He said, 'You've got a lucky face.' "

"What did he say?"

"He said, 'You've got a lucky face!' "

In a few more seconds the room burst into applause, enthralled by John's obscure brilliance. Once again, the king wore no clothes but never caught cold.

* * *

Cynthia, too, became a celebrity as a Beatle wife, and even little Julian was known to all the fans. John's home address could be learned by any fan who wanted to know it badly enough, and by now a constant sentinel of girls waited on the front steps of the Emperor's Gate flat. When Cynthia dragged Julian's pram down the six flights of steps to take him for a walk every day, the girls waiting out front were so anxious to see and touch him that they sometimes pushed Cynthia aside to get to him. It was always frightening, for both mother and child, to see those anxious hands with long fingernails flying into the carriage to pinch his cheek or chuck him under the chin. If Cynthia refused to be touched by them or to sign autographs on demand, the girls would spit and curse at her. At times the crowd was so large she was afraid to go out of the building altogether and stayed home for days at a time.

John's phone number was no less of a secret than his address, and soon a well-orchestrated assault of phone calls was launched, from both male and female callers. Most of them were just pranks, but some of them were obscene and a few authentically menacing. Cynthia became apprehensive about answering the phone, and opening the mail was sometimes not much better. The letters from young women offering to entertain John with various sexual tricks were an education in themselves for the still-innocent Mrs. Lennon. So innocent that she could not understand why their friendship with the young couple downstairs had dissolved in a cloud of disapprobation.

Much to Cynthia's great relief, John announced they were moving out of the maisonette and buying a house. The Beatles' accounting firm, Bryce-Hamner, had advised that they spend some of their untaxed income on real estate and that they should each purchase a home. John found one he liked in Weybridge, a polished little suburb in the "stockbrokers' belt" some twenty miles southwest of London. "Kenwood," as it was called, was a £40,000 mock-Tudor house built on a hill in St. George Hills estates. It was a rambling house, a little run down and in need of renovation. John budgeted £30,000 to fix and decorate it, bringing the price to around £70,000. What pop star John Lennon was doing renovating a home in this fussy neighborhood of manicured gardens and lawns, twenty miles outside of London, where he belonged, no one could guess, least of all John himself, except to say that one of the Bryce-Hamner accountants lived there, and it seemed respectable. Of course for Cynthia the new house was a godsend. It was like a reprieve from prison. Weybridge was a lovely place to bring up Julian and a chance to make a real home for John for the first time in their marriage. The £30,000 budget for decoration and renovation would have thrilled any wife, and she couldn't wait to move in and begin work on it.

4.

*F*AME ALSO HAD COME to Brian Epstein, and his close friends were most fascinated to note what Brian's public reputation was like. Brian had become so world famous as the Beatles' manager, he was photographed almost as much as they were. He was a warm, Christmassy figure to the youth of Great Britain, a kind of loving "inventor" of this great gift to the world. The words "impresario" or "idol-maker" often preceded his name. He was also a symbol of wealth and largesse. If one went into a pub in Kilburn and put a ten-pound note down on the bar, someone might pipe up, "Who do you think you are, Brian Epstein?"

Professionally, he seemed infallible. Cilla Black, his one female act, had scored big for a second time with a Burt Bacharach tune called "Anyone Who Had a Heart" and Billy J. Kramer and the Dakotas had three big smash songs in a row, "Secret," "Back to Me," and their newest hit, "Little Children." In April Brian was asked to write his autobiography to tell the world how he did it all, a suggestion the twenty-nine-year-old greeted with relish.

He proudly mentioned his book project to the Beatles and Neil Aspinall as they were all riding in a crowded elevator together. "Perhaps," Brian said, "one of you could suggest a title."

"Why don't you call it *Queer Jew?*" John suggested.

Brian was so stung by this he was in tears by the time the elevator doors opened, but John was unmoved. Later, when Brian announced that he had chosen *A Cellarful of Noise* as the title, in reference to the Cavern Club, John took to calling the book *A Cellarful of Boys.*

Brian had neither the time nor the disposition to sit down and write a book, so he hired a young journalist to ghost it for him. For this job he chose a young Manchester newspaper reporter named Derek Taylor. Derek was a handsome, clean-shaven fellow who had come to Brian's and the Beatles' attention in the autumn of 1963 in Southport, when, as the theater critic of the *Manchester Daily Express,* he had blithely kicked down their dressing room door to ask them a question. The Beatles were so astonished at his temerity, and his easygoing charm thereafter, they let him in. A few months later when the *Daily Express* asked each of the Beatles to write a guest column, Derek was hired to ghostwrite George Harrison's column for him. When that worked out to everyone's liking, he became Brian's first choice to write his autobiography. Derek was hired for £1,000 plus 2 percent royalties, a handsome fee for a journalist who made only £35 a week at his newspaper job and had a wife and three children.

The book's entire interview and research period took place

over a long weekend at the Imperial Hotel in Torquay in the south of England. On the first day Brian got through his childhood period without much trouble, but on the second day he started having difficulty telling Derek the story of his teens and early twenties. "[He] was at pains to elaborate upon his unhappy, unproductive school days, anxious to dwell on his failure to complete army service, insistent on narrating his inability to succeed at the Royal Academy of Dramatic Art," Derek wrote later. "[He was] determined to discuss his difficulties in relating to the opportunities of his family's prosperous retail furniture business, eager to lay bare his enduring feeling of being 'out of sorts with his environment' and, as if this were not enough, he made it clear that he had problems in making friends."

Brian was in the midst of telling Derek a labored story of an allegedly heterosexual romance when he said, "Switch off the tape recorder and let's have lunch. There's something I must tell you."

Derek says that he listened patiently and compassionately throughout lunch while Brian confessed to what everyone already knew—and wasn't concerned about. Still, Brian was obviously very upset about it himself and Derek indulged him. Derek wanted to comfort him in some way and even thought of taking his hand as an understanding gesture, but he didn't have the courage. "It wasn't until the Beatles taught me that I learned it was permissible to hug another man."

A Cellarful of Noise was a frothy, upbeat volume written in Taylor's poetically brisk style, yet it somehow still captured that curious grandiloquence that Brian emanated. It pointedly avoided any embarrassing revelations, and the most surprising admission in the book was that Brian's relationship with Paul was described as sometimes being strained. Not too surprisingly, the volume became a best-seller in Great Britain shortly after it was published by Souvenir Press.

* * *

5.

*B*Y *NOW,* it was no secret that Paul McCartney was squiring the young daughter of prominent psychiatrist Richard Asher, although the press blithely ignored the fact that Paul was ensconced in the Ashers' guest bedroom. The press also was ignoring the rumors that Paul's amorous adventures had already caused him a great deal of trouble. The rumors were all true. One of the club owners on the Grosse Freiheit in Hamburg was claiming that Paul had made his daughter pregnant and that he was the father of a young child. The mother, a pretty girl with long, straight hair named Erika Hubers, was a waitress in one of the clubs. Paul allegedly had dated Erika during one of his Hamburg stints. Erika claimed that Paul had known she was pregnant and had encouraged her to have an abortion. Erika refused, and a daughter named Bettina was born on the day Paul left Hamburg. Legal documents to the effect were drawn up in Hamburg and delivered to Liverpool, where the matter was quickly turned over to David Jacobs in London. Jacobs instructed Paul to deny any responsibility and sent the documents back to Hamburg unanswered. Jacobs contended that the German tribunal had the right to deal with the matter if they wished, and if the mother continued to press charges the matter could proceed there. Jacobs preferred the slow bureaucracy of the German courts. In England the matter was likely to be given prompt attention and tremendous publicity. The lawsuit, however, would not go away, and the girl's family threatened to file papers in Great Britain. In 1966 Paul allegedly paid a settlement of approximately $27,000 to keep little Bettina's existence a secret. However, in 1981 Bettina Hubers started to pursue the case again, reportedly suing Paul for $6 million.

But that was hardly the end to the complications of Paul's love life. In the spring of 1964, during the shooting of *A Hard Day's Night,* an even more delicate situation of the same nature arose, revealed here for the first time. A young girl in Liverpool named Alice Doyle* had given birth to a baby boy she claimed

* Not her real name.

was Paul McCartney's son. Under David Jacobs' counsel Paul denied being the father, and the young girl was referred to an associate of David Jacobs in Liverpool, a man named D. H. Green. Alice Doyle and her mother visited Green's office in late March of 1964. In a memo Green sent Jacobs he said he found them quite decent and reasonable. He felt that the girl had no intention of trying to hurt Paul and that "her only concern seemed to be getting enough money to buy a pram" for the infant.

Jacobs was in the midst of negotiating a small settlement for this purpose when Miss Doyle's mother confessed her plight to her brother, Joseph McGlynn.* McGlynn went to see D. H. Green, who found him less than savory. McGlynn knew how much the child was worth and intended to see his niece get proper compensation. He was referred to David Jacobs in London, who was waiting for him to call. Jacobs taped the telephone conversation and sent a transcript to Brian.

"I am telling you here and now that all the newspapers that matter have already got this story," Joseph McGlynn threatened Jacobs over the phone.

"Are you pressing me for money or what?" Jacobs demanded imperiously.

The man said the price for the family's silence was £5,000.

When Jacobs told D. H. Green of this demand, Green commented, "There's a nasty word for all this."

Jacobs told Brian and Paul that his greatest concern was that even if they gave the girl a large settlement, it would in no way insure that the uncle would not go to the newspapers, or that he wouldn't be back in a year demanding more. Jacobs advice was that the less money they paid, the less culpable they would appear if the story did come out. Brian agreed that there was nothing worse than falling prey to a blackmail demand and that the best they could do was pay the girl a small sum and hope the family kept quiet.

Jacobs drew up three deeds of agreement. The uncle, Joseph McGlynn, was to receive only £5 for himself in return for signing a vow of silence. The girl's mother was to receive the same amount with the same understanding. For Alice Doyle, with the stipulation that Paul continue to deny being the father of the child, and

* Name changed.

that this sum did not in any way represent an admission, there was £3,000. The deed stated that in the eventuality of a lawsuit and trial that proved to the satisfaction of the court that the child was indeed Paul McCartney's, the maximum payment the court could order for the maintenance and education of the child was £2.10 a week until he was twenty-five. In consideration for the £3,000 paid to her, Alice Doyle was never to make any claim against Paul in the future or allege that he was the father or disclose the terms of the agreement; otherwise she would be liable to return the £3,000.

It wasn't long before it became obvious that the £5 paid to the uncle was not going to shut him up. During the Beatles' triumphant return to Liverpool later that summer for the northern premiere of *A Hard Day's Night*, handbills were distributed through the crowd of 500,000, alleging Paul's paternity, even as the Beatles waved to an adoring crowd from the balcony of City Hall. Jacobs promised to bring the uncle to court on blackmail charges, but for as long as three years later the uncle was still circulating poems about the child to newspapers. One lengthy ode, parodizing the lyrics of several of the Beatles' hit song, reads in part:

> *My name is Mark Paul Doyle, I'm just a little boy . . .*
> *In spite of all her lovin' we got no thanks from him,*
> *It seems he loved my mother, just long enough to sin;*
> *Besides his lust, she took his money, to compensate a lie,*
> *But Mr. Paul McCartney, Dad, you make mother cry.*

By this time, however, the newspapers had heard hundreds of all sorts of crank rumors and accusations about all four of the Beatles, and this one wasn't taken any more seriously than the rest. Coupled with Fleet Street's healthy dependence on the Beatles, the matter was kept from national knowledge. Cynthia Lennon later summed it up: "It appeared from the evidence on the solicitor's desk at this time that Paul had been a bit of a town bull in Liverpool. Claims for paternity suits rolled in. He found himself in great demand in more ways than one. Whether the claims were true is anybody's guess."

Chapter Eight

1.

ON AUGUST 11, 1964, I (Peter Brown) went to London to be Brian's houseguest for a gala celebration he was giving the following evening in anticipation of the Beatles' first major tour of the United States. Brian had been telling me about the party details for weeks, and he was almost as excited about it as he was about their world tour. At that point they had finished three engagements on a global jaunt in which the Beatles were to play fifty cities on four continents. It had begun in early June in Scandinavia and had continued in Hong Kong and Australia. In America the Beatles were scheduled to give thirty performances in twenty-four cities, all in the space of thirty-two days. They were to blanket the country, covering 22,441 miles in the process. Perhaps a world tour of this magnitude had never been attempted before because no entertainment act, save for Elvis, warranted it, or perhaps it was because there had never been a Brian Epstein before to envision it.

So far the tour had been a triumph, although Ringo had come down with 102-degree fever on the eve of the Scandinavian tour, due to a bad case of tonsilitis, and had missed the opening dates in Denmark and Holland, where 100,000 people lined the streets just to get a glimpse of their car. He was replaced by a shy session drummer Jimmy Nichol who was never heard from again. Ringo was well enough to join the touring party, which now included Derek Taylor, as Brian's assistant and publicist, and John's Aunt

Mimi, for the trip to Adelaide, Australia, where 300,000 citizens—the largest group so far—lined the route from the airport to their hotel. In July they stopped traffic back at home at the royal premiere of *A Hard Day's Night*, which was attended by Princess Margaret and the Earl of Snowden. Thousands of fans overran the block of the Pavilion Theater, spilling out into Piccadilly Circus, quite literally bringing the center of London to a halt.

Brian's send-off party for the American leg of the tour couldn't compete with all that, but he was certainly going to try. In that beautiful summer of elaborate entertaining by the Swinging London set, Brian wanted this party for the boys to be the most memorable. For this he hired interior designer Kenneth Partridge to arrange an appropriately elaborate setting. Partridge was a small, wryly funny man who had been recommended by David Jacobs. He understood the scope in which Brian liked to do things, and they got along famously thereafter.

Instead of a restaurant or nightclub, Partridge suggested Brian use his own Belgravia penthouse and set about transforming the apartment and rooftop into a lush party setting. It took five days to build. Partridge started by erecting a mammoth white marquee to cover the roof. The white canvas tent, the size of a small circus tent, was fitted with wooden sides with French windows around the perimeter so the guests could view the city while they dined. A raised floor was constructed over the tar roof and covered with cherry red sisal carpeting. On top of this was built a bandstand and a hardwood dance floor. Several thousand white carnations were ordered to build tall, overflowing centerpieces around the candelabra on the large round tables that dotted the roof. The center pole of the marquee was covered in Spanish moss and intertwined with 700 carnations in the shape of a palm tree. A small society orchestra was hired, as was a caterer to prepare, in addition to filet of beef, cold duck, and lobster, a selection of kosher foods to please Brian's family.

The day of the party was glorious, warm, and sunny, with nary a cloud in sight. Late in the afternoon Partridge was in Brian's flat overseeing the final details with the workmen when Brian arrived with Queenie. "My mother is just coming from the hairdresser," he announced, "and she'd like to see the marquee before anyone arrives."

Partridge led them up to the roof where the florist and his

assistants were just about to leave. Queenie's eyes widened at the sight of the marquee. "Oh no!" she cried, "Red and white! Red and white is very bad luck!" Partridge said he never heard of this particular superstition before, and Brian explained that Queenie was superstitious about a whole, odd assortment of personal taboos, including birds on curtains.

"What can we do? What can we do?" Brian asked Partridge. "It must be changed! We can't have any bad luck just before the boys leave on tour!" Partridge said that he didn't think there was anything that could be done at that point. The guests would arrive in only a few hours. "Then the whole thing will have to be called off," Brian insisted.

Partridge raced out of the flat and down into the street, where he breathlessly caught up to the florist's truck just as it reached the corner. The florist's assistants were sent to the local stationery shops to fetch as much red ink as they could buy. In the interim, Partridge and the florist went upstairs to the roof and took out every single last white carnation from the arrangements and brought them down to the street. They spent the next several hours dipping the white carnations in buckets of red ink. The last, dripping wet pink carnation was replaced in the display just as the first guests started to arrive. Never was Queenie more like the mad Queen of Hearts in *Through the Looking Glass* than when she had her knaves paint the flowers for her.

The party became the most talked about social event of the summer. The engraved invitations went out to all the reigning stars of Swinging London. By eight o'clock that night the mews in front of Wadham House was filled with hundreds of people who turned out to watch the guests arrive. Two uniformed guards stood at the door of the building, demanding to see invitations. Later in the evening, with dinner already being served, one of the security guards came up to the roof looking for Ken Partridge. There was a lady downstairs, he explained, in a mink coat in the middle of the summer, insisting that Brian Epstein had invited her to the party the night before.

Partridge rode down in the lift to find Judy Garland and her then-boyfriend, Mark Herron, standing in the mews. Garland nervously explained that she had been seated at a table next to Brian's at the Caprice Restaurant the previous evening, and Brian had invited her. Partridge turned to the guards and said, "This lady can come in anywhere," and escorted her upstairs. When they arrived in the living room Garland was bewildered to find an empty flat littered with cocktail glasses and dirty ashtrays. Partridge assured her that all the guests were still there, upstairs on the roof having dinner. Having to make a late entrance in front of so many people seemed to terrify her, and she promptly went into the bathroom and threw up. Ironically, Garland needn't have been so apprehensive; except for Brian's personal friends, such as Lionel Bart and David Jacobs, who was her English attorney, Garland was roundly ignored by the Beatles and other pop celebrities, who were totally uninterested in movie stars.

At some point during the party John Lennon was introduced to Ken Partridge. "Did you do all this?" Lennon asked. He was so impressed that he asked Partridge to come out to Weybridge the next day and talk about decorating the new house. Brian accompanied Partridge to Kenwood to supervise the event. They toured the house together, along with Cynthia and John. Cynthia was immediately defensive about some strange man redecorating her home but characteristically kept silent about it. Partridge quickly had a decorator's vision for the house that went way beyond Cynthia's sweet, simple plans. He suggested they tear down walls on every floor and convert the twenty-seven-room house into a cozier eighteen. John said that he wanted the house to be equipped with ultramodern, spaced-age stereo and kitchen equipment. Partridge suggested they build the kitchen on many levels, with floating appliance platforms. Within minutes it was settled. John insisted that Partridge have the drawings ready in thirty-six hours, before he left on the American tour, and Partridge stayed up through the night with an assistant at the drafting table. The following day a series of drawings, along with fabric swatches and colors, were presented to Cynthia and John at Kenwood. Cynthia was devastated at the sight of it; all her plans were ruined. But the only thing she could bring herself to say about the plans was that she could draw better.

John gave Partridge carte blanche with the budget. He had only two small requests: that the artwork of his fellow students at the Liverpool Art College be hung in the bedrooms, and that the music room incorporate the piano from Aunt Mimi's house, which had a wood-cut front with green pleated silk fabric behind it. John said he would be away for two months, and Partridge asked what he should do if there were any questions. Should he consult with Cynthia?

John said, "Don't ask Cynthia. You make the decisions."

The following day John left for America. Cynthia held Julian in her arms at the front door and cried as he got into a limousine and disappeared down the drive. Then she went back into the house, where the decorators and contractors were to relegate her to a tiny servants' apartment at the top of the house while the rest of the mansion was torn away from under her control and kept that way for nearly a year.

2.

*I*F YOU HAD to characterize the Beatles' first tour of America, it would be a sound, a long, high-pitched wailing sound that assailed their ears from the time their plane touched ground in San Francisco on August 18 to the moment they left America four weeks later. It was the screams of hysterical girls at the airport and the whining of their rented Lockheed Electra; it was the wail of the police sirens and motorcycles that escorted them and the shrieking of girls waiting in hallways and the streets. Hoping to see a bit of America, all they got to see were the back seats of limousines, antiseptic hotel suites, institutionalized meals from room service shared with aggressive journalists or loudmouthed disc jockeys, dank dressing rooms in the lockers of athletic stadiums.

As Neil Aspinall described it, "You were so tired you only wanted to get laid and go to bed. Nobody would have understood how awful it really was. No hotel really wanted you; the police wanted you out of town; you'd check into a hotel in the middle of the night, exhausted. On your back, all the time, were the local promoters, the owners of the stadium, the owners of the local athletic teams, the local sheriffs and their wives and kids, all of whom demanded autographs whenever they bloody wanted them."

They brought with them only a skeleton crew. All American

arrangements, from hotels to transportation, had been handled for them by their American booking agent, Norman Weiss at GAC. In addition to regulars Neil Aspinall and Mal Evans, they brought Derek Taylor, whom Brian had hired away from his newspaper job to become his personal assistant and press representative.

The Beatles were playing only the largest stadiums in the country. In this way the promoters could meet Brian's price for the boys and still keep ticket prices low, thus pleasing the fans and the Beatles. Brian was demanding between $25,000 and $50,000 as a cash advance for each appearance, plus upwards of 50 percent of the profits after that, depending on the size of the venue. Although his price was the highest ever quoted for a personal appearance at the time, promoters were clamoring for a shot at booking them. In the end, some of the arenas and promoters were chosen on the basis of the legendary "brown paper bag" money.

The tour turned into a catalog of the incredible. At their opening night concert at the Cow Palace in San Francisco, their limousine driver didn't pull away from the stadium loading ramp quickly enough and the Beatles' car was overrun by hysterical teenagers. The weight of the people began to crush the roof, with the Beatles inside. Only the quick action of the Cow Palace security forces extricated the boys in time. They were then put into the relative safety of an ambulance that was already occupied by several drunken sailors who had gotten into a brawl during the show. Later that night diehard fans kept vigil in sleeping bags and folding chairs in the street below the windows of the Hilton Hotel. The crowds surrounding the hotel wailed so loudly day and night that a woman guest was beaten and robbed while her cries for help went unheard in the din. On August 20 they performed at Convention Hall in Las Vegas, and on the twenty-first they were at Municipal Stadium in Seattle, where a girl climbed high over the stage on a beam to get a closer look at them and fell in a heap at Ringo's feet. On the twenty-second they were at the Empire Stadium in Vancouver, Canada, and on August 23 there was a triumphant concert at the Hollywood Bowl, where the towels they used to wipe their bodies after the concert were cut up into square-inch souvenirs and mounted on certificates for sale. The twenty-sixth found them in Denver at the Red Rock Stadium, the twenty-seventh at the Gardens in Cincinnati, where Brian disappeared for a night and a day, sending the entourage into a state of high anxiety.

That was nothing compared to the night in Indianapolis Ringo disappeared and didn't turn up until seconds before the concert at the State Fair Coliseum, a story told here for the first time. Ringo had been up for three days without any sleep, fueled by "purple hearts," the amphetamine tablets that had replaced Prellys. Speed of every strength and formula was now a necessity for the boys and Brian to keep up with the rigorous schedule. A large supply of these pills was brought with them from England, while others were procured by Mal Evans on the black market, with the help of concert promoters in local towns. The Beatles were on a physical roller coaster, "wired" tight on speed, then buffeted by gallons of scotch and Coke to calm them down. This particular evening the speed got the best of Ringo, who told Neil he was slipping out of the hotel to kill himself. Neil didn't take him very seriously, although he wasn't sure what he meant by "kill myself." He didn't start to worry until the next morning and Ringo was still missing. By the time of that evening's concert, they were frantic. Ringo arrived moments before the Beatles were supposed to go onstage, accompanied by two state troopers. It seemed Ringo hadn't been out of the hotel fifteen minutes when these two young local troopers had picked him out on the street and offered to give him a lift. They gave the speeding drummer a tour of the city, and Ringo casually mentioned he had always wanted to see the Indianapolis auto racing track where the Indy 500 was run every year. The police happily drove him there. The track was officially closed, but the police didn't have a hard time convincing the night watchman to open the gates and let Ringo of the Beatles inside. Ringo spent much of the night driving the police car around the track to his heart's content. At dawn, the troopers took him home with them, and one of their wives cooked him breakfast.

By the time Ringo took his place at his drumkit on stage, his legs were so weak from his seventy-two-hour binge, they went out from underneath him, and he was unable to use the drum pedals for his bass.

The fact that Ringo was too incapacitated to play went unnoticed by the fans, who couldn't hear him anyway. The trials and tribulations of touring might have been made worthwhile by some artistic success, but it was with bitter irony that the Beatles realized their audiences screamed so loudly during their concerts that the music couldn't be heard at all. From the second they were announced, all sound was drowned out by fist-biting, shrieking, crying teenagers. Unless the concert was recorded or broadcast live over a radio station as arranged by Brian, not a soul heard them live—not even the Beatles themselves, whose primitive monitors were too weak to compete with the crowd. This especially depressed John, who felt that he had indeed "sold out" and was nothing more than Brian's puppet on the stage. For some of the concerts the Beatles didn't even bother to sing. They mouthed the words and played the music as fast as they could, so they could get the hell off stage and out of the hail of flashbulbs and jellybeans. Often they were so disgusted, they managed to play fifteen songs in twenty-five minutes.

As the tour progressed the Beatles became aware of a goulish phenomenon. The deformed goblins and cripples of John's schoolboy drawings had come to life to haunt them. Everywhere the Beatles turned they seemed to be surrounded by the unfortunate: children crippled by various horrible diseases, blind children, the retarded, the terminally ill. It was the crippled children who sat in the first five rows of every concert, so the Beatles looked out over a sea of wheelchairs. And it was inevitably the afflicted who got backstage passes. Desperate parents would present these children to the boys, and one of John's primary memories of touring was the twisted hands reaching out for him.

They could take little solace in the girls who were brought for them. The girls on the road consisted of either the professional groupie-cum-call-girl the promoter had arranged to drop by the boys' hotel suite or, more usually, girls Neil and Mal had picked up for them. Supplying girls was one of Neil's and Mal's primary responsibilities on tour, and one that they both went about with great relish. Mal wasn't above the "if you fuck me first I'll introduce you to *them*" routine. The girls were screwed, blewed, and tattooed before Mal and Neil swept them out of the Beatles' suite at dawn. The girls were escorted out the service entrance, each given an autographed picture—forged by Neil and Mal—and told to keep their mouths shut. Miraculously, for no reason anyone can explain, the girls kept their mouths shut. In America, at least, there were no "My Night with Paul" stories in the tabloids, nor were there paternity suits. It was no small wonder either, since it was not uncommon to find fifteen girls waiting on line in Neil's and Mal's rooms, passing the time by ironing the Beatles' stage costumes.

3.

*O*N *AUGUST 28* a small but auspicious event occurred at the Delmonico Hotel in New York that would grow to affect the consciousness of the world: Bob Dylan turned the Beatles on to marijuana for the first time in their lives.

Now, the Beatles did not become marijuana addicts immediately after that—it took at least six months for that transformation to occur—but smoking pot with Dylan gave getting high the Sanctification of the Hip. Before that they had spurned marijuana with a passion; as far as they were concerned, pot smokers were junkies, in the same category as heroin addicts. The pills the boys took were pharmaceutical, illegally obtained but not illegal to take. Shortly after their turn-on with Dylan they began to compose under marijuana's spell. It didn't show very much on the next album, most of which was already composed and recorded anyway, but you could almost smell the pungent smoke on the album that was to follow. There was no doubt about it; Dylan had given them a key that opened a door to a new dimension of pop music, and they took the youth of the world across the threshold with them.

John Lennon had long wanted to meet Bob Dylan but not as badly as he wanted to meet Elvis, however. For John, Elvis was a god who had achieved indescribable sanctity. Dylan was a contemporary, and to John just another competitor, although John was a little envious of Dylan's gift for lyrics. It was only recently that John had begun to take special interest in his own lyrics. His first introspective, autobiographical song, "I'll Cry Instead," had been written for the soundtrack of *A Hard Day's Night* but had never made it into the movie. The lyrics said, "I've got a chip on my shoulder that's bigger than my feet / I can't talk to people that I meet."

That was certainly the case with Dylan. They were introduced by a mutual friend, writer Al Aronowitz, who was one of the first legitimate journalists to write about pop music. Aronowitz had befriended John the previous spring in England, while writing about him for the *Saturday Evening Post.* At that time John had told Aronowitz he wanted to meet Dylan, but only "on his own terms," when John had become his "ego equal." On that August 28, after playing the Forest Hills Tennis Stadium, with the Beatles' smiling faces on the cover of *Life* magazine, John was ready.

Aronowitz rode in from Woodstock with Dylan in a blue Ford station wagon driven by Victor Mamoudas, Dylan's road manager and chum. They parked around the corner from the hotel, and Mamoudas, who's tall, dark, and Sephardic, bombed Dylan and Aronowitz past the crowd of screaming kids into the relative safety of the hotel lobby. There they found themselves with a two-man police escort to accompany them up to the Beatles' floor. When the elevator door opened Dylan and company were shocked to find still more police, plus a dozen people gaily chatting and drinking booze being served out of Derek Taylor's room. Included in this group waiting to be admitted to the Beatles' suite were various reporters, disc jockeys, and the singing groups The Kingston Trio and Peter, Paul and Mary.

Dylan was whisked past these people into the Beatles' private domain. Brian, Neil, Mal, and the Beatles had just finished a room-service dinner around the dining room table when Dylan appeared in the doorway. He was smaller than the boys had expected, with a hook nose and merry, twinkling eyes, like a Semitic St. Nick. After clumsy introductions officiated over by Brian, the embarrassed tension in the room was palpable. Brian moved the guests into the living room, trying to keep the evening afloat. He asked Dylan and his friends what they wanted to drink, and Dylan replied, "Cheap wine."

Brian was embarrassed to admit that there was only champagne, French wines, scotch, and Coke in the suite, and Mal was dispatched to get Dylan's favorite cheap wine. During the wait it was obliquely mentioned that some pills of speed were available, and Dylan and Aronowitz reacted strongly against the idea. Both of them were antichemical at the time, especially speed. In lieu of pills, Dylan suggested, perhaps they'd like to try something organic and green, grown out of Mother Earth's sweet flowing breast.

Brian and the Beatles looked at each other apprehensively. "We've never smoked marijuana before," Brian finally admitted.

Dylan looked disbelievingly from face to face. "But what about your song?" he asked. "The one about getting high?"

The Beatles were stupefied. "Which song?" John managed to ask.

Dylan said, "You know . . ." and then he sang, "and when I touch you I get high, I get high, I get high . . ."

John flushed with embarrassment. "Those aren't the words," he admitted. "The words are, 'I can't hide, I can't hide, I can't hide . . .' "

Dylan couldn't wait to initiate them. The preparations to secure the hotel suite took a half hour before Dylan was even allowed to produce the grass. The doors were closed and bolted, and towels from the bathroom were stuffed into every crevice and crack. The blinds were pulled tight and the drapes drawn against the Park Avenue traffic. Finally, a bemused Dylan was allowed to roll the first joint.

Dylan lit the joint, gave them instructions on how to smoke it, and passed it on to John. John took it from him but was too scared to try it himself and passed it on to Ringo, whom he called "my royal taster." Ringo held onto the joint and finished it himself while Dylan and Aronowitz rolled half a dozen others.

Ringo started laughing first and set the others off. Like many novice pot smokers they found many trivial things funny. Dylan watched for several hours as the Beatles broke each other up, sometimes with something authentically funny, often at nothing more than a look or a word or a pause in the conversation. For a while they all laughed at Brian, who kept saying, "I'm so high I'm on the ceiling. I'm up on the ceiling . . ." After the smoke had cleared out they allowed a room-service waiter to come in to clear the dining room and found everything he did reason to convulse them with laughter. Months later "Let's have a laugh" became the code for "Let's go get stoned."

Paul was overwhelmed with the momentousness of the occasion. "I'm thinking for the first time," he said, "really *thinking.*" So certain was he of uttering gems of wisdom, he demanded that everything he said that evening be recorded for posterity. He had Mal Evans follow him around the hotel suite, writing down everything he said.*

The evening was the start of a long, albeit intermittent, friendship with Dylan, and they made arrangements to see him again when they passed through New York at the end of their tour.

4.

*T*HE CITIES FLEW BY. Milwaukee, Chicago, Montreal, Jacksonville, Boston, Baltimore, and Pittsburgh. On September 19, in an airplane over Houston, Texas, feeling like he was one hundred years old, Brian turned thirty. He was presented with cowboy guns and a holster as a gift. His birthday celebration had been only slightly marred when the Electra aircraft in which they were traveling was overrun by fans on the tarmac at Houston airport just before takeoff. A screaming horde of teenagers broke past security guards and actually managed to climb on the wings of the plane and tried to break the pressurized plane windows with Coke bottles before the airport police could pull them off. It was no less distressing to learn in flight that back at the Houston hotel a chambermaid had been slashed with a knife by a frenzied fan demanding to know the Beatles' room numbers.

When they said they could not go on, would not go on, they did one more date. The people of Kansas City, where the Beatles could not fit in an appearance, felt left out and multimillionaire Charles O. Finley, the owner of the Kansas City Athletics baseball team, promised the city fathers he would get the Beatles for them. Finley had been trying to contact Brian in England previous to the tour, and his requests for a meeting were denied, along with hundreds of other similar requests. In frustration, Finley flew to San Francisco, where through Norman Weiss' intercession he was

---

* Mal Evans kept these notes—ludicrous pontifications in retrospect—with him up until the time of his death in Los Angeles in 1976. They were confiscated by the police and lost with some of his other belongings.

granted a personal audience with Brian. Finley started negotiations for the boys to play in Kansas City by offering the Beatles $100,000 cash, up front, plus any percentage Brian named. A $100,000 fee was unheard-of in 1964, even as a weekly payment in Las Vegas. Brian was impressed, but he still refused; the boys were too tired, he said, and there was no time. Finley persisted, and finally, at a cash price of $150,000 plus expenses—the largest fee ever paid for a performance of a single concert—the Beatles played Kansas City on their last free night in America. This concert held special irony for them, since the audience, like the others, hardly heard a note they produced. When they left town, the sheets on which they had slept in their hotel rooms were removed from the beds in front of witnesses and sold for $1,150 to representatives of Chicago radio station WBKB. The sheets yielded 6,000 one-inch swatches, which were sold at a dollar apiece. As far as can be ascertained, the pillowcases are still in a bank vault, estimated to have appreciated more than the price of gold.

The Beatles' last American appearance of that tour was a charity concert at the Paramount Theater in Brooklyn for Cerebral Palsy in which they were sharing the bill with Steve Lawrence and Eydie Gormé. As soon as the concert was over, Derek Taylor commandeered Brian's rented limousine, which was waiting near the crowded rear stage door. Derek had accompanied a group of important journalists covering the Beatles for national magazines to the concert and wanted to take them back with him to the Idlewild Hotel near the airport, where the Beatles were staying on their last night in town before catching an early flight back to London in the morning. Included in Derek's charge was a young journalist named Gloria Steinem, who was doing a profile on John Lennon for *Cosmopolitan.* But by the time they got back to the hotel, they discovered that the Beatles had already returned and were again sequestered in their rooms with Bob Dylan. Derek and all his disappointed journalists retired to his room for a drink.

It was just after midnight when Brian arrived at the hotel in a taxi. He stormed up and down the hallway in a screaming rage, bringing the Beatles' entourage into the hallway to see what the matter was. Brian was furious that someone had taken his limousine and intended to make a scene about it in front of the gawking journalists. When he found out it was Derek, he ordered Derek into his room and screamed at him, near tears.

"I don't think your behavior is appropriate to the seriousness of the event, Brian," Derek told him coolly. "I didn't take the car joyriding. I used it for important journalists. What was so important about the limousine?"

Brian began to shout, "Get out! Get out!" and Derek crept out the door and down to the bar in the lobby, where he proceeded to get blotto on scotch and Coke. He tried to be entertaining for the journalists who still waited to see the Beatles, but all he could do was sulk about Brian's behavior. How could a man who had come so far on pure gumption get so thrown by a limousine? At dawn Derek wrote a letter of resignation and slipped it under Brian's door.

The next morning, on the plane going home, Brian and Derek sat at opposite ends of the first-class compartment, each suffering from a vicious hangover. Later in the flight Brian sent a note to Derek via a stewardess, asking him to rescind his resignation. Derek read the note and went to where Brian was sitting and sat down next to him. Derek declined to have his job back; the job was too time consuming, and he wanted more time with his wife and children. They both had a good cry over a bottle of champagne, and Derek held Brian's hand. "Well, we can be friends, Brian, but I can't work with you. It was only a limousine, after all."

5.

*B*RIAN HAD WANTED the limousine to go out on the town with a new social friend and impress young boys with it. Losing the limousine put a dent in both Brian's delicate ego and his last night in New York.

Brian's life began to undergo quite a change from the moment he became friendly with Nat Weiss, a successful New York divorce lawyer. Some say Nat was one of the best things that ever happened to Brian, a friend who showed him a way to be at ease and content with himself. Others said Nat showed Brian the path to his own destruction. In truth Brian had long before set down that path, and Nat was just a wise and experienced tour guide.

Nat's booming law practice was due in part to his enormous empathy for people and in part to his shrewd reading of character. Occasionally he would take on an "underdog case"—an accused pornographer or sex offender—just for the fun of championing the underdog. Tall, bespectacled, and slightly balding, he was about the same age as Brian and, like many of Brian's friends, shared a solid middle-class background and had a doting Jewish mother.

They were introduced at a party in the Plaza Hotel, where another business associate of Nat's acquaintance often gave soi-rées for single young men. Nat remembers being fascinated at meeting the manager of the Beatles, but when he tried to engage him in conversation, Brian could not rip his attention away from a young man with whom he was obviously quite taken. The next morning Nat got Brian's phone number from his host and called him at his hotel to ask how the conquest went. Brian said, "The boy was quite boring. He had nothing to say." At first Nat thought Brian was joking, but it turned out that Brian had stayed up all night talking to the boy, pursuing intellectual encounters. Brian never made a move. Nat was mildly amused but disappointed that Brian had deprived himself of so much available pleasure, and he offered to take the reticent but impressionable young man on a tour of some of the delights of the city.

One of their first stops was Kelly's on West Forty-fifth Street, at the time New York's most famous hustler bar. Brian agreed to go to this place of dubious repute only if Nat promised not to tell anyone who he was. But after a drink or two Brian was playing "A Hard Day's Night" on the jukebox twenty times over. Once again, the boy Brian took back to his hotel suite with him was engaged only in conversation. Nat suggested that Brian be more aggressive, but there was no encouraging him. Once Nat even resorted to paying a call boy to seduce Brian, only to learn from Brian the next morning that he and the boy stayed up all night playing music, with Brian lecturing, "Now listen to the chords at the end of this song . . ."

Nat couldn't figure it out. Brian was a lovely man. He was attractive, successful, he was romantic. Nat remembers one night at the Plaza Hotel when Brian ordered thirty-six scoops of ice cream just to delight one young fellow, without so much as hugging him before he left the suite. The only sex that seemed to spark Brian's real interest was rough and degrading, with people who would just as soon as spit on him as touch him.

Brian and Nat's friendship solidified very quickly, in part due to the necessities of business. Nat was just the kind of attorney Brian needed, a New York version of David Jacobs. It didn't take Nat a week of working with Brian to discover that the Beatles' business affairs were a mess in the United States. To begin with, the United States Internal Revenue Service, concerned about all the millions of dollars that were flowing out of the country from their American tour, put a freeze on $1 million in concert proceeds in a New York court. Until the legality of the foreign payments could be sorted out, there would be no payment. This put Brian and the boys in the onerous position of having to float their entire U.S. concert out of their own pockets. The tour had cost them a fortune in expenses, far beyond anything they had imagined, and they needed $500,000 in cash desperately.

Far worse, the problem with Nicky Byrne and the Seltaeb merchandising scheme had turned into a legal fiasco. Brian had insisted that Byrne renegotiate the percentages, which Byrne shrewdly agreed to do. NEMS cut was substantially raised to 46 percent, but even at that rate the Beatles were losing a fortune that could have been theirs. Then, something very odd began to happen. The NEMS offices in London began to issue licenses directly to American manufacturers and started collecting the fees themselves. It didn't take long before several American companies owned duplicate agreements, and the lawsuits began to fly. J. C. Penney and Woolworth immediately canceled $78 million worth of orders for merchandise. Byrne unleashed a reported $22 million worth of lawsuits on NEMS, at which point Brian turned the matter over to their first American attorney, Walter Hofer.

One day Nat was on business at the New York State Supreme Court when he heard through the grapevine that a $5 million judgment had been awarded against Brian and NEMS because no one had answered Byrne's lawsuit against them. To make matters more complicated, Byrne was now reportedly being sued by his own partners, who were claiming that he had spent more than $150,000 of the company's money on entertainment and a charge account at Saks Fifth Avenue.

Brian asked Nat to vacate the $5 million judgment, but Nat advised Brian to hire a high-powered lawyer to end the Seltaeb dispute for good. Nat's recommendation for a man who could handle the chore was Louis Nizer. Although Nizer had recently written a best-selling book about his courtroom exploits and was at least as well known in the U.S. as David Jacobs was in London, Brian had never heard of him. Nat set up an appointment anyway, and a meeting was scheduled before Brian left America.

As soon as Nat and Brian were ushered into Nizer's impressively large office, Nat smelled trouble; Nizer was a diminutive man who sat on a raised platform behind his desk in order to look bigger for his visitors. Chances were, the meeting would be a clash of egos. As things happened, it went quite well. The first thing Brian said was, "Have you read my book?" meaning *Cellarful of Noise.*

"Have you read *my* book?" Nizer asked even more grandly.

After some more posturing between the two gentlemen, Nizer agreed to take on the case. When Brian asked what his fee would be, Nizer said, "Fifty thousand dollars retainer to start." Without blinking an eye, Brian reached into his suit pocket, produced a checkbook, and began writing a check.

"You know, Mr. Nizer," he said as he wrote, "I'm paying you this fifty thousand dollars out of my own pocket. The Seltaeb deal was my fault, and I don't want the Beatles to pay any further for my mistakes."

It would take Nizer two years to untangle the Seltaeb web and vacate the judgment against NEMS. When it was finally settled, in the summer of 1967, it was for only $10,000, which was allegedly paid to Nicky Byrne. The Beatles started over again with their own merchandising company called Maximus Enterprises, of which they owned 90 percent. But by then it was much too late—$100 million had slipped through their hands.

Chapter Nine

1.

THE FOUR BEATLES returned to London physically and emotionally exhausted, wanting only to rest, but they learned they had only eighteen days respite before going out on tour again, this time on a grueling five-week sweep of Great Britain. In the intervening two weeks they were expected to go back to the EMI studios on Abbey Road and record their fourth album. Brian and the record company agreed that it was necessary to have a new LP in the record stores in time for the Christmas gift season. When the British tour ended, the group was booked for three weeks of Christmas shows at the Hammersmith Odeon, until January 16. Over 100,000 tickets had been sold two months in advance. Then they had two weeks off before starting another movie for United Artists and Walter Shenson.

The Beatles were so harried that Brian refused to allow them to appear on their night off at the Royal Command Performance for the Queen, much to the ire of Bernard Delfont. He wrote to Brian in September of 1964, begging him to reconsider his decision and reminding him how thrilled he was to have been asked the first time. When this drew no positive response from Brian, Delfont wrote again, threatening to announce to the press that the Queen had already extended an invitation to the Beatles, in an effort to embarrass them into accepting. But Brian held strong. He replied to Delfont that he didn't see any advantage to the boys repeating themselves, no matter how exalted the event.

The album they were given eighteen days to complete came out in time for Christmas, and it was a wonder indeed, although it contained only eight Lennon-McCartney compositions. The rest of the songs were covers of some of the group's favorite rock and roll songs. Called *Beatles for Sale*, it appeared with none of the earmarks of a hastily prepared album. *Beatles for Sale* replaced *A Hard Day's Night* in the number-one spot on the charts, giving them four number-one albums in a row.

The album's two most notable songs were written by John. The first was a bluesy, waltzlike composition called "Baby's in Black." Pungently unlike the rest of the songs on the album, "Baby's in Black" was a morbid composition about a young girl who refuses to stop mourning the death of loved one. The second tune was even more curious, considering it was penned by a man who was the object of so much public adoration. It was called "I'm a Loser," and it was ostensibly a love song about an affair gone awry but sounded distinctly like a lament. "Although I laugh and I act like a clown," John wrote, "Beneath this mask I am wearing a frown. / My tears are falling like rain from the sky / Is it for her or myself that I cry? / I'm a loser, I'm a loser / And I'm not what I appear to be . . ."

It was easy for anyone who knew John well to see how unhappy he was with his lot. He felt duplicitous in his success, hypocritical with his image of the literary but ultimately agreeable, huggable Beatle. His home life was to him the prime example of this hypocrisy. He was married to a woman he probably never really loved; he was bringing up a child "born out of a bottle on a Saturday night." Even his big house in the country had turned into more of a headache than a joy. The house had been torn apart by Ken Partridge's workmen, and John and Cynthia and the baby were relegated to a small servants' apartment at the top of the house. The house was filled with plumbers and electricians from morning until night, and there was no privacy. One day he gave an old guitar of his to one of the carpenters and started an enormous fight between the carpenter and the foreman, who demanded it for his own children. The carpenter refused to give up the prized guitar, and the argument ended with the carpenter being sacked and leaving the mansion weeping. After that, John locked himself in the apartment and stayed away from the whole thing.

To make matters more claustrophobic at Kenwood, Cynthia's mother, Lillian Powell, left all alone in Hoylake, decided to move to Weybridge, and a small bungalow was secured for her just a few miles away. Mrs. Powell was the archetypical mother-in-law, bossy, opinionated, and omnipresent. She arrived at the house every day along with the workmen and helped oversee the construction and decoration, as well as the rearing of Julian.

Perversely, John refused to let Cynthia hire a nanny to take care of Julian. He insisted he "wouldn't have his son raised by a stranger," and Cynthia was tied to the child most of the time. Fortunately for her, a good housekeeper, Dorothy Jarlett, had been left behind by the previous owners. A hearty and congenial woman, Dot, as she was called, came by in the mornings to help with the cleaning and ironing. When it became clear that more help was needed, John gave in and allowed Cynthia to hire a married couple as cook and handyman. Before long the husband was making passes at every woman in the house, and when John was away, the wife fed Cynthia and Julian hamburgers. At the end of the month, the couple's recently divorced daughter moved back in with them and started making eyes at John. Dot hated the cook and accusations of dishonesty and petty theft were rife. "I was no match for the con agents," Cynthia said. "I was hopeless when it came to standing up to people." Added to this menagerie was a lumbering, unshaven chauffeur named Jock, whose rumpled clothes smelled of cigar smoke. One day a neighbor informed Cynthia that Jock spent the nights sleeping in the back of their Rolls-Royce, which was parked down the block from Kenwood. Eventually, cook, handyman, and chauffeur were duly fired by the NEMS office.

The house began to slowly come together under Partridge's auspices, but Cynthia never stopped believing she could have done better. "[Partridge] having done his job of transforming our mansion into a very plush and modern home, left with, I'm sure, a very healthy bank account. It was very beautiful but my mother couldn't resist buying us more and more junk, and the uncluttered design grew more like home as the months passed." The dining room was furnished with a huge, white, scrubbed-wood table with a dozen antique chairs around it, which John thought looked as if they had been bitten by an angry dog. The master bedroom, which Cynthia thought far too large to be comfortable in, was built from three smaller rooms made into one. Its enormous super-king-size bed had a handpainted headboard ten feet long. The appliances in the kitchen were so "space-age" and complicated that an appliance expert had to come to lecture Cynthia and the housekeeper on their use. Even then they were so difficult to operate that the only machine Cynthia could work was the waffle machine. John eventually called Ken Partridge and told him to come up with another simple machine, because he was sick to death of eating waffles.

The house in Weybridge also had a hidden liability; it turned out that John's long-lost father, Freddie Lennon, was working only a few miles away as a dishwasher in a hotel. John drove past this hotel almost every day on his way back and forth from London. Freddie might never have realized that his son had become a national treasure if it hadn't been for a washerwoman who worked with him at the hotel. One day she came up to him with a picture of John in the paper and said, "If that's not your son, Freddie, then I don't know what." The next day a small dapper-looking man with lush graying hair appeared at the front door of Kenwood and introduced himself as John's long-lost dad. John and Freddie had a polite twenty-minute meeting during which Freddie managed to object to John's life-style, to his music, and to the way his home was decorated. Then he asked for a loan. Freddie was ejected from the house.

Undaunted, Fred turned up again at Kenwood, unannounced, and had the door slammed in his face. He went directly to the nearest Fleet Street newspaper and became an overnight media star, happily granting interviews about his son for a few quid. Fred even managed to sell his life story to a magazine called *Tit Bits* for £40 and recorded a novelty single, "That's My Life." The small record company that distributed the single insisted Fred get his teeth capped so he could make public appearances, and in the end it wound up costing him more to pay the dentist than he earned from his recording career. After that, Freddie drifted back into obscurity.

* * *

2.

THE WINTER of 1965 also saw Ringo become the last Beatle to settle down with one girl. Ringo had entered life in the fast lane with the trepidation of someone who had just received his driver's license. While the other three Beatles had at least learned to order brand-name drinks in bars or a good wine in a restaurant, Ringo was still eating eggs and chips for dinner, because he didn't want to experiment with anything more exotic. With his big puppy eyes and self-effacingness, he seemed an easy target for every blonde bombshell who could get near to him. For a time he was dating fashion model Vicki Hodge, but his friends could see he was going out with her just for the kick of it, and they were hardly the same speed.

The girl the same speed as "Ritchie" had been left behind in Liverpool. Maureen Cox and the girls at Ashley Du Pre's hairdressing salon kept careful track of Ringo's adventures around the world, and tenacious Maureen decided she was not giving up on Ritchie quite so fast. On December 1, 1964, when Ringo had his chronically infected tonsils removed at the University College Hospital in London, Maureen took the long train ride down from London and brought him ice cream. She was still there when he recovered and spent Christmas with him in London. Vicki Hodge went on a vacation to Sweden.

Like any northern girl, Maureen ensnared her man the northern way; by mid-January she was pregnant. Ringo, like any good northern man, did what was expected. One morning at three o'clock, good and drunk at the Ad Lib, he got down on one knee and proposed to her amidst the good-natured catcalls of his friends. They were married at a quiet ceremony on February 11. The newlyweds spent a short honeymoon at David Jacobs' house in Brighton, after which they returned to a small, ground-floor flat they had rented on Montague Square, north of Oxford Street. The flat was small and impractical and offered them no security or privacy from the street, but Ringo and Maureen insisted on it, and it was there they lived for a while. Within a few days the address had leaked, and the street-front of the flat was besieged with fans. The only way to enter and exit undetected was to climb over the sink and out a small window into the mews out back.

Again no trailblazer, Ringo asked Ken Partridge to decorate the flat for them. But Ringo gave Partridge only four weeks to finish, from top to bottom, while he was away shooting the Beatles' new film. The large living room on the first floor was decorated with blue silk wallpaper and white modern furniture. As per Ringo's instructions, the apartment was stocked with the latest electronic inventions, including TVs, stereos, burglar alarms, and telephones. There were telephones everywhere, literally every four or five feet, and there was a red telephone in the bedroom that was connected directly to the NEMS office.

Maureen was more complacent than Cynthia about Partridge's work. He was waiting in the flat for them when they returned from location. Ringo, followed by Maureen, alighted from a limousine. Maureen was carrying a tatty old teddy bear and an overnight case. She went from room to room in the house with a blank look on her face, stupefied that this splendor was to be her new home.

3.

*T*HE BEATLES began work on their second film, tentatively entitled *Eight Arms to Hold You,* in late winter of 1965. Costing three times as much as *A Hard Day's Night,* it took twice as long to shoot and produced only a third of the critical acclaim. It was a convoluted, poorly developed idea, with all the self-conscious anxiety of trying to duplicate their first success. With a final screenplay by screenwriters Marc Behm and Charles Wood, *Help!,* as it was finally called, was a parody of futuristic spy movies like the James Bond series. The silly plot centered around a mad scientist and a Hindu sect in search of a valuable ring that somehow wound up on one of Ringo's fingers. A demented, slapstick chase ensues through the better half of the picture, which included location shooting in Austria and in the Bahamas.

As is revealed here for the first time, the Bahamas were chosen as a location by Dr. Walter Strach of Bryce-Hamner strictly for financial reasons. Strach had finally come up with a solution to the Beatles' enormous tax liabilities. He wanted to divert as much money as possible away from Britain before the tax officials got their hands on it. To this purpose Strach removed himself to the Bahamas and applied for a temporary residency. The Beatles sponsored Strach's trip to the Bahamas, where he then formed an umbrella company with Walter Shenson called Cavalcade Productions. Dr. Strach was named an officer in the company. Gratuitous scenes were shot in the Bahamas purely to impress upon everyone the legitimacy of this venture, i.e., a film being made in the Bahamas and not in England. Although this was unorthodox, Dr. Strach claimed it was not in itself illegal. After a substantial sum had been deposited in a Bahamian bank, a small scandal occurred in London. It was that one of Bryce-Hamner's chief executives, James Isherwood, allegedly had appropriated funds for his own use from Woodfall Productions, the production company that had made the movie *Tom Jones*. Isherwood left the company, but the scandal frightened Brian, who went to Lord Goodman, the Prime Minister's solicitor, for advice. Goodman suggested they dissolve Cavalcade and pay the taxes immediately, which was done. As it turned out, the Bahamian scheme served no purpose, and the Beatles saved not a single penny.

It wasn't difficult for anyone on the set of *Help!* to surmise something was making the boys a little silly. Director Richard Lester certainly knew that the Beatles were stoned on marijuana for most of the filming. Their continuous giggling, plus their periodic trips to the dressing trailer to "have a laugh," was enough of a clue to what was going on without the telltale sweet scent of pot that followed them around. The seeds that Bob Dylan had planted the previous summer had by now blossomed in the minds of four full-blown potheads. The effects of the marijuana, and Dylan himself, are apparent on the soundtrack of *Help!*, because now instead of just laughing on the pot, they were beginning to find musical inspiration from it. John's "You've Got to Hide Your Love Away" was strikingly Dylanesque in its images and vocals, with acoustic guitar chords replacing Dylan's trademark harmonica. For the first time, George Harrison was allowed out of the composing shadows with two tunes on the album, "You Like Me Too Much" and "I Need You."

There were two tunes of special interest. The one written by Paul was a revelation to the public and a milestone for the Beatles. It was early summer of 1965, just as they were finishing up the movie soundtrack, and Paul rolled out of bed one morning and went to the piano and wrote an entire song in one sitting. He used the lyric "scrambled eggs" until he could figure out real lyrics and named the song "Yesterday." As Paul likes to describe it, it was a miraculous creation, like an egg; seamless, flawless, a wonder in itself.* "Yesterday" appealed not only to Beatle fans but to a wide cross section of ages and tastes. It became the first Beatle crossover tune to capture the attention of the adult market and give Paul real validation as a composer. Naturally, the hard-nosed rock press and inveterate noise fans criticized it as a Muzak sellout, and just as naturally it became the single most recorded song in history, with over 2,500 cover versions recorded by 1980.

The other song, lyrics written by John, was the title cut. Since it was, after all, written specifically for the title of the film, no one took special interest in the curious lyrics, a plaintive cry of loneliness and despair much greater than the previous "I'm a Loser," or questioned why the slightly overweight pop star living in the house in Weybridge should be writing them.

When I was younger, so much younger than today,
I never needed anybody's help in any way.
But now those days are gone, I'm not so self-assured,
Now I find I've changed my mind, I've opened up the doors.
And now my life has changed in oh so many ways
My independence seems to vanish in the haze.
But every now and then I feel so insecure,
I know that I just need you like I've never done before.
Help, I need somebody, Help, not just anybody, help . . . help!

* "Yesterday" was not included on the American version of the *Help!* LP as it was in the U.K. It was released as a single by Capitol in September of 1965.

* * *

4.

*I*T WAS IN THE SPRING, during the filming of *Help!*, that John and Cynthia and George and Pattie unwillingly took a leap into the future. George had become friendly with the Beatles' London dentist, Eric Cousins.* Teeth capping and dental cosmetic work had become a major preoccupation for the Beatles since they had become the most frequently photographed entertainers of their time. Cousins was doing a bang-up business with all four of the Beatles and their wives. He lived in a handsome flat on Bayswater Road behind Marble Arch with his girlfriend, Annie, a curvaceous blond who hired the bunnies for the Playboy Club. The Beatles considered the dentist somewhat of a hipster-swinger and were suspicious of his desire to be socially friendly with them, but after much insistence George and John accepted an invitation to dinner at his flat.

The four guests remember seeing the sugar cubes all neatly lined up on the mantelpiece in the lounge as soon as they arrived, but no one ever mentioned them. Dinner conversation revolved around sex and an American fellow named Timothy Leary, whom none of the guests knew about save for John, who had only tangentially heard about a new, awesome drug called LSD. After dinner was served, and without explaining the significance of what he was doing, the dentist ritualistically put a sugar cube in each cup of coffee he served. When Pattie was reluctant to finish hers, Cousins insisted she drink every last drop. "Finish it now, come on, finish it."

When the coffee was all drunk, they retired to the drawing room, and Cousins explained what he had just done. Cynthia and Pattie were terror-stricken, not because they as yet understood the effects of LSD, but because they were given the impression that it was some sort of an aphrodisiac and that an orgy would ensue. George and John and the girls immediately excused themselves, but the dentist insisted they stay put; it would not be safe for them to be on the streets when the effects of the drug took hold. But the Beatles were adamant about leaving, and in a few

---

* Not his real name. As far as the dentist's real name, George, Pattie, and Cynthia all claim that they cannot remember it.

moments they had put on their coats and started down the stairs.

Cousins, concerned for their safety, followed with his girl-friend. George and John and the girls piled into George's minicar, where there was intentionally no room for Cousins and his girl-friend. The dentist said he would follow them wherever they went in his own car, and George drove through the London streets at breakneck speeds, trying to lose him. Cousins managed to keep right on their tail all the way to the Pickwick Club, a popular nightspot where they decided to go to hear Paddy, Klaus and Gibson, an upcoming rock trio, perform. More annoyed than con-cerned, they entered the crowded club with Cousins close behind them, and seats were cleared for them all at a prime, stageside table.

It was at the Pickwick that strange things first began to happen. The room seemed larger, longer, the dark lights dazzling pin-points of fire. The staring crowd around them seemed to swell and pulsate, making them so uncomfortable they all decided to leave after just a few minutes. With Cousins trailing along, advising them to return to his flat with him, the two couples now headed for the Ad Lib club, where they hoped the more familiar surround-ings and faces would help calm them. Along the way Pattie had to be restrained from an inexplicable compulsion to smash all the store windows along the street.

They parked the mini around the corner from where the Ad Lib entrance should have been, but instead of the small marquee, they saw what at first looked like a movie premiere with hundreds of clamoring fans outside. Not until they got up to the door did they realize it was just an ordinary light. "Shit," John thought, "what's going on here?"

"When we finally got on the lift," John said, "we all thought there was a fire, but there was just a little red light. We were all screaming like that, and we were all hot and hysterical, and when we all arrived on the floor, because this was a discotheque that was up a building, the lift stopped and the door opened and we were all screaming."

They were in the Ad Lib only a few moments when the dentist, who had arrived shortly after them, sat down at their table and turned into a pig in his seat. "Then some singer came up to me and said, 'Can I sit next to you?' and I said, 'Only if you don't talk,' because I couldn't think," Pattie said.

Somehow they managed to make it out of the club, leaving

the dentist and his girlfriend behind. George drove all of them to Esher in his mini. The forty-minute trip took hours to make because George couldn't drive any faster than fifteen kilometers an hour. Cynthia sat in the back, sticking her fingers down her throat, trying to throw up the sugar cube. John couldn't stop talking. "I was getting all these sort of hysterical jokes coming out like speed, because I was always on that, too," he said. Pattie, frightened and claustrophobic in the small car, begged to stop and sit in a quiet, open field alongside the road. John kept laughing and repeating, "But you can't play football now, Pattie."

When they finally arrived at George's house, they locked the gate and the door and all the windows. George picked up his guitar and began to play, amazed that the notes came out of the instrument like sheets of colored plastic. John busied himself making drawings. One was of the faces of all four Beatles saying, "We all agree with you." He gave Ringo the originals. "I did a lot of drawing that night," John said. "And then George's house seemed to be just like a big submarine. I was driving it and they all went to bed. I was carrying on in it; it seemed to float above his wall which was eighteen foot, and I was driving it."

But Pattie and Cynthia had not gone to sleep, nor were they having happy hallucinations. Pattie was cuddled with her cat on the bedroom floor, convinced that she had been altered permanently and would never be sane again. She kept thinking, "How will I explain it?" Cynthia lay down on the bed and tried to logically figure out what was happening to them, piecing together the mystery of the sugar cube and Timothy Leary. She was hoping to discover a way to get rid of it, to make it stop, because she too was struck with the terrible conviction that what was happening to her was irreversible. Cynthia stayed awake most of the night, until slowly, slowly, everything seemed to die down, the colors faded, and she dropped off to sleep, more exhausted than she had ever been in her life.

* * *

5.

*I*N THE BEGINNING of 1965, I, Peter Brown, was asked by Brian to move to London to assist him in dealing with John, Paul, George, and Ringo exclusively. For the next five years the Beatles and I lived parallel lives. I supervised and conducted all of their personal and business affairs, from getting their signatures on contracts to getting them out of jail. I helped marry them and divorce them. On my desk was a red phone to which only they had the phone number, and locked in a desk drawer I kept their passports. Yet when I moved to London to be with them, they were only pop stars; we had no idea what was yet to come.

NEMS London office was burgeoning into a miniconglomerate with half a dozen new departments, including travel and booking, and nearly twenty new staff members. By the time I arrived in London the NEMS offices on Argyle Street had become too congested with new staff, so Brian and I moved to a quiet suite of offices in a modern building on Stafford Street called Hilly House. These offices were decorated in leather and chrome furniture with dark wood desks. The location and phone number of these new offices were supposed to be kept top secret according to Brian; he intended these offices as a secret rendezvous point where we could meet with the Beatles without being disturbed by the throngs of fans who were now keeping careful vigil for them at the Argyle Street offices. But only minutes after moving into Hilly House Brian was on the phone in his office, distributing the number and address to all his friends, asking them to come by for a drink and see the office.

Brian's brother Clive was reluctant to leave Liverpool, but he agreed to help Brian with the financial administration of the company, while still keeping an eye on the family stores in Liverpool. To run the day-to-day office administration in London, Brian hired an old Liverpool chum and social confidant, Geoffrey Ellis. An Oxford graduate, Geoffrey had become an executive with the Royal Insurance Company's New York office. Brian had kept in touch during his three American trips and managed to hire Ellis away from the insurance company. Although Ellis had no experience in the entertainment business at the time, he was a precise and meticulous man whose love of detail would serve him well as a chief administrator of NEMS. A creative executive with Redifusion TV, Vyvienne Moynihan, was hired to create a television production division of NEMS and to help develop stage productions. Vyvienne was a small, motherly woman with the air of a stern but kindly headmistress. She became Brian's in-office Queenie substitute; she had Queenie's same forgiving quality yet managed never to overstep her employee's role.

Brian bought outright a small theatrical booking agency headed by a short, round gentleman with a pencil-thin moustache named Vic Lewis. Lewis was an officious type who didn't mind letting you know his opinion. He had booked pop singers Donovan and Matt Monroe among others, and Brian gave him a position on the board of directors of NEMS. This was a gesture he instantly regretted; as soon as the two men were in day-to-day business together, Brian realized he had a terrible antipathy for Lewis. He had a self-aggrandizing, pompous quality that clashed with Brian's own imperial manner. Lewis liked to dispense advice; Brian was overly sensitive and headstrong.

Tony Barrow, the onetime "Disker" record columnist who had sent Brian to Decca when he was trying to get the boys a recording contract, was hired to replace Derek Taylor in dealing with the press. Bernie Lee, another booking agent, was added to the organization, as were, eventually, four more full-time bookers. In 1966 the accounting department was expanded to include Martin Wesson, an executive accountant who had been an administrative assistant to the chairman of the Rank Organization. In yet another office on Monmouth Street, a staff of six ran the *Beatles Monthly Fan Club Magazine*, a profitable business in itself that was selling 300,000 copies a month.

As the corporate size of NEMS grew, so did the roster of NEMS-managed acts. NEMS had become so large and confusing that many of the original Liverpool groups, who had put their personal faith and trust in Brian, were growing increasingly unhappy with the third-level assistants assigned to oversee their careers. During the first year of NEMS' success Brian had paid them all a fair amount of attention, enjoying the grooming process and playing Svengali. But it didn't take long for him to realize that they were only mediocre talents compared to the Beatles,

and one by one they fell by the wayside, languishing from inatten-
tion, or quit, expendable baggage on the Beatles train: Billy J.
Kramer, Gerry and the Pacemakers, The Big Three, Tommy
Quickly.

Only Cilla Black's starlight did not seem to fade in Brian's
eyes. Although her professional success to that point had been
limited, based solely on her cover version of the songs of others—
particularly Paul's "Love of the Loved"—her association with
Brian and the Beatles had kept her prominent in the recording
business, and Brian still had faith in her future as a star. For
anyone who ever saw Brian and Cilla together, it was quite obvious
that his faith in her had nothing to do with her talent. Brian
simply loved Cilla. She was warm, she was funny and dependent,
and she was "safe." She was happily in love with her boyfriend,
a handsome blond Irishman named Bobby Willis, whom Brian
also adored. Somehow, with Cilla, Brian managed to break
through a barrier that existed between him and most women.
Whatever it was, Cilla remained one of the few people in Brian's
life with whom he felt completely comfortable, and he continued
to pursue her career with great devotion.

As if NEMS hadn't become complicated enough, another
scheme Brian implemented that year was to open his own car
dealership, Brydor Auto, in Houndslow, Middlesex. Over the past
year Brian and the Beatles and other NEMS artists had spent a
small fortune on expensive autos, and Brian decided that if he
owned his own car dealership he and the Beatles could get exotic
cars at wholesale prices, while he made a huge profit from cars
sold to other rock stars who would certainly flock to Brydor's
showroom simply because Brian owned it. Lo and behold, this
dubious hypothesis turned out to be absolutely correct, and
Brydor became a thriving business. Brian asked another old Liverpool chum, Terry Doran, to run the dealership for him, and the
name Brydor was a combination of their names. Doran had sold
automobiles in Liverpool, and he became, auspiciously, "the man
from the motor trade."

Through Brydor Brian purchased, in addition to the red Rolls-
Royce he already owned, a silver Bentley convertible and a black
mini-Cooper. Ringo purchased two minis, a Land Rover, and a
Facel Vega, which, he bragged to the press, he could afford to
buy but not spell. George Harrison drove an E Jaguar, then a

white Maserati, like James Bond. He grew tired of the Maserati when it only had 4,000 miles on it and gave it back to Terry Doran to put up for sale. John finally passed his driver's test and bought, on a lark, a green Ferrari and a Mini Minor, which stood in the garage at Kenwood next to his Rolls. The Ferrari was returned to Brydor with only 1,000 miles on it. Neil Aspinall, as a Christmas gift from the boys, was given a gray 2.4 Jaguar.

Still, Brian felt the need to expand his holdings, and on April 5, 1965, he took a lease on the Saville Theater, a cavernous legitimate theater with plush, red velvet seats and scalloped gold boxes adorned with gilt balustrades. Located on Shaftesbury Avenue, on what they called the "wrong side" of Charing Cross Road, the theater was to be run under Brian's personal direction. Brian intended to present a compendium of promising young playwrights and the best of rock music. His financial plan was for the rock performances to subsidize the quality theater. His first production was the West End premiere of James Baldwin's *Amen Corner*, which although a critical flop was a prestigious beginning. *Amen Corner* was followed by a sold-out Sunday night concert by the Four Tops. Once, when the director of another production took ill, Brian took over the direction of the show himself until the director returned.

Unfortunately, we were soon to realize that the rock concerts—although almost always sold out—couldn't possibly offset the cost of a theatrical production, particularly with Brian's deal on the Saville Theater. He had leased the Saville, perhaps in an unconscious, self-destructive gesture, from his old, imagined adversary, Bernard Delfont. Because Brian was too grand to haggle, he signed an agreement in which running and rental costs of the theater were so high it was never possible to make a profit.

In its three years of existence, the Saville became one of the most important places to be seen by the Swinging London set. Every Sunday night was a de rigueur event at which the reigning pop figures, designers, fashion models, and assorted luminaries assembled to show off the latest fashion in clothes and behavior. The center of attraction was the "royal box," from which Brian and the Beatles could watch the performance. This large, gilt-painted box, which hung out over the audience to the right of the stage, was furnished with long, modern sofas upholstered in striking leopard-skin prints. Behind a velvet curtain there was a small anteroom filled with fresh flowers. Along one wall ran an elaborately stocked bar and a refrigerator filled with Moët & Chandon. The box had its own private street entrance down the block from the front-door crowds. Brian and the Beatles would alight from their limousines and be inside the theater in a matter of seconds, before the fans even realized they were there. The assembled audience would glance expectantly up at the box, waiting for the arrival of Paul and Jane Asher or John or George or, often, the esteemed and popular young entrepreneur and starmaker himself.

Yet something all too predictable was happening to Brian now that fame and fortune had become daily realities. They weren't enough. He still felt disappointed. The satisfaction of success proved as fleeting as his first few waking breaths each morning. As with the furniture store in Hoylake or RADA or the record stores, Brian was getting bored. All the theaters and car dealerships in the world could not ease his malaise. Even his love for John Lennon, which had spurred him on during the most discouraging periods, was now flattened and transformed into the same kind of fatherly protective love he felt for all the Beatles.

At night, when the Beatles were off with their wives and girlfriends, after his friends and the staff had gone home, Brian was left to face himself. Speedy from a variety of rainbow-colored biamphetamine pills he'd purchased on the black market, more than a little drunk, he would often read through the night with an insomnia he said he had inherited from Queenie. Indeed, both of them read voraciously at night, devouring four or five biographies in a week. The doctor Brian had been recommended to in London, Dr. Norman Cowan, began to prescribe the barbiturate Seconal for him. One or two of these jam-red capsules would usually put him out at dawn, and he would awake groggy and unhappy late in the afternoon. A handful of illicit biamphetamine tablets would follow and put Brian back in the rut. Dr. Cowan, a married, middle-aged practitioner of sterling reputation, had no idea about Brian's amphetamine use in the beginning of their professional relationship. When Brian finally admitted this to him, Dr. Cowan insisted he stop using the pills, as they were a serious threat to his health. Brian convincingly promised he would never take another one, but, naturally, he only began to take more and more as his tolerance to them increased.

On the nights he was so speedy he needed some action, he would drive his silver Bentley convertible to the Cleremont Club in Berkeley Square. The doorman would keep the car right in front of the white Georgian town house, so all who passed would know the Beatles' impresario was inside. Brian would pass the night playing chemin de fer or baccarat, drinking vintage brandy, smoking a cigar, and nibbling on his collection of pills in an never-ending effort not to be too high or too low. On such a merry-go-round it was easy to lose heavily at the gambling tables; and lose he did, an average of £5,000 a week but often as high as £17,000 in a night. Because of his secrecy about his losses, the total amount is incalculable, but it was certainly several hundred thousand pounds.

To fuel his gambling fever, Brian began to draw heavily on his NEMS personal account, but after only a few months this began to alarm the staff accountants, and Brian had to find another, less noticeable, source of income. He fell into the habit of phoning Terry Doran at Brydor and inquiring if any cars had been sold and paid for. If there was any appreciable sum in the till, Brian would drive out to Houndslow himself in the late afternoon and commandeer the checks or cash. When Brian's brother Clive made periodic trips to Brydor to check the books and sales records, Doran loyally never mentioned the tens of thousands of pounds that Brian had drawn and deleted from the books.

Sometimes when the Cleremont Club had closed, and Brian still could not face going home, he would drive to another gambling club, the White Elephant, for one last drink. Then at dawn he would drive the silver Bentley along the Mall, hoping to spy an off-duty guardsman but more often than not going home alone.

Despite his élan and money and newfound celebrity, Brian was still drawn to the most dangerous and unfulfilling of liaisons, which he knew could be his undoing one day. That day arrived in the spring of 1965, when Brian met and fell in love with an American boy living in London named Dizz Gillespie. Dizz was an aspiring actor-singer in his early twenties, with dark hair, mischievous eyes and an impish, upturned nose. Brian was so taken with him he seized upon Dizz's phantom acting career to play Svengali. Brian had this act down pat. He signed Dizz as a NEMS artist and arranged for a new wardrobe. A press announcement was sent out, and Dizz's picture appeared in several London papers as Brian's new discovery. Using the excuse that Dizz was a NEMS artist, Brian paid many of his debts and began to dole out a small allowance from his own pocket.

Naturally, all of Brian's friends warned him against being used by this boy. "He may be manipulative," Brian said, "but he's different than most. There's something special about him, something that I can't name."

Perhaps it was Dizz's capacity for violence. Dizz and Brian would spend many evenings at Brian's Wadham House flat, ingesting large amounts of uppers, Tuinals, and Cognac. More often than not these drugged, drunken nights ended in some sort of unhappy confrontation. They ran from simple arguments to all-out fistfights, which included breaking vases and mirrors. One night, unhappy with Brian's largesse, Dizz worked himself into a rage. When Brian ordered him out of the house, Dizz raced to the kitchen, grabbed the largest knife he could find, and held it to Brian's jugular vein while extracting an additional sum of money from Brian's wallet.

Brian stopped seeing Dizz after the knife incident, but it was no use, he only pined away for the boy, lovesick over him. One afternoon I arrived at Brian's flat to find Queenie and Harry Epstein on their way out. They had made the trip down from Liverpool because they thought Brian sounded depressed over the phone and were horrified at what they found. Hung over from a drug and booze binge the night before, unable to face the day, Brian confessed to them about his love for Dizz Gillespie. Queenie insisted he take a long holiday in the south of France to forget the boy. That afternoon Brian and I packed our bags and set off for Cap d'Antibes, leaving London and Dizz Gillespie temporarily behind.

On our return to London, Brian decided to rid himself of the Wadham Street flat where he had experienced so much unhappiness with Dizz. Within a few weeks he purchased a £64,000 brick Georgian townhouse at 24 Chapel Street, just off Belgrave Square. This was a lovely five-story building, with private garage, small servants' quarters, formal dining room, and a roof garden. To keep himself busy, and his mind off of Dizz, Brian threw himself into redecorating the house from top to bottom, with the tasteful advice of Kenneth Partridge.

* * *

6.

O *N JUNE 15, 1965,* the Beatles' names were included on Her Majesty Queen Elizabeth's Birthday Honours List. The Beatles were to receive the accolade of Member of the British Empire, or MBE. This is the lowest rank of the Order of Chivalry, an award usually presented to philanthropists, but still an astonishing honor for a rock group or anyone in their midtwenties. "Can there be anything more important than this?" Brian asked. There was some slight surprise that Brian himself had not been named for an MBE, since he was virtually synonymous with the Beatles to the British people. He took it for granted that he had been left out because he was Jewish and homosexual, an accurate assumption. George thought to point out Brian's exclusion by noting to reporters that MBE could have stood for "Mr. Brian Epstein," and Princess Margaret, on the day of their investitures, observed the same thing.

Paul, George, and Ringo were thrilled at this great honor, but not John Lennon. He hated the idea of receiving an MBE. The royals and the class structure of England had always been among his favorite targets, and the thought of joining their ranks filled him with an angry guilt. When he was first informed of the honor in a personal letter from the Queen's spokesman, he was so disgusted he threw the letter in a pile of fan mail and never answered it. Weeks later, after a worried Buckingham Palace queried Brian on John's disposition in the matter, Brian insisted that a letter be sent graciously accepting in John's name.

It infuriated John all the more when the announcement of the Beatles' entrance into the realm of the titled was greeted with revulsion by many older MBE recipients. Author Richard Pape returned his award to Buckingham Palace, as did an army officer who told the press he was sending his MBE back because he didn't want to share the honor with "vulgar nincompoops." Hector Deupius, a member of the Canadian House of Commons, also offered to return his medal. George told a reporter in an interview, "If he doesn't want his medal he had better give it to us, then we can give it to our manager, Brian Epstein."

John was less diplomatic. Army officers, he said, get their

awards for "killing people. We received ours for entertaining. . . . I'd say we deserve ours more." John also pointed out that money was the real reason they were given the award. "We were given the MBE for exports, and the citation should have said that . . . if someone had got an award for exporting millions of dollars worth of manure or machines everyone would have applauded. Why should they knock us?"

The following fall one of the largest and youngest crowds in history surrounded Buckingham Palace on the day of their investiture, crying "God save the Beatles!" The Beatles giggled their way through the elaborate rehearsal and ceremony, just as they had giggled their way through the filming of *HELP!*, high on grass. On the day of the investiture itself, John secreted several joints in his boots. Just before the ceremony they retired to a small toilet off a private anteroom and smoked a joint among them, trying to expel the smoke through the small window. John had brought along an extra joint in the hope of running into Prince Charles, then sixteen and undoubtedly a Beatles fan. Charles was nowhere to be found, however, and history will never know what might had happened if the two had met that day.

Chapter Ten

Nothing, and I mean nothing, *was
ever normal for any of us again.*

—*Neil Aspinall*

1.

*I*N AUGUST OF 1965 John's Aunt Mimi made a
rare trip to London for the opening of *Help!* and
stayed with John in Weybridge. Mimi had acknowledged John's
success with grudging pride but let him know that being famous
didn't make him too grand for her to give him a piece of her
mind. She had reservations about John's fame and all it brought,
not the least of which was the notoriety it had caused her. Mimi
still lived in the neat house on Menlove Avenue, all alone with
a cat. The house had now become the primary stop of the Liverpool tourist trade, and Mimi was subjected to journalists and fans
ringing her front door bell all hours of the day and night demanding to know if this was really John's house and if she was really
John's Aunt Mimi.

John begged her to move out on many occasions, offering
to buy her any house she wanted, or to at least let him redecorate
Mendips for her. But Mimi only smiled at him. "Why should I?
You silly little sausage, there's no need to lift me out of the mire."

The morning after the premiere of *Help!* John and Mimi were
eating breakfast when John said, "Okay, I'm going to find you a
house. Where would you like it?"

Mimi, for want of something better to say, said "Bournemouth," a picturesque, seaside town. John called up his chauffeur,
Les Anthony, and told him to get maps for Bournemouth. They
left within a half hour. Rumseys, the local real estate agency,

was happy to provide them with a selection of available homes. Mimi finally found one she liked, a white bungalow with an unobstructed view of Poole Bay. When she found out the owners were still living in it, she was too embarrassed to go and see it with them there, particularly because John was dressed in jeans with holes in them, a jacket one size too small, and a yachting cap. "This house is far too smart to just land on them like this," she said.

"This is just a ha'penny little bourgeois house, and if you're not careful you'll get a mind to match," John warned her. He got out of the car himself and rang the front doorbell. When the owner and his wife found John Lennon standing on the front doorstep they couldn't do enough for him. Mimi and John toured the house. Her favorite part was the terraced backyard with steps that led down to the waterway where she could watch the ocean liners go up and down the bay.

"Do you like it Mimi?" John asked her. "If you don't, I'll have it myself." He rang his accountant at Bryce-Hamner and bought it for her on the spot. Unenthusiastically, Mimi subsequently sold her house on Menlove Avenue for £6000 but never spent the money, as if one day she might have to return there. She never did, because there was never any going back.

2.

*S*UMMER ALWAYS seemed to revive Brian's spirits. Summer was touring time, and the tours kept him busy with a sense of daily purpose. While the Beatles excluded him from the studios and their film work, the tours were Brian's speciality. He looked forward to tending his flock as they set out around the world for a second time. They began in June with a European tour, starting with a triumphant sold-out appearance at the Palais des Sports in Paris, which was broadcast nationally in France. From there they went on to give concerts in Lyons, Milan, Genoa, and Rome, where Brian disappeared and missed the Beatles' plane when it took off for the south of France. They played the Côte d'Azur, Nice, and Madrid, where Brian reappeared, sporting a black eye and a story about bumping into a closet door.

On a hot and sticky August 13, the Beatles and their entourage arrived in New York to kick off their third concert tour of the United States. This tour the schedule was more leisurely, only thirteen concerts in nine cities, leaving them over a week for relaxation in Los Angeles.

On August 15 the Beatles took perhaps the most breathtaking of their many journeys. A helicopter lifted them from a pad on the East River and flew them over to Shea Stadium, where 56,000 people waited for them in the gathering dusk. The helicopter took them to the World's Fair heliport, from which they were transported in a Wells Fargo armored car to the stadium itself. The truck discharged them on the infield, and they raced across the baseball diamond to a stage constructed at first base. Fifty-six thousand was the largest outdoor concert in history to date, and the humid weather helped induce fainting among the audience, and within ten minutes the emergency nursing facilities were filled to overflowing.

The Beatles performed in Toronto on the seventeenth, Atlanta on the eighteenth, Houston, Chicago, and Minneapolis.

On Monday, August 16, before leaving for Toronto, they were visited at the Warwick Hotel by the Supremes, the Exciters, the Ronettes, and, again, Bob Dylan. The following days, in rapid succession, they hit Atlanta, Houston, Chicago, and Minneapolis. It wasn't until they hit California, where they were scheduled for two nights at the Hollywood Bowl, plus a concert in San Diego, that they took a six-day respite. Brian had arranged for them to rent a large house in Benedict Canyon in Beverly Hills. Before long the address was general knowledge, and the house was a mecca for hundreds of Beatle fans, all of whom came in cars, causing a traffic backup all the way down to Sunset Boulevard. The huge, Spanish-style house was tucked into the side of a mountain. Its smoking green swimming pool seemed to edge its way out over the city below. The steep drop to a certain death did not stop hearty fans from trying to climb the face of the cliff, however, and a special tactical force of the Beverly Hills police was assigned to protect the house and its occupants. The more extravagant Beverly Hills brats simply rented helicopters to fly over the house, so they could take pictures of the Beatles sunbathing in the backyard.

Instead of going out a lot—an impossibility because of the fans—they received guests most of the time. Eleanor Bron, the actress who played the female villain in *Help!* stopped by to spend a few hours with John. Later in the afternoon a few members of the folk-rock group the Byrds arrived, and later in the day actor Peter Fonda turned up. Fonda, who had driven into the Canyon in his Jaguar, was mobbed by fans, who had swarmed all over the car and pounded dents into it.

Fonda picks up the narrative in a reminiscence he wrote for *Rolling Stone* magazine:

> I finally made my way past the kids and the guards. Paul and George were on the back patio, and the helicopters were patrolling overhead. They were sitting at a table under an umbrella in a rather comical attempt at privacy. Soon afterwards, we dropped acid and began tripping for what would prove to be all night and most of the next day; all of us, including the original Byrds, eventually ended up inside a huge, empty sunken tub in the bathroom, babbling our minds away.
>
> I had the privilege of listening to the four of them sing, play around and scheme about what they would compose and achieve. They were so enthusiastic, so full of fun. John was the wittiest and most astute. I enjoyed just hearing him speak and there were no pretensions in his manner. He just sat around, laying out lines of poetry and thinking— an amazing mind. He talked a lot, yet he still seemed so private.
>
> It was a thoroughly tripped-out atmosphere, because they kept finding girls hiding under tables and so forth; one snuck into the poolroom through a window while an acid-fired Ringo was shooting pool with the wrong end of the cue. "Wrong end?" he'd say. "So what fuckin' difference does it make?"

Later in the day the group huddled in the security of a large sunken bathtub in the master bedroom. Fonda got hung up on an anecdote about an operation he had during which he almost died. He kept going on about what it was like to be dead, until

John couldn't take it anymore and barked, "Listen mate, shut up about that stuff."* When one of the group remembered they hadn't eaten anything all day, they tried to rustle up a makeshift meal in the kitchen, but John couldn't figure out how to use his knife and fork, and to stop his food from moving around on his plate he wound up spilling it onto the floor.

This LSD experiment marked the unheralded beginning of a new era for the Beatles. The impact of this LSD trip was not apparent for the first few months, but before long the LSD experience would have a prominent effect in their music and thinking.

Since the band's arrival in Los Angeles, members of Hollywood's film community had made many requests to meet them. The list of inquiries and invitations from the famous was impressive, but not to the Beatles who had no interest at all in meeting "boring" movie actors. Like most rock stars, they were only interested in meeting other rock stars. Brian, however, knew the value of the publicity of Hollywood's royalty turning out to meet the boys and suggested that Capitol Records throw one gala party for them and get it over in one fell swoop. The party was held in the garden of a Capitol Records executive's home in Beverly Hills. The boys were placed on four stools in a row, amused but not especially thrilled as scores of Hollywood royalty and their children lined up to shake hands and chat. Included among the luminaries were Groucho Marx, Tony Bennett, Richard Chamberlain, Gene Barry, Rock Hudson, Dean Martin, James Stewart, Gregory Peck, and Kirk Douglas. Some celebrities were so charmed by the Beatles they got back on line a second time.

The only celebrity the Beatles cared about meeting was Elvis. Brian had been trying to arrange a meeting with Elvis for a long time, but the now-waning King had been unavailable—secretly threatened by the Beatles' enormous popularity. In lieu of a meeting, Colonel Parker had sent Brian and each of the boys impressive suits of cowboy clothing, complete with holsters and real six-shooters. That August Elvis was also living in Los Angeles, shooting *Paradise, Hawaiian Style,* and Colonel Parker prevailed upon him to meet with the Beatles while they were in town. Elvis agreed under the condition that the Beatles come to him.

* The exchange later turned into the John Lennon composition, "She Said She Said": "She said, 'I know what it's like to be dead, I know what it is to be sad.' / And she's making me feel like I've never been born."

The Beatles' meeting with Elvis at his house on Perugia Way has been amusingly recreated in Albert Goldman's book, *Elvis.* The Bel Air police force, alerted to the stellar event, encircled Elvis' house. The Beatles arrived along with Brian and Neil and British journalist Frederick James. Elvis himself answered the door, dressed in a red shirt and tight gray trousers. He was surrounded by his Memphis Mafia of playmates and bodyguards. A jukebox alternated Beatles and Elvis hits. It had been some years since Elvis' mere presence had instigated riots, and almost as long since he had had a song in the top ten, but the Beatles were still in awe of him. Five minutes had passed with the four of them sitting around and staring at Elvis when Elvis finally exploded, "Look, if you damn guys are gonna sit here and stare at me all night, I'm gonna go to bed!"

Colonel Parker, much to Brian's delight, uncovered a roulette wheel hidden inside a coffee table. The Colonel found a very eager gambler in Brian, who felt right in with his element; kingmakers pitted against Lady Luck for high stakes. Later, the Beatles and Elvis jammed. When Elvis played Paul's bass part on "I Feel Fine," Paul remarked glibly, "Coming along quite promising on the bass, Elvis." When the ice had broken a little, the Beatles and Elvis started to compare stories about the trials and tribulations of megastardom. When the Beatles left, they invited Elvis to visit them at their house the next evening, and the Colonel gave them all little covered wagons that lit up as souvenirs.

The following night a few members of the Memphis Mafia showed up, but no Elvis. Paul played the gracious host and showed them around the rented house. He opened one of the bedroom doors to reveal Joan Baez stretched out on the bed, talking to George. Elvis' guys later reported, incorrectly, that she was there to see George, when in fact it was John's bedroom. Baez had developed a wild crush on John and was reportedly following him wherever he went.

It was with great reluctance that they left the house in Benedict Canyon and headed north for San Francisco, where they were to perform the last concert of this American tour at the Cow Palace on August 31.

* * *

3.

A *S THE FINAL DATE* of the tour approached, Brian's spirits fell like a barometer in a desert. It had been a long and arduous August, and Nat Weiss, who had spent almost the entire month with Brian, was beginning to worry about him. Brian had reserved suite 35E in the Waldorf Towers on a regular basis, and Nat was always fascinated to observe him in action there. Brian was the cynosure of attention twenty-four hours a day. His phone would ring constantly, quite literally at any time, with calls from exotic points all over the world. It would be a fan club or a concert promoter or a photographer or a radio station that wanted to give the Beatles a Cadillac car in exchange for some promotion. Brian would laugh at these offers and say, "Only if it's gold," before gently hanging up the phone. Sometimes the phone rang so much that Brian would sneak out of the Waldorf Towers and move into Nat's small, two-bedroom apartment on East Sixty-third Street and Third Avenue for a little peace and quiet. As soon as Brian arrived—ever the Walton Road furniture salesman—he would rearrange every stick of furniture in the apartment until he was satisfied with the way it looked.

It never failed to amaze Nat that Brian could stay up all night talking and playing Beatles records and yet still be so fresh in the morning. One day at lunch, Nat was so tired and hungover from the previous night's revels he couldn't eat. Brian reached inside his jacket pocket to get a pen, and Nat noticed a whole row of little pockets had been tailored into his suit. Brian blithely explained that these were "pill pockets" and that each one was stocked with a different strength biamphetamine or tranquilizer.

Nat only then fully realized that Brian was completely artificially fueled. Pills put him to sleep, woke him up, kept him going. That explained, at least in part, some of Brian's recent erratic behavior and tendency to lose control. One night recently he had made a terrible scene after Cilla Black's opening in the Persian Room of the Plaza Hotel. Cilla had never had a hit record in America, and her career at home was not important enough to warrant her a booking at the Persian Room. But Brian had used his clout with the New York booking agency and had seen to it

190

that she would play the Persian Room the same week the Beatles played Shea Stadium. The day of Cilla's opening, Brian called Nat at his office in a terrible stew. He was angry and peeved that he was being "forced" into taking his secretary to the opening with him, while Nat had the luxury of taking a boy. Brian said being with his secretary would ruin his evening, but he didn't see any choice.

"Take whomever you want, Brian," Nat encouraged him over and over again. "Be true to yourself."

"I can't. I'm the Beatles' manager. If I take a boy with me everyone will talk."

"Then just make sure the boy is beautiful," Nat said.

After Cilla's performance, which was warmly received but obviously was not going to cause a sensation in New York, Brian threw a party for her in a hotel suite upstairs. The party was crowded with press and New York show business personalities when some woman within Brian's earshot remarked that the lobby of the Plaza Hotel looked "Jewish."

Brian flew into a wild rage. The party came to a halt around him as he screamed, "Madame, I happen to be Jewish!" The woman apologized and left, but Brian shook with anger for hours and made himself miserable. It was a small miracle the incident did not find its way into the press.

Yet Brian seemed just as able to prove himself totally in control in tight situations. The very next day after Cilla's opening, Brian took Cilla and her husband Bobby to lunch at "21," one of Manhattan's more intimidating, status-conscious restaurants. After a long and elaborate meal, Brian discovered that he had left his wallet in his suite at the Waldorf Towers and was unable to pay the bill. The furious waiter stormed off to get the captain, who returned with the manager.

Brian met them with an imperious gaze. "I am Brian Epstein," he intoned in his iciest West End accent, "and you shall send this bill to me at the Waldorf Towers."

The three men nodded and left.

It seemed to Nat that Brian's biggest problem was still his personal life. Nat believed that if Brian could only find some personal satisfaction he'd be more at peace with himself and learn to enjoy his professional success more. Yet Brian's romances only seemed to be getting more sordid. He had arrived in New York two days ahead of the Beatles with a terrible dilemma; Dizz Gillespie had reappeared and was in New York at the moment. Brian had lunch with Nat at the Waldorf Towers and recounted for him the entire episode with Dizz, from their first meeting that spring to their last parting over the blade of a knife. Now Dizz had contacted Brian again and wanted to see him. Brian knew he shouldn't, but he had no self-control. With the Beatles coming to town, Brian was afraid that Dizz would do something to embarrass them all, and he needed Nat's help in keeping Dizz away.

Nat agreed to help. It didn't take long for him to track Dizz down and invite him to his office for a talk. Nat sized up the young man the second he walked in the door. "I had met thousands of him," Nat says. "He was the garden-variety type hustler. If you wanted to keep your beer cold you'd put it next to his heart."

Dizz had another version of the story. "I love Brian," he told Nat. "I don't want anything from him, I just want to see him."

"Good," Nat said, "because you're not going to get anything from him, and you're not going to see him. I want you to stay away from him."

"Well, then," Dizz said, "Brian's got lots of money. If he wants me to stay away . . . well, if I had a car I could go away."

Nat Weiss relayed the conversation to Brian, who insisted that Nat give Dizz $3,000 to buy a car. Nat was strongly against this idea; to give Dizz any money at all would keep him coming back for more. But Brian insisted he wanted Dizz to have a car, and Nat struck a deal with the boy. In return for the $3,000, Dizz agreed to be kept locked in a hotel room at the Warwick Hotel on Sixth Avenue—with a private guard hired by Nat—until the Beatles and Brian left town. After that, it seemed, Dizz disappeared. But no one knew for how long.

*　*　*

4.

THE STORY of the prisoners of fame is an old one, but it had never been more electrifyingly played out than by the Beatles. There were moments when, despite their fame and riches and success, I felt sorry for the Beatles. While normal people marked the turning points in their lives with births and graduations and new jobs, the days in the lives of the Beatles melted into one another in a never-ending grind of tours and concerts, separated only by short periods in London when they would record another album. It wasn't until the winter of 1965–66 that the Beatles were able for the first time to spend some months at home and indulge themselves in the spoils of their success.

There were some spoils to be indulged in, too. Northern Songs, the Beatles' song publishing company that had been established in 1963, was turned into a public company and floated on the London stock exchange. It had become clear that while no simple tax savings could be found, John and Paul could at least save a great deal of money by turning highly taxed income into capital gains. Northern Songs was the obvious asset to use, but no one had ever sold what was basically a songwriting partnership as stock before. Although the copyrights to songs had long been making publishers into millionaires, the value to the rights of the fifty-nine pieces of music then in Northern Songs were at first an ethereal entity to the London financial community.

The man who deserved most of the credit for convincing the City that Northern Songs was a valuable commodity was Dick James, the Beatles' music publisher. Dick James knew the value of Northern Songs best of all, because the Beatles music had made him into a multimillionaire. Brian had met James at the start of the Beatles' success, when "Love Me Do" was first high on the charts. "Love Me Do" had been published by EMI's house-owned publisher, which had also put out the sheet music, and Brian was unhappy with the sales. George Martin recommended Dick James who ran a small but aggressive publishing company that would have a real stake in the Beatles' future.

Dick James became for the Beatles a symbol of the music business. He was a balding, Jewish uncle to the boys, a man with a big cigar and a sly smile, who taught John and Paul one of the biggest lessons in their lives. Dick James had been born Richard Leon Vapnick, the son of a kosher butcher. At the age of fourteen, after seeing a Bing Crosby movie, he dropped out of an East End London high school and became a singer. Richard Vapnick became Lee Sheridan, who became Dick James as he worked his way from one dreary dance band to another. In the late fifties, as a session singer, he sang the lead on the theme music for the English TV series "Robin Hood." The song became an international hit, but James was paid a total of only £17 for the session. By the time he was thirty-two years old, Dick James had a pretty good idea of how some people in the music business got rich while others didn't. That's when he went into the publishing business. In 1962, when Brian first met him, he had a small, shabby, two-room office on Charing Cross Road.

James instantly recognized Lennon and McCartney's potential as songwriters and offered Brian a clever deal. John and Paul would form a songwriting partnership called Northern Songs. They would each own 20 percent of this company, and Brian, in lieu of a 25 percent management fee, would own 10 percent. Dick James, in return for his responsibilities as a music publisher, would get 50 percent of the earnings. In literal terms Brian signed over to Dick James 50 percent of Lennon-McCartney's publishing fees for *nothing.* It made him wealthy beyond imagination in eighteen months.

Three years later, five million shares of Northern Songs were being offered on the stock market. In the floatation John and Paul each retained 15 percent of the stock, which was valued at $640,000 at the time. NEMS retained 7.5 percent, and in an act of largesse, George Harrison and Ringo Starr were given 1.6 percent between them. Dick James and his business partner, Charles Silver, were left with 37.5 percent, valued at $1,687,000.

Ironically, although this floatation realized some capital for John and Paul—most of which they used to pay past taxes— George and Ringo, due to their own tax problems, were still in financial straits. Not that you would have known it from their spending.

Ringo became a father for the first time when his son Zak was born, and his apparent contentment seemed complete. In preparation for the baby's birth, Ringo moved out of his compact ground-floor flat on Montague Square* and bought a £37,000 house in Weybridge, just down the road from John's house. Sunny Heights, as it was called, was immediately renovated to the tune of £40,000. Ringo asked Ken Partridge to decorate it for him, but Brian insisted Partridge was already too busy, so the Starrs got another decorator to indulge them in their creative whims. Ringo spent money on the house like a poor man who had just won the Irish Sweepstakes, which in a way he had. For serious construction, Ringo simply formed his own construction company and changed the house as he pleased: a wall there, an extra room here. At the back of the house, which he had landscaped in cascading terraces and ponds, he built a semicircular wall that alone cost him £10,000.** Later came a whole new wing, with an extra living room, a third guest room, a workroom for his video and audio equipment, a screening room, and a poolroom with a pool table flown in from the United States expressly for him.***

The rest of the house was decorated with the same disregard for cost. The chocolate brown Wilton carpet in the main living room was woven to order in one piece, because Ringo didn't like the way seams looked, an extravagance that embarrassed even him at the time. The house was outfitted with six TVs; intraroom stereo systems; over twenty telephones, two to a room, including a hot line to Brian's office; plus every imaginable kind of space-age, remote-control electronic gadget on the market. He bought cameras of every size and description and frantically began to take pictures, like a tourist on vacation in some enchanted land.

George was a bit more practical about his life. He finally proposed to Pattie Boyd on Christmas day of 1965, while driving to a holiday dinner in London. They were married on January 21, 1966, with Paul McCartney in attendance. This was a very happy time for George, the happiest he would know for some

---

* Ringo later rented this flat to Jimi Hendrix, who painted the entire place in black paint, including the furniture and silk wallpaper. Candles were burned on every table, scorching them with hot wax. Ringo sued Hendrix for destroying the flat, and the case was settled out of court.

** After building several suburban homes, Ringo's construction company went broke.

*** There were only billiard tables readily available in the U.K. when Ringo decided he wanted a pool table, and one had to be flown overnight from America at twice its cost. He told this story whenever he played pool on it. Shooting pool became one of Ringo's enduring passions.

years. He was in love and still not too oppressed by John and Paul. He and Pattie were a much-admired young couple. Pattie turned out to be one of the most delightful young women in London. Under her glamourous, high-fashion veneer, she was a warm, caring girl with good sense and good taste. Her modeling career skyrocketed because of her marriage to George, but she turned down almost all work so she could be with him. She occupied her time decorating the bungalow he had bought for her in the country. The house was done in a low-key, eclectic style that was very much a reflection of the handsome newlyweds who lived in it. For all the money John and Ringo spent on their homes, George and Pattie's was perhaps the most admired of all.

Chapter Eleven

*What will I do if they
stop touring? What will be
left for me?*

—Brian Epstein

1.

*I*N TERMS OF CLOUT, the Beatles practically owned EMI's Abbey Road studios. In just the last two years they had recorded at Abbey Road nineteen gold records, of which eighteen had been Number One on most major record charts. When the Beatles said they wanted to record, it was like the sound of some distant giant cash register ringing for EMI, and the studios were cleared for them. Every whim of theirs was catered to, like the royalty they had become, and when Ringo complained of the roughness of the toilet paper in the EMI john, it made headlines in several daily papers.* The Beatles spent most of that winter and spring in the Abbey Road studios, producing their two most important albums to date, *Rubber Soul* and *Revolver.*

These two albums were the first of the minor masterpieces the group would produce. Beatleologist Nicholas Schaffner describes this point in their musical progress as the moment in the movie *The Wizard of Oz* when everything goes from black-and-white to color. Here the simplistic love songs begin to wane, replaced with a dazzling spectrum of subjects and curios, from the banal to the ephemeral. The very sound of the music was strikingly different; richer, more melodious, haunting. Now, in-

---

* The authors were present at an auction at Abbey Road studios in 1981 during which the bidding was fierce and heavy over the roll of toilet paper and its holder that Ringo had complained about. A very happy man purchased it for around £65.

stead of producing an album that was just a disconnected hodge-podge of hit songs (which could be blithely juggled by Capitol Records in America from album to album),* the albums had a sense of collective identity, a mood and a sound linking them.

Yet at the time *Rubber Soul* was something of a critical disappointment. Although it was in the top ten on the album charts for over seven months—four of them in the number-one position—it was a puzzlement to all the confused kids expecting to hear more juvenile "yeah, yeah, yeah" songs. It was the best of the many challenges the Beatles posed to their fans: to keep up. Little could the fans have known that this new musical approach was directly attributable to the Beatles' now habitual use of marijuana. It was in John's songs, seemingly filtered through a haze of marijuana smoke, that the change was most obvious. It was the elegiac "Norwegian Wood" that first made us stop what we were doing to listen to the music. It was on this album that his introspection came to full bloom. "In My Life" was John's first certifiable piece of genius, an autobiographical voyage. This small, deceptively simple song is as superb in its economy as it is in the poignant images it conjures up. John sang it in his sweetest, most hypnotic voice. "There are places I'll remember, all my life, though some have changed./Some forever, not for better;/Some have gone and some remain./All these places had their moments/ with lovers and friends I still can recall./Some are dead and some are living,/In my life I've loved them all."

Naturally, it was Paul who had the biggest commercial success on *Rubber Soul,* called "Michelle." This was another of Paul's saccharine love songs, this time in which he self-consciously lapsed into a French refrain.

It was at the end of the *Rubber Soul* sessions that the Beatles' preliminary LSD experiments began on a fairly regular basis.

---

* In the U.S., Capitol put together an interim LP, *Yesterday and Today.* This was a compilation of various singles and other material left off previously released U.S. albums. The album contained, among notable others, "Nowhere Man," "Drive My Car," and "Dr. Roberts." *Yesterday and Today* had its place in Beatles trivia as the only album to initially lose money. The album was distributed in the U.S. with what was called the "butcher jacket"; a photo of the Beatles in white smocks, with decapitated dolls and red meat strewn about them. Although John thought the cover "as relevant as Vietnam," it was a good example of the Beatles' occasional poor judgment. The record-rack jobbers got so many complaints, they refused to ship the album. Capitol tossed away 750,000 covers and pasted-over many others. A $250,000 advertising campaign was also aborted.

Again the music changed distinctively, this time with a hard-edged, electric sound. "Paperback Writer," with its throbbing chorus written by Paul, was a forewarning of more to come. In John's audiodelic "Rain," augmented by George's Indian instrumentation, the first of the many "backwards" tapes were used. This simple trick of playing a recording backwards through a tape deck and rerecording it had never been considered before as a serious musical technique. John first discovered he liked this slightly unearthly sound when he was tripping one night. He was working late at Kenwood in his little studio at the top of the house, when he put a rough version of "Rain" on the recorder backwards. There are scores of backwards snippets of words and music on subsequent Beatles albums.

The whimsically trippy "Yellow Submarine," with Ringo's atonal vocals, also came out of these sessions, as did "Eleanor Rigby," Paul's eerily compelling portrait of a desolately lonely people. The *Revolver* album also contained, in England, John's drug-dispensing "Dr. Robert," written about a real New York physician who gave "vitamin" shots to the rich and famous, and Paul's pretty "For No One," another effective McCartney tearjerker. George was allowed two songs on the *Revolver* album, the comparatively undistinguished "Love You Too" and "I Want to Tell You," but he was afforded a plum spot in America, where his song "Taxman" was a huge success. This was, for George, an unusually articulate and justified complaint against the English tax system.

Revolver closed with a harbinger of things to come. Other songs on the album had been influenced by LSD, but John's "Tomorrow Never Knows" is the first bona fide, all-out acid trip. Originally titled "The Void," its inspiration came from the Tibetan *Book of the Dead,* which John was reading while tripping. John wanted very badly to record the song with a chorus of a thousand chanting Tibetan monks, whom he no doubt heard singing inside his head.

The Beatles are always second-guessed as not being originators of ideas but, rather, astute followers. Certainly they didn't invent LSD or marijuana, and they weren't the first to take them; but they always managed to be in the forefront of a trend and then popularize it on an international level, until they became associated with the phenomenon itself. Certainly the San Francisco based acid-rock bands did more to proselytize LSD than the Beatles, but it was the Beatles who translated the LSD experience and all that went with it—clothing, grooming, the sexual revolution—into a commercial message. The *Rubber Soul* and *Revolver* albums were the early examples of the Beatles power to lead. A potent and potentially deadly demonstration of this power was soon to come.

2.

*W*ITH THE WORLD exploding and fragmenting around them into the seeds of tangerine trees and marmalade skies, when London was the best place on earth and they were the best people to be, they had to do the one thing they wanted to do the least; they had to leave. It was summer and it was written in the gospel according to Brian that in summer they went out on tour. Nearsightedly, perhaps selfishly, Brian saw no reason to alter this yearly ritual he enjoyed so much, although it was obvious that touring was no longer necessary for the boys' commercial or financial success. It was perhaps the first major indication that Brian was losing his perspective of what the Beatles had become. They didn't need the money, certainly, and they didn't need the aggravation. As far as the Beatles themselves were concerned, their music was so complicated it could no longer be reproduced live on stage.

Yet all the machinery was in motion, and inexorably the familiar entourage was assembled for a June 23 departure for Munich, Essen, and Hamburg, Germany, on the first leg of a world tour. This time Brian insisted that I join them to deal with the Beatles' administrative and personal problems. I was reluctant to leave the London office for so long and wasn't looking forward to the grueling world travel in the summertime, but Brian's behavior and attentiveness had become more erratic in recent months, and I knew I might be needed.

Hamburg was chosen as a stop purely for the sake of nostalgia. We traveled by plane and private train, the Beatles talking excitedly the entire time about old times on the Reeperbahn. But like much of the rest of the world, Hamburg had lost its charm for them. They could no longer walk the streets unrecognized, gaping at the sex shops and the window-ledge hookers. There were no night-long bacchanals, watching the dawn come up over the Herberstrasse rooftops. The bars and clubs where they once played—only a short four years before—were closed; the Star Club was shuttered up with boards. What had once been tempting and exotic in the night was tawdry and tired in the light. Astrid Kirchner, the beautiful young photographer and girlfriend of Stu Sutcliffe, who so dramatically affected the Beatles' appearance, was now a barmaid in a transvestite bar. She had never been paid a cent for the now world-famous photographs she took of the boys in leather and cowboy hats, nor was she in any way recompensed for her famous haircut, which began a revolution in men's grooming. In her small apartment she kept one room shrouded in black velvet where she burned candles underneath a haunting photograph she took of an ethereal Stu Sutcliffe.*

From Hamburg we flew over the North Pole, en route to Tokyo, only to be grounded in Anchorage in the middle of the night by a typhoon raging in the China Sea. It was freezing cold and snowing heavily, and Brian and the Beatles were quite upset at having to be put up in emergency accommodations in a small hotel, as if the typhoon were a personal offense. Brian was claustrophobic and irritable in his small room and decided to ring Nat Weiss in New York City, three time zones and 8,000 miles away. He woke Nat out of a deep sleep, demanding, "Who owns Alaska, Nat?" and "Do you know the name of a good bar?"

We didn't arrive in Tokyo until dawn of the following day, already exhausted, although the major part of our trip was now just beginning. We were looking forward to some relaxation and sightseeing in Tokyo, yet the moment we deplaned we learned there was an ugly surprise waiting for us. A small, officious but polite police commissioner in a business suit ushered us into a VIP lounge and explained that a kamikaze squad of right-wing militant students, who objected to the Western "perversion" of Japanese culture, had vowed that the Beatles would never leave Japan alive. The students were particularly enraged because the Beatles were scheduled for three nights of concerts at the Bu-

* Astrid reportedly now owns two clubs, one of which is a gay bar.

dokan, which was also a national shrine to dead war heros. The commissioner explained that the threats from the student fanatics were not to be taken lightly; they would kill the Beatles if they had the chance, and it was almost certain they would make some sort of an attempt. The Japanese government didn't want to be caught in the middle of an embarrassing international incident, such as having one of the beloved mop-tops murdered in their fair land, and they had dispatched several thousand armed troops to back up the police escort.

Despite all the dangerous episodes and narrow escapes the Beatles had been through, none of them had been as intimidating as this. A cordon of police led us to the passenger luggage area where the well-meaning Japanese promoters had supplied us with two 1950's limousines to bring us to our hotel. Unfortunately, the Beatles' car was an attention-drawing white, while Brian's was an embarrassing pink. There must have been ten thousand fans lining the road on the route into town, who couldn't miss us coming in our bright cars, with a motorcycle escort and police cars in front and behind us. Neither could we miss the chanting students who joined the fans, with signs that read "Beatles Go Home."

The Tokyo Hilton was turned into an armed camp. The entire top floor of the hotel had been cordoned off with army troops, and the elevators were fixed to stop only on the floor below, where a round-the-clock gun-toting platoon screened admission to the penthouse via a single staircase. The Beatles were ensconced in the Presidential Suite, which had six or seven rooms, and Brian and I were in the smaller but equally grand Imperial Suite at the other end of the hall. Once we had checked in to the hotel, the authorities informed us that for security purposes the Beatles were never to leave their hotel suite, except to go to the Budokan for performances. Instead of seeing Japan, Japan was to be brought to them. Disgruntled at what seemed to them to be undue precautions, the Beatles sat around their suite, dressed in ceremonial silk kimonos, and like four young Roman emperors had the riches of the country paraded before them. The directors of the biggest companies in Japan personally came to the hotel to display their wares, and within hours the boys had spent tens of thousands of pounds on cameras, clothing, watches, jewelry, and other trinkets. Sushi chefs appeared in the suite with trays of fish to be carved up for them, and Geisha girls appeared for back rubs and other physical delights.

Late morning of the second day Brian and I were busy tending to last-minute details of the boys' Budokan concert when the nattily-dressed police commissioner appeared at the door. This time he was no longer bowing. He was most annoyed because Paul had snuck out of his suite that morning and had roamed around Tokyo with Mal Evans for several hours, all the while being trailed by undercover security agents. Paul awoke that morning absolutely claustrophobic and couldn't face another day locked up inside, so he and Mal donned fake moustaches and wide-brimmed hats from their collection of disguises and slipped out the service entrance of the hotel. The security agents allowed them a few hours of freedom before they were put under custody and driven back to the hotel in a police car. The police commissioner warned Brian that if any of the Beatles breached security again, all the protection would be called off in the blink of an eye, and the Beatles would be left to their own defenses against the militant students. When the commissioner left the room, Brian's reaction was, "They wouldn't *dare*."

Brian was probably right, although I'm glad we never had to find out. The boys behaved until showtime, when we were whisked to the Budokan along a route that had been closed off to the rush-hour traffic, throwing Tokyo into a gridlock such as they had never experienced before. Army sharpshooters were stationed all along the route, as well as in the orchestra and balconies of the Budokan. The eeriest part of it was the politeness of the Japanese audience. There were one or two screamers, but for the most part the teenaged boys and girls sat politely in their seats and applauded enthusiastically after each number. It was one of the few concerts during which the boys could hear themselves play.

It was without any regrets that we left Japan and moved on to the next stop on the tour, the Philippine Islands. Manila, with its warm sun and exotic scenery, promised to be a welcome change of mood from the tension of the big city of Tokyo. The Beatles were especially popular with the Filipino people and had easily sold out two concerts at the Araneta Coliseum. Indeed, one of the largest airport crowds ever, over 50,000 people, turned out to cheer our arrival. An army escort led our entourage through the crowds into limousines supplied courtesy of the local concert promoter.

Then a most peculiar thing happened, which is revealed here in its entirety for the first time; instead of being taken to the hotel, we were driven to a pier and put on a boat, which took us a mile or two out to sea before returning again. This was neither a reception nor a government ritual but an opportunity to separate us from our luggage for a half hour or so. It was very disconcerting to all of us, for we all knew that the Beatles now traveled with several pounds of marijuana in their equipment cases. Usually, these cases were searched only perfunctorily at customs, if at all, and generally were given the same treatment as diplomatic pouches. We were returned to the pier and handed our luggage, with no explanations offered nor questions asked. We suspected that the drugs had been found and that the government officials were keeping quiet about it as an accommodation. It was assumed that nobody wanted to become involved in an international incident, yet that was exactly what happened.

The following morning half a dozen uniformed aides from the presidential palace appeared at the door of Vic Lewis' hotel room. Lewis was the NEMS booking agent who had arranged for certain parts of the international tour and had joined the touring party in Japan. The military police demanded to know what time the Beatles would arrive at "the party."

"What party?" Lewis asked groggily, "I know nothing of any party." He directed the officers to Brian, who was having a late breakfast with me in the hotel coffee shop. These military police in khaki uniforms had an unpleasant edge to their voices when they again demanded to know what time the Beatles would arrive at the "party." We managed to learn from them that Imelda Marcos, the wife of president Ferdinand Marcos, was giving a luncheon party in honor of the Beatles, and they were expected shortly at the presidential fortress, Malachang. In some quarters Imelda Marcos was more feared than her dictator husband; she was an Eva Peron-like figure with a reputation for being as demanding as she was venal. She had a special taste for the famous and celebrated, and had invited 300 children to the palace to meet the Beatles with her.

Brian claimed that this was the first he had heard of the invitation to the party. He later learned that in Tokyo the publicity man, Tony Barrow, had received such an invitation but somehow nothing had been done about responding. Whether or not it was ever relayed to Brian, by either Barrow or Vic Lewis, was now a moot point; the Beatles were simply not going. They were up in their rooms, fast asleep and in need of rest. Brian wasn't about to have them woken up to be told they were due at the palace in a half hour.

Minutes later, upstairs in our suite, Brian received a call from the British ambassador to the Philippines, who said that he didn't think it was a good idea for the Beatles to miss Mrs. Marcos' party. All the help and protection they were receiving in Manila was courtesy of the president, and this was not the right country to stand on ceremony about an invitation. It was best not to insult them. Brian said he was sorry, but he was adamant they would not attend. Even if they had received the invitation in time to prepare, they would have refused. Long ago, in Washington, D.C., on their first trip to America, he had made it NEMS policy that the Beatles would refuse all official functions, whether given by diplomats, royalty, or dictators.

Ignorant of this turn of events, the Beatles slept peacefully right through the party. They were awakened by Neil and Mal in the afternoon and served breakfast, after which they were escorted to the Araneta Football Stadium in twin limousines. There were two performances, one in the afternoon, one in the early evening, and 100,000 people were shuffled in and out of the stadium to hear the Beatles play two half hour sets, accompanied by the usual happy screaming and hysterics. Meanwhile, back in our hotel suite, Brian and I were watching television when the late afternoon news came on. There on the screen was Imelda Marcos wandering forlornly around her palace, having been snubbed by the Beatles. The commentary explained that they had never turned up at a party held in their honor and, to add insult to injury, the 300 children who were also disappointed by the Beatles were war orphans and cripples. A palace spokesman said the Beatles had "spit in the national eye," or something to that effect.

The moment the broadcast was finished, Brian was on the phone with the manager of the government-run TV station, determined to make an explanation to the people of the Philippines. He and I rushed right over to the TV station, where, much to our surprise, he was brought into the studios and put in front of a camera. Regular programming was then interrupted, and Brian went out live all over the country. He had only started his apology when word was received from the Malachang fortress to disrupt the sound portion of the broadcast. Brian's explanation and eloquent apology were never heard.

The Beatles were totally ignorant of any of this. After their concerts they were brought back to the hotel in their limousines. The evening proceeded normally with a card game, a few scotch and Cokes, and a shared joint. The boys decided to turn in early, as we were due at the airport first thing the next morning to make an early flight to New Delhi, India, where we intended to vacation for a few days.

In the middle of the night, Vic Lewis was dragged from his hotel room by three army policemen and brought to a police station. He was interrogated for most of the night by two Gestapo-like officers who kept demanding, "Why did you not go to the party?"

Early in the morning the Beatles were awakened by Neil and Mal in time to get dressed for their plane. Neil ordered a room-service breakfast for all six of them, and the boys showered and dressed while they waited for it to come. When breakfast didn't show up, Mal called down a few times but couldn't seem to summon anyone at the desk. Finally he went down to the lobby to see what was the matter. The lobby was eerily quiet, without a hotel employee in sight. All the police protection and security men usually lurking around the lobby were gone. Out front the two limousines rented for the Beatles and their touring party were waiting without any escort, just two solitary drivers. When Mal finally raised somebody at the front desk, the man was gruff and angry; there was no more room service for the Beatles. In fact, some unnamed authority had wiped out all services for the Beatles, including bellhops. Mal was extremely puzzled by this, until he spotted an English-language newspaper in the lobby. The headline read, BEATLES SNUB PRESIDENT.

By the time Mal returned to the Beatles' suite with the newspaper, the boys had turned on the TV and found themselves the subject of a national news story. We decided the best thing was to get the hell out of the country, and Tony Barrow, Mal, and Vic Lewis began to hand load all the equipment and luggage themselves into a hired van to take it to the airport. KLM flight 862 for New Delhi was waiting for us, and without any assistance it was certain we would be late and miss the plane. Brian called the KLM office and asked to be directly hooked up to the plane's pilot by skyphone. He made a personal plea to the pilot not to leave us stranded in the hostile country, explaining that we were rushing to the airport. The pilot agreed to wait as long as he could before the plane would need refueling to make it to India; then he would leave Manila, with the Beatles on board or not.

Now the race was on. Without the police escort it seemed to take hours for us to get to the airport in the morning traffic. Accidentally or on purpose, the non-English-speaking drivers seemed to lose their way once or twice. When we finally came in sight of the airport there was no sigh of relief from the touring party; the once civilian-run airport had been turned into an armed military camp. Aside from what appeared to be thousands of soldiers with rifles and bayonets, there was also a mob of several hundred very angry citizens milling outside the terminal building, waiting for us. When our cars stopped outside the terminal, the crowd formed a gauntlet for us to pass in order to get to the door. They punched and kicked at us as we rushed by, trying not to panic and break into a run.

Inside the terminal we found the escalators, elevators, and flight departure information boards had been turned off. Many precious minutes elapsed as our entourage began to rush around the terminal trying to find out at what gate the KLM plane was waiting. Abruptly, an army officer commandeered our group and herded us into a customs room adjacent to a departure lounge. As he slowly and deliberately went over the details of our passports and visa, up above us on a glass-enclosed observation balcony, the angry mob from outside was allowed in to watch. Within moments they were pounding on the glass, screaming for blood. Down below the soldiers began ordering us from one side of the room to the other, poking us with wooden clubs and gun butts as the shouting from the balcony grew louder. At one point Mal tried bravely to intervene by putting himself between the soldiers and the Beatles, and the punches started to fly. Mal was overwhelmed by six soldiers who punched him and knocked him to the ground. Brian was punched in the back and shoulders several times, and Ringo was slammed so hard in the back he stumbled forward and dropped his traveling case.

After what seemed an eternity, during which we all wondered if we were going to be turned over to the screaming crowd above us, we were allowed to board the airliner. The atmosphere in the plane was not much friendlier, however, as we were confronted by a planeful of frightened and angry passengers, impatient to leave for New Delhi. We sank into our seats, thinking the ordeal was over, when an army officer appeared on the plane and demanded that Tony Barrow disembark and have his passport rechecked. Tony was duly escorted off the plane. At this point the pilot asked to see Brian, and I went up to the cockpit with him. The pilot said he had waited as long as possible, and we would have to take off without Tony. Brian made an impassioned plea to the man not to leave Tony behind, since he would certainly be put in jail or be stranded. Brian kept the pilot busy arguing until Tony was finally returned to the plane. The pressurized doors were quickly sealed, and the huge airliner started to pull away from the terminal.

Our touring party clustered together in the first-class lounge and tried to stop shaking. Outside the windows we could still see the angry mob, now allowed out on the tarmac, where they continued to shake their fists and yell curses at the plane.

Brian took it very badly. He was perspiring profusely, mopping at his face with a handkerchief as we waited for the plane to take off. "How could I let this happen to the boys?" he asked me plaintively. "How? I'll never forgive myself. I put the boys in physical danger. I'll never forgive myself for that."

Unexpectedly, Vic Lewis appeared in the aisle. While a stewardess admonished him to sit down in his seat and fasten his seat belt, he leaned across me and demanded from Brian, "Did you get the money?" The money was the "brown paper bag" money that Brian had collected from the Manila promoter in cash, this time almost 50 percent of the performance fee. The rest of the guarantee had already been reported to the Inland Revenue Service and deposited in a London bank.

Brian was enraged that all Lewis could think about was money. Here the boys had almost been hurt, we all had narrowly escaped what seemed to be great physical danger, and all Vic Lewis could think about was the money. "Who was it that screwed up the party invitation?" Brian shouted at him. *"Don't talk to me about money!"*

I tried to calm Brian so that the Beatles and the other passengers wouldn't hear them, but it was too late. Vic Lewis blew up at him. "I'll talk to you about money!" Lewis shouted, reaching across me and grabbing Brian by the throat. "I'll fucking kill you!" As the plane hurtled down the runway, I managed to wrestle Lewis' hand from Brian's throat and force him down the aisle.

Only a few minutes airborne Brian started to vomit and run a high fever. By the time we reached New Delhi he was sick enough to need to be helped from the plane to a waiting car. He was attended to by a physician at the Intercontinental Hotel every day of our four-day stopover.

The Beatles were furious with Brian. They blamed his ineptitude for the entire incident. Down the hall from Brian's suite, in their own interconnecting rooms, they drank scotch and Cokes and passed joints as they discussed the terrifying events in Manila and the hysterical scene on the plane. It was the general consensus that Brian had "fucked up" and was no longer in control of the situation.

"And he's got another world tour already booked for next year," Neil said, "We've gotta do this again."

Everybody in the room groaned. "Is this touring a fucking annual event?" George asked.

"Nobody can hear a bloody note anyway," John said. "No more for me. I say we stop touring."

They told Brian of their decision on the BOAC plane from New Delhi to London. After the American part of the present tour was over, they did not want to go out on the road again, at least in the forseeable future. This upset Brian so much that by the time the jet reached Heathrow Airport his body was covered with hives and welts in an almost uninterrupted pattern. Brian was so sick that the plane's pilot radioed ahead for an ambulance to meet us at the airport. "What will I do if they stop touring?" Brian asked me feverishly. "What will be left for me?"

"Don't be ridiculous," I said. "There's lots for you to do." I meant it, too. Brian had more exciting options open to him than almost any man in show business. But without the Beatles to actively consume his time, Brian saw nothing ahead of him. The Beatles decision to stop touring was an enormous blow. The hives proved to be glandular fever, and Brian was put to bed for a month. Dr. Norman Cowan prescribed a quiet vacation after that for Brian to convalesce. He went by himself to a luxury hotel in Portmerion on the northwest coast of Wales that overlooked the sea and windswept beach, as remote a place as he could get from London. Everyone's advice was the same: "Try not to worry."

3.

*B*UT POOR BRIAN WAS in Portmerion only four days when word arrived from America that the Beatles were in the midst of a terrible scandal. It had started innocently enough several months before with a profile on John Lennon written by the *Evening Standard*'s pop journalist, Maureen Cleave. The previous spring she had been allowed into each of their homes to interview them extensively and observe them with their wives. These rare and fascinating portraits of the Beatles ran one a day for a week, including one on Brian. In John's profile, Cleave got him to wax philosophical on those topics not usually discussed with a pop star. In talking about the futility of organized religion, John mused, "Christianity will go. It will go. It will vanish and shrink. I needn't argue about that. I'm right and I will be proved right. We are more popular than Jesus now. I don't know which will go first—rock and roll or Christianity. Jesus was all right, but his disciples were thick and ordinary."

In England these comments went unremarked by the public and press, by now innured to John's irreverences, but several months later, when the quote was reprinted in an American teen magazine called *Datebook,* a firestorm erupted. The American religious community was up in arms. The Bible Belt was so infuriated by John's remarks, they had come out gunning for the Beatles, literally as well as figuratively. Beatles records were being burned by the truckloads. Church rallies were being held in at least six southern states to collect Beatles memorabilia. Garbage cans were being distributed in a house-to-house canvass. Record stores, including large chains, were refusing delivery on Beatles records.

In the first five days of the controversy, over thirty-five radio stations banned all air play of Beatles records, bowing to pressure from religious groups. The Reverend Thurman H. Babbs, the pastor of the New Haven Baptist church in Cleveland, threatened to excommunicate any member of his congregation who went to a Beatles' concert. In South Carolina the Grand Dragon of the Ku Klux Klan nailed Beatles' albums to burning crosses and made dark threats against the Beatles' safety when—and if—they ever arrived in America. Even the Vatican newspaper felt it necessary to comment on John's remarks, warning that "some subjects must not be dealt with profanely, even in the world of beatniks."* Worse, promoters across America who had lined up dates for the Beatles' upcoming summer tour were threatening to cancel the concerts.

Brian lurched from his convalescent bed in Portmerion and was driven directly to the Chester airport, where he was met by a private plane to fly him to Heathrow. From there he took the next flight to New York, where a limousine met him at the airport and brought him directly to Nat Weiss' office. Not twelve hours had gone by since the first phone call informing him of the trouble.

"What will it cost to cancel the tour," Brian asked Nat. "The boys have suffered enough abuse this year already."

Nat didn't think that Brian was being realistic. "With a million dollars in cash you could probably pay back the promoters, who in turn would probably have to refund millions of dollars," Nat told him.

"I'll pay it," Brian said. "Cancel it. I'll pay every cent out of my own pocket. If anything ever happened to them I couldn't live with it."

Nat pursuaded Brian that there was no need to cancel the entire tour. The whole thing could probably be settled if John made a public apology. Brian used the phone on Nat's desk to call John in Weybridge and tell him the plan. John was furious at the thought of having to apologize for what he felt was simply

---

* One of the most curious side effects of John's "Jesus" remarks was that the South African government banned all sales and radio play of Beatles albums. This ban was kept in effect until 1970, when it was lifted for Paul, George, and Ringo. John Lennon's music, at this writing, is still forbidden. Despite the American boycott, their new album, *Revolver*, sailed to the top of the American charts and remained there for two months.

true, that the Beatles *were* more popular than Jesus. He told Brian he would prefer not to go out on tour rather than apologize. After much arm twisting, Brian got John to agree to at least try to explain what he meant at a press conference.

In the meantime Brian held his own press conference in New York and announced to the assembled newspaper reporters, "The quote which John Lennon made to a London columnist nearly three months ago has been quoted and misrepresented entirely out of the context of the article, which was in fact highly complimentary to Lennon as a person and was understood by him to be exclusive to the *Evening Standard*. It was not anticipated that it would be displayed out of context and in such a manner as it was in an American teenage magazine." Back in London Maureen Cleave, who regretted having caused so much trouble, made her own statement to the press: "[John] was certainly not comparing the Beatles to Christ. He was simply observing that so weak was the state of Christianity that the Beatles were, to many people, better known. He was deploring rather than approving this."

When the Beatles arrived at O'Hare Airport on August 11, a mob of hostile newsmen and disc jockeys was waiting for them. Later that night the media was invited to the hotel for a press conference. John appeared pale and nervous as he took the microphone. "If I said television was more popular than Jesus, I might have got away with it," he said. "As I just happened to be talking with a friend I used the word Beatles as a remote thing, not as what I think—as Beatles, as those other Beatles like other people see us. And I just said 'they' as having more influence on kids and things than anything else, including Jesus. But I said it in that way, which was the wrong way. But, I'm not saying that we're better or greater or comparing us with Jesus as a person, or God as a thing, or whatever it is. I just said what I said and it was wrong, or it was taken wrong, and now there's all this."

The reporters glanced at each other, baffled and unappeased. The very next question was, "But are you prepared to *apologize*?"

That was exactly what John thought he had just done. Now his temper was rising. "I'm not anti-God, anti-Christ, or antireligion," he said firmly. "I was not saying we are greater or better. I believe in God, but not as one thing, not as an old man in the sky. I believe that what people call God is something in all of us . . . I wasn't saying the Beatles are better than God or Jesus. I used 'Beatles' because it was easy for me to talk about Beatles . . ."

But the questions persisted. Was he or wasn't he going to eat crow? Brian gave him anxious looks from the sidelines.

"I wasn't saying whatever they're saying I was saying . . ." he insisted, and then he broke down. "I'm sorry I said it, really. I never meant it to be a lousy antireligious thing . . . I apologize, if that will make you happy. I still don't know quite what I've done. I've tried to tell you what I did do, but if you want me to apologize, if that will make you happy, then okay, I'm sorry!"

John had reached a turning point; he was tired of selling out, pandering to the press and public, of suppressing his feelings and thoughts. He made himself a solemn promise that it would not happen again. Indeed, it went almost unnoticed when a few minutes later in the press conference John took his first public political stand, coming out against the Vietnam war and America's recent involvement. This remark did not go unnoticed by Brian, who mentioned it to John later and asked gently if John would refrain from choosing sides in this hotly contested issue. John just glared at him in return.

John's "Jesus" apology helped soothe some of the troubled waters, but it still left a nasty tension in the air. The American tour now took on the same nightmare quality as the Japanese and Manila dates that had preceded it. On August 14 the Beatles played the Municipal Stadium in Cleveland in the pouring rain on an uncovered stage with poorly grounded electrical equipment. Brian had to stop the show ten minutes into their set to prevent their being electrocuted. They gave tired, lackluster performances in Washington, D.C., and Toronto before going to Tennessee, where the KKK picketed the Memphis Coliseum on August 19. It was at this date that the possibility of a sniper in the large audience was most feared, and police were asked to keep a lookout for firearms. Midway through the performance, a firecracker was thrown out of the bleachers onto the stage where it exploded, and George Harrison very nearly fainted from fright. On the twentieth, in Cincinnati, Paul was so nervous he threw up backstage. On the twenty-fourth they were back in New York for another sold-out show at Shea Stadium. When they were presented with an enormous cake in the locker room, John asked if there was a naked lady inside of it. When he was told there wasn't, he said, "We don't want any of your fucking cake," and stalked off. The twenty-fifth of August they played Seattle and then flew to San Francisco for the final date of the tour at the Cow Palace.

4.

"*I* HAVE AN announcement to make," Brian said to Nat Weiss in the living room of a bungalow at the Beverly Hills Hotel. Nat, who hated Los Angeles, had been coerced by Brian into accompanying him for a short holiday. "Tomorrow night in San Francisco is the Beatles' very last concert," Brian intoned gravely.

"I don't believe you," Nat said, dismissing it as one of Brian's fatalistic predictions. Of late Brian was always saying dramatic things. He had never completely recovered from his glandular fever, and his poor health was complicated by his habitual use of uppers and downers. He had missed a slew of dates on the Beatles' American tour, more often than not stoned in suite 35E at the Waldorf Towers. His liaisons were much more open now but also much more dangerous. The night manager of the Waldorf Towers stopped more than one surly-looking visitor to Brian's apartment. Brian would come down to the lobby himself to straighten the matter out. "This man is unquestionably my welcomed guest," he would say, showing the young construction worker into the elevator. By the end of his stay the Waldorf billed him for the marks left by the dirty construction shoes on the white carpet in front of the living room sofa.

"But it's true, they're going to stop touring after tomorrow," Brian insisted as he fixed Nat a scotch. "It's very sad, I think, but they say they don't want to do it anymore."

"They'll change their minds," Nat assured him.

"There is also something to cheer me up," Brian said. "Dizz Gillespie called me. He's here in Los Angeles."

At first Nat was incredulous, then angry. "Brian, you must not have anything to do with that boy—"

"Now, now," Brian interrupted, "he came all this way to find me. He said he came because he loves me."

Nat sighed but said nothing. As preposterous as it was that Dizz Gillespie had any real affection for Brian, Nat could see by the smitten look in Brian's eyes that he believed it. He wanted to believe it, for better or for worse. Anyway, Brian had been so skittish lately that one wrong word could send him off on a three-day snit. Over the next twenty-four hours Nat watched in silence as the inevitable drama was played out.

They met with Dizz at a house in Beverly Hills that the Beatles had vacated for a concert date in San Diego. Nat and Brian moved in for the day. For Brian it was one brief idyllic moment in a hideous tour. Brian took Dizz from room to room and showed him the Beatles' clothing and where they slept. They sat by the pool in the hot and nourishing California sunshine. They were alone for the first time; there were no servants, no press, no Beatles. Later in the day Brian and Dizz went shopping for dinner together at a local supermarket, and Brian made his roast chicken with vegetables speciality for them.

During dinner, Brian again said, "I have an announcement to make. Tomorrow night is the Beatles' last concert, and I want you both to come." Nat still didn't believe him, but he agreed that if it was their last he'd want to join Brian and Dizz in San Francisco the next day.

The following morning, after spending the night in the rented house, Dizz went off early to the bungalow at the Beverly Hills Hotel, where he had left his suitcase. When Brian and Nat arrived at the bungalow later in the morning, Dizz was gone. So were Brian's and Nat's attaché cases. Nat's case contained important business documents, and its loss was a major inconvenience, but Brian's attaché case was a witches' stew of enormous ramifications. First, there was his large and questionable supply of pills, obviously the property of a junkie. Then there were half a dozen or so billets-doux containing explicit references to his conquests, along with Polaroid photographs of his young friends. Lastly, there was $20,000 in brown paper bag money skimmed from concert funds to be distributed as a bonus. The revelation of any of these items would make John's "Jesus" furor seem like an Easter pageant.

Nat had seen Brian through many mercurial moods, but he

had never seen him come crashing down so quickly or so hard. It was more than he could deal with that he had been fooled again, that he had been caught in another self-defeating scandal. By nightfall he had turned into a mass of self-loathing, lashing out at anyone who tried to console him. Ironically, he was too heartsick to make it to the Beatles' last concert.

Nat Weiss insisted that they notify the police, but Brian wouldn't hear of it. He could not risk the possibility of a scandal. It was better to let Dizz keep the lot, the papers and the money and the pills, than to chance the press getting wind of it. Brian could just see the headlines. "Good riddance to bad trash," Brian told Nat. The next morning, a little feverish, Brian was on a flight with the Beatles back to London.

By the time he arrived at his Chapel Street town house—for the first time in two months—there was an urgent phone call waiting for him from Nat Weiss, who had returned to New York. Nat had received a blackmail letter at his office from Dizz Gillespie. The note demanded an additional $10,000 in cash for the return of Brian's photographs and letters. "Pay him the money," Brian insisted. "Just give him his blood money." Brian got so agitated that Nat didn't press the point, but he had no intention of becoming a blackmail victim himself. Without telling Brian, Nat hired a private detective in Los Angeles and set up a phony ransom rendezvous with Dizz to take place behind the Union Station in L.A. Dizz Gillespie himself didn't turn up, as Nat had hoped, but sent instead a young accomplice who was easily apprehended by the private detective and turned over to the police. The accomplice led them to the attaché case in exchange for a promise not to press charges. The case still had $12,000 in it but no pills or incriminating letters and photos. Dizz had taken the $8,000 and disappeared.

When Nat informed Brian what had taken place, he was beyond solace. Now he lived under the constant threat that one day Dizz would turn the letters and photographs over to some newspaper. Brian was so despondent that his personal physician, Dr. Norman Cowan, asked me to find an excuse to stay at Chapel Street for a few days, so Brian would not be alone. This suggestion was met with great enthusiasm by Queenie, who hoped I would be a good influence on Brian.

Influencing Brian, however, was easier said than done. He

languished in the house all day, sometimes not even getting out of his pajamas for dinner. His conversation was morbid and nostalgic, that of a man who had given up. He stayed up until dawn every day and then slept until five in the afternoon, avoiding his business responsibilities.

One night, directly after finishing his dinner, Brian disappeared to his room. Since this was not his usual behavior, I checked on him in a half an hour and then again later. Brian was asleep both times, but when he was still in the same position, I tried to wake him. He was out cold. When slapping him didn't bring him around, I called Dr. Cowan from the phone next to Brian's bed. Dr. Cowan's service located him on call in a hospital a good thirty-five minutes away in Richmond. When I described Brian's color and shallow breathing to Dr. Cowan, he advised that I call an ambulance and take Brian to the nearest hospital, St. George's, just around the corner from Chapel Street, to have his stomach pumped.

I considered this carefully for a moment and refused. From my experiences with the Beatles, I knew that hospitals and police stations always had a paid informant on staff who would notify the press if any noteworthy personalities turned up. If whatever Brian had taken to put him to sleep didn't kill him, the publicity the next day would. I made the dangerous and frightening decision not to take him to the hospital. I told Dr. Cowan that I would continue to try to revive Brian while waiting for him to arrive from Richmond.

It took Cowan nearly an hour to get there, and all that time I was not able to bring Brian around. With the help of Dr. Cowan and Brian's chauffeur, an ex-guardsman named Brian Barett, we carried Brian out the front door of the house and gently loaded him onto the backseat of his waiting silver Bentley. I followed in Dr. Cowan's car as the chauffeur drove the Bentley at breakneck speeds all the way to Richmond Hospital, while Cowan kept Brian breathing in the backseat. At Richmond, Brian's stomach was pumped, and he was put to bed semiconscious.

"What's the matter with you, Brian? How could you try something like that? You have so much to live for," I said to him.

"It was a foolish accident," Brian answered feebly. "I just took one pill too many. I didn't mean to do it. I promise I'll be careful from now on."

But when I returned to Chapel Street that night, I learned it was no accident. On Brian's night table, next to an empty bottle of pills, was a suicide note I had not noticed before. It said, in part, "This is all too much and I can't take it anymore." A short will and testament followed, in which he left his house and business and money to his mother and Clive. I was also a small beneficiary.

The next day I took the letter to Brian in the hospital and confronted him with it. He was grateful I had not told anyone about it, but I had my doubts I was doing him a favor by not showing it to Dr. Cowan. In any event, Brian took the letter from me, saying he was going to burn it. He never did. I guess he thought it might come in handy some other time.

When Brian was released from the hospital, it was decided he should go away for a short time to an exclusive "drying-out" clinic in Putney for detoxification and rest.

Chapter Twelve

I think the problem was
we underestimated this crazy
little Japanese lady.
                    —*Neil Aspinall*

1.

*I*N THE FALL OF 1966 the Beatles each went their own seperate ways. For the four young men who had been locked up together for so long under such extraordinary circumstances, being apart for the first time in nearly ten years was an odd and wrenching experience. They intended to reconvene sometime in December to begin work on a follow-up album to *Revolver,* but that left four months for them to occupy on their own.* In a perhaps odd coincidence, although they were apart, they each grew moustaches and longer hair without consulting the others. Suddenly, everywhere you looked young men had moustaches and long hair.

Paul adjusted the best. He found lots to keep him busy. He and Jane were the essence of the glamourous young couple in Swinging London. Too old to still be living in the guest room at the Ashers', Paul bought his first house. Distinctly unlike the other Beatles, Paul bought an urban house, on Cavendish Avenue in London's smart St. John's Wood. It was a square white Georgian

---

* Making a third movie was an option, but a suitable script could not be agreed upon by the four Beatles and Brian. Instead, an animated feature-length cartoon was licensed to King Features in the U.S., eventually called *Yellow Submarine,* which Brian hoped would satisfy the terms of the U.A. contract. The Beatles had virtually nothing to do with this animated film, aside from composing a few songs for it when it was almost completed. Although U.A. rejected *Yellow Submarine* as the third film, it went on to become a commercial and artistic success. Ironically, U.A. later acted as a distributor of the film in the U.S.

minimanse, protected from the street by high brick walls and electronic gates. The old house had three baths, two guest bedrooms and separate quarters for the couple who came to take care of Paul and Jane's needs. Instead of turning the decoration over to professionals, they decided to furnish it themselves. They took pleasure in shopping for each piece individually, sometimes buying used furniture at secondhand shops and refinishing it themselves. Paul was proud to point out that the Victorian clock on the mantel cost only £7, and the sofa and armchairs, which he had reupholstered in a bottle green velvet, cost only £20 together. Of course, there was also a gleaming bronze Paolozzi sculpture called "Solo" worth many thousands of pounds and an 1851 clock and a collection of Tiffany glass that were priceless. The floors were covered in deep-pile carpets in sedate tones of brown and gray, and Paul's bedroom, which faced the front courtyard, had a king-size bed covered in Porthault linens, which were changed almost daily by his loyal housekeeper, Rose. Paul also had a closet built that ran the width of the twenty-two-foot room, which he stocked with the latest fashions from King's Road and the top tailors. In the master bath, completely tiled in imported blue and white mosaics, he had built a sunken tub big enough for two.

Jane also encouraged him to find a hideaway from the world, a place for just the two of them, without autograph-seeking fans or the constant ring of the telephone. Paul purchased High Park, an isolated but beautiful farm in the boggy moors of Scotland. High Park was a very simple place, just an old wooden farmhouse and some barns, surrounded by miles of open fields. No outsiders, not even other Beatles, were invited up for a visit. Paul, it should be noted, was the first Beatle to show any distance or privacy from the others. One rare visitor to High Park was Alistair Taylor, the loyal office manager and general fixer at NEMS. Paul summoned Alistair to High Park so that he could pay a visit to the local pharmacy for him. According to Alistair, Paul had the crabs and needed a pesticide to shampoo with. Being Paul McCartney, the neighborhood celebrity, Paul was too embarrassed to ask the pharmacist in the small town for the pesticide himself, so he sent Alistair. There was also a sense of urgency to this mission, lest Paul give the tiny parasites to Jane, who would most certainly realize he had been unfaithful to her. The town pharmacist was baffled by Alistair's request. He had nothing for that purpose other than "sheep dip," which was used to delouse cattle. Paul presumably made do with that.

Paul also persevered with a vigorous self-improvement program. He read, he went to foreign films, he became sophisticated and, in a certain sense, very bourgeois. While the others went on vacation to sunny isles, Paul went on an educational safari to Africa, with Mal along to protect him from lions and cannibals. He also set to work writing a very ambitious motion picture score for the Boulting Brothers' new movie, *The Family Way*, which starred the very popular young Hayley Mills. It was the first solo work by a Beatle.

George Harrison also blossomed once taken out of the vacuum created by John and Paul. As the years passed it had become clear to all of us that as far as John and Paul were concerned, George was only a third-class Beatle, and there was nothing he could do about it. His music was summarily dismissed at recording sessions, and his few songs to appear on Beatles' albums were relegated to filler positions. Only his song "Taxman" had been a commercial hit. In public popularity as well, George seemed to be stuck in third place, in a tie with Ringo. The one talent that set him apart from the others was his growing ability in Indian music. Since he had first heard the sitar on the set of *Help!*, where Hindi musicians were seen playing in one scene in the Bahamas, George had been diligently studying the twenty-one-string, guitar-like instrument. It first appeared on John's "Norwegian Wood" song and then in "Rain," which closed with one of George's neo-Indian ragas.

One night at a London dinner party, George was introduced to Ravi Shankar, India's best-known sitar virtuoso, who was then little known by the Western world. Shankar invited George to come to India to study with him. It marked the beginning of a long, fruitful alliance for the two musicians. In the years to come, George would make Indian music (and Shankar) part of the commercial music mainstream. In October of 1966 the Harrisons left London for Kashmir for a two-month study vacation. They spent the first night at Shankar's home in Bombay, but the house was surrounded by the inevitable frantic Beatles fans, and Shankar and his guests were forced to move out. They lived for the next seven weeks at Shankar's Himalayan retreat, where George and

Pattie studied Indian mysticism and religion, and George worked at mastering the new instrument.

Ringo, who needed much less out of life than it already seemed to have handed him on a silver platter, felt no unrest that autumn. He tinkered with his expensive toys and his cars and enjoyed the London nightlife. Maureen, his loving and dedicated wife, waited up for him no matter how late he came home, always with a hot meal ready if he was hungry. By winter she was happily pregnant with their second child.

2.

OF ALL THE BEATLES, John Lennon suffered the most from the abrupt separation. He felt some relief from the pressure, but most of all he felt lost. "It seems like the end," he said later. "No more touring. Life without the Beatles . . . it's like there's a black space in the future." He considered leaving the Beatles altogether at that point and striking out on his own, but he depended on Paul too much, if not musically, for spirit and industry. "What will I end up doing?" he wondered. "Where will I wind up when it stops? Las Vegas?"

Life with Cynthia in Kenwood was stultifying. She cooked dinner for him every night and brought it to him in the sunroom, where they watched TV as they ate, changing the channels every few minutes, not speaking. A chilling portrait of them was drawn in Hunter Davies' authorized biography of the Beatles:

> John then opened the large sliding window and sat on a step to get some fresh air, looking down upon the pool. Round and round the surface of the pool went the automatic filter, like a space ship which had just landed. Julian came out and went down to the pool. He threw some oars in, then got them out again and came back to the house. Cynthia cleaned up.
>
> Terry Doran arrived and was greeted warmly by all, including Julian, who sat on his knee.

"Do you want your dad to put you to bed?" said Cyn, smiling at John, who grinned back. "Or do you want Terry?" Julian said he wanted Terry. But she picked Julian up herself and put him to bed.

"Are you going to roll us a few, then?" said John to Terry. Terry said yes. John got up and brought out a tin toolbox, which he opened for Terry. Inside was some tobacco wrapped in silver tinfoil plus some cigarette papers. Terry rolled a couple of cigarettes, which they smoked, sharing them.

This was during the pot-taking period. John was keeping it in a toolbox as he'd decided to hide it in the garden in case the police came. He had a box, but hadn't gotten around to digging a hole.

Cyn came back. The television was still on. They all sat and watched it, still changing programs all the time, until about midnight, when Cyn made some cocoa. Terry left and John and Cyn went to bed. John said he was going to read a paperback book someone had given them. Cyn said oh, she wanted to read that first.*

Although John was deluged with offers for his individual services, he did nothing. He was begged to write books, movie scores, to supply lyrics, to write plays for the National Theatre, to execute drawings for an art exhibit, to design greeting cards. Not knowing "what the hell to do all day," he took a small role in the Richard Lester antiwar movie, *How I Won the War*. John felt comfortable working with Lester again, since Lester knew the extent of his acting talents, and the locations, a brief stop in Germany and then two months in Almeria, Spain, sounded interesting. John

---

*Journalist and author Hunter Davies had been commissioned by Brian to write the Beatles' authorized biography. It was published in the U.K. and the U.S. in 1968. All of the Beatles, including their families, had final control over what appeared in the book. Davies says the book went through wholesale censorship, with the Beatles tearing out pages they didn't like as they read the manuscript. The only parent who asked for changes was John's Aunt Mimi, who "went mad" according to Davies when she read the manuscript. Among other changes, all curse words were deleted, the drug use was toned down, and Mimi insisted that her sister Julia had married "Twitchy" so that no children were born out of wedlock. Queenie insisted that a reference to Brian's homosexuality be deleted. She said it wasn't true. Another story not even considered for inclusion in the book was John's trip to Spain with Brian. John admitted to Davies that he had slept with Brian "to see what fucking with a guy was like."

took Cynthia with him, along with Neil Aspinall and a suitcase full of drugs. In Germany they cut John's famed Beatles locks into an army crew cut, a daring and symbolic break with tradition. He also dispensed with his contact lenses for the first time since he became famous, replacing them with oval, wire-framed, army-issue spectacles from the first World War. The glasses became as much of his trademark as his Beatles haircut had been, and around the world, "granny glasses" became the rage.

In Almeria, a coastal town on the southeastern tip of Spain, they rented a palatial villa in the mountains with co-star Michael Crawford and his wife. Although Ringo and Maureen came for a visit as a diversion, the month and a half in Almeria turned out to be a lesson in boredom for John. Most of his time was spent sitting in a canvas chair in a dressing trailer or waiting in the hot sun in his army uniform for the next shot to begin. It was far worse than any Beatles movie, where he was the star. His role of Musketeer Gripweed turned out to be small and uninteresting. Though he garnered fair reviews, the most fun he had making the movie was playing a death scene after being shot. When he and Cynthia watched a screening of the movie, she broke down and cried hysterically. She told John it was exactly the way he would look when he died.

By the time John and Cynthia returned to London, it was late autumn and the long holiday season was already underway, the perfect backdrop for John's unrest. There seemed to be a never-ending round of cocktail parties, crowded Chelsea "happenings," psychedelic club openings, or literary parties in basement Hampstead flats. That fall was also the beginning of his heavy experimentation with psychedelics. Swinging London was just as much about acid as it was about anything else that year. Acid was the perfect drug for the moment; it gave the already shimmering world just the right effervescence. Naturally, John went overboard and took acid almost every day—by his own admission he experienced *thousands* of trips. He became convinced that through acid he would find the key, the answer. Acid was a tool through which problems could be solved. This was when John added his mortar and pestle to the sunroom shelf, with its compound of various drugs that were either purchased or given to him as gifts. Drugs were laid on John wherever he went, like laurel wreaths thrown in his path, for to say that you had turned on John Lennon was a badge of honor.

At night he would roam the city in his chauffeur-driven SS Mini Cooper, with its black-tinted windows so no one could see in, taking along with him one or another of the many nonessential employees of the Beatles organization, usually Terry Doran. For many people it was difficult to fathom that the twenty-six-year-old man so stoned and unhappy in the backseat of the Mini Cooper had that autumn appeared solo on the cover of *Look* magazine in America as one of the prominent leaders of the "youth generation."

John gravitated not so much to the fast crowd in Chelsea as he did the struggling Bohemian artists, a fringe element always in pursuit of the next buck, the next lay, and the next drug. Somewhere in the ever-changing crowd he was introduced to John Dunbar, the twenty-four-year-old owner of the Indica Gallery, an avant-garde art gallery in Mason's Yard. Small, attractive, and shrewd, Dunbar had once been married to Marianne Faithfull, the sexy, blond, somnambulistic singer who was now famous as Mick Jagger's girlfriend. To make the circle even smaller, Peter Asher, Jane's younger brother, who had by now become a major pop star in his own right, had invested in the Indica Gallery, and Dunbar had been a childhood friend of the Asher family. In fact, unknown to Jane, Paul had once "dated" one of Dunbar's and Faithfull's babysitters.

Dunbar was a Cambridge graduate who had hitchhiked across America in 1964 and had returned to London to open the Indica as a sort of salon for underground artists to meet and display their wares, artistic or otherwise. John liked Dunbar's glib and easy banter and was eager to meet more of Dunbar's circle. For a time Allen Ginsberg lived in a flat next door to the gallery, and Roman Polanski, who was a good customer, often appeared in the middle of the night to purchase whatever the gallery was selling from the many passing vendors.

One of the vendors was John Alexis Mardas, a thin, twenty-one-year-old Greek youngster with sandy brown hair. The son of a Greek military officer who had just come to power in the recent junta, Alex, as he was called, spoke heavily accented English at breakneck speed, although his tongue tripped over every syllable. His accent, however, was no impediment to his gift for gab. He billed himself as a world traveler and electronics genius just passing through London on a holiday, although his real story was decidedly less glamourous. Admitted to England on a limited student visa, he claimed that his passport had been stolen from his luggage and had subsequently expired. When he reported this dilemma to the Greek Embassy, an attaché accused him of having sold the passport. In the interim, to feed himself, Alex took an illegal job as a television repairman in the basement of a TV repair service called Olympic Television. About this time, John Dunbar, through his ever-widening circle, got to know Alex and decided his knowledge of electricity and electronics could be put to good use. Kinetic art and sculpture were all the rage, and a young artist named Takis had recently made a fortune with a show comprised of kinetic light sculptures. Dunbar suggested that Alex go into business with him, and Dunbar became his "agent." Alex's first project was a box filled with flashing lights, covered in a transparent membrane. They called it a "psychedelic light box"—a brand-new idea at the time—and sold it to the Rolling Stones, who immediately added it to their act. Brian Jones, the Stones' doomed, baby-faced lead guitarist, took a special liking to Alex. It was through Brian Jones that Alex was introduced to the Beatles, first John, then George.

Both Beatles, by now wary of loquacious strangers with grand designs, were completely taken up with Alex's charms. He was a fascinating companion. He had an encyclopedic knowledge of an endless variety of subjects. For George he spun stories and lectures on India, mysticism, and religion. For John he was full of ideas for magic inventions, incredible things he had figured out how to make: air colored with light, artificial laser suns that would hang in the night sky, a force field that would keep fans away, and wallpaper that was actually a paper-thin stereo speaker. One day, when Alex brought John a plastic box filled with Christmas tree lights that did nothing but blink on and off randomly until the battery ran down and the thing blinked itself to death, John was thrilled. It was the best gift an LSD freak could want. In thanks, John elevated him to the royal circle as the Beatles' court sorcerer and dubbed him "Magic Alex." John also solved Alex's work and immigration problems with a phone call to me. I was asked to make arrangements through an attorney for Alex's legal immigration to Great Britain.

Magic Alex made Cynthia Lennon's skin crawl the moment she met him. He radiated trouble to her. It wasn't that she disbelieved the fantastic promises of inventions, it was his possessiveness of John. No one could know better what a fierce competitor he was for John's attention. Although it was decidedly not sexual, Alex courted John like any female power-and-stardom groupie she had ever observed at work around the Beatles. He became John's unshakeable, constant companion. He was always polite and considerate to Cynthia, but she nevertheless watched carefully for the day Alex might try to stab her in the back.

3.

*O*N NOVEMBER 9 I could no longer put off the worried phone calls from our English tour promoter, Arthur Howes, about booking future Beatles' concerts. Brian, who couldn't bear to admit the truth, finally called Howes and told him that the Beatles would no longer accept any bookings. Within the hour word leaked out to the press, and the office was deluged with calls. It was reported in most papers the next day that the Beatles intended to exist solely as recording artists. No entertainment act had ever attempted this before, and the implication of many of the articles was that that was the first step in their long-expected demise.

While Brian and I were on the phone with various reporters, assuring them that the Beatles were far from having broken up, John Dunbar was on the phone with John Lennon, who was crumpled on the curved sofa on the sunporch at Kenwood. He had been up for three consecutive days, tripping on LSD, and he had not washed or shaved in seventy-two hours. Dunbar wanted John to come to a private preview that night of a show opening at the Indica. Dunbar's description of the show sounded very sexual to John, vaguely like an orgy. There were to be all these beautiful young people laying around in a big bag or something. The exhibit was titled "Unfinished Paintings and Objects by Yoko Ono." John agreed to go.

Later that evening, at about ten o'clock, John arrived at the Indica in his chauffeur-driven Mini. Dunbar met him at the door of the gallery and took him around to see the exhibit. It was unlike anything John had ever seen before. The displays were so simple and arbitrary that it seemed some sort of put-on. There was an ordinary apple on a pedestal with a £200 price tag on it. John assumed one paid £200 for the privilege of watching the apple decompose. There was also a stepladder with a spyglass attached to the top step with a chain. If you climbed the ladder and looked at a circled spot on the ceiling, you could read the word "Yes" printed in a tiny scrawl. And there was a board with several nails hammered partially into it, with a note that said, "Hammer A Nail In."

Dunbar led John downstairs to the basement to see the live part of the exhibition. Several long-haired young men and women were sitting around the floor, darning the rips in a large canvas bag. Dunbar went across the room to get the artist. "Go and say hello to the millionaire," Dunbar whispered pointedly to her, and presently a remarkable figure appeared before John.

She was a tiny Japanese woman, less than five feet tall, dressed in black pants and a tatty black sweater. She had a very pale, grim-looking face, set off by two thick columns of black hair that streamed over her breasts nearly to her waist. Her name was Yoko Ono.

"Where's the orgy?" John asked her, slightly disappointed that nothing sexual was happening. Wordlessly, she handed John a card. On it was printed the word "breathe." "You mean like this?" John said, and panted. The small Japanese woman seemed unimpressed.

They wandered around the exhibit together, Dunbar speaking for the two of them. When John asked if he could hammer a nail into one of the boards, Yoko said no. The exhibit didn't officially open until the next day, and she didn't want it tampered with. Dunbar was embarrassed. "Let him hammer a nail in. Who knows, he might buy it," he encouraged. After a short conference with Dunbar, Yoko agreed to allow John to hammer a nail in— for five shillings.

John was both irked and amused. He'd take her up on her game. "Okay," he said, "I'll give you an imaginary five shillings, and I'll hammer in an imaginary nail."

Yoko Ono finally smiled.

Yoko Ono—her name means "Ocean Child"—was born in Tokyo on February 18, 1934, the eldest daughter of a prominent banker and a cold, aristocratic mother. Her mother's socially conscious family, the Yasudas, were, according to Yoko, the Japanese equivalents of the Rothschilds or the Rockefellers, and they resented her mother's marriage to her bourgeois father. Yoko herself was never very close to her father, who moved to San Francisco to head a branch of the Yokohama Speci-Bank before she was born. She didn't really get to know him until she and her mother joined him in San Francisco in 1936. The Onos lived in San Francisco and New York for four years, until the Japanese attack on Pearl Harbor made the family less than welcome in America, and they were sent back to their native country, a matter of no small bitterness to them.

Back in Japan, Yoko and her younger brother and sister moved to a farmhouse her mother had rented in the countryside for their safety away from the wartime cities, but when they arrived at the farmhouse it turned out to be just a shack, with no food or supplies. Yoko's mother went back to Tokyo, leaving her children with the servants, who soon abandoned them, penniless. Yoko was forced to forage for food and clothing for herself and her siblings until after the war, when she was reunited with her parents.

In 1951, the war over and all forgiven, Yoko's father was named president of the New York branch of his bank, now renamed the Bank of Tokyo, and the family once again moved to New York, this time to a large house in Scarsdale. Yoko attended three years of college at Sarah Lawrence as a philosophy major before getting bored with the regimentation of school and dropping out. When she was twenty-three, much to her parents' distress, she eloped with a penniless Japanese composer and pianist named Toschi Ichiyananagi, and her mother promptly cut her off without a penny. It was years before they spoke again.

She stayed married to Ichiyananagi for seven years, living in various cheap apartments in the West Eighties near Riverside Drive. Now an aspiring avant-garde musician and artist herself, her husband encouraged her into composing with him. Trying to gain a foothold in the fast-moving, competitive art world as an avant-garde artist was not easy. For a while she fell in with musicians John Cage and La Monte Young. Her first displayed art was created to be burned or stomped on. In 1960 she had her first show at a small Madison Avenue gallery owned by George

Marcunia. Marcunia was one of the inventors of a live event he called "Flexus," the forerunner of the popular "happenings." Yoko's show at his gallery was comprised of conceptual art pieces designed with her trademark brand of ironic humor. One of the pieces was called an "eternal time clock," which was a clock with only a second hand encased in a plastic bubble. The ticking could only be heard through a stethoscope attached to the sculpture. She also presented a stage piece at Carnegie Recital Hall in which as part of the performance performers were strapped together back-to-back and instructed to walk across the stage without making any noise. At another "concert" held at the Village Gate, microphones were hidden in the toilets so the patrons could be heard urinating and flushing on stage.

Try as she might to be different, Yoko was soon swallowed up by the harshly competitive art world. In 1961 she joined her husband in Tokyo, where she staged musical dance programs. "I got terrible reviews," Yoko remembers. "The conservative elements—men artists and critics—decided to boycott me. The press wrote snide remarks all over the place. I just felt terrible." When a Tokyo critic accused her of plagiarizing her ideas, she tried to kill herself. "As a teenager I was always trying to cut my wrists or take pills," she said. "And later . . . I was always feeling frustrated as an artist. I felt I was not being accepted by society, work-wise."

When she was twenty-nine she divorced Toschi Ichiyananagi to marry avant-garde artist Tony Cox, whom she met in Japan. On August 8, 1963, a daughter, Kyoko, was born. Yoko didn't really want to have this baby. She said she wasn't ready. Her mother had always warned her that marriage and children would ruin her career, but she had already had so many abortions in the fifties that the doctors advised her not to have another, and Kyoko was born. "I thought, 'Maybe if I have a child, I'll feel differently,' because society's myth is that all women are supposed to have children. But that was a myth. So there was Kyoko, and I did become attached to her and had great love for her, but at the same time I was still struggling to get my own space in the world."

She moved back to New York with Cox, this time to a cold-water loft decorated with orange crates in the then unfashionable factory district of downtown Manhattan known as Soho. "I felt stifled in New York," Yoko said. "I wasn't sure what to do." Then, in early 1966, an English journalist included her in an article on avant-garde artists published in England. Soon after she and Cox were invited to London to attend a symposium called "The Destruction of Art." They arrived in London in October of 1966, nearly penniless. As soon as they got to town, she called an old American friend from the art world, Dan Richter, to find a place to stay. Richter got them the flat next door to his in a big Victorian building on Park Row. Yoko emptied the apartment of furniture and spent her last money on carpeting it wall to wall; she said she liked living in the barren space. A few weeks later she met John Lennon at the Indica Gallery.

Yoko's second meeting with John Lennon was much less memorable than the first. It was at a Claes Oldenburg art opening of soft sculpture. John, stoned as usual on a mixture from his mortar, was wandering past a giant fabric cheeseburger, drinking white wine, when he spotted Yoko across the room, a small, striking figure again dressed entirely in black. They nodded at each other shyly, but both were too embarrassed to speak, and they spent the rest of the evening frozen in place, yards from each other.

One morning weeks later, Yoko turned up in the waiting room of the Beatles' office, demanding to speak to John. She needed financial sponsorship for one of her conceptual projects; she wanted to wrap one of the lions in Trafalgar Square in canvas. The closest she got to John that day was an accidental encounter with Neil Aspinall. Neil came away from the encounter with the impression she might have been making a play for him. Yoko also managed, in passing, to collar Ringo, but her philosophical and conceptual ramblings about her art were so obscure to Ringo that she might as well have been speaking Japanese to him.

Eventually, she sent John a copy of a little book she had published in a limited edition of 500 copies by the Wunternum Press in Tokyo in 1964 called *Grapefruit.* The book was a collection of "instructional poems." On each page there was a suggestion: "Draw a map to get lost" or "Smoke everything you can, including your pubic hair" and "Stir inside of your brains with a penis until things are mixed well. Take a walk." John was at first annoyed by the book, then outraged, and finally amused. So amused he agreed to speak with her. Yoko convinced him to finance her next show at the Lissom Gallery, which was entitled "The Half Wind Show" and which was comprised of half-things; half-a-chair, half-a-bed, half-a-cup. John, cautiously, would not allow his name to be used in the catalog, and the sponsorship of the show was credited only as "Yoko plus me." Later in the year, he noticed, she had one of her shows at the Saville Theater, where members of the audience came up and cut off pieces of her clothing, while she sat stoic and immobile on the stage. One night he asked her back to Neil Aspinall's flat, but they only talked. Yoko curled up to sleep on the divan, while John slept alone in the bedroom.

Instead of a passionate, physical affair, John and Yoko simmered intellectually for over a year. John became a benefactor to the struggling artist, an elusive but important sounding board. She found him kind of square in a rock and roll way, a world from which she felt removed, but he somehow managed to keep one up on her. His mind was like quicksilver, and she admired that. John was teased and titillated by her, and her new art projects never failed to make him laugh. A major film project she was making with her husband was called *Bottoms*. John read a piece about it that Hunter Davies wrote in the *Sunday Times*. Yoko and Cox had rented a room at the Park Lane Hotel and were actively soliciting people to drop their drawers and pose for a few seconds of 16-mm film of their bare asses. Still, he never took her seriously. She wasn't the answer to whatever it was he was looking for. She was just another bird.

On most nights he went back to Kenwood, still high on his drugged jaunts. Upstairs Julian lay sleeping in the nursery, and Cynthia was in the big bed in the master bedroom, waiting for him. Sometimes, at dawn, he would lay down beside her. But most often he would curl up on the too-small wicker sofa in the sunroom and look at magazines and picture books of surrealist painters. He wrote down words and sentence fragments, such as "I am the walrus" from a Lewis Carroll poem, or things that came to him in acid flashes, like the propaganda-spouting Hare Krishna devotees that became "elementary penguins." Often he would stare at the blinking "nothing box" Alex had presented to him or at the walls and shadows until the drugs wore off. Somewhere, in the back of his mind, he heard with dim irony the question-and-answer pep chant the Beatles once used to console themselves in hard times.

"Where are we going fellows?"
"To the top, Johnny!"
"Where is that, fellows?"
"To the toppermost of the poppermost."

4.

A S WINTER DRIFTED into spring, Brian seemed to deteriorate even further. His misadventures continued. A guardsman he picked up one night turned violent and broke the bannister on the staircase as he was forcibly rejected. Another time Brian brought a young man home with him for £20. The boy took with him Brian's £1000 gold watch when he left and sold it hours later in an underground station for £5. When the unsuspecting buyer realized that the name "Brian Epstein" was engraved on the back, he brought it to the Savile Row police station, where it was returned to Brian. Brian gave the man back the £5, plus a £10 reward, ironically less than he had paid the hustler who stole it from him.

Edgy and easily bored, Brian began to travel restlessly, making the same loop from London to New York to Spain every few weeks. For a time he entertained himself by managing his own bullfighter, who was an Englishman improbably named Henry Higgins. Brian's favorite recreation was drugs, however. That winter he discovered LSD for the first time. One Saturday night when Brian returned home to Chapel Street, I confessed to him that I had just started my first trip, and Brian insisted he be given some acid for himself. He downed it on the spot, and we stayed up all night tripping. He enjoyed the experience so much that he immediately took another dose upon waking up on Sunday afternoon. I felt no regret that I had given Brian his first acid but did regret that he chose to do it so frequently and incautiously.

The psychedelic mixed with the uppers and downers and booze were taking quite a toll on Brian. Sometimes he was up for three days at a time without sleep. He was psychologically and physically on the edge of collapse. It was obvious that he was in desperate need of professional help, but Brian wouldn't even discuss the subject. He was fanatically against psychiatry, especially after his experience with the court-enforced psychiatric treatment he underwent in Liverpool after his first blackmail experience. We continued to gently hint that Brian seek help, but there were some subjects one did not press too heavily with him, no matter how close you were, even if you were willing to dare.

I dared one morning in New York in suite 35E at the Waldorf Towers while accompanying Brian on one of his three-pronged trips. Brian was due that morning at a live interview with disc jockey Murray the K at the WNEW studios. Brian intended to again allay the public's fears that the Beatles were breaking up. When Brian didn't awake in time for breakfast, I knocked on his bedroom door and went in. He was sound asleep; he had taken so many Tuinals to get to sleep just a few hours before, he was too groggy to sit up. Nat Weiss arrived in the suite to accompany Brian to the radio studio, and he was enlisted to help revive him. As soon as Brian was conscious and lucid, I started screaming at him with such rage that it even shocked Nat. "Don't you realize how sick you are?" I shouted. "You can't go on like this! You have to stop! Do you hear me Brian? Go to a doctor, go to a hospital, but get help!"

"Calm down," Brian said weakly. "Calm yourself."

"No I won't. I won't have it. I can't stand by and watch you do this to yourself."

Brian stood, clutching the night table, and made his way slowly to the bathroom. "I'm going to have a shower and get dressed for my interview," he said.

"You can't go to your interview," I said. "You'll make a fool of yourself. You're full of pills and slurring like a drunk."

But Brian would have it no other way. He showered and dressed, and Nat helped him down to the waiting limo. I refused to have anything to do with it and swore I wasn't even going to listen to the live broadcast on the radio. In the limo Nat steadied Brian on the drive to WNEW and sat next to him in the studio to prop him up in case he keeled over. Murray the K, who couldn't possibly have missed how zombielike stoned Brian was, pretended it just wasn't happening and played the whole scene in his usual strident way, calling Brian "Eppy" like a close friend.

Back at the Waldorf Towers I tuned into WNEW despite myself. Murray the K's first question was about the future of the Beatles. Brian's voice came over the speakers slurred and deep, the syllables attenuated, yet what he said was undeniably eloquent. "I think they might play together again," he said, "but in another concept entirely. . . . At the moment they're doing great things in the studio. They take longer nowadays, of their own volition, to make records . . ." As the interview continued Brian's words became clearer, his conviction stronger in the future of the Beatles, the youth movement, virtually everything we wanted to hear. Even I was enthused.

Toward the end of the interview, Murray the K asked Brian what "the next big thing" was going to be, and I could almost see Brian smiling wearily in the studio as he said, "A good tune. A good tune is always the next big thing."

When Brian returned to the Waldorf, the incident was never mentioned again. We left New York for some rest and recreation in Acapulco and Mexico City, where we stayed for nearly three weeks. Brian went back to New York for a time, while I flew to London to sign the papers for him on a country estate he had recently purchased. Kingsley Hill in Sussex was a lovely, £35,000 brick and wood eighteenth-century country house that was going to be Brian's retreat, the place where he could get away from it all.

5.

THAT SAME AUTUMN, when the Beatles first went their separate ways, and with much of his responsibility taken away from him, Brian made the most implausible of his decisions to date. He decided that the pressure of running NEMS with its many acts and multitude of functions was too much for him, and he wanted to get rid of it all, except for the Beatles and Cilla Black. The boys and Cilla, after all, were all he ever really cared about. The rest had turned out to be very unsatisfying for the most part. Finding a buyer for NEMS would not be a problem. Over the last few years there had been offers for the company practically every day, but none of them by the right people. One American entertainment conglomerate had offered upwards of $20 million the previous year, but the offer included the Beatles and left Brian no further say in their management. Brian needed someone he could trust, someone who would do NEMS justice. One evening that fall, he met just the perfect person at a party.

It was a Saturday night, and Brian and I had heard that Robert Stigwood gave regular Saturday night parties at the large, fashionably decorated duplex flat on Waldon Court he shared with Christopher Stamp, the brother of actor Terence Stamp. Stigwood was a rosy-cheeked, ginger-haired Australian who at the age of thirty-two had already earned himself a formidable reputation as a shrewd and quick-footed business man. As a rock manager, his acts included Cream, an enormously popular new "heavy rock" band, and Graham Bond. He had also set the precedent for an innovation in the English recording-production process with "lease taping." Instead of the record company owning and producing an album with on-staff producers and then doling out a small percentage of the profits to the artists and managers, Stigwood financed and produced his own tapes. He then sold the finished products to the record company, thus retaining a much larger share of the profits—usually 15 percent—for himself and his artists. This eventually became standard in the British recording industry.

However, Stigwood was also known for his grandiose life-style, which reportedly had capsized his last company and thrown it into an undischarged bankruptcy. It was also known to Brian, through Sir Joseph Lockwood, the Beatles' loyal friend at EMI, that only a few days before Stigwood had liquidated his company he had borrowed £10,000 from EMI—allegedly to pay off his personal debts. According to Sir Joe, he took the money knowing the company was going under and that the sum would never be repaid. Sir Joe never forgave him and refused to allow EMI to do any further business with him.

Stigwood had recently formed a new company called the Robert Stigwood Organization. His partner was a small, nervous man named David Shaw, who was a well-known businessman in his own right. Shaw had many times made the pages of the venerable *Financial Times* with a company he ran called Constellation. In a sense, Constellation was like a giant pension fund for show business figures who had short-term, high income that was usually eaten up by the Inland Revenue Service. Instead of experiencing a huge tax bite during the peak years—the way the Beatles had—income would be deferred into the future by careful distribution. Shaw had once approached Brian about the Beatles joining Constellation. We had all met accidentally in Eze, in the south of France, when I went away with Brian after the first Dizz Gillespie incident. Shaw was staying on the Constellation-owned yacht, *Eridiana,* and asked Brian and me to join him for dinner in the hotel restaurant. On his way back from the men's room, Shaw walked through a sliding glass door leading onto the terrace and was badly cut, bringing the business conversation to an abrupt halt. In any event, it turned out that it was a good thing none of the Beatles had ever invested in Constellation. The company was soon shut down by Parliament when a law was passed to close the tax loophole through which it operated. Some tax experts saw Constellation as more of a "pyramid scheme," into which new income had to be continuously generated to keep up the price of the shares, than a sound financial investment.

It was perhaps less well known that in the summer of 1966 David Shaw was made a public scapegoat in a "bond washing" scandal in which the Church of England and the Royal Bank of Canada were also reprimanded. The scandal centered around Toby Jessel, a Conservative candidate from Hull North, who was a director of Constellation. With Shaw's reputation somewhat tarnished in the City, he had to resign his position. It was about that time he met up with Robert Stigwood, and they formed an alliance.

None of Stigwood's and Shaw's previous misadventures put Brian off, however. The first night they met at Stigwood's party a plan was made to go to Paris together for what Shaw called "a dirty weekend." It was in Paris in a three-bedroom suite at the Lancaster Hotel that Brian told Stigwood he was planning to retire because he wasn't enjoying it anymore, and he wanted to go to Spain and manage bullfighters. To Brian, Stigwood and Shaw seemed like the perfect choice to take over the daily operation of NEMS. He felt that Stigwood had the right amount of creative potential and that Shaw had a sharp financial mind. Most important to Brian, Stigwood was intelligent, amusing, and affected an elegance similar to his own.

Brian made the following offer to Stigwood and Shaw: He

would sell them 51 percent of NEMS—a controlling interest—in a reverse takeover to avoid sustaining a large capital gain. Brian would remain chairman of the board and would continue to look after Cilla and the Beatles exclusively. Stigwood and Shaw could have all the rest. The price was an astonishingly paltry £500,000, considering that Brian had been offered $20 million only two years before. The written deadline for Stigwood and Shaw to raise the money was in May of 1967, but when that date passed, Brian made a verbal agreement with them to wait until September. Why Brian would agree to these terms, especially when selling controlling interest, remains a mystery, except to say that Brian was intent on selling the company to Stigwood and Shaw. He was so afraid to confront the staff and executive officers of NEMS with this proposal that he never announced it until it was a *fait accompli*. One night, when the NEMS offices were closed, I secretly met with Stigwood and Shaw at the Argyle Street offices for them to pick out which offices they wanted, evicting a very peeved Geoffrey Ellis the following day.

The news of the intended sale of NEMS to Stigwood and Shaw was also greeted with dismay by the entertainment community. Brian received sharp admonishments from Sir Joe and the Grade Organization, which criticized Stigwood as "an undischarged bankrupt and an Australian to boot."

Chapter Thirteen

Picture yourself on a boat on
a river/with tangerine trees
and marmalade skies . . .

—*"Lucy in the Sky with Diamonds"*

1.

*A*T THE AGE of twenty-five, Paul McCartney had turned into a self-assured, slightly pompous "culture chaser," as the *Evening Standard* called him, noting that he never missed a play opening or declined an invitation to the right party. A young, handsome multimillionaire and idol of his generation, he had been called a genius enough times, justifiably, to believe it himself with a deep conviction. He had, it appeared, everything—his beautiful and famous girlfriend; his beautiful sheep dog Martha; his St. John's Woods home, which was slowly filling with Beardsley originals; the platinum albums he sent to his father's home in the Wirral. He had everything except the one thing every northern man wants most: a wife and children. Because for all the glamour and perfection of his life, Jane Asher would not settle down with him.

He was still madly in love with her. For him she was "Here, There and Everywhere," and she did more for him than just inspire songs. Only Jane seemed to have any real control over Paul. Only she could gently deflate his impossible ego without destroying his pride. She was able to restore in Paul the one great quality that had been destroyed by his success: humility. Jane loved Paul; he was sweet and well-meaning; he would even make a wonderful father. But he could not be her whole life. She could not live in the shadow of a Beatle.

John and Ringo did not have this problem; their women were

northern women and understood. George, who'd married a London girl with a career, simply put a stop to that career when it threatened him. Pattie Harrison told reporters, "A Beatle wife is just baggage. There's no pretending any different." But not Jane. Although they had officially announced their engagement and even had an engagement celebration for the benefit of Paul's relatives in Liverpool over Christmas vacation, and although Jane made cute remarks to reporters like, "I would be most surprised if I married anyone else," he could not get her to name the day. Instead she worked harder at her career, and her accolades and credits grew more impressive by the month. She was now the premiere ingenue of the Old Vic.

To complicate matters, Jane left Britain on January 16, 1967, for a three-month tour of America with the Old Vic. Paul, at a loss without her companionship, threw himself into his work at the Abbey Road studios, where the Beatles were hard at work on their new album, now entitled *Sergeant Pepper's Lonely Hearts Club Band.* The Beatles started work on the album in December, and Paul insisted that all work be finished in time for him to surprise Jane in America on April 5, her twenty-first birthday. Brian, in an attempt to flatter Paul, went through elaborate trouble to secure Paul's transportation and accommodations for the trip, including the rental of Frank Sinatra's private Lear jet.*

Mal Evans accompanied Paul to America on April 3, the day after work ended on *Sergeant Pepper.* At a stopover in San Francisco, Paul met with the Jefferson Airplane, the leading purveyors of American acid-rock. From San Francisco he took Sinatra's Lear to Denver to surprise Jane on her birthday. They spent the next day alone in the Colorado Rockies and later attended the theater in Denver. The next night Paul went to see Jane in a performance of *Romeo and Juliet* and led the standing ovation she received. The next morning the modern-day lovers parted, and Paul was off in the Lear to Los Angeles for a day. In L.A. he met with John Phillips and Cass Elliot of the Mamas and Papas and attended

---

* Nat Weiss handled some of the arrangements in the United States, including the rental of a house for a weekend that Paul asked for in San Diego. Since no house was available for a weekend, Nat rented one for a month. The family who was living in the house happily vacated it for Paul and Jane—at a much greater price. The only problem was Paul wasn't going to San Diego at all—he meant to say San Francisco. "I didn't realize there was that much of a difference," he told Nat. The house in San Diego went unused.

a Beach Boys' recording session, where Brian Wilson was working on his "masterpiece," *The Four Elements Suite.*

On the way home in the plane Paul was filled with visions of all the things he had seen during this trip, his most leisurely trip to America so far. Paul was especially fascinated with what was happening in California, where hundreds of thousands of young people were streaming to San Francisco to live in the dingy Haight-Ashbury district. The strength of the so-called hippie movement in America, which had coalesced with the growing peace movement, was staggering to Paul. There was nothing like it in London. London was all about affluence, stardom, the latest fab gear; because the hippies wore colorful clothes, Paul assumed they were just American cousins to the Swinging London set. It was curious that they both blended under the same, global, peace-flowers-LSD umbrella. It was even more curious how well the Beatles already-finished album—*Sergeant Pepper's Lonely Hearts Club Band*—complemented all of this. Paul left America feeling certain the album would be a hit, never suspecting that it would come to signify one of the most thrilling and turbulent decades of the century.

Thus inspired, on the way home in the plane Paul began to make notes for the *next* Beatles project after *Sergeant Pepper.* This particular idea had been sparked by writer Ken Kesey and his adventures on a bus traveling cross-country with a group of psychedelized hippies who called themselves the Merry Pranksters. The Pranksters sounded like a fantastic collection of clowns and mad magicians, half seen in a colorful daydream. Sitting in the first-class compartment of the plane, Paul began to draw pictures—clowns and fat ladies and midgets. He was going to call it the *Magical Mystery Tour,* and he intended to speak to Brian about starting it as soon as he got back.

* * *

2.

*P*AUL NEVER GOT to discuss *Magical Mystery Tour* with Brian. On Paul's return I had to inform him that Brian was under a doctor's care in an expensive private clinic in Richmond called the Priory. Brian's sleeping and waking cycles were so disrupted that he was going days at a time without sleeping, and he would then suddenly come crashing down from the effects of all the stimulants. The stress was obviously too much, and at the insistence of Dr. Norman Cowan, Brian agreed to see a consulting psychiatrist, Dr. John Flood—"but only this once!" On May 13 Dr. Flood noted Brian's main complaints as "insomnia, agitation, anxiety, and depression." Brian was admitted at once to the Priory, where he was to undergo a "sleep cure." During the cure he would be kept in a state of induced sleep and fed intravenously. When he was awakened he would feel revitalized and refreshed.

The first night Brian was in the hospital the night nurse came into his room to check on him and found him sitting up in bed writing letters, although he had been given a dose of sedatives that would have put three men to sleep. He wrote one of those letters to me that night, in which he said, "If only they knew what it takes to put this poor body to sleep . . ." He finally succumbed to a massive amount of drugs and was kept in induced sleep for nearly a week. When he was revived he called me in London to say that the beneficial effects were marginal at best. Nat Weiss, who was in London on business, made a special trip to the Priory to see Brian, along with Robert Stigwood.

Stigwood and Shaw were apparently proceeding successfully in raising the £500,000 to take over NEMS. Recently, Brian and Robert had had a contretemps over a new group Stigwood had signed to NEMS called the Bee Gees. Three British-born lads from Australia, they had arrived on NEMS's doorstep one day hoping to see Brian. They were routinely referred to Stigwood, who was responsible for signing new acts. Stigwood was so impressed by their beautiful, poignant harmonies and by Barry Gibbs' pop-idol good looks that he signed them immediately. Brian hated the Bee Gees from the start, perhaps because they weren't his discovery. When Stigwood told Brian on the phone that he had bought 51 percent of the Bee Gees publishing for NEMS for £1,000, Brian shouted, "Well that's a thousand out the window!" and slammed the phone down on him. Almost immediately the Bee Gees had a number-one hit single with their own composition, "New York Mining Disaster, 1941," and Brian was even more annoyed.

The day Stigwood arrived with Nat Weiss at the Priory, Brian was cranky and argumentative. His major complaint was that Stigwood had been riding herd on the Liverpool clan. He had been openly critical of Geoffrey Ellis and was hinting he wanted him out. Stigwood was just as contemptuous of Vic Lewis, who, he said, had been gone from the office for weeks, presumably to sign the Monkees for a concert tour of England. Brian launched into a lecture to Stigwood on how to treat the people he worked with. "Be more sensitive to them," Brian scolded from his bed. "I don't want to hear that you've slighted people again."

The lecture was interrupted by the arrival of an enormous bouquet of flowers. Brian eagerly opened the note and read it aloud. "You know I love you, I really do . . ." It was signed John. Brian broke down weeping, and a nurse ushered Stigwood and Nat out to the hallway.

Stigwood turned to Nat and said, "You know we can't listen to a word he says, you know that."

"Why not?" Nat asked.

"Because he's not in his right mind, that's why. I'm going to ignore him completely," Stigwood said, and proceeded to do just that.

It was also from his bed in the Priory that Brian first heard the Beatles' new album, *Sergeant Pepper's Lonely Hearts Club Band.* The Beatles arranged for a special acetate of it to be made, and I brought it to him myself from London, along with a stereo record player. We set it up on the dresser, and Brian sat up in bed as he listened. Both of us marveled at what we heard, just as the rest of the world was about to marvel.

The twelve songs on *Sergeant Pepper* set a new standard of achievement in popular music. It took only four months to record, at a cost of $100,000. It was so different and stunning to hear at first that when the Beach Boys' Brian Wilson first listened to it, he gave up work on his own forthcoming album, thinking that the quintessential album had already been made. *Sergeant Pepper* became not only the album of the summer but the album that most perfectly personified the incense-laden, rainbow-colored, psychedelic sixties themselves. It functioned as an anthem, orchestrating our lives. With *Sergeant Pepper*, the Beatles ascended from pop heros to avatars and prophets. The album was praised and dissected and studied like the Torah or the Koran, and even within our own Liverpool family, we were dazzled by this achievement.

The album was not without its problems. The cover, designed by pop artist Peter Blake, was a collage of photographs, with the Beatles dressed in brightly colored satin Victorian militia uniforms, surrounded by a surreal collage of sixty-two faces, including those of Marilyn Monroe, Marlon Brando, Carl Jung, Edgar Allan Poe, Bob Dylan, and Stu Sutcliffe. Brian hit the roof when he saw the cover and realized the legal entanglements of getting permission to use the photographs. He begged the boys to use a brown paper bag as the album cover instead, but the Beatles insisted it be kept the way it was. In the end, the Beatles had to indemnify EMI for £20 million against possible lawsuits.

Many songs on the album were swiftly banned by various radio stations around the world, including the BBC, because of their alleged references to drug use. "A Day in the Life"* was banned in England because of Paul's lyric, "found my way upstairs and had a smoke/somebody spoke and I went into a dream," quite obviously about pot; although in the same song, "four thousand holes in Blackburn, Lancashire" had nothing to do with tracks in a junkie's arm, as was also alleged. Ringo does sing, "I get high with a little help from my friends," although the Beatles claimed at the time they meant *spiritually* high. Certainly John's dreamlike "Lucy in the Sky with Diamonds" and its "tangerine trees and marmalade skies" were inspired by an acid trip, but it

---

* "A Day in the Life," arguably the best-remembered song of the album, employed the services of a forty-two-piece symphony orchestra, which was assembled at the Abbey Road huge studio number one in black tie for the occasion. George Martin had scored twenty-four bars of music for them, beginning at "pianissimo" with a line right through all twenty-four bars to the highest possible note, ending in "fortissimo." The forty-two pieces were double-tracked again and again into a thundering, shattering finale. The last note of the album trails off for forty-five seconds, and the microphone pots were turned so high to catch the last fading tones, the air conditioning system at Abbey Road is audible. For a final touch, a note of 20,000 hertz was added, which could only be heard by a listening dog.

was only an accident that the title of the song was an anagram for LSD. Lucy was little Julian's school chum, and "Lucy in the sky with diamonds" was a phrase Julian used to describe a drawing of her he made in school one day. Likewise, the hole Paul was fixing in "I'm Fixing a Hole" was not in the arm of a heroin addict, nor was John's "Henry the Horse" in the surrealistic circus of "For the Benefit of Mr. Kite" a code word for heroin. John took the name from a poster for a Victorian circus he had purchased in an antique shop.

3.

*B*RIAN'S HOMECOMING from the Priory was on May 19, the same day of the *Sergeant Pepper* press party to be held at Brian's Chapel Street town house. I organized the event for Brian, trying to keep it small by inviting only the ten most important representatives of the press to listen to the new album and enjoy a "family" dinner with one or two of the Beatles around the Chapel Street dining table. An invitation to such an event for a journalist was worth its weight in gold, and for two weeks before the party I was inundated with requests for invitations.

One of the calls came from a young American girl named Linda Eastman. I had met Linda in New York, where she was a budding rock photographer but better known as an ardent groupie. In 1967, at the age of twenty-five, she was a striking combination of preppy penny-loafers and seductive star-snarer. She was tall and leggy, with straight blond hair. Her father, Lee Eastman, was a well-known New York attorney in the entertainment and art fields, whose clients included Tommy Dorsey, the TV show of Hopalong Cassidy, and the artist Robert Rauschenberg. Linda and her younger brother John were raised on the Westchester-East Hampton-Park Avenue circuit, moving from one of the family's homes to another, according to weather or inclination. When Linda was eighteen her mother was killed in a plane crash, and her father remarried. The loss of her mother affected her deeply, and soon after she enrolled in college in Denver to escape the East. Later she married a geology student named Bob See. In 1962 Linda gave birth to a daughter, Heather, but the marriage soon broke up, and Linda moved to Tucson, Arizona, for a year before returning to New York. In New York she became an assistant at *Town and Country* magazine. One day an invitation to a Rolling Stones press party aboard a yacht arrived at the magazine, and Linda pocketed it. She brought her camera to the party and managed to strike up a friendship with Mick Jagger. After that she was hooked. Photography and rock stars became her consuming preoccupations.

When she wasn't cavorting in Harlem with Eric Burdon and the Animals, she was backstage at the Fillmore East. Heather had an unusual childhood. Linda once bragged that her babysitters included Mike Bloomfield, Stephen Stills, and Al Kooper. Her apartment and portfolio began to fill with rock stars. In May of 1967 she had flown to London to photograph Stevie Winwood and the Animals, which is when she called me.

One night Chas Chandler, the former bass player of the Animals, took Linda to a popular club called the Bag of Nails to hear Georgie Fame and the Blue Flames. Paul and I were at the "Bag" for a drink after he had finished a long mixing session, and I introduced Linda to him. Linda went on with Paul to a second club, the Speakeasy, but they got separated later in the evening as they were joined by Eric Clapton, Keith Moon, Peter Townshend and Roger Daltrey. Linda went home alone. The next day Linda called me in the office. She said she had a new portfolio of Rolling Stones pictures, and since I was a fan, I asked her up to my office to have a look. I admired one of Brian Jones, whom we had coincidentally run into the night before, and Linda gave it to me as a gift. In return, I gave her an invitation to the *Sergeant Pepper* photo session.

The girl who turned up at Chapel Street that May nineteenth wasn't the same sloppily dressed girl I had seen in my office a few days before. Her shiny blond hair was cut and washed and combed in a long, sweeping line under her chin. She wore impeccably applied makeup, including long, fluttering false eyelashes. She was dressed in a King's Road double-breasted, striped, barbershop jacket, with a short skirt that showed off her long legs. She held her Nikon in front of her and used it aggressively, probing with her lens. It wasn't long before she zeroed in on Paul. Paul sat in a chair by the fireplace in the lounge, dressed in pencil-striped trousers and a gray, striped jacket, nervously smoking cigarettes. He watched as Linda sank to her knees in front of the chair and began snapping photos of him. Although she tried to manage otherwise, she left with all the other photographers.

She tried to contact Paul by phone to learn that his unlisted number was billed to Harry Pinsker. Pinsker worked for Bryce-Hamner, and all the Beatles' unlisted phone numbers were billed to him for security reasons. Later that night Linda phoned and asked for Paul. Pinsker explained to Linda that she had the wrong number, but Linda wouldn't believe him. She kept calling back, insisting that it was Paul trying to trick her. Pinsker finally had to unplug all his telephones to get some sleep.

When Linda returned home to America, her close friend, Lillian Roxon, America's doyenne of rock critics, found a picture of Paul and Linda taken by another photographer at the party. She sent it to Linda, who blew the picture up big enough to cover her bathroom door. She looked at it every day for two months, as if she could will him back to her.

4.

*B*RIAN FOUND HIMSELF deluged by ideas from people who knew what the Beatles should do next instead of touring. Many of these people were would-be managers, circling Brian like sharks in the water, waiting for the right moment to come up and take a bite. The most aggressive of these was a man named Allen Klein. He was a fast-talking, dirty-mouthed man in his early thirties, sloppily dressed and grossly overweight. He had recently burst onto the English rock scene with an enormous show of muscle. Brian had met him previously, in 1964, when Klein was managing American R&B singer Sam Cooke. Klein came to see Brian at his Argyle Street offices to discuss the possibility of Cooke's opening the bottom half of the next American Beatles' tour but soon engaged him in another conversation. Klein said that he heard the Beatles' low royalty rates from EMI were "for shit" and that he could renegotiate their contracts. Klein told Brian that he'd get them at least a million pounds guaranteed against 10 percent of their royalties—if only Brian would let him negotiate the deal for them and take a fee.

Brian was royally offended at the suggestion that someone else should do his job for him, and he had Klein shown to the door. In 1964 Klein had taken over the management of the English folk-rock star Donovan, and then in the summer of 1965 he grabbed one of the golden rings: the Rolling Stones. In a splashy move that was reported in all the papers, Klein renegotiated the Stones' recording contracts with Decca and got them a $1.25 million advance, a highly publicized figure that Brian found himself having to live down. When Paul was asked what moment with Brian he regretted the most, he said it was in a crowded elevator with the other Beatles when he said to Brian, "Yeah, well Klein got the Stones a million and a quarter, didn't he? What about us?" To make Brian's paranoia even worse, Klein gave an interview from his suite at the Hilton Hotel in London the winter of 1967 in which he said he would "get" the Beatles. So many rumors followed this announcement, which alleged that Allen Klein would merge with NEMS, that Brian finally issued a formal statement to the press discounting Klein's claims as "ridiculous" and "rubbish."

But in his heart Brian was scared. First of all, he had not told the boys about his plan to sell the controlling share of NEMS to Robert Stigwood. In fact, the Beatles didn't even know of Stigwood's existence. Secondly, he was worried by what he saw as signs of the Beatles' growing discontent. They were slowly hearing bits and pieces of the Seltaeb fiasco, and they were beginning to learn that Brian was unable to get out of bed until five o'clock in the afternoon because of the huge amounts of barbiturates in his system. He was scared most, however, because unknown to almost everyone, the Beatles' management contracts with Brian were up in the fall of 1967. The possibility always lurked that the boys would take one of the many other offers to heart, and Brian would be "fired." Late at night, drunk and stoned, Brian would discuss his fears with Nat. Nat thought the worst that could happen was that the Beatles might demand a reduction of the 25 percent commission they paid Brian to only 20 or 15 percent of the take, since Brian's responsibilities were so greatly reduced without touring. Brian scheduled meetings from time to time to discuss renewing his contracts with them, and once he even assembled everyone at his country house for the express purpose of discussing it, but somehow the subject never came up.

Instead, without telling them, he renegotiated their recording contracts with EMI, which were up at the end of 1967.* Brian had written into the contracts a clause wherein NEMS would collect all monies due to the Beatles, from which Brian would deduct his 25 percent. However, these EMI contracts ran for nine years— a full eight years past the duration of Brian's management contracts. Now, even if they fired him, he would continue to collect record royalties. Brian never pointed this clause out to them. He asked me to get their signatures on the contracts for him while he was recuperating from glandular fever, and I brought the contracts to Spain, where Ringo and Maureen were visiting John and Cynthia while John was shooting *How I Won the War.* I got their signatures with no questions asked and had George and Paul sign the contracts later in London.

I personally believed that Brian was foolish to worry. The Beatles were as loyal to him as he was to them. Of the four, Brian only truly needed to fear Paul, who was outspokenly critical of him. While John could cut Brian with a glib remark, and George remained disturbingly distant, only Paul made him really worry. Paul called him almost daily with some complaint. He had also recently become interested in the day to day operations at NEMS, and he would often turn up at the office to snoop around. He had heard, obliquely, that Brian had lost the Beatles a lot of money through the Seltaeb deal, although it wasn't until years later that Paul found out exactly how much.

When Paul finally made a mistake of his own, it was whopper, but it gave Brian a welcomed opportunity to come to his aid. In an interview printed in *Queen* magazine in England and later in *Life* in America, Paul admitted that he had experimented with the dreaded drug LSD. Worse, he endorsed it. "It opened my

---

* Brian tried his best to show the boys he was as tough as anyone. In a good show he raised the Beatles royalty to 10 percent on all singles and albums sold under 100,000 and 30,000 pieces respectively and 15 percent on all albums and singles sold above that. In America, at Capitol, the royalty rate was brought up to 17½ percent. The new advance, which confusingly included accrued royalties, was approximately £1 million.

eyes," he said. "It made me a better, more honest, more tolerant member of society." It was a moment of unsurpassed folly. When George once capriciously said he liked jelly beans, the Beatles spent three years performing in a perpetual hailstorm of them. If every jelly bean equaled a tab of LSD, there were going to be a lot of psychedelized children around, courtesy of Paul McCartney.

Not owning up to his responsibility in the matter when the daily papers called to question him about his *Queen* interview, he shot back, "If you'd only shut up about it, so will I. It's your fault for putting it in the papers. You've got the responsibility not to spread it."

Brian, too, was besieged with phone calls from reporters at his Chapel Street house. It was too late to issue a denial or to say it was a misunderstanding, as he had done in America about John's "Jesus" remarks, so Brian well-meaningly did the worst thing possible. He admitted that he, too, took LSD and that he saw nothing wrong with it. "There is a new mood in this country re LSD," he told reporters. "I am wholeheartedly on its side." To *Melody Maker*, the teen music paper, he gave a more lengthy interview in which he said, "I did have some apprehension, but I took that risk. I think LSD helped me to know myself better, and I think it helped me to become less bad tempered."

With this, all hell broke loose. Brian was widely criticized in newspaper editorials, TV commentaries, and by parent and church groups for his confession. It was discussed at length on the floor of Parliament, and the Home Office issued an official statement saying it was "horrified" at Epstein's attitude toward this dangerous drug.

Paul himself was the least grateful for Brian's compounding his mistake. Phone calls between them shot back and forth, until they became so abusive in tone that Brian stopped taking Paul's calls, and then he would sulk about guiltily for not having dealt with the problem. And Paul wasn't the only member of the immediate family who was angry with him. Cilla Black and her husband Bobby Willis were furious with him. Cilla's audience was more middle-of-the-road than the Beatles', and those were the people who seemed most offended by Brian's remarks. Cilla was strongly identified with Brian and felt, perhaps unfairly, that her career was not moving ahead as it should have been. The previous sum-

mer Brian had booked her into the Prince of Wales Theater head-
lining a variety show with Frankie Howard for four weeks, but
the run slowly dragged out to nine months before Brian got her
out of her contract. Cilla's next project was her own television
special, the first color TV special ever broadcast in Great Britain
and a great honor. But all throughout the rehearsals Brian had
been in Spain, making a movie of his own about matadors and
bullfighting, while Vyvienne Moynihan at NEMS did his work on
the special for him. When the show was broadcast, to rave reviews,
Brian was nowhere around, and he sent Cilla a color TV as a
gift. Cilla was unimpressed. "I felt like a kid on sports day when
your parents don't show up." Now, to top it off, Brian admitted
he took drugs.

To calm Bobby and Cilla, Brian took them to lunch at L'Etoile.
Brian ordered champagne, but Cilla was not about to be buttered
up so easily. "What about this telling the press you take drugs,
Brian?" she demanded.

"It was the fault of the reporters for publishing Paul's statement," Brian explained lamely. "After the cat was let out of the
bag, I felt it would have been hypocritical for me not to say I
did it too."

"Well, I feel betrayed," Cilla said. "What are me mom and
dad gonna think? That I'm on LSD? It was a very selfish thing
for you to say."

Brian made an eloquent apology. When the champagne arrived, he toasted her and Bobby. He seemed so sincerely repentant
and so sincerely helpless, that she forgave him again.

5.

*W*ITH THE SUCCESS of *Sergeant Pepper*, the Beatles
became even more sensitive to their power to affect
vast numbers of people, and thus we passed over into the era
of message songs. The Beatles had decided that the message that
summer was love. Love was all you needed. It was naive and
banal, but somehow it was so earnest they gave us all hope. That

was part of the magic of the Beatles, to renew our belief and neutralize our cynicism. They made this message into a new anthem, a dirgelike song called "All You Need Is Love," which was premiered to the world on June 25 in an international broadcast called "Our World," telecast via satellite to over 200 million viewers. "It's easy," they sang over and over. "All you need is love."

Brian was inspired to give a party at Kingsley Hill to celebrate this mood of benevolence and love and LSD that was sweeping over us. He didn't intend for it to be an acid party in particular, but there was very little chance it could have turned out any other way that warm June day. At that particular moment there was an abundance of very special LSD in the Beatles' family. It had been prepared to order by San Francisco's famed acid-chemist, "Owlsley." An ingenious plan was devised to get the acid into England. That June the first major, outdoor rock festival was taking place in Monterey, California, not far from Owlsley's laboratory in San Francisco. Although the Beatles knew the film rights to the Monterey Festival had been sold exclusively to an American film company, they sent a large complement of film equipment to San Francisco, ostensibly to film the festival. When the camera crew was refused permission to film, as was expected, the airtight camera lenses were filled with liquid LSD and shipped back to England without any problem. Several pint-size vials of this Owlsley LSD now graced the bookshelves in the sunroom at Kenwood, while others had been converted to more convenient little pink pills, which made their way through the Beatles' inner circle. The acid was especially potent, and tripping on it was very hallucinogenic and "electric."

The guest list for the party included the Beatles and most of their immediate friends, Mick Jagger, Marianne Faithfull, Lionel Bart, London Philharmonic Orchestra conductor Sir John Pritchard, radio and TV personality Kenny Everett, and Nat Weiss, who had flown in from New York for the event.

Derek Taylor and his wife Joan had also been invited to come to Brian's party and were supplied with round-trip, first-class plane tickets from Los Angeles. Derek had moved to California the year before and had opened a successful rock publicity company. His client list included, among others, the Byrds and the Monterey Pop Festival. Brian had run into Derek in the interim at the Polo Lounge of the Beverly Hills Hotel. Brian had just read the good reviews for *Help!* and was in an especially good mood. A little guiltily, he told Derek that the book Derek had ghosted for him, *A Cellarful of Noise,* continued to sell well and that perhaps Derek hadn't been properly rewarded. When Derek told Brian that he had long ago lost his contract, Brian promptly pulled out his checkbook and wrote Derek a check for an additional £1,000.

Derek and Joan arrived at Heathrow shortly after dawn on the Saturday morning of the party. They were greeted by a most incredible sight. John and Cynthia and George and Pattie had come out to the airport to meet them, and they were acting like they had gone out of their minds. They were dressed like wizards and fairy princesses in costumes of purple and yellow satin. They were garlanded with flowers and bells around their necks, which tinkled and shimmered as they moved. With them were the three people who had designed the clothing. This group was referred to as "The Fool." The Fool was Simon Posthuma, a slight ethereal man with curly hair, and his two pretty female companions, Josje Leeger and Marijike Koger. They had been introduced to the Beatles by a publicist for the Saville Theater and had recently become the Beatles' Royal Clothing Designers. The Beatles and The Fool cavorted and pranced around the reception lounge, kissing and hugging Derek and his wife, who couldn't figure out what was happening.

John and George said the plan was to drive directly to Kingsley Hill and arrive before the other guests. All nine of them poured into John's Rolls-Royce, which had recently been repainted by hand in a bright psychedelic design of flowers and scrolls, and set out into the English countryside. Gaily colored clusters of balloons had been hung as signposts along the way to mark the route for the guests, and the roads were lined with smiling towns-folk, peering into the crowded Rolls as it went along the country roads.

Derek found the inside of the Rolls as different as the exterior paint job. John had installed not a tape deck but a studio-quality turntable delicately suspended on a platform. The doors were outfitted with similar quality speakers. John put the new Procol Harum album, *A Whiter Shade of Pale,* on the turntable, sending the Fool into waves of ecstasy. As a thermos of tea was passed around, Derek, too, soon began to notice that the music sounded extraordinary, almost as wondrous as the green hues of the countryside, which had begun to throb and glow. Derek was about to ask what was happening when John said, "This was the first morning I had acid for breakfast. You too. There was LSD in the tea." Joan, who was seven months pregnant with her third child, had been spared this surprise, but when apprised of what was happening, she voluntarily took a dose herself. A small pillbox was produced and an acid-soaked tablet was passed around the car for everyone to further nibble on.

Squashed in the back seat between John and Pattie, Cynthia Lennon was now the only member of the group not tripping. Quietly refusing all offers of the tablet or tea, no one had paid much attention to her. Now she watched the flecked pink pill come her way with trepidation. She had only tripped once or twice since she was dosed by the dentist and she hated it each time. She found no cosmic consciousness like the others, only consuming anxiety. Yet that day in the back of the Rolls, with everyone happy and safe and confident for the future, the balloons marking the way, reassuring her with the promise of the party to come, she decided to try again. "Perhaps this is the time to hear John's drum," she thought. "It's now or never." And when the tab came to her, she swallowed it.

The party had a soft, dreamlike quality to it. The prophets were here, the masters were in control, there was good food and liquor and friends. *A Whiter Shade of Pale,* interspersed with *Sergeant Pepper,* played all afternoon and into the evening. Brian, of course, found something to ruin his fun. Paul had phoned earlier in the day with an impeccable excuse and was not coming. Brian was deeply paranoid about Paul anyway, and with his emotions magnified by the LSD he had taken, he was devastated by Paul's absence. He strode around the living room at dusk and leaned dramatically up against the piano. "Paul . . . didn't come . . ." Brian intoned softly. "This day of all days . . . he should have come . . ."

John and George, who were in the room with him at the time, rushed to where he stood to comfort him. "Come on now, Brian," George said, hugging him, "*we're* all here, and we're good friends, and *we* love you!"

At one point in the party George discovered that Derek and John were curled up in the plush backseat of John's Rolls, listening to *A Whiter Shade of Pale* for the hundredth time, and climbed in with them. The three men felt warm and secure in the backseat and stayed there for what seemed like a long time. Occasionally, John would slip into a bad trip, and Derek would have to talk him out of it. At one point barbed wire formed on the car windows, but it turned out to be Lionel Bart. George said to Derek, "Don't worry, Derek, you'll never have to worry about anything as long as you live. You'll always have us." Nine months later Derek and Joan sold their house and furniture in Los Angeles and moved back to London so Derek could work for the Beatles. Except for short periods, Derek has worked for one or another of the Beatles ever since.

There were two people at the party who were not enjoying the effects of the LSD. One was Brian's assistant, Joanne Newfield, who became violently ill and threw up in Nat Weiss' shoes, which were beside the bed in the guest bedroom. Another, predictably, was Cynthia. From the moment she'd arrived at the party she had been overwhelmed with anxiety. The gardens melted and oozed around her, strangers grinned at her from behind rubber lips, and again she was afraid that it would never wear off, that she would be that way forever. At moments she was so frightened that she was unable to speak or ask for help. At other times she felt physically paralyzed, and the only person whose presence calmed her was John. All she could do to keep her sanity was to follow him wherever he went, wordlessly hanging behind him. John began to glare furiously at her until she finally let him alone and went into the house. She made her way upstairs to the second floor bedroom and sat on the bed for a while, feeling desolate. Then she went to the window and watched the party taking place out on the lawn below her, like a movie; the other guests laughing and having a good time. She drifted in her thoughts. Why was she so different? It wasn't far down, she thought, down to those other people having a good time. She could just step out the open window and float. She opened the window wider and started out.

"Cynthia!" Pattie Harrison called to her from the garden, waving and laughing. "What are you doing up there? Come on down."

Cynthia withdrew back into the room and lay down on the bed. She stayed there until very late that night, until the acid wore off. Only this time she found that it *had* left behind a permanent effect: a sense of dread. One thought filled her mind; there was no hope for her marriage now. If the acid had brought to her one irrefutable truth, it was that she and John were doomed.

* * *

6.

*C*YNTHIA HAD an unexpected ally against drugs in Magic Alex. Although Magic Alex filled Cynthia with the most dread and paranoia of anyone she knew, they were sympathetic insofar as drugs were concerned. For Magic Alex, the mortar and pestle on the shelf of the sunroom was the single greatest cause of John's unhappiness—and of Alex's inability to control him. John under the influence of drugs was not John under Alex's influence.

Magic Alex had seen too many crazy things happen when people took drugs. Once, when John sent Cynthia and her mother away on vacation to Italy to get rid of them for a while, Alex stayed at Kenwood with an Australian girl to keep John company. John encouraged them to take acid with him, but they refused. He took his own dose anyway, and the three of them sat up until early in the morning talking and drinking wine. Alex and the girl finally went to bed, while John stayed up alone, painting the white shirt Alex had been wearing in watercolor doodles. When John got bored with tripping alone, he woke Alex and the girl with a pot of tea. "One lump of sugar or two?" John asked, dosing them.

Alex was annoyed at being dosed, but he was at least familiar with the effects of LSD to some degree. The Australian girl had never tripped before, and she was terrified. When the trip started she became claustrophobic inside the house and ran out into the backyard, where she started to take her clothes off. Then she hallucinated that the pool vacuum cleaner hose was turning into a giant snake and proceeded to climb onto the low rear roof of the house. John and Alex had to climb up after her to get her down. They gave her a tranquilizer and locked her in a guest bedroom to sleep it off.

Fifteen minutes later, much to Magic Alex's dismay, the Weybridge police arrived at the front door. It seemed that the Australian girl, left alone in the bedroom with a telephone, had called a girlfriend in London and told her she was being held hostage by two men, one of whom was impersonating John Lennon. Her girlfriend got the address and called the local police. The Weybridge constables assured the girl that the man at that address was no imposter but decided to go out to the house anyway. John greeted them at the front door, wearing a top hat and evening cape he had put on when he saw them coming up the drive. The police were mildly amused, and when John assured them nothing was wrong, they left without any questions. But it was too close a call for Alex; only a cursory search of the house would have uncovered enough drugs to put both of them in jail for years.

During the summer of 1967 there was another, more important, convert to the antidrug contingent. George Harrison had given up drugs after a short trip to the West Coast of America. When Paul returned from his trip to San Francisco after his birthday visit with Jane, he was full of wondrous tales of the hippy movement and Haight-Ashbury, making it sound like a heaven on earth. On August 1, George and Pattie set off to see for themselves. They were accompanied by Neil, Magic Alex, and Pattie's sister, Jenny Boyd. They arrived on a beautiful, sunny Saturday in a rented Lear jet and were met at the airport by Derek Taylor, who knew his way around San Francisco and offered to act as their local tour guide. No sooner had they settled into the backseat of a rented limousine, then George produced some famous Owlsley acid, and they set off, tripping, to see the blessed hippies.

"I expected something like the King's Road," George said, "only more. Somehow I expected them all to own their own little shops, because I heard they'd all bought out blocks. I expected them all to be nice and clean and friendly and happy."

Instead, from behind the tinted windows of the limousine, all they saw was a depressing slum area inhabited by a multitude of lost and disillusioned kids. They were stoned all right, stoned beyond all comprehension or necessity. They stood on the street corners, begging, selling incense, loafing in the sun. They were, for the most part, barefooted and unwashed. The limousine stopped not far from the famous intersection of Haight and Ashbury streets, and the occupants got out to take a walk. George Harrison alighting from a limousine in Haight-Ashbury, summer of 1967, was akin to Christ stepping out of a flying saucer. The long-haired kids on the streets parted in waves around him as he strolled along. At the first corner, George and his party encountered a Hells Angel named Frisco Pete, a big, burly tattooed guy in a sleeveless denim jacket with a skull and crossbones on the back. The LSD made Frisco Pete seem even larger than his already intimidating size, and George quaked at the sight of him. Frisco Pete, it turned out, only wanted to shake the hand of this young god, just like everybody else, and joined the crowd. Relieved that Frisco Pete meant them no harm, he invited him to London. "Come visit us sometime. We'll put you up." It was an offer George would live to regret.

George and Pattie and friends wandered past the seedy psychedelic head shops, the dingy boutiques selling tattered secondhand clothing, and into Golden Gate Park, site of the famous San Francisco love-ins. The park was swarming with teenagers on this warm summer day, the air filled with a rainbow of frisbees. Word spread like wildfire through the park that George Harrison was in their midst. In the blink of an eye, perhaps a thousand very stoned kids surrounded the tripping celebrity, pushing and shoving. The air was rife with the smell of sweat. Out of the crowd came a guitar, which was thrust into George's hands.

"No . . . no, please," George stammered, trying to return it.

"Play!" someone shouted in the crowd, and then all of them began chanting, "Play! Play! Play!"

George gave Pattie a sick look. He began to strum a few chords, but the acid made the cheap guitar feel like a lump of cheese in his hands. He tried to sing "Baby You're a Rich Man," the Beatles' present singles chart-topper, but he didn't have the heart. The crowd closed in to a little circle five feet in diameter before George insistently returned the guitar, with profuse apologies, and they tried to make a break for it back to the car.

Angry hoots were heard as the mood of the rejected crowd turned malevolent. George and his entourage could practically hear the change in the footsteps as the crowd turned into a mob. George and his friends quickened their pace, so did the mob behind them. By the time they got to their limousine, they were practically running, with Neil bringing up the rear to protect them. They threw themselves into the limousine and slammed the door locks shut. Now the mob surrounded the car, pressed up against the windows, pounding and shouting as they rocked the huge car from side to side. The driver managed to start the car and drive it slowly through the crowds, but the occupants barely escaped unhurt.

When George returned to England, he was so disgusted with what he had seen in San Francisco that he swore he would never take another drug, a promise, of course, he would not keep. Yet this was an important turning point for George, the recognition that LSD was not the key, that there was a higher, purer form of contentment waiting for him somewhere. He told John about giving up drugs, but John only shrugged and said, "Well, it's not doing me any harm, so I'll just go on with it for a while."

7.

Y ET SOMETIMES it was hard to tell what part of their madness was drug induced and what part was pure whimsy. I was in my office one day that summer when the Beatles' private phone rang. It was John calling to say that the Beatles were moving out of England! The idea had come to him the previous night in the studio, when Magic Alex was attending a session. The Beatles were talking about how sick and tired they were of notoriety and were bemoaning how restrictive it was for them to live in London. John suggested they escape it all by creating their own little kingdom, like an island. On the island they would build beautiful houses and the best studio money could buy and even a school, where Julian could be taught in a one-room schoolhouse with the children of Bob Dylan, who would be invited to join. Alex, hearing opportunity knocking loudly, said he knew just the place off the coast of Greece, where there were thousands of islands the Beatles could buy "dirt cheap."

The very next day I dispatched Magic Alex and Alistair Taylor, who was now office manager and took care of sundry chores for the Beatles, off to Greece to find an island. Not forty-eight hours later Alex phoned to say that he had located a place God had created just for them. It was a tiny cluster of islands twenty-five miles out into the Aegean, 100 acres in all. There was a large main island with four secluded beaches and five smaller satellite islands surrounding it. There were also sixteen acres of rich olive groves on the large island, which Alex computed would pay back the cost of the six islands in just seven years' time. All this a bargain at £90,000. The Beatles impetuously agreed to leave for Greece at once.

Magic Alex had not bothered to remind the Beatles that in 1967 Greece was struggling under the power of one of the most repressive military governments in the world. The ruling military junta had banned both long hair and rock music, and a rock and roll group moving to Greece would be viewed with the same suspicion as the long-haired American hippies who were smuggling hashish from Istanbul via Athens. Long-term and life sentences for small offenses were common. Certainly, if any of the Beatles carried drugs into Greece with them, it would be discovered by the customs officers at the airport.

According to Alex, in a story told here for the first time, before the Beatles set out for Athens, he contacted a high government official he identifies as the "vice-president of Greece" and asked the man if he knew who the Beatles were. "Yes, they're a pop group," the man answered. "But what does this have to do with me?"

"They could be of tremendous publicity value to you if you cooperate in making their journey pleasant," Alex said. He struck a deal with the government official; if the Beatles were given VIP treatment, and not searched at the airport, they would pose for a set of publicity pictures for the Ministry of Tourism to show how benevolent Greece was; in effect, diplomatic immunity in exchange for an endorsement of the junta.

Alex warned John by phone before he left England not to criticize the junta to the press, either in Athens or in London, and to behave himself at all times in Greece. But when the commercial jet arrived at the airport, John emerged from the door wearing a military jacket and immediately began saluting every soldier in sight. When Alex got up close to him, he could see by John's glazed eyes how stoned he was and barely got him out of the airport before he insulted the general who had come to greet him.

Alex had gone to a lot of trouble for nothing; John wasn't in Greece five minutes before he discovered he had left his LSD supply in London. He was inconsolable when he realized this.

"What good is the Parthenon without LSD?" he demanded. Magic Alex knew of no LSD in Greece and wasn't about to try to find any. The only way John was going to get any LSD would be to import it from London.

Alex, believing his phone was tapped, made a cautious phone call to Mal Evans at the NEMS office. "John isn't well, Mal," Alex told him cryptically. "You've got to come to Greece and bring his medicine."

"What medicine?" Mal asked, baffled.

"You know, the medicine for his *acidity* . . . ."

Mal was on the next flight for Athens, and John was tripping the next day. The Beatles were unmercifully exploited by the Greek government. They were driven around from location to location in the hot Mediterranean sun without a break for fourteen hours straight. The photographs of them appeared on wire services throughout the world. The Beatles' sudden endorsement of Greece caused some puzzlement but was never explained.

The Beatles loved the islands that Magic Alex picked out for them, and I tried to make the arrangements to purchase them in London. Bryce-Hamner was instructed to purchase the necessary "premium dollars" from the English government to buy foreign property. The Beatles applied for £95,000, on which they had to pay a 25 percent premium per pound. The Beatles' accountant prepared an analysis that showed the Beatles had only £137,000 in cash to spend and that purchasing the islands would be disastrous to their finances. But the Beatles persisted, and arrangements for the purchase were made directly with James Callahan, the Chancellor of the Exchequer. In a letter Callahan sent to the Beatles, he pointed out that £95,000 was the absolute limit to the amount of pounds he would allow to flow outside of the country. He added at the bottom of the letter, in his own hand, "But not a penny more . . . I wonder how you're going to furnish it?"

The islands finally turned into so much of a hassle, like everything else they wanted to do, they quickly tired of the problems and sold the property dollars back to the government at the new going rate of 37 percent, making a handsome profit of £11,400 in the process.

* * *

8.

*I*N HIS DEN at 24 Chapel Street, Brian fretted over the boys' scheme to buy a Greek island. He didn't especially trust Magic Alex, and there was never any suggestion from the Beatles that Brian come to Greece with them. He wrote to Nat Weiss while they were away in Greece that he thought the idea was dotty. "But they're no longer children, and they must have their own way."

Brian had more pressing problems. He had now come to completely regret his option agreement with Stigwood and Shaw. With every day he was growing increasingly more upset over what he saw as Stigwood's personal extravagance: NEMS executives had a charge at a local butcher where they were charging Sunday turkeys; articles of personal clothing were charged to the company account at Harrods; and when Stigwood took the Bee Gees to New York for a promotional trip, he rented a yacht for them to sail around Manhattan Island. Stigwood told Nat to charge the boat to his personal account, and Nat forwarded this information to Brian in London. "What personal account?" Brian fumed. "When the Bee Gees are as successful as the Beatles, then Robert can rent them a yacht around Manhattan!" Brian's personal hope was that Stigwood and Shaw would not be able to raise the £500,000 to close the option. There was some doubt they were going to be able to raise the money in the financial community, but Stigwood insisted there was no problem and that Brian should inform the Beatles of what was taking place.

It was also just at this time that Cilla Black informed Brian that she had decided to leave NEMS. While the Beatles didn't seem to mind Brian's unpredictable hours and behavior, it was an impossibility for Cilla to nurture a still-growing career with Brian so incapacitated. When Cilla called him at home she got either his secretary or a butler, who made embarrassed excuses for him. He canceled or missed half a dozen appointments and sent flowers and candy or notes of apology the next day. Sometimes Vic Lewis would be sent in his place and would refer to Cilla as "my star," affronting her. Cilla didn't even think she was Brian's star.

In a last-ditch effort to save their relationship, Brian sent Clive to make a personal plea that Cilla and Bobby attend one last luncheon at Chapel Street. On the Wednesday morning of the lunch, I called Cilla to make sure they were coming. Brian was very nervous all morning, and I joined them at lunch for moral support. Brian had the butler lay out the best silver and china and served fillet of beef and champagne. No mention of Cilla's departure was made at all. Later, just Brian, Cilla, and Bobby went up to the roof garden and stood at the railing, looking out over the city. "There are only five people I love in the world," Brian said, tears coming to his eyes. "And that's the four Beatles and you, Cilla." Cilla hugged him tightly. "Please don't leave me, my Cilla, please . . ." he whispered.

The next day Brian arranged a meeting with the BBC to produce a new TV series for Cilla. It went on the air a few months later, and became a sensation. "The Cilla Black Show" was one of the most successful female variety TV shows in British history, winning Cilla the TV Personality of the Year award for several years in a row and establishing her as a major star.

It must have seemed to Brian that whatever tenuous hold he had on those around him was slipping. That July his father died of a heart attack while away on vacation in Bournemouth. A badly shaken Brian returned to Liverpool to be at Queenie's side for the funeral. Queenie was deeply depressed at this tragic end of her thirty-four-year-long marriage. When Brian and Queenie returned home from the funeral together, they sat on a sofa in the living room of Queenie's house.

"What will you do now, Mother?" Brian asked her quietly.

"I don't know," Queenie said.

"Come to London, then," Brian begged her. "Come to London to live. What do you want with Liverpool? I'll find a flat for you near my house, and we'll decorate it splendidly. We'll have the best time!"

Queenie hugged him and wept. "I need you Brian," she told him. "I do so need you."

"Now, now, Mother," Brian said softly, "I need you more than you could ever need me."

On August 14 Queenie arrived in London to stay with Brian at Chapel Street, and an immediate change came over him. Queenie woke him each morning by coming into his room and pulling back the drapes to let the sun in. He showered and dressed, and they ate breakfast together in his room while discussing his plans for the day. He went to the office every day and worked diligently. At night he took Queenie to the theater or a restaurant. His use of barbiturates was discreet, and he didn't seem to let it interfere with his work or his sleep. He was clearly a man more in control of himself, and his close friends felt a sense of relief. One day Cilla Black and Bobby Willis were pleased to find him waiting for them at Euston Station when she returned from a visit to Liverpool. Brian said he had come by just to show her how much he loved her. He took her out to lunch that day, and it seemed like old times for a while. Then he told her he had a surprise for her; he had arranged for her to appear on the Eurovision TV contest, which was broadcast all over the continent. Cilla and Bobby were surprised at what they thought was a ridiculous decision. Only the year before another English female singer had won the contest. To think Cilla could win was hopeless. But Brian insisted; he knew what was best, and she would appear on the show. Cilla and Bobby left lunch that day, determined that her management contract had to be terminated.

On a warm Sunday night near the end of August, Brian was leaving the Saville Theater with his mother when the paparazzi closed in around them, strobe lights flashing like so many excited fireflies. "When will I see these photographs?" Queenie asked, getting into the backseat of Brian's Rolls-Royce with him.

"Either when I'm bankrupt or I'm dead," Brian told her.

Queenie left London the next day, August 24.

9.

*A*S QUEENIE sat in the train on the way home to Liverpool, John, Paul, and George were on their way to the Park Lane Hilton Hotel to hear the Maharishi Mahesh Yogi speak his wisdom. They had first been alerted to the Maharishi through Pattie Harrison, who had been introduced to Transcendental Meditation as a way to get "high" on her first trip to India with George. Although George had become an aficionado of Indian music and food, the religious aspects of the culture still eluded him. Pattie taught herself mysticism and TM from books, and that previous February she had surprised George by enrolling in the Spiritual Regeneration Movement. She attended these meetings once a week without him. When Pattie told George that she had been "indoctrinated" and given a "mantra"—a secret word to chant—George felt left out. "What kind of scene is this if they make you keep secrets from your friends?" When Pattie heard that the Maharishi Mahesh Yogi himself would lecture on August 24 at the Hilton, she started a ground-swell movement to get the Beatles to go. As an added inducement, Magic Alex had heard the Maharishi lecture years before at a university in Athens, and he helped Pattie lobby for all the Beatles to hear him speak. John brought Cynthia, Paul took Jane Asher and his brother Michael, and George came with Pattie and her sister Jenny. Ringo, the only Beatle who did not attend, was at Queen Charlotte's Hospital visiting with Maureen and his newborn second son, five-day-old Jason.

When they arrived at the Hilton, the Beatles were immediately shown to the front row of the ballroom, where there were over 1,000 people in attendance. The Maharishi turned out to be a tiny, brown-skinned man with a squeaky, sing-song voice, who wore flowing white cotton robes that further dwarfed his small frame. His dramatic gray and black mane of hair flowed into a long beard with a white fringe below his bottom lip, which made him look like a beatific nanny-goat. He spoke to the Beatles of Jesus, of Buddha, of God; of eternal happiness and peace; of the inner self and of sublime consciousness; about reaching a state of nirvana—all without the use of messy and illegal drugs. His sales pitch, in short, was that Transcendental Meditation, when practiced twice a day, would make you a better, happier person at whatever it is you do.

The Maharishi was only scratching the surface of this complicated and subtle ancient Hindu practice, but he couldn't have been more on target for the Beatles. He offered them a brand of instant relief and salvation, like a psychic Band-Aid. To demonstrate this method, the Maharishi went into a deep, trancelike state for ten minutes right there in front of them. The Beatles were overwhelmed. A holy man who could give you a magic word to chant; a mystical trance that sent you into a psychic dreamland. John in particular was swept away by his emotion. He had found it! He had found the key, the answer, what he had been looking for! The Next Big Thing.

The Maharishi may have seemed like a deeply spiritual, unworldly little guru from the Himalayas to the Beatles, but he was far from being a country bumpkin. He was a college graduate with a degree in physics. After college he learned Sanskrit and studied the scriptures with Guru Dev, the most famed of the Indian sages. The title Maharishi, meaning saint, was reportedly self-adopted. In 1959 the Maharishi moved to various Western countries, where for eight years he had been selling his potent brand of mystic salvation when not on international lecture tours.

After the lecture the Maharishi—not unaware of the Beatles' publicity value should they become disciples—invited them up to his hotel suite for a private audience. He told the Beatles, "You have created a magic air through your names. You have got to use that magic influence. Yours is a tremendous responsibility." When John left the Maharishi's suite that night, all he could say to reporters was that "I'm still in a daze." The following day the press was informed by the Maharishi's representatives that the Beatles and their friends had been invited to enroll in a ten-day meditation course the Maharishi was giving in Bangor, North Wales, at Normal College, and the Beatles had accepted. They would leave, along with 300 others who had signed up for the course, not by limo with an entourage and bodyguards but alone, for the first time in memory, on a public train from Euston Station.

The Friday afternoon of their departure was also the beginning of the long weekend bank holiday that marked the end of the summer, and the normally crowded Euston Station was almost impassable with dense throngs of holiday travelers, including many families with suitcases and screaming children. Added to the crush was the appearance of film crews and reporters who were giving up the holiday weekend to trek after the Beatles to Bangor. Fleet Street knew a delicious story when they saw it, and they didn't intend to let the Beatles get out of their sight. The story seemed to get even better when the Beatles were joined by Mick Jagger and Marianne Faithfull.

Although the Beatles had arranged to get to Euston Station

by themselves, I thought that as a precaution Neil and I should show up there anyhow and make sure the boys got on the train without any trouble. John and Cynthia were driven to the station in his Rolls-Royce, which was instantly recognizable to the crowds. As the chauffeur let them out of the car, John pushed his way determinedly into the crowds, pretending to be just another citizen off on vacation. A wave of flashbulbs went off in Cynthia's face, temporarily blinding her. By the time she could see again, she had lost John. First she went to platform 8, then she realized it was number 12 and began to fight her way through the thick crowds. The "Mystical Express," as the reporters had dubbed it, waited on the platform with the Maharishi himself sitting cross-legged on a white sheet in the parlor car of the first-class compartment. Conductors up and down the platform were shouting, "All aboard!" as John swung up on the train. Suddenly, the train lurched forward with a jerk. John looked around him and realized that Cynthia was missing.

"Where is she?" he shouted, sticking his head out of the window of the slow-moving train. The other pop stars on the train followed suit, much to the delight of the photographers. There on the station, being held back by policemen and fans, was Cynthia. "Tell him to let you on," John shouted. "Tell him you're with us!" But Cynthia could only burst into tears as she finally broke free and raced after the train. "Run Cynthia! Run!" John shouted, but it was no use. Cynthia broke her stride and came to a defeated halt as the train pulled out of the station. I caught up with her just at that moment. The next day the newspapers all featured a front-page photograph of the young pop stars departing for spiritual heaven on a parlor car, while Cynthia sobbed on my shoulder. I promised her that Neil would drive her up to Bangor, and she would probably get there before the train.

But Cynthia wasn't crying anymore about getting to Bangor. "I knew in my heart," she wrote in her memoirs, "as I watched all the people that I loved fading into the hazy distance, that that was to be my future. The loneliness I felt on that station platform would become a permanent loneliness before very long, and I shivered at the thought."

Bangor, North Wales, was a seaside town with rolling green hills that met the water. The Maharishi's meditation course was being held during the summer recess at a spartan teaching college, and the 300 enrollees, including the Beatles, slept in college dormitories. For the Beatles this only increased the sense of adventure, and a warm wave of camaraderie from the old times washed over them. The first night, after dinner at a local Chinese restaurant, they discovered that none of them had any cash to pay the bill; like the Royal Family, they never carried any. George Harrison saved them from having to wash dishes when he confessed to keeping a ten-pound note hidden between the layers of one of his sandals. He pried open the false heel with a table knife and managed to cover the check.

The following morning, at a press conference encouraged by the Maharishi, the Beatles made a startling announcement: They were giving up drugs. John, George, and Paul explained that it was impossible to achieve spiritual harmony with foreign substances in one's system, and since they wanted to give the Maharishi a fair shake, they were giving it all up. John seemed as sincere as the rest. And for a few days, at least, he kept his resolve.

10.

B RIAN HAD NOT given up drugs. John and Paul had halfheartedly invited him to join them on the trip to Bangor, because they thought the rest and meditation would do him some good, but they knew he wouldn't come. That bank-holiday weekend, Brian intended to spend a quiet three days at Kingsley Hill with me and Geoffrey Ellis. Brian had been on his best behavior while Queenie was at Chapel Street, and now he was looking for a little *divertissement.* Some new acquaintances were promised as weekend houseguests, and while I put the Beatles on the train to Bangor, Brian set out for the country in a mood of happy anticipation.

By the time Geoffrey and I arrived at Kingsley Hill, in time for dinner, Brian was in a dark mood; the other houseguests had called to cancel, and Brian faced the prospect of spending the holiday with two old chums. After a quiet meal of roast loin of pork and many bottles of wine, Brian went to the phone and began calling around London to find some amusing company to come to Kingsley Hill. But everyone was already busy or gone for the holiday weekend. It was ten o'clock on Friday night when Brian announced that he was going to take a drive around the countryside. This hardly surprised Geoffrey and me; we were by then innured to Brian's moods and disappearances. I did say I thought it was a foolish idea for Brian to drive after drinking so much, but once Brian made up his mind there was no way to discourage him, and in another moment he walked out the door, started up his silver Bentley, and drove off into the night.

I assumed that Brian would just drive around the countryside and come back, but when he didn't return by midnight, I phoned Brian's private number at Chapel Street. After many rings it was answered by Antonio, the Spanish butler, who said that Brian had come in a while ago and gone directly to bed. The Bentley was parked in the street in front of the house. Antonio tried to rouse Brian on the house intercom for me, but Brian was obviously fast asleep. Since it was best for him to get his rest, I told Antonio to leave him alone. We let him sleep all the next day.

It was five o'clock in the afternoon when the phone rang at Kingsley Hill. It was Brian. He had just woken up and was feeling very groggy. He was going to have some breakfast, read the mail, and watch "Juke Box Jury" on TV before driving back to Kingsley Hill. I suggested that instead of driving back he should take the train since he was still groggy from Tuinals. Brian agreed this was a more sensible idea and said he would call back later to say on what train he would be arriving. He never called.

Sunday at noon, when Brian's car was still in the same place in front of the house, Antonio and his wife Maria tried to rouse him on the house intercom. When he didn't answer they called me at Kingsley Hill, but Geoffrey and I had gone to lunch at a local pub. Antonio then called Brian's secretary, Joanne Newfield, who called Alistair Taylor and asked him to meet her at Chapel Street. By the time they arrived at Chapel Street I was back at Kingsley Hill, and they summoned me to the phone. I told them not to call Brian's doctor, Norman Cowan, who lived far away, but to get my own personal physician, Dr. John Gallway, who lived only two blocks away in Belgravia. By the time Gallway arrived—fifteen minutes later—Joanne, Alistair Taylor, and Brian Barrett, the chauffeur, were all waiting outside the still-locked, double oak doors to Brian's bedroom. Dr. Gallway called me and asked me what to do. I said to break down the doors. I remained on the line in Sussex, listening to the grunts of Antonio and Brian Barrett as the double oak doors splintered and caved in under their combined weight.

The drapes were drawn and the room was dark. In the light from the hallway they could all see him, lying on his right side, his legs curled up in a fetal position. Saturday's mail was open on the bed next to him. Everyone in the room knew instantly that he was dead, but nevertheless Joanne said, "It's all right, he's just asleep. He's fine."

A moment later, I could hear Maria screaming, "Why? Why?"

Clive Epstein's phone rang in Liverpool. It was Geoffrey Ellis with the news. "It's a lie! You're lying!" Clive screamed into the phone hysterically. Sobbing, he raced to his mother's house. Queenie collapsed when he told her and had to be put under sedation. Then she pulled herself together and flew to London to be with her son.

Simultaneously in Bangor, North Wales, the Beatles had just finished a late lunch and were strolling around the green campus grounds, enjoying the last weekend of summer and toying with their new mantras. Inside the dormitory a pay phone on the wall in the hallway began to ring incessantly. The phone was the only access to the Beatles from the outside world. I had made Pattie Harrison swear that the moment they arrived in Bangor she would call me with the number of the nearest phone in case of an emergency. It turned out to be the pay phone of the dorm. The Beatles could hear the phone ringing from the campus, and finally Jane Asher answered. "Call Paul to the phone," I told her.

"I've got bad news," I told Paul. "Brian is dead. They found him at Chapel Street just a little while ago. The press is on to it, so you'd all better get back to London."

Paul was shocked and saddened but strangely sedate, as were the rest of the Beatles. More than anything, they seemed confused. Like little children whose parents have suddenly disappeared, they turned to the logical authority figure of the moment for comfort and leadership, the Maharishi. The Maharishi had a lot to say to them about Brian's death. He said, in effect, that Brian's passing was a good thing and not to be mourned. He gave them a thumb-nail description of the material world versus the spiritual world and had each of them hold a beautiful flower in the palms of their hands and crush it to see that the beauty was only an illusion of a few cells and water. He told them to laugh, because laughter would clear the bad karma and help Brian's spirit on its journey. He sent them giggling and smirking out to meet a swarm of reporters in Bangor who had learned about Brian's death.

"Our meditation has given us the confidence to withstand such a shock," John told reporters coolly, although he had only been meditating two days. Cynthia stood nearby, weeping into a handkerchief.

Paul was wooden. "It was a great shock and I am very upset," he said as he and Jane climbed into the backseat of a chauffeur-driven car.

"This is no such thing as death, only in the physical sense," George told the group of reporters. "We know he is okay now. He will return because he was striving for happiness and desired bliss so much."

That was the extent of the eulogy Brian was to receive from the Beatles. Within a few days, when the shock had worn off, they made foolish jokes about him.

Another phone call went out to David Jacobs, Brian's attorney, who was spending the weekend at his country house in Brighton. Jacobs got on the next train for London. By the time David Jacobs, Geoffrey, and I converged on the house at Chapel Street, the press had assembled on the front doorstep. Jacobs most likely had called them himself, as it was he who took over making statements to reporters. Jacobs' legal officiations at Brian's death were some of his last duties as NEMS chief solicitor. Two autumns later Jacobs would die under mysterious circumstances. He was found hanging only a few feet off the ground from a satin drapery sash tied to a low beam in his garage.

In Monte Carlo, Robert Stigwood was on a yacht he had rented for the Bee Gees, who were celebrating the end of the work on their first album. Stigwood sent his assistant to the phone box on the pier to check his answering service in London. He was sitting on the aft deck of the yacht, having lunch with the Bee

Gees and their girlfriends, when his assistant came running down the pier screaming, "Brian's dead! Brian's dead!" David Shaw arrived in Monte Carlo a few hours later for a meeting with Stigwood. It turned out that they wouldn't have to make the £500,000 option in just a few days after all. The Beatles and NEMS could be all theirs.

North of London, at a private cricket club, a man came running out of the clubhouse and across the field to Vic Lewis. He was out of breath and ashen. "Mr. Lewis, I'm sorry to tell you that Brian Epstein is dead."

"There wasn't much I could do," Lewis said, "so I finished the game."

In New York City, Allen Klein was driving across the George Washington Bridge to his home in New Jersey. Behind him, Manhattan was glittering like a diamond diorama. Just then there was a news flash on the radio: Brian Epstein was dead.

Klein snapped his fingers. "I've got 'em!" he said.

11.

S TRICTLY FROM the point of view of selling a newspaper, the story of Brian's death was a gold mine. It was the best media free-for-all in England since the Profumo-Christine Keeler scandal. Brian's life had all the elements of a great story: money, glamour, pathos, and tragedy. It was a pitiful story in the end, but nonetheless it left the public strangely satisfied and reassured. Many people even gloated. Here was a man who had power and fame and success, and none of it was enough; he was still unhappy. For the really pious, it was another good example of how God punishes homosexuals. The public verdict was that Brian died a suicide, even though at the lurid inquest that followed, the coroner ruled that he had died of an accidental overdose of carbitol, a component in his sleeping tablets that had built up in his system for many weeks. The suicide assumption by the press was compounded by the rumor that a suicide note had been found. In truth, a note was found, but it was from his previous attempt, and only discovered later among his possessions.

Brian was given a quiet and dignified funeral in Liverpool. The Beatles were asked to stay away so it wouldn't turn into a media circus. He was buried at the Longlane Jewish Cemetery, not far from his father's fresh grave. Queenie never fully recovered from the shock and spent many years in psychiatric treatment, blaming herself for his death. She still lives in Liverpool in a small house adorned by too many pictures of Brian. In her bedroom closet is a carton filled with mementos that she hopes she can bring herself to look at one day. She calls it her "memory box," and in it are the pictures taken the night she and Brian left the Saville Theater together.

Nat Weiss, who flew in from New York, tossed a sunflower given to him by George Harrison into Brian's open grave. Rabbi Samuel Wolfson, the minister of the Greenbank Drive Synagogue in Liverpool, who hardly knew Brian, spoke at the service. "Brian Epstein was a symbol of the malaise of our generation," he told the mourners.

Nat Weiss sat in the chapel and wept bitterly. The most tragic part of Brian's death was just beginning to dawn on him. Here was a man whose passions had sparked an entertainment phenomenon, who had influenced the course of history, but the world would only remember his unhappiness and not the dreams that filled stadiums.

Chapter Fourteen

> You know, where they turn
> over the last page of one
> section to show you they've
> come to the end of it before
> going on to the next. That
> was what Brian's death was
> like. The end of a chapter.
>
> —George Harrison in
> **The Beatles** by Hunter Davies

1.

*B*RIAN'S EARLIER SUICIDE NOTE and the will
that accompanied it remained a secret shared only
by Clive, Queenie, and me. In it he had designated that all his
holdings go "to my family," and since by English law everything
went to Queenie anyway, we all felt his wishes had been fulfilled.
However, there were other bequests in the will, and without explaining to anyone what they were doing, Queenie and Clive decided to fulfill each of the other gifts. Geoffrey Ellis and I were
given a generous cash gift and, along with Nat Weiss and each
of the Beatles, we were asked to choose something from Brian's
possessions.*

The value of Brian's estate was purposely underestimated for
the purpose of "death duties," an opportunity for Inland Revenue
to plunder the dead as well as the living. Still, at roughly £800,000,
the estate taxes were backbreaking, and Clive had to start selling
off Brian's personal holdings to pay it. He got rid of the lease
on the Saville, he sold the silver Bentley, the house in the country,
the furniture, and the crystal chandeliers. Last to go was the Chapel Street town house, where Clive even weighed the coal in the
basement so he could charge the new owners.

At NEMS there was a wild scramble for power. The old guard
Liverpool contingent, which included me, Geoffrey, and Neil,

---

* I took a favorite Queen Anne chair, John took two paintings by a northern England
painter named Lowry, and Nat took a blackamoor table.

274

among others, lined up against the newer partners like Stigwood and Shaw who had been brought into NEMS later. The entire burden of the Beatles' personal management fell on my shoulders, much to my distress. I suddenly found myself the object of much resentment from employees who thought I was eagerly stepping into Brian's shoes. Nothing could have been further from the truth. I did what I had to do simply because there was no one else who knew how to do it.

Stigwood and Shaw continued to insist that Brian's death would not interfere with their option to buy NEMS. Vic Lewis, on the other hand, hinted in an interview with the *London Times* that he might take over. "Brian Epstein designated the operation of much of our company's overseas business to me." Clive called for a meeting of the board of directors of NEMS, hoping to block Stigwood and Shaw's takeover, and Stigwood told reporters that if a boardroom battle developed, he felt he had a "tough ally in Mr. David Shaw." Stigwood and Shaw had one major problem though: they had to convince the Beatles to stay with them. Stigwood hardly even knew the Beatles. In fact, the Beatles were shocked to learn that Brian had planned to sell NEMS. In any event, as far as the Beatles were concerned, Brian's option agreement with Stigwood didn't include them anyway. When they heard that Stigwood and Shaw were claiming otherwise, they met with Stigwood to set him straight. "We weren't about to be sold, like some sort of chattel," Paul said. "Not to Robert Stigwood, not to the Queen Mum."

A diplomatic effort was arranged by Clive Epstein and Stigwood and Shaw's quick exit was negotiated. It was agreed they would stay with the company only until they were able to raise enough money to start their own company, the Robert Stigwood Organization, which was backed by Phillips, the German entertainment conglomerate. Stigwood insisted on some sort of severance settlement from NEMS and he was paid £25,000 just to get out of the company quietly. He took his office furniture and the Bee Gees with him. The Bee Gees, of course, turned out to be one of the biggest pop acts of all time, and Robert Stigwood became an international impresario and producer of *Evita*, *Jesus Christ Superstar*, and the movies *Saturday Night Fever* and *Grease*.

* * *

"No one could possibly replace Brian," was what Paul kept saying. Except, perhaps, Paul himself. On September 2, only six days after Brian's death, Paul took the reins and set us off at a wild gallop. He requested that I arrange a meeting with all the Beatles at his house in St. John's Wood to discuss their next project. Paul's idea was to go right on with the *Magical Mystery Tour* that he had dreamed up on the plane coming home from America. He had decided it would be an hour-long special for TV. He had already written part of the title song, and with an addition of six or so other new songs, they would make a film to go with it, a kind of *Sergeant Pepper* with pictures. The project was to be recorded, produced, scripted, directed, and edited by the Beatles—namely Paul himself.

"I knew we were in trouble then," John later admitted. "I didn't have any misconceptions about our ability to do anything other than play music, and I was scared. I thought, 'We fuckin' had it . . .' and I thought, 'fuckin' I've never made a film, what's he mean, write a script . . .' Then George and I were sort of grumbling, you know, 'fuckin' movie, oh well, we better do it,' we felt we owed it to the public that we should do these things."

A formal script was never prepared for the project. Instead there was only an outline, sketches of dwarfs and rewarmed Fellini characters out of Paul's comic-strip imagination. John halfheartedly contributed a dream sequence with fat ladies and spaghetti. The closest to a written synopsis was the press release, which said, "Away in the sky, beyond the clouds, live 4 or 5 musicians. By casting wonderful spells they turn the most Ordinary Coach Trip into a Magical Mystery Tour."

Magical Mystery Tour was a mess. If Brian had been alive, it never would have happened the way it did. On Monday, September 11, a sixty-seat yellow and blue coach festooned with signs that identified it as the Magical Mystery Tour took off for Devon and Cornwall with a cast and crew of forty-three aboard. Following them was a procession of carloads of Fleet Street reporters, plus ten or fifteen fans in their own cars. The *Magical Mystery Tour* stopped in Devon, where they hoped to find the Devon Fair but found only a town. At Teigen the local constable chased them on for disturbing the peace. They changed directions and headed for Brighton, where they filmed two cripples sunning on the beach. When they stopped for a lunch break, they discovered they were thirty lunches short to feed the cast and crew. The first night on the road the sleeping accommodations had been underbooked and Paul and Neil spent hours sorting out fights between fat ladies and dwarfs who did not want to share rooms. Heading north the next day, their caravan caused mayhem and traffic jams wherever they went, not just because of the procession of cars that followed them, but because a line of cars now preceded them for a mile. Unable to take another second of it, John ordered the bus to stop, stormed out the door, and ripped the signs from the sides of the coach in a fury.

"They should have filmed *that*," Neil barked.

Paul had planned to shoot the finale, a top hat and cane dance number, at Shepperton Studios outside of London, but no one had thought of booking time on the sound stage. In desperation they leased an old airfield in West Mailing, Kent, where a huge set was built. The climactic Busby Berkeley episode employed more than forty dwarfs, a dozen babies, and a military marching band in full costume. Paul took all the developed footage and disappeared into an editing room he'd hired on Old Compton Street to piece it together. Each Beatle had a say about the film, and it was edited and reedited and tinkered with a thousand times. Often it was changed back and forth four times in the same day, with Paul countermanding John's suggestions of that very morning.

One day I received a phone call in my office on the Beatles' private line. It was Paul and it sounded like long distance. "Where are you?" I asked him.

"I'm in Nice, France," Paul told me, "with a camera crew. We found the perfect hill, but we haven't brought the right lenses. Do you think you could have them shipped out to us, along with some money?"

I was baffled. "Nice? Perfect hill? What are you talking about? How can you be in France? I have your passport."

Paul explained that he wanted to include a scene in *Magical Mystery Tour* of him sitting on a picturesque hill singing a song he had written called "The Fool on the Hill." He took off for France without telling anybody and bluffed his way past the English authorities at Heathrow, saying his passport was waiting for him in France. In Nice he told the French officials the passport was arriving later by messenger, and they agreed to allow the celebrated visitor into the country by special dispensation until his passport caught up with him. By the time Paul and the crew returned to London, it had cost £4000 just for the one shot of him sitting on the hill in Nice.

When *Magical Mystery Tour* was finally finished, Paul screened it for everyone at NEMS. The reaction was unanimous: it was awful. It was formless, disconnected, disjointed, and amateurish. I told Paul to junk it. "So what, we lost £40,000," I said. "Better to junk it than be embarrassed by it."

But Paul's ego wouldn't let him consider this. He was positive that *Magical Mystery Tour* would be as warmly greeted by the public as all the Beatles products that came before it. Reluctantly, we sold the TV rights to the BBC, who put it on the air on December 26, Boxing Day in England, when millions of Britons were at home celebrating the holidays.

The critical reaction was truly remarkable. The critics pounced. ". . . blatant rubbish" cried the *Daily Express*, ". . . the bigger they are the harder they fall . . ." Nine thousand miles away, in Los Angeles, *Daily Variety* covered the reaction with the headline, "Critics and Viewers Boo: Beatles Produce First Flop with Yule Film." The press was so unaccountably mean and vindictive that for the first time in memory an artist felt he had to make a public apology for his work. The next day a picture of Paul in a sweater and herringbone jacket, on the phone to journalist Ray Connolly, ran on the front page of the *Evening Standard*. The headline was, "We Goofed Says Beatle Paul." "It was like getting a bash in your face," he told Connolly. "You know [better] the next time. It annoys some people that we always jump in the deep end without knowing what we really want, but that's the way I like to do things. I suppose if you look at [*Magical Mystery Tour*] from the point of view of a good Boxing Day entertainment we goofed really."

As *Time* magazine subsequently noted in a report on the failure of *Magical Mystery Tour*, the film managed to gross $2 million from rentals to colleges. In America the *Magical Mystery Tour* album grossed $8 million in its first ten days of release. In England, where *Magical Mystery Tour* was released as an EP, it also hit the number-one spot. As usual, whatever they touched turned to money. And money began to be their biggest problem.

* * *

2.

*A*ND STILL the money rolled in. Or did it? When Brian was alive, as far as the Beatles were concerned, all they had to do was pick up a phone or sign a bill and everything would be paid for. They never gave a second thought to how much they spent or where it was coming from. Suddenly, with Brian gone, they had to come face to face with a lot of hard facts. They were being taxed at a 96 percent rate. While the flotation of Northern Songs had given John and Paul some untaxed income, Ringo and George were poor in comparison. In any event, everyone had spent well beyond their means. Documents prepared in June of 1967 showed that they had spent approximately £750,000 on homes, cars, and luxury living. Because of the 1965 finance tax, it was no longer possible for them to advance money from their various companies without incurring an immediate tax liability. Also, a payment of £1 million in advances and royalties was due them by EMI.

The advice of the tax experts was simple. Expand. Invest in related businesses with practical real estate values and then go public in four or five years. This was a solid, long-term plan to insure the Beatles wealth as they got older. For the Beatles, the message was simple: spend.

For several months the Beatles toyed with the idea of a related business, but for the Beatles the very word "business" had terrible connotations. There was something about business that was like going to school. Businessmen were derisively called "the men in the suits," and even associates like me, who were close to them, were considered men in suits. Why couldn't business be fun? they asked. Why couldn't business be called something pretty like, say, "Apple." Apple. Everybody knew the children's nursery poem, "A is for apple . . ." Apple, said the Beatles, would be a place where business could be fun.

From their old company, Beatles Ltd, a new company was formed called Apple Corp., a pun of Paul's, which was to "manage" a new partnership called Beatles and Co. I was asked to become administrative director of Apple, plus operate and run Beatles and Co. Neil Aspinall was named a managing director of Apple Corp. Apple Corp. in turn purchased 80 percent of the stock of the old company. The formation of the new company also included what was to become a crucial partnership agreement, which they all signed. As it turned out, John was so stoned at the time he later couldn't recall having signed any partnership papers at all.

The catch to investing money was that in order to get the tax break it had to be invested in a "related field" or, loosely interpreted, in whatever it was the Beatles did. The first idea was to open a chain of record stores called Apple, not so much to sell records as to be able to buy up valuable real estate for each store. But selling records was dismissed as too commercial for the Beatles. Apple had to reflect the spirit of the times we were living in. It had to be something bigger, more encompassing than just becoming shopkeepers. Overnight the idea mushroomed, as was the Beatles wont, and Apple became bigger than life, just like them. Apple became a multi-faceted source of endowment and financing in all areas of creativity: music, filmmaking, publishing, design, and electronics.

There were two perfect examples to invest in right under their noses: Magic Alex and The Fool. Magic Alex would be given a workshop in which to research and develop all of his wonderful inventions, including the paint that plugs in and lights up the wall. The Fool could design and manufacture clothing on a mass level and sell it in their own store. In September, while filming *Magical Mystery Tour,* the Beatles allocated £100,000 to the Fool to design and open a clothing line and boutique, "a beautiful place where you could buy beautiful things." It didn't seem to faze the Beatles that The Fool's previous experience in the retail business, an Amsterdam barber shop they had converted into a boutique, reportedly went bankrupt because The Fool's personal expenses ran so high. Magic Alex was commissioned to design the store's lighting, and he spoke of hanging a sun in the street to light up the night sky for the opening.

The Beatles discovered that their accountants had already purchased for them, as a long-term investment, a building on the corner of Baker and Paddington Streets, on the "wrong side" of Oxford Street, just off the beaten path of shoppers, where the design and construction of the Apple Boutique could begin. In the floors upstairs from the store they opened other Apple offices. Terry Doran was made managing director of Apple Publishing. John's childhood pal, Pete Shotton, who was running a supermarket John had purchased for him, was asked to apply his retail expertise to the Apple Boutique. When the Oxford Street building became too crowded, additional offices were opened on a large floor of an office building on Wigmore Street. Here Ron Kass, the vice-president of Liberty Records in Europe, was hired away to run Apple Records. Jane Asher's brother, Peter, was asked to head the company's talent division. Apple Films was established, to be presided over by Dennis O'Dell, a former associate of Richard Lester's. Brian Lewis, a prominent entertainment lawyer, ran the legal and contracts department. Stephen Maltz, an accountant from Bryce-Hamner, also joined the firm. Most everyone hired assistants, and the assistants hired secretaries.

The construction of the boutique took a little longer than was expected. A group of art-school students was hired to repaint the five-story exterior of the building in a psychedelic motif designed by The Fool while the interior of the store was being redesigned. Paul would arrive at the store every morning bright and early and ask the workmen to literally move the walls around. The same afternoon John would appear and say to move the walls back the way they were. In the interim tens of thousands of pounds' worth of merchandise and fabrics began arriving at the cutting rooms upstairs where tailors busily turned out Fool clothing.

The boutique finally opened its doors on December 7, 1967. The all too self-conscious invitation to the opening read, "Come at 7:46, fashion show at 8:16." Only George and John bothered to attend. Alex had hung no magic lighting in the street; it had proved too complicated, and the lighting in the store was expensive but not very unusual. The painting of a woman's face with stars in the background and a rainbow swirl of colors below her that had been executed on the building might have been attractive to some, but not to the local business community. The Civic Association started suit to have it removed. As the press and public wandered around the newly opened store, they were clearly confused as what to think. The store was stocked with trinkets similar to those found in any "head" shop. The incense, bracelets, and wild velvet and satin clothing seemed slightly stale, like props left over from last summer's flower-power vogue. The huge dressing rooms of the boutique were only good for one thing: shoplifting. From the day the store opened its doors, it started losing money.

But losing money was what it was all about, in a way, and the Beatles remained undaunted.

3.

*I*T *WAS IN FEBRUARY* of 1968, just as Apple was about to go into full swing, that the Beatles informed me they intended to finish the Transcendental Meditation course they had begun the previous August in Bangor, North Wales. But this time the Beatles had agreed not to just a ten-day course but to go off to Rishekesh in the remote wilderness of north India for three months of serious study. The mastery of Transcendental Meditation, they hoped, would give them the wisdom to run Apple. In Rishekesh, they said, they would live in an ashram—without any drugs or alcohol.

The Beatles' faith in the tiny Maharishi seemed unshakeable. Through the winter they had remained serious devotees of the guru and visited him frequently in his London digs in South Kensington. They still went to his lectures, and George and John became vegetarians, although John had almost immediately gone back to his regimen of drugs after Brian's death. The Beatles were even contemplating, as an offshoot of Apple Films, to finance a major motion picture about the Maharishi, the proceeds of which would fund a Transcendental Meditation University in London.

I had my doubts about the efficacy of the Beatles going off to India with the Maharishi in the middle of the formation of Apple, particularly because of certain incidents that led me to believe the Maharishi was using the Beatles' name for his personal gain. One day I received a call from the lawyers for ABC Television in America. They said that the Maharishi had been negotiating with them for a TV special that he said would include an appearance by the Beatles. ABC's lawyers were calling me to confirm the Beatles' cooperation. I told them that the Beatles had no intention of appearing on the Maharishi's show. But only a week later the lawyers were back on the phone; the Maharishi was insisting he could deliver them.

I called the Maharishi in Malmö, Sweden, where he was lecturing at the moment, and explained the problem to him, but his answers were obscure and indefinite. I decided to fly to Malmö to insist he not represent the Beatles as being part of his projects. In Malmö the Maharishi greeted me warmly but only giggled and nodded and chattered on like a mouse on speed as I laid down the law. The following week in London I was again contacted by ABC's lawyers, who said the Maharishi was still insisting the Beatles would appear on his TV show and was soliciting sponsors with this understanding. I went to Malmö again, this time with Paul and George in tow. We met with the Maharishi and tried to explain to him that he must not use their names to exploit his business affairs, and that they definitely would *not* appear on his TV special, but the Maharishi just nodded and giggled again. "He's not a modern man," George said forgivingly on the plane home. "He just doesn't understand these things."

On February 16 the Beatles set out for Rishekesh. The traveling party consisted of John and Cynthia, George and Pattie, Paul, Jane Asher, Ringo and Maureen, Jenny Boyd, Donovan, and Mal Evans. They traveled first by jet to Delhi, then by taxi and jeep and eventually on the backs of donkeys. When the road became impossible for even the donkeys to navigate, they walked the last half mile, crossing a narrow rope bridge over a muddy chasm before they reached the gates of the ashram. Their luggage followed later on ox-drawn carts. For the first time in years, the Beatles were cut off from the world—and the press from the Beatles. The absence of news of what was happening in the ashram tantalized the public. The whole world seemed to know that the Beatles had gone off to India to discover the "truth," and millions waited expectantly for them to come down from the mountain and spread the Word. Here, told for the first time, is what really happened in the ashram.

The Beatles were joined at the ashram by Beach Boy Mike Love, jazz musician Paul Horn, American actress Mia Farrow, her sister Tia, and her brother John, plus some twenty other noncelebrated students, an assortment of discontented Americans from California, and some aging Swedish widows.

The ashram turned out to be more like a hotel than the spartan guru's camp the Beatles expected. The sleeping quarters were in a complex of picturesque stone bungalows with four or five bedrooms in each. The Beatles' rooms had four-poster beds and solid English furniture. Each was equipped with a modern bath and toilet, and there was even an electric fire for cold nights. Meals were eaten communally at long, hand-carved tables under a vine-covered trellis next to the Ganges. Food was served to them by a large staff of servants and prepared in a completely modern kitchen by a trained chef. The Maharishi's house, a short distance away from the rest of the compound, was a long, low, modern building with its own kitchen and staff. There was even a woman to give the girls a daily massage. The most eyebrow-raising of all the luxury accoutrements was the landing pad for the helicopter used to ferry the Maharishi in and out of the compound on his appointed rounds throughout India. This was the man whom George had excused to me as "not a modern man."

Once settled into the ashram they began to study in earnest. They woke at dawn each morning for an early breakfast, then went to long lectures, and spent the afternoons in meditation sessions. A friendly competition started among them to see who could meditate the longest, and there were heated debates at dinner every night about "who was getting it" and who was not. John seemed really into it, others thought he was faking it and that George was the most readily spiritual of the group. They dressed in traditional Indian clothing, and although they had shaved their moustaches shortly before the trip, they let their hair grow. It was the end of the rainy season when they arrived, but in a few weeks it turned warm and balmy, and they were able to bathe in the Ganges River, still clear and clean in the late winter. At night in their bungalows they could hear the river crashing rhythmically on the banks.

Every evening after dinner, without the aid of drugs or alcohol, the boys would take their guitars out under the moonlight and sing and write songs. The quantity and quality of the songs composed in India was staggering, even to those who knew them. Thirty of the songs would comprise their next album. Everyone in the compound seemed touched by the muse. Donovan wrote his most beautiful song, "Jennifer Juniper," for Pattie Harrison's sister Jenny. The mood was loving and mellow, and perhaps the best celebration the Beatles had in years was George's twenty-fourth birthday party, when the Maharishi presented him with a seven-pound cake and a fireworks display.

When they'd first arrived at the ashram, Cynthia had been stung to learn that John had arranged for them to sleep in separate quarters. John explained that the distance would be good for meditating, and anyway they would see each other constantly in the small camp. Despite the unromantic arrangement, Cynthia relished being in Rishekesh. The Maharishi's retreat was her one last hope for their marriage. Her life with John was in a shambles. He was little more than a frequent visitor to their home, and when he was there the house was filled with drug dealers and other smarmy "international leeches" as she called them.

And recently Cynthia had become aware of the presence of a small Japanese woman named Yoko Ono in their lives. She seemed to be everywhere; waiting in front of the house for them, or sitting in the back of the car. Her little book of instructional poems was left on the night table on John's side of the bed, like an omen. Although John swore to Cynthia over and over that he had no romantic interest in her, Cynthia was as relieved to get him away from Yoko Ono as she was from the drug dealers.

Little did Cynthia realize that John had considered taking Yoko Ono with him to India instead of her, or even in addition to her, if he could have figured out how to pull it off. It would have been much more fun to go to Rishekesh with Yoko. He felt no guilt about Yoko, because he had not lied to Cynthia; it was an intellectual relationship, not a romantic one. Yoko's galling wit and gentle craziness titillated him. She was smart and opinionated, a grateful distraction from Cynthia's cloying kindness. Whenever John was about to tell Cynthia their marriage was over and he had to get away from her, she would look up to him with those sad, blue, believing eyes, and he didn't have the heart. So off they went to Rishekesh together, while Yoko waited impatiently for John's return.

Rishekesh gave Cynthia a chance to regain a sense of herself, away from the pressures of Kenwood. She meditated and returned to the easel, where she spent hours drawing and painting. She watched from a distance as John became healthier and stronger without drugs.

For one brief moment the Maharishi was even successful in raising some optimistically romantic sounds from John. Cynthia and John had told the Maharishi that Julian, who was staying with Lillian Powell and Mrs. Jarlett while they were gone, was celebrating his fifth birthday in a few weeks. The following week they were asked to the Maharishi's house where they were presented with a made-to-order wardrobe for Julian befitting an Indian prince. The young couple was moved by the Maharishi's thoughtfulness, and on the way back to the student compound they held hands while strolling along the Ganges. John was filled with warm, paternal feelings. "Oh Cyn," he said, "won't it be wonderful to be together with Julian again. Everything will be fantastic again, won't it? I can't wait, Cyn, can you?"

But the momentary surge of warmth soon passed, and John began to drift further away from her. Even in the small ashram he sometimes managed to avoid seeing her for days. He spent more and more time locked away in his room. Cynthia assumed he was meditating. He was not. He was writing long, rambling diatribes to a Japanese artist waiting for him in London. He got up early each morning and went to the mail drop to collect letters from Yoko, who wrote just as faithfully. "Look up at the sky," she wrote him, "and when you see a cloud think of me."

"I got so excited about her letters," John said. "There was nothin' in them that wives or mothers-in-law could've understood, and from India I started thinkin' of her as a woman, not just an intellectual woman."

On the tenth day Ringo and Maureen left for home. They told the reporters who greeted them in London they had to leave because Ringo's delicate stomach couldn't take the spicy food, but it was also because they hated the ashram. The clincher was Maureen's aversion to flying insects. The banks of the Ganges are not a good place to visit if one is afraid of flying insects. Each night before Maureen went to sleep, she would make a hapless "Ritchie" kill every fly and insect in the room and dispose of the carcasses. Back in London Ringo told friends that the ten days he spent in the ashram weren't as much fun as Butlin's Holiday Camp.

Paul and Jane stuck it out for six weeks. Paul simply wasn't getting it. Or believing it either. The mock seriousness of the Maharishi and the tediousness of meditation were too much like school for him. Paul and Jane were much too sophisticated for this mystical gibberish. But when they were greeted by the press at Heathrow, they said none of this, only that they missed London and wanted to get home.

John and George, however, remained true believers, despite the growing skepticism of their friends, Neil Aspinall among them. Neil was flying in and out of London to the ashram at regular intervals, keeping the Beatles informed on the progress of Apple. One of these trips concerned making a deal with the Maharishi for a film about him. Neil expected to have a hard time explaining the business arrangements to the spiritual man, only to find the Maharishi employed a full-time accountant. For a long while Neil and the guru haggled over an additional two and a half points. "Wait a minute," Neil thought, "this guy knows more about making deals than I do. He's really into scoring, the Maharishi."

The Maharishi's most powerful critic turned out to be Magic Alex. Alex was summoned to Rishekesh by John, who missed his company. When Alex arrived at the ashram, he was appalled at what he found. "An ashram with four-poster beds?" he demanded incredulously. "Masseurs, and servants bringing water, houses with facilities, an accountant—I never saw a holy man with a bookkeeper!"

According to Alex, the sweet old women at the ashram Cynthia liked so much for their warmth and openness were "mentally ill Swedish old ladies who had left their money to the Maharishi. There were also a couple of second-rate American actresses. Lots of people went to India," he said, "to find things they couldn't find at home, including a bunch of lost, pretty girls." Alex was disgusted to observe the Maharishi herding them together for a group photograph, like a class picture, which he would use for publicity.

It was also quite apparent that John was totally under the Maharishi's control. John had been completely free of drugs and alcohol for over a month by the time Alex arrived, and he was the healthiest he had been in years, but Alex still felt the Maharishi was getting more than he was giving. Alex was at camp for only a week when he heard that the Maharishi expected the Beatles to tithe over 10 to 25 percent of their annual income to a Swiss account in his name. Alex reproved the Maharishi for this, accusing him of having too many mercenary motives in his association with the Beatles. Alex claims the Maharishi tried to placate him by offering to pay Alex to build a high-powered radio station on the grounds of the ashram so that he could broadcast his holy message to India's masses.

By the end of the tenth week, Alex was bent on undermining the Maharishi's influence. He began by smuggling wine into the compound, having secured it on trips to the local village. The men would not drink, but the girls did. Late at night Alex would distribute the wine to the women while John and George were writing songs. During one of these late night, secret drinking sessions, a pretty blond nurse from California admitted that during a private consultation with the Maharishi she had been fed chicken for dinner.

The Maharishi's menu became a subject of great debate over the next week as word spread through the ashram that someone had accused him of smuggling chicken into the vegetarian community. Oddly, whether or not it was appropriate for Alex to be smuggling wine in was never questioned. In general nobody at the camp cared if the Maharishi had a little chicken on the side once in a while, but then, in the eleventh week, the story got worse. The same girl confided to Alex that not only had she been fed chicken during one of her private consultations but that the Maharishi had made sexual advances toward her. The Maharishi began by asking to hold her hand so that his spiritual power would flow between them. It soon developed that he had a more complicated but very old-fashioned method for facilitating the flow. On five separate occasions, eager to please the great teacher, the girl lay back, closed her eyes, and thought of California while the little guru ministered to her flesh.

When Alex transmitted this information to all the other women the following day, they were appropriately horrified. The thought that the Maharishi was not only a religious phoney but also one of such seedy proportions made some of them break down and weep. Cynthia, for one, didn't believe a word of it. She had long ago become acquainted with Alex's jealousy over anyone who had John's attention, and she didn't doubt that Alex would lie to destroy the Maharishi's hold. As for the testimony of the American nurse, Cynthia claimed to have seen the girl in Alex's room sitting at a candlelit table one night. While anyone else would have jumped to a sexual conclusion, Cynthia became convinced that Alex was using "black magic" to bewitch the girl.

Alex decided to set a trap for the Maharishi. On the nurse's next trip to the Maharishi's house, it was arranged for several "witnesses" to hide in the bushes outside the Maharishi's windows. When the Maharishi began to make advances, the girl was to scream, and everyone would come running to her aid. The Beatles and their wives, when told of this plan, strongly disapproved of Alex's tactics and would have nothing to do with it, but the plan proceeded nevertheless.

Late that night Alex and the nurse returned from the Maharishi's house with another tale. The girl was again served chicken, after which the Maharishi made sexual advances, but for some reason the girl did not call out for help as planned. As the scene and the Maharishi began to unfold before Alex's eyes, Alex made a loud noise outside the window to distract him. Afraid they would be discovered by an intruder, the Maharishi fixed his clothing and sent the girl away at once.

John, George, and Alex sat up arguing about it all night. George didn't believe a word of it, and he was furious with Alex. John had serious doubts. The Maharishi had indeed turned out to be as worldly and mercenary as the rest. John had expected a ticket to peace, but it turned out that the little LSD pills he nibbled on at home were more effective in the long run. The decision was made to leave early the next morning. Alex was afraid that the Maharishi might try to block their way by refusing to help them find transportation, and there was such urgency to their departure that Cynthia and Pattie were ordered to leave behind all their accumulated souvenirs. Shortly after breakfast, the Maharishi entered the compound and took his place, cross-legged, under a little grass canopy. Cynthia could see he was far from giggling. The three men went up to see him. John had been elected as spokesman, although he hated the task. "We're leaving, Maharishi," he said.

The little man looked pained. "But why?" he asked.

John didn't have the courage to confront him. Evasively, he said, "You're the cosmic one, you should know." The Maharishi looked as if he wanted to kill him. The guru said all he could to persuade them to stay without discussing the true reason they were leaving. As far as his unnamed tresspasses went, he said that the truth was like an iceberg with only ten percent showing. It was not enough. Alex was dispatched to the nearby town of Deradoon to fetch taxis.

According to Alex, just as he had predicted the Maharishi had put the word out in the small adjacent town that the Beatles were not to be assisted in leaving. Alex was made to understand by the townspeople that the Maharishi would put some sort of jinx on them if they helped. Alex even offered to buy two taxis and finally managed to rent two old cars and their drivers. He had them driven to the ashram, where they loaded whatever luggage could fit in the trunks. They piled into the cars and drove off with the Maharishi watching sadly from the gates.

The cars broke down every few kilometers, and John and Cynthia's car got a flat. Everybody thought the Maharishi had put some sort of curse on them. There was no spare tire, and while Pattie and George went ahead for help, John and Cynthia and their driver sat alongside a deserted road in the baking heat for more than three hours before two Eastern-educated travelers recognized John and stopped to give them a lift.

Exhausted and angry when they finally reached Delhi, they checked into the Hilton and were immediately recognized. It was only a matter of twenty minutes before foreign correspondents and reporters from every wire service were milling about the lobby of the hotel, trying to get a statement from the Beatles about why they were leaving the ashram. Wisely, it was agreed that while they were still in India they would say nothing of what had transpired. John and George told the press they had left because they had pressing business in London, and they did not wish to be in a film the Maharishi was planning to shoot.

Back in London the Beatles decided to observe a code of silence about the incident. They decided that if the story were told in full, it would only reflect poorly on them. In later years bits and pieces of the story did get out but were greatly distorted. One widely circulated and believed story incorrectly names Mia Farrow as the Maharishi's corespondent. Individually the Beatles had predictable reactions to the Maharishi incident. Ringo was benign, Paul was smug in an I-told-you-so sort of way, and George remained a stubborn believer and determined follower. To this day George is one of the many convinced that Alex was lying and trying to slander the Maharishi in order to get John away from him. John had the strongest reaction of all; he felt duped. He felt used, for the millionth time, and he was angry as hell. He took some of his anger out in a song about the Maharishi, but at the last minute he changed the title to "Sexy Sadie" to avoid a possible libel suit. The Maharishi was added to his long collection of disappointments, and John was once again open and gullible for the Next Big Thing to come.

4.

*L*ITTLE COULD ANYONE, not even Cynthia, have expected the Next Big Thing to be Yoko Ono. It was on the airplane going home from Delhi that John and Cynthia first had that little talk about their marriage. Cynthia doesn't remember exactly how they eased into it, but it started with lots of scotch and Cokes, which they hadn't had in a long time, and ended with John making the most remarkable admission to her; he hadn't been faithful to her throughout their married life.

"I don't want to hear about it," Cynthia said, staring out of the plane window with a sad, distant look on her face. "It's worse knowing than not knowing," she said. She also worried that John's sudden need for confession was a bad omen of things to come.

"But you've got to bloody hear it, Cyn," John said, putting his hand on her arm. "What the fuck do you think I've been doing on the road all those years? There was a bloody slew of girls—"

"In Hamburg," Cynthia interrupted. "Yes, I knew that—"

"In Liverpool, too! Dozens and dozens, the whole time we were going together."

Tears welled in Cynthia's eyes and spilled out onto her cheeks. She wiped them away with one finger under her glasses.

"There were an uncountable number," John insisted, "in hotel rooms throughout the bloody world! But I was afraid for you to find out. That's what 'Norwegian Wood' was all about, the lyrics that nobody could understand. I wrote it about an affair and made it all gobbledygook so you wouldn't know. And do you remember whatshisname and his sobbing wife turning up at the door while I was away on tour? Yeah, her too."

"I don't want to hear any more," Cynthia pleaded. But John

had caught fire with the idea, the flames fanned by winds of release and honesty. He went on to claim affairs with a well-known English journalist and in America with Joan Baez, among others. There had also been an intermittent affair with an English actress. The rest were one-night stands, sometimes Playboy bunnies set up for him at the homes of friends in London.

By the time their plane landed at Heathrow, Cynthia was in a panic. John's confession had made her so insecure, it was all she could do to stop herself from clinging to him in the terminal. She worried herself sick over his infidelities, and in the coming weeks she became impossible for him to be with. The following weekend John went away by himself to visit with Derek Taylor and his wife and four children. He spent the day tripping on LSD, one of the first trips since returning from India. Derek spent the day feeding John's ego, reminding him of how lucky and talented he was. The day with the happy family in the country lifted John's spirits temporarily. He returned home that night still tripping, ebullient about having more children. He hugged Cynthia to him and said, "Christ, Cyn, it was great. We've got to have more children!" Cynthia was so disheartened by this sudden burst of affection, which she knew was only a side effect of the LSD, she burst into tears.

"What the hell's the matter with you?" he shouted at her.

"One LSD trip isn't going to guarantee *my* future!" she shouted back at him. "What's that going to solve?"

"Goddamn you Powell!" he shouted at her.

"It's not me you want, it's that Japanese woman, Yoko Ono," Cynthia said through her tears. "Maybe you're right, maybe she is the woman for you."

John said that was ridiculous. Yoko Ono was crazy. He had no interest in her.

The atmosphere in the house became impossibly tense. Cynthia was nervous and depressed, on the verge of a breakdown. "I felt . . . as though I was sitting on the edge of a volcano," she said. "John suggested that as he had to work for long hours in the recording studios for a few weeks, I should accompany Jenny and Alex on a holiday to Greece."

Julian was packed off to live with Mrs. Jarlett, and John sat alone in the house. He dipped his fingers into his magic mortar, wandered around London, and had a few laughs with his mates

Terry Doran and Derek. He called up Pete Shotton at the Apple Boutique and asked him if he would like to spend the night at Kenwood with him, so he wouldn't have to watch TV alone. Late that night they sat in the sun room at the back of the house, the TV on with the sound off, music on the stereo, shooting the bull about their favorite conquests. Suddenly, John said, "I've met this woman called Yoko. She's Japanese."

It was nearly the middle of the night when John called her up and asked if she wanted to make the trip to Weybridge. Yoko arrived in a taxi an hour later. They had always been so shy around each other John wasn't sure what to do, so he took her on a tour of the house, which included a stop at the mortar and pestle, where they both took LSD. Later John took her upstairs to his studio and played some tapes of electronic music he had been experimenting with. John had, on occasion, tried to play these tapes for the other Beatles, suggesting they be included on a cut on an album, but Paul wouldn't even bother to listen to them. Yoko, however, loved the tapes; they didn't sound very different from her own avant-garde "music" of howls and screams. She giggled and smiled, and it pleased him no end.

"Let's make one ourselves," he said.

Fused on acid, they spent the rest of the night recording together. Yoko's Oriental sense of metric time challenged and confused John, mocking his commercial approach to music. The recording was like an aural doodle of a man and woman in heat late at night, naked and high. When the sun rose they made love and named the tape *Two Virgins,* for both of them felt reborn.

It was a few days later that Cynthia came home from Greece with Magic Alex and Jenny to find John and Yoko sitting so comfortably in her kitchen.

To this day Cynthia still regrets having gone to bed with Magic Alex that night, but at the moment it must have seemed the perfect revenge. She awoke the next morning in Alex's bed, disgusted with herself and determined to fight for her husband. A few days later, when Cynthia returned to Kenwood to pick up more of her clothing, there was a reconciliation of sorts. Yoko was gone— John said he had gotten bored with her—and Cynthia was invited to move back in if she wanted. She was only there a few days when John said he had to go to New York on a business trip with Paul to announce the opening of Apple. Cynthia begged to accompany him on this trip, but John said he would be too busy, and anyway, when he got back to London he had to return to the studios to work on a new album. Once again, John packed her off, this time with her mother and Julian, to Pesaro, Italy. Reluctantly, Cynthia kissed John goodbye for what was to be the last time.

Pictures taken in concert at Munich in 1966. Above: Ringo sings "I Wanna Be Your Man"; Below: John and Paul joke with the audience, George looks on. (*Beat Publications, Ltd.*)

Pattie and George in a rare photo taken of them during their first trip to India, where George went to study the sitar with musician Ravi Shankar. (*Beat Publications, Ltd.*)

John and Cynthia leaving the New London Synagogue after a memorial service for Brian Epstein. (*Pictorial Parade*)

John and three-year-old son Julian play with a top. (*Transworld Features Syndicate, Inc.*)

This 1966 photo shows Ringo playing with his firstborn son, Zak, held by wife Maureen in the den of their Surrey home. (*Beat Publications, Ltd.*)

On the phones at Apple, four conversations go on at once. From left: Dennis O'Dell, Paul McCartney, Peter Brown, and Neil Aspinall with his back to the camera. (*Transworld Features Syndicate, Inc.*)

Officially announcing the opening of Apple. From left: John Lennon, Peter Brown, Paul McCartney, Derek Taylor (back to camera), and Neil Aspinall. (Heads chopped off, left to right: Dennis O'Dell, Brian Lewis, and Ron Kass.) (*Beat Publications, Ltd.*)

John Lennon, so stoned that he's recording *Abbey Road* lying down on the floor. (*Beat Publications, Ltd.*)

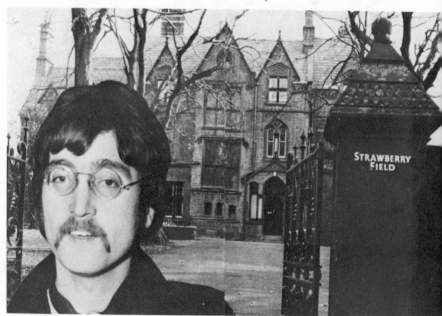

A photo montage of John in front of the children's orphanage after which he named his famous song. (*Beat Publications, Ltd.*)

Paul explains his shots to a technician, while cast and crew follow him onto an open field for the shooting of *Magical Mystery Tour*. That's Magic Alex with the moustache on the left. (*Beat Publications, Ltd.*)

George's mom, Louise, and father, Harold, look on as their son shows off the gold wedding band on his new wife's finger. (*Beat Publications, Ltd.*)

Jane Asher and Paul with the sheep at High Park, Paul's Scottish retreat. (*Pictorial Parade*)

Cynthia Lennon wipes a tear from her eye after missing the "Mystical Express" to Bangor, North Wales. Crowds of fans and police held her back from boarding the train that contained the Maharishi, the four Beatles, and Mick Jagger. (*United Press International, Inc.*)

In Malmö, Sweden, where George and Paul have gone to ask the Maharishi Mahesh Yogi to stop using their names in his business dealings. The Maharishi smiles happily as George, Paul, and Peter Brown follow him out of the meditation center. (*Lennart Gullberg*)

Magic Alex, AKA Lexis Mardas, the Beatles' controversial electronics genius and John Lennon's close friend. (*Transworld Features Syndicate, Inc.*)

John smokes a cigarette and Yoko fidgets as the local authority marries them in Gibraltar. Peter Brown bears witness as best man. (*David Nutter*)

Yoko dreamily waits for takeoff aboard the private plane that took her and John to Paris after their Gibraltar wedding. (*David Nutter*)

A rare photo of Yoko, John, Kyoko, Tony Cox, and his second wife, Belinda. This was taken in Denmark's North Jutland at an experimental center dedicated to studying peace. A few days later John and Yoko would cut off all their hair. (*Pictorial Parade*)

John and Yoko in the kitchen at Tittenhurst. This photo was taken shortly after the two had cut off all their hair in Sweden. (It was at this table that Cynthia first caught John and Yoko in their bathrobes.) (*Richard DiLello, Camera Press, Ltd.*)

The curved wicker sofa in the sunroom at Kenwood, hardly big enough for one, now holds two. (*Camera Press, Ltd.*)

Paul and Linda are mobbed after their wedding at the Marylebone Registry. In the crowd are Peter Brown, Paul's brother Mike McGear, and Mal Evans. (*Wide World Photos*)

Heather Eastman, Paul, Linda, and Doll are exhausted after Paul and Linda's wedding at the Marylebone Registry. (*Camera Press, Ltd.*)

Paul gives the thumbs-up signal
outside the gates of his Sussex
country home shortly after his
release from a Japanese jail.
(*Transworld Features
Syndicate, Inc.*)

George shares a joke with racing car driver Jackie
Stewart. The thrill and danger of fast cars became
a counterpoint to George's spiritual endeavors in the
late seventies. (*Transworld Features Syndicate, Inc.*)

During Ringo's jet-setting period he frequently returned to London to visit with the kids. From left: Zak, Lee, and Jason see him off at the Heathrow airport on his way back to Los Angeles. (*Transworld Features Syndicate, Inc.*)

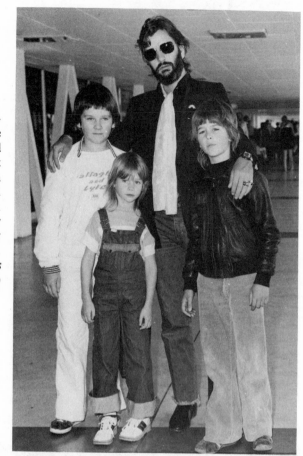

The surviving Beatles reunite for Ringo's wedding to actress Barbara Bach in 1980. From left, George and Olivia Harrison; Ringo and his new bride; Paul, Linda and James McCartney, the youngest of the McCartney brood; and Gianni, Barbara Bach's eight-year-old son from a previous marriage. (*Beat Publications, Ltd.*)

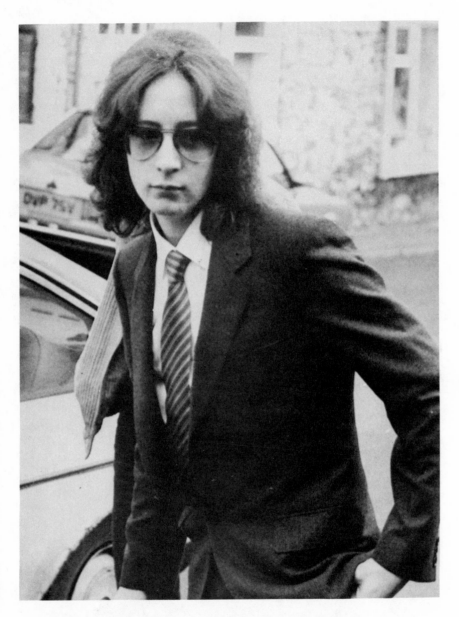

Julian in 1982 leaving a court in Ruthin, North Wales, where
he admitted to the Forestry Commission that he had caused
£10 damage by burning some wooden stakes at a birthday
party. "There were times when I wish I had been born Joe
Average," he was quoted as saying. (*Transworld Features
Syndicate, Inc.*)

The chic, skinny widow, Yoko Ono, accepts a cultural award from New York City on John's behalf. To her right is Mayor Ed Koch. (*United Press International Photo*)

Chapter Fifteen

I was used to a situation where the newspaper was there for me to read, and after I'd read it, somebody else could have it. . . . I think that's what kills people like Presley and others of that ilk. . . . The king is always killed by his courtiers, not by his enemies. The king is overfed, overdrugged, overindulged, anything to keep the king tied to his throne. Most people in that position never wake up. They either die mentally or physically or both. And what Yoko did for me, apart from liberating me to be a feminist, was to liberate me from that situation. And that's how the Beatles ended. Not because Yoko split the Beatles, but because she showed me what it was to be Elvis Beatle and to be surrounded by sycophants and slaves who are only interested in keeping the situation as it was. And that's a kind of death.

—John Lennon
Newsweek, October, 1980

1.

*T*HAT MAY, when the Beatles met again with George Martin at the Abbey Road studios to record the material they had accumulated in India, they discovered an unexpected presence in their midst: Yoko Ono.

Yoko was at John's side at all times. Literally at his side, as if she had been surgically attached to him. It was bizarre to see, this small figure with all the wild hair, dressed in black, sitting, standing, walking next to John, peeking out from just under the neck of his guitar as he played. At first we thought Yoko would leave when the album's work began in earnest, but it soon became clear that John intended for her to stay.

This was more than unusual; it was in defiance of one of the Beatles' most carefully kept covenants; nobody was allowed in the studio while they were working, save for Neil and Mal. When Dick James showed up at the studio, he was politely asked to leave. Even Brian was encouraged to get his business over with and get out. Once, when Brian brought with him a young man he wanted to impress, he made a musical suggestion to John over the intercom from the control room. John shot back, "You stick to your percentages, Brian. We'll look after the music."

Yoko might have been more tolerated if she had kept a discreet distance, but instead she was in the middle of everything. If she had an opinion about their music, she offered it. Not just once, but insistently. She spoke with the conviction of the ignorant, because she knew nothing about rock music, and it galled them. One night the Beatles were reminiscing about a concert at Shea Stadium, and Yoko asked what the boys were doing at a baseball stadium. When told they had sold out Shea Stadium, twice, Yoko said, "That was 1966? Well, that year I gave a concert in . . ." Her story was greeted with stony silence.

At first Paul tried to understand about Yoko and not make a big crisis about it. Paul was a showman, and the album came first. But Yoko wore him down. He and the others soon lost their patience, and the hostility poured out. To her face they were sarcastic and cold; behind her back they called her the "Jap Flavor of the Month" and made jokes about her vagina being slanted like her eyes. When someone asked Neil if he had forgotten to shave or was he growing a moustache, Neil said, "We're all trying to grow one, even Yoko." There was also some conjecture as to why Yoko followed John into the men's toilet every time he went. It was assumed she assisted him in his chore.

Ringo even went to see John at Weybridge. "Listen, John, does Yoko have to be there *all the time?*" he asked.

"You just don't understand," John told him. "It's different with Yoko and me."

For John, each nasty crack about Yoko was like the thrust of a knife in his back. The omnipotent northern men were clearly threatened by this small woman and closed off to her. As far as John was concerned, it was completely their loss; for in the past few weeks together with Yoko, she had given John more alternatives in his life than the Beatles had in eight years. She revitalized his rebellious nature, awoke in him the stirrings of the artist he once wanted to be in Liverpool Art College. She confirmed to him the hollowness of being a pop star. Life with Yoko was like living one of her instructional poems—whimsical, silly, often provocative. Yes, he misused her to rile the other Beatles, but she was much more important to him than they could ever realize. She was his staff, his strength, his new lease on life. What John and Yoko were developing between them was a love of classic proportions, a legend as big as the Beatles themselves.

In early May, with Cynthia still tucked safely away in Pisaro, John brought Yoko out of the background and into the public eye. They staged their first art exhibition together at the Drury Lane Arts Lab consisting of wooden "objects to be taken apart or added to," which were speedily disassembled and carted off by the public. Later in the month Yoko attended a press conference with him to publicize the opening of Apple Tailoring, and on June 18 she attended the opening of *In His Own Write,* John's book of doodles and drawings that had miraculously been adapted and directed for the stage by John's friend, actor Victor Spinetti.* *In His Own Write* was opening the summer season at the National Theatre.

The Fleet Street press had been aware of Yoko's presence but not of her importance. Since he was ostensibly a married man, Yoko had not been photographed or publicized. But by the night of his opening at the National Theatre, the press's curiosity had peaked. As John and Yoko stepped from John's Rolls, followed by Neil Aspinall, the flash cameras exploded around them.

"Where's your wife?" a reporter shouted. "Where's Cynthia?"

John was so stunned he was speechless; it never crossed his mind that he would be challenged in his love for this woman or even called upon to explain it. He assumed Yoko would be remarked upon by the press but not challenged. Again came the question. "Where's Cynthia?" "Where's your wife?" "What happened to your wife, John?"

"I don't know!" John exploded, pressing his way into the theater.

On June 15 they appeared together at Coventry Cathedral at an exhibit of recent British sculpture. Yoko had managed to wangle an invitation to participate in the exhibit. Yoko and John's idea was for a "living sculpture," the ceremonial implantation

---

* John had met with Sir Laurence Olivier, then the director of the National Theatre, but John turned up at the meeting tripping on LSD and Olivier couldn't figure out a word he was saying. The project was summarily turned over to Victor Spinetti.

of two acorns, over which they would place a brass plaque declaring, " 'John' by Yoko Ono, 'Yoko' by John Lennon." When they arrived at the cathedral for the acorn-planting ceremony, they were met by Canon Verney. "Unfortunately," the canon told them, "the cathedral authorities have decided they cannot permit you to put your work in the main exhibition area, as it is on consecrated ground." The canon didn't consider acorns real sculpture in any event.

Yoko turned into a sputtering little volcano of rage. She launched into a red-faced harangue, insisting that all the leading sculptors in England be telephoned to testify to the validity of her acorn idea. She actually got through to Henry Moore's house, but fortunately for the great sculptor he was out at the moment. A compromise was finally reached when permission was granted to plant the acorns on a lawn *near* the cathedral where new-generation sculptors were being displayed. A week later the acorns were dug up and stolen in the night. John and Yoko sent a second set, and a security guard was hired to stand watch over them for the duration of the show.

On July 1 John made a public declaration of his love with an art exhibition he sponsored entitled "You Are Here," dedicated "To Yoko, from John, with love." A gala celebration was held for the opening at the Robert Fraser gallery off Oxford Street, with all the major art critics and Fleet Street regulars in attendance. John and Yoko arrived dressed all in white, the beginning of their color-coordinated phase. John wore a wide-lapeled Tommy Nutter shirt and suit, his hair crookedly parted down the middle of his head; Yoko wore a matching bell-bottom trouser and tunic outfit. They grinned at the guests and reporters like two cats fresh from swallowing canaries.

I remember wandering through the exhibit wondering, "What in blazes could John have been thinking?" The show was an exhibition of collection boxes: charity boxes for the blind, the spastics, the preservation of donkeys, for birds, and for lepers. A mechanical dog, when fed a sixpence, barked, wagged his tail, and lifted his leg. The only vaguely original piece of art in the gallery was a white circle six feet in diameter in the center of which was carefully printed, "You Are Here." The event was also being videotaped and shown on a TV monitor as it happened. Art students from the Hornsey College of Art who attended the opening were so disgusted with the exhibit they delivered a rusty bicycle to the Fraser Gallery with a tag explaining, "This exhibit was inadvertently left out." John put the bike on display with the rest and left a pair of shoes in front of it with a note, "I take my shoes off to you."

The climax of the opening was the release of 365 white helium-filled balloons that were launched into the London sky. Each balloon carried a tag reading, "You Are Here, please write to John Lennon care of the Robert Fraser Gallery."

The reviews and press coverage of the exhibit were more savage than the reviews for *Magical Mystery Tour* but no worse than the hundreds of letters from people who found the white balloons. Most of them contained seething racial epithets against the Japanese woman who had suddenly appeared at their hero's side. What was this nonsense about acorns and collection boxes and balloons? everyone wondered. The public sentiment was, *Bring back the old Lennon!* Most of all, everybody wanted to know, *What happened to Cynthia and Julian?*

It was the beginning of a 180-degree turnaround for John, from favorite son to an object of derision and controversy. "I suppose the trouble is I've spoiled my image," John told a journalist. "People want me to stay in their own bag. They just want me to be lovable. But I was never that. Even at school I was just 'Lennon.' Nobody ever thought of me as cuddly!"

In Pisaro, at the Cruiser Hotel, Cynthia saw the photographs of John and Yoko together in the British press and tumbled into a black well of depression. She took to bed in her hotel room and stayed there for days, not eating or sleeping. It wasn't until the beginning of the second week that her mother talked her into leaving the hotel to have dinner. She was accompanied by Roberto Bassanini, the attentive son of the hotel owners, and a waitress from the resort who had befriended her. Bassanini had on an earlier trip to Pisaro rescued little Julian from a mob on the beach that had wanted to touch the "Beatle bambino." Cynthia's first night out she threw herself headlong into the task of drowning her sorrows. Cynthia and Bassanini and the waitress went from club to club, drinking until the small hours of the morning, not returning to the hotel until sun-up, laughing as they came down the street.

Magic Alex was waiting on the pavement in front of the hotel.

He had arrived earlier in the evening expecting to find a spurned and disconsolate wife and had learned that Cynthia was out on the town with an eligible bachelor. He told Cynthia that John would be very interested to learn this. John had sent Magic Alex with an ultimatum; he wanted a divorce so he could marry Yoko Ono, and if Cynthia didn't cooperate and made a fuss, he would take Julian away from her and ship her back to Liverpool.

"Suing *me* for divorce!" she shouted. "On what grounds is he suing me?"

"John is claiming adultery," Magic Alex said coolly. "I have agreed to be corespondent and testify on John's behalf." Alex pointed out he had slept with her, after all, and now, after catching her coming back to the hotel at dawn with Roberto Bassanini, Alex wasn't so sure he was the only one.

Cynthia rushed back to London to try to explain to John about Magic Alex, but it was two weeks before she could get in to see him, and then they weren't alone. John insisted Yoko be present during this difficult husband and wife confrontation. While Cynthia choked back tears, mostly at the humiliation of having to discuss the matter in front of Yoko, she tried to explain that Magic Alex had bewitched her with candles and black magic, just as he had hypnotized the American nurse in Rishekesh to lie about the Maharishi. John simply reiterated the terms of the divorce; there was bound to be a lot of bad publicity, and Cynthia should keep her mouth shut and let him claim adultery. He would give her a small settlement and let her go her way. Their meeting ended when John excused himself to go to the bathroom, and Yoko followed him out of the room.

Cynthia kept her mouth shut and let John sue her. I was asked by John to arrange the terms of the divorce. Everything was proceeding smoothly when in early September John confided to me that Yoko was pregnant with his child. I advised him that this should be kept top secret from the press for the moment, but I also explained that with Yoko pregnant, it would make it rather ludicrous for John to pursue his adultery charges against Cynthia. Thus, John's charges against Cynthia were dropped, and Cynthia was allowed to turn the tables and sue John for divorce. It gave her no pleasure. I've rarely seen anyone as distraught. Cynthia was granted a "decree nisi" in November of 1968, which became final six months later. She accepted a settlement of only £100,000, of which she had to use £25,000 to buy a home for herself and Julian and her mother to live in.

Cynthia was amputated from the Beatles and their families with ruthless speed and precision. Few Beatles employees or friends dared to show her support or speak out against Yoko, lest the wrath of John Lennon fall on them. I had tremendous sympathy for Cynthia, but although I was unhappy about the way John was handling it, I knew it was best for both of them. Arranging the divorce was an unpleasant task. The only Liverpool chum who was able to give Cynthia any real support or sympathy was Paul. He drove out to Weybridge in his Aston Martin to visit her and Julian. On the way he made up a song to cheer the little boy. It went, "Hey Julian, it's not so bad. / Take a sad song, and make it better." This was, of course, to become one of the Beatles' greatest hits of all time, "Hey Jude."

Cynthia's best friends became strangers to her now. She bought a house in Kensington and spent a lonely summer packing and moving out of Weybridge. Months later she tried to give a dinner party in her new home for the people with whom she had shared so unique an experience, but her guests were so uncomfortable the party was a disaster. We rarely heard from her until she married Roberto Bassanini on July 31, 1970. Cynthia and Bassanini opened a London restaurant, but it was not very successful. Nor was their marriage. She divorced Bassanini in 1974 and moved to Ruthin, North Wales. Four years later she married restauranteur John Twist, and they opened a small restaurant and inn in Ruthin. Two years later she divorced Twist. She would always believe, up until John's death, that one day they would be back together again.

Just as I was finished arranging the terms of John's divorce from Cynthia, I was asked to arrange the terms of Yoko's divorce from Tony Cox. Charles Levinson, a London lawyer, handled the divorce for us, although most of the negotiations were done in my office at Apple, where John, Yoko, Cox, and the lawyers met amiably to discuss the settlement. John agreed to pay all the joint debts of Yoko and Cox, which came to approximately $100,000. This included back rent, bills from various film labs, and the repayment of personal loans. John also agreed to pay for the cost of the divorce, which included moving Cox to the Virgin Islands, where he could establish residency.

In return, Yoko and Cox's child, Kyoko, was to be remanded to Yoko's custody at will.

Months before John and Cynthia had picked out a black £6,000 Italian Revolto automobile at an auto show. When it was delivered, John had it sent to Magic Alex as a token of his appreciation for his troubles. Magic Alex remained a close friend to John for a while—for as long as Yoko let him.

For several months John and Yoko lived out of suitcases, like homeless waifs. "We were shoved around a bit," Yoko says. "We were basically two illicit lovers without anyplace to go." They spent a few days at Paul's house on Cavendish Avenue, but Paul's presence loomed too large for them. They passed a night or two at my flat and then went on to Neil Aspinall's for a week. Eventually, they ended up in Ringo's old flat, the vacant basement apartment on Montague Square.

It was at Montague Square, feeling more than a little bruised and already like outlaws, Yoko says, that they began to take heroin. As Yoko later put it, they took heroin "as a celebration of ourselves as artists." "Of course," Yoko says, "George says it was *me* who put John on heroin, but that wasn't true. John wouldn't take anything he didn't want to take." Still, many of John's intimates saw heroin as the way Yoko could gain complete control over John. If there was one single element that was the most crucial in the breakup of the Beatles, it was John's heroin addiction.

"John was very curious," Yoko explained. "He asked if I had ever tried it. I told him that while he was in India with the Maharishi, I had a sniff of it in a party situation. I didn't know what it was. They just gave me something and I said 'What was that!?' It was a beautiful feeling. John was talking about heroin one day and he said, 'Did you ever take it?' and I told him about Paris. I said it wasn't bad. I think because the amount was small I didn't even get sick. It was just a nice feeling. So I told him that. When you take it—'properly' isn't the right word—but when you do a little more, you get sick right away if you're not used to it. So I think maybe because I said it wasn't a bad experience, that had something to do with John taking it."

Whatever it had to do with, it wasn't a passing fancy, and before long they were hooked. They lay in the basement of Montague Square almost all July that simmering summer, submerged in a self-inflicted stupor.

* * *

2.

*J*UST AS JOHN was taking up with Yoko Ono, Paul McCartney's five-year romance with Jane Asher was coming to an end. Jane was back at work again, much to Paul's chagrin, this time touring Great Britain with the Bristol Old Vic. Paul very obviously always needed to be with a woman, and when he wasn't you could see the unhappiness in his face. In fact, when Paul first played "Hey Jude" for John in the studio without telling him he had written the song for Julian, John mistakenly thought that Paul was writing about the end of his romance with Jane. "Hey," John thought, "he's going through the same thing as I am."

On May 12 Paul and John went to New York to join me and other officers of Apple to officially announce its inception. The trip was basically a five-day publicity blitz arranged by the public relations firm of Solters and Roskin. It included a press conference; a meeting of the board of directors of Apple, which I chaired aboard a Chinese junk in Manhattan harbor; a photo-layout in *Life* magazine; and an appearance on the "Tonight Show," with an estimated audience of 25 million.

John and Paul were disappointed to learn that Johnny Carson, the show's regular host, was being substituted for by retired baseball player Joe Garagiola. Garagiola was a pleasant, straightforward guy who was obviously pleased to have the Beatles on his show, but just as obviously confused as to what they were talking about. They explained to him in earnest their plans for Apple. "It's a controlled weirdness," Paul said, "a kind of western communism. We want to help people but without doing it like a charity. We always had to go to the big men on our knees and touch our forelocks and say, 'Please, can we do so and so . . . ?' We're in the happy position of not needing any more money, so for the first time the bosses aren't in it for a profit. If you come to me and say, 'I've had such and such a dream,' I'll say to you, 'Go away and do it.' "

Garagiola grinned at them. He continued to grin as John went on, "The aim isn't just a stack of gold teeth in the bank. We've done that bit. It's more of a trick to see if we can get artistic freedom within a business structure—to see if we can create things and sell them without charging five times our cost."

All across America, the word went out. Every dreamer, every crook, rip-off artist, and sham entrepreneur understood just one thing: The Beatles were so rich they were giving away money. All you had to do was come to them with a plan, and they'd say, "Go away and do it!" John and Paul had no idea what they had unleashed that night.

After the show Paul McCartney went off by himself to meet Linda Eastman. Linda had appeared earlier in the day at the Apple press conference and had boldly slipped Paul her phone number. He called her later and made plans to see her that night, but he was afraid they would be photographed together if she came to his hotel suite at the St. Regis, and Jane Asher would see the photos. Instead, he arranged to meet Linda at Nat Weiss' East Side apartment, where they spent the next few days together.* One night when Paul told her how fond he was of children, Linda produced her daughter Heather, then six years old. Paul happily babysat for the child while her mother went off to photograph a rock act at the Fillmore. When Paul returned to London later that week, Linda sent him a huge blow-up of himself, lips pursed, on top of which she had superimposed a photo of Heather kissing him.

A few weeks later Paul was back in America, accompanied by Ron Kass. This trip was made expressly for him to speak at a record convention for Capitol Records in Los Angeles. Paul was the only Beatle who would consider addressing a business meeting attended by beer-bellied rack jobbers in polyester leisure suits, but Paul knew the value of good public relations. He also wanted his "western communism" to work, and he knew that as far as Apple Records went, the Capitol distributors were in a position to help him do it. Much to Ron Kass' amusement, Paul spent the day glad-handing distributors and signing autographs for their children back home. He did everything except hand out cigars.

But all work and no play makes Paul a dull boy, and he found plenty of time to amuse himself in a bungalow of the Beverly

---

* They signed the door of the bedroom they occupied. That door now hangs on a wall in Nat's apartment.

Hills Hotel. He staged that weekend what Ron Kass called "The Paul McCartney Black and White Minstrel Show." In one bedroom Paul installed a beautiful young Hollywood starlet. In the other bedroom he kept one of L.A.'s most famous black call girls. Kass, who was sharing the three-bedroom bungalow with Paul, got to watch his juggling act. He spent the weekend making trips from one bedroom to the other, stopping only to sign room-service bills. On Sunday morning a ringing telephone interrupted the proceedings. It was Linda Eastman. She had flown to California at her own expense and was at that moment in the hotel lobby, speaking to Paul from the house phone.

Paul didn't skip a beat. He told her to come right on over to the bungalow. She appeared at the door a few minutes later, and Paul brought her right into the sitting room. He knocked on the door of each occupied bedroom and told the girls to dress and split. He and Linda chatted away nonchalantly on the sofa while the Black and White Minstrel Show packed and left in tears. Linda and Paul couldn't have treated the situation more casually. They seemed just as blasé when Peggy Lipton, an American actress who at the time was filming the popular TV series *Mod Squad*, appeared unannounced on the doorstep of the bungalow to make a declaration of love for Paul. Paul explained he was busy and shut the door in her face. Linda spent the night, and the next day Paul took her sailing with him on the yacht of John Calley, then head of production at Warner Brothers.

It was also Linda Eastman who accompanied Ron Kass and Paul back to New York and brought with her a bag filled with marijuana. This was the first of many of Linda's pot follies, which would lead to numerous ugly scrapes with the law. Marijuana, it turned out, was one of Linda's favorite vices. Ron Kass became aware of this while the three of them were waiting in the VIP Ambassador Lounge at the Los Angeles International airport. It was announced over the public address system that because of a bomb threat all carry-on luggage would have to be searched.

Kass immediately turned to Paul and said, "Do you have anything in your bag that would embarrass us?" Paul shook his head. Then Kass turned to Linda Eastman. She seemed surprisingly complacent as she informed him that she had "a couple of kilos" in a Gucci bag sitting at her feet.

Kass went to the airlines supervisor and complained that

searching Paul McCartney and his friend in public would cause them great embarrassment. Certainly they didn't think Paul McCartney was carrying a bomb and could an exception be made? The officials were adamant; everyone would have to be thoroughly searched. However, to avoid embarrassment, Paul and Linda could be searched in a private office. When Kass went back to the Ambassador Lounge to collect them, he kicked the Gucci bag underneath a long row of plastic turquoise chairs and left it there. It went unnoticed during the general search. After Paul, Linda, and Kass were politely searched, Linda retrieved the bag and carried it on the plane. Kass was so furious with her he couldn't wait until they got rid of her in New York before he and Paul caught a flight home to London.

When Paul arrived home, Linda mounted a transatlantic campaign of phone calls and letters, but there was little any girl could do to keep his attention three thousand miles away.

Still, Paul pined for Jane, wishing she would come home from tour, yet he managed to keep himself distracted. One day that summer an American girl from New Jersey named Francie Schwartz turned up at the Apple office. She wore jeans, no makeup, and her hair needed to be washed, according to Barbara Bennett, the secretary who was at the reception desk at the time. Just like a thousand other girls, she had a letter and a script she wanted Paul McCartney to read. Barbara usually sent these girls on their way, but in some unexplained gesture of kindness, she told Francie Schwartz to come back in the afternoon when Paul was in.

The girl who returned to the office several hours later was completely transformed from the ragamuffin who had come through the door earlier. Francie had spent the day buying a dress and having her hair done. Barbara Bennett introduced her to Paul, who took her into his office. Later they went out for cocktails and dinner, and then she spent the night at St. John's Wood. Within the week Paul requested that Francie be given a job at Apple, and amidst much resentment she was installed at a corner desk in the publicity department. Three weeks went by as Francie served no special purpose other than being Paul's bird. It seemed she was firmly ensconced in the house on Cavendish Avenue. Until one night Jane came home unexpectedly.

The regular crew of groupies who stood in front of Paul's

house when he was in residence tried to warn him over the house intercom, but he thought they were playing a joke on him when they told him that Jane had returned from her tour and was letting herself in with her key. Just as had happened to Cynthia before her, Jane discovered another woman in her bathrobe. Jane stormed out of the house a few moments later and drove off in her car. Mrs. Asher arrived later that night to pick up Jane's clothing, dishes, and pots and pans.

Although Paul and Jane were seen together once or twice after that, and Paul dutifully attended the opening night of her new play at the Fortune Theatre so that questions concerning his absence would not detract from the happiness of the evening for her, they were finished. A month later the public learned of this when Jane casually mentioned on the BBC's "Simon Dee Show" that their engagement had been broken—by Paul.

Jane rarely saw or spoke to Paul again. As the years went by, she began to resent fiercely her public association with him and refused to discuss the subject in interviews. Today she is one of England's most highly regarded actresses. She is married to political cartoonist Gerald Scarfe, and they and their son and daughter live in London.*

Francie Schwartz was soon sent on her way. Back in America she wrote a book about her short affair with Paul, called *Body Count,* which was published by the Rolling Stone Press.

Linda Eastman kept the calls and letters coming. In early autumn Paul invited her to London to see the house at 7 Cavendish Avenue, and she never left.

---

* When Jane walked out on Paul, he came into the office the next day determined to have Peter Asher fired in retribution. Ron Kass was able to talk him out of it. The following year, on May 2, 1969, Dr. Richard Asher was found dead in the basement of his Wimpole Street home after being missing for six days. The police found Dr. Asher lying on the cellar floor with half a bottle of whisky by his right hand. Dr. Asher had recently suffered some professional setbacks. The cause of death was attributed to a mixture of alcohol and barbiturates.

* * *

3.

*A*S THE CASH FLOW reports crossed my desk, it became apparent that the Apple Boutique had turned into an enormous drain of money. In seven months the operation of the boutique lost nearly £200,000. Everything about it seemed to be a disaster of poor planning and incompetence. The Beatles and The Fool had since parted acrimoniously. The previous January, John Lyndon, who replaced Pete Shotton as the manager of the boutique, sent angry letters to The Fool and their management threatening to bar them from the shop if they removed any more garments from the premises or charged any further debts to Apple. The Beatles, who felt justified in taking legal action, dropped the whole matter quietly so as to avoid public embarrassment. The Fool subsequently moved to America and signed a recording contract with Mercury Records as a singing group. They were never heard from again.

The local citizens committee had succeeded in having the garish mural that graced the walls of the boutique scrubbed off. The customers seemed to be there only to shoplift or to stare at Jenny Boyd, Pattie's sister, who was working there as a salesperson along with a self-styled mystic named Caleb. Caleb slept underneath a showcase during one of his many breaks. The store was also sometimes tended by a fat lady who dressed in authentic gypsy costumes. The inflatable furniture with the exaggerated price tags now sagged in the corners, the Hobbit clothing, a nostalgic reminder of the previous summer's fashions, hung unpurchased on the racks. In the large stockroom on the floor above stood row upon row of unopened bolts of raw silks and lush velvet fabrics that had been ordered by The Fool. In the basement, hundreds of Nothing Boxes constructed by Magic Alex waited in the darkness, having blinked themselves to death.

The final blow came when the boutique caused them to be publicly embarrassed and derided. A newspaper column criticized the Beatles for having turned into shopkeepers. This infuriated John and Paul so much they decided to close the store without delay. Characteristically, they decided to liquidate the stock, not through sale but by giving it away. I was told that John and Paul had decided that on Wednesday, July 31, the entire contents of the store and stockrooms was to be opened to the public, who could take whatever they wanted.

The Monday night before the giveaway, Yoko Ono and John arrived at the shop. Before the amazed employees, Yoko spread large swatches of fabric out on the floor and began to pile merchandise into it waist high. Then she knotted the corners of the fabric hobo-style and dragged it out of the store on her back, like an Oriental Santa Claus, into John's Rolls-Royce.

The morning of the giveaway, which had been well publicized in newspapers and on TV, there was a queue three blocks long. The basement door was opened so that people could walk in the front way, wander around, and then exit from the other end. According to the Beatles' strict instructions, there was to be no restriction on the amount any one person could take. As much as you could carry was the rule. Rack after rack of Hobbit clothing was brought down and fed to the ravenous public. People got back on line two and three times, snatching at articles like sharks at a frenzied feeding. When all the merchandise was gone, the bolts of raw silks and velvets were torn apart by the crowds. They took the hangers and the store fixtures, too, and no one stopped them until one woman tried to pry the carpeting off the floor. By noon it was all over.

Less than a month later, Apple Corp. moved into new headquarters more befitting its grandiose intentions. The Beatles purchased, at a cost of nearly £500,000, a beautiful five-story Georgian town house at 3 Savile Row, in the heart of the custom tailoring district. This imposing brick structure was once a popular gambling club called the Albany and was rumored to have been the sometime love nest of Lady Hamilton and Lord Nelson. Gamblers and lovers that the Beatles were, they set about transforming the building into their new home.

Each executive was given his own spacious office and allowed to decorate it. On the first floor, just off the glittering mirrored reception foyer, Ron Kass had a gleaming white office with a white desk and liquor cabinet and white leather Wasirly chairs. On the second floor, up a flight of apple-green carpeted steps, was a large office for the Beatles and Neil, overlooking Savile Row. This office was never completely decorated, for as was the Beatles' wont, they changed their minds so many times about what it should look like they never made any progress. I remember that only a short time after wall-to-wall carpeting was installed, they had it pulled up and the wood-plank floors polished. On the third floor was the press office, now presided over by Derek Taylor. My own office was across from the Beatles, on the second floor rear. It was a huge rectangular office with elaborate, handsome moldings around the ceiling. In lieu of a chandelier, Ringo had given me a huge lighting fixture of chrome headlights, designed by a firm he had invested in. At one end was a marble fireplace and four comfortable armchairs, and at the far side of the room there was a large, octagonal rosewood table. It was around this table that the dissolution of the Beatles would occur, as well as hundreds of other unhappy meetings over the next two years. On the higher floors were the A&R offices, a film department, accounting offices, music publishing, a film library, and an office for office management, headed by ever-loyal Alistair Taylor. In the deep basement Magic Alex set to work with a construction crew to build the Beatles' own private studios, complete with, he promised, 78-track recording.

There was also, for executive use, a stately wrought-iron lift, and on the third floor, a well-appointed kitchen and pantry stocked with everything from bacon butties to caviar. Two Cordon Bleu chefs prepared an endless array of dishes all hours of the day, including ham and eggs for Ringo and roast leg of lamb for business lunches. The front of the building was sandblasted and whitewashed, and a flagpole was installed so that it looked like an embassy. A full-time footman-bouncer was hired and dressed in a Tommy Nutter frock coat. On the front steps, in every possible kind of weather and at any time of day, waited four girls the Beatles nicknamed the Apple Scruffs and whom George later immortalized in song. They stood vigil on those front steps as the weirdos and wackies of the world descended upon us.

In addition to John's and Paul's incautious proclamation on the "Tonight Show" in America soliciting projects for Apple, a poster and newspaper campaign appeared that summer asking aspiring artists to bring their wares to Apple. Alistair Taylor was recruited to appear in the advertisement costumed like a "busker" or street musician. He was pictured playing a guitar with a harmonica braced to his mouth, a drum hanging from his back, and a washboard glued to his foot. The headline announced, THIS MAN

HAD TALENT. The copy read, "One day he sang his songs to a tape recorder (borrowed from the man next door) . . . sent the tape, letter and photograph . . . if you were thinking of doing the same thing yourself, DO IT NOW! This man now owns a BENTLEY!"

Lots of people wanted Bentleys, it turned out, and most of them appeared at 3 Savile Row.

The list of people with schemes and plots and plans is as long as it is sometimes astonishing. There was an American man who wanted the Beatles to purchase anonymously six square miles of Arizona land to hold a three-week rock and roll orgy attended by three million people to climax in a live performance by the Beatles. There was a man with a formula for a pill that could make you into whomever you wanted to be. There were several messiahs and one or two prophets of doom. There was a plan to save whales and a plan to build a commune in India. There was a woman who made tactile art from patent leather covered in oil. There were people who had seen flying saucers and God and needed money to go up, or down, or around in circles. Often they were stopped at Heathrow airport for having no money or passports, and they simply gave John Lennon's or Paul McCartney's name as their sponsor. A family of psychedelized California hippies virtually moved into the Apple building, en route, they said, to the Fiji Islands, and they needed John's aid in setting up a commune. The mother, a fortyish woman named Emily, would blithely breast feed her youngest in the reception room, while a half dozen other totally naked children ran from office to office. The proposals and schemes sent to the office could fill a volume in themselves. They were piled into stacks in a storage closet nicknamed the Black Room, where they threatened to bury anyone who got near them.

If there was a source of energy at 3 Savile Row, it was Derek Taylor. In some ways Derek was the most brilliant choice of all the department heads, and in other ways he was the worst. On the good side, he was one of the few people who could plausibly and concisely encapsulate the purpose and idealism of Apple Corp. Derek believed in the Beatles' good intentions, and his enthusiasm was infectious. He was also blessed with the gift of charm, wit, and imagination. But Derek, at the time, was also a man with a great capacity for alcohol and drugs. As a kind of inebriated, psychedelic visionary, he was the dispenser of Apple's good vibes, and it became Derek Taylor and his brand of inspired lunacy the world saw as Apple's best foot forward. It was hardly the best foot. From his second-floor office, Derek encouraged a kind of benevolent anarchy to develop. Derek's specific responsibility was to deal with the press, enough of a chore in itself; but since no one in the organization could really deal with the collection of freaks who turned up in the entrance hallway, Derek took it upon himself to screen these people, too. He sat behind a large desk in a fantail wicker chair, cigarette or joint in hand, scotch and Coke before him, greeting a never-ending stream of visitors. The office shades were always drawn, and the majority of light was contributed by a light show of a giant amoeba projected on the wall.

Derek had all the screwballs. When someone came into the building announcing he was Adolf Hitler, Derek might invite him up for a drink and ask about Eva's health. Someone, or something, nicknamed "Stocky" was allowed to sit on the file cabinets all day and draw pictures of genitalia. The receptionist at the front desk didn't even blink when one day a young donkey named Samantha was walked into the lift and sent up to Derek's office. Derek and I only now remember the persistent phone calls from someone named Squeaky Fromme in Los Angeles to talk to us about Charles Manson. I took many of those phone calls or transferred them over to Derek. Derek's bushy-haired assistant, a young American lad named Richard DeLillo, began squirreling away notes and clippings about the Apple madness for an hysterically funny book called, quite appropriately, *The Longest Cocktail Party*.

And a party it was. The kitchen was kept busy preparing snacks and elaborate lunches. A fifteen-day tally of the supplies for Derek's office alone included 600 packs of Benson and Hedges cigarettes, four bottles of Courvoisier brandy, three bottles of vodka, two dozen of ginger ale, one dozen of tonic water, two dozen of bitter lemon, one dozen of tomato juice, three bottles of lime, and four cases of lager. The office manager, Alistair Taylor, noted with relief that the provision list had decreased; the previous one had included two cases of J&B Scotch. The liquor bill eventually peaked at £600 pounds a month.

At the beginning of Apple's inception on Savile Row, the Beatles took great interest in the company, particularly Paul who acted like a kid with an expensive set of new trains. The first few months he arrived at the office bright and early every morning and went over details of running the company, including whether there was enough toilet paper in the bathroom. His personal pride and joy, however, was the record division. Paul insisted that the company be a class production. Ron Kass struck a distribution deal with EMI in Great Britain. EMI was not particularly happy when he informed them the Beatles intended to start their own record label. At the time the Beatles were still being distributed on the Parlophone label in Great Britain, a label that existed virtually for their benefit. For EMI to let them out of their contracts to distribute the Beatles on their own label was of no value, and they were reluctant to change the structure without a fight. To put pressure on them, Kass threatened to sign Apple in American distribution to a company other than the EMI-owned Capitol label. In the end the EMI executives gave in and signed a new agreement to release Apple records worldwide. Kass's next task was to buy back George Harrison's publishing in America, which had been sold off to Terry Melchior by an inexperienced Terry Doran.

Audition tapes for Apple Records arrived by the tens of thousands at Savile Row, so many that Ron Kass estimated that five men in five years couldn't finish listening to them all. In general, the prevailing attitude at Apple Records was "Sign 'em up!" With the newfound power of being starmakers themselves, almost everybody in the entourage believed he had "discovered" the next major pop star. Terry Doran signed a group of teenagers called Grapefruit, who set about recording an album; Mal Evans discovered the Iveys, who were signed on the basis of a demonstration tape and sent into the studios; George signed Jackie Lomax, a singer from Liverpool, the singers of the Hare Krishna Temple, a husky-voiced black American R&B singer named Doris Troy, and noted session keyboard player Billy Preston; a Swedish group called Bamboo was flown to London for a live audition; John gave a contract to a group called Contact, who sang a tune called "Lovers From the Sky" about flying saucers. To give the Apple label "broader appeal," Paul signed the winners of the English brass-band competition, The Black Dyke Mills Brass Band, and the prestigious Modern Jazz Quartet. A "spoken word" series was created to record famous writers and poets reading their own works, and Ken Kesey, the American writer who had in part inspired Paul's conception of the *Magical Mystery Tour,* was imported to London and given a typewriter and a recording contract.

Some of Apple's discoveries were especially promising. Peter Asher had signed a young American boy named James Taylor. Taylor played acoustical guitar and sang bittersweet love songs with a world-weary resignation, although at the time he was so young his father had to cosign his contracts. Asher believed so strongly in Taylor that he wanted to manage him too. The only reluctance in awarding Taylor a contract was that his sporadic heroin use was not a promising addiction for a young musician. Taylor was eventually signed and sent to the studios to record a single, "Carolina on My Mind," and later he made an LP. Paul also had high hopes for a seventeen-year-old Welsh singer named Mary Hopkin. Hopkin had been brought to Paul's attention by the model Twiggy as the three-time winner of a TV talent show called "Opportunity Knocks." Paul was producing a single with Hopkin called "Those Were the Days," a folk-rock song with an eastern European flavor, written by songwriter Gene Raskin. "Those Were the Days" was being included in a specially boxed introductory set of new Apple releases called *The First Four.* A copy of *The First Four* was dutifully delivered by hand to Buckingham Palace. The other tunes were a George Harrison composition entitled "Sour Milk Sea," sung by Jackie Lomax, and the Black Dyke Mills Band playing a Lennon-McCartney composition called "Thingumybob."

The Beatles' personal contribution to *The First Four* was the single "Hey Jude," backed with John's "Revolution." "Hey Jude" had turned into a pop epic. Beginning with Paul's plaintive voice against simple instrumentation, it built to a melancholy anthem of forty instruments and a chorus of one hundred voices chanting a four-minute coda. To help publicize the release of "Hey Jude," Paul decided to put the closed boutique at Baker and Paddington Streets to some good use. Late one night he snuck into the store and whitewashed the windows. Then he wrote HEY JUDE across it in block letters. The following morning, when the neighborhood shopkeepers arrived to open their stores, they were incensed; never having heard of the song "Hey Juden" before, they took it as an anti-Semitic slur. A brick was thrown through the store window before the words could be cleaned off and the misunderstanding straightened out.

As it turned out, Paul need not have worried about such a small publicity gimmick; "Hey Jude" became one of the biggest selling singles in England in twenty years. Mary Hopkin's "Those Were the Days" sold almost as well, and throughout the summer both songs fought for the top spot on the record charts, selling a combined thirteen million copies in all.

In its own right, the Beatles new double album was no less successful. Entitled *The Beatles,* the album became known to the public as the *White Album,* because of its stark, glossy-white laminated jacket, with the words, "The Beatles," in almost invisible raised lettering. It was Paul's idea to have each album individually numbered, like fine lithographs. And indeed, the *White Album* was a work of art. The thirty songs on the two-record set took them an unprecedented five months to record and mix. The critics were ecstatic at the huge selection and diversity of taste on the LP, ranging from John's "Revolution 9," a taste of his experimental tapes with a strong influence from Yoko, to Paul's pudding-sweet "Ob-la-di, Ob-la-da." Tony Palmer, in the *London Observer,* raved, "If there is still any doubt that Lennon and McCartney are the greatest songwriters since Schubert, then . . . [the *White Album*] . . . should surely see the last vestiges of cultural snobbery and bourgeois prejudice swept away in a deluge of joyful music making. . . ." None of the critics noted, however, that perhaps some of the album's diversity was due to the work of individuals rather than the four Beatles working in collaboration. By the time of the *White Album* sessions, the Beatles' working relationship had disintegrated to the point where the only way for them to get anything accomplished in the studio was for one of them to wrest control for the recording of his own composition while the others played "backup band." This put Paul at the controls most of the time, with John in second place, and George in a poor third with only four of his own compositions on the finished album. George had so much trouble getting John and Paul's attention that he even brought famed guitarist Eric Clapton into the studios with him to use as his "session guitarist."

Ringo contributed hardly at all. He had finally become superfluous to the Beatles. Most of the time he spent in the studio he sat in a corner playing cards with Neil and Mal. It was a poorly kept secret among Beatle intimates that after Ringo left the studios, Paul would often dub in the drum tracks himself. When

Ringo returned to the studio the next day, he would pretend not to notice that it was not his playing. The fans never knew, but it must have cut him terribly. The message from Paul and the others was clear; this little man who had lucked into the group and sailed with them to the big times was not good enough musically to play with them.

One day Ringo arrived home after a recording session during which Paul had lectured him on how to play, and he told Maureen tearfully that he "was no longer a Beatle," that he had quit. Maureen was terrified at first. Ringo sat at home for the next few days and brooded or played with his kids while the recording sessions went on without him. When he got bored and peeved that the others had not attempted to draw him back, he sheepishly announced that he was "returning to the Beatles." The evening he arrived back in the studios the other three arranged to have his drum kit smothered in several hundred pounds' worth of flowers. Ringo was delighted and all was forgiven, but the rot had already set in; the foundation of the group was cracking, and no amount of flowers would be able to cover it up.

Chapter Sixteen

*And they were both naked,
the man and his wife, and
were not ashamed.*

—*Gen. 2:25*

1.

IN OCTOBER of 1968 the Fleet Street gossip mill had uncovered an item that brought cries of moral indignation from kitchens and living rooms all over Great Britain: Yoko Ono was pregnant with John Lennon's child. The public was outraged, fans as well as parents; first John had ditched his good English wife to take up with this interfering foreigner, now she was pregnant out of wedlock. To top it off, unknown to the public, the police were apparently tipped off that John and Yoko were using heavy drugs.

The establishment came down on them with an iron fist.

It was about eleven-thirty on the morning of October 18 that there was a knock on the door at Montague Square. John had just woken up and was trying to get himself in shape to appear at Apple for a press conference about his upcoming single. He was pale and felt sickly that morning; his hair hadn't been washed in days. When he opened the door he was faced with Detective Sergeant Norman Pilcher of the Scotland Yard Drug Enforcement Squad, along with six policemen, one policewoman for Yoko, and two drug-sniffing canines. As John and Yoko sat next to each other, this team tore through the apartment, turning it upside down as they searched for contraband. One of the police dogs sniffed out some marijuana residue in a binocular case on the mantle, and some marijuana seeds were found in a forgotten rolling machine hidden on the top of the bathroom mirror. A larger quantity of marijuana was later found in a film can inside an old camera case in a rear storage room.

John and Yoko had already heard about Detective Sergeant Norman Pilcher, who was making quite a name for himself as an antidrug zealot. Pilcher had launched a vigorous campaign against drugs in this very druggy era, and his primary targets were those he saw as the foremost purveyors of drugs to teenagers: rock stars. Mick Jagger and Keith Richards had already fallen victim to the Drug Enforcement Squad. The previous spring they had raided Keith Richards' country house in Witterlings, known as "Redlands." Pattie and George Harrison had spent all that day at Redlands, along with Jagger, Marianne Faithfull, art dealer Robert Frazer, and a big-time international dealer to the rock trade. Some of the guests passed the day tripping on LSD or dabbling in heroin. Pattie and George left rather hurriedly in the late afternoon when Marianne Faithfull appeared naked after a bath and wrapped herself in a tawny fur rug. Pilcher raided the house shortly after they left. Some newspaper accounts intimated that a famous rock star and his wife were at the house all day but that the Drug Squad had waited for them to leave before raiding the house. This was presumed to have been in deference to Brian Epstein's reputation, as well as David Jacobs' expertise as an attorney. But they were both dead now, and an open season had been declared on pop stars. John was the next righteous target.

I was at a rehearsal hall watching Mary Hopkin prepare for an appearance on a TV show, when I received an emergency phone call from Neil. Neil said he had called the Montague Square flat and a strange man had answered the phone and said John was not there. "Who are you?" the man asked Neil. "Who the fuck are *you?*" Neil demanded. After a few moments John was put on the phone. "You better cancel the press conference for today," John told him.

"Okay, but why?"

"Imagine your worst paranoia," John said. "Because it's here."

I set off for Montague Square at once and arrived just as John and Yoko were being formally charged with possession, with a charge of willful obstruction of search added for good measure. John, in a black army jacket, black pants, and white sneakers, was ashen-faced and frightened and chain-smoking cigarettes. Yoko was also dressed in black. They were marched out of the flat to a waiting mob of photographers, a pitiful sight as they were led to a police car, with Yoko trailing behind in the custody of a stern policewoman.

Informed at his home that John had been taken to Marylebone Station to be booked, Paul McCartney loyally came to John's rescue. He placed an emergency call to Sir Joseph Lockwood at EMI, asking him if he could use his political influence and connections to help John. Sir Joe agreed to call Marylebone Station and advise John. By this time, John had regained his composure, and he answered Sir Joe's phone call, "Hello! This is Sergeant Lennon, can I help you?"

Later that afternoon John and Yoko were released, and on the way back to the apartment, John filled Neil in on the details behind the day's events, which are told here for the first time. Actually, John and Yoko had been tipped off days before that there was a rumor they were targeted for a bust. John had decided to "clean house" and dispose of any large amounts of drugs—larger than could be disposed of at a moment's notice. That's why no heroin was found and also why a charge of obstructing the search was pressed; John wouldn't let them in while he flushed the remnants down the toilet. John also told Neil that he was high on heroin when the police knocked on the door, but Yoko later denied that this was so. As far as the marijuana they found, John had no idea it was there. He had been so meticulous in his housecleaning that he even had washed the bowl they kept the marijuana in. The film can the police found hadn't been touched in two years. It had been moved into the storage room by the chauffeur, and John didn't have a clue it was there.

A few hours after the harrowing arrest, Yoko almost miscarried and was confined to bed. On October 18 she was rushed to the Queen Charlotte's Maternity Hospital for a series of blood transfusions. John insisted on staying with her in the hospital at all times. For the first few nights he slept in the next bed in her room, but when the hospital needed the bed for a real patient, he slept on pillows on the floor. On November 21, when it became clear that Yoko would not carry to term despite all the emergency medical treatment, and that their unborn child would die inside Yoko's womb, John asked that a Nagra tape recorder be brought to the hospital. Using a stethoscopic microphone, he recorded the embryo's last fluttering heartbeats as it died.

Since the dead baby was old enough to legally warrant a death certificate, they had to name it. John called it John Ono Lennon II. He ordered a tiny coffin for him and had it buried in an undisclosed location without telling anyone but Yoko. That night at the hospital he cried himself to sleep on the floor at her bedside.

The *Times* treated the loss with brevity, but it was certain to note that on November 22 "Yoko Ono, the Japanese artist and friend of John Lennon and the Beatles, has had a miscarriage in Queen Charlotte's Maternity Hospital. Mr. Lennon has said he was the father."

Later, on November 28, still weak and sick, Yoko appeared with John at the Marylebone Magistrates Court. They clung to each other, depressed and beaten, glassy-eyed with the pain of the world's persecution. John pleaded guilty to possession of cannabis, with the understanding that his guilty plea would absolve Yoko of any responsibility. He was fined £150. It seemed like a small price on the surface, but in John's and Yoko's minds, at least, the arrest had cost them their child.

The same day John was found guilty at Marylebone court, he and Yoko gave the finger to the establishment with the release of their first joint album, *Unfinished Music No. 1—Two Virgins*. This was an album comprised mostly of tapes they had made together their first night in Kenwood while tripping on acid. The long, seemingly endless tracks were filled with Yoko's peculiar screaming and John's earsplitting feedback. But it wasn't the album itself that was so controversial, it was the cover. When the photographs first arrived at Apple I thought it was a joke. The photos were so scandalous I locked them away in my desk drawer and didn't share them with anyone. Weeks later John called to make sure they had been put into production. I tried to convince him that he was making a mistake, that the pictures would cause untold legal problems and general aggravation, but he wouldn't listen.

The photographs were taken in the basement bedroom of the Montague Square flat by a remote-control camera. The bedroom is a pigsty, a junkie's haven of rumpled sheets, dirty clothes, newspapers, and magazines heaped all over the floor. In one picture John and Yoko are grinning over their shoulders at the camera, stark naked. In the second shot, they face the camera, holding hands. Yoko is smiling coyly, her breasts sagging toward the floor, a courageous display.* John, glassy-eyed and heroin-stoned, is grinning idiotically, so proud to be exposing to the world his shriveled, uncircumcised penis. Two virgins indeed.

That this was the Lenny Bruce of rock and roll, that John was a madcap yet destructive genius, never crossed anyone's mind at the moment. No one at Apple was amused. Paul McCartney hated the cover beyond words. He took it as a personal affront, probably just as John had planned it. When Ringo saw the photographs he just rolled his eyes and told everyone not to get upset. "It's just John being John," he said. When the cover was forwarded to Sir Joseph Lockwood, he refused to believe that John actually intended to manufacture an album with such a cover. He called John and Yoko and begged them to change their minds. "Why do you want to do something like this?" he asked. Yoko said it was art. "Well, then, why not show Paul in the nude? He's so much prettier!" Sir Joe's final decision was that although he deeply regretted turning John down, he could not allow EMI to distribute an album with such a cover—although EMI was perfectly willing to manufacture the record for them at its usual fee. The record was reluctantly released on the Apple label and distributed by Track, a maverick label owned by the rock group the Who. The album cover was wrapped in a plain brown wrapper wherever it was sold, like a piece of pornography, which is how it was treated throughout the world. In America, the New Jersey police confiscated 30,000 copies waiting for distribution in a Newark warehouse. But copies sold quicker than they could be pressed, while people everywhere wondered why John would do such an outrageous thing.

The day the album was released, Harry Pinsker, the sober, waistcoated head of Bryce-Hamner, the Beatles' accounting firm since the start, resigned his position as financial advisor to Apple Corp. and washed his hands of all Beatles affairs. Now that John and Yoko, in defiance of all moral authority, were involved in drugs and nudity, Pinsker no longer cared to be associated with the group. He was the first of many supporters and friends to break away. Sides were being drawn.

* It is probable that Yoko was pregnant when this photograph was taken.

* * *

2.

*O*N DECEMBER *4, 1968*, the Apple staff received the following memo from George Harrison: "Hell's Angels will be in London within the next week on the way to straighten out Czechoslovakia. There will be twelve in number, complete with black leather jackets and motorcycles. They will undoubtedly arrive at Apple, and I have heard they may try to make full use of Apple's facilities. They may look as though they are going to do you in but are very straight and do good things, so don't fear them or uptight them. Try to assist without neglecting your Apple business and without letting them take control of Savile Row."

It seemed that George's encounter with Frisco Pete, the Hell's Angel who had accosted him on the Haight-Ashbury street corner, was bearing nightmarish fruit. Frisco Pete had actually taken George up on his invitation to visit him in London. Fortunately, not twelve but only two Hell's Angels arrived at Heathrow: Frisco Pete and his swastika-tattooed pal, Billy Tumbleweed. The others were refused visas because of pending criminal charges against them or because they were out of jail on probation. Frisco Pete and Billy Tumbleweed brought with them two motorcycles—which arrived collect at a shipping cost of £250, which Apple paid—and a traveling entourage of smelly, stoned, long-haired California hippies in bells and love beads. These were dubbed the California Pleasure Crew by the press office.

The arrival of the Hell's Angels and the California Pleasure Crew stopped all activity dead at Savile Row. The employees gathered in doorways and corners and tried not to stare as the contingent marched up the green-carpeted stairs, past the vulnerable gold records on the walls, and into the press office, where I waited with Derek Taylor.

After a slightly horrified pause, I extended my hand to Frisco Pete and said as pleasantly as possible, "It's a pleasure to make your acquaintance, I'm sure," and promptly left the room.

Derek headed for his scotch and Coke. "Well," he said hurriedly, "you are here and so are we and this is Sally who has just joined us and that is Carol who has always been with us and Richard you know and if you'd like a cup of tea then a cup of tea it is but if you would rather have a glass of beer or a bottle of wine or a scotch and Coke or a gin and tonic or a vodka and lime then that it is because it is all here and if it is not then we will come up with something but have a seat or have a cigarette or have a joint and I will be back in three minutes so please don't go away because there is a lot to talk about and more to find out and stranger days to come!"

Derek had matters of much greater consequence on his hands at the moment. A few months before he had slightly overstepped his responsibilities by promising a monthly magazine that he would obtain for them an original recorded message from John and Yoko. This message was to be pressed as a "flimsy," a pliable plastic record that could be stapled into the magazine. The text of the message was to be a plea for world peace and an end to the war in Vietnam. It sounded like a stroke of genius at the moment, but throughout the fall, when the recording should have been prepared, Derek was unable to get in touch with John. We assumed that most of the time he was too drugged to come to the phone. Soon, it was the beginning of December, the magazine had been advertising the flimsy for a month, and there was still no message. The magazine's solicitors had already been on the phone with me, threatening an expensive lawsuit.

After Derek practically begged the household staff, John finally came to the phone. Derek explained the problem to him and the urgency of taping a simple message, even if it was over the phone. John sounded very tired and stoned. "I have a recording for you," he told Derek. "Have somebody come here and pick it up."

A few days later Derek invited the magazine editors and their lawyers to 3 Savile Row. Derek asked them to sit in a row of chairs in front of huge, studio-quality speakers. He said, "This is John and Yoko's contribution for a Christmas message," and turned on a tape. The room was filled with the sound of a baby's heartbeat growing fainter and weaker until it slowed to silence. Derek said, "And then the baby died."

The magazine people were incredulous. "This has to be some sort of monstrous joke," one of them said.

"No, it's no joke," Derek said. "It's unique, it's them, it's authentic, and it's yours for free. What can I tell you? That's my story."

Apple was sued by the magazine for damages. The case was

eventually settled out of court. At the time of the settlement, Derek wrote a memo that was circulated throughout Apple. It said: "If I'm to be held responsible for this, take it out of my salary. You know where to find me. Derek."

3.

*T*HAT NEW YEAR'S EVE was rather sad. It didn't really dawn on them that the end was coming yet, but it was obvious that things weren't what they used to be. It had become a New Year's Eve tradition for all of us from Liverpool to celebrate together, frequently at Cilla Black's large terraced flat on Portland Place. These celebrations were befittingly warm, noisy affairs. In the northern tradition, just before midnight the "darkest" member of the house is sent outside with a piece of bread and coal, symbolizing food and warmth, and is then the first person let inside after midnight. The previous year Ringo had been sent out into the snowy London street and we had been having such a good time, we forgot about him for half an hour, until the sound of the doorbell was finally heard over the revelry.

But this year the celebratory mood was subdued. Cynthia was gone. So, of course, was Brian. John and Yoko didn't show up. Ringo was growing bored with Maureen. And now Jane Asher was missing, too. In her place was Linda Eastman, whose tenacity had triumphed in landing her a Beatle. And now George and Pattie seemed to be having a hard time of it. Rumors were rife that George had lots of girlfriends on the side, while Pattie sat home and played the good hausfrau. The young couple spent most of New Year's Eve arguing, and at midnight Pattie was locked in the bathroom, crying.

The Beatles' spirits were not much higher when on January 2 they assembled at a cold and dreary sound stage at the Twickenham Film Studios to begin work on a new album and documentary tentatively titled *Get Back*, later renamed *Let It Be*.

Get Back was once again mostly Paul's idea. Paul increasingly regretted the Beatles' decision to stop touring. The Beatles had lost contact with their audiences, and he felt that was a mistake. His creativity was nurtured by the immediate feedback of a live audience. That public adulation was half the fun of being a musician, he felt, and his need for the sound of applause was so strong that one day, high on LSD, he stopped at a roadside pub in Bedfordshire and played the piano for the delighted patrons. Paul had decided that it was important for the Beatles to "get back to their roots," and that's what *Get Back* was supposed to be.

However, the idea of a huge tour was greeted with great reluctance by the others, and it was whittled down to having a documentary filmed of them making the album, capped by a single live performance. Paul wanted to justify the idea of one show by holding it in some grandiose location. A Tunisian amphitheater was considered but dismissed as impractical, as was holding the concert on an ocean liner in the middle of the Atlantic. John's personal suggestion was that they hold the concert in a "lunatic asylum," and perhaps he was right. The Beatles needed their heads examined to embark on such a project.

An angry and tense atmosphere hung over the whole project from the start. Twickenham Studios was an awful place to be in early January. The Beatles were brought there early every morning—while they preferred to meet at night—and put under the scrutiny of two 16-mm cameras filming their every move. "We couldn't get into it," John remembered. "It was a dreadful, dreadful feeling in Twickenham Studios being filmed all the time. You couldn't make music at eight in the morning, or ten, or whatever it was, with people filming you and colored lights."

Paul played the part of the schoolmarm, coaxing them to work. He took it upon himself to tell John, George, and Ringo just what to play on each song, explaining each drum set, guitar line or vocal. He blatantly treated the others as his backup group. It was all the more insulting because the cameras were rolling all the time. Most of the vitriol among them was cut out, but the finished film captures Paul lecturing, "We've been very negative since Mr. Epstein passed away. The only way for it not to be a bit of a drag is for the four of us to think: Should we make it positive or should we forget it? Mr. Epstein said, sort of, 'Get suits on,' and we did. We were always fighting that discipline a bit, but it's silly to fight that discipline if it's our own. I think we need a bit more if we're going to get on with it."

In ten days at the Twickenham Studios the Beatles ran through scores of songs from their roots, most of them, like "Johnny B. Goode" and "Roll Over Beethoven," dredged up from the Hamburg days. But it soon became apparent they were going nowhere. They all agreed that recording on a mobile unit at Twickenham was impossible and that they'd better move into either EMI's Abbey Road studio or their own newly built one in the basement of Apple.

When they arrived at the Apple studios to begin recording, they were in for a shock. The 78-track studio that Magic Alex was building wasn't exactly ready. In fact, not only weren't there 78 tracks, there were no tracks at all. The recording machines that Alex was purportedly building for them from scratch had not been installed. Not only that, they had arrived direct from a German manufacturer with the manufacturer's name on them, although Alex had claimed the machines were being built to his specifications. Added to that, the heating and ventilating equipment for the entire building was located in a corner of the studio; it wheezed and hummed so loudly that it precluded any recording in there. Alex had even forgotten to install an intercom system between the studio and the control booth.

A team of acoustical experts and sound technicians were rushed to 3 Savile Row to correct all the problems. To save time a mobile unit was moved in to record on. Once again the cameras and lights were turned on, and the Beatles returned to the studio. After spending another week or two laying down some basic tracks, it became apparent things weren't going much better than at Twickenham. A kind of a hostile lethargy characterized the sessions. One morning Paul stopped everything and said, "We've been going round and round for an hour. I think it's a question of either we do it or we go home." Then he told George how to play the guitar, and George cracked.

"Look," he said angrily, "I'll play whatever you want me to play, or I won't play at all. Whatever it is that'll please you, I'll do it!" When they broke for lunch, George got in his car and went home to Esher. When he walked in the door he said to Pattie, "I've quit the group. The Beatles are over."

Like Ringo before him, George sulked at home while recording and filming were delayed. But when they had a business meeting a few days later, George showed up with the rest of them as if nothing had happened.

The final concert that was to end the movie was not held in some grand location but only on the rooftop of 3 Savile Row. Braving the bitter cold, they ran through a few numbers, giving a frozen, ironic performance. The noise from the rooftop brought a crowd of pedestrians to the street below, and eventually a bobby arrived and tried to stop it all. But by then it was too late. The Beatles had given their last public performance.

At the end of the filming they had twenty-nine hours of raw tape and ninety-six hours of sound film. The film, the tapes, the bad vibes, all went on a shelf for a long, long time. "Nobody could look at it," John said. "I really couldn't stand it."

Chapter Seventeen

I'm not the new Epstein,
I'm the old Allen.

—Allen Klein

1.

*T*RYING TO CONTROL the spending at Apple was like riding the back of a tiger; it's hard enough to hold on, but if you let go the tiger turns around and eats you. It wouldn't have been so bad that Apple had turned into a three-ring circus if at least there had been a ringmaster to run the show. But with no final authority to control the cash flow, money was simply pissed away. The Beatles had already spent £400,000 earmarked for investments by the accountants, mostly on undeserving or farfetched schemes. Among other fruitless projects, they had sunk money into the design of a new "demobilization suit" and a puppet show in Brighton. Individually the Beatles had overdrawn their company accounts as well. John was £64,000 in the red, Paul £66,000, and George and Ringo £35,000 each.

The largesse of the Beatles, combined with the willingness of those who benefited from it, bordered on organized crime. The liquor continued to flow, as did the fancy lunches from the Cordon Bleu chefs. Caviar was stocked at all times for Yoko Ono, and the charge account at Fortnum and Mason was used daily. Magic Alex had so far produced nothing of any value. He had been loaned a £20,000 home to live in and was given his own laboratory on Boston Street in which to invent. After the Apple Boutique closed, Pete Shotton left with a Jaguar automobile owned by the company. It was missing for months before anybody noticed. Promotional records were disappearing by the gross, to be sold on the black market to unscrupulous record stores. Television sets vanished out the front door, as did an occasional pay packet left on some trusting soul's desk. With all the traffic in the building, even the messenger boys were stealing by peeling the lead roof right off the building and hauling it out the front door in huge sacks to be resold to metal dealers.

The vast expenditures had already been brought to the Beatles' attention by Stephen Maltz, the young staff accountant who had resigned the previous October in protest over the way the Beatles were handling their finances. In a letter sent to each of the Beatles, Maltz wrote, "After six years' work, for the most part of which you have been at the very top of the musical world, in which you have given pleasure to countless millions throughout every country where records are played, what have you got to show for it? . . . Your personal finances are a mess. Apple is a mess . . ."

Thus began the ill-fated search to find someone to head Apple. Paul decided that if Apple needed a chief, they should get the biggest chief of all. In Paul's mind that was, improbably, Lord Beeching. It was Lord Beeching and his "Beeching Axe" that had consolidated British Railways and made it financially healthy. The Beatles extended an offer to him, but he immediately declined. Next they turned to Lord Poole, chairman of Lazard's Bank, who offered to sort out Apple's finances for them at no charge without becoming officially involved. But Paul quickly lost interest in the generous but formal banker and never called him back. They also consulted with Lord Goodman, the lawyer to the Prime Minister, and with Cecil King, the newspaper baron, but both men declined. Ronan O'Rhielly, the visionary who had started Radio Caroline, was invited to attend a meeting at Apple to discuss the possibility of his becoming involved, but he was voted down when Caleb, the former salesman at the Apple boutique, consulted the *I Ching* and found that Ronan O'Rhielly didn't have the right "vibes." In fact, Caleb and his pickup sticks were being consulted with such great frequency that Caleb was making as many important decisions as anyone else.

Then one day Paul realized that he had the perfect Big Daddy for Apple right under his nose. Linda Eastman's father, Lee, had recently been giving Paul advice on his personal and business holdings, and Paul liked what he had heard. Lee was a sound and conservative lawyer whose legal background in the music business had been with the big bands, including Tommy Dorsey. When Paul mentioned to the other Beatles that perhaps Lee Eastman would be able to help them, the suggestion was met with groans of disbelief. Paul was informed that he was sadly mistaken if he thought he was not only going to run the group musically but also arrange for the financial management to be taken over by someone who seemed likely to be his future father-in-law. Characteristically, Paul dug in at this challenge and insisted that at least they all should have a meeting with Eastman to hear what he had to say.

Lee Eastman misjudged the importance of this meeting and never showed up. Instead he sent John Eastman, his twenty-eight-year-old son and partner in his law firm. John was very different from his wilder younger sister. He reeked of urban sophistication and old money. He was clean-cut and handsome in a "Kennedy" sort of way. He represented many of the things Paul aspired to himself—and at the same time everything that would turn the other Beatles off. At their very first encounter, John and Yoko pegged him as a phony intellectual when he tried to engage them in esoteric conversation about Kafka.

John Eastman's legal advice, however, was not pretentious. It was first class and intelligent. He suggested that the very first thing they do was to buy NEMS, now renamed Nemperor Holdings. Clive Epstein was desperate to get Nemperor Holdings off his hands. The death taxes were due by March 31, 1969, and there was very little in ready cash to pay for them. To make the situation more urgent, John Eastman pointed out to the Beatles that although Nemperor Holdings provided no services for the Beatles, they continued to deduct a whopping 25 percent income from their recording royalties. Indeed, Nemperor Holdings was entitled to collect 25 percent of their earnings for *nine more years,* even though Brian was dead, even if Clive sold the company to total strangers. Since Clive had to sell Nemperor, they damn well had better buy it from him themselves.

Clive Epstein, in the meanwhile, had put the word out in the City that Nemperor and its 25 percent cut of the Beatles was for sale. It wasn't long before he got a serious bid from Leonard Richenberg, the aggressive managing director of a successful company called Triumph Investment Trust. Richenberg offered one million pounds for Nemperor, which would pay the death taxes and guarantee a handsome profit to boot. Clive dutifully reported this offer to the Beatles; if they wanted to match it, Nemperor was theirs. Clive said he would wait a few weeks for the Beatles to make a firm counteroffer. All they needed was the money.

The Beatles asked for a meeting with Sir Joseph Lockwood at EMI. The four of them, plus Yoko and John Eastman, had tea with Sir Joe in the EMI conference room. After some small talk, John Eastman told Sir Joe why they had come. "We need an immediate cash advance against royalties for one million, two hundred and fifty thousand pounds."

Sir Joe didn't blink. "When do you want it?" he said.

And Eastman said, "Wednesday afternoon."

2.

*I*T WAS JUST at this moment that Allen Klein arrived on the scene. A few weeks before, John had told an editor of Britain's *Disc* magazine that "if Apple goes on losing money at this rate, we'll be broke in six months . . ." While most dismissed the statement as typical Lennon hyperbole, Allen Klein recognized it as a signal that his services were needed, and in he swooped to the rescue.

Since Brian's death, Allen Klein had called the Apple office frequently, and I had many phone conversations with him. I once even acquiesced to a meeting with him, one that Clive Epstein also attended, but he was so foul-mouthed and abusive, I ended the meeting in a few minutes and had him shown to the door— just as Brian had done years before. After John's "bankrupt" statement, Klein unleashed a new barrage of phone calls to Apple. I would dutifully return the calls, but Klein was now insisting that he would only speak to one person—John Lennon. I told him this was impossible.

One day in early February, Tony Calder, the former co-manager of the Rolling Stones, gave Derek Taylor a lift to the train station on the way to work in the morning. Calder had recently heard from Klein, who was under the impression that it was Derek

Taylor who was standing in the way of his getting to John. Derek hated being characterized as the bad guy and said he would speak to me about it. Later that day, Derek asked me as a personal favor to turn Klein's phone messages over to John and I relented.

Unbeknownst to the other Beatles, John and Yoko went to meet with Klein in his suite at the Dorchester Hotel that very night. John had met Klein once before at the filming of the Rolling Stones' *Rock and Roll Circus,* but John didn't remember him. John couldn't understand why. The man who confronted John and Yoko in the Dorchester Hotel was truly memorable. He was short and fat, with a sallow complexion and several chins that came over a dirty stretched-out turtleneck sweater. His socks hung around his ankles, his shoes were scuffed and worn. He was bigger than life. He talked loudly and incessantly in grandiose generalizations and with a New York Jewish accent that made John's scouse sound like the King's English. John and Yoko liked him. In some ways Klein had many of the same ethnic elements as a Liverpudlian; he was blunt and he was common. This kind of crass honesty, even his frequent use of four-letter words, appealed to Yoko, too, who admired Klein as one street fighter does another. Most of all, John and Yoko were impressed by Klein's true appreciation of John's music. Klein was, at his deepest center, a true-blooded record business man; he loved his clients and he loved their music. He was able to quote from every song of John's already large body of work. This left John feeling terribly flattered and slightly softheaded, a bit of putty in Klein's hands.

They spent the night talking over a long dinner of macrobiotic rice that Klein had thoughtfully arranged to be served by the hotel. Over the course of the evening, Klein's fascinating story unfolded. Like John, he was an orphan who had lived with an aunt, but Klein's story was even more dramatically tragic. The son of a Hungarian butcher from New Jersey, Klein's mother had died when he was only a few months old, and his distraught father had put him in an orthodox Jewish orphanage in Newark, where he lived until he was fifteen, when an aunt took him in. He worked his way through accounting school at night, a profession for which he had perfect affinity. Numbers added, subtracted, and divided magically in his computerlike mind, which was full of schemes for ways in which numbers could be put to use. As an accountant he had the best pitch for prospective clients. "You should be rich," he would say, stabbing the air with a pudgy finger. "Let me make a lot of money for you."

One night Klein was a guest at a wedding where pop singing star Bobby Darin was the best man. Klein introduced himself to Darin and said, "How would you like a hundred thousand dollars?"

Darin said, "What for?"

"For nothing," Klein told him. "Just let me go through your accounts."

Klein moved his wife and mother-in-law into Darin's offices as assistants and reportedly found misappropriated royalties. From there his fame as a business barracuda grew with his client list, which soon included Connie Francis, Steve Lawrence and Eydie Gorme, and finally, as manager, Sam Cooke, which was when he first met Brian. In 1965 Klein ingratiated himself with the Rolling Stones business office, then attended to by Andrew Oldham and his partner Eric Easton. Shortly after Klein took the reins, he pounced on Decca, the Stones' record company, and came up with the much discussed advance of $1.25 million that had irked Brian and the Beatles so much.

Klein promised John and Yoko that he would do the same thing for them. He would renegotiate for the Beatles a much higher percentage of royalties from EMI, plus a huge cash advance that would solve all their financial problems. On top of that, he would get Nemperor Holdings for them—but he would get it for *free;* don't ask how, just rest assured that he would do it. He would also, he promised Yoko, get United Artists to distribute the films she was making with John, and he would get her an advance of a million dollars, a figure that John repeated to me in the office the next day with pride. I found this quite astonishing, considering that John and Yoko's latest cinematic venture was a long film of them smiling at each other in soft focus.

Before John and Yoko left Klein's suite that night, John wrote a note in longhand. It said, "From now on Allen Klein handles all my stuff." The next day at the Apple offices, he dictated another memo, this one to be sent to Sir Joseph Lockwood at EMI, who was in the process of loaning them a million pounds. It said, "I don't give a bugger who anybody else wants, but I'm having Allen Klein for me."

Now the war began in earnest. As John later admitted, he

wanted somebody to go after Paul and the Eastman family for him, and Klein obliged him with a vengeance. John insisted that just as the Beatles had met with John Eastman, they would meet with Allen Klein, and a conference was arranged in Klein's suite in the Dorchester Hotel. George and Ringo arrived with John and Yoko; Paul arrived with John Eastman. Klein started the meeting by telling them that they should hold off buying Nemperor Holdings from Clive Epstein until he had finished an audit of their books. He said that John Eastman's idea to buy Nemperor for a million pounds was "a piece of crap." He said that in order for Sir Joe to loan them a million pounds against royalties, the Beatles would have to earn approximately two million pounds before taxes to pay it all back. He called John Eastman a fool and a "shit head." Eastman gritted his teeth and didn't answer, but when he went to the bathroom he emerged holding a glass jar full of suppositories left there by Klein. "Why Allen," Eastman said, "I thought you were the perfect asshole."

Paul and John Eastman left the meeting early. It was a poor tactic, because once Klein was alone with George and Ringo he was able to say to them all the things he had been saving up to say since he had heard about Brian's death. First, there were *four* Beatles, not one Beatle with a backup group. If Klein had his way, there would be no more secondhand citizenship for John, George, and Ringo. Secondly, he would make them rich again. He would start with an audit of the books, and then he would fire all the deadwood they had brought with them from Liverpool. It sounded good to them.

Suddenly there were three Beatles behind Klein, and it was arranged for him to go over the books. Shortly thereafter, on February 14, 1969, Clive Epstein received the following letter from John Eastman: "As you know Mr. Allen Klein is doing an audit of the Beatles' affairs vis-à-vis NEMS and Nemperor Holdings, Ltd. When this has been completed I suggest we meet to discuss the results of Mr. Klein's audit as well as the propriety of the negotiations surrounding the nine-year agreement between EMI and the Beatles and NEMS."

Clive and Queenie were infuriated by the implication of the note. Clive shot back a letter which said in part, "Before any meeting takes place, please be good enough to let me know precisely what you mean by the phrase, 'The propriety of the negotiations surrounding the nine-year agreement between EMI and the Beatles and NEMS.' "

At this point John Eastman's father decided he'd better fly to London and have a meeting with Klein and the four Beatles. Lee Eastman, distinguished and unflappable, intended to put Klein straight. The meeting took place in my office. Neil Aspinall and Yoko came along, too. The proceedings got off to a roaring start. Klein had done some research on Lee Eastman and had turned up the information that his name had allegedly been changed a long time before from—of all things—Epstein. Klein had also armed John with this intelligence, and throughout the meeting the two of them referred to Eastman as "Epstein." If Lee Eastman managed to remain calm in the face of that affront, he was unable to contain himself when Klein began interrupting everything he said with a string of the most disgusting four-letter words he could tick off his tongue. Finally Lee Eastman leapt out of his chair and got into a childish screaming match with Klein. He lost the battle at that moment. He and Paul stormed out of the office. After that, Paul stopped attending most meetings and sent in his stead a lawyer named Charles Corman who had been hired to represent his interests by the Eastmans.

Three days after receiving John Eastman's letter questioning the nine years left on the Nemperor contracts, Clive Epstein quickly and quietly sold Nemperor Holdings and its 25 percent share of the Beatles' earnings to Leonard Richenberg at Triumph Trust before the tax year ended. According to the terms of the deal, Triumph became a 90 percent holder of Nemperor. Clive Epstein, relieved, packed his belongings and went back to Liverpool to raise his children in a house near Queenie's. He lives there still, a successful and contented businessman.

The Beatles were stunned that they had lost Nemperor, and a finger-pointing, name-calling match ensued. Klein, the three Beatles, even Leonard Richenberg put the blame on John Eastman for being too young and too soft. Klein told them not to worry, though, he would get Nemperor back for them—for free. On February 25 Klein arrived at Leonard Richenberg's office in the City, dressed in a wrinkled plaid sportsjacket and one of his turtleneck sweaters. Richenberg thought that at first Klein might have been mistaken for a "nasty little gangster."

"You're very smart to have jumped in first and bought NEMS,

but what you don't know was that the Epsteins owed the Beatles huge sums of money from road shows," Klein told him. Klein then proceeded to make all kinds of dark threats about lawsuits that would destroy both Triumph and "Rikenboiger," as he liked to call him. Richenberg, however, was unfazed, and again Klein was shown to the door.

Klein then went back to the Beatles, including Paul, and got them to sign a letter to EMI which said, in part, "We hereby irrevocably instruct you to pay Henry Ansbacher and Co. all royalties payable by you directly or indirectly to Beatles and Co. or Apple Corp." A letter to Richenberg at Triumph followed, informing him that Nemperor no longer acted on behalf of the Beatles.

At EMI Sir Joe had his hands full. First, Allen Klein's timing was perfect; there were £1.3 million in royalties due to be paid shortly to Nemperor. Secondly, Sir Joe knew that Klein intended to renegotiate the Beatles' recording contracts for a higher royalty and didn't want to make an enemy of him just now. Trying to be fair, and perhaps a little "chicken" as Richenberg called him, Sir Joe decided not to do anything; he "sat" on the money at EMI.

Richenberg did not wait a day to take the case to court. Once again, the Beatles found themselves the unwitting subject of inch-high newspaper headlines. In a packed courtroom, Mr. Jeremiah Harmon, counsel for Triumph Trust, told Justice Buckley that Apple appeared to have recently fallen "under the influence of a Mr. Allen Klein. He seemed to have a somewhat dubious record." It was believed that if EMI paid the royalties to the Beatles, they might turn the money over to Klein, who might abscond with it. Klein's threatening meeting with Richenberg was cited in court, as were other legal proceedings against him in America and England. Harmon ended up saying, "If some manipulator arrives on the scene and causes trouble between the Beatles and Nemperor, we are justifiably apprehensive."

Sydney Templeman, counsel for EMI, protested that "such allegations were irrelevant and unfair to someone [Klein] who was not a party to the proceedings." EMI made clear their position that after March 5, 1969, they would pay the royalties to no one. The judge, in turn, saw no reason not to freeze the funds.

Now Richenberg was really angry. If Klein's forum was street fighting, then a street fight he would get. Richenberg secretly paid to have a Bishops report done on Klein. Bishops was a detective service that ran financial and legal checks on individuals for the big banking firms of the City. They didn't have to dig deep to find a lot of information about Klein. Richenberg had a report on his desk within the week, and after reading it he happily turned it over to reporters at the *Sunday Times.* On April 13, 1969, an article written by John Fielding appeared in the investigative column called "Insight." "The Toughest Wheeler-Dealer In The Pop Jungle" was the headline. It began by saying that Klein's operations were "a startling blend of bluff, sheer determination, and financial agility, together with an instinct for publicity and the ability to lie like a trooper. He is a veteran of some forty lawsuits, and dealings in one of his shares was halted by the American Stock Exchange. In one of his better known achievements he himself took over one of his own companies and saw the value of the stock go up by $15 million." The article alleged that Allen Klein and Co. had bought 297,000 shares of a near-bankrupt company called Cameo-Parkway for only $1.75 each. Rumors began that Klein would take over the giant Chapell Music corporation, and the Cameo-Parkway shares rose to $72. It soon became apparent that Cameo had no resources to make such a bid. In the end the only acquisition made was of Allen Klein and Co. in a reverse takeover. At one point the Cameo shares were suspended, but the ban was later lifted. Klein had been sued for over $5 million over the Cameo deal, but the suit had been dismissed.

The story of Klein's relationship with the Rolling Stones didn't sound very pretty either. Klein took over the Stones in the summer of 1965 and got them a $1.4 million advance against royalties, but the Stones weren't to see any of it very soon. The Stones expected the money to be deposited into their business account, Nanker Phelge Music Ltd. The money was deposited into such an account all right but to a company called Nanker Phelge Music Inc., which Klein had formed in the United States. It was later disclosed that all the money had been invested in General Motors stock, which although it produced a high income did not make its way into the Stones' pockets. Klein pointed out that his contractual agreement with them only obligated him to pay the $1.4 million over a period of twenty years. The article closed by noting many other pending or dismissed lawsuits against Klein, and that

Klein somehow continued to own a piece of the singer Donovan. A share of all Donovan's publishing and recording royalties was paid directly to Klein's company, "a situation in a certain way like the Beatles, which Klein finds so deplorable."

Klein sued the *Sunday Times,* but it was too late; he was already smeared.* But he wasn't vanquished. Now more respectful of Richenberg, he agreed to a quick compromise with him. The Beatles bought back Triumph's 90 percent of Nemperor stock for £800,000 cash plus a quarter of the frozen assets of £1.3 million, along with £50,000 additional for Nemperor's share of Suba Films, the Beatles' film company. On top of this they had to pay Triumph 5 percent of their gross royalties from 1972 to 1976. Richenberg outdid himself, however, when he convinced the Beatles to trade the 10 percent of the stock they already owned in Nemperor for nearly a million dollars of Triumph stock, neatly making the Beatles shareholders in Triumph.

Klein triumphantly took credit for the event, claiming that his masterful dealing had won their 25 percent back for them, but John Eastman was quick to point out the reality of the negotiations. "Before memories become too short," he wrote each of the Beatles, "I want to remind everybody that we could have settled the NEMS affair for very little. Klein killed my deal, claiming all sorts of improper acts of NEMS which his investigations would disclose and promising to get NEMS for you for nothing. We all know that no improper acts were found by Klein, if, in fact, Klein made an investigation at all.

"We do know, however, that NEMS tied up £1,400,000 of Beatles phonograph recording royalties which Klein has been unable to free. . . . These are the facts, I shall be more than pleased to give you chapter and verse if you desire. . . ."

But that was only the beginning.

* The suit against the *Sunday Times* was later dropped. The research file, including the Bishops report, is missing as of this writing. The journalist who wrote the piece, John Fielding, later went to work for Klein on the picture *The Greek Tycoon,* which Klein produced.

* * *

3.

E VENTS suddenly began to accelerate.
On the morning of March 12, 1969, I witnessed
Linda Eastman and Paul McCartney's marriage. Sometime the
month before Linda had learned she was pregnant, and just like
two other Beatles before him, Paul agreed to do the northern
thing and make the girl his wife. They arrived at the Marylebone
Registry a little before ten in the morning in a black Daimler.
There was a cold drizzle that day, but that didn't stop scores of
weeping, breast-beating young women who had turned up to protest this great loss, the last available Beatle. Aside from Paul's
brother Michael, who was best man, and Mal Evans and me, none
of Paul's dear friends attended.

John and Yoko said they couldn't come because they were
putting the finishing touches on an album called *Unfinished Music
No 2: Life with the Lions,* which they had recorded at an avant-
garde jazz concert at Lady Mitchell Hall at Cambridge University.
Ringo and Maureen were occupied at home, and George Harrison
mumbled something about attending to work at 3 Savile Row.

On that same morning Pattie Harrison drove to London to
pick up a new dress to wear to a "Pisces" party that artist Rory
McEwen was throwing in Chelsea that night. Princess Margaret
and Lord Snowdon were expected to attend, and Pattie had picked
out a special dress at designer Ozzie Clark's showroom. Pattie
parked her car on the street down the block from Clark's salon
and went inside to pick up the dress. When she emerged a short
time later, she found that someone had put a pack of Rothman's
cigarettes on the dashboard while she was gone. Inside the cigarette pack was a phone number and a man's name with the message, "Phone me." There was also a gift: a tiny piece of hashish.
Pattie put the cigarette pack in her pocketbook and returned to
Kinfauns, their home in Esher, to have a bath. She was just drying
off when the doorbell rang. She looked out the window and saw
three or four cars pulling up the drive. "That's strange," she
thought, "I wonder who's here?" and went to open the door.

Detective Sergeant Norman Pilcher was waiting for her, along
with eight policemen and a drug-sniffing canine named Yogi. Sergeant Pilcher said, "We're looking for dangerous drugs."

Pattie said politely, "I'm terribly sorry but we don't have any." They searched the house thoroughly nevertheless, almost making a beeline for the chip of hashish in the Rothman's cigarette pack. It dawned on Pattie that perhaps she had been set up, and she patiently explained to them how she got it. Then she went to the phone and called my office. I was still out with Paul and Linda, so they put her through to George. "Guess what?" she said gaily. "It's a bust."

"No stop it," George said. "Don't joke."

"I'm serious. Who would you like to speak to?" She handed the phone to Sergeant Pilcher, who told George it was no joke. George said he would leave for Esher immediately, but with traffic it took him over two hours to get there.

In the interim Pattie asked Sergeant Pilcher why he was doing this. "To save you from the perils of heroin," he told her. Before George arrived, one policeman came up with a small brick of hashish that Pattie had never seen before. It weighed 570 grams. Sergeant Pilcher claimed that Yogi the dog had found it in the bedroom closet in one of George's shoes.

"You're lying," Pattie told him sweetly. "If we had that much hash we certainly wouldn't hide it in one of George's shoes. And if you're looking for grass, we keep it in the sitting room on a table in a cigarette box."

When George himself arrived the policemen began elbowing each other out of the way to get near to him and have a closer look. George and Pattie were surprised they didn't ask for autographs.

They were hauled off to jail for arraignment, and Martin Polden, the lawyer who had handled John and Yoko's case, got them out. That didn't stop them from rushing back to Esher to bathe and change and go off to the Pisces party as planned. When they arrived at the party, Princess Margaret and Lord Snowdon were already there. George and Pattie went directly over to their little circle and said hello. "Hey, you can't believe what happened," George said. "We got busted. Pilcher planted hash in my shoe."

"Oh my, what a shame," Princess Margaret said politely.

"Can you help us?" George asked her. "Can you sort of use your influence to eliminate the bad news?"

"Oh, I don't think so," said the Princess, appropriately horrified at the suggestion.

Just at that moment Pattie's youngest sister, Paula, joined the group. Much to everyone's wide-eyed embarrassment, she produced a joint from her pocketbook and lit it. When Paula realized everyone was glaring at her, she thought she was being discourteous by not passing the joint. She extended it to Princess Margaret and said, "Here, do you want this?"

Princess Margaret turned and fled the party with Lord Snowdon following her.

Pattie and George were fined £500 for possession of drugs on March 31. Mr. Michael West, the prosecutor, noted to the judge that Pattie and George were of impeccable character. On the steps of the courthouse, Martin Polden told reporters, "The police might now accept that this is a closed season for the Beatles."

But John and Yoko were about to give them even bigger targets.

4.

ON MARCH 20, only eight days after Paul and Linda were married, John and Yoko took the plunge themselves. Yoko's divorce from Tony Cox had become final on February 2, and she was free to do as she pleased. John opted for a private small ceremony at a place where he could get married quickly, without posting banns or alerting the press. He had seen what a media circus Paul's wedding had turned into and wanted to avoid a similar scene. I was asked to find a location for the "secret" wedding to take place. John and Yoko were in Paris on vacation when I learned that as a British resident John could get married immediately in Gibraltar if he wished. I chartered a plane for them from Paris and met them at the Gibraltar airport with photographer David Nutter, who had no idea what kind of event he had been hired to photograph. I was honored to be John and Yoko's best man.

John and Yoko arrived at the small Gibraltar airport dressed in wrinkled matching white outfits, Yoko with her skirt halfway up her thighs. The ceremony took less than ten minutes, after which we went directly to the airport. They were on the ground only a few hours.

As private and simple as they wanted their wedding to be, they had planned to turn their honeymoon into a public piece of buffoonery. Quite suddenly, it seemed, John took up the antiwar banner and became overnight one of the most vocal and relentless nonviolent peace advocates known to the media. This was most peculiar to those who knew him, for although the anti-Vietnam War movement had long been a just and fashionable cause, this sudden dedication to it could only be attributable to Yoko's influence. It seemed a safe and admirable choice in any case, because there was hardly anything morally outrageous about peace, and perhaps being a peace advocate would keep John out of bigger, more serious trouble. We hoped that John's pacifist stand would deflect some of the hostility that John and Yoko were experiencing from the press, but characteristically, John made peace a holy crusade and turned his honeymoon into a side show.

John and Yoko flew to Amsterdam, where they checked into a one-hundred-pounds-a-day luxury suite at the unsuspecting Amsterdam Hilton Hotel and staged the first of their infamous "bed-ins." Scores of journalists and photographers from newspapers all over the world were invited to see the two in bed. Many of them rushed to Amsterdam expecting to see some sort of sexual act take place à la *Two Virgins,* but they were gravely disappointed. A bed-in was simply John and Yoko sitting up in bed in clean pajamas, clutching flowers, espousing peace, and eating plentiful orders of the food served to them by white-jacketed emissaries from room service. John and Yoko allegedly left bed only to go to the bathroom. This in itself didn't seem to be the grist for headline-making news, but the amused members of the world press helped turn it into one of the most widely reported stories of John and Yoko's adventures to date. The newlyweds welcomed reporters and photographers into their suite practically any time of the day or night to give interviews and pose for pictures. At home in England the progress of the bed-in was reported to fans with snide benevolence. A favorite headline was "John And Yoko Are Forced Out Of Bed By Maria The Maid."

John was lying in bed in Amsterdam one day, reading about his own adventures in the English papers, when he came across an article that said that Dick James, the Beatles' longtime music publisher, was selling all of his 37 percent of Northern Songs stock to Sir Lew Grade at ATV. Grade presumably wanted to gain control of Northern Songs by buying up any remaining stock he could find. This was a remarkable testament to the longterm worth of the Beatles' songs; ATV's bid for undeclared Northern Songs stock came to a staggering £9.5 million.

John was shocked, as was Paul when he heard. How could Dick James, the Beatles' sweet, cigar-smoking "uncle"—whom they'd helped make into a multimillionaire—sell out Northern Songs without first informing them, or at least asking them if they wanted to buy it themselves. To John and Paul, Northern wasn't just a collection of 159 compositions, it was like a child, creative flesh and blood, and selling it to their business antagonist, Sir Lew Grade, was like putting that child into an orphanage.

But Dick James had seen the writing on the wall; it was written in Allen Klein's handwriting, and James was determined to pull out. He had greatly enhanced the value of Northern Songs by his hard work and by diversifying the catalog with the purchase of such songs as "Stardust" and "Those Were the Days." But he also knew that the value of Northern Songs depended not only on the 159 Lennon-McCartney tunes it already owned but also on the willingness and ability of Lennon and McCartney to continue to compose together. Already John and Paul had refused to sign an extension on their songwriting contract with Northern Songs, and Dick James had good reason to doubt the longevity of their relationship. On one of his rare visits to see the Beatles at work, at the Twickenham Studios during the filming of *Let It Be,* not only did the Beatles ask him to leave but the icy tension between John and Paul made the freezing studios seem warm in comparison. Yet Dick James might have stuck it out if it hadn't been for the injection of Allen Klein into the already volatile situation. James knew of Klein's propensity for lawsuits and tearing up contracts, and in the few meetings James had with him, Klein's behavior had been characteristically harrowing. This was clearly the time to abandon ship. After all, James had Northern stockholders to consider. So he sold his stock to Lew Grade—without ever mentioning it to any of the Beatles.*

---

* Geoffrey Ellis, who still sat on the board of NEMS, had knowledge of the sale, but because NEMS no longer worked for the Beatles, he never informed them either.

With John and Yoko in Amsterdam, Paul and Linda in East Hampton, New York, on their honeymoon, and Klein on vacation in Puerto Rico, that left only George to go see Dick James to ask him to postpone the sale until Paul and John could return to London. Neil Aspinall and Derek Taylor accompanied George on this sensitive diplomatic mission. I counseled them all not to get into any trouble, but Derek and Neil seemed hell-bent on giving Dick James a piece of their minds and had a few scotch and Cokes before leaving the office.

They weren't in Dick James' Charing Cross Road office two minutes before things got out of hand. James said he had no intention of waiting for John to get out of bed; he said he had to move his shares quickly or the price might fall. "It's a very serious matter," he told them solicitiously.

George lost his composure, jumped up, and began to scream, *"It's fucking serious to John and Paul is what it is!"* Derek and Neil happily chimed in, and the meeting turned into a verbal bloodbath during which George, Neil, and Derek got out all the animosity they had been saving up for James over the years. It ended with them storming out of the office and James warning them, "You're getting a lot of very bad advice, if I may say so."

Again the Beatles rode into financial battle, this time with Allen Klein leading them. Klein enlisted the aid of Bruce Omrod, an officer with the merchant bank of Henry Ansbacher and Co. "Sergeant" Omrod, as he was nicknamed, was a tall, distinguished gentleman experienced in takeover battles. But Omrod had no idea what he was letting himself in for in agreeing to make a counterbid for Northern and supervise the purchase. On Friday, April 11, the Beatles formally announced their plan to fight the ATV bid. Newspaper advertisements appeared urging undecided shareholders not to accept ATV's offers. Omrod told the *Financial Times* that the Beatles would make a substantial counteroffer. "Finding the cash is a detail, but no more than a detail."

It was that detail that put the final wedge between John and Paul. In order to raise the money for a counteroffer, John and Paul would have to put up their shares in Northern Songs as collateral. Even Klein was chipping in by putting up 145,000 shares of his prudently held MGM stock. But under the advice of the Eastmans, Paul refused to put up his stock. At first he said it was because the Eastmans said it was too risky, until the reason became clear at a meeting at Ansbacher on April 20. When the Beatles' Northern Stock holdings were tallied, it was disclosed that Paul had 751,000 shares of Northern Songs versus John's 644,000. At Paul's direction, I had been purchasing shares secretly for him in his own name. Paul had recently learned a greater appreciation for the value of a copyright, especially his own. As he put it, "It was a matter of investing in something you believed in instead of supermarkets and furniture stores . . . so I invested in myself."

"You bastard!" John spit. "You've been buying up stock behind our backs!"

Paul blushed and shrugged limply. "Ooops, sorry!" he smiled.

"This is fuckin' low!" John said. "This is the first time any of us have gone behind each other's backs."

Paul shrugged again. "I felt like I had some beanies and I wanted some more," he said.

Without informing ATV or the Beatles, the brokers on the London market identified the holders of the outstanding shares in Northern Songs, and a meeting of the three largest shareholders was arranged to protect their investment. It was agreed to pool all the shares in a consortium representing nearly 14 percent—the decisive hand.

John's and Paul's first tactic was to imply that if the sale to ATV went through, they would stop composing together and not fulfill their six songs a year minimum stipulated in their Northern contracts. An exasperated Lew Grade felt it necessary to reassure the stockholders in a statement to the *Financial Times* saying, "I have every confidence in the boys' creativity. They would not possibly be able to sit still and write only six new songs a year. Apart from that, songwriting plays an important part in the boys' income."

Another point of contention was that if John and Paul gained control of Northern Songs, who would sit on the board? Allen Klein? With Klein's reputation, his presence would probably not be agreeable to the stockholders. By Easter it seemed that the consortium would throw their shares in with the Beatles on the basis of an extended songwriting contract with Northern—but only on the condition that a new board of directors would be elected. This board would be comprised of three directors—none of whom could be Allen Klein. One suggestion for a board member acceptable to both the stockholders and John and Paul was David Platz, the respected head of Essex Music Corporation and the fourteen-time winner of the Ivor Novello Award for Great Britain's best music publisher. A second suggestion was Ian Gordon, one of the managing directors of Constellation, who had an easygoing relationship with what the consortium regarded as "show business types" like John and Paul.

On May 3 ATV made front-page financial news when they announced they were extending the date on their bid for Northern Stock until May 15. If they had not won control of the company by then, they intended to turn the tables on the Beatles and accept their partial bid of forty-two shillings, sixpence a share.

The next day Northern Songs' price rose by nine pence.

Two days before the ATV deadline it seemed they had failed in their takeover bid, and a statement to that effect was drawn up and released to the press. In a front-page article in the *Financial Times* ATV announced they had come within 150,000 shares of owning 47 percent of Northern Songs. It appeared the Beatles had won.

Meanwhile, as Ian Gordon, officers of Astaire and Co., Eastman, Klein, John, Yoko, and Paul were tied up in a five-hour meeting, trying to come to terms with the consortium, John lost his temper. "I don't see why I should work for a company in which I have no say," he told those present. "I'm not going to be fucked around by men in suits sitting on their fat arses in the City."

John's statement effectively threw the consortium into ATV's hands. On May 19, although ATV had already admitted defeat in the papers, the consortium signed a deal with them shortly before the Beatles' own bid expired at three P.M. With some additional machinations and business details, the deal dragged on until October, when it was finally closed. But as far as John and Paul were concerned it was all over now except for the mopping up. They had lost their child. To pour salt in the wound, ATV appointed Dick James to sit on the board of directors.

John and Paul were left with a £5,000 bill for Ansbacher and Co.'s services.

* * *

5.

NOW WAS THE TIME for Klein to try to renegotiate the Beatles' contract with EMI and Capitol and get them one of those huge advances he was famous for, except for one small detail—he didn't legally represent them. All this time Klein had been operating on the Beatles' behalf without a signed contract. He had long ago drawn up a contract for them to sign, but so far none of them had actually put his signature to it. The terms were for a three-year period, cancelable by either side at the end of each year. Klein's fee for managing them, however, was not to be the standard 20 percent of their income—income which they were already earning before Klein appeared on the scene—but 20 percent of whatever increases he made for them. Therefore, renegotiating their recording contracts was a potentially large source of income to Klein.

As far as Paul was concerned, the Eastmans wouldn't even consider letting him sign a contract with Klein under any circumstances. Paul still clung to the hope that he could get the other Beatles to see Klein's evil ways before it was too late, but no matter what the evidence seemed to be, they stuck with Klein rather than cast their lot in with the Eastmans. As John told Paul about Klein, "Anybody that bad can't be all that bad."

One night in early May, on one of the rare occasions all four Beatles were in the Abbey Road studios together, there was a rumor going around that Klein was going to appear that night for a showdown. Paul dreaded having to speak to Klein. He even was having nightmares in which Klein was a dentist chasing him with a drill. Sure enough, late that evening Klein appeared with a set of management contracts under his arm.

He stuck the contracts under Paul's nose and said, "I gotta have dis ting signed. I gotta have you guys on contract."

"On a Friday night?" Paul asked innocently. "What's the big hurry? Give me the contracts and on Monday—"

Everybody groaned. "Uhhh, there he goes again," John said. "You're stalling again, Paul."

"But what's the big hurry?" Paul insisted.

Klein explained that he was on his way to the airport to catch a plane for New York, where there was an ABKCO board meeting over the weekend. ABKCO was Klein's personally owned company—the initials stood for Allen and Betty Klein Company—and according to Paul, "Klein was the 'board,' the tables, and the chairs." Paul insisted he could not sign any contracts without first showing them to his London attorney, Charles Corman. But since Corman was an orthodox Jew and this was the Sabbath, it would not be possible to reach him until Sunday.

"Oh yeah? Well, we can't wait. If you won't sign dis, den we gotta do majority rules." Klein was blatantly trying to turn the three other Beatles against Paul.

"Forget it," Paul said. "You'll never get Ringo." Paul turned to wink at Ringo, but the drummer only gave him a sick look.

"I'm in with them," Ringo said.

"It's like bloody Julius Caesar!" Paul said. "I've been stabbed in the bloody back! So it's come to this . . ."

Paul never got any sympathy from the other Beatles, particularly in light of his having bought up Northern Songs' stock without telling anyone. Klein flew out of London that night without Paul's signature, but it didn't matter. While his plane was still in the air, I received a phone call in New York where I happened to be on business with Neil Aspinall. It was John. He was with George and Ringo, and they were instructing Neil and me to sign Klein's contracts in our capacity as directors of Apple Corp. Thus on May 8, 1969, Paul was effectively caught in Klein's web.

Much to Paul's discredit, his onerous relationship with Klein didn't stop him from standing behind the man when it came to the renegotiation of contracts with EMI and Capitol. Although Sir Joseph Lockwood was not happy about the idea of paying the Beatles more money, they had already fulfilled their minimum number of albums and singles, and Sir Joe didn't think it unfair if they got a commensurate increase for additional product. One day in May, Allen Klein appeared in Sir Joe's office with all four Beatles in tow. "I don't mind talking about this," Sir Joe said, "as long as there's some benefit to both sides."

Klein chuckled. "You don't understand," he said. "We get everything, and you get nothing."

Sir Joe thought that the man was surely joking, but as the minutes passed Klein became more threatening and crass. Sir Joe called an end to the meeting and asked Klein to leave. Klein marched out the door with John, Yoko, George, and Ringo behind him. Paul hung back, making apologetic faces at Sir Joe behind the others' backs.

"That's all right," Sir Joe said to his assistant. "They'll be back." Sure enough, half an hour later Klein called to apologize, and negotiations later resumed. The deal wasn't finished until September, but when it was done the Beatles were mighty impressed. Under the new terms two new albums were due each year until 1976. All the new albums would net them an unprecedented 58¢ royalty until 1972 and a 72¢ royalty thereafter until 1976—an increase from a previous 39¢ royalty per LP. To boot, reissues of early recordings would garner a 50¢ royalty until 1972 and 72¢ thereafter. However, for the first time in the Beatles' history, Klein agreed to re-release old material, a marketing ploy that Brian swore he would never agree to. Now the record stores would be flooded with "Best of" albums and cheap compilations. Still, because of this repackaging, the Beatles' royalty incomes soared.

Paul was as impressed as the rest of them, albeit grudgingly. Paul never complained about making money. "If you're screwing us," he told Klein, "I can't see how."

But that didn't mean the Eastmans were going to let Paul sign the new recording contracts that Klein had negotiated. They feared that if Paul signed them it could be legally interpreted that Klein represented Paul, and he would therefore be entitled to 20 percent of Paul's increased earnings. Hypocritically, Paul attended the photo session to commemorate the contract signing. He was photographed standing around a table with Klein and the three other Beatles, as if his signature was on the contract with the rest of them. Thus, as far as the outside world knew, the Beatles were still whole.

* * *

6.

*W*ITH KLEIN now in power there followed a blood-letting that no one could have anticipated. Klein's first task was a mass firing. Paul also backed Klein in this endeavor. For months Paul had been announcing his intention to clear Apple of deadwood. He had asked several of the executives for a list of all Apple employees who weren't essential, but the request so distressed us that we put off the task and pretended the list was forgotten or misplaced when Paul demanded to see it. Now such a list was no longer necessary. Klein was making his own decisions.

Brian Lewis in the contracts department was one of the first to go. The publishing office was closed down, and Dennis O'Dell of the film division resigned. Magic Alex, away on a trip to Paris, returned to London to find himself locked out of his Boston Place laboratory and his precious inventions sold to an electronics scrap dealer. Klein had computed that Alex had cost the company a reported £160,000, aside from the £20,000 paid for the Boston Place property. Of the 100 patents Alex had applied for through EMI's helpful patent attorneys, every single one of them had been turned down as not being an invention but just an embellishment on an already patented idea.

Some of the dirty work was left to me. I have been criticized for serving Allen Klein in this task, but I unhappily agreed to do the job only because I hoped the news could be delivered with kindness and dignity, instead of from Klein's mouth.

Six employees and their staffs went in one afternoon. One of the most regrettable firings of the day was Ron Kass. Since it was such a nice sunny spring day, I asked him to take a walk with me and told him the bad news on Savile Row. Kass was deeply hurt but not surprised. Klein had seemed especially resentful of Kass all along. Kass was doing an excellent job with the record company and ran the division with pride—and corresponding autonomy as far as Klein was concerned. But Kass believed that Klein's resentment over him was due less to a power struggle in business than to the fact that Klein wanted to live in the luxurious town house Kass occupied. Apple was picking up the tab, as part of Kass' contract, on a picturesque town house on South Street in Mayfair, and Klein was searching for a permanent place to live in London.

Klein had launched an out-and-out campaign against Kass. One day Klein had requested a meeting in my office with all four Beatles, Yoko, Neil, and Ron Kass. Klein opened a folder and produced a check that looked vaguely familiar to Kass. It was from Capitol Records in New York, and it was made out to Kass for $1,250. Kass remembered the check after seeing the date. It was made out on the first official day of his employment with Apple Records, on the day that John and Paul had arrived in New York to publicize the opening of Apple. The English currency laws allowed an English resident to take only £50 in cash out of the country, and the two Beatles needed more spending money than that. Kass had requested that Capitol Records advance them some cash, but the accounting department refused, afraid of getting involved in English tax matters. Instead, they agreed to give Kass a check made out to him, which Kass could cash at their New York bank. The $1,250 would subsequently be paid back to them by Apple in London.

"What happened to dis money?" Klein demanded, waving the check in the air.

Kass recounted the incident, ending by turning to Neil to whom he had given the $1,250 on the Chinese Junk in Manhattan Harbor. Neil shrugged. "I hardly remember being in New York let alone taking the twelve hundred dollars," he said.

Ron was indignant. "Surely you don't think I stole twelve hundred and fifty dollars on my first day of work?" The Beatles all said they believed him, but Kass could see from the expressions on their faces that Klein had planted a seed of doubt, and they would never fully trust him again.

When we returned to 3 Savile Row, I signed over the lease of the town house that Klein wanted so badly to Ron Kass. Klein never forgave me, and that was probably the moment he put me on his hit list, but it didn't matter. I got supreme pleasure in seeing Kass get that town house. He lives there to this day with his wife, actress Joan Collins, and their two daughters.

Another poignant redundancy that day was Alistair Taylor, who had been at Brian's side the first moment he laid eyes on the four boys in the Cavern Club. Alistair had not only been a loyal friend and supporter, but he was probably the most frugal of all their employees. When I broke the news to him he choked back tears. At first he refused to believe it and spent the rest of the day on the phone in his office trying to reach Paul or John to hear it from them directly, but neither of them would take his calls. Alistair never heard from or saw any of them again, except indirectly through an article in the *Daily Mail.* A reporter came to 3 Savile Row to interview Alistair as he cleaned out his desk. "It was a hell of a blow," he said, shaking his head. When Paul was asked for comment, he said, "It isn't possible to be nice about giving someone the sack," and I wondered how he would know since I was the one who was doing it.

Klein's number-one man, Peter Howard, moved into 3 Savile Row and took over financial expenditures. The waiting room was cleared of loonies and eccentrics, and the feeling of joy that had once pervaded the building descended into gloom. All the employees were now asked to sign in and out on time cards. When Klein and his staff would pull up at the front door in his limousine, the Apple Scruffs would stick their heads through the front door and yell, "Mafia's coming!"

An associate of Kass' named Jack Oliver was named head of Apple Records. Shortly after, Peter Asher resigned his position, taking James Taylor with him. Asher went on to become one of the music business's premier record producers, noted in particular for his work with Linda Ronstadt.

Three Savile Row had turned into a mausoleum just waiting for a death.

Chapter Eighteen

*Yeah, sure I know John thinks we <u>hate</u> her and
that we're all a bunch of two-faced fuckers running
around behind his back sniveling and bad mouthing
her, sticking pins in our homemade Yoko Ono
voodoo dolls, but you know and I know what's
happening, and that's not happening at all. No one
in this building <u>hates</u> her. <u>Hate!</u> That's a very
strong accusation and an extreme assumption. I
can't say as I blame him for thinking that sometimes,
but the reason he feels that way is because we don't
<u>love</u> her.*

—Derek Taylor

1.

*T*HROUGH ALL THIS, through the in-fighting and
the hectic meetings and the fiascos of Nemperor
and Northern Songs, John and Yoko managed to keep involved
in a myriad number of astonishing projects. These included recordings of experimental music, 16-mm films, and the continua-
tion of their peace campaign in which acorns were solicited from
fans all over the world and mailed to the heads of governments.
There was also more baggism, in which the couple appeared inside
large canvas bags and made noises at public events, and the purchase of an island called Dornish, intended as a retreat but quickly
given away to a band of traveling hippies to use as a commune.
Also during this time, on April 22, 1969, John changed his name
from John Winston Lennon to John Ono Lennon in a brief ceremony on the roof of 3 Savile Row presided over by the Commissioner of Oaths. John happily told an attending reporter: "Yoko
changed her name for me; I've changed mine for her . . . It gives
us nine O's between us, which is good luck . . . Three names
is enough for anyone, four would be greedy."

John and Yoko also formed their own company called Bag
Productions and took over what had been Ron Kass' ground-floor
office. The once shining white room was slowly transformed into
a messy assemblage of magazines, newspapers, memorabilia, gifts

from fans, spilled coffee, and butt-filled ashtrays. The white walls were strewn with handwritten signs saying "Peace," "Hair Peace," and "Baggism Peace." In this office they continued to welcome the curious press and were available to any qualified journalist providing them a platform from which to further their dogma. John's hair grew longer and stringier, and at times he and Yoko looked like refugees from some poor hippie commune.

On May 9, 1969, on the small Apple subsidiary label called Zapple, John and Yoko released *Unfinished Music No. 2—Life with the Lions.* This album was presumably the next edition in the musical diary of the couples' adventures, this installment covering the time from her first miscarriage up to the present. It had another unfortunate cover. The front was a dismal shot taken in the Queen Charlotte's Maternity Hospital, with John lying on the floor next to Yoko in her hospital bed. The back cover was the pitiful photo of them surrounded by police after their drug court appearance. The album inside was no less unpleasant than its package. The first side featured a twenty-six-minute live recording of John and Yoko's performance at Mitchell Hall in Cambridge the previous March in which Yoko yodeled and shrieked in counterpoint to John's syncopated guitar feedback. It also included the debut of what was to become Yoko's signature piece, the astonishing "Don't Worry, Kyoko, Mummy's Only Looking for Her Hand in the Snow," written for Yoko's daughter. Side two included Yoko singing stories from a newspaper, with John chanting in the background, and a four-minute segment of the heartbeat of the baby that Yoko miscarried. The album was scathingly reviewed and largely ignored by the public, except as a curiosity. The other Beatles, although they obviously hated it, kept silent.

The following month John and Yoko indulged themselves further by releasing yet another musical tale about their adventures, this one a commercial single called "The Ballad of John and Yoko." This lyric drama about their tribulations was practically a solo recording by John. When John wanted to go into the studios to record it, George was conveniently busy recording chants with the Radha Krishna monks, and Ringo was pursuing his movie career, co-starring with Peter Sellers in *The Magic Christian.* Paul was the only one still gracious enough to come to the studio to help John record. He played the drum part, the only instrument John could not play himself. Aside from the vanity of the subject matter, "The Ballad of John and Yoko" was a good old-fashioned Lennon rocker and an instant hit. I was immortalized in the verse that goes, "Peter Brown called to say you can make it okay; You can get married in Gibraltar near Spain."

Unfortunately, the refrain of each stanza, "Christ you know it ain't easy," caused the song to be banned on the BBC, as well as on several Bible Belt stations in America, all in light of John's previous "Jesus" statements.

Without pausing to take a breath, John and Yoko decided to pursue their peace campaign by staging another bed-in. The perfect opportunity presented itself when Pattie and George and Ringo and Maureen booked passage on the *Queen Elizabeth II* to America. Ringo was scheduled to shoot additional scenes for *The Magic Christian* on board during the crossing. John and Yoko decided to join them on the journey, after which they would open their peace campaign in New York where it could reach the widest, most receptive audience.

But John and Yoko were in for a nasty shock when they arrived at the Southampton pier accompanied by Kyoko, Derek Taylor, their new personal assistant Anthony Fawcett, a two-man film crew to record all of their activities, and twenty-six pieces of luggage; John was refused a temporary visa to the United States because of his 1969 drug conviction. He was turned away from the boat, rejected as a criminal. Disappointed and bitter, John was convinced this was just a simple matter that Allen Klein and the immigration lawyers could clear up. Refusing to be totally defeated, he and Yoko went directly to Heathrow airport from the pier and boarded a flight for Freeport in the Bahamas, twelve hundred dollars overweight. The Bahamas were chosen because they were in the British Commonwealth, and John could not be refused admittance. They were also selected because the Bahamas were close enough to the United States, John thought, for them to have access to the American media.

But the Bahamas didn't turn out to be the most readily accessible place to stage a bed-in. Its proximity to the U.S. still didn't make it a hub of international journalism, and most American newspaper editors were not about to come up with airfare for reporters and photographers to go look at John Lennon and his wife sitting in bed. Worse, the hotel only had rooms with twin beds cemented to the floor with a three-foot gap between them, a distance the size of the Grand Canyon to John and Yoko. As it turned out, sitting in bed all day when it was so beautiful and sunny outside was just a trifle too perverse, even for them, and two days later they were off to Toronto with all twenty-six pieces of luggage and their entourage.

Again, at the Toronto airport, John was detained by immigration officials for almost four hours before he was allowed to enter the country on a provisional visa. After one restless night in Toronto, while Allen Klein made a last-ditch effort to get John into the United States, they moved on to Montreal where they began a ten-day bed-in at the Queen Elizabeth Hotel. This one was more of a circus than their Amsterdam stint. The easy access of the American press did bring scores of reporters to their bedside, as well as such luminaries as poet Allen Ginsberg and cartoonist Al Capp who came to heckle them. They gave some sixty interviews in those ten days, including many live radio broadcasts beamed to a large American audience. Again, the press treated them with amused curiosity, but no one doubted the sincerity of their convictions.

The Montreal bed-in climaxed with a Saturday night sing-in, attended by, among others, Tommy Smothers, Timothy Leary, Rabbi Abraham Feinberg, and the entire Canadian chapter of the Radha Krishna Temple. The event was photographed by three camera units, one from the BCB, one from the BCBC, and one from Murray the K's production company, in addition to John and Yoko's own crew. A new song written by John called "Give Peace a Chance" was recorded live in two sessions in the hotel bedroom on a Nagra tape recorder. "Give Peace a Chance" was later released on Apple, credited to Lennon-McCartney under the musicianship of something called the Plastic Ono Band. The song became the utopian theme music of the era, replacing "The Ballad of John and Yoko" on the record charts as the world continued to tune in on what was becoming an international soap opera.

*　*　*

2.

THE SUMMER of 1969 was the last big whimper of the sixties. That summer seemed to sum up all we had learned and all our dashed dreams. In the summer of '69 half a million disciples of the rock generation assembled on Yasgur's farm in Woodstock in a three-day celebration of music and love. U.S. astronaut Neil Armstrong became the first human to set foot on the moon. In London, Brian Jones, the former member of the Rolling Stones who was coldly ostracized by Mick Jagger, was found floating dead in the swimming pool behind his mansion, bloated with barbiturates and booze. In Los Angeles, having heard what he believed was a call to destruction on the Beatles' song "Helter Skelter" from the *White Album*, Charles Manson and his gang of lunatics slashed their way into infamy with the Tate-LaBianca murders.

That summer was also a turning point for John and Yoko. Worn out from their bed-ins, which might have looked like restful experiences but were actually exhausting, they decided to get away from it all and take a real vacation. They invited Kyoko and Julian to go with them and rounded the children up from Tony Cox and Cynthia. It was John and Yoko's earnest hope that the two kids would get to know and like each other, and then they could all be together like a modern-day nuclear family. They decided on a simple motor trip to visit one of Aunt Mimi's sisters in Scotland. Although John never drove himself because he couldn't see much beyond the hood of the car, he insisted on driving all the way to Scotland in an Austin Mini. I tried to dissuade John from this, but it was no use, they were off. Three days into the trip I got a call from John asking me to arrange for his chauffeur, Les Anthony, to deliver a larger car, an Austin Maxi, to John somewhere on the road. A day later I received a most alarming call; John had driven the car off the road headfirst into a ditch. All of them had been injured and had been rushed to a hospital in Scotland. John was the most severely gashed and received seventeen stitches. Yoko received fourteen and Kyoko four.

Within an hour it was on the wire services and a very concerned Cynthia was on the phone. I agreed to take her with me up to

Edinburgh the next morning so she could fetch Julian, but by the time we arrived, he was already gone; Aunt Mimi's sister had collected him and taken him to her house in Edinburgh. Cynthia was a pitiful sight in that hospital corridor, her injured child having been snatched away from her like that. She asked to see John and Yoko, but a nurse returned from their room saying they didn't want to be disturbed.

Yoko, whose back was severely wrenched in the accident, was taken by stretcher to a private helicopter on the hospital lawn. From there she was transferred to a private jet John had rented for her and transported to Heathrow. Another helicopter completed the trip home to Weybridge. The Austin Maxi automobile, complete with Yoko's and John's bloodstains still on the front seat, was crushed into a cube and shipped to Kenwood, where it was put on a platform and displayed in the garden as sculpture.

Later that summer, still recuperating from the accident, John and Yoko moved into their real first home, "Tittenhurst Park," a £150,000 estate John had purchased just outside of Ascot. This stately white mansion was situated on seventy-four acres of prime wooded hills and gardens, featuring its own lake and over fifty varieties of exotic trees and flora. Even before they moved in, massive interior renovations were undertaken on the house, including a large, modern kitchen and a well-equipped, sound-proofed professional recording studio. All the business areas of the house were repainted and carpeted in black; all the living areas were done in pure white. John and Yoko also had a small island with a gazebo on it built in the middle of the lake, so they would have somewhere to row on sunny summer afternoons and eat a picnic lunch.

Except they didn't do much picnicking that summer. After moving to Tittenhurst they virtually disappeared, not just from public view but from everyone. This sent the press office at Apple into a tailspin, as they were publicizing the "Ballad of John and Yoko," which was making a strong showing on the charts. They had disappeared like this once before, at Montague Square, and that meant only one thing: heroin again. Told here for the first time, Yoko says it was the accident that put them back on heroin, as an antidote to the back pain. They sequestered themselves in the master bedroom of Tittenhurst Park and never came out. They took all their meals in the room on trays. The only messages in or out were transmitted by Val, the cook; Anthony Fawcett, their new assistant; or Yoko's friend Dan Richter, who was now living at Tittenhurst in one of the guest bedrooms.

It was Paul who finally compelled John to come out of that bedroom in Tittenhurst Park. Paul with his irrepressible enthusiasm for the Beatles had gone ahead with plans for a new album, to be titled *Abbey Road.* Despite the fact that their kingdom was crumbling down around them, despite almost unbearable acrimony among them as a group, Paul had managed to assemble all the weary Beatles, plus George Martin, Neil, and Mal, into the studios for one last hurrah.

Yoko was there, too. She was pregnant again, it was announced, and in delicate health. John refused to be separated from her, so a bed was moved into the studio, where she napped or read or knitted while John worked with Paul.

Back at Tittenhurst Park by August, John and Yoko decided they had better get off the heroin before they got even more deeply addicted. They decided to do it alone, without any help at all—"cold turkey" as the addicts call it. "We were very square people in a way," Yoko says. "We wouldn't kick in a hospital because we wouldn't let anybody know. We just went straight cold turkey. The thing is, because we never injected, I don't think we were sort of—well, we were hooked, but I don't think it was a great amount. Still, it was hard. Cold turkey is always hard."

John and Yoko's intimates that summer, particularly Magic Alex, Ray Connolly, and Neil Aspinall, remember the events of this summer differently from Yoko. They remember visiting John and Yoko at the London Clinic, where they say both of them were undergoing treatment for heroin withdrawal. Alex, who was around Tittenhurst Park a great deal, also remembers seeing syringes in the house.

In any event, it was all over by the morning of August 24, when John composed the song "Cold Turkey" in one creative outburst. He rehearsed it all afternoon and recorded it that evening, with Ringo and Klaus Voorman assisting. The song was appropriately harrowing, and John got right to the heart of his subject matter with his usual simple clarity: "Temperature's rising, fever is high, can't see no future, can't see no sky: / my feet are so heavy, so is my head; I wish I was a baby, I wish I was dead." John naively suggested to Paul that "Cold Turkey" be released as the Beatles next single, and Paul was understandably incredulous. John said, "Well, bugger you," and he released it himself as a product of the Plastic Ono Band. The critical response was predictable, and John was lambasted for "Cold Turkey." Ironically, while "Cold Turkey" may have been musically abrasive and not the happiest subject for a pop song, it was again another example of John's bravery and honesty, an attempt at making his work into a reflection of his life, just like any painter or writer. The public didn't buy it though. It was banned from airplay by the BBC, and in America it struggled its way up the charts to number thirty before dropping off. In England loyal but confused fans brought the single into the top twenty before it disappeared altogether.

3.

*I*N EARLY SEPTEMBER John received a telephone call from concert promoter John Brower who was holding something called the Toronto Rock and Roll Festival in Canada on September 12. Brower was only calling to ask if John wanted to attend the concert as part of the audience; on a whim John agreed to accept Brower's offer of free plane tickets only if he and Yoko could *appear* on stage. John almost immediately regretted this offer, since he had no backup band, no material rehearsed, and he was still very sick from drugs. Nevertheless, with Eric Clapton's encouragement, John rounded up several musicians, including Klaus Voorman, and went to Toronto. Because they missed their original flight, they arrived at the Varsity Stadium in Toronto a scarce half hour before they went on. There was no time for anything more than a tune-up session. John, nervous and sick to his stomach from drugs, vomited profusely backstage before the impromptu group went on. He knew as he went onstage that he would be heavily judged for this performance; it was the first time that any Beatle had appeared in a solo performance and the first performance by any Beatle since the rooftop set for *Let It Be.*

John and Yoko's mere presence on the stage caused a near-riot in the stadium. The frenzied crowd was ecstatic at John's surprise appearance. When the crowd quieted down, John timidly went to the microphone and said in a voice quavering with fear, "We're just gonna do numbers that we know, y'know, because we've never played together before." There followed a third-rate, pell-mell performance by some of the world's finest rock musicians rushing through unrehearsed old standards like "Blue Suede Shoes" and "Dizzy Miss Lizzie." The crowd didn't mind how awful they were; they loved every second. Then came the world premiere of "Cold Turkey," which had not been released to the public as yet. The audience was as confused as they were stunned by this number but applauded it enthusiastically anyway. Then, to everyone's amazement, the stage was cleared of all musicians, except for John, at which point Yoko Ono emerged from a large canvas bag that had been sitting at the side of the stage. They launched into a seventeen-minute version of "Don't Worry Kyoko, Mummy's Only Looking for Her Hand in the Snow," complete with Yoko's blood-curdling howls, screams, and shrieks. It left the audience completely baffled, but they certainly got their money's worth.

Surprisingly, John was elated over the performance. He remembered the thrill of performing live again, and this time the speaker systems were advanced enough to be heard. He was so happy with the experience that on the plane ride home he decided he was going to formally announce to the press that he was leaving the Beatles and starting his own band with Eric Clapton and Klaus Voorman.

Allen Klein, who had joined John and Yoko in Toronto for the plane ride back to London, dissuaded him from this. The new recording contracts Klein had negotiated for the Beatles with EMI and Capitol weren't in effect just yet, and the huge advances hadn't all been paid. Klein asked John to wait until the contracts were finalized before he started talk that the Beatles were disbanding.

But that didn't keep John from enjoying the satisfaction of telling Paul. Shortly after John's return from Toronto, he demanded a meeting at Apple. Paul arrived, his usual magnanimous self, full of plans for new Beatles projects. But no matter what Paul suggested, John kept saying, "No, I don't want to do that," or "No, I'm not interested." The discussion finally dissolved into a mean argument, which Paul finally recovered from by launching into one of his Beatle pep talks, one of those "Toppermost to the Poppermost" things. "When everything is said and done," he summed up, "we're still the Beatles, aren't we?"

"Aw fuck," John said, "I ain't no Beatle."

Paul wouldn't hear it. "Of course you are—"

"I'm not!" John shouted, "Don't you understand? It's over! *Over!* I want a divorce, just like the divorce I got from Cynthia! Can't you get it through your bloody head?"

The meeting ended shortly after with John rushing down the stairs, Yoko right behind him, shouting, "It's over! Finished!"

Still, John said nothing to the press, and when he and Yoko left Savile Row that afternoon in their white Rolls-Royce, Paul still somehow believed that John would calm down and there would always be the Beatles.

4.

*O*N OCTOBER 9, the day of John's twenty-ninth birthday, Yoko was rushed to the Kings College Hospital in Denmark Hill, London, for a series of emergency blood transfusions. Four days later it was quietly reported in the daily papers that she had miscarried again.

Depressed and exhausted from this second loss, John and Yoko took a Greek vacation with Magic Alex. They rented a yacht with a small crew and set out into the Mediterranean, with no destination except to get away from the rest of the world. John and Yoko vowed to use the ten-day cruise to purge their bodies of all the poisonous drugs and alcohol they had been using, and they went on a total fast except for water. Instead of improving their health, this radical approach only seemed to do more damage to their bodies and their temperaments. Alex was witness to all manner of physical violence between the couple and substantial damage to the boat. More than a few times John hauled off and gave Yoko a good walloping—just as he had done to Cynthia years before.

Upon returning to London, John released *The Wedding Album* on Apple. This was another experimental album, consisting of some recordings made at their Amsterdam bed-in, including a long selection in which John and Yoko repeat each other's names in a chant. The expensively boxed album, which sold for nine dollars at a time when most LPs cost four dollars, contained newspapers clippings, a plastic facsimile of a piece of wedding cake, and a copy of their marriage certificate. The release of this album was quickly followed by the release of the single, "Cold Turkey."

On the morning of November 26, while reading stories in the daily papers about the war in Vietnam and the starving children in Biafra, John decided that he was ashamed to be an MBE and that he would return the award to the Queen in protest. He ordered his chauffeur, Les Anthony, to drive to Bournemouth and fetch the MBE from where it sat on top of Aunt Mimi's television set. Mimi later said, "If I knew what John wanted it for, I never would have given it to him."

John dictated a letter to the Queen on Bag Productions stationery, saying, "Your Majesty, I am returning this MBE in protest against Britain's involvement in the Nigeria-Biafra thing, against our support of America in Vietnam, and against 'Cold Turkey' slipping down the charts. With love, John Lennon of Bag."

The mention of "Cold Turkey" was added as an afterthought, one that John would seriously regret. It cheapened the whole gesture of returning the MBE, turning it into another John Lennon publicity gimmick. John and Yoko delivered the medal themselves to the tradesmen's entrance at Buckingham Palace. A spokesman for the Palace told the press that it was ironic "that he should return the medal, as the first MBEs that were returned were from people protesting that Mr. Lennon . . . was given the award in the first place."

"I don't think the Queen will be embarrassed," John said.

"The Queen is above embarrassment," replied the spokesman.

Soon after returning his MBE, John stepped up his peace activities. This was launched with an international billboard campaign, in which billboards in twelve major cities around the world carried the message: "War Is Over—If You Want It—Happy Christmas John and Yoko." This campaign was kicked off with a charity concert for the United Nations Children's Fund held at the Lyceum Theater in London. The day after the concert, John and Yoko were off to Toronto again, this time to help instigate plans for a mammoth free "peace concert" to be held at an as yet undetermined site the coming summer. The concert was to be promoted by John Brower and his partner Ritchie Yorke, who had arranged John and Yoko's appearance at the Toronto Rock and Roll Festival. More than thirty billboards blanketed Toronto for John and Yoko's arrival. The Canadian press covered their every move from the time they entered the country, and John and Yoko kept them busy. They held a press conference at the Ontario Science Center to announce the peace concert would incorporate a worldwide "peace vote" in which the audience would vote for peace or war on a ballot, and then John and Yoko would "give [the ballots] to the United States." John and Yoko were also filmed during a meeting with Marshall McLuhan at the University of Toronto. They then hired a glass-roofed observation train to take them to Montreal, where their Rolls-Royce had already been shipped for their use. In Montreal they had an hour-long meeting with Canadian Prime Minister Pierre Trudeau, which gave their campaign enormous credence and energy. "If there were more leaders like Mr. Trudeau," John told the assembled press corps after their meeting, "the world would have peace." Yoko added, "It was a beautiful meeting. We got good incentive."

John and Yoko returned to Tittenhurst Park for Christmas, then jetted on to Aalborg, Denmark, on December 29, where Tony Cox had moved with Kyoko and his new wife, an American girl named Melinda. For several months now Tony had been reluctant to let Yoko see her daughter. There had been no specific custody agreement when they were divorced. Tony knew of John and Yoko's drug addiction and didn't like the idea of Kyoko being exposed to them in that state. Also, he was now very angry about the car accident in Scotland in which Kyoko was injured. At first Cox said that it could have happened to anybody, and that it was Kyoko's "karma" that she was hurt, but now he was complaining that she was permanently injured and had difficulty breathing at night. John and Yoko insisted they wanted her to spend the spring with them at Tittenhurst and went to Denmark to convince Cox.

When they got to Cox's farmhouse in the frozen wastes of Aalborg, they found that Cox was on his own trip. He was vehemently opposed to the use of any drugs, cigarettes, and alcohol, and they were forced to empty their pockets and luggage of any of these evils before being allowed into his farmhouse. Cox was also involved in a group called the "Harbingers" who were some sort of cosmic commune, and two of the members named Hamrick and Leonard were fetched to hypnotize John into giving up smoking. John, who was rarely without a cigarette in his hand, agreed to this ritual, in part to please Cox. Then, to make the event seem even more surreal, John and Yoko agreed to have all their hair cut off by a woman barber in Cox's barn. The haircuts were skinhead short, and the two of them never looked more awful and waiflike. The clippings were saved in plastic bags for later use.

In the interim, concert promoter John Brower and his partner Ritchie Yorke flew to Aalborg to get John and Yoko's official approval for the plans for the upcoming peace concert. Allen Klein, who had appeared in Aalborg to help negotiate Kyoko's move to Tittenhurst, presided at the meeting. Brower and Yorke were ordered to empty their pockets at the door and then were led into Cox's simple country kitchen to find John and Yoko, practically bald, with a bewildered Kyoko pulling at Brower's jacket and whispering, "I'm a girl, I'm a girl."

John and Yoko were reading over the advertising material about the peace concert that Brower and Yorke had brought with them, when John came across a flyer that said, "Free (for one dollar) John Lennon Peace Festival. Toronto, July 3, 4, 5, to celebrate the year 1 A.P. War is over if you want it."

"No! No! No!" John shouted. "Free means free, man! Not one bloody dollar!" Brower and Yorke argued that it wasn't feasible to set up a concert to be attended by hundreds of thousands of people without some way to pay for sanitation and portable toilets. They said that a business office called Karma Productions had already been set up to sell tickets. John flew into one of his more vicious rages. He refused to give the concert his sanction or authorization unless Brower and Yorke could come up with a positively one hundred percent free concert for people dedicated to peace. Hamrick and Leonard, the hypnotists from the Harbingers, were appointed as John's liaisons with Karma Productions.

A month later John was back smoking cigarettes and taking drugs at Tittenhurst Park; Kyoko was still with Cox; and the peace concert was dead. Brower and Yorke could find no plausible way to give a free concert, and Leonard of the Harbingers was giving press conferences saying that flying saucers would appear at the peace concert as a featured event and that John and Yoko would arrive in an "air car" that ran on psychic fuel. John shot off a telegram to Brower and Yorke in Toronto saying, "We do not want to have anything to do with your festival. Please do not use our names or our ideas or symbols. John and Yoko Lennon."

That was the end of the nonviolent peace campaign for John and Yoko.

On the morning of January 26, John wrote a song called "Instant Karma." This was a little warning from him that all those bad people he kept running across were going to be punished for their deeds. Phil Spector produced the song for him, which was released on Apple and credited to the Plastic Ono Band. The song was a substantial commercial success, particularly in America, where it sold over a million copies. Most of the credit, however, was given to Phil Spector for broadening and enriching John's sound. As a gesture of gratitude, John gave Spector the raw *Let It Be* tapes, which had been sitting on a shelf in a vault, and asked him to make an album out of it.

John was willful, he was brilliant, and he was lost. There are men who at times are in need and who have kind and loving friends who come forward to give them aid and advice and encouragement. John was such a man with friends like these, but John was also unapproachable. Endowed with enormous wealth and power, there was no control over him, not a chance of affecting his behavior by good advice. His wife really had that responsibility, but Yoko seemed only to egg him on. In some odd way, John enjoyed the pain of being the outcast, it fed his martyr complex, as well as the Quarry Bank Ted in him.

Unfortunately, there was a point in early 1970 when John became such a pathetic and silly figure that he destroyed his last shreds of credibility with the press. The coup de grace was a press conference that John and Yoko called to announce the opening of the Black House. This was a black cultural center in Camden Town, sponsored by Michael Abdul Malik. Malik was better known to the public as Michael X, one of the controversial and feared leaders of the Black Panther movement in London. John and Yoko had befriended Michael X and taken him to their bosoms, agreeing to help raise money to support the Black House. With Derek

Taylor's coaxing, the press dutifully assembled on the roof of the Black House to witness a short ceremony during which John and Yoko would present Michael X with the bags full of hair they had cut off at Tony Cox's farm in Denmark. Michael X intended to auction the clippings at Sotheby's auction galleries and turn the proceeds over to his "brothers."

The ceremony would have been laughable if it hadn't been so sad. The press watched in silence, John obviously in a bad way, his hair still short from the severe haircut, his eyes glassy little marbles. Derek Taylor looked around the crowd of journalists and could see that there wasn't one person present who didn't know exactly what it was that John was stoned on. The next morning, for the first time in Beatles history, not one photograph of the event appeared in any of the London papers.

By the middle of March of 1970, Yoko was pregnant again. The doctors quickly remanded her to the London Clinic, an exclusive private hospital, for treatment. This hospital visit was a top-secret matter, unknown to the other Beatles and Apple employees. As top secret as the hospital stay might have been, it didn't stop John and Yoko from having a few trusted friends visit them, including Magic Alex, journalist Ray Connolly, and Michael X, who brought to the hospital with him as a gift a suitcase full of marijuana. Yoko insists this hospital stay was purely for medical reasons connected to her pregnancy, but Magic Alex remembers Yoko being given methadone, a heroin substitute used in withdrawal treatment. At one point when Ray Connolly was in Yoko's room, the doctors arrived to give Yoko some medication, and John stopped them, shouting, "Don't give her that! She's a junkie!"

Yoko's difficult pregnancy continued back at Tittenhurst Park. With Yoko confined to bed in poor condition, John felt as if the walls were closing in on him. Extensive renovations were still underway at the house, and there was the constant noise of hammering and sawing. They began to have violent arguments, none of which did Yoko's health any good. "We'd been together twenty-four hours a day," John said of this unhappy period. "That was our love, to protect our love—we were really beginning to choke each other . . . We were in danger of being, I don't know, Zelda and Scott . . . We would have blown up in a few years, couldn't have kept up the pace we were going at."

What saved John was the Next Big Thing. It appeared one

morning in the mail at Tittenhurst Park. It was a book called *The Primal Scream, Primal Therapy: The Cure for Neurosis.*

"Just the words, the title, made my heart flutter," John said. "I mean, Yoko's been screaming for a long time. Then I read the testimonials—you know, 'I am Charlie so and so. I went in and this is what happened to me.' I thought, *that's me, that's me.* Okay, it's something other than taking a tab of acid and feeling better, so I thought, let's try it."

The book's author, Arthur Janov, was one of the more prominent new-wave therapists who were flourishing in California in the late sixties. Janov's theory was that the "primal scene," which occurs in everyone's life around the age of five, is the single most shattering moment of our lives. Since we repress negative emotion, almost from the time of birth, a patient must be taken back to the moment of his primal scene to reexamine and reexperience the trauma and release it. When the "primal state" is achieved, the session ends in hysterical fits of screaming and rage as the patients release all the bitterness and hatred they unconsciously harbor toward their parents.

It was an epiphany for John. "I thought it was like Newton's apple. 'This must be it' I said. But I'd been so wrong in the past, with the drugs and the Maharishi . . . that I gave it [the book] to Yoko. She agreed with me, so we got on the phone . . ."

In fact, Janov's primal therapy, however valid, was for John exactly like the Maharishi and drugs and Magic Alex, another panacea. Janov himself sensed this in John's transoceanic phone call and insisted that John and Yoko think first about what they were doing. He also insisted they write lengthy letters about their childhoods, examining what they hoped to attain through primal therapy. Janov must have been very impressed with the letters, because a few weeks later he temporarily left his practice in Los Angeles and moved into Tittenhurst Park with John and Yoko. "He came on like a silver-haired Jeff Chandler," John said, "impressed with our celebrity."

Janov directed that for twenty-four hours before his arrival John and Yoko separate into distant rooms and have nothing to do with each other. He stipulated that they must use no drugs or any kind of chemicals and not speak on the phone or listen to the radio or watch TV. The therapy sessions themselves were grueling. John would lie on his back spread-eagled in the middle of the floor while Janov took him back through all the hurt and rejection of his childhood. His heartrending screams could be heard all over the house. After a week at Tittenhurst Park the therapy sessions were disrupted by the noise of the construction, and the sessions were continued in a large suite at the Inn on the Park in London. At the end of three weeks, when Janov thought they were making progress, he invited them back to California with him, where they would officially enroll at the Primal Institute in Los Angeles and undergo a four- to six-month course of intensive therapy—shades of the Maharishi. In fact—and for John this was the nifty part—John's immigration problems in the U.S. could be temporarily solved by Dr. Janov; one of the few ways he could be allowed in the country was for specialized medical treatment.

Just before John and Yoko were to leave for California, Janov suggested that it would be helpful for John in his therapy if he resolved some of his own ambivalent feelings for Julian, who was living with Cynthia and Roberto Bassanini. John hadn't seen Julian since the car accident the previous July. A meeting was arranged, and John came alone in his Rolls to Cynthia's Kensington home to see the little boy. "He was surprisingly pleasant," Cynthia recounts. "He almost immediately went upstairs to Julian's room, where they spent several hours playing together. I was delighted and so was Julian. Later, John came downstairs to have a cup of tea with me and tell me about primal therapy. Yoko was never mentioned. Just then the phone rang. It was the housekeeper at Tittenhurst Park, hysterical because Yoko was threatening to take an overdose of sleeping pills because John was spending so much time with me and Julian. John slammed down the phone and shouted, 'That silly bitch! She's threatening to kill herself!' "

After that, all communications and arrangements about Julian were made by Yoko Ono. Cynthia never heard the sound of John's voice again.

The next day they were off to Los Angeles, where they rented a small house with a manicured lawn in Beverly Hills. In Los Angeles, according to Yoko, she promptly miscarried John's third child. After a few days bedrest to regain her strength, she joined John in primal therapy. For nearly three months they spent two half days a week in therapy with Janov. The screaming sessions, which John found very effective, usually left him a wailing, hysterical puddle of misery on Dr. Janov's office floor. "We'd go down to a session, have a good cry, and come back and swim in the pool," John said. "And you'd always feel like after acid or a good joint, you know, sort of in the pool tingling and everything was fine. But then your defenses would all come up again—like the acid would wear off, the joint would wear off—and you'd go back for another fix."

Yoko didn't buy Janov's therapy at all. John later claimed that she only went along with it from the start to satisfy him, that in her heart she felt John was only searching for another "Daddy." But she also thought the therapy was useful for men who needed to be able to cry and release themselves. This form of expression was quite familiar to Yoko, who would not only scream and cry in her private life, but perform it on records and the stage.

As with the Maharishi, there came a moment of disillusionment with Janov. According to John, one day Janov appeared at a therapy session with two 16-mm cameras. John wouldn't even consider having his session recorded. "I'm not going to be filmed," John said, "especially not rolling around on the floor screaming."

According to John, Janov started to berate them. "Some people are so big they won't be filmed," Janov said. Janov said that it was coincidental that he was filming the session, and it had nothing to do with John and Yoko's fame. "Who are you kidding, Mr. Janov?" John said. "[You] just happen to be filming the session with John and Yoko in it."

John and Yoko had many discussions about Janov's professionalism. "I was rather cynical about it," Yoko says. "I observed the relationship between Art Janov and his wife, Vivian, as a couple, and I felt that Vivian was rather unhappy. But we both decided that the therapy was beautiful but that people who were doing it didn't have to be perfect. We wondered when it would end, and one day in the pool we looked at each other and realized that we were the ones who were going to say when it was over. John said, 'Oh, if we're the ones who are supposed to walk out I'll tell them.' "

One day in June John turned up at the Primal Therapy Center and said to Janov, "Well, we're cured. Thank you." They left Los Angeles the next day.

If primal therapy did not turn out to be the magic elixir that John sought, it was one of the few Next Big Things to leave him with lasting value and improvement. Primal therapy put him much more in touch with his fears and angers, burdens that he had been carrying around with him his whole life. Being able to deal with his feelings in such an explicit way unleashed the artist in him, sending him back to the easel and canvas to translate his emotions into terms he understood best. The results are evident in John's first solo album, the so-called "primal" LP, *John Lennon/Plastic Ono Band*. This album is one of the most powerful and effective autobiographical works to be produced in any medium. John used the studio for a musical exorcism. By far one of the most disturbing songs on the album is called "Mother," a far different tribute to his mother than "Julia" had been. In this taut, funereal song, John sings, "You had me but I never had you,/I wanted you but you didn't want me . . . / Father, you left me but I never left you . . ." The song culminates in a series of pitiful cries, as piercing as they are somehow poetic, of John calling, "Moooooooother! Moooooooother!" Just so nobody missed the point, there was also a short chant to the tune of "Three Blind Mice," with the lyrics, "My mummy's dead."

John Lennon/Plastic Ono Band also included John's "Working Class Hero" song, with the Janovian lyrics, "As soon as you're born they make you feel small/by giving you no time instead of it all . . ." The most commercially successful cut on the album was a song called "God," a simple litany of John's disappointments. "I don't believe in Jesus," he sings, "I don't believe in Bible . . . I don't believe in Elvis . . . I don't believe in Beatles . . . I just believe in me . . . The dream is over."

5.

*T*HROUGHOUT THE YEAR Paul followed the adventures of John and Yoko in the newspapers with a growing sense of dismay and disgust. John was making a fool of himself, and it was time for Paul to break away, otherwise John would pull him down with him. Since it was foolish for Paul to continue to think there would ever be another Beatles album, Paul decided the first step in breaking away was to make an album on his own. That autumn, amidst all the bad vibes at Apple, Paul gathered his wife, their precious daughter Mary, Linda's daughter Heather, and Martha the sheepdog and headed for his remote farm, High Park, in Scotland to record his first solo album. He left without telling anyone, except for Derek and me, where he was going.

One reason why Paul was so eager to get out of town was because of the recent runaway success of the Beatles' swan-song recording sessions, *Abbey Road*. This album turned out to be the last of the Beatles' masterpieces, with most of the seventeen cuts a group effort, truly a minor miracle. The album was rhapsodically reviewed, for both its rock and roll and progressive pop cuts, all populated by some of the Beatles' more astonishing musical characters, including Mean Mr. Mustard and his transvestite sister, Polythene Pam. George Harrison had the biggest breakthrough of his career on *Abbey Road* with "Something," a beautiful love song he wrote for Pattie. This song went on to become one of the most widely covered of any Beatles song and one of the largest selling singles. *Abbey Road*, boosted by Allen Klein's masterful, high-powered promotion and hype campaign, became the Beatles' most successful album ever, selling over five million copies the first year, which was two million more than *Sergeant Pepper*. It was the enormous popularity of *Abbey Road* that was focusing more attention on Paul for the moment instead of John, and Paul made a rare attempt to dodge the limelight by slipping away to High Park.

This little secret vacation of Paul's had a morbid side effect. On October 12, 1969, an American disc jockey named Russ Gibb on Detroit station WKNR-FM claimed to have received an anonymous phone call saying that Paul McCartney was dead. The proof, in part, was allegedly wedged into the end of the song "Strawberry Fields," which when played backwards could be deciphered as John chanting, "I buried Paul." As much as this might have been John's sentiments at the time, it was hardly true.

Soon after Russ Gibbs' broadcast in Detroit, the Apple switchboard in London was deluged with calls from reporters and fans asking if it were true that Paul was dead. None of us found the rumor at all amusing, and we very sternly assured all the callers that Paul was alive, in good health, and enjoying himself, but to protect his privacy, we declined to say exactly where he was. But this only fueled the mystery of Paul's whereabouts, and before we knew it the Paul-is-dead rumor became an issue of international conjecture. It seemed as if a Paul-is-dead mini-industry developed overnight. One of the more ghoulish entrepreneurs published an entire magazine devoted to the subject. According to the extensive lore that developed, Paul had been killed in a traffic accident, a tragedy portrayed in "A Day in the Life." This occurred in November of 1966, the "stupid bloody Tuesday" in "I Am the Walrus." Paul "blew his mind out in a car" because he "hadn't noticed that the light had changed"* and was decapitated.

Among the thousands of alleged clues and symbols, the *Sergeant Pepper* cover was said to depict Paul's funeral, with the Beatles standing around his freshly dug grave. The Paul McCartney in the photograph was supposed to be an actor named William Campbell, who had undergone extensive plastic surgery to fool the public in an attempt to keep the group going, an ironic counterpoint to real life. The cover of *Abbey Road* was alleged to be a funeral procession, with Paul—barefoot because he's a "corpse"— out of step with the other Beatles. Also, the Volkswagen license plate in the background, which reads 28 IF, was supposed to mean that *if* Paul had lived, he would have been twenty-eight. Unaccountably, he was only twenty-seven if he was still alive, but then not many of the clues made much sense.

Derek Taylor finally started telling reporters that Paul was on his farm in Scotland, but that didn't satisfy their curiosity either. I finally called Paul on his private line at the farm and told him that work at Apple was being disrupted by the thousands of queries about his health. I asked him what he wanted to do about it, and he said, "Nothing, just let it go." Which is what I did. But in a few days the situation had grown even worse, and I rang him back, telling him that we had to make a statement or in some way show that the rumor was nonsense. Paul was determined; he was going to say nothing and stay in Scotland and that was that.

That wasn't good enough for *Life* magazine, however. The

---

* It was actually John Lennon who blew his mind out in a car. John and Terry Doran were driving into London from Weybridge one night with John at the wheel, so stoned on acid he couldn't figure out if the traffic light had changed. However, the song for the most part was based upon the death of Guiness heir, Tara Browne, who was killed in a traffic accident.

editors at *Life* were determined to publish photographic evidence that Paul was alive and dispatched a team of photographers and reporters to Scotland to track Paul down and bring back a photograph. The hearty group trooped over four and a half miles of marshy land on foot until they were in sight of Paul's farmhouse. They were quickly discovered by Martha the sheepdog, whose barking brought Paul running. Enraged at this blatant invasion of his privacy, as well as at their trespassing, Paul ordered them off his property, but not before they got their cameras out and started shooting scores of photographs of Paul yelling at them. Angrier still, Paul grabbed a bucketful of water he was using to feed the farm animals and tossed it at a cameraman, who took a picture of that, too.

Moments after the *Life* representatives left, Paul realized what he had done. He quickly recovered, jumped into his Land Rover jeep, and chased the photographers and reporters across the Campbelltown hills. Once again his old charming self, Paul apologized for his outburst and asked if they could come to a compromise; in return for the exposed film of his temper tantrum, he would give them an exclusive interview, plus exclusive photographs of him and his newborn daughter Mary—taken by the family photographer, Linda. The resulting interview and picture became the cover story of *Life* magazine. It amused us at Apple when Paul was quoted as saying, "The rumors of my death have been greatly exaggerated. However, if I was dead, I'm sure I'd be the last to know . . ."

In March of 1970, after nearly six months away, he returned to London with his solo album, *McCartney*. While no tour de force, it was a pretty, worthwhile album, which contained the hit songs "Maybe I'm Amazed" and "Every Night." Paul had improvised studio effects with home remedies, including recording in the bathroom and the living room for different echos. On some cuts you can hear the front door slamming or the children playing in the next room.

As soon as Paul hit London, he rang up John. "I'm doing what you and Yoko are doing," he said. "I'm putting out an album and leaving the group."

John couldn't believe that Paul even thought there was still a group left to leave. "Good," he said. "That makes two of us who have accepted it mentally."

Paul then informed me and Allen Klein that for personal reasons he wanted his album released on April 10 through Apple. Klein explained that April 10 was out of the question. April was the release date of *Let It Be*. Phil Spector had done such a good job on John's "Instant Karma" single that John and Klein had given him all the dusty *Let It Be* tapes that had been locked in a vault for over a year and had told him to make an album out of it. The album was going to be released in time to back up the finished *Let It Be* documentary, which was to be released in theaters on May 20. Since it was a United Artists film, the date could not be changed. Also, Ringo had recorded a solo album, an innocent but mawkish album called *Sentimental Journey,* of classics sung off-key like "Love Is a Many Splendored Thing." Ringo's album would have to be released next, after *Let It Be.*

Paul would just have to wait his place in line.

Paul called Sir Joseph Lockwood at EMI in a rage. "I'm being sabotaged, Sir Joe, that's what they're doing to me!" he ranted. Sir Joe said he would see what he could do to help, but in the end it was up to the other Beatles.

Ringo went to see Paul one night at his home in St. John's Wood. Ringo was the least volatile of them all and the best mediator to effect some sort of compromise. Ringo was at Paul's house only a few minutes when Paul flew into a rage and, according to Ringo, "went completely out of control." He shook his finger in Ringo's face and screamed, "I'll finish you all! You'll pay!" He gave Ringo his coat and threw him out of the house.

Ringo, reasonable fellow that he is, told the others that if it meant so much to Paul to have his solo album released in April, they should let him do it, just to show friendship. Ringo's own solo album was pushed back and the release of *Let It Be* pushed up. As it turned out, all three albums hit the market within three or four weeks of each other, flooding the record bins with Beatles products. It was a dismal marketing decision.

Paul was angry but not as angry as he was when he eventually heard the *Let It Be* album. Spector had completely bastardized the Beatles sound. Although it had certain merits, *Let It Be* was purely a Phil Spector Wall of Sound Production, with his inimitable backdrop of vast choruses and lavish orchestrations. Paul was mortified by the kitschy female voices—the first female voices ever on a Beatles record—and by what Spector had done to one of his prettiest songs, "The Long and Winding Road," which Klein had earmarked as the album's first single. Paul had originally recorded the song with just an acoustic guitar, similar to the way he sang the song in the finished documentary, with just his sweet voice carrying the song along. Spector had turned it into a monumental pile of mush, complete with strings, horns, and an ethereal chorus in the background.

Paul tried everything in his power to get it changed, first through Spector, then through Klein; but it was too late, the record was already being pressed. This desecration of his work was the final straw.

On May 20, at the gala premiere of *Let It Be* at the London Palladium, none of the Beatles showed up. Instead of a film about the making of an album, it was a portrait of the dissolution of a group. Even more painful, it was about the dissolution of a friendship into animosity and hatred.

The night of the opening, George Harrison went into the studios with Phil Spector and began what was to be six months of work on his own solo album, *All Things Must Pass.* Not to be left out, Ringo went into the studios with Nashville producer Pete Drake to work on his next solo LP, *Beaucoup of Blues,* which took six days, instead of six months, to record.

On April 17 Paul McCartney's solo LP, *McCartney,* with a cover photograph of a bowl of spilled cherries, was released to lukewarm reviews from critics. Inside the album package was an interview Paul had done with himself, making up the questions as well as the answers. It was self-serving, vain, and painted him in the poorest light. But it telegraphed one irrefutable message: the Beatles were dead.

Q: What do you feel about John's peace effort? The Plastic Ono Band? Giving back the MBE? Yoko's influence? Yoko?
A: I love John and respect what he does—it doesn't give me any pleasure.
Q: Are you planning a new album or single with the Beatles?
A: No.
Q: Do you foresee a time when Lennon-McCartney become an active songwriting partnership again?
A: No.
Q: Do you miss the Beatles and George Martin? Was there

a moment, e.g., when you thought: 'Wish Ringo was here for this break'?

A: No.

On April 10 Paul announced to the newspapers what John had wanted to announce all along. He was leaving the Beatles "because of personal, business, and musical differences."

6.

*T*HROUGH THE AUTUMN of 1970, Paul and the Eastmans continued to make polite inquiries as to whether the other Beatles were agreeable to letting Paul out of his partnership contracts. The major problem with the dissolution of the partnership was that an enormous tax burden would have to be paid in the near future if all the Beatles funds were divided up. The Eastmans weren't sure how much this tax burden would be, because Klein was allegedly obstructing the Eastmans' access to the account books. "I don't give a damn about tax considerations," Paul said. "I don't want to be an ABKCO-managed industry. It was weird, my albums would come out saying 'An ABKCO Company' and [Klein] wasn't even my manager."

One day, rather offhandedly, Paul said to Klein, "Either let me out of my contracts or I'll sue you." Klein, who had been sued over forty times before, just laughed at him.

Paul once again tried to talk to each of the Beatles individually, but John and George didn't care to listen. He invited Ringo to his house on Cavendish Avenue again to play arbiter. "Look," Paul said, "it's not the rest of the group, it's just that I don't want to have anything to do with Klein. It's Klein that's the problem."

"It's not just Klein," Ringo told him. "It's the Eastmans, too." Then Linda started to cry hysterically, so Ringo shut up. Every time Ringo tried to speak, defending Klein, Linda would dissolve in tears. Thus frustrated in his discussions, the meeting ended without any solution.

Next, Paul tried writing a long letter to John, asking him to agree to a formal dissolution. All he got in return was a cartoon drawing from John with the words "How and Why?" in a bubble.

Paul wrote back, "By signing a piece of paper agreeing to dissolve the Apple partnership. Why? Because we don't have a partnership anymore."

John responded with a postcard. "Get Well Soon" it said. "Get the other signatures and I will think about it."

For most of November and December Paul sat around his house in St. John's Wood mulling over whether or not he had the heart to sue the other Beatles. It was Klein he really wanted, but the only way to get at him was through the others. He kept thinking, "I can't do this. I can't sue my pals. It would ruin my reputation. I'll be characterized as the villain. I can't possibly sue the others . . ."

But he did.

And he did it on New Year's Eve. He had John, George, and Ringo each served with writs on December 31, 1970, and started proceedings in the High Court Chancery Division.

I handed in my resignation that same day. Paul begged me not to do it, because I was his only sympathetic contact at Apple, but I wasn't able to be much help to him anyway. My departure had been coming for a long time. Robert Stigwood had asked me to join his now very successful company, and Klein had long wanted me out of the way. Klein would have tried to fire me and Neil Aspinall if he thought the Beatles would have stood for it, as they had with Alistair Taylor; but we were clearly invaluable to the running of the company, and Neil and I were their last links with Liverpool. In any event, things had become so ugly at Apple over the last year that I was looking for a way out myself. Handing in my resignation was really only a formality.

Neil Aspinall was lost after the lawsuit began. Neil without the Beatles was unthinkable. He seemed like a man who was falling from a great height without ever reaching bottom. At first he stopped coming into the office, saying he was on vacation. He had married Suzie Orenstein, an attractive, petite American girl, in 1968 and was the father of three, so there was much to keep him busy at home. But Neil was soon bored with family life, and he started visiting one or another of the Beatles at their homes almost daily. He settled in for a time at George's place, making

16-mm experimental movies and eventually set himself to the task of editing together thousands of feet of documentary footage on the Beatles that he had gathered over the years, most of it never before seen by the public. It was a pathetic project, Neil standing over an editing machine all day, watching his youth roll by on a small screen. The documentary took years to finish and has never been seen by anyone outside of Neil's immediate circle of friends.

Neil was never taken off salary. Deservedly, too, for although John, Paul, George, and Ringo would deny it, he was as much a Beatle as any of them. And now that it was over, the four others survived intact, as personalities and as stars; Neil Aspinall lived in limbo as an executive of Apple, which is now just a moribund record label, in existence only to collect the substantial royalties from the never-ending sale of old Beatles albums. As Neil put it, "I am the custodian of the graveyard."

The court trial itself began on January 19, 1971, and lasted for nine days. Paul was the only one to show up in court, winning a two-shilling bet with a courtroom attendant who insisted that John and Yoko would be there too, not wanting to miss a chance to have it out with Paul in public. But the three others were represented only by affidavits. These affidavits were read aloud in court, the details of which became the next day's headlines. Some of the less soiled of the Beatles' dirty laundry was thus washed in public, including the Twickenham Studio tensions and Paul throwing Ringo out of his house.

Paul's lawyers, who were very well prepared by the Eastmans, took the position that Allen Klein was unscrupulous and they feared for Paul's interests. They roasted Klein in the process of the trial, bringing testimony to the court that Klein had recently been convicted of ten charges of tax fraud in the United States. The court was urged to appoint a receiver and to freeze the funds.

John, George, Ringo, and Klein's lawyers had a different story; evidence was introduced that Klein himself had drawn only £150,000 commission from the group since he joined them, a nominal sum indeed when it was disclosed that the Beatles' earnings had increased by nine million pounds in the previous nineteen months. In fact, Klein had doubled the Beatles' record royalties of the last eight and a half years. This, it was pointed out, did not include the vast income from John's and Paul's songwriting royalties.

On March 10, the high court appointed Mr. J. D. Spooner as receiver of the Beatles' assets. As a group, at least, Allen Klein no longer represented the Beatles, but he still represented John, George, and Ringo. As large sums of money began to accrue to the receiver, both sides frantically tried to figure out a way to unfreeze them. One major problem, as usual, was the tax. A large tax would have to be paid almost immediately, and John, George, and Ringo wanted Paul to sign a personal indemnification against it. The Eastmans wouldn't hear of it, and so the money sat.

What followed was a barrage of mean and vitriolic interviews. If Beatles fans were disillusioned by the nastiness of the trial, John and Paul proceeded to destroy any respect for them that might have been left. The most notable interview of this period was John's 30,000 word "Working Class Hero" interview with *Rolling Stone*'s Jann Wenner, in which the Beatles breakup was discussed with any truthfulness for the first time. The interview also touched on John's relationship with Brian and Yoko and accounted for the Beatles breakup "because we were tired of being side-men for Paul."

In response, Paul gave a rare interview to England's *Melody Maker* in which he said, "I just want the four of us to get together and sign a piece of paper saying it's all over, and we want to divide the money four ways . . . But John won't do it. Everybody thinks I am the aggressor, but I'm not. I just want out."

John was so infuriated by this interview that he dictated a long letter to *Melody Maker* and asked that it be published in the next edition. Several lines had to be edited out for libel. John asks in the letter, "For the millionth time . . . I repeat, what about the TAX? It's all very well playing 'simple honest ole human Paul' in the *Melody Maker,* but you know damn well we can't just sign a bit of paper . . . If you're not the aggressor (as you claim), who the hell took us to court and shat all over us in public?"

The argument continued on vinyl. Paul, responding to the criticism that his *McCartney* LP was too raw and unfinished, went in the opposite direction with his second solo outing called *Ram.* *Ram* was recorded at Abbey Road with the best studio musicians available. It was a cute, tuneful little album, a bit silly in its musical innocence but not in its lyrical content. The cover featured a

Linda McCartney photo of Paul taking a ram by the horns, with an interior photo of two beetles fucking each other, a not so oblique reference to the way Paul felt his pals were treating him. Lyrically, the references were more direct. When Paul sang, "Too Many People Preaching Practices," John knew he was singing it to him, and that he was just a "silly boy(s) breaking their lucky breaks in two." And it was to John to whom Paul sang, "Dear Boy, I hope you never know how much you missed [me]." *Rolling Stone* called the album "the nadir in the decomposition of sixties rock thus far." One English newspaper posed the question, "How do you tell an ex-Beatle that he has made a lousy album?"

John Lennon was gleeful. In September of 1971 he responded with an album called *Imagine,* recorded during the summer in his studios at Tittenhurst Park. In comparison to the pain of the primal LP, *Imagine* was a pleasantly tuneful album but not without some good old-fashioned rock and roll nastiness. In "How Do You Sleep?"—on which George happily plays guitar—John spells it all out to Paul: "A pretty face may last a year or two, but pretty soon they'll see what you can do. / The sound you make is Muzak in my ears, you must have learned something in all those years. / Ah, how do you sleep . . . The only thing you learned was yesterday, and since you've gone you're just another day . . . Those freaks was right when they said you was dead . . ."

There was also a tune called "Crippled Inside." And just in case anybody missed the point, the album package included a postcard with a parody of Paul's *Ram* cover: John wrestling a big old barnyard pig by the ears.

All this vitriol managed to overshadow one of the most popular tunes of John's career, the title tune, "Imagine," which wasn't even released as a single in England until 1975. "Imagine" is one of John's heartfelt but hopelessly naive visions of a world free from strife. "Imagine," he sings, "there's no heaven, / It's easy if you try, No hell below us, Above us only sky. / . . . Nothing to kill or die for, And no religion too. / Imagine all the people living life in peace, / . . . you may say I'm a dreamer, But I'm not the only one. / I hope some day you'll join us / And the world will be as one."

The *Rolling Stone* critic, Ben Gerson, wrote, "I fear that John sees himself in the role of the truth-teller, and as such can justify any kind of self-indulgent brutality in the name of truth."

Mick Jagger, when asked if the Rolling Stones would ever break up, said, "Nah. But if we did, we wouldn't be so bitchy about it."

Three members of The Beatles pop group yesterday abandoned their appeal against a High Court order putting the affairs of their company, Apple, in the hands of a receiver. John Lennon, George Harrison and Ringo Starr now face a bill for legal costs estimated at £100,000.

—*The Times*
April 27, 1971

Chapter Nineteen

That was your worst mistake.
You took your lucky break and
broke it in two.
Now what can be done for you?
You broke it in two.

—Paul McCartney
"Too Many People"

George

*E*VERYWHERE they went, people on the street, desk clerks, interviewers, all asked the same thing: "When are the Beatles going to get together again?" Each of the ex-Beatles hated the question as much as the frequency with which it was asked. If you said "never," which was the truth, it made you the bad guy, so Paul and George and Ringo just sloughed it off. John had a pat response: "When you go back to high school."

If the dissolution of the Beatles benefitted anyone, it should have been George. George was always complaining about how John and Paul oppressed him, and now he had his chance to show his stuff. Free of the Beatles' yoke, George went into the studios with Phil Spector and spent six months handcrafting his first solo venture, *All Things Must Pass*. This beautifully boxed, three-record set included four sides of new material by George and a third record of a superstar jam session, which included Eric Clapton, Dave Mason, and Billy Preston, who also appear on the rest of the album. Released just before Christmas of 1970 at a record-breaking $13.98 retail price, the album instantly became number one in America and England. It was perhaps the most lavishly praised album since *Sergeant Pepper*, and deservedly so. George proved once and for all that he was something of a musical genius on his own. Bolstered by Phil Spector's highly orchestrated production techniques, *All Things Must Pass* managed to be an uplifting listening experience. As *Melody Maker* said, "Garbo talks! George Harrison is free!"

Despite the sudden accolades and solo credit, George didn't seem any happier than the rest of them. This confirmation of his talent didn't take the edge off his strident personality; if anything he seemed moodier and more dissatisfied than ever. He became inwardly spiritual and turned away from his friends. In one of his more famous quests for religious fulfillment, he spent several days sitting on a mountaintop in Cornwall on a search for "truth."

In 1970 George bought an enormous mansion in Henley on Thames, thirty miles west of London. This $300,000 estate, called Friar Park, was in terrible disrepair and would cost George hundreds of thousands more to put it in shape, yet it was undoubtedly one of the most fabulous and eccentric domiciles in the world. It had been built some eighty years before by multimillionaire Sir Frank Crisp, a lawyer and advisor to the Liberal Party. Sir Frank's sense of humor was obviously as big as the eighty-room house. Each room was more overwhelmingly elaborate than the next. The theme was friars and religion, and there were ornate carved wood moldings and faces everywhere, around all the windows, doorframes, ceilings, and staircases. They were carved into seraphim, serfs, flowers, and thousands of fat little friars' heads. There were friars' heads everywhere you turned, on every door, in nook and cranny, even on the light switches, which were friars' heads cast of brass with the switch sticking out of their mouths. Some rooms were as vast as ballrooms, and the bathrooms were as big as an average flat in London.

The grounds of the house featured three manmade lakes and seven major theme gardens, including one with a replica of the Matterhorn. One of the lakes was equipped with stepping stones just below the surface of the water, so one could give the appearance of walking across the lake. The gardens had some 40,000 different varieties of flowers and trees, which took five full-time gardeners to care for them. There was also a complex of subterranean caves, some with skeletons and distorting mirrors. One was filled with statues of gnomes (which can be found on the cover of *All Things Must Pass*) and one was a wine cave illuminated by glass grapes that were actually tiny light bulbs.

In this bizarre, quasi-religious setting, George continued along his spiritual path, now almost obsessively. He supported the growing Krishna movements around the world and hooked up with a new guru, Bhaktivededanta Swami, the seventy-seven-year-old spiritual leader of the International Society for Krishna Consciousness. He invited the guru and several saffron-robed monks to live in one of the smaller houses on the grounds of Friar Park. He began to rise at the crack of dawn, bathe in cold water, and study the *Bhagavad-Gita.* As time passed he became more and more fascinated by Friar Park's massive gardens and spent hours walking through them, examining the plants and trees. He found particular pleasure in making things grow and began planting and tending the garden himself. He became, to all those he considered less enlightened than he, a stern lecturer. His conversations consisted of long, wandering dissertations on karma and life metaphors to plants. He spouted on about the problems of being a rock-star millionaire confronted with the luxuries of the material world, when the spiritual one was the only one that really mattered. His friends soon began to call him "His Lectureship" behind his back, and his beliefs, however well intentioned, became one big bore.

Pattie Harrison was miserable. After six years of marriage she felt unfulfilled and stifled. Only twenty-six years old, she was forbidden to have her own career and was isolated almost continuously in the big gloomy house with all the friars' heads. She wanted dearly to raise a family, but she never seemed to get pregnant. George was the only Beatle who had never became a father, and in a peculiar way it embarrassed him. Both George and Pattie went for fertility tests, and George, who discussed the problem with a few close friends, said the medical problem was his. But, around Apple, it was suspected that this was not true, that it was Pattie's problem and that George was being gallant by taking the blame.* Pattie was willing to adopt children, but George refused. They had heated arguments over this, and Pattie began to escape him by taking overnight trips to London. Once, after one of their more violent arguments, Pattie climbed onto the roof of the main building of Friar Park, as far as the uppermost cupola, removed the OM symbol that always flew there, and replaced it with a pirate's skull and crossbones. The war was on.

Pattie's strongest weapon against George was the man who had become his best friend now that the Beatles were gone: Eric

---

* George was later to father a son, Dhani, in his second marriage. Pattie is still childless.

Clapton. Clapton's own career had recently skyrocketed, and he had become perhaps the most revered virtuoso rock guitarist in the business, called "Old Slow Hand" because of his distinctive twangy guitar sound. For a long time now it had been obvious to anyone who saw Eric and Pattie together—including George—that Eric was madly in love with her. He turned into a pile of romantic mush in her presence, while she blinked at him with those big blue eyes and giggled. Now that Pattie was so unhappy in her relationship with George, she encouraged the attentions of the handsome and romantic rock guitarist. She began to manipulate Clapton's infatuation with her to control and anger George. "She used me, you see," Clapton later admitted, "and I fell madly in love with her."

That didn't stop the three of them from socializing together, however, and the dangerous chemistry between them led to some explosive moments. One of the worst was on the opening night of *Oh Calcutta!* in London. *Oh Calcutta!* was being produced in London by Robert Stigwood, who was also managing Eric Clapton's career. Since George was toiling in the studios on *All Things Must Pass* on the night of the premiere, I took Pattie to the opening as my date. After the show, Stigwood threw a gala party at his newly purchased £100,000 estate, the Old Barn, on the far side of Stanmore.

When George finished his work in the studios in the early hours of the morning, he set out for the Old Barn to join Pattie and me. Unable to find a parking space near the gate, he drove his Ferrari up the long driveway to the main house. Exhausted from his recording session, he wanted only to find his wife and take her home with him. He searched all over for her, but she was nowhere to be found. George came up to me and asked what had happened to Pattie. I found myself in the difficult position of telling George that I didn't know where Pattie was, but she was last seen with Eric Clapton.

George was furious that the two of them had gone off together so long ago and still hadn't returned. He stalked back to his car and set off down the driveway. He had gone only a few yards when in the early-morning mist his headlights picked out two figures walking hand in hand at the side of the driveway. It was Pattie and Eric. George stopped the car with a screech of brakes and burning tires, flew out of the car, and launched into a terrible tirade that could be heard by the guests in the house. He forbade them to ever see each other again, practically shoved Pattie into the car, and tore off into the night with her.

Eric's consuming passion for Pattie eventually wore him down. He withdrew to his baronial mansion, Hurtwood Edge, in Ewhurst and started to shoot heroin to dull the pain of his longing. In desperation he began a new relationship with Alice Ormsby-Gore, the daughter of Lord Harlech, whom some said bore an eerie resemblance to Pattie. Locked away in Hurtwood Edge for months on end, Eric was ravaged and withered by the effects of the heroin. During this time he read the great Persian love poem, Nazimi's *Layla and Majnum*, about the obsessive love between a lovesick man and a married woman. Pattie became his Layla. Now in perilously ill health, Eric flew to Miami to record his pained but beautiful masterpiece, *Layla*, for her, perhaps the most impassioned love song of the pop era. Even as the album hurtled up the charts, he moved back to Hurtwood Edge and continued shooting heroin. We all worried that he would not survive.

During the summer of 1971, George received worldwide acclaim for his concert for Bangladesh, which took place on August 1 at Madison Square Garden. This charity affair was organized to raise funds for the starving people of war-torn Pakistan, and he invited a sparkling array of superstars to appear on stage with him, including Ringo, Leon Russell, Ravi Shankar, and surprise guest Bob Dylan. The plan was to raise money not only through ticket sales but through the release of a live album and a documentary movie as well. Even Eric Clapton, despite his illness, managed to show up. George had invited the other Beatles to join them, but Paul flatly refused, not wanting to confuse the public with what might seem to be a Beatle reunion. John accepted George's invitation and flew to New York and checked into the Park Lane Hotel with Yoko. The morning of the concert, John and Yoko had a fierce fight. When John got in touch with George, he was infuriated to learn that George didn't want Yoko on stage with them. He thought it would be insulting to ask the greats of the rock and roll business to share the stage with John's wife. John was so angry that he checked out of the hotel within fifteen minutes and took the next flight back to London, leaving Yoko behind to catch up with him forty-eight hours later.

Ostensibly, the concert was a huge success, but the euphoria over this achievement would not last George a fortnight.

Bangladesh had turned out to be something of an embarrassment, too. All the recording artists who had blithely signed record and film releases for the album and movie were now involved in a legal spiderweb with all the different record companies they recorded for. The unraveling and permissions went on for years. So did the tax problems. The Inland Revenue Service insisted that taxes be paid before any money from the album or film could be released, and George wound up paying the taxes himself. On July 25, 1973, he had a meeting with Patric Jenkin, the chief financial secretary to the Chancellor of the Exchequer, at which he wrote a National Westminster Bank check for one million pounds payable to the IRS. There was also more than a touch of scandal when *New York* magazine reported that some of the Bangladesh concert proceeds had allegedly found their way into Allen Klein's pockets. Klein responded with a $100 million lawsuit, which was eventually dropped.

Now came the rub for George Harrison. His long-awaited second solo LP, *Living in the Material World,* released the summer of 1973, was an artistic disaster. Although his spirited "Give Me Love (Give Me Peace on Earth)" single drove the album to the top of the charts, on the whole the LP was a long, repetitive diatribe on God, Krishna, and the Hindu religion. The lyrics were preachy, sanctimonious, and worst of all, boring. It seemed that with *All Things Must Pass* George had put all his eggs in one basket.

Even more painful for George, his marriage had come to an ugly end. His relationship with Pattie ended with such explosive force that it took Ringo and Maureen's marriage with it. George was cheating on Pattie a great deal by then, and it wouldn't be incorrect to say that he had reverted to his old Don Juan ways. He seemed to want to seduce every woman he laid eyes on. He even once suggested to Neil Aspinall that they swap wives. As much as Neil was amused by the offer, he was happily married and said no. In a story revealed here for the first time, another object of George's *amours* was Maureen Starkey. Why he should suddenly want to seduce the wife of one of his closest friends after knowing her for ten years remains inexplicable.

Maureen and Ringo had moved into Tittenhurst Park after John had moved to America, and one night they invited George and Pattie to join them there for dinner. After a hearty meal with much wine, they all sat around the long white dining room table, with George strumming his guitar and singing love songs.

Suddenly, he put down his guitar and blurted out that he was in love with Maureen.

The others were speechless. Maureen turned bright red and shook her head, Ringo stormed off, and Pattie burst into tears and locked herself in the bathroom. The couple left Tittenhurst soon after.

Just a few weeks later, Pattie returned to her own home, Friar Park, from a shopping spree in London, reportedly to find George in bed with Maureen, just as Cynthia and Jane Asher had found their men with other women. Neither Maureen nor Pattie will confirm that this often-reported incident actually took place, but they pointedly will not deny it either. Says Pattie on the subject: "I don't want to get anybody in trouble."

When George was later asked why of all the women in the world he had to choose his buddy's wife, George shrugged his shoulders and said, "Incest."

So much for the spiritual world.

In retaliation for catching George at play, Pattie began to lead an independent life and pursue her career against George's explicit wishes. She agreed to model again and appeared at an Ozzie Clark fashion show. She had her first extramarital affair, with Ron Wood, the pixiesh guitarist from the group the Faces (and now with the Rolling Stones), and not long after packed and left Friar Park while George was in London. She told him she was taking a vacation, and he never questioned it. Pattie moved out of England altogether for a while, to settle in Los Angeles with her sister Jenny, who had married rock star Mick Fleetwood. It was no coincidence that Eric Clapton was also living in the United States, in Miami.

Eric Clapton had made a near-miraculous recovery from heroin. Concerned friends led him to Dr. Margaret Patterson, who had experienced promising results in treating heroin withdrawal symptoms with electro-acupuncture. This reportedly not only eased the pain of withdrawal but was an invaluable aid in staying off the drug. Clapton, encouraged by the reports of the breakup of George and Pattie's marriage, went through Dr. Patterson's treatment. He was finally "clean" in 1973 when he went back to Miami to record what they were calling a "comeback" album, *461 Ocean Boulevard*. The album was an enormous success and gave Clapton the confidence to launch a national tour of the U.S.

and England. When Clapton went out on tour, Pattie joined him on the road, and they have been together ever since. They were finally married on March 27, 1979, but that was only a formality, for rarely have two people ever been so deeply committed to each other. To this day they continue to be as romantic and playful as they were at the start. They still live in Hurtwood Edge, and Clapton continues to pursue his successful career.

For a short time after Pattie moved out, George took up with a twenty-four-year-old girl named Kathy Simmonds, reportedly a onetime live-in of Rod Stewart's. George's drinking increased, and he became more gloomily religious than ever. Although he considered himself a great cocksman, he was very much alone. In an attempt to rejuvenate his career, he launched another album in the fall of 1974, *Dark Horse,* and embarked on a twenty-seven-city tour of North America, making him the first solo Beatle to tour the United States. The album and tour were equally disastrous. The album was yet another religious tract, the tour more of a Hindu revival meeting than a rock concert. The show opened with Ravi Shankar conducting twenty-four Indian musicians in an hour of pretty but boringly esoteric Indian music. The young audiences, anxious for their first chance to see a real live Beatle on stage, were at first politely restless, then resentful. When George finally took the stage himself for the second half of the show, he tried to coax his audiences into chanting mantras with him and singing Hare Krishna. When they wouldn't respond with gusto he chastised them like a schoolmarm. He changed the lyrics of his best songs to reflect his religious beliefs and turned his performance into a pseudoreligious experience.

In October of 1975 he followed up with an equally boring and pedantic album called *Extra Texture—Read All About It,* but that didn't stop A&M Records in Los Angeles from signing a $2.6 million deal to distribute George's newly created record label, Dark Horse. The major attraction on this label was to be George himself, who was scheduled to deliver an album of his own in January of 1976, after his contracts with Apple Records ran out. When George's first album for them, *33⅓,* was seven months late, George got a note from A&M President Jerry Moss saying either he turn in the album or they'd sue him for $10 million in damages. It was Warner Brothers Records that came to George's rescue by offering to buy the album from A&M. Warner's rushed the record into the stores, but *33⅓* was another qualified flop.

But George had yet to face what was perhaps the single greatest embarrassment of his career. It had been widely remarked in the years following the release of *All Things Must Pass* that the big hit single, "My Sweet Lord," bore an uncanny resemblance to the Chiffons' hit single of the early sixties, "He's So Fine." In 1976 the publisher of "He's So Fine," Bright Tunes, brought a plagiarism suit against George. In the widely publicized trial, George appeared in court with his guitar and demonstrated for the judge how he had composed the song in the first place. George was found guilty of "unconscious plagiarism" and eventually paid $587,000 in damages to Bright Tunes. The great irony was that by the time the settlement was made, none other than Allen Klein had purchased the Bright Tunes catalog, and the money ended up in his company.

On George's frequent visits to A&M Records before his legal run-in with the company, he made the acquaintance of a twenty-seven-year old, Mexican-born secretary named Olivia Trinidad Arias. She was sweet, dark, and pretty, and it wasn't hard for a man with even the most cynical heart to fall in love with her. George's relationship with Olivia was probably the first time in his life that he was truly in love and not simply infatuated with a Brigitte Bardot look-alike. She moved into a rented house in Beverly Hills with him and later they traveled to Hawaii and London. They were together for over four years before, much to George's great pleasure, Olivia gave birth to his first child, a son named Dhani, on August 1, 1978. George and Olivia were married a month later in a quiet ceremony at Friar Park.

Olivia remains a distant figure to all of George's associates. He guards his relationship with her carefully, and perhaps wisely so. She is kept away from his celebrity life and is introduced to only his closest friends. The couple lead a quiet life at Friar's Park, just the way George said he always wanted it, with plenty of time to spend with Dhani or at work in the garden.

Nevertheless, George doesn't seem very content. As with the other Beatles, there is something gnawing away at him. One would like to think that it is the absence of his former associates or the loss of his glory as a Beatle, but it is not. Just the opposite, it is probably the omnipresent shadow of the four moptops still hanging over everything that he does. He has been unable to solve his problems with his spiritual tools, although he is as fervent as ever in his Hindu beliefs. The last time I saw him at Friar

Park, he rattled on about Karma and gardening and will still lecture anybody who will sit still long enough to listen to him. Alas, he doesn't record much anymore. He has recently developed a penchant for racing cars and has driven at several charity events. George is the third richest of the Beatles and has become a shrewd and successful investor in motion pictures. One of his more profitable investments was Monty Python's *The Life of Brian,* which he helped bankroll to the tune of $5.5 million. The film grossed upwards of $70 million as of this writing. George's other film investments, *Time Bandits* and *The Long Good Friday,* were relatively just as successful.

In 1981 George published an exorbitantly expensive, leather-bound edition of his autobiography with a small, exclusive publisher in England. The book was ghost written for him by Derek Taylor, who works for him still. The volume is mostly full-color reproductions of the original lyrics to his songs, along with a few photographs, but precious little text. In his reminiscence of his days with the Beatles, he omits all reference to John Lennon, as if he never existed. Once, long ago, in what seems like another time altogether, young George Harrison worshipped John so much he followed him everywhere he went, dressing in similar clothes and combing his hair like him. Now the two of them had no use for each other during what were to be the last five years of John's life.

Ringo

*W*HILE *JOHN AND PAUL* were fabulously rich, and George was about to be, everybody worried about what would happen to poor Ringo. Although a millionaire in his own right, he was by far the poorest, and he was a man of expensive tastes. His first two solo albums, the only major source of revenue for him, were hardly successes. So the three other Beatles decided to help him with a record. This was as close as the four Beatles would get to a reunion, a collaboration on tape but not in the same place at the same time. The Beatle magic was still working on this album, even long distance. Under producer Richard Perry's excellent direction, each of the ex-Beatles contributed at least one song. *Ringo* became one of the most popular albums of the year, ringing up three hit singles, including two number-one singles, "Photograph" and "You're Sixteen." The success of the album both surprised Ringo and made the other Beatles a little jealous. John, half kidding, sent Ringo a telegram that said, "How dare you? Why don't you write me a hit song?"

Heady with the success of *Ringo*, Ringo started putting out an album a year. With minor exceptions, each of these albums was so undistinguished that none of them would ever have been given any airplay if it weren't for the fact that Ringo was an ex-Beatle. In December of 1974 the overhyped *Goodnight Vienna* album was released, with its moronic "No No" novelty song that became a short-lived hit single, and "Only You." In 1975 he formed his own, ill-fated record label, Ringo Records, but closed the company down when running it turned out to be too much hard work with no immediate results. Ringo also invested in a furniture design company with Robin Cruikshank called Ringo or Robin Limited, which featured items like a Rolls-Royce Grille table or chrome-plated circular fireplaces. This company, too, met its demise.

By 1976, having been released from his Apple recording contracts, Ringo signed a deal with Polydor Records in England and released another solo album called *Rotogravure*. Although the album sold reasonably well, it, too, was considered a commercial and artistic failure. In 1977 *Ringo the 4th* appeared, a desperately trendy disco album that was not only a failure but an embarrassment. His 1978 entry, this time on Columbia's Portrait Records, *Bad Boy*, was equally unsuccessful, and his contract was canceled. *Rolling Stone* reported, *"Bad Boy* isn't even passable cocktail music."

Ringo acted in a few bit parts in films, most notably *That'll Be the Day* and Mae West's last movie, *Sextette*. Although he received some warm reviews, it was obvious he was no actor. He tried his hand at directing for a time and produced and directed glitter-rock star Marc Bolan in a concert film called *Born to Boogie*, but that, too, was doomed to failure.

So there was poor Ringo, a cameo part player without a part.

He was an international celebrity and a wealthy man, but he had little daily purpose in life. Always fancying himself the lady's man, he divorced Maureen in 1975. The poor girl was devastated. Even if it were true that she had gone to bed with George, even if she had strayed, Maureen still loved her "Ritchie" with as much passion and dedication as any northern girl could muster. She was his faithful servant and friend, always there for him, to cook and clean, to soothe him when he was tired and cranky. She turned her head when he started to fool around with other women, but she couldn't hold him. Ringo made Maureen a wealthy woman with the terms of their divorce settlement, giving her a cash settlement of £500,000 with more to come as it was needed over the years. A short time later, when Maureen wanted to live in London, Ringo bought her and the kids a £250,000 house in Little Venice. He also bought Tittenhurst Park from John and Yoko and turned it into a rental property and recording studio. Then, for tax purposes, he signed the $1.7 million property over to his kids. Maureen pines for him to this day, and in the same sense that Cynthia waited for John, Maureen dreams that one day Ritchie will come home to her.

Ringo gave up his English residency because of the prohibitive tax laws and became a tax exile. He bought a lavish condominium in a luxury building on the side of a cliff in Monte Carlo, where he took up residency, but he was really a man without a country or a home. Ringo was always attracted to life in the fast lane, and he threw himself into a high-speed, jet-setting existence with a vengeance. He had a penchant for beautiful young women and took up for a time with American model Nancy Andrews. He gambled heavily in Monte Carlo's Loews Casino and jumped from continent to continent at whim. It seemed Ringo was always in a plane, looking for the next good party. "Well, I am a jet-setter," he said. "Whatever anyone may think and whoever puts it down, I am on planes half the year going places . . . Wherever I go it's a swinging place, man." Nancy Andrews soon grew tired of the pace and went back to Los Angeles, where she later slapped him with a $7 million palimony suit. Ringo also bought homes in Amsterdam and Los Angeles, where he rented a $300,000 home in the Sunset Hills just above Sunset Boulevard, and frequented his favorite haunts, like the private rock club, On the Rox. He caroused around Los Angeles with some of the more hell-bent rock stars, including Keith Moon and Harry Nilsson. There was always another beautiful young woman on his arm, including actresses Vivian Ventura and Shelly Duvall and singer Lyndsey De Paul.

One of Ringo's frequent nightclubbing pals turned out to be none other than Mal Evans, the Beatles' road manager. When the Beatles disbanded, Mal was at a loss for something to do. As Neil Aspinall put it, "He went from fixing telephones to Shea Stadium, overnight. He lived with the stars for a decade, and then suddenly he was an ordinary man again." Bored with his wife and children, he left England and moved to Los Angeles in the early seventies, following the rock and roll action. But no work he could find in the U.S. equaled the exhilaration of working with the Beatles, and Mal's life began to disintegrate. By 1976 he was living in an apartment complex in West Hollywood with some young girl, drinking and drugging heavily, seeing Ringo or John or one of the guys as they passed through town.

Because Mal was so big, he always thought he needed twice as much as anybody else; twice as much food, twice as much booze, and twice as many drugs. Neil remembers that when they first discovered LSD, Mal took five tablets at a time and was up for two days tripping. He did the same sort of thing one night in Los Angeles, except with downers. They made him drunkenly angry, and he got into a terrible row with his girlfriend. Allegedly, he pulled a gun on her, and she called the police. When the police arrived, pounding furiously on the door of the apartment, Mal barricaded himself inside. When the police broke down the door, this drunken giant was standing there with a gun, and they opened fire on him, killing him instantly in a barrage of shots. His girlfriend sent the bill for the cleaning of the carpet to Apple, but Neil refused to pay it.

There is a macabre twist to this already terrible story: Mal was cremated, and his ashes were lost in the mail. When John Lennon heard the story, he couldn't help but quip that Mal had wound up in the dead letter department.

Life in the fast lane finally sidelined Ringo in late April of 1979, when he was rushed to a Monte Carlo hospital in critical condition. His fragile stomach, still sensitive from his childhood illnesses and operations, had given out from the large quantities of harsh substances he was ingesting, and doctors in Monte Carlo were forced to remove part of his intestines. Yet when he recovered after several months of rest, Ringo returned to the party circuit as if nothing had happened. Too much time on his hands was his greatest problem, and he seemed to straighten up a little in the late winter of 1980 when he went to Mexico to star in a spoof of caveman pictures, called *Caveman*. This clever yet simple film had no real dialogue; the actors talked in prehistoric grunts and pieces of made-up language. Ringo's major task was to be a clown, and he was brilliant at it. He received glowing reviews and felt a sense of real achievement.

It was while he was filming *Caveman* that he met Barbara Bach, the leggy, buxom actress who co-starred in the picture with him. Bach was best known for her co-starring role in the James Bond movie, *The Spy Who Loved Me*. Like Ringo, she was divorced with children, and despite her glamourous image, she seemed to be a dedicated mother. They started dating during the filming, and the following month Ringo took her to London to meet his children—much to Maureen's great distress. Ringo and Barbara Bach were nearly killed in an automobile accident on this visit, when Ringo's car went out of control in South London and cut through three lampposts before it came to a halt. Ringo had pieces of the shattered windshield set in little gold lockets, which he and Barbara wear around their necks. Like John had done several years before, Ringo had the twisted wreckage of the car compressed into a cube, and he displays it as sculpture.

Ringo and Barbara were married in London at the Marylebone Registry on April 27, 1981. It was a Beatle reunion of sorts, because Paul and George both attended the ceremony with their wives. John was the only one missing.

Paul

*P*AUL McCARTNEY was thrown into serious doubt about his own talent. Not only were John's barbs about him being "the rock version of Engelbert Humperdinck" sticking to his flesh, but his first two solo albums, *McCartney* and *Ram*, were the objects of particular derision by rock critics. Indeed, the rock critics were flailing Paul's flesh over the breakup of the Beatles. For the most part rock critics take personal delight in being able to castigate their heroes when disappointed. Because Paul (along with Yoko) was being labeled as the villain in the Beatles breakup, his reviews became so pejorative that they would have killed the career of a lesser artist. "It became a challenge to me," Paul said. "I thought either I was going to go under or I was going to get something together."

All along, even when he was with the Beatles, what Paul wanted to do was start all over, to get back to his audience and just be in a little rock band again; this seemed like the perfect moment to try and do it. With great courage, Paul formed a new band from scratch and named it Wings. No superstar group this, he hired all unknown musicians and paid them salaries, as little as $450 a week. His first hiring was a New York session drummer named Denny Seiwell, who auditioned for Paul in a decrepit New York loft. His second hiring was Denny Laine, a former vocalist with the Moody Blues and a sometimes competent, creative guitarist. The last member of the group, on the keyboards, was none other than Mrs. Paul McCartney herself, much to the delight and ridiculing of the rock critics.

Paul figured if John could do it with Yoko, he could do it with Linda. Of course, Yoko at least had some musical ability and aspirations; Linda was a photographer. But he insisted on injecting her into his professional life. If Paul thought the rock critics had been mean to him, they were downright cruel about Linda. Her ability at the piano was minimal, her vocal was worse, and she was even criticized for her clothing and appearance, right down to the hair on her legs. There was a popular joke going around London: "What do you call a dog with wings?" "Linda McCartney."

Paul almost immediately found himself in a legal battle with Lew Grade and Northern Songs over Linda's musical ability. The call to arms came with the release of a single called "Another Day." Authorship of this tune was attributed to "Mr. and Mrs. Paul McCartney," as most of the *Ram* album would be. This meant that a pure 50 percent of the publishing rights—millions of dollars in the long run—would go directly into Linda's pocket, bypassing Northern Songs. Lew Grade was furious at what he saw as a deception on Paul's part, for Linda had not been and was obviously not now a musician capable of composing with Paul. Grade maintained that 100 percent of the songwriting credit deserved to go to Paul, and he took the case to court. Yet another painful public trial unfolded in the daily newspapers. The essence of Grade's lawsuit was that Linda had no musical ability, and this was what the attorneys had to prove. Linda took the witness stand to testify to her minimal talent, bravely sticking the trial out to the end. Paul's lawyers maintained that Linda's musical ability was not the point of the case and that it was his privilege to compose with absolutely anyone he wanted to compose with, regardless of their musical experience. It was to everyone's surprise and delight when Paul and Linda won the suit. To smooth over the decision with Lew Grade, Paul agreed to star in a Lew Grade–produced TV special for ATV, *James Paul McCartney*, which turned out to be to their mutual benefit.

If the rock critics were waiting to feast on Paul, he served himself up to them on a silver platter with Wing's first group album, *Wild Life*. This was a trivial, sophomoric LP, seemingly bereft of any redeeming melody or lyrics ("bip, bop bip bom bop bip bop bip bom bam"). Without pausing to take a breath, Paul added guitarist Henry McCullough to the Wings lineup and went back into the studio to record a new single, "Give Ireland Back to the Irish," which he composed in the wake of the "Bloody Sunday" shooting in Londonderry. This single was seen both as a ploy to regain credence with a hip audience and as a weak attempt at making some serious political statement (as John was doing with no problem in America). The song was declared too incendiary to be played on British radio and television, and although it sold several hundred thousand copies in Great Britain, it was also considered a failure.

In early February of 1972, Paul and his new band set out into the English countryside in a van, just as the Beatles had done in Neil Aspinall's van eleven years before. Without any advance warning, Paul turned up at the administration offices of Nottingham University and asked if he could set up his equipment and give a free concert for the students the following night. His only request was that the students not be told nor the press notified. On February 8, Paul gave a surprise concert for 700 deliriously happy students on what was the eighth anniversary of the Beatles' first appearance on the "Ed Sullivan Show."

Paul loved every minute of it. There was a thrill and satisfaction from entertaining a live audience that he could get nowhere else. He and Linda and Wings spent the following summer and fall touring around England and Europe in a double-decker bus painted with rainbows and clouds. It was their practice to turn up unannounced at various colleges and towns and offer to play. They took their meals on the road, often only bread and cheese and wine, and were a happy bunch of minstrels. Paul and Linda were enjoying themselves thoroughly. "We've no managers or agents," Linda told *Melody Maker*, "just we five and the roadies. We're just a gang of musicians touring around."

And like any "gang of musicians," they were traveling around with a stash of marijuana. Pot still remained Paul and Linda's favorite recreational drug, and they were rarely without it. Since they were traveling on their own, with no more Neil or Mal to carry it through customs for them, they arranged to either carry it themselves or have friends mail it to them in various hotels around Europe throughout the summer. The McCartneys made it through France, Germany, Switzerland, and Denmark without any trouble, but their luck ran out in Gothenburg, Sweden, on August 10. The local police and customs officials had intercepted a reported half pound of grass that had been mailed to them at their hotel from London. Paul, Linda, and Dennis Seiwell were brought to the police station directly from the stage of the Scandinavian Hall, where they performed that night. After several hours of questioning, the three allegedly "confessed" to smoking pot and were fined £800. The public prosecutor said that formal charges would be brought against them later, but none were ever lodged.

Their arrest was widely reported in the press back home, and in a move that only seemed to exacerbate the incident, Paul's next Wings single was called "Hi, Hi, Hi," which was understood to be a drug reference. The song was banned by the BBC and was a relative commercial failure in America. To pour salt in the wound, a few months later a local constable in Campelltown, Scotland, snooped around Paul's farm when he wasn't there and found marijuana plants growing in the greenhouse. With the utmost of leniency, the courts fined Paul only £100. Paul testified that an American fan had sent him the seeds, and he didn't know what they were when he planted them.

Always the workaholic, Paul kept busy with a second Wings

LP entitled *Red Rose Speedway*. Although not very distinguished by Paul's standards, it was a million selling commercial hit and spawned another one of Paul's brilliant, albeit saccharine, love songs, "My Love." Paul also composed the internationally acclaimed theme music to the James Bond movie *Live and Let Die*, which was produced by George Martin in his first work with a Beatle since the breakup. "Live and Let Die" was one of the biggest singles of the year and earned Paul an Oscar nomination for best song. In late spring of 1973, Paul also undertook the first scheduled commercially booked tour of an ex-Beatle in Great Britain.

It was on this British tour that Paul's overbearing nature started to cause him trouble again. During their off hours much of the band's time was spent composing and rehearsing Wings' next album, this one to be recorded in the exotic surroundings of Lagos, Nigeria, just for the fun of it. One day during rehearsals, Paul insisted that Henry McCullough play the guitar part in just a certain way—the way *he* wanted it—something Paul used to do quite often to superstar George Harrison. Well, McCullough wasn't a superstar, but he was no sideman either. He tried to avoid a head-on confrontation by telling Paul that the guitar bit couldn't be played the way Paul wanted it. "I, being a bit of a guitarist myself," Paul said, "knew it could be played, and rather than let it pass, I decided to confront him with it, and we had a confrontation. He left rehearsals a bit choked, then rang up to say he was leaving . . ."

To complicate matters, Denny Seiwell also rang up Paul in London just hours before they were supposed to leave for Lagos to tell him that he couldn't face playing with him any longer. Characteristically determined, Paul left for Lagos anyway with Linda, the children, and Denny Laine. They rented a two-bedroom house near the airport at Ikeja and drove to a recording studio nearby in the late afternoons. They would record far into the night, just the three of them, with the occasional help of an African drummer Paul hired for a few sessions.

Even this did not go well. The local gossip was that Paul had come to Lagos to steal the black man's rhythms. One night a fight developed in a local nightspot, and Paul reportedly told one of the owners, "I've done perfectly all right without your music so far. Nobody's gonna steal your bloody music." Lagos didn't have the prettiest terrain or the most pleasant weather, either. It was a steamy, dirty, often frightening place. The humidity made Paul think he was having a heart attack one day, and Linda summoned a doctor. On another occasion late one night, while returning from the studios, they were chased by several black men in a car. Trapped on a dark street, the men herded them into a doorway and held them at knifepoint while they searched them and stole their wallets and jewelry. Linda kept screaming at them, "Don't hurt him! He's Beatle Paul! He's Beatle Paul!" The authorities later said it was a fortunate thing Linda had done this, otherwise they most certainly would have been killed.

The tension, danger, and sense of furtiveness of Lagos, combined with the success of Paul's James Bond theme music, gave him a sense of confidence and power in these recording sessions. The results are evident on the album, appropriately entitled *Band on the Run*. Released in December of 1973, this is an inventive and unique album, which spawned three hits singles, including the title song and "Jet," which were both number one on record charts the world over. *Band on the Run* sold six million copies, the highest amount of any ex-Beatle and an amount equaling the group's biggest success, *Let It Be*.

Rejuvenated by the success of *Band on the Run*, Paul formed yet another band called Wings. The new drummer was named Geoff Britton, who was perhaps best known for representing Great Britain in an international karate tournament with Japan. Britton auditioned with fifty-two other drummers for the job. The new guitarist, Jimmy McCulloch (a name strikingly similar to the McCullough he replaced), was only twenty years old and had played with several second-string rock groups since he was thirteen.

Paul spent the next year traveling extensively with his new group. He passed the summer of 1974 in Nashville recording singles and then went on to New Orleans in January and February of 1975, where he recorded Wings' next LP, *Venus and Mars*, another best-selling, workmanlike LP that spawned the hit single, "Listen to What the Man Said."

That same summer I heard from Paul unexpectedly one Sunday night. I was staying in the Beverly Hills Hotel on business for the Robert Stigwood Organization. Paul and Linda and the kids were living in a rented house in Los Angeles and vacationing around southern California in a rented car, just like any family from Orange County. It was near midnight when the phone rang in my room. Paul was calling from the house phone in the lobby. He said there was a bit of trouble and asked if he could come up to my room to see me. When he appeared at the door I could see he was as pale as a ghost and very upset. He and Linda and the kids had been returning from a day's outing, driving along Sunset Boulevard in their rented car, when they jumped a red light. Two officers of the L.A. Police Department pulled them over to the side of the road and asked Paul to produce his license and registration. By the time the officers realized who it was they had pulled over, they also had taken a good whiff of the marijuana odor emanating from the closed car. The police conducted a spot search and found marijuana in the glove compartment. Because Paul was a foreigner on a visa—and already had two pot busts on his record—Linda took the blame, saying the grass was hers. She had been arrested and was being held at the station house. Bail had been posted at five hundred dollars, but Paul had only two hundred dollars in cash and travelers checks with him and needed to borrow the rest. Unfortunately, I had only one hundred and fifty dollars in cash with me, and the hotel cashier, although sympathetic, was unable to help because the safe was locked on a timing device. I finally borrowed the money from a friend, and Paul went off to get Linda out of jail. John Eastman flew out to Los Angeles to handle the case. The judge at first suggested that Linda see a psychiatrist for drug rehabilitation, but the case was later dismissed.

This third pot bust was enough to mark Paul as an habitual drug offender by most authorities, and he began to experience difficulties getting work visas in foreign countries. In fact, an elaborate tour of Japan had to be canceled because the authorities would not grant Paul a visa. It took three years before the Japanese would relent and allow Paul into Japan, in January of 1980, for what was to be the first Wings tour there. You would think that Paul would have learned his lesson, but upon arriving at the Narita Airport, nearly a half a pound of marijuana was found in their luggage. Allegedly, this was marijuana that Linda had picked up at a stop in New York on their way to Japan, and Paul knew nothing about it. He was handcuffed and led away by the police, begging the photographers not to take his picture as he was escorted into jail. Paul was in for one of the worst nightmares of his life. At first it was reported that he would be treated like any drug smuggler, and he might face a long prison sentence. His clothes and belongings were taken from him, and he spent his days sitting on a mat in a prison cell, writing a diary to keep him calm. Linda and the kids checked into a hotel and frantically tried to obtain his release through both lawyers and political diplomacy. Paul spent a total of ten days in jail, after which he was deported from the country on January 26. He intended to publish his diary, which he titled *Japanese Jailbird,* but thought better of it. It was reported that Paul was at the end of his rope with Linda and that their marriage was going to split up, but if anything their relationship seemed stronger than ever.

Curiously, while so many drug arrests would smear the public reputation of most artists, Paul's image as a kind of goody-two-shoes family man remains intact. He is the most commercially successful of any musician in history, a certified *Guinness Book of Records* entry. His personal worth is estimated at close to $500 million and climbing. Among his other profitable investments, he has purchased many valuable music catalogs, including all of Buddy Holly's music, Paul's special favorite.

In the beginning, after their breakup, Paul tried to keep in touch with John, but there was never a renewal of their friendship. Once, early on, Paul was in New York and he called John at the Dakota to say hello. Not more than three sentences were exchanged before the conversation disintegrated into a screaming match about lawsuits and tax liabilities. "But what about the fuckin' tax!?" John screamed at him. Paul slammed down the phone and then quickly looked through his phone book for the number of John Eastman, but in his haste he mistakenly called John Lennon's number again. John picked up the phone on the first ring.

"John?" Paul said. "This is Paul. You wouldn't believe what that fuckin' asshole John Lennon just said—"

"Fuckin' *who?*" John demanded. "*I'm* fuckin' John Lennon!"

Paul, realizing his mistake, slammed down the phone again.

As time passed and the lawsuits were settled, things cooled down and the two of them visited from time to time in Los Angeles and New York, but never more than an hour or two and never to effect any great reconciliation. The last time I saw Paul was at his country home, Waterfall, some 90 miles south of London. The house is circular, like a large gazebo, with the rooms cut up like pieces of pie. This odd architecture leaves little privacy, as you can hear every sound from room to room. There are few trappings of a rock star or even of a rich man. The gold records and expensive stereo equipment are in his offices in London. The furniture in the house is simple and well-worn, the floors littered with newspapers, magazines, and children's toys. There are so many books and plants and knickknacks everywhere that it's easy to miss the black baby grand piano in the corner.

Paul spends most of his time in this house with Linda and his three young children. He is a caring and attentive father and is particularly attached to his young son, James. It was amusing to watch him trying to discipline the children while remaining Beatle Paul. While I was there, Heather, who is now a young woman and living in her own apartment in a nearby town, brought her boyfriend home to meet her dad. I suppose it's hard enough to meet your girlfriend's father without him being a Beatle. To top it off, the young man was an aspiring musician himself, just starting out with his own band. As he was introduced to Paul he stared down at the floor and shuffled his boots nervously. Paul was charming. "What's yer band called, son?" he asked. It was a long way from the cherub-faced skirtchaser I knew at the Cavern Club.

That same visit John's last album, *Double Fantasy*, was about to be released. It was his first record in over five years, and Paul was curious to hear it. I could see he was still threatened by John. John and Yoko had recently given an interview to *Newsweek* magazine and for no reason had lashed out at Linda and Paul. In the interview John mentioned turning Paul away from his door. Linda said to me, "Is this new album all of John's music or does it have *her* on it too?" When I said it was half Yoko's music, Linda sneered at the thought.

I asked Paul if John had really turned him away, and he told me the story. He was in New York on business, and he had his guitar with him. He felt a few pangs of nostalgia and decided to take his guitar and just drop in on John at the Dakota. Paul went past the guarded gate, through the arched entranceway, and into a small, mahogany-paneled office where another guard sat behind a switchboard. John didn't believe it was really Paul

McCartney at first, but when Paul got on the phone to confirm it was really him, he was greeted with a cold silence on the other end of the phone. "I'm sorry," John finally said, "but you can't come up now. You just can't drop in on people in New York like you did in Liverpool. The old times are over."

Chapter Twenty

I am convinced of the fact that Lennon perhaps has a career whose balance is somewhat more delicate than the career of other artists. Lennon has attempted a variety of ventures both in popular music and avant-garde music. Lennon's product tends to be somewhat more intellectual than the product of other artists. What this means in my view is that Lennon's reputation and his standing are a delicate matter . . .

—Justice Thomas P. Greisa
New York Federal Court
July 13, 1976

1.

*B*ETWEEN RECORDING albums and singles, bed-ins, concerts and various other international shenanigans, John and Yoko managed to turn out a prodigious number of 16-mm films. These films were sometimes aired on European TV or shown at minor film festivals. One of their early attempts was entitled *Rape*, a metaphor for the media's treatment of them. In *Rape* a camera relentlessly pursues a young girl, finally reducing her to tears. *Erection* was only a movie of a building being constructed in stop-action time, but *Self Portrait* turned out to be the real thing. This is a short film of John's flaccid penis, in close-up, almost imperceptibly growing tumescent in slow motion. The special slow-motion effect was achieved with a Milliken high-speed camera. This noisy camera sends film through the gate so fast that there's no way to shut the camera off once it's been turned on until the film runs out. This meant that John had to become erect on cue. John stood poised in front of the camera and lights, thinking erotic thoughts, and said, "Hit it!" But every time the camera went on he panicked. Thousands of feet were wasted without any results. Finally, the crew was asked to leave the room, while Yoko posed erotically for him. Still no erection. Finally, John was given a copy of *Playboy* magazine, and that did the trick. When Yoko and John were interviewed about the film in their office at Apple, Yoko innocently told a reporter, "The critics wouldn't touch it," and she was right.

There was another film that John and Yoko made that disturbed one person in particular: Tony Cox. This was a short film made to commemorate Kyoko's seventh birthday, which she celebrated at Tittenhurst Park. Only instead of a birthday party and cake with candles, it was a film of Kyoko and John bathing nude together in the same tub. Cox was reportedly furious over this film, and he vowed not to let John and Yoko get near his daughter again.

Things had been deteriorating anyway over the past year. Intermittently, Cox would call to say he needed money to pay his bills. In exchange for whatever sum of money was needed at the time, Cox would allow Yoko a few days with her daughter but always under his careful supervision. Then he would vanish for a time, only to resurface a few months later when he needed more money. By mid-1971 Cox and Kyoko had disappeared altogether, and John and Yoko were determined to find them.

They hired an elite team of private detectives to track Cox down, but he kept hopping from continent to continent in an effort to evade them. In April they were tipped off that he was living on the island of Majorca, off the coast of Spain, attending a course given by none other than John's old friend, the Maharishi Mahesh Yogi. John and Yoko rented a plane, and along with Dan Richter, Yoko's American friend, they slipped onto the island of Majorca. Without attracting any attention, they managed to check into a suite at the Melia-Mallorca Hotel and started to search the island for Kyoko. They learned that during the day, while Cox studied with the Maharishi, Kyoko stayed in a communal children's camp just outside of town, guarded by the Maharishi's disciples.

John and Yoko arrived at the camp later that day to find Kyoko frolicking in a playground with the other children. According to Yoko, all she did was extend her arms to the child, who ran toward her. They then spirited her to their rented car, and with Dan Richter at the wheel they sped off through the countryside with the Maharishi's disciples chasing after them on foot. Fearful of road blocks by police, John and Yoko laid down in the rear of the car with Kyoko between them so it looked as if Richter were driving alone. They made it back to the hotel with no trouble and rushed the little girl up to their suite. It was only then that they realized that Kyoko wasn't wearing any shoes, and they sent Richter out to buy some. By the time the elevator brought him down to the lobby, the hotel was crawling with police.

The following day the London tabloids carried a front-page picture of John carrying the frightened nine-year-old Kyoko over the threshold of the police station, with Yoko, Cox, and a phalanx of police close behind. John and Yoko were kept fourteen hours on suspicion of kidnapping. "I'm not exactly being detained," John told reporters who assembled outside the courthouse. "I'm trying to sort this matter out."

Cox was furious at the alleged kidnapping. "I've got John by the balls this time," he said at the station house. "This will cost him millions." When the Lennons were finally permitted to leave the station, it was without Kyoko. The judge pulled the same rotten test on them that Freddie and Julia Lennon had pulled on John when he was a little boy; he asked Kyoko whom she wanted to stay with. Kyoko said, "My daddy."

"We will be back for her, wherever she is," Yoko told the reporters, her voice quavering emotionally. "But now we must get a legal ruling. How can you kidnap your own baby?" she demanded. "I did what any mother would have done."

"We've done everything we can to come to an amicable agreement with the father," John said. "In all it's cost us a lot of money and a shaft of broken promises. Yoko loves her daughter, and I can't let her suffer like this any longer. What effect can all this be having on Kyoko? I remember it was happening to me . . . I was shattered."

The Lennons jetted back to London, where their lawyers advised them to get a legal writ of custody in the same court where the original divorce had been granted in the Virgin Islands, a U.S. possession. Late that August they flew to the Virgin Islands, where an attorney entered a plea for a custody order, which was summarily granted. Now all they had to do was collar Tony Cox. Cox had now reportedly moved to America. Cox's move to the U.S. was to their great advantage, for the writ obtained in the Virgin Islands was good only on U.S. territory. This meant, of course, that in order to continue the search for Kyoko, the Lennons would have to move to America themselves.

John was delighted at the prospect of moving to New York.

He wasn't very much liked at home, and he had recently begun what would be a long-term love affair with Manhattan. Since his visit to Los Angeles for primal therapy, the United States Department of Immigration had let up on him and was allowing him into the country on a temporary basis. On these numerous trips to New York, John met with Jonas Mekas, the dean of underground filmmakers, and made several films. One, called *Up Your Legs*, consisted of a camera pan of bare legs up to a bare behind. Three hundred volunteers were assembled to be photographed, and John met a whole spectrum of New York society, including actor George Segal and artist Larry Rivers. He was suddenly exposed to a whole new cast of characters, more artists, poets, musicians, and assorted loonies in one single city than in all of Great Britain. In John's two-part *Rolling Stone* "Working Class Hero" interview, he virtually spouts odes to New York. "America is where it's at. I should have been born in New York. I should have been born in the Village, that's where I belong. Why wasn't I born there? Paris was 'it' in the eighteenth century. London—I don't think had ever been 'it' except literary-wise when Wilde and Shaw and all of them were there. New York was 'it.' I regret profoundly that I was not an American and not born in Greenwich Village. That's were I should have been . . . this is where it's happening . . ."

At the end of August 1971, John's immigration lawyers had arranged a six-month visitor's visa for John, and in September he arrived in New York to settle. He checked into the St. Regis Hotel for a few weeks until he rented a brownstone apartment on Bank Street in Greenwich Village. He was never to see England again.

2.

*B*Y THE TIME John and Yoko moved to Manhattan, I was already living in New York in my position as president of the Robert Stigwood Organization. RSO, as it was known, had become as diversified and sprawling as Apple had been, and in many ways it was much more successful. There was an RSO recording label, which featured many RSO-managed acts, including the Bee Gees and Eric Clapton; there was a TV division that produced "Movies of the Week" and licensed such American TV shows as "Sanford and Son" and "All in the Family"; a stage division produced *Jesus Christ Superstar* and *Sergeant Pepper's Lonely Hearts Club Band* for the theater; and a film company produced the movies of *Jesus Christ Superstar* and *Tommy* while I was with the company. As the chief operating officer in America I traveled extensively between Los Angeles and London, but I considered New York my new home, and I took an apartment there overlooking the park on Central Park West. I remained a close friend to all of the Beatles, particularly John and Paul, and saw all of them frequently as they passed through the city.

Life in New York held great promise for John and Yoko. New people. A chance at starting over, a city where you could be anonymous if you wanted to be, even if you were John Lennon. A place where the press would leave him alone if he didn't call attention to himself. John was also in a vulnerable position in America. He was an already controversial figure with many illegal vices and addictions. He was allowed into the United States only by the good graces of the Bureau of Immigration, even though he was a convicted pot felon. So what does John do? Sit back and keep his mouth shut so he can look for Yoko's kid?

John took on the U.S. Government. He became, overnight, one of the most vocal political activists in the country, a powerful and feared rock and roll rabble-rouser. It wasn't John's fault, it was just the Next Big Thing.

The Next Big Thing happened "right off the boat," as John put it. "I landed in New York," John explained, "and the first people to get in touch with me were Jerry Rubin and Abbie Hoffman. It's as simple as that. It's those two famous guys from America callin, 'Hey, yeah, what's happenin', what's goin' on? . . .' And the next thing you know, I'm doin' John Sinclair benefits and one thing and another. I'm pretty movable as an artist, you know. They almost greeted me off the plane and the next minute I'm *involved.* "

John forgot to mention that "those two famous guys from America" were also two of the most rabid political activists in the United States. Abbie Hoffman and Jerry Rubin had gained international fame as two of the convicted members of the "Chicago Seven," the group that was blamed for disrupting the 1968 Democratic Convention in Chicago. Hoffman and Rubin were aggressive, unattractive, and intentionally aggravating at every turn. In retrospect they may seem absolutely benign, but at the time they were an alarming example of radicalism for the so-called "Silent Majority" and considered a direct threat to national security by the Nixon administration.

John was just ripe for this far left, publicity-conscious brand of politics. His personal failure in his peace endeavors with Yoko had hardened his line. His early vision of a pacifist revolution— "All You Need Is Love" or "Imagine"—was slipping into a more active mold. The public had already tasted this new, aggressive political stance in a single released that spring called "Power to the People," a proletarian anthem that begins with a chorus of marching feet. Politics was also one of John's ways of struggling with being rich. In a sense, being rich to John was selling out. He was by instinct part socialist, part right-wing Archie Bunker; to be an indolent, wealthy rock star would have made him feel guilty as sin. Yet the passionate politician he was to become was also a phoney pose, possessed with the guilty enthusiasm of a hypocrite. Years later John would disclaim the radicalism of this period, saying that an ideological breach between him and the other activists existed from the start, but if this was John's attitude at the time, it was impossible to tell by his actions.

John threw himself into the world of radical causes with all the enthusiasm he had poured into previous Next Big Things. The mayor of the East Village, David Peel, who sang "The Pope Smokes Dope," threw a Welcome-to-New York parade for John and Yoko through the streets, singing "You also met an underground, welcome to a freaky town." They began hanging out at Max's Kansas City, a once superhip club patronized by Andy Warhol that had turned into the home of underground rock, where John began practicing with an unknown band called Elephants Memory. They set up command headquarters in the bedroom of their Bank Street apartment and turned it into a salon for the leaders of every potentially unpleasant political and social cause in America. No matter how far-out you were, John and Yoko would embrace you. They did all their business from bed, and they quite literally invited the diminutive Jerry Rubin into bed with them, right in front of a delighted reporter. "You should be a member of the band," John told Rubin. "If you're gonna work with us, you should play music with us."

Under Hoffman and Rubin's tutelage, John "came out" politically. In October he appeared at a protest on behalf of the American Indian's civil rights; in November he appeared at the Attica Relatives Benefit at the Apollo Theater in Harlem for the relatives of the men in the bloody prison riots. He wrote guest columns for an underground magazine called *Sundance* and made the trip all the way to Ann Arbor, Michigan, to appear at a John Sinclair rally. Sinclair, founder of the White Panthers, had been given ten years in jail for selling two joints to an undercover cop. John also wrote for the *Gay Liberation Book* and spoke out to the press loudly in support of Angela Davis, the accused murderer and Black Panther leader.

Then John made a near-fatal mistake; he took on the paranoid Nixon White House directly. Rubin and Hoffman were working on a master plan for a demonstration at the Republican National Convention, which was going to be held in San Diego in the summer of 1972. Rubin and Hoffman intended to sponsor a rock concert, which they hoped would draw upwards of 300,000 antiwar demonstrators, bringing the convention to a standstill. Of course, gathering a few hundred thousand war demonstrators together, convention or not, wasn't going to be easy without a big-name drawing card for the rock concert.

Enter superstar John Lennon.

In the autumn of 1971 John and Yoko attended a meeting about such a concert to be held in San Diego. Present at the meeting were Rubin, Hoffman, Allen Ginsberg, and John Sinclair. Says John, "When they described their plans, we [he and Yoko] just kept looking at each other. It was the poets and the straight politicals divided. Ginsberg was with us. He kept saying, 'What are we trying to do, create another Chicago?' That's what they wanted. We said, 'We ain't buying this. We're not going to draw children into a situation to create violence—so you can overthrow *what?*—and replace it with *what?*' "

But if John and Yoko refused at the time to go along with the plan, that wasn't the way it was reported to the press. According to John, it was Jerry Rubin's fault for blabbing about the concert to *Rolling Stone,* which published a small piece about it.

John was angry with Rubin for announcing his presence at the concert, but he never denied his participation, and thus he gave the plot his tacit consent.

The Nixon administration immediately labeled John a threat and set about to remove him from the country. In January of 1972 the Senate Internal Security Subcommittee of the Judiciary Committee researched and wrote a classified memo on John Ono Lennon and his wife. It was six paragraphs long and delivered to Senator Strom Thurmond. It listed all of John's activist causes and his alliances with Jerry Rubin, Rennie Davis, Leslie Bacon, Jay Craven, and "others." The memo stated that "This group has been strong advocates of the program to 'dump Nixon.' They have devised a plan to hold rock concerts in various primary election states for the following purposes: to obtain access to college campuses; to stimulate eighteen-year-old registration; to press legislation to legalize marijuana; to finance their activities; and to recruit persons to come to San Diego during the Republican National Convention in August 1972 . . . Davis and his cohorts intend to use John Lennon as a drawing card to promote the success of the rock festivals and rallies. The source feels that this will pour tremendous amounts of money into the coffers of the New Left and can only inevitably lead to a clash between a controlled mob organized by this group and law enforcement officials in San Diego. The source felt that if Lennon's visa is terminated it would be a strategy counter-measure."

On February 29, John's immigration attorney filed for a routine extension to his six-month nonimmigration visa, which was granted. In the interim, Senator Thurmond forwarded the Judiciary Committee memo to Attorney General John Mitchell, along with a note: "This appears to me to be an important matter and I think it would be well for it to be considered at the highest level as I can see many headaches might be avoided if appropriate action be taken in time." Across the bottom, in his own hand, Thurmond wrote: "I also sent Bill Timmons a copy of the memorandum." Timmons was on the White House staff; John Lennon's troublemaking had found its way directly to the top.

On February 14 Deputy Attorney General Kleindienst, who didn't even realize the Lennons were already in America, sent the memo to Immigration and Naturalization Service commissioner Raymond Farell with the note; note, "Ray, please call me about the attached. When is he coming? Do we—if we so elect—have any basis to deny his admittance?" If Kleindienst had turned on the television set in his den in Georgetown, he would have been able to see the enemy of the government beamed into tens of millions of American homes all week as co-host of the "Mike Douglas Show."

On March 2, Farell's associate commissioner, James Greene, told the New York INS district director to "immediately revoke the voluntary departure granted to John Lennon and his wife." A few days later, on March 6, John's visa extension was summarily canceled. The official reason given was John's 1968 pot bust in London. John and Yoko didn't believe that was the real reason, but they still didn't seem to connect it with their political activities. They guessed they were being asked to leave because in January they had given a concert at Alice Tully Hall without INS permission. They had no American work permits and were forced to perform from their seats, where Yoko conducted the band with an apple instead of baton. John's lawyers appealed the case and applied for a temporary extension on his deportation date. The case against Yoko, who had no criminal record, was dropped, and John became the solitary target.

Ironically, getting a permanent visa was supposed to be John and Yoko's primary concern. In order to get final custody of Kyoko, Yoko had to live in America. Through all their political activities, John and Yoko hadn't abandoned their search for Kyoko. Again through a series of private detectives, they learned that Cox had moved to Houston, Texas, where his second wife, Melinda, had been brought up. Now the story had taken yet another bizarre turn; Cox had given up the Maharishi and become a born again Christian, as fervent an apostle of Christ as he had been of the guru. He had legally changed Kyoko's name to Rosemary and had applied to Houston Domestic Relations Court for legal custody.

Upon learning of this, John and Yoko flew to Houston in December of 1971 and presented their custody order from the Virgin Islands to Justice Peter Solito. Judge Solito, faced with the choice of giving the child to her Bible-spouting father or to John and Yoko in bed with Jerry Rubin in New York, quickly overrode the Virgin Islands order and gave custody of the child to her God-fearing father. However, the judge added that Yoko could see

Kyoko-Rosemary frequently—as long as she posted a $20,000 bond in case she "kidnapped" the child again.

John and Yoko would have quickly forfeited the $20,000 bond to have Kyoko back—$20,000 didn't mean that much to them—but there was no amount worth the legal problems if they broke the law in the United States. They agreed to a ten-day visitation period over Christmas, during which they wanted to take Kyoko-Rosemary back to New York and the Bank Street apartment with them. It was suggested that before they hustled Kyoko-Rosemary away from her father, that they first spend the weekend with her in Houston so she could get used to being with them again. But when it came down to the moment for Cox to hand the child over to them, he just couldn't do it and refused to let Kyoko-Rosemary come out of the house.

With this clear-cut defiance of Yoko's custody rights as ordered by Judge Solito, John and Yoko summoned up a team of high-priced lawyers who got a court order for contempt of court against Cox. On December 22 he was arrested and put in a Houston jail, shouting, "Pray for me all good Christians!" The following day Cox was released on his own recognizance on $5,000 bail. On Christmas Eve, he and Kyoko-Rosemary and his wife Melinda vanished into the night, never to be seen again.

In the ensuing years John and Yoko dropped their search for the girl, now in her early twenties. Since 1972 Yoko has heard from Kyoko-Rosemary only twice, in two spontaneous phone calls. As of this writing, Yoko has never seen her daughter again.

3.

*T*HROUGH THE SPRING and summer of 1972, John felt the unmistakable heat of Big Brother breathing down his neck. It began with a certain hollowness on the phone; the soft clicking noises and the vacuum of a third person listening. He began to think people were following him, serious-looking men in suits and ties. When he talked about politics or drugs in hotel rooms, he sometimes went into the bathroom and ran the water in the sink in case the room was bugged. He told everyone who would listen to him that something weird was happening to him, that he wasn't imagining it, that he was the victim of some baroque plot brewed up in the Oval Office of the White House. ". . . It was really gettin' to me," John said. "There was a period where I just couldn't function, you know. I was so paranoid from them tappin' the phone and followin' me . . ." John even appeared on the "Dick Cavett Show" to publicly confess his paranoia, saying that his phone was tapped, much to Cavett's quiet bemusement. For most people who watched this broadcast, it sounded like more of John's provocative ramblings. John had cried wolf too many times.

Paranoia had long been a constant in John's life. Drugs and paranoia went hand in hand, and John was taking drugs again. Yoko claims that whatever this drug was, it was not heroin. However, it was a drug (possibly methadone) they found it necessary to "kick." By June of 1972 it was perilously dangerous for John, under constant government surveillance, to be fooling around with drugs again. Afraid of checking into a hospital or staying in their apartment, which was bugged, they came up with the extraordinary, if ingenuous, plan to kick in the back of a limousine during a cross-country trip. Since George and Ringo were due in New York that month and expecting to see them, John and Yoko seized on this as the time to escape. John later told Tony King, who worked for him, that he and Yoko were ashamed to see George and Ringo in their condition. They spent over a week in the backseat of the limousine, traveling across the country, withdrawing. The identity of the limousine driver remains a mystery, but he was either a friend or very well paid. When they reached the Coast they stayed several weeks in a rented house with a pool in Ojai, outside of Santa Barbara, and then spent a month at the Miyako, a traditional Japanese hotel in San Francisco, where they saw a Chinese acupuncturist. By mid-summer they returned to New York, ready to face the foe again.

In the interim, John's lawyers fought for various continuances and appeals to extend his visa. John lived constantly on the edge, facing deportation orders every sixty days. It didn't help his cause any when on June 12 he released his new album, *Sometime in New York City*, a shrill and abrasive catalog of protest songs. This two-record set contained titles like "Attica State," "Born in a Prison," "John Sinclair," and one for Angela Davis, called "Angela."

For good measure there was a version of "Cold Turkey" and a seventeen-minute live cut of Yoko doing "Don't Worry Kyoko, Mummy's Only Looking for Her Hand in the Snow." Needless to say, even superstar John Lennon couldn't make this kind of music sell at the record stores. *Sometime in New York City* sold only 164,000 copies, compared to John's *Imagine* album which sold 1,553,000.

The Republican National Convention came and went that summer without John's appearing at any provocative concerts. The only place he did appear was, by contrast, quite admirable, and that was at the One to One Concert at Madison Square Garden, where he and Yoko helped raise $1.5 million for retarded children. Also, to their great pleasure, a host of credible character witnesses came forward on John's behalf, including New York's mayor, John Lindsay, Dick Cavett, artists Larry Rivers and Roy Lichtenstein, United Auto Workers president Leonard Woodcock, Congressman Ed Koch, and columnist Pete Hamill, who wrote in the old *New York Post,* "John Lennon has improved this town just by showing up."

But John had already lost the fight. He was a nervous wreck, pale and puffy with that unhealthy white complexion that comes from rising at dusk. He chain-smoked unfiltered Gitane cigarettes from the moment he woke up, drank his fair share, and remained almost perpetually stoned. To add to his troubles, he began to have violent disagreements with the way Allen Klein was handling his business matters. Foreseeing a protracted legal fight, John and Yoko arrived at Klein's office unannounced one day and raided the files for their personal records while he wasn't there. In June of 1973 Klein and John let fly with major lawsuits, claiming assorted mismanagement practices and breaches of contract, not unlike the previous accusations made against Klein. Nobody got much of a chance to tell John "I told you so." In November Paul, George, and Ringo joined in the suit against Klein, alleging that he took excessive commissions and practiced fraud. This was in addition to George's claim that Klein had mismanaged the Bangladesh concert. Klein responded with another lawsuit against John, George, Ringo, Yoko, and Apple for a total of $63,461,-372.87 in claims. In a separate suit against Paul, in which he accused him of conspiring against him in business, Klein claimed damages of $34 million. The lawsuits were just another stone around John's neck.

He tried to distract himself by working on a new album in the studio, but the album he produced for Christmas of 1973, called *Mind Games*, was one of his weakest, most submissive works. "Yes is the answer," John sings on the title cut, tired of fighting. *Mind Games'* twelve selections are so offhand and low-key that critic Nicholas Schaffner called them "a collection of out-takes ranging over the past six years . . ." *Mind Games* also had hopelessly banal liner notes, left over from the days of flower-power, that proclaimed a "Nutopian nation" governed by cosmic law. "The Nutopian International Anthem" was one of the more readily forgettable cuts on the album.

In early 1973 John and Yoko visited me in my apartment and fell in love with the view of Central Park. A few weeks later Yoko called to say they had purchased their own apartment with a park view at the Dakota, a gothic fortress on the corner of Central Park West and Seventy-second Street. This forbidding-looking building, with its gargoyles and sinister dormer apartments at the top, was one of the most desirable on the Upper West Side and boasted a long tenant list of celebrities, including Lauren Bacall, Leonard Bernstein, and Rex Reed.

John wasn't at the Dakota for long, however. He and Yoko had been feeding off each other with an exclusivity that would have long ago devoured any other couple, and they were due for a separation. They were bickering almost constantly, and when epic lovers fight, the fights are of epic proportions. In particular, Yoko was critical of John's drinking and drugging. She thought that with the heat on it was time for him to really clean up his act. Yoko insists that there was never one big argument but that their parting was amicable, though unexpected. "One night John and I were lying in bed in the Dakota," Yoko said, "and John kept saying how miserable he was, how he needed to get away. I said that we had been together twenty-four hours a day for five years and that I needed some time apart for myself. I told him, 'Why don't you go to Los Angeles?' "

"What would I do there?" John asked.

"Make an album. Call Phil [Spector] and make an album."

"But who would I go with?" John said. "I can't go by myself."

According to Yoko they discussed several possibilities, including Mal Evans, the Beatles' loyal road manager and bodyguard who had moved to L.A., and Tony King, a close friend of John and Yoko's who was then working for Apple Records. But John fancied May Pang, a shapely twenty-three-year old secretary who worked for them for years out of Allen Klein's New York office. Hard as it is to believe, Yoko says she gave this union her blessings. Whether the relationship was going to be physical or not did not faze or interest her.

May Pang first met John and Yoko in December of 1970 when they had come to New York to meet filmmaker Jonas Mekas and help make an underground movie called *Fly*. One day John and Yoko walked off the elevator into Klein's offices on Seventh Avenue, and May happened to be in the reception room. May Pang became their de facto assistant and was dispatched to a Chinese restaurant to collect hundreds of live flies for use in the film they were making. Pang also accompanied John and Yoko to England for the shooting of some footage to complement John's *Imagine* album.

"We decided on May," Yoko says, "because she was the most efficient secretary available. It was not a love affair, although the relationship might have been physical. But then, John had a lot of girls. . . . May remained on salary the whole time she was with John, and she reported to me almost daily."

Needless to say, being the wet nurse-paramour of a rock star on the skids was a thankless job; for the next year May Pang would be the sole comfort to a man trying to exorcise his worst demons. John used to refer to this nightmarish period in L.A. as his "Lost Weekend." "My goal was to obliterate the mind so that I wouldn't be conscious," John said later. "I think I was maybe suicidal on some kind of subconscious level." Indeed, it was probably the closest John ever came to suicide in a real sense. The prodigious quantities of alcohol alone—there are stories of John's polishing off fifths of Rémy Martin in one sitting—were enough to kill the average man, to say nothing of the increased danger of mixing the booze with his usual assortment of drugs, plus an L.A. specialty, coke. John fell in easily with a certain L.A. group, most notably Harry Nilsson, Who drummer Keith Moon, old buddy Ringo Starr, and sometimes Alice Cooper. "I was like an elephant in a zoo, aware it's trapped but not able to get out."

He had gone to L.A. ostensibly to record a new album with Phil Spector. This was going to be a "return to roots" album for John, tentatively titled *Rock and Roll*. John had made a list of his old favorites, songs like "Be Bop A Lula," the Gene Vincent song Paul was playing the moment they met, and Ben E. King's "Stand By Me." John anticipated giving Spector all the responsibility, hoping he could sit back and relax, to be used like a superstar session singer. But when John arrived in L.A., he found Spector was more out of control than he was. A legendary rock and roll eccentric in his own right (it is Spector who appears in the back of the limousine at the beginning of *Easy Rider* to collect the dope), Spector's own vices had sent him over the edge. Spector's peculiar behavior began from the moment they got together at Spector's Beverly Hills mansion. Spector promptly locked John and May Pang in the house and kept them prisoner for nine hours.

Spector and Lennon in the studio together weren't much more winning. Spector acted flakey and weird all the time, and John's voice was too laced with brandy. The sessions climaxed one day when Spector fired a revolver into the ceiling of the control booth. He disappeared shortly after, taking all of John's tapes with him. When John protested that *he* owned the tapes, not Spector, he was informed that Spector had personally paid for the sessions through Warner Brothers, and John would have to get the tapes from Spector. Spector literally barricaded himself in his Beverly Hills mansion, and whenever John called, a servant informed him that "Mr. Spector is ill" or "Mr. Spector has died in an accident."

"I'm crazy, he's crazy," John said. "And he's crazier than me, that's all." A custody battle over the tapes developed, which only depressed John even further; there didn't seem to be anything he could do that didn't disintegrate into lawsuits. Without the regimen of the studio to keep him on at least a minimal schedule, John slipped further into his binge. During this period John's public behavior got correspondingly more desperate, the kind of things an unhappy man does as a cry for help. These incidents were widely reported in the papers back East and in England. In one of the more famous incidents, John was thrown out of the Troubadour, a nightclub on Sunset Boulevard, for heckling the Smothers Brothers show. It seems that John and Harry Nilsson got blitzed on Brandy Alexanders, and John couldn't restrain himself from interrupting the Smothers Brothers act with wisecracks. The show was brought to a complete halt until John and Harry Nilsson could be ejected from the club. On the way to the parking lot, a shoving match with the club's manager and a photographer ensued. An ugly photo of Nilsson about to throw a punch, with John trying to hold him back, was on all the wire services the next morning.

Another famous incident, often repeated, occurred at a small restaurant on Santa Monica Boulevard called Lost on Larabee. John, drunk again, returned from the rest room with an unused sanitary napkin stuck to his forehead. When the waitress came to the table, John demanded, "Do you know who I am?"

"Yes," said the waitress. "You're some asshole with a Kotex on his forehead."

One morning John turned to Harry Nilsson and said, "What are we doing? Why don't we do some work instead of getting into trouble, you know? My name gets in the paper, you never get mentioned and I get all the problems, and *I'm* the one with the immigration problem—so let's do something constructive!"

Like little boys setting out to build a tree house, John and Harry decided to occupy themselves by recording an album for Harry, which John would produce. They rented themselves a vast beach house in Malibu and moved in together. It couldn't have been a worse arrangement. Harry was John's partner in crime, and John had to literally lock himself away in his bedroom not to drink. Harry's voice was almost gone from cigarettes and alcohol, and it was to John's credit that an album was produced at all. Entitled *Pussycats*, it was released on RCA to no big fanfare.

Meanwhile, back in New York, Yoko's so-called friends dropped her like a hot potato, figuring she was washed up without John. The phone at the Dakota stopped ringing, and Yoko became a virtual recluse. No longer under the protection of John's effective tongue, Yoko now took the full blast of hostility from the rock press, who still blamed her for breaking up the Beatles. After a few months of hermitage, she forced herself out of the apartment and became a regular browser in the many antique stores that lined nearby Columbus and Amsterdam avenues.

I was touched by a phone call I received from her that winter, asking me to please include her in my social calendar. I made sure that Yoko knew she was a welcome visitor in my home. She was always a fascinating yet slightly intimidating dinner guest and a worthy conversationalist. However, she declined more invitations than she accepted, and when she did come by, she was more retiring than I had ever seen her. The fire was still there, but it had been turned down low. People gossiped constantly about whether or not John would ever take her back.

Little did anyone realize at the time that it was Yoko's decision whether or not she would take John back and that she spoke to either John or May Pang almost every day. Yoko got reports from Pang on John's daily behavior and mental condition. Often Yoko would give some specific advice on how to handle John in a sticky situation. It was a most sophisticated relationship. John would often say he missed the Dakota and wanted to come back to New York, but Yoko would say "No, you're not ready" and would encourage him to stop drinking and using drugs.

In August of 1974, after eight months in Los Angeles, John returned to New York. "I sort of woke up, still very fuzzy, because I'd been drinking like a lunatic, and it takes it out of your body. And so then I finished what I could of the work in L.A. and dragged it back to New York. Even though [Yoko] said I couldn't come back, I had to get back to New York anyway and get rid of Harry and this business, and then see where I'm at. So the first instinct was to stop drinking and playing around with the guys, and the thing was to finish off the responsibilities I had, which was my own album and Harry Nilsson's album, which was very difficult because everybody else was still loony."

John checked into a suite at the Regency for a while and then into May Pang's apartment, until he found a large place on East Fifty-third Street and the East River. As soon as he arrived in New York, he felt a creative outburst and in one marathon writing session he composed all the songs for a new album, this one entitled *Walls and Bridges*. "I'm surprised it wasn't all bluggghh," John said. "I had the most peculiar year. I'm just glad something came out. It's describing the year, in a way, but it's not as schizophrenic as the year really was . . . only the surface had been touched in *Walls and Bridges*." Along with Klaus Voorman, Jim Keltner, and Nicky Hopkins, John recorded the album in a creative frenzy at the Record Plant Studios on West Forty-fourth Street. *Walls and Bridges* was an important album for John, a revelatory one in which he comes to terms with himself, similar in a way to his primal LP. Two of the more obvious instances of this are "Scared" and "Nobody Loves You (When You're Down and Out)." "Whatever Gets You Through the Night," which made it to num-

ber one on the lists as one of the most popular light-
hearted hits of the year, is a brilliant bit of hip philosophy. The
critics were rapturous, as were fans, and having a number-one
single out of the clear blue was an enormous boost to John's
confidence and spirits.

The day before he began work on *Walls and Bridges,* the tapes
of the Phil Spector album were returned to him. Capitol Records
president Al Coury paid Spector $94,000 for their release. John
put them on the console and listened to them. According to John,
only four cuts were salvageable, and he didn't know what to do
with them. "Some were all right, but I didn't feel confident about
'em. So I thought, 'Oh, I'll record some more.'" John went back
to the Record Plant and in five days recorded ten more classic
rock and roll songs, using the musicians he had assembled on
the *Walls and Bridges* album.

Now a typically Lennonesque complication arose. Years before,
John and the Beatles had been involved in a minor plagiarism
suit over a passage in "Come Together." Morris Levy, publisher
of Big Seven Music, felt "Come Together" sounded suspiciously
similar to Chuck Berry's "You Can't Catch Me," which Big Seven
owned. It was one of many annoyance suits the Beatles had to
contend with, and it was settled out of court in October of 1973
in Levy's favor. In the settlement John agreed to record three
Big Seven oldies on his next album. These Big Seven songs were
to be recorded on the *Rock and Roll* album in L.A., but Spector
had kidnapped the tapes, so when John's "next album"—*Walls
and Bridges*—appeared and only one song, a cover of Big Seven's
"Ya Ya," was to be found, Levy was angry. Somehow, John took
over the negotiations with Levy himself, and John allegedly made
a verbal promise to record an album of oldies for Levy's Adam
VIII label. Adam VIII was a TV mail-order company that usually
advertised on the late-night movies. Whether or not this is so,
John did send Levy a raw tape of his *Rock and Roll* album, albeit
only on 7½-inch per second tape and hardly of broadcast quality.
Levy packaged this as an album called *Roots* and started hawking
it as a TV mail-order item.

When Capitol learned of this album, they rush-released a version of the Phil Spector *Rock and Roll* tapes into the stores, although at a dollar more in price than the *Roots* album. Levy responded with a $42 million lawsuit for damages. The trial started

in January and dragged on for three months. The first trial ended in a mistrial when Levy's lawyer, William Schurtman, allegedly prejudiced the jury by holding up the *Two Virgins* nude album cover. The case was finally settled in July—in John's favor. Big Seven was awarded $6,795 for John's breach of contract, and John was awarded $109,000 in damages for lost royalties on *Rock and Roll* and another $35,000 in compensatory damages for the damage his reputation suffered by the release of *Roots*. John was more than happy with the results. It wasn't the money, and it wasn't even winning the case exactly, but for once in his whole life, the powers that be, the schoolmasters, the police, the judges and the jury, had found in his favor. There was some justice in this world after all, he decided, and renewed his determination to fight for his immigration clearance in the U.S.

During this period, as John began to take more responsibility for his life, he had three meetings with Yoko. She invited him to the Dakota for tea on three specific occasions. Each time John brought a chum along with him for confidence, usually Harry Nilsson. On the first visit conversation was warm but awkward and kept to generalities. At a signal prearranged by Harry and John, Harry stood up and said he had to leave for an appointment. Yoko walked him to the door, while John sat where he was, hoping Yoko would invite him to stay awhile. But no such invitation was forthcoming; Yoko stood holding the door for him, while Harry waited in the elevator. Yoko remembers how guilty she felt when John called sadly after Harry, "Hold on, wait for me. I'm comin', too."

On another visit John looked out the tall windows overlooking the Central Park skyline and said, "I forgot how beautiful it was."

"Don't start that again," Yoko said, tears in her eyes. She sent him away quickly before her resolve broke.

The first real glimmer of reconciliation occurred at the Elton John concert at Madison Square Garden on Thanksgiving of 1974. This was a particularly festive holiday concert at the height of Elton's popularity, and John was rumored to be making a surprise appearance on stage with Elton in payment of a happy debt. Elton had helped out by singing and playing piano in the sessions for John's "Whatever Gets You Through the Night." When Elton recorded John's "Lucy in the Sky with Diamonds" for his own album, John sang in the backup chorus. At that recording session

Elton asked if John would appear live with him on stage if "Whatever Gets You Through the Night" became a number-one hit. "I said 'Sure,' " John said, "not thinkin' in a million years it was gonna get to number one." The single indeed hit number one, and Elton was calling in the chips. John was expected to appear in the latter half of the show as a poorly kept surprise.

When Yoko heard about this she called Tony King, who happened to be working for Elton. "I would like to go to Madison Square Garden to see John, but I don't want John to know I'm there," she told Tony. "I want to sit somewhere where I can see him but he can't see me." This was arranged, and Tony ushered Yoko to her seat just after the lights went down in the Garden.

Just before John and Elton were about to go on stage, two gift boxes containing white gardenias were delivered to their dressing rooms backstage. Both notes said, "Best of Luck, all my love, Yoko." John rushed into Elton's dressing room and said, "Oh, look what Yoko sent me!" and Elton said, "Me too!" They both pinned them on their lapels. "Thank God Yoko's not here tonight," John said. "I couldn't go on I'd be so nervous."

Elton smiled knowingly.

When Yoko first saw Elton wearing her gardenia she broke into a broad smile. She applauded excitedly throughout the concert, beaming in the dark. Finally, Elton introduced his surprise guest. All the lights in the Garden went up, a blinding white light that illuminated 22,000 fans in the huge rotunda, and then John appeared on the stage. The impact of recognition was breathtaking. The crowd burst into cheers and applause that far exceeded anything heard in the sports arena that night. There was an outpouring of love and respect for him that would have melted the coldest heart. In her box seat, lost among the waving mass of fans, Yoko burst into tears. All these people worshipping and loving the man, and yet he was still alone.

When the show was over, she asked Tony King to take her backstage to see John. Tony knocked on the door to John's dressing room and said, "I've got a surprise for you," and in walked Yoko.

"Oh hello," John said coyly, smiling. "Were you here tonight?"

Yoko smiled back at him as if she were still very much in love.

May Pang, dressed in black from head to toe, like an oriental leopard, sat in a corner of the dressing room and watched her job and relationship ending before her eyes. "Nobody likes to see their situation disappearing," Yoko says diplomatically.

John's return to the Dakota was not immediate. Two more months of bartering and demands between them were necessary, during which he spent Christmas at Disneyworld in Florida with May Pang and Julian. Some of the agreements they came to during this period were old promises, ones that somehow had to stick this time; no drugs, no drinking, a healthy diet. The last prerequisite was that John give up smoking his Gitanes. He went to a hypnotist for this, and the snide joke in Beatles circles was that Yoko had John hypnotized into coming back to her. But nothing could have been further from the truth. John started smoking again, but he and Yoko will always be together in history. As of this writing May Pang is a secretary at a record company.

In one of his last interviews, John told Barbara Graustark, a *Newsweek* magazine reporter, that "[a] baby thinks that when you go out of the room you vanish . . . the moment that overwhelmed me, that I couldn't get through to [Yoko] on the phone, it was overwhelming—I just felt completely out there . . . It described that situation, too, of being kicked out of the nest and being dead. Or being not connected is like being dead. There's that difference—being alone and being lonely is two different things. Something I've learned in the past ten years. What I did in the past ten years was rediscover that I was John Lennon before the Beatles, and after the Beatles, and so be it."

Chapter Twenty-One

1.

WHEN JOHN finally returned home to the Dakota he was completely detoxified. He and Yoko went on a forty-day liquid fast to cleanse their bodies. John emerged whippet-thin but strong. For the most part, it was the end of his drug use. Grateful to be back in the womb, he was just as anxious for Yoko to take over in her role as earth-mother. Yoko consulted a Chinese acupuncturist who put them on a diet of fish and rice, gave them acupuncture treatments, and promised that if Yoko followed his regimen, she would become pregnant again, although she was now forty-two. John was only home a few days when, just as predicted, Yoko became pregnant early in 1975. John had been planning to return to the studios to record a new album, but when Yoko told him this last chance at parenthood together had blessed them, he changed his mind. He arrived home from the studios one night and said, "I've got a surprise for you, Mummy." They had taken to calling each other Mother and Father upon John's return.

"What is it, Daddy?" Yoko asked him.

"I'm going to cancel the new album and stay home with you while you're pregnant."

"Oh, gooooood, Daddy!" Yoko said.

This was the beginning of what was to evolve into John's "househusband" stage. The doctors insisted that Yoko have complete bedrest, and John took care of her from morning to night.

When she had to leave the bed, John pushed her around the Dakota in a wheelchair. He took over all the household chores and began running the kitchen.

It was during Yoko's pregnancy that John's long immigration battle with the government came to a triumphant end. The Nixon White House, embroiled in Watergate, had already fallen. On John's return to New York that previous summer, his lawyers had applied to U.S. District Court Judge Richard Owens for permission to see his confidential immigration files. In his affidavit John claimed, "I have been the subject of illegal surveillance activities on the part of the government; that as a result my case and the various applications filed in my behalf have been prejudged for reasons unrelated to my immigration status." But the Department of Immigration lawyers insisted that John's files were privileged information.

In December of 1974 *Rolling Stone* magazine printed a revelatory article, in which the dirty mechanics of John's deportation saga were described in detail for the first time. Encouraged by this, John began attending court hearings himself, fighting for his own cause for the first time. He even cut his hair short and wore a tie to the courtroom. In June of 1975 John's lawyers lodged a suit against former U.S. Attorney General John Mitchell and former U.S. Attorney General Richard Kleindienst, charging that deportation actions they took against him were improper.

On October 7, 1975, the U.S. Court of Appeals overturned the order to deport John Lennon. In a thirty-page ruling, the court noted that "Lennon's four-year battle to remain in our country is testimony to his faith in this American dream."*

Two days later, at one in the morning, on John's thirty-fifth birthday, Yoko went into premature labor and had to be rushed to the hospital, where she went into convulsions. John stayed by her side through the night, as they kept her alive with transfusions. Late that morning she gave birth to a healthy, eight-pound, ten-ounce baby boy. They named him Sean Ono Lennon.

Sean Lennon gave John renewed hope; here was a tiny mortal through whom he could recreate his own life, solve all the mysteries, and soothe all the hurt of his own childhood. Baby Sean became the Next Big Thing, one of the few that would never

---

*John received his "green card" as a permanent resident on July 26, 1976.

fail him. John gave himself over to Sean's childhood. "I wanted to give five solid years of being there all the time," he said. "I hadn't seen my first son, Julian, grow up . . . I was not there for his childhood at all. I was on tour. And *my* childhood was something else. I don't know what price one has to pay for inattention to children. And if I don't give him attention from zero to five, then I'm damn well gonna have to give it from sixteen to twenty, because it's owed, it's like the law of the universe."

John woke each morning at six to get the household chores started and to fix Sean and Yoko's breakfast. He cared for the child all day and bathed with him at night. As the boy got older they had romps in the park, and John fretted over his diet. He began the boy's education by answering all his questions, tenderly and carefully. Sean was showered with all the love and attention and material comforts a child could want. He even had Elton John as a godfather.

As John started to learn how to bake bread, Yoko gravitated to the business end of things. Yoko turned out to be a canny investor and formidable negotiator. She dug into the Beatles' various lawsuits and negotiated a reported five-million-dollar settlement with Allen Klein. Klein credits this completely to Yoko's diplomacy; but there were also times when Yoko very undiplomatically wore Arab costumes to a meeting with six Jewish lawyers. Yoko also made a series of profitable, if sometimes peculiar, investments. She began buying up apartments in the Dakota as they became available, until they owned five of the choicest layouts in the building. They opened up a production office in a professional office on the ground floor, called Lennono Music. Yoko went to work here every day in an office with a ceiling painted in blue clouds. Yoko also purchased a 316-acre farm in the Catskill Mountains of New York, along with homes in Japan, Oyster Bay, Long Island, and Palm Beach. She also invested in cattle, and one of their cows sold on the auction block for a record-breaking $250,000. John's worth soared to $250,000,000 under Yoko's guidance.

Yoko's business acumen was a combination of street smarts, guts, and the forces of magick. Yoko had always been very into astrology, numerology, psychics and mediums, but never more so than at this period. Everywhere she turned, the psychics all saw trouble ahead. "They said that John had lots of bad luck,"

Yoko said, "and we needed to give him all the luck we could."
This luck came in the form of "directional moves." Yoko, like a
sorceress with a formula for a spell, would send John around
the world in forty-eight hours or tell him he had to be 1,843
miles to the northeast, or sometimes she would send him to a
specific spot. They spent four months in Japan in the Hotel Oku-
ra's Presidential Suite on such a directional trip, while John waited
impatiently till the numbers and spirits said it was good luck to
go home.

Yoko talked of one such trip, to Hong Kong and Macao. "I
knew that astrologically, directionwise, Hong Kong was a good
trip, that it would put him in the best possible position, so I
told him to go, alone."

John said, "Really? By myself? Hong Kong? Singapore? . . .
I hadn't done anything by myself since I was twenty. I didn't
know how to call for room service, check into a hotel . . ."

John arrived in his hotel room in Hong Kong in a state of
high anxiety at being so isolated and so far from Yoko and Sean.
"So sitting in this room," he said, "taking baths, which I'd noticed
Yoko do, and women do, every time I got nervous, I took a bath.
It's a great female trick . . . I must have had forty baths . . .
and I'm looking out over the Hong Kong bay, and there's something that's like ringing a bell, it's like what is it? And then I
just got very very relaxed. And it was like a recognition. God!
It's me! This relaxed person is me. I remember this guy from
way back when! This feeling is from way, way, way back when. I
know what the fuck I'm doing! I know who I am—it doesn't rely
on any outside agency or adulation, or nonadulation, or achievement or nonachievement, or hit record or no hit record. Or anything."

This ephiphany—so long overdue—brought John tremendous
peace and relief. For the first time, he experienced serenity and
confidence in the future. He didn't have to prove himself anymore;
the pressure was off him; he could create when he felt like it
and become the public persona of John Lennon at times and
the househusband at others. "The feeling in the music business,"
John said later, "is that you don't exist if you're not in the
gossip columns, or on the charts, or at Xenon with Mick Jagger
or Andy Warhol. I just wanted to remember that I existed at
all."

At this point John and Yoko became frantically private, almost secretive. They drifted apart from many of their friends and acquaintances. Those who were loyal understood and waited patiently for an unexpected phone call, others were insulted and went away angry. When not living in some hotel room on a "directional trip," John spent almost all of his time in the bedroom of their apartment at the Dakota. This room was decorated all in white, with white stereo speakers, a white "staircase to nowhere" leading into a blank wall, and a white, king-size bed. The only other furniture in the room was a wicker chair for Yoko on her side of the bed. John's side of the bed was his little inner sanctum, with his ashtray and cigarettes and a Sony Stratocaster TV set that was inevitably always turned on.

The summer of 1980 John took a "directional trip" to Bermuda. He enjoyed it so much he asked Yoko to send Sean, who arrived with a nanny. One day John and Sean were strolling through the Botanical Gardens, when John noticed a lovely, white flower called "Double Fantasy." The pretty name inspired him to write a song, and back in his hotel room, he called Yoko and played it for her over the phone. She said she had been writing a song also, and she played it for him. Suddenly John decided that they would make an album together, his first in nearly six years. Yoko was thrilled at the prospect and set about making a recording deal with a major company for them. On the eve of John's fortieth birthday, they signed a deal with Geffen Records to distribute the album, and John spent the early fall at the Record Plant studios recording the *Double Fantasy* album.

The release of the album was greeted by a flurry of publicity and renewed interest in John and Yoko. *Newsweek* did a special interview with them, *Playboy* asked them to be the interview of their big Christmas issue, and *Esquire* did a cover story. The single from the album, "(Just Like) Starting Over" was headed right for the top of the charts. The album itself was fresh, upbeat, and critically well received. John was so pleased with the response that he returned almost immediately to the studios to work on a new single, "Walking on Thin Ice." Things couldn't have been more perfect. His career had had an unexpected resurgence, he loved his wife and his child, and he felt at peace with himself. For a brief moment, it looked as if John had everything he wanted.

* * *

2.

*O*N OCTOBER 23, 1980, as "(Just Like) Starting Over" was shooting to the top of the record charts, a twenty-five-year-old security guard named Mark David Chapman signed out of his job at a high-rise condominium in Honolulu. The name he signed was "John Lennon." Later that day he called his employment counselor and quit his job. "Are you looking for something else?" she asked him.

"No," Mark said, "I already have a job to do."

On the surface, Mark Chapman was just like millions of other kids who had worshipped John Lennon and the Beatles while growing up. There was no way of telling that one day he was to split apart and become two people, himself and John Lennon, and then feel the compulsion to reduce the number to one again. Chapman fit the psychological profile of many presidential assassins. They are men of low self-esteem, bitterly disappointed with their lives. They attach themselves to heroes with what historian Christopher Lasch has called "a deadly intimacy," first as a fan, then as an imitator, inevitably as a killer.

Chapman was born on May 10, 1955, in Fort Worth, Texas, the son of a retired air force sergeant, but he grew up in a suburb of Atlanta, Georgia, where his father worked as a credit manager at an Atlanta bank. Chapman was an average, quiet teenager, whose interests ranged from flying saucers to the Beatles. He loved the Beatles, much to his parents distress, and grew his hair long and learned to play the guitar. In high school he joined a local band and worked as a camp counselor at the South DeKalb branch of the YMCA. His aspiration was to become a YMCA director.

Then in 1969 Chapman underwent a radical transformation. Introduced to psychedelic drugs in high school, he took every kind of hallucinogen he could get his hands on, often having bad trips. His parents tried to put a stop to it, but it only ended up with Chapman running away for two weeks. Then, just as suddenly as it had started, it stopped, and Chapman became a fifteen-year-old Jesus freak. He sold his Beatles records, cut off his long hair, put on a white shirt and black tie, and wore a large wooden cross around his neck. His friends remember him spouting passages from the Bible, which he now carried around with him. At school he spent free periods studying the Bible, and at prayer meetings Chapman once renounced the Beatles because John Lennon had once said they were more popular than Jesus. The song "Imagine" became one of the prayer group's pet peeves, and they sang it with the lyrics, "Imagine John Lennon was dead."

After graduating from high school, Chapman enrolled at the DeKalb Community College for a short time and then dropped out. He went to work at the YMCA camp for a while, until a friend told him of an available full-time job at the YMCA in Beirut, Lebanon. Chapman saved enough money for his airfare by washing cars and bagging groceries, and by June of 1975 he was off. Chapman wasn't in Lebanon two weeks, when a fierce civil war started, and he had to be evacuated with other Americans. He taped the sound of gunfire on a cassette recorder before he left and played the tape over and over again for his friends back in Atlanta.

It was later that year that he fell in love, with a pretty girl with long dark hair named Jessica Blankenship. It was a thoroughly unrequited relationship, and Chapman went to all sorts of extremes to impress her, including having "Happy Birthday Jessica" spelled out on the marquee of the local Holiday Inn. He even enrolled at Covenant College, a strict, Presbyterian school, to impress her. His dream was that they would become Christian missionaries together and go off to some exotic place to live. But Covenant College was too hard for him, and when he dropped out Jessica saw him as a failure. A job at the Fort Chafee Vietnam refugee placement center in Arkansas buoyed his spirits temporarily, but when that was over, in December of 1975, he was lost.

In 1977 he moved to Hawaii, where his mother had moved after divorcing his father. Shortly after his arrival, he attached a pipe to the exhaust of a car, fed it to the interior, and tried to kill himself. He was found in time and was hospitalized for psychiatric treatment at the Castle Memorial Hospital, but he was soon released. He later worked at the local Y and in the print shop at Castle Memorial. In 1979, with some money his father gave him, he took a trip around the world and visited various YMCAs in Tokyo, Hong Kong, Bangkok, Paris, and London. Upon returning to Hawaii in June of 1979, he married Gloria Abe, a Japanese woman four years his senior who had booked his world tour for him at a local travel agency. Although he held only a four-dollar-an-hour job as a security guard, he managed to bankroll enough money to collect lithographs. His first was a Salvador Dali called *Lincoln in Dalivision,* which Chapman purchased for five thousand dollars. He later traded that in for a Norman Rockwell litho, entitled *Triple Self-Portrait.*

By this time something had transformed Chapman into an overweight, irrascible young man. He was curt and snubbed co-workers and developed a sudden interest in firearms and guns. At home he became testy with his wife, refusing to let her listen to the radio or read a newspaper. Scientology became a favorite hate for him, which he saw as a type of brainwashing. His security job was across the street from a Scientology headquarters, and every day someone would call them and whisper into the phone, "Bang, bang, you're dead." He was also once seen wearing an identification tag at work with the name John Lennon written on a tape and placed over his own. But there was nothing Mark David Chapman had said or done that would have led anyone to believe he was going to kill John Lennon.

Sometime in October, Chapman read the latest issue of *Esquire* magazine, the one with John as the cover story. The article, a piece of nonjournalism in search of a subject who had refused to be interviewed or cooperate, portrayed Lennon as "a forty-year-old business man who watches a lot of television, who's got $150 million ($250 million according to the *Fortune* 400), a son whom he dotes on, and a wife who intercepts his phone calls." John had sold out. "That phoney," Chapman thought.

On October 27 Chapman went into J&S Sales, Ltd in Honolulu and purchased a Charter Arms .38-special revolver. He had applied for a gun permit earlier that month for his job as a security guard and had no problem obtaining the gun.

In November Chapman made a pilgrimage to Atlanta, Georgia, to see his father and friends. Then he went to New York. He spent a few days at the Waldorf Astoria Hotel on Park Avenue, before checking into the Hotel Olcott, not far from the Dakota. Chapman allegedly later told a minister that during this period he was wrestling with "good" and "evil" spirits. Evidently the good spirits won out, for the time being, because Chapman suddenly boarded a plane for Atlanta, staying there only a few days before he went home to Hawaii. Finally, Mark headed for New York for a second time on December 5. His total journey at this point had taken him 17,000 miles.

The first night he checked into the Sixty-third Street YMCA, just nine blocks south of the Dakota, and then into the Sheraton Centre Hotel at Fifty-second Street and Seventh Avenue. The next day he took up vigil in front of the Dakota. He carried with him some cassettes of Beatles songs, a copy of J. D. Salinger's *Catcher in the Rye,* and his .38 revolver. Chapman was not noticed in the changing guard of fans who often waited outside the Dakota, hoping to catch a glimpse of Lauren Bacall or Gilda Radner on their way in or out.

Monday, December 8, was an unusually warm winter's day in New York, the perfect day for waiting in front of the Dakota and celebrity watching. No one is quite certain how long Mark Chapman was there that day. When John and Yoko left for the Record Plant at five P.M. John's limousine was at the curb, instead of inside the entrance gates of the Dakota, and as he strode to his car, Chapman thrust a copy of the new album, *Double Fantasy,* into his hands. John obligingly stopped and signed the cover for him, "John Lennon, 1980." Another fan ran up and snapped a picture. Mark Chapman was ecstatic as John and Yoko got into the limousine and rode off. "Did I have my hat on or off?" Chapman asked excitedly. "I wanted to have it off. Boy, they'll never believe this back in Hawaii."

John and Yoko returned to the Dakota at 10:50 P.M. in the limousine, John carrying the "Walking on Thin Ice" tapes. The tall security gates were still open, but again the limousine pulled to the curb, and John had to walk from the sidewalk. Yoko preceded him into the entranceway. Just as they passed into the dark recesses of the archway, John heard a voice call to him, "Mr. Lennon?"

John turned, myopically peering into the darkness. Five feet away, Mark Chapman was already in combat stance. Before John could speak, Chapman fired five shots into him.

Yoko heard the shots and spun around. At first she didn't realize John had been hit, because he kept walking toward her. Then he fell to his knees and she saw the blood. "I'm shot!" John cried to her as he went down on his face on the floor of the Dakota security office.

The Dakota doorman, a burly, bearded, twenty-seven-year-old named Jay Hastings, dashed around from behind the desk to where John lay, blood pouring from his mouth, gaping wounds in his chest. Yoko cradled John's head while Hastings stripped off his blue uniform jacket and placed it over him. John was only semi-conscious, and when he tried to talk, he gurgled and vomited fleshy matter.

While the police were called, Hastings ran outside to search for the gunman, but he didn't have far to look. Chapman was calmly standing in front of the Dakota, reading from his copy of *Catcher in the Rye.* He had dropped the gun after the shooting. "Do you know what you just did?" Hastings asked him.

"I just shot John Lennon," Chapman said quietly.

Yoko screamed hysterically until the police arrived. The first at the scene was Patrolman Anthony Palma. Against Yoko's wishes, he turned John onto his back. "Red is all I saw," Palma said. "The guy is dying. Let's get him out of here." By then a police cruiser had arrived, and Palma and Officer James Moran carried John to the backseat. They took off for Roosevelt Hospital with their sirens blaring. Yoko followed in a second police car, repeating over and over, "It's not true, tell me it's not true!"

On the way to the hospital, Officer Moran looked down at John Lennon in his lap and couldn't believe it. "Do you know who you are?" Moran whispered to him. John moaned and nodded his head. It was his last gesture. By the time they reached the emergency room of Roosevelt Hospital, over 80 percent of John's blood volume had been lost from seven massive wounds in his neck and shoulder. They raced him into the emergency area, and several surgeons and nurses worked on him feverishly for half an hour. According to Dr. Stephen Lynn, the hospital's director of emergency services, "It wasn't possible to resuscitate him by any means."

When Dr. Lynn went out into the waiting room, Yoko asked frantically, "Where is my husband? I want to be with my husband! He would want me to be with him!"

"We have very bad news," Dr. Lynn told her. "Unfortunately, in spite of massive efforts, your husband is dead. There was no suffering at the end."

"Are you saying he is sleeping?" Yoko sobbed.

She was back at the Dakota shortly after midnight. Alone.

She called three people that night. She called Julian, who had lost the father he had never known; she called Aunt Mimi, who lost the little boy she once pretended was her own; and she called Paul, who lost the chance to redeem part of his soul.

On December 10 the following letter appeared in newspapers around the world. It was from Yoko and Sean.

I told Sean what happened. I showed him the picture of his father on the cover of the paper and explained the situation. I took Sean to the spot where John lay after he was shot. Sean wanted to know why the person shot John if he liked John. I explained that he was probably a confused person. Sean said we should find out if he was confused or if he really had meant to kill John. I said that was up to the court. He asked what court—a tennis court or a basketball court? That's how Sean used to talk with his father. They were buddies. John would have been proud of Sean if he had heard this. Sean cried later. He also said "Now Daddy is part of God. I guess when you die you become much more bigger because you're part of everything."

Yoko still lives at the Dakota, though many of her friends imagine it would be too painful to pass every day the spot where John was killed. Indomitable and determined, she leads a busy, productive life. Often she returns to the studio to work on old tapes she made with John, or to record new songs herself. A few months after John's death she began an unlikely friendship with a young man named Sam Habitoy, a sometimes antique dealer and interior decorator. For a time rumors were rampant that Yoko would marry Habitoy, or that they were already married, but Yoko denies all this. She has a full-time job living with John's memory, and no man will ever replace him, in any way.

John's shadow, his very presence, is inescapable wherever she goes. Indeed, she speaks of John all the time, always in the present tense, as if he's just in the other room, about to knock on the door. She is publicly very philosophical about his death. When asked why all the psychics and astrologers hadn't warned them about the night of December 8 under the archway of the Dakota, she says they had. Not that specific date, perhaps, but that John always had bad luck in his future. Some fates, she says, cannot be changed.

I can't remember anything
without a sadness
So deep that it hardly
becomes known to me

—From a poem John wrote in a letter
to Stu Sutcliffe in 1961

Index

McCartney, Mary Patricia Mohin (mother):
   death of, 26
   marriage and pregnancies of, 25
McCartney, Michael (brother), 339
   early childhood of, 25–26
McCartney, Paul (James Paul), 42, 239–241,
   319, 321, 359–360, 361–362, 396–405
   birth of, 25
   on Brian's homosexuality, 74
   death rumor about, 372–374
   directorial efforts of, 276–278, 324–327
   early compositions of, 27
   film scores of, 221, 400
   formal withdrawal of, 374–377
   George's early relationship with, 34–35
   High Park home of, 220
   John's death and, 437
   John's early relationship with, 27–29, 32,
      34
   marijuana incidents of, 399, 402–403
   marriage of (see McCartney, Linda
      Eastman)
   new group of, 396–401
   in Northern Songs takeover bid, 343–346
   Oscar nomination of, 400
   paternity suits against, 144–146
   personal wealth of, 403
   romantic life of, 98–100
   solo albums of, 371–377, 380–381
   St. John's Wood home of, 219–220
   twenty-first birthday of, 96–97
   as virtuoso, 24
   Waterfall home of, 405
McCulloch, Jimmy, 401
McCullough, Henry, 398–400
McFall, Roy, 50
McGlynn, Joseph (pseudonym), 145–147
McKenzie, Phyllis, 11
McLuhan, Marshall, 364
Macmillan, Harold, 107, 131
Magic Alex (see Mardas, John Alexis)
Magical Mystery Tour, 241–242, 276–278
Magic Christian, The, 354, 355
Maharishi Mahesh Yogi, 368, 369, 370, 407
   ashram of, 282–291
   Beatles' first encounters with, 264–268
   Brian's death and, 270–271
   exposed as phoney, 288–291
Makin, Rex, 56–57, 62, 67, 69, 73, 76, 97
Malik, Michael Abdul (Michael X), 366–367
Maltz, Stephen, 281, 329
Mamoudas, Victor, 156
Manchester Daily Express, 106, 142, 278
Manson, Charles, 357
Man Who Gave the Beatles Away, The
   (Williams), 53
Marcos, Fernando, 204
Marcos, Imelda, 204–205
Marcunia, George, 229–230
Mardas, John Alexis (Magic Alex), 265, 359,
   362, 367
   antidrug feelings of, 256–257
   in Apple Corp., 280–281, 308, 310, 326,
      328, 350
   Beatles' first meetings with, 225–227
   in Greek island scheme, 259–261
   in John and Cynthia's divorce, 300, 302
   in John's estrangement from Cynthia, 1,
      2, 4, 8, 292–293
   on Maharishi's ashram, 281–291

Margaret, princess of England, 106, 148,
   184, 339–341
Marsden, Gerry, 90–91
Martin, Dean, 188
Martin, George, 77–78, 84, 90, 105, 107,
   295, 359, 400
   first recording sessions with, 86–89
   recording contract offered by, 78–79
   role of, 87
Marx, Groucho, 188
Mason, Dave, 383
"Maybe I'm Amazed," 374
Meggs, Brown, 109
Mekas, Jonas, 409, 419
Melchior, Terry, 313
Melody Maker, 88, 89, 250, 380, 384, 399
Mersey Beat, 35, 71
Michael X (Michael Abdul Malik), 366–367
"Michelle," 198
Milligan, Spike, 78, 87, 134
Mills, Hayley, 221
Mind Games, 418
Mitchell, John, 413, 428
Modern Jazz Quartet, 313
Monroe, Marilyn, 244
Monty Python, 392
Moon, Keith, 246, 395, 419
Moore, John, 32
Moore, Tommy, 37–38
   John's relationship with, 38
Moran, James, 436
Morris, Brian, 131
Moss, Jerry, 390
"Mother," 371
Moynihan, Vyvienne, 176, 251
Murray the K, 119–121, 234–235
"My Love," 400
"My Sweet Lord," 391

NEMS (Nemperor Holdings), 66, 110, 249
   as concert promoters, 88, 90, 104
   diversified operations of, 175–179, 235
   as lever in recording contract search, 71,
      72
   in merchandising business, 128–129,
      162–163
   offered to Beatles, 330–331
   opening of, 62–63
   power struggle at, 262, 274–275
   sale of, 235–241, 248, 330–331, 335–337
Newfield, Joanne, 255, 269–270
New Record Mirror, 88
Newsweek, 125, 134, 404, 426, 431
New York, 388
New York Post, 417
Nichol, Jimmy, 147
Nilsson, Harry, 419, 420–421, 422, 424
Nizer, Louis, 163
"Nobody Loves You," 422
"No No," 393
Northern Songs, 193–194, 397–398
   takeover bids for, 343–346
"Norwegian Wood," 198, 221, 291
Nureyev, Rudolf, 131
Nutter, David, 341

"Ob-la-di, Ob-la-da," 315
O'Dell, Dennis, 281, 350
Oh Calcutta!, 386
Oldenberg, Claes, 231

COLD STORAGE, ALASKA

Also by the Author

The Woman Who Married a Bear
The Curious Eat Themselves
The Big Both Ways

COLD STORAGE, ALASKA

JOHN STRALEY

For Sophie Rosen

@

Copyright © 2014 by John Straley

First published in the United States in 2014
Soho Press, Inc.
853 Broadway
New York, NY 10003

Library of Congress Cataloging-in-Publication Data

Straley, John, 1953-
Cold storage, Alaska / John Straley.
p cm

ISBN 978-1-61695-306-5
eISBN 978-1-61695-307-2
1. Ex-convicts—Fiction. 2. Small cities—Alaska—Fiction.
3. Alaska—Fiction. 4. Domestic fiction. I. Title.
PS3569.T687C65 2014
813'.54—dc23
2013019796

Interior design by Janine Agro, Soho Press, Inc.

Printed in the United States of America

10 9 8 7 6 5 4 3 2 1

CHAPTER ONE

ANNABELLE HAD PUT the tea kettle on just moments ago. Now it was whistling, yet she didn't get up to attend to it. Recently the past had become a hallucination constantly intruding into the present moment, so she wasn't certain what really needed doing.

She had been thinking about Franklin Roosevelt: the grinning man with the cigarette holder who was never photographed in his frailty. But now it was early spring in the last year of Bill Clinton's presidency, and all the news was about the president's failings. Flawed men kept ruling the world, and the radio in the corner with the long antennae squealed on and on about it. Not that the news mattered much to Annabelle now. It was raining hard, and all of the events of her life—past, present, and possibly future—were taking on the quality of a slightly malevolent screwball comedy.

She sat in her chair looking out the window. She had been distracted by so many things lately: presidents, family members, and lost animals all swirling around her. The glass on the door rattled, and she looked up expecting to see her uncle, Slippery Wilson, walk in slapping his wet leather gloves against his pants, even though Slippery Wilson had been dead for more than three decades. She found herself listening for crying from the crib, even though both her boys were grown men. The younger one, Miles, was down at the senior center cooking dinner, and Clive was getting out of prison.

"Never matter," Annabelle said aloud to herself. She got up and turned off the radio in the corner.

Throughout the afternoon, she had been trying to remember the joke she had heard the day before. It was good, she remembered, and she thought that it would have been good to tell Miles. But the joke eluded her in its detail.

Out her window, the hillside fell away to the inlet. Alder trees grew quickly on the disturbed ground where the boys had built her house. A gust of wind came, and she thought she saw some darting color. A flash of yellow, she couldn't be sure, but it seemed like a match head exploding. Yellow with red sparks flaring in the trees. She slid her glasses up her nose and was almost certain that she saw the bird fluttering up and away.

"Buddy?" she said aloud, as the kettle boiled over and doused the flame.

ON THAT SAME day in April 2000, Clive McCahon, Annabelle's oldest son, was released from prison. He was thinking about his plan to get home.

He had hated living in Alaska as a kid. His father had assumed he would become a fisherman. His mother had assumed that no matter how he made his living, it would be made right there in Cold Storage. Only his grandma Ellie had told him not to listen and to dream his own dreams. Having grown up on an island on the North Pacific, Clive had longed for the great American highway. He dreamed of cars and deserts and long, straight roads. Ellie had always given him books about cars for every birthday and Christmas. Cars and guitars, he dreamed of, bands he heard on the radio and beautiful girls who didn't know everything about him. Ellie had understood his itch to move on. Only she seemed to understand that living in Cold Storage, Alaska, was like being born into a small maze where everyone constantly bumped into one another. As soon as his father died in the Thanksgiving Day storm, Clive had left. He had flown north to Haines, bought a car without ever owning a license, without ever learning to drive, and took off. He was fifteen. Ellie's ashes had been scattered at sea and his father's body had never been found, so he didn't consider that he had anything holding him to his cloistered island town.

Clive was thirty-five now. It was early April, and the clouds were clearing away after a morning rain. The air was so clean it almost burned his lungs. Clive had served seven out of his ten-year sentence in McNeil Island Penitentiary, and he was wearing his old court clothes: a dark blue suit his mother had bought him on one of his few visits home as an adult, now far too tight in his shoulders and upper arms. Feeling the sun cut through the trees, he set his cardboard box on the ground, slipped off the coat, folded it neatly, and placed it on top of the box. He had called ahead to order a cab.

There were only a few people getting off the prison boat, mostly staff members carrying lunch boxes and rain gear. There was one other inmate, a skinny white kid with red hair who walked down the dock to meet an old man waiting beside a sputtering Ford LTD. The convict approached, the man opened the passenger side door, and a woman in a blue house dress got out and threw her arms around the boy before he could put down his gear. She cried and snuffled into his neck, while the old man rubbed the back of his shoulders.

Clive shifted from one foot to another, waiting for his ride. A yellow minivan finally rolled up.

"You Stilton Cheesewright?"

Clive was still watching the kid being greeted by the old couple. He wondered if he had seen the kid inside but didn't recognize him. He hadn't recognized the false name the cabbie was saying, either.

"You're Stilton Cheesewright, yeah?" the driver said again. He reached behind and opened the back door of the van.

"Absolutely." Clive didn't know why he'd given the cab company a false name; it was simply the first name that popped into his head and had nothing at all to do with the plan. He set his box of personal effects in the back seat, slammed the door, and walked around to sit in the front passenger seat.

"You want to go to a grocery store?" He squinted at his run sheet.

"That's right," Clive said. "If it's not too much trouble."

"No problem, Mr. Cheesewright. Would you like me to wait while you shop?"

"Naw . . . just drop me. I might be a while," Clive said, but then added, "You know a place with really fresh lettuce?"

The driver smiled. "I think if you want the really fresh stuff you should go over to the Farmfresh store down Sixth. It's good, you know. They really do buy it from the farmers and everything. It's a couple of miles out of town, but it's worth it."

"Perfect," said Clive. The driver punched the meter and wheeled to his left, down the road away from the prison.

Clive watched the fence posts stutter by. He watched the sunlight filter through the evergreen trees, and he watched a cow eating in a green field, a rusty bell hung from her neck. She lifted her head as the cab sped past, and Clive could imagine the soft clonking of her bell. Clive asked to stop for a moment; the driver put on the turn signal and eased the van to the gravelly edge of the road. Clive thanked him, leaned back in the cab's mildewed seat, and smiled. He sat that way for a few moments, smiling and listening for the cow's bell.

"You do a long stretch?" the driver asked.

Clive nodded, his eyes closed. "Yes," he said. "It's time to go home, I guess."

"You want me to get going?" the driver asked.

Clive nodded again, his eyes still closed.

"Let's go get you some lettuce then," the driver said, and pulled the blinker all the way down, rolling the cab back onto the road.

CLIVE WAS BOTH happy and nervous. He had looked forward to this day with an urgency that few people who haven't been in prison could know. But just as it was happening he felt a kind of raw anxiety. He could not go back to crime, and although he had scrubbed his mind clean, he knew that in this world of free men he understood little else besides crime. Crime was now, in his new state of mind, too chaotic, too unpredictable. Clive wanted to be rooted to something as certain as the rising of the sun.

McNeil was an old federal prison that had been remodeled as a medium security jail when it was turned over to the state of Washington. The Birdman of Alcatraz had actually done most of his time at McNeil. The main building had the original feel of the place: thick iron doors, WPA-style murals on the walls of the mess hall. It could have been a large public library in some small Midwestern town if it weren't for all the sex offenders.

In jail, Clive had been known as the "Milkman," for that's what the newspapers had dubbed him. He had been a semi-famous drug dealer when he had been caught—famous for his method of delivering his drugs and famous for never snitching on his customers or his partners.

He had seen arterial blood spurting and painting the shower floor red. He had seen the black holes that handmade knives leave in young white skin. He had heard all the swearing that there was in the world and the blubbery threats made through spit-stuffed lips. All he wanted now was peace. No grittiness. He was done with it. He would always be a sinner, he knew that, but he could at least try not to sin as much. He had thought that even if he could cut back on his sinning by ten percent, that would still leave him plenty of room, while giving him a shot at some minor redemption at least.

In the last three years, he had purposely kept himself in segregation. He told the jailers he was going to be killed and that was the truth of it, but that was not what mattered. He wanted the quiet of the stone slice of ten by ten, the only noise a basketball bouncing on echoing concrete in the exercise yard where they let the segregated inmates out, one at a time, an hour and fifteen minutes every day.

All he took into segregation with him was a Bible and a pencil. He kept his journal in the margins.

It wasn't until the beginning of his third year in segregation that he started listening to bugs. A blue fly landed on the edge of the Bible page, which was open to Numbers. The fly twitched what he imagined to be its filthy legs. The spidery printing of the first word was almost the size of the fly itself:

How can I curse whom God has not cursed?
How can I denounce whom the Lord has not denounced?
For from the top of the crags I see him,
From the hills I behold him;
Behold a people dwelling alone,
And not counting itself among the nations.

"What?" Clive said aloud, leaning even farther toward the book. "What was that?" But the fly had not said anything.

THERE WERE TWO picnic tables beside the store where Clive was going to eat his salad. Cigarette butts fanned out on the pavement. An overflowing garbage can sat next to a bike rack. Clive brought his packages out and set them down carefully. He had asked the produce manager to wash all of the vegetables. He had bought a plastic bowl, a cutting board, a knife, and some bottled oil and vinegar dressing. He reached inside his bag and took the knife and the cutting board out first. A kid, riding a trick bike in the parking lot, stopped long enough to stare at the skinny man in the dark suit smelling a tomato, then hopped the bike onto the rack, skidded down the top pipe on his cranks, landed, and wheeled away.

The spring weather in western Washington was strangely warm. Clive sat and slowly cut the vine-ripened hothouse tomatoes. He washed all the vegetables under the outside spigot once again, just to be certain. He peeled the carrots and sliced them into thin strips. He had two kinds of lettuce, one red pepper, a bottle of artichoke hearts, and one fresh avocado. He spoke to no one, but chopped and sliced with great deliberation. After all the vegetables were laid out in his bowl, he stared at them and licked a bit of ripe avocado off his fingers. He added the fresh Dungeness crab meat to the salad. He opened a bottle of white wine and poured himself a glass. He said a short prayer, swore that he would never eat canned spaghetti or unidentifiable meat ever again, and ate his first meal in the free world.

The bottle of wine was three-quarters empty by the time the cabdriver came back to check on Clive. He was sitting at the picnic table with his back against the building; long shadows from the poplar trees next door played out across the parking lot. The salad was gone, and Clive had the wine bottle stuck down between his legs and a plastic fork in his mouth.

The cab rolled up on the crunching gravel and came to a stop. The driver lowered his window.

"You got a place for tonight, Stilton?"

"No, I guess not." Clive pulled the fork out of his mouth.

"You got a plan?" He fished out his smokes.

"Oh yes, I have a plan. " He looked back at the cabdriver. "Foolproof."

It was only then that Clive noticed that the driver had brought a little dog back with him. The corgi stood now on the driver's lap, sniffing the damp air through the open window.

"What's your dog's name?" Clive asked.

"Bandit," the driver replied, and the dog wiggled up and put his whole head out the window.

"You haven't got a plan," the dog said.

"Excuse me?" Clive said, a little distressed, for never before had he heard an animal speak so clearly. But then again it had been a while since he had seen such a large non-human animal.

"You got a place to go?" the driver asked.

"Sort of. I'm going to pick up my dog." Clive offered the driver the bottle of wine. "Then I'm going back to Alaska."

"It's a long way to Alaska," the driver said, and took a drink from the bottle. "You're going to need some money for that."

"Well, that's what the plan's about," Clive said. "I've got my money the same place where my dog is."

Bandit sniffed the air again and shot his ears straight forward. "You don't have a plan," the corgi said again. Which distressed Clive all the more. The dog was telling the truth.

"I got a little travel trailer out back of my place. You can spend the night there if you want," the driver said as he stroked the little dog's head.

"No. I'll be all right," Clive insisted.

"Get in," Bandit said, and Clive gathered his things.

CHAPTER TWO

THE JOKE WENT like this: The doctor comes back into the waiting room and tells his patient, "I'm sorry, Mr. Smith, but I have some bad news. It appears you have only eleven minutes to live." The horrified patient beseeches him, "Please, doctor, isn't there something you can do for me?" The doctor looks around the room and at his watch and says, "Well, I suppose I could boil you an egg."

The joke was everywhere on the boardwalk. It seemed to Miles McCahon that it had infected the residents of Cold Storage like a flu virus. He heard it everywhere, and he was beginning to wonder why.

Maybe it was the darkness or the rain. Maybe it was the fact that almost everyone in Cold Storage was either clinically depressed or drunk most of the time. But they *loved* that joke, and Miles was beginning to take it personally.

Miles had spent most of his life in Cold Storage. There had been trips out for a few years in college and his years in the Army Rangers. When his brother had gone to jail in 1993, Miles had been in Mogadishu as a medic with his delta team and had mustered out soon after that well-publicized mess. He had told himself he was never again going to leave the quiet of Cold Storage, but now he was beginning to wonder.

Miles was the medical technician and physician's assistant

in a village without a doctor. He splinted broken bones and stopped bleeding. He stitched up severe cuts and treated people for shock. He monitored medications and researched medical issues for the 150 residents of this failing fishing village on the outer coast of southeastern Alaska. He was the closest thing to a doctor they had, and maybe it was for this reason he didn't get the same amount of glee from the joke as everybody else obviously did.

Miles was cooking Sunday dinner at the community center. He had used some of the money left over from a health and prevention education grant the previous PA had written. That PA had tried to hold classes on heart disease and diabetes; he had started "Healthwise" informational gatherings to which only a few people came, but none of those people were the ones who really needed the information. The principal of the school and the secretary came to the first two classes, the city administrator and her husband came to a few more, and then nobody came. The PA left town after six months.

But the money had to be spent because the administrators in Sitka could not show unspent money in their program at the end of the fiscal year. They phoned Miles and told him to do whatever he could to clear the account. The administrators had kissed a lot of ass in Washington to get these funds, and it would be an insult to leave them unspent. So Miles started hosting dinner parties on Sundays. He tried to cook reasonably healthy food, but health concerns couldn't get in the way of turnout. This Sunday he was cooking three meat loaves, each roughly the size of a carry-on luggage bag.

"I don't see why you can't buy us some beer," complained Ellen from her wheelchair next to the Jell-O molds.

"Ellen, I can't buy alcohol with the health education and

prevention money. We've been through this. I'm already on thin ice for the cheesecakes and heavy cream."

"That's just like government thinking," the old woman wheezed. "I mean, what if—I'm saying *what if*—I'm going back to my place for a beer and I slip and break my hip? What the hell kind of health education is that?"

Bob Gleason piped up, "You're not going to break a hip. You always drink someone else's beer." Here he nodded toward Miles. "Besides, you ride that frigging wheelchair everywhere you go, even though there's not a frigging thing wrong with your legs."

Ellen didn't give even a hint she'd heard Bob's comments. "Miles, you could at least buy us some beer," she insisted, "if you were really serious about doing a good job."

"Listen, Ellen, next week I could maybe include some non-alcoholic beer in the order."

Ellen stared up at him with strange, squinting eyes as if he had suddenly started speaking Japanese. "Non-alcoholic beer?" she asked feebly. She reached a claw-like hand for something to hang on to, accidentally landing it in a bowl of raspberry Jell-O with bananas hovering at the top.

"Somebody better get her medication," came a wheezing voice from over by the furnace.

"Take more than near-beer to kill her. Better men than us have tried." Bob levered a shingle-sized slice of meat loaf onto his plate, set it next to the pond of gravy in the potatoes. "Goddamn, this looks good, Miles. Don't have any boiled turnips, do you?" He held out his plate.

As luck would have it, Miles did, and he ladled them out quickly. Bob's hand wavered, and hot water slopped against the side of the old man's thumb.

"Christ, Miles, watch what you're doing, would ya?"

"I'm sorry." Miles handed him a napkin. "I'm just kind of in a hurry."

"I heard." Bob nodded knowingly, staring down at his plate of food. "There's a cop here to talk to you." He reached onto his plate, fingered a slice of turnip up into his mouth. "It's about your brother."

Miles wiped his hands on a dishcloth and took off his apron. He walked out the door without saying a word to anyone.

The police officer, Ray Brown, had sent word to Miles that he was in town as soon as he'd gotten off the floatplane. Miles had been in the middle of getting the giant meat loaves ready and so had arranged to meet with the trooper at the clinic later in the day, just before Brown's plane took off for Juneau. That way, he thought, he could talk with the officer and then walk him back to the hall to check on the community dinner. It might be a good thing to have a police officer with him when he returned, in case any fights broke out in his absence.

Miles wasn't eager to show that police officer around. No matter where they were from, visitors always wanted to ask questions. They started with history: why is this place here? To this Miles would usually answer, "Fish . . . mostly." He longed to tell the whole story but the truth was people didn't really want to know.

What they really wanted to ask was, "Why in the hell would anyone live here?"

But to truly understand, it helped to know the whole story. Just walking around town you wouldn't feel the history of the place, wouldn't know its old jokes or see the ghosts who still roamed around in everyone's memory.

Cold Storage, Alaska, was first settled by white men in 1934. These white men were a group of Norwegian fisher-men looking for a place to ride out the storms on the outer coast. They drove a few pilings and ran a boardwalk along the edge of a steep-sided fjord. They chose it because of the good anchorage with protection from all four directions of the compass. But as one of the Norsky fishermen put it, "She's hell for snug except when it's coming straight down."

Cold Storage got approximately 200 inches of rain a year; the exact number was subject to debate. That rain led to the second reason the old Norskies chose to build on this particular spot: a natural hot spring just off the beach where the thermally heated water dribbled out between the rocks. The old fishermen cribbed up some walls and a roof and made a quite passable tub where they could lounge in the warm water while watching their wooden boats ride at anchor out in the bay.

In 1935, the town got an infusion of energy when a bat-tered logger, a woman Wobbly, and her little girl with glasses fled the mine strike in Juneau in a leaky dory and made the place their home. The logger was named Slippery Wilson. The woman was named Ellie Hobbes. She was a pilot and a committed anarchist. The little girl with the thick glasses was Annabelle. When Slip and Ellie built the first store, the old fishermen complained that the town was growing too fast. But when Ellie turned the store into a bar a few years later, the complaining stopped.

No one in his family had been fond of the police. It wasn't an active antagonism, it was more of a wary indifference bol-stered by living in a town some ninety air miles from a police station. There had been the old man who ran the supply boat who had been some kind of detective in Seattle. But that was long ago, and he had never done any policing in Cold Storage. The old Seattle detective was dead now, and only a few of the older people remembered the stories about him.

Miles stopped at the door of the clinic and put his hand on the cold metal knob. He didn't want to go in, but as he considered going back to his meat loaf, the door jerked open, and Ray Brown stood before him in an immaculate blue state trooper uniform. He was pressed and tidy. His round, brimmed, Mountie-style hat had gold braid laid out against the blue. He was imposing, like a patriotic monument of some sort. It made Miles feel a little like Jeanette MacDonald.

"McCahon!" Brown barked, as if giving Miles permission to have the name. He jutted out his hand. "Ray Brown. How are ya?"

"I'm doing well, thanks," Miles began. He was about to mention the fine weather for flying and maybe add something about going fishing if there was time.

"Two things," Brown lumbered on. "First, a little bit of shop and then some personal business."

"Personal business?" Miles walked around the big trooper to pick up the coffee pot sitting on a table in a corner of the waiting room. The coffee had been reheating for weeks as far as Miles knew. He just turned the same coffee on and off every day and evening. It didn't matter because no one ever drank it. He kept it there only to chase people out of the clinic.

"That's second. The first thing has to do with Harold Miller. Do you know him?"

"Coffee?" Miles held out the pot.

"No, I'm topped off." Brown patted his flat stomach. "Harold Miller?"

"I know a Mouse Miller." Miles put the pot back into the plastic coffee maker.

Brown unsnapped the breast pocket of his shirt, took out a small notebook and flipped through the pages. "I think that's him. Fisherman." Then Brown rattled off a social security number.

Miles looked for any trace of humor, any sign that the trooper was going to relax. It didn't seem likely. "I don't know Mouse's Social Security number, but the date sounds like it matches his age. How can I help you, officer?" Miles sat down on a chair next to the coffee pot.

Brown remained standing, and for a second Miles worried he was going to click his heels together.

"Harold Miller has been reported missing. I'd like to get some information together."

"I haven't seen Mouse around. Have you been down to his boat?"

Brown had started writing in his notebook, didn't answer the question. After a long silence, he lowered the notebook and asked, "When was the last time you think you saw him?"

"Geez . . . I don't know, couple of weeks ago. I don't know if he even has family here in town. I think I heard he was going to fly in to Juneau for some change of scenery for his drinking."

"Ex-wife," Brown said to the notebook, "he had an ex-wife."

"Really? I didn't know Mouse was married." And then in a bright voice, a bit curious, "Who's his ex?"

The trooper was writing again. He looked up with a vaguely thoughtful expression on his face. "So, would you say it was two weeks ago that you saw him last?"

Miles leaned back and scanned the paint on the ceiling. "I don't remember exactly." If Trooper Brown had shown any trace of humor or humility, Miles might have offered to look at his calendar to see if there were any notations, but he didn't.

"Okay." Brown stabbed a period emphatically onto a page. "It's just a formality. He's probably sleeping it off somewhere." He clicked his ballpoint pen as if unchambering a round, put the pen and notebook back into his front shirt pocket, and pulled another chair away from the wall and around to face Miles. He sat down, knee to knee with the PA. Miles sat up straight and put his coffee cup down.

"Now, two," Brown said. "I believe you have a family member who is incarcerated?"

Miles waited, wondering if that was the final form the question was going to take. "Actually, if you include my extended family, I have several relations who might still be serving time. Maybe you could be a little bit more specific."

"So, that's the way it's going to be." Brown stared down at Miles for several long moments.

"Excuse me, Trooper Brown, is there some reason that you're being rude?" Miles smiled and tried again to be friendly.

Trooper Brown didn't hesitate and didn't smile. "I don't like drugs, and I don't like Satan worshipers."

Miles looked perplexed. "Wow! No. I mean, who does? Well, drugs . . . I assume you are not opposed to penicillin, unless you are a Christian Scientist?"

The Trooper waved him off. "Your brother worked for a major drug dealer in Seattle. I don't want him moving his business into Alaska."

"First thing, Trooper, I haven't heard from Clive in years. I have no reason to think that he's going to come to Alaska after his release. Frankly, I doubt it, and even if he does, I have absolutely no reason to believe that he will be engaged in any illegal activity. This is not exactly a promising spot to go into the drug trade. Unless you had some blood pressure meds or fiber supplements you wanted to move."

"You are a veteran . . . Army Rangers, is that right?" Brown said.

"That's right," he said patiently.

"*You* were the guy in that photograph?" This was neither a question nor a conversation starter; it sounded more like an accusation.

"I know the one." Miles's flat voice did not invite further comment.

"That was some shit, huh?"

"Yes, it was some shit, all right."

"But that doesn't mean I want your brother up here selling drugs."

Miles was beginning to wonder if Trooper Brown had some kind of neurological damage or perhaps a kind of Tourette's syndrome that manifested itself in non sequiturs. "Trooper Brown, does this somehow tie back around to Satan worship? If not, I'll keep my eyes open for Mouse Miller and if I find out anything, I'll be sure to let you know. And if my brother shows up and is involved in any illegal activity, I'll let you know that, too."

Brown leaned forward. "I've heard things. I've heard things about a Weasel character and about drugs off shore and about his sick movies and about his gatherings of men. Listen, I don't care if you are some kind of war hero. If I get one whiff that you're allowing some Satanists to use drugs or that your brother is back in business, if he gets one strange package, if he makes one phone call to his old associates back in the Seattle area, I'll have him and anyone who helps him"—Trooper Brown paused and stared at Miles for emphasis—"back in jail so fast it will make their head swim."

A swimming head, Miles thought to himself. What does that really mean anyway? "Look, we've gotten off to a bad start." Miles tried to brighten the tone of his voice. "You've never been here before, have you? Let me show you around town. I'll give you the whole tour. It will help you get to know the place. We can ask around about Mouse."

"Thanks for the offer." Brown's smile was icy. "But I can do my own legwork. I was born in Alaska, you know."

"Ah!" Miles said, as if long-term residency explained and forgave everything. He walked over to the door of the clinic and opened it.

"Let me explain something to you." Brown loomed over Miles. "Your brother has an old associate named Jake Shoemaker. He's a smart guy, he has a lot of holdings in Seattle, and a lot of money. Your brother never gave up this Jake Shoemaker, and let's say Jake owes him now."

"All right, let's say that," Miles said, smiling to the scowling face of the trooper.

"We have reason to believe that right now your brother is looking to reestablish contact with Jake Shoemaker. I also have reason to know that law enforcement in Washington is very interested in taking Jake Shoemaker down. So if you hear from Clive, you tell him to talk to me right now. You understand? If he sells one ounce of product in this state, he's going away for much longer than the seven-year bid he just did. But if he helps us put Jake away, he can breathe easy for a long time. You understand me, Miles?"

"I understand, Trooper, but this is all theoretical as far as I'm concerned. I have not heard from my brother, and I honestly doubt that I ever will."

"Really!" the Trooper boomed. "Well, we know that there are people right now bringing drugs in off the coast of this town. Right this second."

"This second? Wow. You better get to arresting somebody then!"

The Trooper put his hand on the doorknob to leave. "Your mother's name is Annabelle. Isn't that right?" asked Brown, as if he knew every thought Miles had ever had.

"That's right, it's Annabelle. You know, that's a great idea. You should go talk to her."

Not expecting this answer, Brown squinted at him.

Miles walked over and tapped the big blue policeman on the chest hard enough that they could both feel the bullet-proof vest underneath the uniform. "But I'd be sitting on this if you're going to talk shit about Clive to Annabelle." Miles raised his eyebrows, faintly nodded. "And while you're at it why don't you ask her about Satan worship?"

Brown turned and walked out the door.

"I've got to get out of this town," Miles sighed to himself. The only thing keeping him from walking down to the boat dock right now and striking out was the possibility of being there when Annabelle gave Trooper Brown a monumental ass chewing.

Annabelle lived alone in a damp frame house near the end of the boardwalk and up a set of stairs into the hillside. She had not been feeling well for the last three months, and Miles had tried to talk her into going to the hospital in Sitka. She had chronic heart disease and diabetes, but lately she'd been losing weight and her color was not good. Miles suspected she had something new, something more serious going on, but he didn't know. Neither did Annabelle. Miles wanted to find out, but Annabelle did not.

Miles thought about that as he watched Brown's lumbering figure barrel down the boardwalk. Miles had tried to talk his mother into moving to Arizona where the hospitals were clean and warm, where they could sort out what was going on with her health, where she could eat avocado sandwiches and watch the Mariners on TV.

"I don't even like avocados. What in the heck are you talking about?" She'd shaken her head bitterly. "Besides Arizona? What do I look like? A cactus?" She shook her head again and looked out the window, closing the book on the subject.

Miles knew it wasn't Arizona that was the problem. Annabelle didn't want to leave Cold Storage because she was waiting for Clive. She imagined seeing her older son, tall and rangy, walking in the door of her house. He would have some outrageous story to tell about who he had met on the road and what adventures they had gotten him involved in. Miles was a good boy, but Clive made her laugh. Clive would lift her off her feet and swing her around the kitchen while Miles fretted about what might get broken.

Recently, Annabelle had been considering the possibility that she might not be alive by the time Clive walked through her door again. Still, she did not want to leave Cold Storage. She suspected the weight loss and the weakness was cancer, but it didn't matter that much to her. She liked the taste of the meals Miles cooked. She liked to watch the tapes of old movies she had flown out from town. She liked to do needle-point in the late afternoon while the tea kettle rumbled on the oil stove, and she liked listening to the rain. Death was no big deal, she told herself. At least she was under her own tin roof and not in some concrete jail.

Miles waited a few minutes before walking back up the boardwalk. As far as Satan went, there were only two signs of the Dark Lord in Cold Storage. One was a band that two kids had tried to start called the Boomerang Bombers, which had caused quite a stir in the school about six years ago. The boys, Ajax and Billy, painted pentagrams on the school district's drumheads and had to write a letter of apology and work at the school for two weeks during spring break. As far as Miles knew, the Boomerang Bombers had never played a public performance, but out of solidarity for the only death metal band along the coast, the man named Weasel had the band's name and a pentagram tattooed to his shoulder, fostering the rumor that Weasel was some kind of Satanist mentor to the boys. Which was dismissed as far too ambitious for Weasel by anyone who knew him.

By the time he got within sight of the community center, Miles could tell Trooper Brown was ready to leave. A loud screeching voice was issuing from the windows like smoke. Miles couldn't make out the words, but old people were steadily streaming out of the front door. Some were using their canes, a couple had walkers, but they were making remarkably good time. They moved as if flames licked their heels.

Miles reached the door just as Trooper Brown hurried out. His face was scarlet, almost as if he'd been burned, and he was trying to put his notebook into his pocket but seemed to be having trouble finding the front of his shirt. Miles didn't say a word. The trooper looked at him momentarily, averted his eyes, took two steps away from the community center.

"Did you find Mom? I think she's in here," Miles said evenly, without sarcasm.

But Trooper Brown was in some sort of preverbal state of rage or perhaps shock. He had never before been tongue-lashed by an old lady in a wheelchair. Annabelle was probably lucky he hadn't pepper-sprayed her.

"D . . . D . . . D . . ." the trooper tried to say.

"Don't leave town?" Miles offered. "Don't worry, we'll be here. We'll keep an eye out for Mouse. Have a safe flight." Miles waved, turned, and walked into the community center.

Bob Gleason was standing by the door, eager to greet Miles. "By God! You missed it, Miles. She unloaded both barrels on him. I'm telling you, I've worked in logging camps some thirty years and I've never heard the likes." He grinned.

Miles looked over to where Annabelle sat by herself, tears rolling down her cheeks. He walked over and handed her a paper napkin. "Got something on your chin." He didn't look at her, didn't draw attention to anything in particular.

"You're a doll," the old woman said. She took the paper napkin and held his hand for a moment, took several deep breaths as if shaking off some great exertion or bad dream. "That wasn't really a cop, was it?" she asked.

"State trooper. I guess he found you, huh?"

"Oh my God, Miles." Annabelle smiled up at the younger of her two sons. "You know what your father would have called someone like that?"

"Well, there are several names I think he might have used." He smiled back, remembering.

"He would have used some choice King's English on him," sniffed Annabelle.

"Yes, I suppose he would have." Miles laughed.

"My God," she huffed. "You remember Uncle George?"

"Dimly," Miles said. "I was just tiny when he died."

"Well, he was a good man, and he had been a cop. I told you about how he didn't arrest Slip and Ellie, haven't I?"

"Yes, you have, Mom." Her son smiled and stroked her thin arm.

"If that flibbertigibet of a cop thinks I'm going to drop a dime on Clive before he's even done anything wrong, then . . . well, then . . . I just don't know."

Miles smiled at her. His mother had always peppered her speech with crime jargon she had gotten mostly from Travis McGee novels. But he noticed she used more of it after Clive had gone to jail. Miles thought it was her way of showing loyalty to her wildest son.

She sat smoking her cigarette, remarkably tranquil for a woman who had apparently used some choice King's English on an officer of the law.

"You really think Clive will be here soon?" She stared out into the swirls of smoke surrounding her head.

"I don't know, Ma."

She looked around the room at the dishes of uneaten food sitting right where people had left them before fleeing: meat loaf and cooked cabbage, potato salad, and gelatin. She smiled.

"Say, Miles?" Annabelle looked up at her son. "Can you do something for me?" She snubbed out her cigarette and slid her glasses up her nose.

"Sure, Ma." They both knew he worried about her. "What did you have in mind?"

"Could you boil me an egg?"

Bob Gleason broke into applause.

AFTER THE DUST settled, diners started creeping back into
the community hall; they hadn't forgotten their free dinners.
Miles sat by himself in a corner, listening to people talk, eating some of his own meat loaf and mashed turnips. Bob and
a friend from Juneau were doing the dishes, laughing, joking,
calling out to people in the hall. When they were done, Miles
made himself an extra sandwich and wrapped it up. He waited
until he heard the trooper's floatplane take off, stuffed the
sandwich into his wool coat, and walked down to the floating
dock where his skiff was tied.

It had been years since Miles had caught a king salmon.
He had spent hours in his boat dragging a line through the
water. He used the right gear, fished at the right depth, trolled
at the right speed, and still he had been denied. He had a
subsistence permit and had dipnetted enough sockeye salmon
to smoke up for the winter. He had brought in coho salmon
and chums when they were running. But there was nothing
quite like catching a king salmon. The electric tug and the
zing of line spooling off into the deep green. It had been so
long since he had had that feeling. He longed for it like an old
man longing for youth.

Tonight as he scanned the sky and checked the wind fluttering through the pennants in the rigging of the few boats
left in the harbor, he was—despite all odds—flush with optimism.

He walked down the boardwalk, noticing the soft spots in
the planking. Rot was creeping up from the water through the
pilings and in around the edges of the entire town. He could

smell mildew, sooty diesel stoves venting out of broken stacks, a whiff of fish slime, and the egginess of the thermal water trapped in the old, concrete bathing tub.

It was early spring; he would have enough daylight for fishing. The herring had been spawning late on the outer coast, and he had heard people were catching king salmon out at the mouth of the bay. He was determined to bring one home.

Miles had an aluminum skiff with a temperamental outboard motor. He had fought the engine, sworn at it, even threatened it with violence. Only in the last three months had Miles's relationship with the cranky piece of equipment changed; he now tried to think of it as a kind of teacher, one with the temperament of a wild animal. If you wanted something from an outboard such as this, you had to display the virtues of understanding and patience. If you rushed up to it and started jerking on the starter cord, the soul of the machine would immediately fly out into the cold air and what would be left on the stern was an inert pile of metal. You could pull on that cord until your knuckles bled. You could change plugs and clean the fuel filters. It would not matter. The engine was no longer of this earth. It was as if the outboard were watching him from the trees as he pulled and swore and pulled and swore until steam rose from his sweater and sweat stung his eyes.

Miles arranged everything in the skiff carefully; the trooper had put him in a bad mood. He took a deep breath and slowly let it out before speaking softly and gently to all the equipment.

"Well, old girl, I've heard there are fish out there. What do you say to going out there with me?" He patted the machine, checked the mixture of the fuel. Whenever he could, he'd add some of the fresh gas stored in a sealed jug under the hatch. He pumped the bulb on the fuel line and pulled the choke halfway out. He pulled three times until the engine sputtered.

Closing off the choke, he opened the throttle halfway, then paused to say a few words he had settled on months ago and never changed. In a perfectly serious voice, free of irony, he spoke: "I want to thank you for all the hard work you've done in your life. I promise I'll treat you well today."

The sun hung behind thin and ragged clouds. Across the bay, Miles saw a raven watching him, sitting all by itself, shrugging and ruffling its feathers in the wind. Lonely, Miles thought. Lonely for the irascible soul of the outboard engine.

The light at the head of the bay was silver grey now above the dark green sea. Beyond the few islands to the west lay only the Gulf and distant Kamchatka in Asia. To the east, mountains rose up two thousand feet on both sides of the inlet and eased back against the more fractured and eroded slopes of the outer coast. Here the sky widened, and the wind freshened. Here the swells were larger, and the breeze carried the smell of waves broken apart on the shore. As he ran up and over the smooth swells coming in off the coast, Miles passed through occasional warm pools of air; they carried the scent of cedar trees from the outer islands.

Just ahead, gulls circled a tight ring of water, and Miles began to slow the motor. He saw dark squalls rolling in toward the coast from the north, but to the south, clouds floated almost white, threaded with blue. The gulls were diving on some tiny silver fish. Herring, Miles guessed, although he couldn't see them clearly enough to tell for sure.

He quickly rigged his salmon pole and lowered the

throttle on the skiff's engine as far as it would go. He picked up a green hoochie, a small plastic squid surrounding a hook that danced behind the twisting motion of a silver flasher. Miles watched the progress of the dark squalls to the north; he didn't want to be caught in the rain. He let the flasher drag out perhaps thirty-five feet behind him, snapped his line onto a downrigger with a small cannonball attached to a wire cable pulled by a hand crank, and adjusted his reel's drag, keeping his thumb on the spool of monofilament line. He lowered the cannonball to sixty feet beneath the boat, played out the line from his reel; the tip of his pole bent over from the weight of the rigging.

Miles put his rod into the pole holder and navigated a course through the circle of feeding birds. If a fish didn't bite, he would move, change depths, change gear. For now, though, he let out a long breath, eased back against the plastic seat bolted onto the hard wooden bench built into the skiff.

Miles loved this kind of slow fishing. Since returning to Cold Storage, he had rediscovered his respect for the uneventful life.

Miles had served in the first Gulf War. All it had left him with was an almost unquenchable thirst and a sliver of metal in his shoulder. There had been a photograph of him in a national news magazine, the one to which the trooper had referred. The image of Miles helping another bleeding man into a helicopter had spun its way around the world. The image meant nothing to him now. He could not, nor did he want to, recognize himself in the photo.

Miles's father had been a good fisherman who had disappeared off the coast in a storm while Miles was a small boy. But he didn't dwell on grief. He had been satisfied with where he was. Even as a fatherless boy, Miles had loved the little cabin on the water and the thousands of acres of ancient forest just up the hill. In this he was like his old Uncle Slip, who had loved every unchanging stone and tree of the place. Though Slippery Wilson was good with tools and hard work, he was uninterested in catching fish, and Miles was beginning to think he might have inherited some of the old man's bad luck.

Somewhere near his skiff, a loud exhalation of breath woke Miles from his thoughts. Miles fussed with the drag on his reel. First he tightened it, and then he loosened it back up. He unscrewed the top of his water jug and drank about half of it down.

He heard the loud breath again and scanned the waves. The western sky glowed with a pink haze above the wavering line of the horizon; the view of the outer coast was blocked by islands, their humps glowing with silver and tipped with red as the sun washed over the curve of the ocean.

Underneath his boat, a cloud of silver fish roiled in the green. He could hear them boiling up on the surface. He reached over and turned off the motor. The sea was thick with herring pushing their quicksilver bodies into the air and slapping them down on the surface. The air smelled cold, oily. Down below, he could see large slices of silver shoot under his hull.

Miles, twitching with energy, lifted his pole from the holder. The drag was rolling, and he tightened it down slowly. A large salmon leaped into the air a hundred feet from the boat, a rail of pure lightning coming up out of the darkness of the water. Miles pulled back hard, felt a sudden and heavy jerk; his fish was gone.

The water was quiet. The cloud of silver had moved on.

But he heard the breath again, and he held tightly to the side of his skiff, half expecting to be nudged by an orca whale chasing the school of fish.

He looked in all directions, even peering into the sky, until he caught sight of a sea lion some twenty feet behind him, its head steady above the water, seemingly impervious to the motion of the waves. Its eyes glowed milky brown with sympathy and from its mouth drooped a king salmon, graceful as flowing mercury.

"Goddamn it!" Miles shouted.

The sea lion looked at him for a long moment, shook itself, huffed a short breath, then dove under the waves.

"You son of a bitch!" Miles yelled out over the cowling of the outboard to the ripple of water left on the surface. "Bring me back that fish."

But the sea lion was gone, and Miles was left with the food in his freezer. Muttering about bad luck, he tied off the loose end of his line, lay his pole down on the floor of the boat, and jerked on the starter cord. No response. He pulled again. Silence.

He shouldn't have been swearing. Miles knew that. And now he knew he might as well get used to the idea of sitting out in the bay for a long time. He would sit and take some deep breaths, try to get his mind right so he could coax the soul of the cranky machine back into the boat.

CHAPTER THREE

LESTER FRANK WAS the only Tlingit Indian living full-time in Cold Storage. There were traditional native villages elsewhere in the area: Hoonah, Sitka, Juneau, Angoon; even Pelican had native communities. Cold Storage had Lester Frank, a contemporary artist who lived next door to the clinic. Miles had asked him once why he had moved to Cold Storage, and Lester had given his characteristic answer: "I study white people."

Lester carved wood and silver. He painted in acrylic and even sculpted in stone. He said he was writing a book about white people called *Circling the Wagons*, but no one had ever seen even a scrap of a manuscript.

Lester's house was one large, square room with a smoky wood stove sunk down three steps in the center. His bed was high up in one corner, a kitchen was in another corner, and everything else was desk, bookshelves, and studio space. As Miles walked up the boardwalk from the dock, Lester stuck his head out the shoreside window and yelled down, "Oy, Doc! Where's all the fish?"

"In the sea where they belong." His voice was barely loud enough to carry.

"I got tacos. Plenty of them and good tomatoes, too. You come up and eat." He shut his window without waiting for a reply.

Miles went into the clinic and checked the bulletin board for messages. He looked at the answering machine to see if anyone had called. The relay towers up on the ridges were always being blown over and phone service was sketchy; there would be weeks in the winter without any telephone contact at all. Tonight there was a fine, strong dial tone but no messages.

The sky was almost dark, and the air thick with moisture as Miles walked up the stairs to his apartment. He hung his wool coat in front of the oil heater, reached into his refrigerator to grab a bottle of sparkling apple cider, and went back next door for dinner. He could barely see Lester standing at the far end of the room, laying a warm flour tortilla on a plate.

"Just in time. I got venison. I got cheese."

"I'm not too hungry. I ate at the center before I went fishing."

"You never eat your own cooking. I know that. Eat a taco, for Pete's sake."

Miles took the plate and ate the taco. Arguing with Lester was like arguing with the weather.

"I saw you, you know. I saw you in your skiff before you went fishing." Lester walked down three steps to a seat in front of his cast iron stove.

"You saw me doing what?" Miles tried to flatten his voice.

"I saw you praying to that piece of junk engine." Lester shook his head, held up an empty glass.

Miles walked down and poured sparkling cider into the cup. "It's not a prayer exactly."

"It's some goofy new age prayer." Lester snorted into the mouth of his glass. "I'm telling you, man, you are going to be a whole chapter in my book about white people: the man who makes devotions to recreational equipment." Lester smiled.

"It's not recreational equipment," Miles mumbled from his seat on a round of wood next to the woodbox. "It's a thinking thing."

Lester rolled his eyes, slapped his friend on the shoulder. "A thinking thing? I don't know about that. That engine was owned by an Indian. It just doesn't care for white people is all."

"Why not? What did white people ever do to that engine?"

"How should I know?" Lester said. "Do I look white?"

They sat silently while the fire inside the cast iron box popped, sucked air through the draft. Lester was comfortable without words spoken every second, which suited Miles; he sat and ate his venison taco.

They finished and started eating cookies that Lester had had flown in from Juneau. He probably could have afforded the most expensive cookies on the market, but he preferred cheap, off-brand things bought in bulk. At first they appeared to be brand cookies you could recognize, but once you bit into them you were reminded that you were in bush Alaska and a long way from the centers of culture where people probably ate a better class of cookie.

Miles washed the dry crumbs down with juice. Lester took a bite and stared at the grate on the front of the stove. The fire rumbled, and a gust of wind pushed against the sides of the old frame house.

"So, you going to the movies tonight?" Lester asked.

"What're they showing?" Miles held little hope of surprise.

"*The Bad Lieutenant.*"

"Ah, Christ, isn't that the third time?" He picked up a stick of wood to feed the fire.

"I think it might be the fifth time in, like, six months. It's Weasel. He loves it. I think it makes him happy or something." Lester opened the door to the stove, and Miles threw a piece of wood on the fire. "I think Weasel wishes he were Harvey Keitel," Lester added, shutting the door. "Harvey Keitel lets ugly white men think they're still sexy."

The Cold Storage Film Society was made up entirely of men. After a truly horrendous argument about *Reservoir Dogs*, the women had splintered off into their own film group and had "Movie Tuesdays" instead. Now an insurrection was starting up again in the men's group.

"Naw, I'm not going," Miles said. "Are you going?"

"I might."

The two men sat for several minutes, listened to the fire hiss and suck at the grating; the new stick of wood was damp. A gust of wind slapped against the house, and Miles looked toward the dark windows to see the reflection of a tiny light above Lester's workbench.

"Have you seen Mouse lately?" asked Lester.

"No." Miles didn't look away from the window. "Didn't he fly to Juneau?"

"I don't think so. I went down to his boat a couple of days ago, and his stuff was all there like he had just walked out."

"You tell that to the cop?"

"Hell no. Mouse doesn't need to be found by a trooper." They both sat looking into the fire box for a few more moments before he added, "He wasn't looking so good when I saw him last."

"Not so good . . . like how?" Miles turned his face away from the window.

"Not so good like drunk, pale, thin, and about ready to fall over."

"That doesn't really distinguish him from many people around here."

Both men let the silence sit between them again while wind pounded against the window.

"I didn't even know you had a brother, let alone a high-ranking crime boss brother," Lester said.

"Yeah, well, you learn something new every day."

"Your brother going to come here?"

"I have no idea."

"I hope he does." Lester looked over at him.

"You do?" Miles kept his eyes on the floor. "Why?"

"You know, for my book." He laughed, stood up, and slapped Miles on the back. "I better get after it." Over at the bench where his jeweler's vise held a thin strip of silver, he picked up a tool and started working. He sold his work in two galleries—one in Seattle and one in New York—and a shipping deadline was coming up for each one.

Miles rinsed off his plate, dried it, and placed it back in the cupboard. He walked out of the house.

SO SURE WAS Clive that he had money waiting for him at this last stop, he gave fifty dollars to the driver for the ride. He scratched the corgi's head as he was getting out, but the dog seemed to be ignoring him now.

Clive's dog, Samson, was the kind of golden retriever who got progressively wider and wider. Eventually, he could have been used as an animate end table. Samson was sweet-natured and loyal beyond all reason. Clive remembered Samson lying on the rug, watching baseball on TV. Any time Clive made the slightest move, the dog would lift his head and stare, sometimes worried, sometimes excited, but always with the knowledge that something good was going to happen and it would start with Clive. Samson was an optimist.

During the early years in prison, Clive had not dared to think about him. He'd left Samson with Oscar because there was no one else; he'd told himself that Oscar could be trusted and that he loved dogs. But during those early years the goal was clear: everything good on the outside had to be buried away and hidden from the life inside, the life that circled the concrete hole of protective segregation.

Oscar worked for Jake Shoemaker, though it would take a lot of digging to figure that out. The warehouse where Oscar was the manager was called Little Switzerland. It sat in the Never-Never Land of warehouses and sketchy motels and iron-barred bodegas in the neighborhood you get lost in when you miss the turnoff for the Seattle-Tacoma airport. Stunted pine trees were planted in a border around the edge of the paved parking lot, and Oscar sat in a windowless office inside the first door of the building, the one closest to the chain-link fence. He was a short man with a full moon face and a thin covering of mouse brown hair swept back over a bald spot.

He sat back in his chair, flicking a butterfly knife back and forth with a quick clicking sound. His feet rested on an open desk drawer, and the light made him look even whiter than Clive had remembered.

"Hey, man, your dog's dead." Oscar made it sound as if they were in the middle of an argument.

"What do you mean, dead?" Clive reached over, grabbed the front of his shirt, pulled him to his feet.

"Don't put your fucking hands on me." Oscar's teeth were clenched, and he held the knife blade up to Clive's ear awkwardly.

"Just tell me what happened." Clive didn't pay attention to the knife. He was looking at the pudgy man's mouth instead, noticing the missing tooth.

"What can I tell you, man? He was old, and I got a ton of fucking vet bills. If you want to get snotty about it, I suppose I could let you pay me back for them. I mean, you were the model of a concerned pet owner. Fuck!" Oscar threw the knife on top of the desk, and Clive eased him down into the seat. "Just don't touch me again. All right?" Oscar added, reminding himself that he wasn't a man to be messed with.

"Did you want me to break out of McNeil, swim across the Sound, and take him to the vet?" Clive sat down on an overturned wastebasket in a corner, his body sagged, and tears came to his eyes.

Clive hadn't cried when he was arrested or when he was sentenced. He hadn't cried on the DOC bus that drove him out to McNeil. He hadn't cried that first night in the dorms when men rustled around his bunk like bears at the dump. He hadn't even cried the first time he was assaulted in the sign shop and had spent those weeks in the infirmary.

But now he was out of jail, Samson was dead, and he was going to cry like a baby. "He was a good dog," he said in a thickening voice.

"Yeah, he was." Oscar pretended to read some invoices. He didn't want to watch Clive cry; he didn't like to witness any kind of weakness. He waited a second. "I got another dog. You want him?"

Clive didn't say anything for quite a while. He was thinking about Samson, curled up those last few months on the blanket of his cell. He was thinking about the look in the golden retriever's eyes and thinking that even then Samson was probably already dead. He looked around the messy office, covered with old cardboard cups and circle-stained copies of *Soldier of Fortune* magazine; he was amazed that he had ever thought this life of crime was anything but pathetic.

"What kind of dog?" Clive wiped his eyes.

"He's an ugly son of a bitch." Oscar looked at Clive. "A guy left him here in trade on a bad debt. He said he was a fighting dog. He said he'd be a good guard dog for the warehouse. I mean, the fucking dog is ugly and scary enough to chase anybody off, but he don't listen to a goddamn thing anybody says." Oscar got up and grabbed a large ring of keys off the desk. "Let's go look at him. You can have him if you want."

Outside, Oscar opened up a chain-link gate with barbed wire coiling along the top. Clive's stomach tightened.

Oscar laughed. "Hey, dude, we got the keys. No worries. I'm not locking you up." He jingled the keys and laughed again.

"I got to get into the locker, Oscar," explained Clive. "Can you arrange that for me?"

"Is it cool with Jake?"

"Of course it is. I did his time, didn't I? I should think it is very cool with Jake. Call him if you want."

"I don't know. There's nothing much in there anymore. But still, Jake would take my nuts if I let you in."

"Oscar, man, it's all my stuff. Jake's just been paying the storage bill."

Oscar stopped, jingled his keys again, shifted his weight from foot to foot. "So," he asked, "you aren't going to mind sharing whatever's in there?"

"Sharing? What, like the United Fund or something?"

"I thought you'd want to cover the vet bills I fronted. Shit. You know, I don't have to let you in that locker." He looked Clive in the eye.

"We'll work something out." He put his hand on Oscar's shoulder and turned him back in the direction they'd been walking. "Let's go take a look at that dog." Gently, he put a little pressure on the small man's back.

"Don't fucking touch me," said Oscar with enough bluff to maintain his dignity.

They came to another fenced area. Inside was a shack and tied to it was a strange gangbanger mix of rottweiler, pit bull, and wolf, a brindle-dun carnivore without an ounce of extra fat and with chewed-off ears.

"Lord have mercy," Clive said under his breath.

The dog was 120 pounds of head, jaw muscles, and shoulders. His eyes scanned the yard and stopped on the men. Slowly, he walked forward with the off-kilter stare of a Mexican street dog charged up on a jolt of methamphetamine. He did not look anything like Clive's golden retriever. He looked like something that fed on golden retrievers.

"What's his name?" There was a degree of awe in Clive's voice.

"Well, his father was supposed to be a real good fighting dog. That dog was called Big Brother, and I guess he made a ton of money for the guy. When he dropped this dog off, he said his name was Little Brother, but it doesn't matter. He won't come to anything."

"Does he bite?" Clive walked around the fence; the dog's dark eyes followed him.

"I don't give him the chance," said Oscar. "When I want him out, I open the gate to his pen. He wanders around inside the fence. When I want him back in the morning, I carry this and he goes back in." He reached over and picked up a wand with a battery pack on the end. "It's a cattle prod. They use 'em for loading bulls into trucks."

"Then how do you get the chain on him?"

"I put this on." Oscar picked up a single sleeve attached to a thick glove that looked like a piece of hockey equipment. "Got this from a guy who trains attack dogs. I put it on and clip the chain to his collar. This dog's never actually bitten me, but shit, I mean look at him."

"What do you mean, 'actually' bitten you?" Clive inched closer to the fencing.

"He's never bitten me, man, but I know he really wants to." He touched the switch and there was a metallic buzzing sound; the dog cowered in a corner. Oscar walked closer and jabbed the end of the probe through the fence; the dog started snarling, thick saliva falling through its teeth. Oscar kept pushing the probe further until it hit the dog; there was a sharp yelp and the animal fell to the concrete.

Clive put his hand on Oscar's elbow and pulled him back.

"I said don't fucking touch me, man!" He swung around and glared at him. Clive recognized that look: Oscar both did and didn't want to kill someone right now. Clive hoped Oscar never went to jail, for prison was the place where cowards learned to kill.

Clive slowly took the prod away. "It's okay." He smiled. "I'll take the dog."

As he got closer to the fence, the dog got to his feet, sniffed the air in front of him as if there were a frightened cow being lowered into the pen. Clive saw deep scars around his throat and shoulders; his back leg had a crook to it like one that had been seriously broken and badly set.

"Little Brother . . . That your name?"

The dog's expression didn't change. He said nothing. Clive leaned in to listen carefully.

Nothing. Silence like looking down a well.

"Well, I guess I'll take you with me, dog." Then he turned to the ugly man and fished his wallet out of his pocket.

"Here's fifty bucks for nothing, and there is nothing more. Now open my locker."

Oscar snorted, grabbed the bill and backed slowly away, keeping his eyes on the big boulder-headed dog, who watched him like raw meat.

THE NEXT MORNING, Miles walked down the boardwalk from the café to his clinic. Several appointments were penciled in that day, but the calendar didn't really matter because most of the people in Cold Storage couldn't be bothered with making and keeping appointments. Most of the patients simply showed up any time their aches or pains occurred. Miles turned a corner to find Billy Cox sitting in the doorway. Billy was squatting, eating an apple. His large green poncho spread over his shoulders and hung to the ground like a tent. Billy was a fisherman now but had once been the lead vocalist and percussionist for the short-lived death metal duo Boomerang Bombers.

"Hey, Billy!" Miles greeted him and reached into his pocket for the keys.

Billy didn't speak at first. He was eating his apple with such concentration it seemed that if he turned his attention away, even for one moment, the apple might disappear.

"Miles, have you ever gotten a really, really good apple when you were expecting a crummy one?" Billy finally asked just as Miles opened the door.

"Yeah, I have." He wanted to get to the point. "How are you doing today, Billy?"

"I mean, you bite into a series of soft mushy things and you kind of get used to them, but then you get a really good one." He stood up, his poncho rolling water off onto the deck. "And it makes you both kind of happy and sad." He put the last of the core into his mouth.

"Come on in, Billy." Miles switched on the lights inside. "Sit down a second and I'll get things going here. You want to make the coffee?" He was already tipping water into the coffee maker.

The entire clinic was about twenty feet by thirty. It was built on pilings out over the inlet, on the water side of the boardwalk. Miles had a small office, a storeroom, a drug locker, a very small meeting room in the back corner with space for four people, a waiting room with a coffee pot, and an examining room. The clinic was clean and decorated; health posters and framed wildlife photos hung on the freshly painted walls.

After the incident with the trooper, Miles had decided to make a fresh pot of coffee. The thick liquid burbled down through the grounds, and its tropical steam rose up into the room. Billy took off his poncho.

Miles turned on his new computer in the office, checked to see if the fax machine had spit out any indecipherable messages. He did a quick walk-around to make sure nothing had been disturbed and double-checked the fastenings on the red metal drug locker holding the sedatives and narcotic pain killers. There weren't many. Miles didn't like the responsibility of keeping a large supply, but there were some people in the fishing fleet who thought of Miles's red drug locker as a kind of cornucopia of pleasure, and he'd once been asked to donate a tour of his drug locker as a prize for a local fundraiser. Not samples, just a simple look inside. Miles declined.

"How's the coffee coming, Billy?" Miles scrolled down through the emails, mostly tasteless jokes or boring drafts of policies that didn't apply to his practice, pausing only long enough to read the headings and hit the delete icon.

"I'm making up some Colombian. That okay with you, Miles?" Billy called. "Looks like you're out of the Deadman's Reach."

"I got more on the way from Ketchikan. Why don't you pour us both a cup, and I'll meet you in the exam room?"

Going through the stack of mail, Miles's eyes stopped on the return address of one envelope. It came from the probation office of McNeil Island Correctional Facility in Washington state. It read:

The Probation Department is sending this message to inform you that you have a family member by the name of Clive J. McCahon, who has stated his intention of residing with you upon his release. Please review all information below concerning the mentioned inmate. If you cannot, for any reason, abide by all the listed conditions of probation for your family member, please contact this Department immediately. If you are willing to assist the Department in the supervising of this inmate you must provide your name, Social Security number, and physical address by return mail. This is your responsibility and the Department will take no further action.

Beneath this message was a list of data: Clive's birth date, his Social Security number, and his record of conviction. At the end, like a fishhook, was the release date. He saw it and looked at his cartoon desk calendar; Clive's release date had already passed three days ago.

"Miles, you're out of sugar. You want me to run down to the boat and get some for you?"

Miles stared at his desk calendar.

"Miles, it don't matter to me, man. I don't do sugar in coffee, you know, but if you want some, I got some down on the boat. It's probably hard as a brick, but I could break you off a chunk."

Miles shook his head as if waking up from a dream. "Naw, that's okay, Clive."

There was a long silence in the waiting room. "Huh? Whatchya call me?"

"I'm sorry, Billy." Miles clicked out of his email and left the office. "I was thinking of somebody else."

"Hey, Miles?"

"What?"

"Did you know that trooper was asking everybody in town about your brother?"

"Yeah, I know."

"He even said there'd probably be some kind of reward if we turned him in."

"I don't think that's true, Billy," Miles said sadly.

"Miles?" Billy asked again. The coffee machine gurgled.

"Yeah?"

"Your brother doesn't sound all that bad to me."

"He's not a bad guy." Miles smiled. "You know, for a career criminal."

Miles put away the letter from the Washington Department of Probation. He decided there was nothing he could do about Clive at the moment but there might be something he could do for Billy, but even that was uncertain for many of Billy's problems were metaphysical.

Billy had been born in El Cajon, California, but had come to Alaska with his parents when his dad went fishing. His pop earned money by fishing for salmon from his own small wooden boat and by fishing for halibut and black cod with a couple other guys who had more expensive permits. When his father grew sick of it, he left for California. When Billy's mom grew sick of the rain, she did, too. Billy was sixteen. The transition wasn't as hard as people from the outside would expect. Billy just stayed on the boat. Guys from the fleet gave him a hand with chores he couldn't do alone. He finished high school and worked hard maybe sixteen weeks a year and spent the rest of the wet months reading and volunteering in the school. His health insurance was covered by the local tribe in Sitka because his mother had been a tribal member from California. A good thing, because his new religious interests had caused him to come into the clinic more often.

Billy was twenty-four now and had decided he was a Tibetan Buddhist. The little library didn't have many books on Tibetan Buddhism, so he settled for a few books about the Dalai Lama and the movie version of *Seven Years in Tibet*.

After seeing pictures of the Dalai Lama smiling, Billy

asked the librarian at the school in Cold Storage to find out
how his name was written in the Tibetan language. She surfed
around on the Internet, printed out a copy of the script, and
gave it to Billy the next day; she told him the Dalai Lama's
name translated into something like "Ocean of Wisdom."
Billy painted the Tibetan symbols onto the blades of his kayak
paddle and believed that each time he dipped his paddle into
the sea, he was in effect saying a prayer.

It was this new form of prayer that had been causing Billy
to come to the clinic. Billy was paddling more than anyone
could remember. He was off for days at a time; sometimes he
would take off at the height of the worst storms of the season.
When he came back to the docks in Cold Storage, he was
soaked; apparently he never got out of his boat to rest.

Miles flattened Billy's palms to examine the ulcerated blis-
ters that covered his hands. "Billy, why don't you wrap your
hands or wear some kind of gloves?"

"Gloves get wet, then they rip and make it worse. I just
need to toughen the skin a little more."

"You could at least get some better kind of seat in that
thing. These sores on your tailbone aren't healing. I'm telling
you, why don't you find another way of getting around and
let your skin heal a bit? Is your shoulder still bothering you?"

Billy shook his head; he wasn't even listening. He really
came to talk to the only person in Cold Storage who seemed
interested in him.

"I've decided," said Billy. "I'm going to do it." He rubbed
some ointment into his hands.

"Do what?" Miles was hopeful. "Give up paddling for a
bit?"

"No," he replied. "I'm going to take my kayak to Seattle."

"You mean on the ferry?"

"No." Billy sounded serious. "I'm going to paddle to Seattle."

"Really?" Miles said, trying his best to keep a sarcastic tone out of his voice.

"His Holiness is going to be there. In Seattle. He's going to make an appearance at the Opera House or something. He's going to give a talk, and I'm going to be there." Billy's eyes, wide and unwavering, looked straight into Miles's.

"Why do you have to paddle?" Miles motioned him up so he could look at the infected sores on his tailbone.

"I'm going to raise money to free Tibet. You know, like a walk-a-thon or something, but paddling. I'll get people to pledge money for each mile if I can make it all the way."

"You'll get folks from Cold Storage to pledge?" He tried to hide the note of skepticism starting to sour his voice. "Christ, Billy, I don't know . . ."

"Listen, Miles, they only have to pay if I make it, right? It's about eight hundred miles. Nobody will think I'm going to get there, right? I mean, make it in time to see the Dalai Lama in four months. They'll sign up. I get just five or six of them to sign up and that makes a few grand to give to His Holiness."

Miles looked at him, trying to form an objection to this plan, but the battered young man continued. "The money's not the main thing. I'll be praying the entire way. By the time I get there, I'll be ready. I'll have some dough to give him, and I'll probably have a shot at getting to meet him." He stopped to breathe. "He's a good guy, Miles. He'll meet me if I come all that way."

Billy lay on the examining table, his butt in the air, and

Miles cleaned the infected ulcer on his tailbone. He didn't say one word while he washed the wound with water and alcohol and wiped the blood away from the edges of the sores.

"What do you think, Miles?"

"I think you ought to stick around and meet my brother."

MILES WASHED HIS hands and checked his watch; he had to walk from the clinic down to his mother's house. The boardwalk ran about a quarter of a mile south along the coastline from Cold Storage; there the wooden ramp ended and a gravel trail wound through the woods to an estuary of a little stream. The school was built on the flat area to the north of the stream, and a hundred yards back to the north, just before the boardwalk ended, sat what was left of Ellie's Bar. The tin roof was sunk down in the back corner, and the front windows were broken with a few torn tarps nailed over the openings. Even though the bar was closed, it was still the preferred residence of several of the outer coast's most dedicated drinkers.

Mouse Miller had a small wooden troller and slept in the bar whenever he was in town. He was a tiny man, fitting for the size of boat he ran. He had a long beard and wore one shirt for most of a year. He had loved one of the last barmaids who had served drinks in Ellie's, had loved her with an ardor that was unmatched up and down the coast. The majority of bills tacked to the dripping ceiling of the fallen bar were his.

When he was in town, Mouse would often drink to the point of blackout. He would light candles and kerosene lanterns in the bar, and drink brandy that he'd brought up from the boat. He would drink and carry on conversations with the dead barmaid off and on for days; he would moan and bang on the bar, and he would pin more money up on the ceiling. Miles thought about Mouse and knew he should ask around town, but then he had plenty of walk-in traffic at the clinic; he didn't have to go hunting up a drunken fisherman.

The wind blew a squall of light rain, and the steep hill on the other side of the boardwalk moaned, sizzled as the wind pushed through the trees. Miles put up his collar and walked up the stairs toward his mother's house.

The faint smell of mildew and boiled cabbage filled the kitchen. In a corner sat a diesel stove, a large square metal box with chrome grillwork that could have come off a '49 Ford coupe. On top of the grillwork sat a copper tea kettle, and above the stove, dishtowels hung drying over metal rods hinged to the wall. The edges of the dishtowels swung slightly in the rippling heat.

Beside the electric range, an electric percolator bubbled quietly.

"Get yourself a cup of coffee," Annabelle called from the other room. "Then come in here and sit with me."

Miles poured himself a cup, carried it into the living room.

Annabelle lay back in a recliner. She wore a sweater over her nightgown and housecoat and heavy wool socks and strange-looking slippers that had the heads of two cartoon mice jutting out of the toes.

"Hi, honey! What's going on with you?" Her voice creaked.

"Not a lot, Mom." He took a straight-backed chair from the card table, set it close to the old woman's feet, and sat down. He looked at the stuffed mice slippers for a long moment, caught himself staring at them, and didn't know what to say.

"I've never seen you wearing mice on your feet before," he managed.

Annabelle wiggled them from side to side. "Oh, I know they're ugly as sin, but they go on easy over my socks. I been feeling a little chilly in the mornings."

"Uh, Mom . . ." he started. "I really think you should go into Sitka and see the doctor. I mean, you know, it might be something simple. Might be a couple of pills. I really wish you would let me get you in to see your doctor." He took a sip of his coffee; his tone was easy. This was as hard a sell as he was going to make.

"Yeah, and I wish I had a million bucks. I'm not going to spend that money flying into Sitka." She reached over and touched Miles's hand as if to reassure him, but then her small frame shook and pumped with coughing, frighteningly deep and strong coughing, and Miles thought she could break a rib coughing this way.

"You know, I can arrange to have the clinic pay for the flight," he said. He put down the coffee cup and handed her a tissue from the little box with a crocheted cover standing on the nightstand next to her chair.

Annabelle spat into the tissue, quickly covered it and threw it in a wastebasket near her feet.

Miles reached into his pocket and felt the message from the probation department, the news about Clive getting out of prison. He knew he should tell his mother the news. He even felt his hand starting to bring the paper out of his pocket, but he stopped.

"Mom," he stammered, "I'm sorry, but I get the idea you don't want to go to Sitka because you are just waiting for Clive, and if that's the case . . ."

She held up her hand to stop him. "I saw the darnedest thing. Just the other day. I'm certain I saw that old bird of mine. I saw Buddy in the trees. That can't be right, can it?"

"No. I don't think so," Miles thumbed the letter in his pocket. He didn't tell her about Clive. He was not sure why. He told himself it was to protect her, but truthfully, he wasn't sure.

The water continued to rattle against the sides of the pot, and he could hear the greasy flame flutter down in the oil stove. Out in the inlet, a trolling boat was working its way out toward the coast. Miles could hear the old engine labor away, and he could almost hear the gulls crying out as they wheeled over the stern. Up on the mountains, the wind wheezed through trees that had been there for eight hundred years; some had blown over and were rotting back into the ground. Everything was old up on the hillsides, but the rain was older than all of that and it was falling again, as it always had, as it always would.

They said nothing. The wind blew, and a limb kept ticking against the window.

"You don't know anything about him coming back, do you?" she said suddenly.

"Who?" he said with a start.

"Buddy," the old woman said, and looked up at him through her thick lenses. "They can't live that long, can they?"

She sat forward, started coughing so hard that he leaned her even farther forward, causing her thick glasses to fall into her lap. He rubbed her back between her shoulder blades until the coughing subsided. He got her some water to drink, and after putting on her glasses, she looked up into his eyes as tired as he had ever seen her.

"Just get me some pills," she spat out, "or some heavy-duty cough syrup."

"Okay, Ma." He stood up.

"Do me another favor, would you, pal?" Her voice was weak.

"I'm not going to boil you an egg, in case you are going to ask."

"No." She smiled. "Pop in that movie there. I was watching it last night and fell asleep."

Miles wheeled the television closer to the recliner, straightened out the cords, turned on the TV, and pushed the button on the VCR. The dusty screen on the TV flickered and glowed silver. There was Bedford Falls, and there was Jimmy Stewart, madly looking for the eight thousand dollars Uncle Billy had let slip out of his hands. There was Uncle Billy's raven hopping on the counter of the failing Building and Loan.

Annabelle waved at her son as he walked toward the door, and he waved back; neither said anything.

Miles walked down the boardwalk toward the clinic, thinking about his brother's return, knowing that, despite what the probation department said, there was still less than a fifty percent chance that his brother would actually show up. At least he could always hope.

A light rain was falling, and the sun was beginning to rise above the ridgeline to the southeast. Shafts of light cut a silver highway across the water. Gulls chattered as they sat near the pilings of the fish plant built in the 1950s on the site of what had once been the Norwegian fishermen's bathhouse. Miles felt deep down in his bones with a kind of mortal finality that he was home from the war.

He would open up the clinic, but nothing much would happen today. He'd call the hospital in Sitka, and a few people would come by the clinic with their simple and sociable complaints. Nothing would happen today, and nothing much would happen tomorrow. Even if his brother were to come to town, there was not enough to keep Clive busy. Clive would have to bring his own excitement to Cold Storage, which might be exactly what the trooper was concerned about.

CHAPTER FOUR

"I'M SORRY," JAKE Shoemaker simpered in an uncommonly polite voice. "I know this must be inconvenient for you." Oscar sat on the couch, his hands tied behind his back. "I mean, it's more than just inconvenient; this is frightening, I'm sure."

Oscar's mouth was covered with a strip of silver tape, his skin was white, his eyes wide open and red-rimmed. Spattered across his yellow polo shirt was his own blood.

Jake didn't like this kind of scene. He knew that when it came to violence, he was being blown forward by some old fear. It was probably as simple as a fear of failure, but he didn't want to think about that very deeply.

Jake's father had been a logger in the eastern Cascades. He had wanted to leave the woods, but he never did. Sometimes after work he would gather Jake and the gear into the truck and head up to a green lake surrounded by dusty hills. The wooden rowboat they pulled up into the weeds had more than a little rot around the oarlocks. Jake would sit in the stern while his father gingerly pulled on the oars, not wanting to rip the locks out of the boat.

Jake remembered his father wearing an oil-soaked hickory shirt opened down to show a chest burned mahogany red from the sun. He remembered his father opening a beer, making his first and only cast, leaning back and saying the exact same words every single day: "Hey boys, chow!" Jake couldn't understand what in the hell he and his father were doing there. They never caught any fish, and it made him angry.

When Jake thought of his old man, he remembered his smell: sweat and saw gas. It was the smell of failure, rising like steam.

Jake was wearing a black silk shirt with no tie today, a soft leather jacket and wool slacks. He sat and picked lint off the front of his trousers while Oscar struggled on the couch.

He watched Oscar tip onto his stomach. The old man's cheeks puffed out against the silver tape wrapped around his thinning brown hair. His hands were shaking and turning blue from the tightness of the cords bound around them.

"I'm just in a bad mood," said Jake. He didn't like watching the man on the couch so he spoke up into the air, as if addressing someone in heaven. "I know I shouldn't take it all out on you, but this is business. This is a lot of money we're talking about."

Jake hated this part of his job. He had nothing personal against Oscar, but missing from his storage unit was a large amount of money and, worse, some important business records. Even though he was certain Oscar hadn't taken it, he was almost positive that Oscar knew who had, and, more importantly, knew where that someone was heading. This unpleasantness was just some stupid business foul-up. Jake was a writer, and this was only his day job; like most day jobs, his had its share of irritations.

Jake had been irritated for weeks. Everywhere he went he saw the advertisement for *Stealing Candy*. It seemed like half the buildings in Los Angeles were plastered with billboard ads for the movie. It galled him to no end. Jake could hardly drive anywhere without eventually banging his head against his walnut steering wheel.

Jake had written several films; two of them had been produced so far, erotic films that some people had inaccurately called soft-core porn. He had hoped viewers would have been able to see past whatever label brainless money men put on his work. Both of his films had gone directly to video release, a major disappointment. His dream had been to attend a premiere of one of his own films; the limo ride and the flashbulb walk up the roped-off carpet, standing with the stars, waving, laughing, making sly, private jokes with the director. But that was not going to happen any time soon. *Stealing Candy* was scheduled for its premiere, and he would not be invited. He wouldn't even be comped a ticket to the show. It set his teeth on edge.

Oscar struggled to speak, but the silver tape held fast. Jake stood up and threw a windbreaker over Oscar's head. Oscar rolled onto the floor and started thrashing violently back and forth.

"Gracious!" he said, as if calming a feverish child. "Just settle down. Nothing bad is going to happen." He took a couple of wraps around the man's ankles with a spare electrical cord.

Jake had originally written both the treatment and the first draft for the movie that became *Stealing Candy*. Jake's script, called *Who's Your Daddy Now?*, had been well-received by a producer at Paramount; Jake had even negotiated a six-month option and a development deal with Viacom. He hadn't had a star, of course, and he'd foolishly trusted the earnest young Harvard graduate he'd hired to flesh out the script. Now everywhere he turned, he was seeing seven-story likenesses of a Cameron Diaz clone holding a bloody knife.

Jake loved the movies. He loved the feeling inside a darkened theater: the cool air, the expectant rustle of people settling into their seats, all of them facing the same direction, all of them waiting for a new world about to shine right there in front of them. He hated the moment after the film ended, and the lights came up on the spilled sodas and sticky boxes of candy on the floor. This was too much like real life, like the smell of a dirty hickory shirt or the sound of a nagging cough. This was a life he rejected. He preferred success. He preferred the movies.

Oscar had wet himself, and the urine was running in a slow yellow stream across the floor toward Jake's desk.

"I'm sorry," he said, and looked at his watch. He was supposed to be meeting a friend for lunch in thirty minutes. He picked up the nine millimeter in his desk drawer, racked a round into the chamber, and stepped over the stream to shut the door.

"Don't worry, Oscar," he said, a trace of genuine sympathy in his voice. "When the bullet hits your skull, it won't really hurt. You're going to feel a little bit of pressure and maybe some stinging, but not for long."

Oscar shook off the coat covering his head. He looked up into Jake's eyes and seemed to relax; his hands unclasped, his wrists stopped tugging against the cords cutting into him. He just lay there, waiting for the big wind to blow through his skull.

"Wake up now, Oscar!" Jake said softly, as if he really were waking him up. "If you didn't take the money, all you have to do is tell me who did, and we can work together to find it. You hear what I'm saying?" His voice was urgent.

Oscar shook his head violently, nodded up and down to indicate he understood, and Jake reached down and pinched the edge of the tape.

"This is going to hurt a bit," he warned and jerked the tape away.

"Clive McCahon!" Oscar sputtered. "Clive took the money. Three days ago. He said he was picking up some gear for you. He said I could call you if I wanted to, but you know . . . I thought, shit, it's Clive, you know, he's one of your boys. I mean, I know that. He was one of yours. He went to the joint and never gave anybody up. I thought it was all his stuff in the locker anyway. Shit, Jake! I had no idea he was going to rip you off. I had no fucking idea. You got to believe me. Really . . ." Oscar kept babbling.

Jake reached down and patted him on the cheek. "Clive McCahon? He's in jail." He lifted the gun to Oscar's eyes.

"No, no! He's out," Oscar sputtered. "He just got out. You can check that. Really, check it."

Jake stood up straight. He rubbed his chin with the front sight of the gun. "I believe you. I do, Oscar, but still you owe me. You're going to have to give me something, Oscar. You hear me now?"

"Anything," he puffed, struggling to sit up.

"Do you ride a bicycle?" asked Jake, tapping the pistol against his leg.

"No . . . no, I don't." He looked up with a twitchy kind of panic, a tone that hinted he was willing to start riding a bike right away.

"No bike, huh? Do you play basketball?"

"No . . ." Oscar tried to push his way back up on the couch. Jake lifted his foot and shoved down on his shoulder.

"What do you mean, you don't ride a bike or play basketball? Do you jog or anything like that?"

"No, Jake. I don't jog." His voice shook.

"Then this is a piece of cake, buddy." He lifted his gun slightly and fired one round into Oscar's left knee.

CLIVE WAS ON his knees in the Seattle airport in front of the oversized baggage desk; he was trying to load Little Brother into an expensive, brand-new kennel. It appeared he might never set foot in it.

Clive had tried crawling into it himself. He thought if he showed the dog how easy it was, he might convince Little Brother to load up. The tactic wasn't successful.

"Won't you even consider getting into the crate?" Clive asked politely. The dog stood, his head bowed toward the slick linoleum floor, and said nothing, which frankly relieved Clive because he was afraid of what would come out if the dog did speak.

"Well, I guess we could travel by ship." Clive backed out of the crate. "But I think they will still make you get in a box."

Behind him, a security man, clearing the area for some VIP passing through, grabbed Little Brother's studded leather collar. The growl grew as loud as gears grinding in a Sherman tank; the hair along the ridge of his back stood on end and every muscle was taut, as clearly defined as on a wet, brown bear charging up a river bank.

Every person waiting in line took a step back. The security guard put his hand on his gun. Clive put his hand on the guard's elbow and spoke to him in a friendly, even tone to show he wasn't kidding around.

"Don't do that."

"Yeah . . . Okay." The guard looked shaken, waved to his partner to route the procession to the other side of the concourse. "But if this dog isn't out of here when I get back in five minutes, we'll have to call in the animal control people."

"I think that would be a good plan," Clive said. "Do they have a fire hose? Maybe we can spray him inside the kennel."

Clive was about to say more when the echoing voice of a disembodied pleasant woman came through the air: "Clive McCahon, Clive McCahon, please meet your party at the Alaska Airlines Board Room." Clive looked around and took out a hundred dollar bill and gave it to a Vietnamese man with whom he had struck up a conversation earlier.

"Make sure no one shoots my dog, okay?"

"No problem. He's good here," the man said with no evident concern, and Clive took off down the pre-security hallways of the Seattle airport. He introduced himself to the polite staff behind the Alaska Airlines desk, who showed him to the small board room where sat Jake Shoemaker and the eminently efficient Miss Peel.

Clive nodded to each of them. "Jake. Miss Peel." Everyone in the room knew Jake had once actually had sex with Miss Peel, a fact that she immediately regretted and which he would never let her forget.

"Clive boy, sit the fuck down. You can't steal money from me. What the hell are you thinking? You, you of anybody, know what I have to do to you." Jake had a briefcase in front of him. He was fingering the latches. Miss Peel had not said a word.

"Miss Peel," Clive said, turning to her, "you are looking well. Have you been swimming in the warm ocean regularly?"

"Clive." She looked at the black expanse of desk between them. "I see jail has agreed with you."

Miss Peel—whose first name was Ann, although he had seldom ever heard it used—was a truly glamorous human being. She looked to be of some indeterminate Hispanic descent. Her lustrous, raven black hair was down to her shoulders and clipped up in the front. Her dark eyes were wet and sparkled like wells. Looking at her made men a little crazy, which was why Jake took her to business meetings. But the fact that he never made advances on her led many men to think he might be gay. Clive thought that he might truly be a gentleman, or he was just frightened by that much beauty.

"Anyway, it's good to see you," Clive told her, then turned to Jake. "And you, you little fuck. A: it's my money, it's my paperwork, not yours. B: you are not going to shoot me in the Alaska Airlines Board Room because I know what kind of frequent flyer miles whore you are. I know. I *know* that you gave them your real ID card checking in here, so you can't blast me and walk out. It's stupid. Besides you know they have a camera that photographs each and every one of us when we walk in here and that means that most likely the Port of Seattle Police have probably started asking for the tapes already after hearing your discreet little page of my fucking name. Jesus. How did you ever get this far in crime anyway?"

Jake sat up straight. "Look, man, we talked before. Crime money is hard money. It's stressful. All the fucking assholes— no offense—all the guns, who needs it? You know what I'm saying? Me, I'm taking crime money and putting it into non-stressful businesses. Everyone else is making money. Computers, what a load of bullshit. Dot-coms. Christ! Companies full of zitty kids who sleep till eleven in the morning and produce nothing you can understand and want a million dollars, and they fucking get it. I don't get it. I'm going back into real estate. You can't go wrong buying buildings, you know what I'm saying? Nothing less stressful than that."

"Your stress level concerns me how?" Clive was still looking at Miss Peel, who would not look up at him.

Jake kept fidgeting with the latches on the case. Clive could see Jake's stress now, and it concerned him. "There is this pain-in-the-ass DA. Federal guy. They can make your life miserable, you know what I'm saying? What you have—my money, how you got it . . . The gun stuff, the drugs . . . That could do me in. Twenty years, they are saying."

Clive leaned toward him. "You got no gun stuff. You were strict about that. You never killed anyone. That one thing a couple of years ago, with the Filipino salesman in Yelm, that was a total accident and everybody knows it."

"I know. I never sold to gangs, I never supplied gangs. I only ever sold to these rich dot-com yuppies. But these feds say they can track gangbanger guns to me."

"That's crap. That was your father's bird hunting gun that was stolen out of the milk truck. I told them that, and it's on one of the tapes. They can't use that."

"But if you go backward on me they can put me away."

"Jesus, Jake."

"Listen, kid, keep the money."

"Shut the fuck up, Jake. Don't you hear how you sound? It sounds like you are bribing me to lie. I'm keeping the money and the documents because they are mine. I'm keeping the documents and the money because I'm getting out of the business. I'm retiring. I'm going back to Alaska to get away from you and the life. I'm *not* taking the money to lie for you. If asked, I'll tell the truth that you were not into drugs and guns. You were only into drugs. The Feds love drugs and guns. Well, you were only into drugs. That's it. Sure, you had a gun, but that's, you know, Second Amendment shit." Clive stood up and looked down at Miss Peel. "That's a – m – e – n – d – m—"

"Oh my Lord." She finally looked up at him. "Were you the spelling bee champion of McNeil Island I read so much about?"

"Ann, if you were to marry me, we would have enough leverage with the Feds to get a free home in American Samoa. What do you say?"

"Mmmm, tempting. Unrelenting heat, dysentery, and you. Let me think about it."

"Do that," Clive said. Jake, staring forlornly at his briefcase, didn't say anything. Clive gave Miss Peel a little bow.

"See ya, kids. Got a plane to catch."

As he walked out of the Board Room, Miss Peel put a tidy "X" at the end of the last line she had written. She shut her pad, straightened her skirt, and stood up without looking once at Jake.

WHEN CLIVE RETURNED to check in and pick up his dog, Little Brother was waiting inside the kennel, apparently having decided it was time to lie down with his new sock toys.

At Clive's seat in first class, the flight attendant wanted to take his heavy parka, but Clive kept it on his lap. She brought him a gin and tonic in a heavy imitation crystal glass.

Clive looked out the window. Outside the plane, the city of Seattle was a tangle of wires and flat concrete. There were homes and sheds and stores and shopping malls all connected by an interlacing web of crushed rock and paving tar. It reminded him of a tangled blackberry patch full of blackbirds hunting through the vines for food.

There was minor damage on one of the cargo hatches, and they were going to have to wait a couple more minutes while it was repaired. Clive heard the captain chuckle; a mouse had somehow crawled up and chewed a tiny part of the rubber seal around a hatch. It would just take a second to get that fixed, and they would be on their way.

For a moment, Clive believed he could hear the merry laughter of mice and raised his glass in a solitary toast.

Soon the plane accelerated down the runway, pushed into the exhaust-scented air, and banked over the bay while the sun set in a red gaseous plume. On the purple sea, an oil tanker ploughed north. Far below him was a cardboard box with his name and his prisoner number written on one end; he was leaving his old clothes and his time in jail all behind.

The captain's voice interrupted his thoughts. The plane was going to have to turn back to Seattle. It appeared there was a caution light indicating a problem with one of the cargo doors. There was no need to worry; he would have them back on the ground in Seattle in just a short while, and after a minor repair they would be up in the air in an hour or two.

Clive took another long drink of his gin and tonic. He pulled his bulky new parka tightly around his knees to warm his legs and lap.

MILES WALKED BACK down the boardwalk toward the clinic. Every time he passed Ellie's Bar, he wondered about Mouse Miller. He had seen for himself that Mouse's boat was in the harbor. He had even asked the harbormaster and a couple of other fishermen who lived on the boats whether anyone had seen him.

In the morning Ellie's Bar seemed haunted, but now in the afternoon the old building was unrelievedly lifeless, a corpse with broken-toothed windows that didn't sparkle. A light rain was falling but not enough for water to drip off the eaves; no boards pushed up with the wind, no rusty nails shrieked, no cats hissed. But to Miles, this was when the old bar was at its most frightening.

He hurried along the boardwalk, lifting his collar against the chill. There was no point getting bogged down in useless worry. He had things to do, and he wouldn't be slowed down by ill-considered options.

The rain had stopped; the sun was cutting down through the clouds, and the woods to his left lit up as the clouds moved in the sky. Berry bushes held tiny pearls of rainwater that sparkled like diamonds. The alder trees were starting to show tiny green buds, and the salmonberry brambles had tight fists of well-spaced green leaves at their tips. A varied thrush whirred and chirred up under the dark canopy of the old spruce. A river otter scuttled under the boardwalk and set loose a small cascade of stones back down to the beach. Miles took it all in and was happy to be just where he was.

He got back to the clinic, wrote his notes, went upstairs to the apartment. He put on his sweatpants and flip-flops, gathered up clean work clothes and some shampoo, and headed for the bathhouse.

Like most of the structures in Cold Storage, it was an old plank building sagging on its timber frames. There was a small entryway and a second door leading to a dressing room where painted wooden walls were ringed with benches and hooks.

A set of clothes was scattered on the bench, and a pair of red rubber boots sat underneath. The smell of marijuana smoke overwhelmed the egginess of the bathhouse, and Miles knew exactly who was inside.

Mouse Miller's one deckhand was Weasel, who had taken the name after signing on with Mouse and kept it long after he quit fishing on the tiny trolling boat. He liked being called Weasel much better than he liked being called Julius, which was his birth name. Weasel lived ashore now. He spent most of his time smoking marijuana and watching movies he had flown in from Juneau on scheduled food flights. He grew his pot hydroponically on his float house and always seemed to have a good crop.

His electrical power came from an old hydroelectric complex that the cold storage plant had put in years ago. As long as the rain kept falling, there was power. And as long as there was power, Weasel could keep running the massive lights hanging above the flat tubs of his growing operation. When they started putting a drain on the town power supply, he was told his rates would quadruple in keeping with a new "prorated" energy policy. He cut back on the lights.

Some people in town considered Weasel a genuine gangster. A logger named Tiger Johnson was convinced Weasel was one of the major dope operators on the entire West Coast. He had a theory about him that included black boats, helicopters, and midnight runs to private submarines off the coast. All of that sounded too rigorous for Weasel.

Besides, it had been made clear to him quite forcibly by Miles that if any of his pot showed up in the possession of any of the school kids, his float house would suffer from an accident involving either fire or flooding. Weasel took the message to heart.

Miles had poked around. It was pretty clear that Weasel sold his crop to a select clientele: familiar adults without kids and visiting fishermen coming in to sell their catch or ride out the bad weather on the coast. The rest of the marijuana Weasel saved for himself.

So while some people had tried to run him out of town and some had tried to turn him in to the drug authorities, Weasel didn't scare off. The drug cops were not interested in coming all the way out to Cold Storage merely for a marijuana bust— or at least they hadn't been before Trooper Brown and his hunt for Satanists. Miles wondered if Weasel's lifestyle would be affected by the trooper's new interest in Cold Storage.

In the bathhouse, Miles crossed the grey-green concrete floor of the main room, passed the old-fashioned claw-footed cast iron tubs against the wall, and headed toward the main pool. A solitary bare electric bulb twenty feet above him shone like a midwinter sun lost in fog.

"Hey, what's going on?" Weasel, a skinny man with hair tied back in rubber bands, sat on the edge of the pool, feet dangling in the water. He smiled up through the steam. "You want some?" He held out a fat, soggy-looking joint to Miles. A sense of propriety made him offer even though he knew Miles didn't smoke or drink.

"Naw, thanks, Weaz." Miles thought about how Weasel could have written a Miss Manners, handbook for stoners. "Hey, Weaz," he asked, "do you know where Mouse is? I haven't seen him around."

"I don't know." Weasel let out a long plume of smoke. "I wouldn't worry or anything, Doc. He's been getting stuff out of his boat. I've been checking, and it looks like he's been going in and out. I bet he's shacked up down at the bar, you know?"

"I was just thinking that I hadn't seen him around." Miles studied the green and white lines left on the wall by the condensed steam sliding down.

"Well," Weasel said, "if I see him I'll tell him to come by and see you."

"That would be great." Miles draped his towel over the stair rail and eased into the hot water. He leaned his head against the concrete step, closed his eyes, and let the heat begin soaking into his bones.

"Missed you at the movies last night," said Weasel on an exhalation of breath.

"I've seen *The Bad Lieutenant*, Weaz." Miles kept his eyes closed. "I wasn't in the mood for it again."

"Naw, we watched *Get Carter* with Stallone. I don't know. No one else was into watching *Lieutenant*. I had just gotten the Stallone tape and I figured, you know, what the hell?" Weasel took a long thoughtful drag on his joint, squinting and cocking his face away from the fire. He washed his armpits with a soapy rag.

"How was it?" Miles asked. "*Get Carter*, I mean. Any good?"

Weasel stepped back from the tub and dipped his head in a plastic bucket of fresh water. He threw his head back in one long wet rope of blond hair. "I liked the original better," Weasel opined. "I mean, this was a fashion show. The guy never mussed his hair."

Miles shook his head. He trusted Weasel's appraisal on this. He might have an unhealthy interest in Harvey Keitel, but Weasel knew how to judge an action film.

"Hey," Weasel changed the topic. "Did you meet Officer Friendly when he was in town?"

"Oh yeah."

"I never even knew you had a brother, man. That's cool."

Miles stepped out of the tub, soaped and rinsed himself with fresh water. "Yeah, it is," he asserted. "It's pretty cool."

Weasel had a limited number of subjects he liked to discuss in the bathhouse: movies, the history of the Industrial Workers of the World, the solo music of Robbie Robertson (after he left The Band), the industrial uses of hemp, and—most recently—the novels of Haruki Murakami. He discussed those stories as if they were holy texts.

Miles didn't think any of these topics would be of particular help with his family problems, so he got back in the tub, submerged his head in the hot water, and stayed there as long as he could.

When he came up, Weasel was speaking as if he'd never stopped. "Hey, you wanna hear something really wild? You know your mom? She came by the boat today and asked me if she could have some pot."

"You're kidding," Miles floated away from the edge of the tub. "No way."

Weasel went on. "She said she had cancer, and she wanted some pot. I didn't know she had cancer, man. That sucks."

"I don't think she knows for sure." Miles tried to be professional, to keep what he felt was confidential information to himself. "Did you give her any?" he asked.

"I kind of felt bad but you know, I thought she might be setting me up or something. I told her I didn't know what she was talking about. She looked sad." Weasel's hands were white and wrinkled from the water now, and he inspected them as he kept talking about Miles's mother. "I almost gave her some after that; she looked so bummed, you know? That sucks big time. Cancer . . . shit!"

"Yeah." Miles looked up into the gloomy steam rising up the concrete walls. "Yeah, it sucks all right."

Weasel dunked his head in the hot water and came sputtering out. "Hey, Miles, have you asked Mouse's ex-wife about him? I bet she might know something."

"Who's his ex-wife?"

"Come on, man," Weasel said. "Mrs. Cera down at the fish plant. She was married to Mouse for years. You know, she dumped him because of his drinking, but she always kind of looked out for him."

"Thanks, Weaz."

The only light came from the cracked skylight above the tub. They both sat silently for a few moments. Fat drops from around the edge of the skylight plopped noisily in the pool.

"Hey, Miles?" he asked.

"Yeah?" Miles reached for his towel.

"Let me know when your brother shows up, man. I'd like to meet him."

"I'll do that, Weaz," he said, toweled off his hair and stretched.

AT THE NORTHERN end of the boardwalk sat the old plant, a collection of buildings covered with green and white wooden siding that looked like they'd grown up out of the ground. The old people in town always referred to the color as "oil company green." The main building was built like a barn with large sliding doors on the ocean side where fishing boats tied up to unload their catch.

In 1952, Old Country Seafoods had built a cannery on the site of what had been the fishermen's bathhouse and recreational camp. The old detective was hired as the manager, and the battered-up logger ran a fishing boat. Over the years, the founders' children stayed on, tinkered with their lives on the inlet. The cannery was changed over to a cold storage when the market for fresh and frozen fish overpowered the canned market. When the fresh fish market became the most lucrative, fishermen started keeping fish on their boats, selling directly to towns like Sitka and Juneau that had airports and jet service. The result was that Cold Storage had been born, thrived and started to wither, almost all within the lifetime of her oldest citizens. That their children lived to see the decline in their parents' paradise gave the town a melancholy atmosphere.

In front of the main building was a small store where you could buy bait and milk and canned stew along with a few belts for your diesel engine. There were a couple of bins of apples and a stack of newspapers by the door. In the main part of the plant, bright lights lit up the stainless steel slides, bins, and work tables; the air held the wet smell of disinfectant and cold fish; generators and compressors hummed, but all Miles heard as he walked in was the guttural throbbing of a boom box.

The cold storage had a skeleton crew of workers who bought fish from a few boats. Recently there'd been some black cod. The crew cleaned and headed the fish, and then sent the commercial meat on a packer down to Sitka.

The matriarch of the large Filipino family was Mrs. Cera. She ran this branch of her family like a crew boss, although that title was technically her nephew's. Her current husband worked for the State Department of Corrections in Juneau as a cook at the Lemon Creek prison; he got good pay and benefits. Her son had been living with his dad and going to high school in Juneau, but three weeks ago he'd got into trouble and Mrs. Cera had made him come out to Cold Storage to go to school even though he was a football player and a wrestler with a statewide ranking. If Anthony worked hard and stayed out of trouble for the spring and summer, she'd let him go back to Juneau in the fall in time to tryout for the team. He'd tried to argue with his dad before being flown out, but he did not bother to try that with his mom.

Mrs. Cera was having a work party. The black cod collars, thin lines of dense meat between the most forward fins and the gills, had to be cut off the heads. The meat was rich with oil, and even though the strips of meat were too small for the commercial plants, they made a good meal if you had enough fish heads and enough time to cut the collars out.

A couple of teachers, Ed and Tina, who were married to each other, stood around a high white table carving up the reptilian-looking heads. Miles's neighbor Lester, the silver carver, was cleaning some of the fish collars while Anthony sulked and smoked a cigarette by an open window in the back of the plant. He considered himself an urban boy now, which made his internment here painful. Mrs. Cera filled out paper work in the office. Three others were stripping out of their work clothes to go rest and eat some dinner; maybe they'd cut cod collars later again, after their Auntie's guests were done.

Tina and Ed had been in Cold Storage for three years, the first teachers to last so long and the first husband-and-wife team at the school. They split all the teaching for the thirty students, dividing kids into classes not so much by age but by temperament. Tina was good with mathematics at any grade level, kindergarten to grade twelve, but lost her patience with the sloppiness of little kids and their endless art projects.

She wasn't a finger paint kind of teacher. Ed was. He'd take classes out to trap bugs and make clay models; he'd get them on fishing boats to study the environment; he loved traipsing through the tide pools and didn't mind getting water in his boots to give a third grader a chance to hold a crab or watch the blowing scarves of sea anemones. Tina stayed dry and took field notes. She loved watching her husband, though, loved seeing him in this wild and incalculable classroom. She loved his ability to rekindle wonder in these drowsy kids.

They had been cutting up black cod heads for half an hour when Ed reached into the box beside the table and held up a red fish with a massive round belly. The head alone was almost the size of a football helmet; it had a scary looking snout.

"Isn't this a beautiful thing?" Ed's voice held wonder. "It's a short raker rockfish, a red snapper. This very animal was swimming around before airplanes crossed the oceans. He was alive when Amelia Earhart disappeared in the South Pacific and when the Japanese bombed Pearl Harbor. He might even be older than that. Some people think they could get to be two hundred years old."

Miles and Lester looked at the strange fish Ed was holding up close to his face. Miles thought of Annabelle. He thought of Ellie Hobbes, who had raised Annabelle. Ellie had loved Amelia Earhart.

"Did they ever find Amelia's plane? I thought I saw something on cable TV about that."

"I don't know." Lester shrugged. "I don't have a TV."

Mrs. Cera walked out of the office. A tiny woman, still in her apron and work clothes and her short hair in a net, she smiled broadly at her friends working at the table. She scowled, though, at Anthony in the corner and the music stopped, as if by magic.

"You go on." She gestured to her son. "Go get clean and have dinner. Yes?" Her voice was soft but direct.

Anthony picked up the folder of CDs and walked up the stairs to the workers' cottages on the edge of the woods. Mrs. Cera walked over to Miles and pulled him toward the door of her office.

"Miles," she said quietly, "people been saying that policeman is giving you trouble. I'm so sorry."

"It's not a problem."

"I'm sorry I called him, but I'm worried about Mouse. I really think his drinking might have killed him. I was hoping that policeman could find out where Mouse is." She finished in almost a whisper. "But I didn't want him to make trouble for you or your mother."

"Forget about it," he said. "When was the last time you saw him?"

"Ten days ago. He looked bad, you know. He looked skinny, and his face was white."

"Did Mouse say anything to give you any idea where he might go? Did he mention any friends or anything?"

"Miles, Mouse has got no friends on this side of the grave. You know? Mouse doesn't have anymore real friends. Will you keep an eye out for him, Miles?"

"We'll find him." Miles stood up straight. "Don't worry about it."

He glanced toward the door, but she said, "No. You stay. Get some collars. Get some collars." She gestured toward the cutting tables and raised her voice so everyone could hear her. "Take what you want," she called and pointed to the fish tote of black cod heads next to the table. "We've got some already. Just come up to the house when you're done so somebody can come back over to lock up, okay?" She closed the door.

Miles put on an apron and grabbed a knife.

It was quiet in the old plant. The compressors had cycled off, and all Miles could hear was the hum of the lamps above the table and the rain hitting the tin roof. They worked in silence for several minutes, cutting into the fish heads for the oily strips of meat, each lost in their own thoughts.

Ed's knife slipped off a tough piece of cartilage, and the blade slid down through his rubber gloves. He jerked his hand back and held on to his thumb, afraid to look. Gently, Tina took his hand, opened it and smiled. The blade had only scraped the skin, not even drawing blood.

It was a little miracle, Miles thought. Evidence of the surfeit of good fortune here in Cold Storage. If he had been in Oakland, Ed would have sawn his thumb off, and Miles would be packing the severed digit into an ice bag right now.

He started working on another fish head, smiling to himself.

After a while, Ed spoke. "Holy cow, Miles, that policeman doesn't like your brother."

"I heard."

"Is he really going to come here?" Trepidation hovered in Tina's voice.

"I don't know," Miles said, "but it's not like he's rabid or anything."

"Oh, I didn't mean it like that, Miles. I think it's wonderful that you have a brother." She flipped a chunk of flesh into her plastic bag. "I don't know; that policeman made him sound kind of scary is all."

"Clive's not scary," Miles said. "He's . . . intense and maybe kind of odd, that's all."

"Nobody like that around here." Lester wiped a bit of gill material off his knife.

"Not to change the subject, but," Ed's tone of voice sounded like he wanted to change the subject, "I heard Clint Eastwood was going to come here on his yacht."

"No way," said Tina.

This new kind of gossip had almost become the default setting for conversation around town. The international yachting set had discovered the outside coast, and every summer there were more and more reports of movie stars being seen in unlikely places: Russell Crowe in a fly-fishing shop in Sitka, Minnie Driver at the health club in Juneau. There had been a persistent rumor that Clint Eastwood was scouting locations for some future project from the decks of a yacht; someone mentioned that he'd bought a fishing lodge in south Chatham Strait.

"Well, the truth is my brother is coming to town." Miles hadn't left the first conversation. "He's coming to town and I'll be responsible for him, so you don't have to worry. It will be all right." His voice was more stern than he wanted it to be.

Tina scowled and brushed a strand of hair from her eyes; she looked for a moment at Miles. Ed stopped his work, took his gloves off, and tucked his wife's hair back into her beret.

"It's all going to be fine," Tina finally said by way of not saying much of anything at all.

Miles tried to think of something to say, but Lester beat him.

"I hear Annabelle has cancer."

"She's got a lot of things," Miles replied.

"Weasel is telling everybody in town about it." Lester kept working on his fish.

"Is it true she bought some pot from him?" whispered Ed.

"Well, if she has cancer it makes sense," Tina broke in. "I say good for her."

Miles didn't say anything. He didn't feel like gossiping about cancer, and he didn't know if his mother had cancer. But he knew better than to try to fight the tide of gossip, particularly considering his own ignorance. In Cold Storage, gossip was a semi-official medium of exchange; residents looked to gossip for social context, if not necessarily literal truth. Weasel had become the expert on his own mother's sickness, and Miles had nothing to offer, no expertise, no direct experience to counter Weasel's claim.

"To hell with it," Lester said, and he put down his knife. "I'm going home for dinner. I'll feed any three white people who want to come, but that's it. I'm cooking up a few of these collars—just a few, you understand. It's not the first Thanksgiving or anything." And with that he picked up his bucket of collars and left. The rest of them nodded and kept cutting.

"Thank you for the invitation, Lester, but we've got rice on already," Tina called after him.

"I'll be by later with some shiny trade objects," Miles said, and Lester grunted as he shut the door.

THE RAIN WAS falling again, but not hard. The inlet was dark, and Miles could hear a stream rattling down a rocky chute on the black hillside; he heard the wind pushing the trees around and the faint threads of someone's FM radio leaking through a cracked window.

He turned from the boardwalk and started up the steps.

How had Annabelle made her way up and down these last few weeks? He had seen her almost pulling herself up the rail, but the one time he offered to help, she brushed him away as if he were trying to snatch her purse. Miles was going to talk to her one more time about going into Sitka, but if she had enough vitality to climb these stairs, if she had enough vitality to go down to Weasel's float house to buy some pot, maybe she wasn't that sick after all.

Miles had been considering leaving Cold Storage in the last few months. The lack of age-appropriate single women, his bad luck at catching fish, and increasingly, this sense of responsibility for the health of a town that gloried in their bad habits, all of these things made him watch the big blue ferry boat coming in and leaving each month. But each month came and went, and he was never ready to buy a ticket. He was from here. His people were from here and truth be told he didn't feel as good anywhere else in the world. There was no sense in ever loving or hating the place. It was who he was, and that would change only in its own good time.

He walked and thought. Maybe all she needed was an adjustment in her medications and a change of diet. Maybe she was simply out of compliance with her heart medicine and felt depressed. Maybe a lot of things.

But one thing was certain: going to Weasel for drugs was not going to lengthen her life span or even help her with her symptoms if she really had cancer. Miles was going to be firm with her. He went over all the things he wanted to say. He wasn't going to leave with some vague promise from her to "give it some thought." He was going to get her in for some tests.

He rapped on her door, let himself in, and rounded the

corner of the kitchen. The tea kettle was sitting on a lit burner, all the water boiled out and the bottom burning black. He turned the burner off. The room was hot, and there was no steam on the windows. He could just see his mother's mouse slippers propped up on the end of the recliner.

"Ma?" he whispered, worried about waking her.

He put the black cod collars in the refrigerator and walked into the front room. His mother sat in her recliner, the remote control for the television resting in her right hand. Her eyes were open, and her mouth gaped wide as if gasping for breath. She was dead.

Miles felt for a pulse, but her flesh had already cooled to a stiff clay. So he sat for several minutes, trying to decide what to do.

He turned on the VCR. There was James Stewart running through the snowy streets of Bedford Falls; there was the front door of his drafty old house, already filling with friends.

The phone rang on the counter in Annabelle's kitchen, but Miles did not move to pick it up. It rang eleven times, but still he did not answer.

CHAPTER FIVE

THE PLANE DIPPED into the clouds, rocking from side to side so hard that the seats in the first-class cabin creaked in their moorings. Clive looked out the window and saw a grey world of stone and water below. The waves foamed white on the rocks. Small boats tugged on their anchor lines. The plane buffeted through the wind shear, curling up from the peaks. It shook, banked several times, and landed with a gentle thump. Clive opened his eyes, grateful but regretting that he now had to transfer to a smaller plane.

In the Juneau airport, Clive sat, drank espresso, pushed some muffins through the bars of the kennel. Little Brother's lurid, pink tongue licked up the crumbs, swept across his fingers. All the while, Clive talked to him in a calm, almost confessional tone:

"You are going to like Alaska. The climate is a bit standoffish at first, but you are going to like it."

The ugly earless dog lifted his head and stared at him. Clive leaned in close, listening, but all he heard was his snuffling breath. The dog's silence was irritating to Clive, like a manhole in the dark with the cover taken off by vandals.

"And I expect you to be wildly popular," he finally said.

ⓒ

CLIVE HADN'T BEEN able to reach his mother out at Cold Storage, though. He'd called her number several times, but there had been no answer. It had been at least ten years since he had been home. He didn't know anyone in Juneau anymore, and frankly he had only assumed that his mom and his brother were still out on the inlet.

Clive and Miles had grown up around planes and bad weather. Their grandmother had been a fine pilot; she had run a small flight service. It irritated him that there was no one he recognized at the airport. But it didn't surprise him. He had always hated flying. He had never exchanged stories with the ramp rats who loaded gear into bush planes. He never bragged about his grandma's exploits. He had never cultivated his faith in the physics and mechanics of flight. He wasn't a puker; he just didn't believe it was possible, no matter what the available evidence told him.

He had just decided to call a cab, stay in a hotel for the night, and try to fly out again the next day, when a woman came around the corner and told him that they were "going to give it a try." Clive didn't particularly like the idea of a small plane "trying to fly," but he raised his hands, palms up and shrugged. "Let's go!" he said.

The pilot, a Howdy Doody in a plaid shirt and dungarees, smiled sweetly. "I don't think the kennel is going to fit in the Beaver like that, but the dog can be in the seat with you," he said. Even though he didn't like the sound of it, Clive had long ago given up on confrontation.

The de Havilland Beaver was a single engine prop plane with landing wheels tucked under the aluminum floats on the undercarriage. It could land on the runway in Juneau and then land on the inlet at Cold Storage. To

Clive, this particular floatplane looked like a piece of farm equipment.

He walked around the tail of the airplane and saw two men loading what looked like his dog kennel, except the kennel was in two pieces; the men had made a nest from the two halves and set Clive's suitcase inside. They were stuffing the whole thing into the cargo compartment behind the passenger seats.

Little Brother stood by himself on the tarmac, his choke chain glittering in the milky sunlight that filtered through the clouds.

"I don't know . . ." The pilot's head poked out from the doorway of the plane. "I guess your dog wants to wait for you . . ." His voice sounded wary. "He seems kind of touchy."

"I think he's just sensitive."

"Well, he's going to love the trip. I bet he sleeps right through until we land; they usually do." He paused and looked at the dog. "You can handle him, right?" he asked.

"Oh, yeah, no problem. Don't worry about a thing."

"He's kind of . . ." The pilot hesitated. ". . . impressive."

"Impressive is a good word," Clive said, starting to climb into the plane without his dog. "Vicious might be another."

A kid loading baggage walked toward Little Brother and stopped about ten feet from the working end of his anatomy. The kid turned his head toward Clive and yelled, "You going to load him on up there with you?"

"I don't think so." Clive kept climbing.

"What do you want me to do?" His voice quavered.

"Well, if he's still there after we take off, you can keep him." On the tarmac, Little Brother looked sleepy. He turned his head one way and then the other. Then he lowered his head and took a small step toward the plane. The luggage kid turned away, and the pilot started to crank the engine and close the side door.

Little Brother came bounding up the stairs, clambering up the ladder, jumping into the seat next to him. Clive carefully patted the muscled hump between his dog's shoulder blades, and the thin creature settled into the seat, his head on Clive's lap, his breath filling the cabin with the smell of raw hamburger.

The trip west was noisy and bumpy. The plane bucked, the single-radial engine blared, and Clive put his fingers in his ears. Things didn't smooth out as they entered Icy Strait and headed toward the ocean; the plane dipped and rolled against the strong southwesterly wind. Clive watched the pilot scan the water and the clouds and try to adjust his altitude to find smoother air. It was going to be rough.

According to the pilot, everything would be fine as long as the visibility stayed good. Clive quietly gripped Little Brother's collar and stroked his ears. His head—big as a fishbowl—settled down to rest on Clive's new parka. The plane jolted up and down, and the two of them closed their eyes. They might be rattled apart before they got to Cold Storage.

The plane bounced over the mountains of Chichagof Island. The world below them looked like a cauldron of rock, water, and wind. Waves rolled and battered the outer islands, and sweeping spumes of water broke off the tops of the waves.

Clive was about to suggest that someone should either lend him a parachute, or they should all turn around and fly back to Juneau. He opened his eyes, but before he could open his mouth to say anything, the pilot pointed to the water, gave Clive a thumbs up, and put the plane into a dive.

Clive gripped his knees and kept his eyes open. Waves bombarded the aluminum floats, the plane bounced, and they came to rest on the surface. They were in Pelican.

Clive and Little Brother watched silently as the pilot threw a line out to a bald-headed man in a red raincoat. Slowly they were pulled up to the dock, and the pilot handed the man a padded mailing envelope.

"Great, Tommy!" he said. "Thanks for dropping it off. You headed over to Cold Storage?"

"Yeah, Harry, I am, as long as the ceiling holds. You got something?"

The man reached down and lifted a garbage bag off the dock. "You got room to take this salmon over to Miles? I told him I'd give him one this spring. Poor bastard can't seem to catch one."

"Yeah, I've got room. But if we don't get in," he added, "I'm keeping it. That okay with you?"

"Fair enough."

The man held out a black bag, and the pilot shoved it in under his seat. Tommy would take off again and make the short hop to Cold Storage and then back to Juneau and his home. Clive looked out. He remembered Pelican. Everything in Pelican was pushed together along one boardwalk, like some kind of Russian fishing village. Cold Storage wasn't anything like Pelican. Pelican had smart children and beautiful girls. At least that's what Clive had always felt. Pelican felt like the Paris of southeastern Alaska to a kid scraping along the boardwalk of Cold Storage.

@

LITTLE BROTHER COULD smell the fish. His nose came up off Clive's lap. His eyes narrowed, started to look almost primeval, and his muscles tightened. He hadn't eaten well in either of the airports. He tried to get down onto the floor; he rooted and pushed against the seats and against Clive.

"Is there a problem?" Tommy yelled over his shoulder.

A rocky ridgeline lay a few hundred feet below them.

"Just a few more minutes, and we'll be down," Tommy said. "Can you keep control of that dog?"

"We're doing fine," Clive called. "We're having the time of our lives!"

He tried to wrap his new coat up around Little Brother's shoulders, but the dog seemed to be growing. He would soon be the size of a buffalo, Clive thought.

Looking over his shoulder, all Tommy could see was a massive rump of brindled dog pushing against the seat. Above the roar of the engine, he could hear deep growling.

"Just a few more minutes," he said in a weak voice.

Clive pulled against Little Brother's collar, but the dog wasn't interested in calming down. He reached back, and with his teeth he grabbed the coat from around his shoulders. He began to furiously tear at the parka; feathers and dog slobber flecked against the windscreen.

Tommy started pumping the flaps and leveling off for a landing, but hundred dollar bills were floating up over his shoulder and landing in his lap. He pushed the plane down on the water. Feathers and paper money fluttered through the cabin. The dog snarled, Tommy shrieked, and Clive closed his eyes.

When they got to the float, no one was there to meet them. Tommy jumped down; he tied the plane off to a cleat and sat down on the dock with his head in his hands. One thousand dollars in assorted bills were plastered to his hair, and his neck was covered with feathers and dog slobber.

Coming down the boardwalk to meet them ran a flock of children, squeaking with short joyful cries like small seabirds. Miles was walking soberly in their wake.

Inside the plane, Little Brother had finished tearing up Tommy's seat and was busy ripping into the salmon. Blood, scales, and red bits of fish spattered the windows. Bills that had been sewn into the coat's lining fluttered like leaves.

Tommy picked himself up, turned back, and opened the passenger door. Little Brother, the king salmon firmly in his mouth, bounded up the ramp, crossed the boardwalk in two strides, and ran up into the woods. Everyone could hear him breaking through the brush, turning over the stones. No one offered to go after him. No one called or whistled for the dog to come back. They acted as if he were just another spell of bad luck that had happily just passed them by.

Clive clutched the ripped bundle of his coat and jumped down onto the floats. He'd cut his hand on one of Little Brother's teeth and was slathered with drool, feathers, large denomination bills, and his own blood.

Miles pointed to the water beside the dock. A slobbery clump of one hundred dollar bills floated toward the Aleutian Islands and Japan. "That would be your money, I take it?" he said without irony.

"Miles," Clive said softly and opened his arms wide. "Come here and hug me, you lug!"

Miles shook his head slowly from side to side. Behind him over his shoulders trees trembled on the hillside where the big brindled dog was charging up the mountain with the dead fish.

CHAPTER SIX

J AKE SET DOWN his menu and waited for the waiter to come. It was a fine spring evening in Seattle with the smell of rain on dry pavement drifting in from the parking lot. Jake looked around the restaurant at the young millionaires in T-shirts and jeans. All of them drinking coffee with their meal. All of them giving the impression that they had another eight hours of work to do back in some loft on the waterfront where they were planning the initial public offering of some bullshit idea that would make them dozens of millions of dollars.

Jake was eager to get out of the drug business, and more and more he was eager to get out of computers. It was beginning to have the same kind of tension of the high stakes big deal where you didn't really know what was in the other guy's briefcase until you handed your case over to them. There was too much trust based on bullshit reputations, and the reputations were built by liars or, worse, young cokeheads.

He had understood the drug business. It was substantial and easy. There was a seemingly inexhaustible need for people to get high. There was a substance they wanted, and he provided it by the pound. Classic entrepreneurial supply and demand. But all this computer stuff . . . People were investing in things that had not made—would not make—money.

People were sinking money into imaginary products that no one really understood, for Christ's sake. There was a company who hooked up people on the Internet to give and receive free things. Free: as in no money exchanged hands. This was a bad business for a drug dealer.

Jake's first love had been in films. But so far making films had been a money hole. Worse than owning a dozen boats. Films, like computers, had been bad business for a drug dealer.

The waiter brought the calamari and a bottle of Washington Zinfandel. Jake spread his linen napkin evenly on his lap. He slowly expelled his breath and took a sip of wine. Miss Peel had given him a list of subpoenas a private detective had managed to get from the grand jury who had convened on a number of criminal enterprises in the south end of Seattle in which he was included. It was a federal grand jury and a CCE—Continuing Criminal Enterprise—investigation, in which he understood that he was not the main target but was presented as one of the "Capos."

Jesus, he thought, *these fucking guys. How they love Francis Coppola. That guy changed the world. Not one of these Northwest guys is even Italian.*

Jake was anxious to get started on a new script. He had six strong ideas. All he needed to do was flesh them out, send out a few feelers, then take the strongest idea on through to a final script. One was a comedy about a single dad adopting a kid who was psychic. Jake was most hopeful, though, about his story of a husband-and-wife hit team going for marriage counseling; everybody would want this. In fact, he was thinking of shit-canning all the other story ideas and just moving on the hit team story. He'd already titled it *Till Death Do Us Part*.

"Tarantino is a pussy," he said, and took a long drink of wine. It was a tart white, with just a hint of lavender. "I can write violence," he said to himself. *But first I'd better kill Clive,* he thought as he swallowed some more.

He needed to get back on solid ground. He needed money for this enterprise. Clive had taken money from him . . . but even Jake had to admit that Clive had earned at least part of it. The money had come from Clive's milk truck profits. The whole milk truck thing had been his idea and a damn good one. Looking nice, presentable, you could wander around those neighborhoods in the early morning hours and no one gave a fucking thought. But Jake needed the money, and he couldn't risk the liability. Jake exhaled, shook his shoulders loose, and realized that he was nevertheless going to have to kill Clive, even if Clive had kept his mouth shut after getting busted. Crime is almost as dangerous as high tech. That's just the thing you have to accept about being a criminal.

Jake bit into his calamari and calmly scanned the room, as if he had just heard the voice of a good friend over in a corner. He didn't want to look like a gawker, but he had heard that Bill Allen liked to come to this restaurant.

One of the reasons Clive had been such an excellent business partner was that he didn't snort coke. He was also smart and careful, which was unusual for a criminal. Clive wouldn't blow the money; he'd squirrel it away someplace clean and retrievable, so Jake didn't have to worry about that. What he had to worry about was the cops putting pressure on him. Clive was not a natural snitch, but he was not really in love with the life. Jake knew that. Clive was a wild man but not naturally dishonest. He was Alaskan, and once he was home, he wouldn't want to go back to jail. Once he was home the

threat of getting sent back inside could make him say anything. It was one of those things that was going to make Jake
worry no matter how much comfortable soothing money he
had. No matter if he put all his money out of high tech and
into real estate and gold bars. Clive McCahon, whose name
just happened to show up on this list of subpoenas to be
issued, was just going to have to go.

The waiter set a dish of swordfish with mango chutney
in front of him. Jake looked down at it. An abstract painting.

"What is it with this town?" he complained to himself.
"The portions have gotten so goddamn small." He forked
a bite into his mouth, closed his eyes, and imagined buying
acres and acres of land inside the lines of America's most prosperous cities. Nothing was more secure than real estate. Real
estate never went down. It was as restful as the afternoon nap
he was going to take every day when he could finally work on
his script full time.

First, though, he had to find Clive, get the drug money,
and kill that motherfucker.

THE SENIOR CENTER in Cold Storage was still draped in
pink and white crepe paper from the last birthday party. Elo-
ise had torn down half of the decorations before Gary decided
they should leave them up; since there was no middle ground,
they argued until it was time for Annabelle's memorial service
to start. The hall stayed half-decorated.

Clive wore a Hawaiian shirt under a blue sweater he'd
bought in Seattle and stood in a corner drinking punch from
a paper cup. A heater kicked in, and dust swirled through the
room, rustling the remaining strands of crepe paper hanging from the ceiling. Miles had hardly spoken to his brother.

He hadn't asked about the dog, or the money, or what Clive planned to do in Cold Storage. He had walked Clive up to their mother's house, showed him how to work the oil stove, brought down some old photo albums, and piled them on the kitchen table.

"You might like to look at these," he said, and headed toward the door. His hand was on the knob before he turned around. "If you want to see her . . . her body . . . you can come down to the clinic. She has to be flown out to Juneau and then Anchorage tomorrow. She'll have an autopsy and will be cremated up there." He stopped and stared at the floor. "So," he finished, "I'll see ya."

Clive watched the door close. He stood there looking at it while familiar gulls called out over the inlet. "Hey . . . Hey . . . Hey . . ." they said.

"Good talking to you," Clive said to Miles through the closed door.

By midmorning the next day, the hall was beginning to fill. Men and women carried plates of food, laughed and nodded to neighbors still arriving. Alice brought a baked salmon, and Terry arrived with a pan of halibut enchiladas; there were scalloped potatoes, strips of smoked salmon, a smoked ham, and blueberry pies. The buffet table began to sag in the middle. Ellen came walking in the door with a bag of chips and headed straight for the beer.

Annabelle had been there at the very founding of the town. She had actually witnessed the changes others only remembered through stories. Annabelle's mother had built Ellie's Bar, which had brought Cold Storage its modicum of regional fame. Ellie's was a destination drinking establishment. Alaska had had only seven governors since statehood,

and all of them had had a drink at Ellie's. Anarchists and
libertarians drank there. Democrats had their pictures taken
sitting at the bar, and Republican legislators wore Ellie's silk
bar jackets in the capital offices. This rightly should have been
a watershed event in Cold Storage, but Miles was worried it
would devolve into another boozy afternoon of overblown
memories and bickering.

Chairs had been set up in the center of the room. Miles
had wanted the local minister to say a few words about
Annabelle, but he was on vacation down at Six Flags in Los
Angeles with his niece. Miles had thought of opening the
floor to remembrances from people instead but had thought
better of it. For one thing, Weasel would be there, and he'd
probably bring up the movie club's problems and ask people
to pay him the money he was owed. Miles remembered when
people were asked to speak at Bob William's memorial. Two
had spoken lovingly about their memories of Bob, but then
someone mentioned that he had sometimes let his dog run
loose on the boardwalk, and the memorial broke down into a
melee of charges and countercharges until a fight broke out
in the receiving line, which caused the widow to leave early
with a sprained elbow.

A Cold Storage crowd needed more structure, but Miles
didn't have enough energy to design much of a service. He
thought of a few words to say and resigned himself to letting
everyone drink as much beer as they brought in for themselves.

Now he looked around the hall. People were already starting to drink. Clive was standing in a back corner talking to
Tina; she stared up into his eyes, absently reached behind her
head, and pulled a strand of hair away from her neck. Clive

looked up to see Miles on the other side of the room; he smiled and then went back to talking to Tina.

Ed sat over by himself on one of the chairs set up for the service. His elbows rested on his knees, and he stared down at his shoes. A little kid ran by and clipped his knee, and he stumbled out of his reverie.

Weasel sauntered into the cold storage wearing a light tan sports coat, and Billy Cox almost spit up his beer. Weasel shrugged and lifted the lapels with the tips of his fingers.

"Yo, check it," he preened. "White Elephant shop. Sitka. Last halibut trip."

Mrs. Cera came in carrying a large tray of smoked black cod collars with Anthony slumping in behind her. Before she had even set it on the buffet table, Weasel had a black cod collar in one hand and a sweaty bottle of beer in the other.

Miles decided he'd better start before people got going on their second beer. He was walking up to the front of the room when he saw Lester come in. He was wearing clean work clothes, pressed and neat; his hair was tied back with a silver clip, and he wore a black silk tie and one of his own silver bracelets. He looked like a delegate from another, more dignified country.

He nodded to Miles. "I meant to give this to her." He took the bracelet off his own wrist and handed it to Miles. It was a thick piece of silver with a traditional salmon design carved into the surface. Before Miles could say anything, Lester softly spoke again. "I can't stay." He gestured around the room as if it were evident. "But come by later if you've got time."

Miles put the bracelet in his coat pocket and continued toward the front of the room. On the table by the flowers someone had put a picture in a frame, a photo of Annabelle as a girl standing at Ellie and Slip's cabin site. She was squinting through the thick lenses of her glasses. Her pigtails were tightly braided, and behind her Ellie and Slippery Wilson sat on the second level of logs laid down and notched into their home.

Miles had scribbled some notes about his mom's life. But these people knew all the details. He could have said how he had enjoyed having a mom who could catch a fish in any season. Or how she could laugh at a dirty joke, eat her own cooking, and burp loudly after drinking a soda, or how she knew more facts about animals than any person he had ever known. Or how she loved his father even after death and the wild north Pacific separated them.

But of course he said none of these things. He stood and muttered his "thanks-for-comings" and looked at his notes. He finally wiped his eyes and turned away. He wanted to be somewhere else.

Then he felt an arm on his shoulder and heard Clive's voice.

"What my brother wants to say is that Annabelle was a good person. She loved her friends. She loved this place. She had two sons, one who is a good guy and likes to take care of people . . ." Clive gripped Miles's shoulder and continued talking. ". . . and another who usually makes a mess of things. But even so, she was proud of her family. And she liked a good party; she liked to eat and drink, and she would hate for us to let this food go to waste. So, let's get started!"

With that, a third of the people in the room lifted their bottles into the air and said, "Annabelle," in loud voices, unashamed and unafraid of the distance that separated them from her. Others called out, "Hear, hear."

@

BOB GLEASON, USING his walker, pushed his way up to Miles and jutted out a wobbly hand.

"Best memorial I've been to in a good long while," he said. He turned away, but before he got more than two steps away he doubled back. "Did you hear the story about her beautiful yellow bird?"

"Of course, Bob. That was a famous story. Grandma Ellie told it all the time, about how Mom brought her cockatiel up the inside passage in the dory—"

"And about how it flew away somewhere down south of Dixon Entrance?" Bob Gleason interrupted. "You know I think she half expected that bird to come and find her. Nearly all her life. I really think she did."

"Maybe so, Bob," was all Miles could offer.

"She was a fine gal. I always liked her. I always wanted to kind of steal her away from your father for a little while."

Miles grimaced, even though this was well-known information to him now. He tried to walk away, but Bob's skinny claw of a hand clamped down on him.

"And after your dad's boat went down and she was . . . you know . . . available, well, it just never seemed right after that."

"Yes. I suppose that's true, Bob." Miles took a step away, and the old man turned again.

"But she was a hell of a fine gal," he said, and toddled off toward the food.

Tina came, put her arms around Miles, and kissed him on the cheek. "She did a good job with you, Miles," she said.

"Thanks." He tried to stuff his notes into his pocket, but Tina kissed him again, and he felt the strong muscles between her shoulders holding onto him and he felt the air slowly slide out of him as if he wanted to stay right there in her arms.

But a line of people were waiting for him. Some, it was true, were simply grateful that they didn't have to sit through a bunch of speeches, but all of them knew what Miles was feeling because speechlessness was something they recognized in themselves and each other.

So Miles stood there, hugging people one by one. Friends and people he barely knew: drunks he'd sewn together after countless falls off the boardwalk, angry women who didn't like the tone of his voice or the selection of magazines in the clinic, fishermen who thought he was soft and inept. All of them came with their hugs, their beery breath, sour perfume, cigarettes, and fish slime. They were hugging him because he was burying someone he loved, someone he felt responsible for, and this, too, was something they understood.

Old Walter Williams came up and shook Clive's hand.

"You just got out of jail, huh?" He fixed a stern but wobbly eye on him.

Clive stood flat-footed and stared him right back in the eye. "That's true, Walter, and I've never been happier."

"Well, welcome home, buddy boy." His palsied hand gestured weakly around the hall. "Hell, you know, half of us have done a jag or two, and the rest of them just never got caught. Now get me a beer, would you?" He sat down, and a young girl handed him a plate of food and kissed him on his cheek.

Someone gave Miles a beer, and Tina brought him a plate of food. He sat down in an empty chair and let his eyes roam through the crowd, hoping Mouse Miller might wander in for some free food and beer. Other freeloaders smiled weakly and shouldered their way into the food line, but Mouse wasn't among them.

Clive hadn't eaten yet. People kept shaking his hand and talking to him. The idea of shaking the hand of a man you knew as a kid and was now an ex-con apparently was just too interesting to let go of easily. Kids and old men crowded around him, and some of the younger women stood watching from a distance.

For twenty minutes, Weasel backed Clive into a corner and tried to engage him in a discussion about the films of Harvey Keitel. The problem with Weasel's conversational strategy was that he never paused or asked questions. He lectured. And now he lectured Clive on the subject of Harvey Keitel and America's dark underbelly, which left little for Clive to add.

Mrs. Cera came over to Miles and gave him a special plate of black cod collars. She said some of them "came out of the smokehouse just perfect," and she wanted him to have them. He thanked her, and she held his face in her hands and disappeared back into the crowd.

People who had already had enough to eat were starting to leave. But someone came in with more beer and someone else plugged in a tape player and suddenly the room was full of Glenn Miller. Weasel took his sports coat off and started swing dancing with Tina. Ed undid his tie and began talking to Mrs. Cera about the subtleties of smoking black cod. Miles drank some more beer, even though he hadn't drunk much beer since he got out of the Army.

Now the old people were telling stories. Many were about Annabelle. Miles and Clive walked around the room, sitting on the edge of a group of two or three. They sat and listened. Old women would place their old hands over the boys and leave them there. There were stories of picnics and big salmon. There were stories of bears and long snowy winters. There were stories of unexplainable kindnesses and debts that would never be repaid. Clive and Miles went from group to group, and each group folded them into their own loving company. Glasses clinked. Laughter burbled up, and old friends and people said the names of those who had long left this stormy coast.

The room was quieting down, and most of the older folks had headed home. Clive was talking to a young woman working in the cold storage for the summer; he was eating huckleberry pie and drinking black coffee and watching her sway in her chair and hold onto her beer with both hands. Tina was sitting with Miles and listening to Weasel tell her about the John Sayles movie *Matewan*; she was laughing at what he said but her arm was draped over the back of Miles's chair, and he could feel her forearm against his back.

Billy flopped down with a cup of coffee, a bottle of brandy, and a plate of sugar doughnuts. He poured brandy into his coffee and ate one of the doughnuts; powdered sugar dusted his chin as he chewed and drank and looked at Miles but didn't say a word.

Tina got Miles up to dance to "Pennsylvania Six Five Thousand," and they spun around the room, bumping into the folding chairs only once. It was dark outside when the song was over.

The people left in the hall sat at a long table where Billy was still eating doughnuts. Miles sat down between Tina and Clive. The cold storage girl was sleeping against Clive's shoulder.

"Forty-nine days," Billy blurted.

"What?" Tina asked.

"Forty-nine days," Billy repeated. "She's got forty-nine days to get a new body."

"Ah!" said Miles.

Tina leaned over to explain this to Clive. "Billy's a Tibetan Buddhist."

"Ah!" said Clive.

"And he's going to paddle his kayak to Seattle so he can meet the Dalai Lama," Miles added.

"I'm going to raise money to free Tibet," Billy said with a mouthful of doughnut.

Clive looked at him and smiled broadly. "Christ, something should be free in this life." He reached into his pocket. "Give this to him for me," he said, and handed Billy ten hundred dollar bills.

"Excellent! Lemme get a picture . . ." Weasel stood up and wove over to the counter for the Polaroid camera kept in the supply drawer. They bunched around the table with Clive and Billy in the center of the group, and Clive handing the money to Billy as if he were a lucky sweepstakes winner. Weasel snapped the picture and waved the exposed print in the air as if he were fanning himself.

"Billy," he said, "you take this with you so the Dalai Lama can see who we are." He lay the print out on the table, and they watched the images ease into being, watched the white sheen of light spread over the slightly overexposed photograph.

Billy took it and held it gingerly in his sugared hands. "I will give this to him myself," he said with purpose.

Billy kept staring at the picture and at the hundred dollar bills. He grinned and put the money and the photo in his front pants pocket, finished his coffee nudge, brushed the powdered sugar off his hands. He licked one fingertip and smiled again. "Sweet," he said.

OUT ON THE boardwalk, rain had started to fall through the dark. Clive had helped the young girl find her feet and handed her off to Tina, who promised to get her back to the bunkhouse. Everyone said goodnight and started to go, but Tina doubled back to give Miles one last kiss, holding up the drunken fish slimer with one arm.

"Have a good sleep, bud," she said.

"Thanks."

"I love you so much!" blurted the drunken girl.

"Thanks," Miles said, and patted her on the back.

The brothers turned to walk to their mother's house.

"You shouldn't have dismissed her like that," Clive said, and turned up the collar of his Hawaiian shirt, shrugging.

"Like what?"

"Like that!" Clive's voice was affronted. "Hell, she spent the entire evening telling me about her deep longing for you."

Miles spun around and watched her staggering home to the bunkhouse. "I don't know that girl," he said. "She was probably in grade school when I went in the army."

"You need to pay a little better attention, brother." He stepped around a spilled can of paint lying on the boardwalk, red drops falling through the cracks. Delicate paw prints ran through the scarlet puddle and along the boardwalk, fading into the darkness.

"You've been here, what . . . a couple of days and already you're critical?" Miles couldn't keep his voice friendly anymore.

"What do you want, Miles?" Clive asked. "You want me to leave right away?"

Miles didn't say anything, and they walked along the slick planks.

"Screwy things happened after you went away." Miles was quiet for a bit. "Pop died . . . and then you just left . . . and then it seemed like all she ever talked about was you."

Wind shushed through the trees, and a raven stood on a rail beside the boardwalk, scratching its beak.

"And I was right here." Miles's voice was tired. "I'm tired of all the attention you got around here," he said.

"I haven't even been here," Clive said.

"I know." Miles turned away from his brother.

Clive wanted to walk away. He wanted to walk back into the silence that had enfolded him in the protective segregation cell. There was no use in explaining anything to a brother who was angry with him. Who had good reason to be angry with him.

"Jesus! You were a dope dealer," Miles said. "While I was in Somalia!"

"I know, Miles," Clive said. "It's not right. I wasn't right. I'm going to try to be better, a better brother."

The raven jerked its head back and forth between the two brothers as if deciding whose side he was on. Clive watched him for a moment. He turned and walked over to the black bird. The bird looked up at Clive and said very succinctly, "Just tell him the truth."

"Cocaine," Clive said finally. "I sold flake cocaine. When I was doing it, I told myself that it wasn't crack. Pure rationalization, it's true. I sold to a select group of rich clients. I delivered early in the morning and they left me cash, and I told myself that at least I didn't sell to kids or people who were reckless around their kids."

"Do you know how you sound?"

"I do," Clive said. "Listen, I'm sorry for leaving you. I really am. I thought about you all the time. But . . . you know those people who talked about me all the time? They didn't know who they were talking about."

"Just as you didn't know the little brother you say you were thinking about."

"What's it like being a hero?" Clive asked.

"Shit," Miles said, looking up and down the inlet. For a moment he thought of brushing his brother off with a canned answer he usually gave about training and instant response, but instead he said, "When it's happening to you, it's kind of a dumb surprise. You just wonder, 'Is this it? Is this what I've been worried about?' And then you see people dying and you kind of figure . . . yeah, this must be it. But there is no music like in the movies, and there is no time to take it all in, you just keep moving and reacting . . . You just go, go, go, and when you make it—if you make it—that's when you get scared. It's weird. You never feel like a hero, you really don't, you just feel bad that you made it and the other guys who must have done that one thing more, that one brave thing, or mistaken thing, that you didn't. I don't know."

They walked on in silence. In the distance, the wind scoured over the trees and out into the darkness. A street lamp cast a shaky pool of light onto the boardwalk.

Miles thought of his mother's empty house. He thought of her being forever gone, and he hunched up his shoulders to the wind.

"I realize that there is so much I don't know about you,"

Clive said finally, "and that can be added on to the list of things that are my fault." Then he held out his hand to Miles. "I was a criminal, but now I'm not and I'd like to get to know you."

"What are you now?" Miles asked, still a little shaky on his feet.

"I'm not sure, brother."

"Is that money from your coat going to get us in trouble?"

"Us?"

"Well, you."

"No. I don't think so. It's my money. Even the guy I stole it from knows that."

Miles looked up at his brother. "Somehow I don't find that very comforting."

"Money doesn't really belong to any one person. That's why they call it money. But we're splitting hairs. Tell me the truth: have you seen my dog?" Clive smiled at his brother.

"That is an ugly dog, Clive."

"I didn't ask for your opinion of his looks," Clive said. "Have you seen him?"

"No." Miles said. "No, I haven't seen your dog."

They looked at each other. The wind washed up the hillside in a wave, and the trees flung their arms in the dark. Fat raindrops started falling, sounding like a gamelan hitting the tin roofs and the buckets all around town. "We can look for him tomorrow." He stepped forward to put his hand on his brother's shoulder. "Thanks for helping me out back there at the memorial," he said, "when I froze up."

Clive returned the gesture so they were arm in arm as they had once been walking down the boardwalk. "Don't worry about it."

They started up the stairs to Annabelle's house. The wind

was shrieking now, and a branch of a tree scraped against a metal roof. They stopped in the dark and looked up toward the noise. There, at the peak of the roof, sat a strange yellow bird with orange dots on its cheeks. Clive saw it clearly as a fever dream. He pointed without saying a thing, and the bird flew away.

"Look," Clive whispered even though the bird had flown.

"What?" Miles said, following his brother's gesture but seeing nothing.

"I must be imagining things."

Just as they reached the dark porch they heard a deep-throated growl. Miles pushed past Clive, picked up the flashlight stored on a shelf, and pressed the switch. He swept the beam of light into the darkness.

Twenty feet away was Clive's brindled dog. Black tree limbs swirled above him. He sat, the stubs of what were once ears erect, taking short puffs of breath and holding a dead cat in his jaws; red paint daubed the pads of the cat's feet.

"I would like to take this opportunity to apologize for my dog," began Clive.

"Whoever owns that cat is not going to be happy," Miles said, as if to himself.

"Well, they can take that up with the dog." Clive turned to go into the house.

"What's his name?"

"Little Brother!" Clive called through the closed door.

"Perfect," said Miles. The sigh of the wind in the trees blended with the growl of the ugly dog with a dead cat in its mouth.

CHAPTER SEVEN

IT WAS A clear morning; the sun hadn't risen yet above
the ridgeline, and the sky flared blue and silver above the
inlet. Out to the west, a layer of fog rolled in from the coast.
It should burn off by the time Billy reached it, but if it didn't,
he could hug the shoreline of the outer coast.

His kayak, loaded and heavy with gear, was tied up at the
floatplane dock. She sat low in the water, but every inch of
her looked buoyant, long and narrow like a eucalyptus leaf
caught in a back eddy. Billy had built her from strips of Sitka
spruce and canvas following a modified plan of an Aleut
design, and the bow swept up to a large, flat holding point
shaped like a dragon's head. Billy had painted a pair of eyes
up there to watch over his progress.

He had packed a few clothes, a small tent, a sleeping bag,
and some charts. He planned to build fires most of the time
but had a small gas stove along, just in case. He had dehy-
drated pinto bean flakes, rice, cheese, vitamins, and chocolate
bars. He had a small fishing rod and a spinning reel with a box
of lures, since he was almost certain he could jig up rockfish
just about anywhere he put in. On top of the boat, he'd lashed
two extra paddles.

Tina had given Billy a gift for this trip. She had wrapped
it in a waxed canvas bag and tied it up with a length of

tarred twine. *The Tibetan Book of the Dead*. It was an old library book by Dr. W.Y. Evans-Wentz. Billy flipped through the pages, scanning each page as if he were reading a map.

"I thought you might need it."

"Cool!" He hugged her and closed his eyes as if he were committing the moment to memory. "I knew you believed in me."

"I never said that." She whispered into his ear, "I just want you to come back, one way or another, and this might help." She held him a little longer than usual.

Billy had ordered a brand-new dry bag from Seattle. It was bright yellow and carried all of his most important papers: his passport, his money for the trip, Clive's money for the Dalai Lama, and some flyers he'd made that described his trip and requested donations. Inside all of these papers, he had placed the photograph taken at Annabelle's wake. He added Tina's new book to the bag.

Billy took off his boots, rolled them up, tucked them behind his seat. He put on his warm slippers, eased into the kayak, and wriggled around in the tight cockpit as if he were putting on a new pair of blue jeans. He put a bottle of water on his lap and slid his rolled up slicker under his thighs. He pulled his spray skirt over his head, stretched it tight over the hole in the cockpit; he slipped wrist gaiters over his long-sleeved shirt and looked around.

A few gulls were floating like chips of ice on the surface of the inlet. Tina had disappeared. A couple of kids were running up the boardwalk pulling a red wagon, clattering like a bucket rolling on its side. Smoke was sliding out of the chimney of Lester's house and rising up, ghostly white, against the sides of the mountain. Billy undid the painter line from the dock and pushed away.

He had hoped a few more people might have come down to say goodbye, even though he knew that his sentimentality about the place was an illusion. He had Clive's money and two thousand dollars in pledges if he made it all the way to Seattle, but he knew that was an illusion of sorts, too. The substance of this trip was compassion. And even though compassion was supposed to flow from him and not toward him, he was still a little ticked off that no one had noticed his leaving.

He pulled his paddle through the water. "I take refuge in the Dharma," he murmured sadly, thinking that he must still be a pretty crappy Buddhist.

He pulled his way through the water and past the pilings of the cold storage. Fat drops of water plunked into the water from a broken pipe. With each new stroke, his boat felt sleeker and stronger as if she, too, were looking forward and pushing ahead. A fat raven flew down from the roof of the cold storage and landed on the bow of his kayak, and he stopped paddling, sat still. The bird cocked its head from side to side and looked at him expectantly. Billy had a peanut butter sandwich in his coat pocket; he fished it out, broke off a corner, and tossed it toward the raven. It made a loud cry, jumped, caught the bit of bread in midair, and flew low over the water back to the shadows under the wharf. Billy watched it weaving between the pilings. He could hear the air pushing past its wings as he started paddling toward Seattle.

He made it around the first point out of town in a few minutes. A squall from the west was blowing through, and fog lay ahead. Should he cross the inlet? He looked to his right and saw the sign.

They had hung the sheet about twenty feet up in the trees at the end of the boardwalk. A white sheet with some kind of red design that was hard to decipher because the wind pushed the tree limbs around and pulled the sheet in all directions. He tried to identify the pattern but couldn't, so he turned to face the sheet head on and stopped paddling.

The squall passed. The branches hung motionless. A group of people stood beneath the sign, and Billy saw Tina reach up and pull on a rope tied to one corner of the sheet. The red lettering on the sign snapped into focus; it read: "We love you, Billy. Whatever is here, that is there."

The kids who had been running along the boardwalk were now standing on their wagon and waving, as if he were floating away in a hot air balloon. Clive was standing beside his brother, and Billy heard Miles call out over the water, "I put some extra medication in your boat. Some ointment and antibiotics. I thought you should have some just in case."

Billy raised his hand and shook it in a short embarrassed wave.

Weasel pulled his pants down and mooned him.

"Meeeee, tooooo!" he screamed. And the children started swaying with laughter, almost falling out of their wagon.

Clive was waving as if he were the Prince of Wales.

Someone shouted, "Give our best to His Holiness!"

And the girl from the cold storage yelled, "You go, boy!"

Billy waved again and started paddling toward the head of the inlet where fog was easing in from the coast.

CLIVE DRANK A cup of coffee, walked along the boardwalk, and tried to decide what to do. Radio reports had tracked a storm off the coast, but for the time being the air was clear. A light breeze drifted across the inlet, teasing the steam rising from his mug.

Clive had spent a week going through his mother's house. Some evenings Miles would come over, and the two of them would start packing boxes and end up cross-legged on the floor or parked at a table, flipping through piles of loose photographs. They would talk, try to help each other remember names or places, and drift back into their separate reveries.

Only a few boxes were filled. Annabelle's clothes still hung in the bedroom closet, and her sheets lay untouched in the linen closet. Clive slept in her bed but borrowed bedding from Miles because he didn't want to use hers. There had been no more discussions about Clive's past or about the money sewn into the down parka.

Little Brother ranged on the hillside and over in the far river valley; Clive left food in a bowl and found it empty in the mornings. No cats were reported missing, not even the white cat that had been killed the night of the wake. Clive had been prepared to make a substantial payment to the aggrieved cat owner, but none appeared and Miles wasn't surprised. Most of the cats in Cold Storage belonged only to themselves; they had to survive on scraps from the fish plant and from the garbage cans along the boardwalk.

MILES WAS AT the clinic tending to Teddy, whose knees and elbows were full of splinters from a particularly spectacular bicycle wreck.

Clive was restless. He didn't want to look at pictures and the inside of Annabelle's house was beginning to feel close. A storm was expected to blow through soon, and Clive felt a headache coming on.

He eased around the southern border of the boardwalk and walked into Lester, who'd clamped a music stand onto the top rail of the walkway to make himself an easel. He had a piece of fiberboard set up and was scratching at it with a tiny putty knife.

"Hey, Clive," Lester murmured.

"Lester," Clive nodded.

He squinted at the drawing on the board. It was a traditional Tlingit design of a raven; thick black lines surrounded the stylized ovoids, the eyes and the beak reflecting the same circular forms.

A raven flew across the tide flat, back around the point and out of sight. Lester wiped the palette knife on a rag, then daubed at the canvas, watching the bird. Clive looked at the stylized drawing, then to the bird, then back at the canvas. He started to ask why he was watching a raven when Lester obviously wasn't drawing from life. But he held his tongue, remembering enough of the manners he learned from before he left Alaska the last time.

"Can I ask you a question, Lester?" he finally said.

"I don't suppose it would hurt," the artist replied without taking his eyes off of his work.

"Do you think animals can talk to people?"

Lester put aside his palette knife on the top of his supply box. "Before I get into that let me ask you something."

"Okay."

"Were they giving you some medication in jail that you stopped taking? You know what I'm asking? The pills that made the voices stop?"

"I don't need medication, Lester."

"At the risk of employing a cliché, Clive—that's what they all say."

"Come on, Lester. What about all the old stories? Animals used to talk to people, didn't they?"

Lester wiped his hand on an oiled cloth. "You are serious about this, aren't you?"

"Yeah, I guess I am."

"And you're not talking about parrots and mynah birds, are you?"

"No. I'm not."

"Because there is a girl up at the cold storage who has lost her parrot, and she's going crazy looking for it."

"Somebody really lost a parrot?" Clive thought back to the vision on top of his mother's house.

"Okay . . ." Lester bullied his way through the silence. "It's not like the animals talked to people. It's more like people used to be animals. It wasn't such a big deal. Like you talk to your dog, you don't really expect the dog understands everything you say, but you talk and the dog gets your meaning because . . . I don't know. Because you have a relationship. It used to be that way with animals and human beings. They all were related somehow. They talked to one another, and even if they knew all the meaning wasn't getting through, they could still understand each other."

"Could it happen now? Could someone start understanding the animals now?" Clive asked in a low voice, obviously embarrassed now.

"Are we back talking about the pills thing? Maybe you should talk to someone about that."

"No. I want to know. Could it happen to someone now?"

"Why the heck are you asking me?" Lester snorted. "You're not some new age nut job who is going to ask me to lead them on some frigging dream quest, are you?"

"No. I just remember the old people talking about it when I was a kid. Even some of the old Norwegian fishermen, they'd tell stories about hearing seals talk and the birds. I remember the Indians talking about how to act around bears and what to say and stuff. I'm . . . I'm just . . ." And he stopped speaking and turned to walk away.

"Hold up," Lester called to him, and Clive turned. "Yes. Yes, it can happen now."

"What would cause it?"

"All it takes is getting over yourself as a human being. Living with animals for a long period could do it."

"Is it a bad thing?" Clive asked.

"Are any animals telling you to start killing Indians?"

"No."

"Then it sounds fine." Lester snapped shut his supply box. "But again, I'm not sure why you are asking me."

"All the square-headed Norsky fishermen are dead." Clive smiled.

"You'll be fine," Lester said as he unscrewed his makeshift easel. "Just don't try and go Native. That's just so eighties. Schizophrenia is what's happening now. Go with that."

"Thanks for the tip," Clive said, then waved and walked down the boardwalk.

Up to his left, he could hear a large animal walking along the rocks of a steep-sided stream bed; he had heard that there had been a bear in the garbage cans out in front of the restaurant, and in fact had heard dogs barking in alarm early in the morning when he was cooking his breakfast. The trees rustled fifty feet away, and Clive started whistling the tune to "Don't Fence Me In," hoping that the bear would recognize him as a kindred spirit and give him a wide berth.

So he was whistling when he turned the corner and saw the fallen-down bar. Actually, he saw Little Brother sitting on a loose piece of roofing lying out in front of a salmonberry thicket some ten feet from the boardwalk. The big dog was lying in the sun with his head on his front paws; his eyes were barely open, and he seemed to be content.

"It's good to see you," said Clive as if greeting an old friend at the post office.

The brindled dog lifted his head just slightly, turned, and said nothing.

Clive headed toward the dilapidated structure. The sun was breaking over the ridgeline, and the building started to glitter; steam began to rise from the roof. Clive stopped and watched for a moment. The thicket came up and around the back of the roof; just up the hillside, two gnarled hemlock trees leaned out from the forest with their trunks almost shading the bar. This was a magician's hiding place, Clive thought, and something he later recognized as optimism rose in his chest.

This was Ellie's Bar. The wildest and most storied drinking spot along this stretch of coast. From World War II and onward, fishermen had yearned to make port here. Now its spongy boards were melting into the moss. All he had to do was push the wooden door aside, and it came off of its hinges. He ripped some of the plastic off the windows to let the light in, and when he had, he knew he had taken the right path. Chairs were stacked on tables in the center of the room and old high-backed booths lined the walls; dusty bottles stood at the back of the ebony bar; the ceiling was water-stained plaster. Wet dollar bills hung over the room like wilted leaves from tacks that had been pinned there years before.

All around the bar and on the edges of every booth, people had carved the names of their boats: *The Defiant, The Lisa M, The Samuel R Wiks, The Point Hope, Willie's Raider.* There were hundreds of names of fishing boats carved around the room. There were tin beer signs, and an old horsehair dart-board, green with mildew. At the back was a slate pool table with leather pockets; one of the legs had broken through the flooring and the whole table listed forward like a ship gone aground; colored balls rested in the leather pockets, mossy with neglect.

Clive pulled a chair off the top of one of the tables and sat staring. He could smell something underneath the mildew and spilt heating oil. He could smell burgers cooking, and perfume; he smelled beer foaming over thick glass mugs. He could hear the gurgling of the coffee maker as morning regulars came in to chat; he heard music and women laughing at badly told jokes. Something about the bar's decrepitude attracted him. This was the opposite of his old concrete bunker in protective seg. This was some place the forest was going to eventually get back; this was only a temporary shelter from the storm. Unlike prison, this place was designed for impermanence and escape. Clive sat with his eyes closed and imagined such a thing.

Little Brother walked in and lay down on a mat at the end of the bar.

"You want to be a bouncer?" Clive asked the big dog. "You are family now. I could probably put you on."

Little Brother raised his head and looked down behind the bar, whimpered softly, and put his head back down on his front paws.

Clive went over to where the dog lay. A pad and a ring of

candles in shot glasses rested on the floor; a fairly new sleeping bag was spread out, and a backpack stuck out from under the bar where the garbage cans had been. A sour smell of rotten meat reached out and enveloped them both.

There was a foot in a rubber boot, attached to a leg.

Clive walked past the dog and over to the body. Half of the sleeping bag was resting over the shoulders of the short, bearded man. Clive rolled him over. The body was stiff, hard as wet clay under the damp wool jacket; small animals had already started in on the exposed flesh of the face, but Clive could still make out the features.

"You must be the famous Mouse Miller everyone's been talking about," said Clive. He patted the old fisherman's shoulder and eased him back down.

A gust of wind rattled through the bar and sent a flurry of dry alder leaves swirling behind the bar. One landed on Mouse Miller's dead open eye just as the storm from the outer coast announced its arrival.

CHAPTER EIGHT

BONNIE HAD BOOKED an Alaskan cruise on board the SS *Universe* as a last attempt to bring order to her life. It was beating down on her, like a hard rain, just how mistaken she had been.

She was standing on the port side of the lower stern deck dressed as Little Bo Peep and carrying the empty swimming pool's lifesaving hook as her shepherdess crook. The ship was on the first sailing of the season, southbound from Valdez. By nine o'clock, the seas were darkening to a bruised color, but the steep slopes of the Fairweather Range still shone with a brilliant, rose-colored light. On the deck above, the band from Oberlin College was playing "You've Got to Ring Them Bells," and a tiny boy from Belgium, dressed as some kind of fuzzy space monster, was boxing with two Japanese girls dressed like lambs.

Bonnie had seen whales spouting near the ship that afternoon, rubbery grey forms with slick backs slowly lifting their tails up in the wake of the ship, then disappearing into the white-washed foam. She thought she could hear one of them make a long groaning sigh, almost impossibly low and mournful.

She looked down at herself, at the blue Bo Peep dress billowing out away from the rail in the brisk wind. "How stupid is *this*?" she asked the sea, hissing below her.

Bonnie's mother had insisted that she take the Alaskan cruise, had sent the ticket for her twenty-seventh birthday. It wasn't lost on her that her mother hoped she'd meet a man, and she had met men, almost all of them over fifty and traveling with their second or third wife. All the forced gaiety of the cruise made her feel sad: the dances where retired people swayed to big band tunes, the lectures where retired professors and engineers dominated the question-and-answer sessions, trying, Bonnie supposed, to regain some of the authority they'd left behind in their old jobs.

But why was she sad at this particular moment? She didn't know. She'd just started to cry while sitting on the bench before the costume parade, sitting by herself, waiting alongside three people in black garbage bags who were planning to dance to Marvin Gaye's "Heard It Through the Grapevine" like the California Raisins. She hated herself for being sad and judgmental. After all, she was dressed as Little Bo Peep, and no one had made her wear a costume. But still, she hated herself and these people she didn't know.

She took a bottle of vodka out of the front pocket of her pinafore, took a long drink. She looked down into the grey water curling around the stern of the ship; no fish cut the surface, no life rose up from the darkness. She felt something lift inside her chest. Her right foot began to rise up to the lateral rail support, but as she felt her weight come down on the raised foot, she knew she wasn't going to climb over the rail. She couldn't kill herself because she knew her problems didn't have the gravity of a suicide. Her vague sadness now wouldn't compare to her mother's grief later when she heard from the Coast Guard that the search for her daughter's body had been suspended. Even though there wasn't a clear reason to go on living, there wasn't a clear enough reason to take her own life.

The sun sank over the starboard side; the Fairweathers darkened and stepped back into the grey-greenness of southeastern Alaska. Bonnie looked out to sea. The band barreled into a medley of songs from *Cabaret*; a balding man with a cardboard shark fin taped onto his head peered over the railing above her, scanned the horizon, took a sip from his glass, and stepped back inside the deck lounge; and Bonnie imagined her life proceeding at its own implacable pace throughout the rest of the evening, the rest of the voyage, on and on through a long cycle of years. She'd live her life, learn to pull up her socks, accept whatever fate brought her.

She started to turn toward the stairway but something caught her eye; about fifty yards from the ship, a long ridge cut the water from beneath the surface. Another whale, she thought, but no blow appeared, and the ridge was straight, not nearly as pliable as the backs of whales. She looked again and made out the straight line of a piece of wood, a drift log perhaps. But then a pale arm reached up out of the water.

Bonnie screamed. She threw the useless shepherdess crook overboard toward the figure fading behind the ship; she threw an emergency life ring hanging from a nearby wall. And as two of the California Raisins came out on the upper stern deck, she jumped from one foot to another and screamed, "Man overboard!" and various unintelligible syllables in a high-pitched voice.

The emergency beacon lit up as soon as the life ring hit the water. The Raisins saw the small blinking light lost in the darkening Gulf of Alaska and heard the loud blast of the ship's whistle. They cupped their gloved hands over their ears and

looked at each other in dull surprise as the engines of the
Universe started to slow.

BILLY WAS NOT making great progress down the coast. The
prevailing winds had been against him the entire week.

"I take refuge in the Buddha, I take refuge in the Dalai
Lama, I take refuge in the Dharma, I take refuge in the
Sangha," he repeated to himself as he paddled.

His boat rode low in the sea. Billy was not a big man so his
torso above the spray skirt didn't make up a lot of sail area.
Even so, the weight of the wind pushing against his chest felt
like a hand holding him back.

The clouds were spun from iron filings, silver to grey to
black. They smeared across the pale grey, sunless sky. The
wind shrieked across the top of the waves, drew claw marks
across the water.

Billy rode up the waves, topped the broken whitecaps as if
sledding down a fast river. His spray skirt filled with water at
his lap, but no water came into his boat.

"I take refuge in the Buddha, I take refuge in the Dalai Lama,
I take refuge in the Dharma, I take refuge in the Sangha."

Billy had to make a decision. He could try to find a safe
place to land, but then he risked getting caught in the big
surf the storm was throwing up against the rocky bluffs to the
west; a ten-fathom shelf caused ocean swells to steepen dramatically on this part of the coastline. He could try to paddle
out past the shelf where the swells would flatten out, but then
he'd have to battle the wind to stay upright until he could find
a headland to hide behind or a broad passage he could take
back to inside waters.

He stopped paddling. He rode the waves up and down;

steadied himself with his paddle and kept his bow pointed into the wind. If the wind built much more, the waves would start cresting hard enough to roll him down the face of the swells. He'd rolled his boat before, first in a swimming pool in Sitka and then a couple of times in a lake for practice, but he didn't know how long he could maintain his strength in cold water. He didn't think he could fight the storm all night long.

He thought he was going to die. He thought about his parents back in California, about the early mornings when he was a baby and his baby feet left faint impressions on the lawn and how his footprints were never there just a few moments after. He pushed his paddle into the waves and felt himself growing weaker, felt himself fading away just like those footprints. He felt sad. Then angry. Then he heard easy laughter, the low rumble of the storm, and . . . "No fighting," he said to himself. He turned his boat with the wind and spread his shoulders to catch the storm.

The wind blew straight onto the steep coastline; the sea pounded against slick rocks, sending the broken teeth of the waves thirty feet into the air; white foam churned up, and Billy tasted saltwater in his mouth as his slender kayak plunged through the tumult.

He floated giddily above his fear. He shifted his weight almost imperceptibly; the boat cut into a wave and sledded down the slope.

He pulled the boat toward a narrow channel of green foam-mottled water and felt the sudden boost of a shore wave building beneath him; he cut back. He slid down a broken wave, and just before the white water tumbled over his shoulders, he and his boat were tossed out into an eddy of water behind a bluff.

It was like walking into a quiet room off a busy street—suddenly calm. The green sea rose and fell with the swells, but no water broke through the mouth of the small bight. Billy's hand shook; he reached under the spray skirt for a bandanna to wipe the seawater from his eyes. High above him in a cranny in the bluff, a peregrine falcon split the wind with its call. Three hundred feet up the rock wall, Billy saw trees surging back and forth in the wind.

There was no flat beach from which he could crawl out of his boat, and so he floated on water relentlessly rising and falling against the steep walls of the island. He ate flakes of fish that he'd caught and cooked the previous night; he lay them out on top of his spray skirt and ate them with two pieces of soggy pilot bread and half a piece of chocolate. He washed it all down with the last of his fresh water. And his boat dipped into the trough of a wave.

The wave didn't break, but the force of it slid up the side of the bluff, rebounded; rocks appeared and water eddied in circles. The tide was rising. The small ledge protecting the tiny bight was about to become awash and time was running out for Billy. In a few minutes, the waves would break through and his little seedpod of a boat would be ripped wide open. If he had to ride out a night at sea, he'd have to stay well clear of the rocks.

Billy hadn't thought of trying to get on the *Universe*, although he'd seen it moving down from the north; its lights had served as a frame of reference in the descending darkness. But it was lit up like a birthday cake in the tenebrous night, and its resplendence seemed remarkably close, and so Billy paddled. He pulled his boat up over the swells until the booming and sucking shoreline was behind him, and the wind died.

The lights came nearer. Billy saw the railings, the lights from the portholes, the lone figure of a woman in a long dress standing on the back deck of the ship and holding some strange kind of fishing pole. He felt like he was on a collision course with the *Universe*.

He didn't want to be caught in the wake, in churned waters that would snarl the already confused sea. But his hands shook and his spray skirt was undone; his legs were wet and he shivered. The adrenaline that had rushed through his body and carried him through the surf was leaving, and he felt light-headed, weak, and cold. The flakes of fish, the bread, the chocolate had been burned up half an hour ago, and now his teeth chattered.

"No fighting," he said out loud and reached for another chocolate bar. His paddle dropped. He reached for it reflexively, and a wave crested. He felt his boat give way and he tried to recover, but another wave slapped him in the face, then pulled him into the sea.

His gear drifted out of the boat. Sealed food bags, half-filled with air, floated like jellyfish; his yellow bag of documents drifted downwind, and he tried to swim after them but the water was too frigid, his strength was too feeble, and he felt the weight of his body pull him beneath the surface. He turned, raised his arm high into the air, and brought it down on the overturned hull of his floundering boat.

The lights of the ship spilled out over the water. Billy heard the engines churn, felt the wake of the bow wash over him, and threw out his arms to grip onto something in a world turning black.

@

THE *Universe* HAD come to a stop, and Bonnie stood on the deck pointing and shouting. A boat crew began lowering a lifeboat from station number eight, and before they could stop her, she jumped down into it. The crew wanted to lift the boat back up, but the sailor in charge motioned to lower away and another crewman put a life jacket on Bonnie. She allowed him to attach the straps but continued to point out into the darkness where just moments before she had seen the human arm rise up out of the water.

The lifeboat floundered in the water until they were able to start the motor and pull away from the ship. The waves rocked the little boat from side to side, but even so Bonnie stood on top of the middle seat pointing. Three crewmen held onto her legs, asking her politely to step down and be careful.

The lifeboat motored out into the darkness and as soon as it did, a spotlight on the deck of the *Universe* flashed a burning hole into the night. Bonnie could see a kayak overturned in the water, and the boatman steered toward it. But a half-dozen yards upwind, Bonnie could see someone floating just under the surface of the water. As soon as she saw it, she dove into the water and swam.

The water was so cold she felt as if she would pass out. The cold coursed through her body almost immediately, as if it were a drug being pumped into her veins. She flailed her arms, trying to swim, but the bulky life jacket kept her from moving well, so she unhooked the jacket and swam free. The sounds of the men on the boat were a slurry of voices. She found herself fighting back against a kind of sleepiness that was overtaking her. She started slapping the water with her arms, aware of breathing each new breath and pulling herself toward the man sinking in the water.

The spotlight followed her progress through the waves. The shaft of light turned the black water green and when she stopped swimming, she opened her eyes and saw a man with pale white skin suspended just underwater. With his arms out at his sides, he drifted there as if the light were holding him up. A few bubbles came from his mouth, and he looked up at her as if he had been waiting for her. What she remembered most clearly before she dove down to grab hold of his jacket was that he was smiling like a saint.

THEY BOTH WOKE up in the infirmary on the boat. They were covered in warm blankets that felt as if they had just come from the dryer. Hot pads sat on their chests and bellies, the extension cords running out from under the blankets.

The ship's doctor leaned over Billy and asked him if he knew where he was.

"I'm in the *Universe*," Billy said with a smile on his face.

"Exactly," the doctor said, and patted the shivering man's shoulder.

ALL OF BILLY'S gear scattered in the darkness that had closed in around the wake of the ship. Once the lifeboat crew had gotten both of the people out of the water, their only thought had been to get them back on board the SS *Universe*. Billy's tent, sleeping bag, the paddle, and the boat itself lay to the stern on top of the water. The bags of food had been wrapped too tightly to maintain buoyancy and drifted down and settled some six hundred feet below the surface where only the long-lived short raker rockfish swam among the bare stones.

But the yellow package with the money for the Dalai

Lama, Billy's passport, the photograph of his friends, and his unread copy of *The Tibetan Book of the Dead* floated on the surface of the great black sea, mindless and undisturbed.

CHAPTER NINE

THERE WAS BARELY a memorial service for Mouse Miller. Some of his friends brought the leftovers from Annabelle's service down to the deserted bar. Mrs. Cera brought some fresh black cod and some potato salad, but she did not stay. She hugged Miles and Clive, thanked Clive for finding Mouse, and left. Her eyes were rimmed red, and Miles thought that he had never seen the strong woman look so sad. He walked her to the boardwalk and touched her on the elbow as she turned silently toward home.

Weasel had a forty-five pound white king salmon that he brought straight up from the docks and laid on the bar with the shaved ice still stuffed into its belly. Within an hour, someone had set up the half-barrel grills in the yard, and the coals were almost ready for cooking. Someone had put a photograph of Mouse over the bar.

Fishermen balanced themselves on the uneven floor and passed around a bottle of schnapps. In a corner, a deckhand from Juneau played cribbage with Jerry Hughes. Miles and Clive walked in, and since it was only ten in the morning, both of them asked for a cup of coffee. Weasel poured some from his insulated jug, and the three of them toasted the portrait above the bar.

"Here's to strong hearts," Miles said, and drank his coffee.

"Was that it?" asked Weasel. "His heart gave out?"

Miles nodded. Mouse's body had been shipped to Anchorage the same morning Clive had found him, and they had gotten the report two days later. Mouse had died of a heart attack. "He ate badly, drank two fifths of whisky a day, and had a history of heart disease in his family. He was what they call in the trade 'at risk.'"

"Aw," said Weasel. "That's not it." He took a long pull on a bottle of beer. "He loved Ellie's barmaid, Kelly. She had black hair and a huge"—he held his hand out in front of his chest—"vocabulary, she really did. She was a master of the crosswords," and he laughed. "It near killed him when she died. You know how he liked the crosswords." He belched and wiped his mouth with his forearm.

"Did this Kelly with the huge vocabulary ever love Mouse in return?" Clive asked over the lip of his coffee mug.

"Not really. I mean she liked him and all. But you know, she basically ran the bar and Mouse liked to drink. It was more or less a professional relationship."

"To unrequited love," said Clive. He raised his cup, and the three of them drank. "The glue that holds us all together." They banged their drinks on the bar.

"What's up with this place?" Clive asked Miles. "Who owns it now?"

"Aw, it's a mess, like most every piece of property in this town. Mom didn't want it so she sold it to a guy who got divorced and his ex-wife's daughter sold it on a contract to some guy from Juneau who said he was going to open up a hotel, but of course he quit making his payments after the bank disapproved his loan for the hotel, and she's never gone through the process to call in the note."

"You think I can find the guy's name in the city office?"

"I suppose so." Miles stood up from the bar. He intended to go back to work. "Why do you want it?"

"I'm going to buy this place," said Clive, "and I'm going to open up my own bar slash church."

"A *what?*"

Clive explained. He had looked into getting a liquor license when he first came to town, but the town council, which met on a semi-regular basis, had discovered an old ordinance that allowed only as many liquor licenses as there were churches. The hardware store had a liquor license and sold beer and hard liquor, mostly by the case, to people in town and on the fishing boats; there was one church that allowed the town Catholics, Lutherans, and Unitarians to hold Sunday services, in that order. When Ellie's bar had closed down last time, so many people had moved out of town that the second church had closed. In order for Clive's new bar to receive a liquor license, there needed to be another church in town.

Of course Clive could have asked the town council to change the ordinance, but since there hadn't been a quorum at any of the last two dozen council meetings, this seemed a poor option. But the idea of closing down for drinking on Sunday and opening up for worship instead didn't seem like a bad one to him.

"I've seen you studying the Bible," Miles said. "Do you mind if I ask you, are you a Christian now that you got out of jail?"

Everyone at the fallen down old bar leaned in. Most of them had expectant smiles on their faces.

"Brother. I'll tell you," Clive said. "I love Jesus the way Mouse loved Kelly. Unabashedly. I love Jesus like I love Duke

Ellington and the great Satchmo, like I love the music of Bonnie Raitt and Joni Mitchell. I love Jesus like I love the opening
paragraph of *One Hundred Years of Solitude* and all the books
of P.G. Wodehouse. I love Jesus like Elvis loved his momma.
For in Jesus is forgiveness, love, joy, and happiness." Clive
lifted his beer as if to toast them all. "That love will always
be unrequited for the gift has already been given, and we just
have to get used to it. So one more time to the great Mouse
Miller, to his love, the beautiful and unattainable Kelly, and to
Ellie Hobbes, the anarchist mother of us all!"

The beers went up and a loud cheer could be heard far
back up the hill into the forest.

MILES WAS OF two minds about his brother's attempt to
buy Ellie's bar. It was a good idea, and he knew that Clive
would do a fine job of running a bar. But the money still
bothered him. Miles knew that somehow or another the cash
sewn into the jacket would eventually bring a storm of bad
luck down on all their heads.

But Clive had no such concern. For some reason the conversation with Lester and the finding of Mouse Miller had put
Clive's life in a new perspective. He was either suffering from
some new psychosis or he had developed a superpower, one
that allowed him to hear animals speak. And neither possibility frightened him, as long as the animals didn't start telling
him to kill people or to start picking random numbers for a
distant lotto. So three days after Mouse Miller's wake he flew
to Juneau and found the current owner of Ellie's bar sitting
in the Triangle Club downtown. He spoke to him about a
price, and when the owner said he was asking four hundred
thousand dollars, Clive held up an envelope with twenty-five

thousand dollars in cash and a contract to take over all payments and liabilities (which included several tax liens and a potential disastrous environmental clean-up necessitated by the fuel oil spill under the building). The owner took the cash, signed the contract, and ordered a round for the house.

Clive had already contacted Ellie's former legal representative. She was living down in Lewiston, Oregon. He proposed that he begin making payments on the property where the former buyer had left off, and she agreed, figuring some money coming in was better than no money, lawyer fees, and a rotting bar a thousand miles away.

MILES TOOK THE news of this new venture with a mixture of strong emotions. The thought of his ex-con brother in a legitimate business, most likely a very lucrative business, created in him a kind of giddiness that only other worried siblings may know. But on the other side of the emotional color wheel there was the rising of a kind of sharply focused dread. Clive was spreading the money around the region with equanimity, which was sure to attract attention: the attention of the police and eventually the attention of the original owner of all the parka money.

Clive continued with his project, showing little concern for his brother's fears. He began work down at the site in early June. He had rough-cut yellow cedar brought in by a young boat builder down the inlet, and he bought new pilings to shore up the foundation. He had an engineer come and give an estimate for cleaning up the spilled oil, and he paid a couple of local kids to dig out the contaminated soil with shovels for less than half the estimated cost.

Clive patched the roof, and any afternoon that had more than an hour of sunshine, he scraped and painted the outside of the building. He painted it white, added red trim, and hung a new sign over the door. The sign was much larger than the old one, and it hung prominently over the boardwalk. Clive called the new bar Mouse Miller's Love Nest.

BILLY ENDED UP enjoying life on the *Universe*. He was given a room in the crew quarters right next to where the members of the orchestra bunked, and he was allowed to eat in the dining hall with the passengers. After being fished out of the north Pacific, Billy seemed to have developed a large appetite. He ate as if he could end all suffering at the three offered meals and lined up for every midnight buffet and sundae bar.

Bonnie had never saved anyone's life before, and she wasn't quite sure of the protocol. The captain was horrified that she had gone into the water and threatened to fire every member of the lifeboat crew. But the cruise director eventually convinced him of the public relations value of declaring them all "heroes" and even agreed to have Bonnie and Billy sit at his table two evenings in a row, nodding and making a show to each of the passengers who passed and stared, some of them being bold enough to come and shake Bonnie's hand and marvel at her courage.

Both Bonnie and Billy were dumbfounded. Billy was mostly overwhelmed by rich food and sat at the captain's table in a caloric haze. Bonnie meanwhile was on new emotional ground, having saved someone's life. After coming out of the ocean, her old life, her old melancholy, seemed to have been left behind somewhere in the wake of the lumbering ship.

She liked this new feeling, but she couldn't quite give words to it. She couldn't describe it to her mother when she talked to her on the ship's satellite phone. She could not describe the feeling to herself.

And so, she fell in love with Billy, thinking that since he was the most tangible evidence of her adventure, she had to keep hold of him if she were going to preserve this new life in its current form.

She moved out of her room for the rest of the cruise and bunked down in the crew quarters with Billy.

"It's not like love," she said to him as she squeezed into the narrow metal bunk bolted to the bulkhead, "it's more like waking up from a dream."

She kissed him, and they took each other's warm breath into their own lungs, and their hands felt the warmth of skin created by their bodies' burning calories. They were alive again, together, and this was something Billy enjoyed. Looking back on it, he saw that he enjoyed eating crab cakes and fresh asparagus. He enjoyed making love to a beautiful woman who had saved his life.

The four noble truths taught that life was suffering, and suffering could be overcome by overcoming desire. But he had to admit to himself that he didn't simply enjoy this new life, he craved it now, all the more so because he had spent his entire life not knowing that there was such pleasure possible on this earth. He craved the feeling of his own warm body after he had been taken out of the Pacific. He suspected all the more now that he was a crappy Buddhist. He still wanted to meet the Dalai Lama, but there was no getting off the *Universe* until it came into port. So he kissed Bonnie and lay in that narrow bed beside her as if he had fallen out of the sky from a jet airplane and had landed safely beside her. So they drank and ate and slathered their skins against each other's in the narrow bunk. At night they clattered up the metal stairs in borrowed formal clothes and danced to the ship's little orchestra.

The kids in the band were all music students from Oberlin. There were only seven of them, but the ship insisted on referring to them as "the orchestra" even though they were clearly a band. Rick was the tenor sax player and had put the band together after the Christmas break the year before. He had cajoled, and sometimes bullied, his friends into joining him on this northern gig. Rick looked a bit like Bono, and he knew how to work any room made up of any age group. Earl was the drummer. He was black and had a wispy goatee and horn-rimmed glasses. Nix was a young white girl who played the bass as if she were dancing with it. She had short brown hair and multiple piercings, all of which she had to either hide or allow to heal up while she worked on the ship. Rick had explained that you simply couldn't play Cole Porter while wearing a goat head stud through your tongue. Nix had rolled her eyes but took the stud out. The rest of the band reminded Billy of children attending a wedding, faces flushed from their ill-fitted formal shirts.

But they loved to play. They performed three sets a night and then backed up various solo performers. They played '40s music at seven, '50s music at nine, and something called "contemporary" music at eleven. Every other night they played for the cabaret singer or did the Broadway medleys for the operatic duo from San Francisco.

The band was intensely interested in Billy. The idea of him paddling through the dark of the north Pacific struck them as something almost mythic. Late at night, they would pile into the tiny room and hunch onto the floor to eat junk food (which the band seemed to prefer over the ship's cuisine), smoke pot, and talk about Alaska. Billy held court during these sessions, and he relished the role of the story-teller pulled from the sea.

Nix, particularly, was interested in the stories about Cold Storage. She liked hearing about Lester and Clive. She tried to imagine a community clinging to the side of the mountains with no roads, no cars, and virtually no sense of the outer world. She ate handfuls of greasy cocktail peanuts and leaned her head against the hard bulkhead and tried to imagine such a place.

Nix had a boyfriend in Portland. He was a fiddle player, and sometimes he would fill in on guitar. He would play any-where but preferred traditional Irish music. There was a big Irish scene in Portland, and Nix had sat in on many of the all-night sessions in one of the three pubs that hosted them. She liked the sessions but was getting tired of her boyfriend, who was in danger of becoming an IRA-style Catholic. Nix had taken the Alaskan gig with her old schoolmates as an easy out from the situation. She had moved all of her things out of their apartment and into storage before her boyfriend had noticed anything was wrong. She had said goodbye over the phone from a booth in Vancouver.

Billy would sometimes tell stories well into the early morning. He'd talk about whales rubbing their backs on the bottom of his fishing boat, and about the fights in the movie club, and the time a brown bear got into the café and had actually crawled into the chest freezer. He told about Mouse Miller being in love with the barmaid and disappearing from sight, and he told about the time a fisherman was beaten to death by a giant halibut that had landed in his boat, and how they had served the same halibut at his wake.

The band from Oberlin listened and snacked and dreamed their own Disneyfied version of Billy's adventures. Earl beat his sticks against his thighs. Nix practiced her finger exercises. Bonnie sat up on one elbow with a blanket covering her bare body and played with the ends of Billy's hair as Billy told story after story about the world he had left behind.

The boat put into Vancouver on the last day of the cruise. Billy found out that afternoon that the Dalai Lama had canceled his appearance in Seattle after some security issues were discovered, and Billy breathed a sigh of relief. He knew he wasn't worthy. He hadn't been meditating, he hadn't finished his journey, and he had lost all the money, anyway. He felt a certain sense of peace when he learned the Dalai Lama's plans had also changed.

So Billy decided to stay on the *Universe*. The band hired him on as a percussionist and backup vocalist. There was not much of a problem getting on the band's roster, because they had sailed with one musician short when the original trombone player broke his leg skateboarding the week before the first sailing. Billy just had to fill out a few pieces of paperwork, and he was on.

Bonnie got a job in the ship's library. This job was a little harder to get, but Bonnie had dropped a couple of hints that she might have suffered a back injury as a result of her rescue from the water. The ship's lawyers claimed not to be concerned about any liability, but when an assistant librarian quit because of seasickness, Bonnie was offered the job.

On that afternoon the *Universe* sailed from the dock at

Vancouver with Bonnie and Billy as staff members, the sun was glittering off the water, and a few people waved from the dock. Bonnie stood out on the deck and waved to her mother, who had flown to Vancouver to try and take her daughter home. Bonnie waved and blew kisses while her mother wept. Billy was looking resplendent in his new black pants, white shirt and formal red bow tie. He was knocking on a wood block as the quartet played a samba on the back deck. And so the *Universe* moved slowly away from the dock for its trip back toward Alaska.

CHAPTER TEN

I T WAS THE second week of June, and Jake Shoemaker was sitting at his breakfast table in Seattle harassing Miss Peel over the telephone. Miss Peel was upset; Jake was trying to calm her down. The police had been around again. They'd raided the warehouse and hadn't found anything incriminating, but they kept coming around trying to bully everyone into snitching off their boss, and Jake was having to do a lot of hand-holding.

Clive had been right about one thing: Miss Peel needed to be kept happy. She knew so much that she could put Jake away for a very long time. He also knew that she was smart enough to have hidden copies of everything in some safety deposit box somewhere. Miss Peel had many admirers—sports stars, several of them, famous men who were in the papers nearly every week. One of them clearly loved her and sent her flowers as often as he was in the paper. If anything bad were to happen to Miss Peel, it would be noticed. It would be investigated vigorously. Also, Jake was sure there were portions in her will and testament that read, "If anything of a suspicious nature should happen upon my death . . ." At least she could be trusted. The ballplayers were insurance both ways; she wouldn't want her gangster connections coming out while she was still in play.

Jake had been riding a seesaw with his fortunes. On one hand, it turned out to be a good thing that Clive had cleared the money out of the unit; if he hadn't, it would be sitting in some evidence room right now and Jake would have no hope of ever seeing it again. On the other hand, it was a bit of bad luck that he had shot Oscar in the knee because it had pissed the man off and sent him running. He suspected Oscar had snitched him off; the cops kept asking about a gun and about Oscar's whereabouts.

Jake said that he'd be happy to talk with the police and get all of this mess cleared up; they just needed to set up an appointment with his lawyer; and the cops took that and walked away, lumbered down the steps leaving Jake smiling at their back. They'd soon discover that his lawyer would no more set up an interview to talk with the police than waive his fee.

Life in Seattle was heating up. Real estate was looking good. Banks for some reason were loving to lend him money. But the computer kids were total pains in the asses. When they weren't sulky about not having a basketball court in their office suites, they would complain about the coffee, for Christ's sake. Jake was ready to drown the whole lot of them like kittens.

Adding to his peevishness was the fact that Jake's lawyer had started hinting around that he should be putting together cash for bail money, and had flat-out advised that it might be a good time to go on a long fishing trip in Mexico. But Jake didn't want to leg it; start running and you have to be ready to keep running, and he wasn't ready. He had to be somewhere his agent could find him; he had to be somewhere where he could entertain producers and money men if they ever became interested in one of his scripts. So he smoothed Miss Peel's feathers and helped her get the bail money together from his various interests.

He was focusing most of his creative energy into *Till Death Do Us Part*. He'd decided to make it a bit more topical by making the lead roles—a couple who worked together as covert CIA operatives—Jewish, while their therapist would be Arab-American. He'd already drafted the early scenes where the husband and wife go to the marriage counselor for the first time, and it was funny—or it would be as soon as he smoothed it out. He could see any number of stars fighting over it. He just had to get away from the cops, lawyers, and the cokeheads for a few months. And if he could just get that money back from Clive he could solve all his problems in one fell swoop. But no one knew where Clive was.

Jake put out feelers. His lawyer's investigator had contacts at McNeil, where Clive had been inside. No one had a line on him. The investigator had run records and talked to the usual jailhouse snitches but had come up dry. Jake had received a report from the investigator, along with his last outrageously inflated bill. The only information in the report was from a cabdriver who had given someone who matched Clive's description a place to stay for the night, someone who called himself Stilton Cheesewright, which was no doubt Clive. The cabbie mentioned something about this Cheesewright going to pick up his dog. Jake snorted and tried to rub the sleep from his eyes. He knew for a fact that Clive's fleabag of a dog was dead, and the ugly new guard dog was missing.

Jake was angry. It wasn't easy to find someone who had no home, no car, and no mailbox or email address; it was even harder to find someone who was traveling on cash. The investigator had worked a source in the probation department but had come to a dead end. They wouldn't give up any addresses, just told the investigator that Clive had family in Alaska. But unfortunately Alaska covered a lot of fucking real estate.

He was in a situation where he was spending money to recover money. This was not something he enjoyed. He considered making another call to this shit heel of an investigator and telling him to get back on it, get him a name of a relative or something. Jesus! How hard could it be?

But he didn't want to bring on any more unnecessary stress. So he took some deep breaths and a sip of fresh orange juice and opened the paper. It was there on the third page of the second section in a two-column AP story that Jake found the answer to what he was looking for. His eyes widened, and he started smiling in a grateful kind of disbelief.

"I'll be a son of a bitch!" he said, reached for his orange juice and knocked it over in his excitement.

IT WAS THE first week of June, Billy was in the middle of his third cruise of the season. He was standing on the bandstand up in front of the band, singing, "Do Nothing Until You Hear From Me." He was singing more and more solos on each trip, and he loved it. He loved standing in front of the band with his eyes closed and his hands gripped around the mic stand. Billy sang, and he felt the ship sway under his feet. As he sang, he imagined the *Universe* flying through the green water of Dixon Entrance north of Vancouver Island; he imagined the flat, sandy bottom of the ocean three hundred fathoms below his feet. He felt his mind unspooling as he sang. He glimpsed the dancers, felt the sway of the ocean in his legs.

He imagined the waves, and the whales swimming through the gloom beneath the ship. He imagined his lost gear—the kayak, the packet of money for the Dalai Lama—floating over the north Pacific, and he felt no yearning, no loss, only a sense of lightness as if the top of his head had been removed and his mind were able to rise up out of his body.

So it was more than a surprise—it was almost a collapse of his imaginative world—when he went to the Vancouver Post Office three days later and opened an envelope that contained his battered passport, *The Tibetan Book of the Dead* and a letter.

THERE ON PAGE three of Jake's copy of the *Seattle Times* was a somewhat overexposed picture of some people jammed together around a table. In the center of the group was a goofy long-haired man being given some money. Two things struck Jake immediately: the first was that the man handing the money over was Clive McCahon, and the other was that it was *his* fucking money Clive was giving away.

The headline above the article read: "Lost Donation Finds Its Way to the Dalai Lama." Above the first photo was a larger one of a smiling Tibetan described as "a secretary to his Holiness the fourteenth Dalai Lama happily displaying the watertight package found in the Pacific and forwarded to Dharamsala, India."

A quote in a box next to the article said, "Good fortune has allowed this small package to survive a dangerous and uncertain journey. His Holiness is grateful to Mr. William Cox of Cold Storage, Alaska, and to the person who sent his generous donation on to India."

The article described how the package appeared in Dharamsala with a postmark in Kodiak. Some anonymous fisherman had apparently found the waterproof pack and sent it on to the Dalai Lama. The reporter noted that William Cox had been located and was working as a shipboard musician on an Alaskan cruise ship. He had not been contacted for comment. The photograph represented friends and well-wishers from the small fishing village, and one resident, the local health care provider, Miles McCahon, was quoted as saying, "We're happy that Billy is all right and glad that the money found its way to His Holiness."

"Son of a bitch!" Jake said once again and reached for his telephone.

IN COLD STORAGE, it was a beautiful summer day. Clive was finishing up the painting on the outside trim and playing an old vinyl record of Spike Jones. He smiled, bounced on his feet in time to the bicycle horns and slide whistles squealing out from the rattling big band panic. Little Brother lay on a piece of tin roofing, soaking up the heat of the day, slowly raising his head as a raven hopped along the railing of the boardwalk with a brown strip of a potato peel drooping out of the side of its beak. The raven strutted along the rail and teased the big earless dog.

"Ugly. Ugly. Ugly," was all the bird said.

Clive waved his paintbrush at his dog. "You're scaring the customers, you know." Little Brother glanced over at Clive, saying nothing, then went back to languidly watching the big black bird.

"Your job is to throw them out when they get rowdy, not keep them from coming in."

He put his brush into the paint can and walked over to Little Brother, came to within three feet and started to put his hand out. But the brindled dog stood up. He backed away, the heavy roofing underneath him buckling. He didn't growl or show his teeth, but he stared at Clive with eyes that burned like cigarettes.

"All right, all right. I was just asking you to consider the options." Clive turned to go inside.

At the bar, unofficially open now, five men sat and talked about Billy's amazing rescue; dance music loped in and out of the open windows. It was a fine sunny day in rain country.

"The lucky bastard was flopping around out there in the dark, and he gets scooped up by a cruise ship."

"How'd you hear that?" asked Clive.

"Are you kidding? Reporters have been calling all over town. They're loving this story. Haven't you talked to any of them? They'll talk to anybody who will pick up the receiver."

"Reporters?" Clive watched the raven outside; it stood barking at the big dog, taunting him with his prize potato skin.

"Yeah, reporters. They're loving this story about how the money you gave to Billy found its way all the way to India."

"They asking about me?" Clive asked tentatively.

"They don't know your name, but they want to know who was in that picture. But you know, we don't say anything about you or nothing. We just say the money was raised by the community. That's okay, don't you think, Clive?"

"Yeah . . . yeah . . . sure, it's okay." Clive watched the raven drop the potato peel, bark twice at the woofing dog, and fly up into the blue summer sky, saying, "Bye. Bye. Bye."

"Yeah, that's fine," he repeated.

"Good, now can we try some of that new tap beer? You know, for quality control purposes."

"Absolutely." Clive reached down for the hose attached to

the rusty keg beneath the bar. Little Brother came back inside and sat on the sleeping bag laid out in the spot where Mouse Miller had died.

BILLY READ THE letter from the Dalai Lama's secretary with a mixture of panic and amazement. Billy had been living on the ship for the last forty-nine days like a man who had been born again into a life of satiated desire. He had been pulled from the sea by a woman who wanted to love him; he had been eating his fill of rich food and telling stories of his old home, embellished stories to feed his ego, and they had started to become almost like fables in his mind.

But now here was his old passport—his old identity—and it smelled like home. He held the passport up to his nose, picked up a whiff of sulfur water and fuel oil. He flipped through the pages and inexplicably felt as if he had been taken prisoner by that village. The stories in his mind sank away into his chest, where the reality of that place—the rain, the bickering, and the depression—seemed to have always resided. Unlike a cruise ship, Cold Storage was well-suited for the life of denial.

In the letter, the secretary explained that he'd gotten Billy's new address in Vancouver from a member of the press; he'd assumed that "Mr. Cox" would want his official papers and reading material back. The secretary thanked him for his kind donation and wished him health and good fortune on his journey.

Inside the book, the secretary had placed a small photograph of His Holiness. It was a postcard-size official portrait of the Buddhist monk in his robe sitting and staring at the camera with an expression of dignity and intelligence. But staring at the photo, Billy knew the Dalai Lama had been suppressing a laugh, as if he knew exactly how silly Billy looked in his tuxedo. He slid the picture back into his book and, with a heavy heart, took the longest possible route back to the ship.

ON THE NIGHT after Billy had recovered his passport, the fabric of his new life began to come unraveled.

There had been dissension in the band before this. The cruise director, a perky Australian who had been a singer in a dinner theater company in Key West before signing on the *Universe*, felt directly responsible for the enjoyment of every single passenger who came up the gangplank. She took her job very seriously. For the last two trips, she had been forwarding complaints about the band to Rick and saying that the "contemporary" music was getting "a bit wild." There had been reports that they'd done a version of "Roadrunner" by Jonathan Richman.

"Do you really think that was appropriate?" she'd asked the band leader.

"Roadrunner" had been Nix's idea. She was going stir crazy. On each cruise, she made friends with the two or three younger passengers and encouraged their requests for newer music. She'd tried everything, even ska versions of rhythm and blues tunes and playing Richard Thompson's waltz time numbers with horn accompaniment. She watched couples in knitted Irish sweaters and deck shoes happily dancing, not paying the least attention to the twisted lyrics about red hair and black leather. But the cruise director heard.

Billy and Bonnie's cabin had become the unofficial club room of the band, and it seemed the best place to clear the air, even though Bonnie was in bed trying to recover from a cold.

"Listen, Rick, I never signed up for this kind of gig." Earl threw a stick onto the dresser. "You told us there would be a variety of material. You told us it wouldn't be a painful boom-chuck–Imperial Room–cocktail lounge-off-the-interstate kind of scene. Christ! It's way worse. You said we would have one set a night where we could choose the material. If that's not the case anymore, I want to know right now."

"We signed a contract," Rick sighed. "We work for the cruise director, and she told me we would have one set, but she also told me the music had to suit the audience, that we couldn't play free jazz or experimental music."

"This is hardly Sun Ra," Nix said. "We're just talking about something with a few different rhythms. They could have gotten a polka band if that's really what they wanted. Besides, there are plenty of people who like Richard Thompson." She sat beside Bonnie, who rolled over and put a pillow over her head.

The argument sprayed out. They discussed the subtleties of the tunes in their repertoire; charges and countercharges were laid, the trumpet player threw some cheese curls at Rick, and Rick's face darkened in anger.

Outside, Dall's porpoises played in the wake of the ship. They pushed through the water like torpedoes and burst onto the surface, their black and white bodies shooting into the sunlight. Passengers on deck cheered while the musicians argued about the changes in their arrangement of "Stardust."

"Listen, Rick!" Nix said. "I'm not saying Hogie Carmichael isn't a fucking genius. I just want to play some different tunes." She bounced up and down on the bed, her arms held tightly to her sides, like a child about to break into tears.

"Wait," Billy said from the upper bunk. He had not said one word so far throughout the entire argument. All the players stopped, stared up at him. "I know exactly what we can do."

CHAPTER ELEVEN

B Y LATE JULY, the salmon were starting up into the rivers to spawn and die. Once in fresh water, they became humped and hook-nosed, their bodies already beginning to rot. But out in saltwater, these late season fish were bright and quick. These were the fish Miles was determined to catch.

Miles had heard nothing from Trooper Brown, but he knew that there was a visit coming. Clive had been making too many things happen not to be noticed. There was the liquor license, and the business license, and money changing hands. And Weasel seemed busier than usual: talking on the public phones at the head of the dock, using the one computer at the library, even taking his old wooden boat out past the inlet. Each day that he didn't see Trooper Brown walk into his clinic, Miles felt lucky; each moment that he didn't need to be in the clinic, he wanted to be out in his skiff, if for nothing else than to be somewhere else when Brown did blast through his door.

Besides the occasional prayer made to Japanese outboard engines, Miles was extremely practical when it came to fishing. He was good with all manner of salmon but king salmon, and this flaw was irritating him. Lester had told him that Tlingit elders believed that the fish only came to those who were worthy of catching them. This, Miles believed, was a faith promulgated by a core group of successful fishermen. He was beginning to wonder if there was a religion for the consistently unlucky.

He rounded the point and ducked into the lee of two small islands out near the northern opening of the inlet. He could feel what was left of the swells moving from the outside; these little swells were lifting his boat up and down, but there was hardly a breath of wind on the water. Miles went about rigging his gear and lowering it into the water; he set the engine on the lowest possible idle and started pushing along at a moderate trolling speed.

It was then, with the motor geared down and his line taut against the pull of the flasher, only then that he forgot about his brother's criminal enterprise. He forgot about his mother's sudden absence from this world, and he had finally forgotten his bad luck as a fisherman. He was just sitting in the sunlight, empty headed, and here, as if empty headedness was the one element that was necessary for his good luck to come, was the exact moment when it did.

The line pulled tight as hard and fast as if the whole world were on the other end. He jerked back on the pole. He cranked on the reel, and the pole bowed. He reeled, and the drag spun, letting the fish run; he tightened down the drag and pulled harder. Thirty yards off, the salmon broke the surface of the water and flashed in the sunlight. Miles breathed hard, his knuckles white from the pressure he was putting on the pole.

The line twitched and jerked, and Miles leaned back. The salmon dove under the skiff and for a moment Miles thought it was off, but he kept reeling, putting more and more strength into his grip until he saw a flash of silver close to the rail. He reached over carefully with one hand for his net. He held his pole up high and gently pulled his net toward the head of the tired fish from behind.

There was a flash, and a tug, and all of the shaking, silver energy of the ocean teetered on the lip of the net. With one arm, he tried lifting the big fish. He struggled. He lifted again, but his line went slack and the hook flipped out of the lower jaw; Miles dropped his pole and lunged with the net.

But the fish was gone, the pole was in the water, and all of the earth's slippery energy dissipated into the dark.

"Fuck it!" Miles said, and threw the pole out of the boat. "Goddamn son of a bitching motherfucker," he swore. He slapped his hands against his thighs. He looked at the engine and slapped the housing. "And you shut up!" he threatened.

But then, of course, when he pulled on the starter cord hoping to recover the pole floating thirty feet from the boat, the engine would not start.

"I'm sorry," Miles said. His voice had the faint quaver of a man who was either going to find religion or give up fishing.

"I'm sorry," he repeated and sat there waiting for forgiveness.

THE OPENING DAY of Mouse Miller's Love Nest took on the atmosphere of a solstice festival in Cold Storage. Flags flew from porches all around town, and from the flagpole in front of the bar flew both an American and an Alaskan flag. Clive had given six tours to groups of citizens, including one group of kids from the school.

Into this atmosphere, Trooper Brown arrived for a second visit. The plane landed just after nine in the morning, and Miles had come down to pick up some clinic supplies arriving from Juneau. The pilot was handing Clive his three boxes from the cargo hold when Ray Brown stormed down the ramp in his blue uniform.

Clive looked up, smiled and put his hand out. "I'm Clive McCahon. I bet you want to talk with me."

Trooper Brown skidded to a stop, and all the creaking leather on his utility belt became silent.

"Yeah, well, I have a federal subpoena for you to appear and produce records for the US attorney in Tacoma, Washington."

Clive looked at the papers. He looked down at the ground around him. "What do you think, Trooper? Are we above mean high tide?"

"What do I care?"

"Just wondering," Clive said as he fished into his own jacket pocket. He pulled out some old paperwork sealed in the kind of plastic bag that one might freeze salmon in. "It just means that as long as we are above mean high tide we are on Township land, which is good for you on one hand but bad for you on another."

"Cut the crap, McCahon. The US attorney in Tacoma wants you down there pronto, and I don't have to waste any more time with you."

"Now that's true, Trooper. But have you ever met Willa Perlmutter in Anchorage, Alaska? She's a lovely woman. Are you single, Trooper? Willa Perlmutter is single, I believe. At least she was when I went into the joint. Lovely woman, the mind of Voltaire and the body of a Brazilian swimsuit model."

"I'm married, wise guy."

"Too bad. A runner. Very spirited. Hardly rests in the pursuit of the interests of her clients. Willa Perlmutter of Anchorage, Alaska, is my attorney."

"Listen, I don't really care."

"I realize this. But for one thing, you have no fucking authority to be serving a federal subpoena on township land, flat foot. And for another, if you can read, which I doubt, the US attorney has been notified by the lovely Willa Perlmutter, as noted and acknowledged by the US attorney himself, that she herself—the lovely W. Perlmutter—would be the point of service for all legal notices and subpoenas for said Clive McCahon in perpetuity or, as far as your fat ass is concerned, until hell freezes over."

"Bullshit, McCahon, this is a Washington case." Trooper Brown started frowning now so that great deep furrows of fat curled above his nose.

"Not that this matters in the least in this instance, fat boy, this being a federal case, but did I tell you, Trooper, that among all of Willa Perlmutter's lovely features, the loveliest is the fact that she is a member of the bar of both Alaska and Washington? So, you can take this subpoena and hip hop on up to Anchorage, and/or Bremerton, where the LWP has one of her fine-ass offices, and serve her there. And when you do, she and I will begin the months-long process of asserting my Fifth Amendment right against self-incrimination by whittling away what questions I can and cannot answer and, when it comes down to it, I will answer the big payoff question that everyone wants to ask and the answer to that is this: Jake Shoemaker is a doof who wants to make easy money and watches too many movies. He is not a federal grunt or a gangbanger. He loves his Second Amendment, but he is no gangster."

"So you must of shot the warehouseman?"

"What the fuck?"

"Oscar Laurentis, if Jake is such a Gandhi. You must have blown Oscar Laurentis's knee off."

Clive wasn't feeling so smart now. "I don't know anything about that. Talk with my attorney, talk to Willa. This conversation is over."

Brown grunted, turned toward the waiting airplane and slammed the door shut. Clive watched the thin door bow out as Brown fumbled for the seat belt and got the ends connected. The trooper slapped the pilot on the shoulder, and the engine sputtered to life.

AT TWELVE NOON, when Mouse Miller's Love Nest's doors officially opened to the public, a crowd of people poured into the bar. The turntable was spinning an LP of the Turtles singing "Happy Together," and Weasel was sitting there at the corner of the bar wearing aviator sunglasses and his best Hawaiian shirt, looking for all the world like a Jimmy Buffett-style drug runner. By twelve thirty, people were dancing to Kitty Wells. By two, they were listening to The Doors, The Kinks, and Marvin Gaye. People brought food, the barbeque was once again set up in the front yard, and Tina and Miles helped tend bar. Ed was learning his way around the tough lies on the pool table, and Clive was behind the bar thumbing through the Bible, brushing up for his first service.

He had considered showing a church service from a television broadcast since he could hook up on satellite, but he decided he was going to refuse to allow a television or any high-tech entertainment in the Love Nest. The Love Nest was to be a haven away from American pop culture. If someone wanted to listen to a sporting event, Clive would try to find it on the radio, but people were going to have to look at each other while they listened. He had an expensive stereo system with a shortwave and FM receiver, as well as a new turntable. Carl Erickson, who had been a logger until he was laid off three years ago, had volunteered to climb the spruce tree behind the Love Nest and place an antenna at the very top. This dramatically improved the radio reception. The first night Clive had tried the shortwave, he listened to dance music from Cuba while finishing the plumbing repairs under the bar.

Since televangelism was out of the question for this church service, he flipped through Luke and John, cruising through the New Testament hoping to find a long passage about the power of love without referring to the need for obedience. He didn't want to scare off potential customers with his first sermon.

But the music kept distracting him. His head bobbing along with Marvin Gaye, he considered playing "What's Going On" at the service and throwing the floor open to discussion. He slammed the Bible shut and started thumbing through the LPs.

In his mother's house, he had found a large collection of vinyl, including his old records from childhood. He envisioned keeping these in a cabinet next to the bar; if customers wanted to hear a particular record, they could ask whoever was working to put it on for them. There would be no video games to ruin the solemnity of the atmosphere.

Clive had done his best to recondition the ancient pool table. The floor had been shored up and the table itself was level, but the felt and the slate top had somehow warped slightly and developed some interesting characteristics that greatly improved the playing advantage for players with local knowledge. One had likened it more to putting on an undulating green than playing pool.

Clive had reattached the money that had once hung from the ceiling, and people were encouraged to stand on the bar and pin up more. The beautiful barmaid loved by Mouse Miller had died of breast cancer, so Clive pledged every dollar on the ceiling and some percentage of the opening day's receipts to a women's health center in Sitka, and he had hung a picture of Kelly at one end of the bar with the only known portrait of Mouse beside it. The photographer had caught Kelly standing behind the bar, gently scolding him, trying to avoid having her picture taken. Her awkward pose and laughing face told Clive that she was a woman almost certainly worthy of Mouse's unrequited love. She looked both intelligent and modest, a woman with whom it would have been a pleasure to spend a couple of hours on a stormy afternoon. There was also a photograph of Ellie Hobbes and Slippery Wilson, the original founders, at the crest of the roof beams.

The portrait of Mouse was some twenty years old and showed a healthy young man wearing a dirty white cap and grey halibut coat; he was standing in the trolling pit of his little wooden boat and working the gear. He looked strong and capable: one of the last hunter-gatherers. In the photograph, the sun was painting strips of light up the side of the boat and onto the fisherman at work.

The night before the bar was to open, Clive had mounted the two portraits with heavy screws that showed through the frames; he intended them to be a permanent fixture in the bar. He drove the last screw and put the driver into his back pocket, looked at the interior of his new life's adventure, wiped his hands on a bar rag he had stuck in the front of his belt, and gave a satisfying sigh. The Love Nest would be a dignified shelter for both drinking and prayer.

After dinner, the bar thinned out, and kids ran back and forth with plates of food. Clive changed records, and Weasel kept asking for Frank Sinatra doing "Fly Me to the Moon"; Clive played it twice but when Weasel asked for it a third time, he exercised his imperial discretion.

"No," he declared. He played one entire side of The Band's *Music from Big Pink* while Weasel sat quietly on his stool.

Little Brother didn't seem to notice all the people. He stayed close to his pad near the corner of the bar, slept sometimes but raised his head whenever he sensed a cross tone of voice or heard the sharp thump of a chair.

"That dog's going to eat somebody," observed Lester.

"I just hope it isn't somebody I like." Clive set a glass of iced tea in front of him and waved off Lester's gesture to pay.

"Don't take this the wrong way . . ." Lester paused a moment. "But I've been thinking about what you asked me about a while back."

"About the animals . . . umm . . . talking?"

Lester nodded and looked around the bar to see the happy faces of the patrons. "You talk to anybody else about that?" He steadied his eyes on Clive.

"Just a couple of mice in my room." Clive smiled.

"You ever get anything out of the ugly mutt?" and he nodded toward Little Brother. Neither Lester nor the dog were smiling, and both of them were staring at Clive.

"It's a funny thing . . ." Clive leaned in and spoke softly. "The big dumbbell never says a thing. Silent like a tomb."

"Dumb . . ." Lester said, almost as if to himself. "It's just this . . . If he does ever say anything, will you let me know?"

"Sure, Lester, but . . ."

"To the owner of the Love Nest!" Lester lifted his glass of iced tea, raised his voice. Everyone looked toward him as he said, "And to the best bouncer on the coast."

"To the Love Nest!" Voices roamed around the room, fell silent. Everyone swallowed and slammed their glasses down.

The evening wore on peacefully enough. The opening day crowd gradually wandered out, and a core group of drinkers and pool players were left listening to Dolly Parton on the record player. Robbie Robertson and Pearl Jam were replaced by *West Side Story*. Clive cut some drinkers off before they were ready, but no insolence lasted long in the festive atmosphere.

By closing time, Clive was serving more free coffee and soda pop than mixed drinks. Tina and Miles had gone home. Weasel and Ed had left to watch some movies that had come in on a plane that afternoon; they'd invited Clive over to watch *The Piano* after he got off work, but he'd told them not to wait up.

Finally the place was quiet, and Clive turned off the stereo to listen to the wind washing through the tree limbs above the bar. The place smelled fine, more like coffee than cigarettes, and the furniture didn't seem tired yet after this first night.

"Good night," he said aloud to the room and turned to the dog. "What are you going to do? You can come up to the house if you want. Or you can stay here. What will it be?"

Little Brother stood up, stretched. He too cast a glance around the room, although more suspiciously, and walked to the front door and stood there, staring straight ahead.

"Home it is, then." Clive grabbed his cash bag full of the night's receipts, and they walked out into the night.

The late summer sky was dark. There was a hint of silver on the western edges of the horizon, and Clive stood for a moment looking at the dark outlines of the islands humped up to the west. The wind continued sighing, and he thought for a moment about going to watch the movie with Ed and Weasel; then he thought of hunting up the girl who worked at the cold storage but he had heard that she had found her parrot and had gone fishing with a guy from the longline fleet and wouldn't be back until the fall, if she came back to Cold Storage at all.

So he turned and walked south toward his mother's house. The alder trees and the thick bramble of salmonberry vines darkened the way, and the great ugly dog stopped at the steps to Annabelle's house to wait for Clive.

Except for when they'd flown into town six months ago, Clive had not touched Little Brother, nor had anyone else in Cold Storage as far as Clive knew. Little Brother was clearly a fixture at the bar and it could not be said he was a feral dog, but neither could it be said that he actually "belonged" to Clive.

Now he saw the dog watching something hidden ahead of them. A deep growl, like grinding rocks, came from his chest. His eyes were fixed on some phantom in the brush. Clive moved to walk around him, but the dog took two steps ahead and blocked his way.

"I'm going to go to bed. You can take care of whatever's out there." He stepped around the bristling dog. "But if you kill another cat, it's coming out of your wages." He tried once more to walk around him, but the dog would not let him pass.

Clive reached out and nudged him three times with the toe of his right shoe, but the dog would not move.

Clive took a step back and raised his leg as if to actually kick at him. That's when Little Brother turned and looked straight at him and said, "What have I done to you that you have struck me these three times?"

Clive froze. Along the boardwalk, footsteps padded toward them.

"What did you say?" Clive asked, surprised mostly by the dog's strange diction.

Then Little Brother said, "Look up."

And he did, straight into the high-caliber revolver at the end of Jake Shoemaker's outstretched arm.

"Hey, Clive," said Jake, businesslike. "I really need to talk to you about something."

Little Brother showed an alligator smile of teeth.

"You should have stolen a better dog." Jake pulled back the hammer on the big six-shooter. "He's sure enough ugly, but he isn't worth a damn for protection."

"What did you say?" Clive asked again.

CHAPTER TWELVE

L ITTLE BROTHER LEAPT for the arm holding the gun.
Clive ducked and rolled off the stairway into a tangle
of salmonberry bushes, rolled until he came up hard
against a thorny stalk, and looked back to where the big
dog was standing over the fallen Jake, shaking the man's
arm back and forth as if it had come unhinged at all of its
joints. Jake was crying out in a wordless howl, his head
thumping on the decking, while the dog worked almost
silently, breath heaving out of nose and jowls as he tore at
the limp man's arm.

Clive circled back down under the boardwalk near the
water, taking his time, listening to the animal grunting into
his work. Jake's voice became more and more faint.

For a moment, Clive considered walking down the beach
to Miles's house, letting the dog finish what he had started.
He even considered going back to the bar and listening to
records for a while.

But then he heard Jake's voice floating out over the tide
flat, calling for help in the same kind of faltering voice Clive
used to hear from under the door in his old cell block. It was
the last bleating of a dying animal. Clive didn't want to have
to explain to anyone how his former partner in the drug trade
had had his throat torn out on the steps of Clive's new home,

so he walked back toward the boardwalk, found a cross brace to climb, and lifted himself back onto the decking.

The gun lay just under the stairs of the house; Clive stepped over Jake and picked it up. The dog had stopped trying to tear Jake's arm away, but he still clenched what was left of the arm between his teeth. In the thin light from the porch, Clive could see that the forearm was broken, the wrist and hand flopped at an unsettling angle, and the shoulder was dislocated. Little Brother blew air from his massive lungs like a racehorse at full sprint.

"Get . . . him . . . off," Jake managed.

"Jeepers, Jake!" Clive knelt down beside his head. "I'm sure he'll let go when he's ready. There's not that much I can do."

"Shoot . . . it," Jake wheezed.

"Aw, cripes! I can't do that, Jake. I mean, you were going to shoot me through the head. Probably would have, too, if my dog hadn't helped me out. I can't just shoot him now that he saved me. That just doesn't seem fair."

"Do something . . ." Jake's voice grew fainter.

"I tell you what." Clive sat cross-legged on the decking with the pistol resting in his lap. "This dog likes to hear good news. You can't boss him, but you can use a nice tone of voice on him and tell him that all the money in that storage container was rightfully mine."

"Fuuuugghhhyewwww," Jake sighed.

"And tell him that I will be keeping all that money to help run our new enterprise here in Cold Storage."

"Fine," he said weakly.

"And that you will never ever try to hurt me again for the rest of your life."

"Yes . . . I will never try and hurt . . ."

Little Brother still held on.

"Then I don't know." Clive shrugged. "You could tell him he's a good dog."

"Good dog." Jake's eyes closed. His head rolled to the side, his cheek nearly flat against the planking. Little Brother's breathing eased, and the boardwalk grew silent; Clive could hear the wind in the trees up the hill but nothing from his former employer.

Clive looked over at the dog. "I think you killed him." His voice was somber.

Little Brother stared up with sad brown eyes, looked almost sheepish. "No," was all the dog said.

Once Jake's body had gone limp and the tension of the fight was over, his floppy arm had dropped from the dog's jaws and fallen to the deck with a slap like a dead fish.

Little Brother studied Jake, contemplated Clive. He looked tired of the conversation. Without saying another word, the ugly dog shouldered past Clive, padded up the steps, scratched the outer door open and went inside.

"I'M SURPRISED HE didn't kill him!"

Clive stood under the clinic's unduly bright lights and watched Miles wipe away the blood on his former partner's arm.

"This is an amazingly clean break," Miles was saying. "I mean considering that the dog snapped his arm, then pulled his shoulder out of the socket."

Jake was hooked up to an IV and a blood pressure monitor. His eyes weren't focusing; they were open but rolled around as if he were lying back in a convertible, driving through a tunnel of trees in autumn.

"I've got him on so much Demerol that he shouldn't be feeling much of anything," continued Miles, "which is a good thing because he's got a little bit more to go through before we get that shoulder back in place."

"Well, I'm just going to leave him here," said Clive. "I need some sleep before I have to open up in the morning."

"I need you here." Miles's voice was calm but firm. "First to stitch him up and watch his BP, but then to pull this shoulder back so we can pop it in. It's going to take at least two of us." Miles looked around. "Unless you can get your dog to do it."

"Come on, I can't get that dog to do anything." Clive took his jacket off. "Except eat and pass gas."

"That," Miles added, "and chew up men who want to kill you."

"Hey! I had nothing to do with that. Whatever happened was between Jake and the dog. They had some old business."

"All right," said Miles. "Just stick around to pop his shoulder back in."

"Sure. I'll help. Just lose the tone with me, okay? I didn't do anything criminal."

"I'm sorry, brother. I know. Let's just get this back in, then do the stitching, all right?" Miles stood up on a chair, grabbed the injured arm below the break and wedged his knee behind Jake's shoulder. "You better hold him," he said gently to his brother. "He's apt to flop around some."

BY THE NEXT afternoon, Jake's eyes were beginning to focus. He writhed, tried to get away from where his splinted arm was suspended, and saw Clive and Miles standing at the foot of the bed; they were smiling. Jake closed his eyes and reopened them; felt as if half his body had been stung by bees;

closed his eyes again. The room spun, and a vague electric current pulsed up and down his arm.

"I'm going to have to get you to a hospital so they can take a look at my handiwork," Miles was saying. "Get you a bed where you can heal up for a bit before you travel."

"No," breathed Jake. "No police."

Miles turned to his brother. "I take it this is the owner of the money?"

"Former owner, Miles." Clive looked over at the bed. "We've worked all that out, haven't we, Jake?" He leaned across the broken arm while Jake recoiled, tried to move to the other side of the bed. He was pulled up short by the tension on his elbow and winced, rolled back in agony.

"More drugs," he pleaded.

"Soon," said Miles.

"I am the sole proprietor of the money, and all she has purchased. Well, me and the dog. I think I'm going to have to cut him in for a full share after what he did for me."

"This guy could turn you in to the cops, Clive. I mean, your dog did mess him up pretty bad." Miles directed a sympathetic glance toward Jake, huddled at the far end of the bed.

"First off, somebody is going to have to prove I'm responsible for that dog. I mean, he lives on his own. But more importantly, if Jake goes to a hospital and says one word about that ugly meat-eater being my dog, I'm going to have to give federal law enforcement the whole poop on Jake. I don't have anything to lose. I've got old business records that can account for all that money. My records might not stand up for long, but they will stand up long enough for the cops to get a load of Jake's interest in me. I've done my time. I haven't violated parole . . . at least, the spirit of my parole. I've got a new life going, and then this drug dealer came and attacked me. So my dog ate him." Clive tapped Jake's splinted arm. "Well, ate half of him anyway."

Jake sucked air through his nose, tried again to escape to the far side of the bed.

"No," Clive went on, "if federal law enforcement puts his name into their computer, the thing will light up like a pinball machine. Jake's not going to a hospital if he can help it."

"We've got to put him someplace." Miles was running out of patience.

"Can I say something?" Jake whispered.

"He could stay with me." Clive turned to face Miles. "But I don't think the dog would care for it. I don't know, that ugly bugger might wake up feeling peckish in the middle of the night." Clive smiled at the thought.

"Excuse me," Jake's voice quavered.

"He can't stay with me. I do not take patients home. Christ, if I did that I'd have half the town wanting to bunk with me. I'm not doing it, Clive." Miles was turning away from the bed as if he were going to walk out on the conversation.

"The more I think about it, I'm certain he can't stay with me," said Clive. "What would our buddy the trooper think of me living with this chewed-up old crook? I've got my new, clean reputation to think of. No way, he's not moving in with me."

"You. Doctor. Listen to me!" Jake yelled, hauling his head up from the pillow. "If you don't scurry around and get me some more pain killers, I swear to God when I get up out of this bed I'm going to shoot your nuts off."

Miles glanced at his wristwatch. "I suppose I can give you some more Demerol. But listen, you are not staying with me. I don't care which body part you threaten to shoot off."

Jake lay his head back down and let out an exhausted moan.

A FEW HOURS later, Jake sat in a sturdy camp chair in front of Lester's wood stove.

"This is one chewed-up-looking white man," observed Lester. "Did your dog eat him, then spit him back out?"

"I tell you, Lester, he's not really my dog." Clive carried in a bag of groceries, set them on the counter. "I got some hamburger and some canned stuff. There's milk and cereal and some bread here. I think there's a jar of peanut butter. Hell, Jake's not a picky eater." Clive smiled over at the men sitting in the sunken area around the stove. "But I have to tell you, Lester. Little Brother. He speaks."

"What he say?" The Indian man leaned forward.

"The first thing he said was, he complained about me tapping him with my foot."

"You kicked him?" Lester said with alarm.

"No. Cripes. It was just a tap."

"He say anything else?"

"No. He just warned me about Jake."

"Is he an angel or something?"

"Who, the dog? Hell, Lester, he's just a mutt."

The carver sat quietly for a moment, staring at his wood stove. Finally he turned to the injured man and asked, "What brought you to Cold Storage, Jake?"

"I wanted to kill him and get my money back." Jake pointed with his chin toward Clive.

"Oh . . . okay." Lester put some more wood into the firebox. "So you got some assassination travel package: airfare, hotel, ammunition? That sort of thing?"

"Is everyone in this town a goddamn comedian?"

Lester continued feeding sticks into the stove, the flames lighting his face. "No, actually most of the people in this town are drunks or depressives, but we have our funny moments."

No one spoke for a few seconds; the fire popped; Clive folded the grocery bag.

"Like when a hit man gets eaten by a dog," Lester said flatly. "You've got to admit, that's funny."

"I'm out of here," said Clive, but then remembered. "Hey, thanks, Lester." He looked over at Jake. "If you feel up to it, come on down to the bar. I'll buy you a cup of coffee." He started to leave but doubled back again. "You don't keep any guns here, do you, Lester?"

"I've got a deer rifle and a bear gun. But I keep 'em locked up."

"Good." Clive's hand was on the doorknob. "Just keep them out of reach of old Jake here. We're getting along so well now, but if he gets a little more bounce in his step, he might try to blow my brains out. Okay. See you later." He was gone.

Lester slapped his hands together; he stood up and held them toward the stove for warmth and asked, "What other kind of work you do, Jake, besides killing people?"

"I'm in the movie business." He didn't look at his Tlingit host.

"Get out of here," said Lester. "What were you in?"

"I wrote the script for a film called *Stealing Candy*, but they made a fucking mess out of it." Jake leaned back, but there was no way to sit comfortably in a camp chair, especially with his arm in a fiberglass cast. He grimaced.

"No kidding. I read about that movie. Hell, Jake, you must

be a player. Why you need to keep your day job of killing
people?"

"It's a long story," he lamented.

"Yeah, everybody's got a story." Lester went over to his
workbench, put on his jeweler's glasses. "I got a story. In fact,
I've got a book I've been working on, and it would make a
hell of a movie."

"Oh, Christ." Jake groaned.

"That's okay, I trust you. It's called *Circling the Wagons*.
It's a crime story, but it's really about white people in North
America. There's this Indian undercover cop, see . . ."

Lester started talking; the wind rattled under the eaves; if
he'd been listening, Jake could have heard the yawp of a heron
fishing on the tide flat underneath the house. The fire in the
wood stove popped; the tea kettle rumbled on top of the iron;
Jake closed his eyes and tried to shut out every sound in the
universe.

IN OTHER PARTS of America, August was the height of
summer, but in Cold Storage, it was the beginning of fall.
The first two weeks of steady rain had already fallen. Those
who were not used to this were emotionally pulled up short.
Miles was cleaning up the clinic; he wanted to go home early
and get a nap. He was tying the top of a garbage bag when the
bell above the clinic door clanged. He put the sack in a box for
burning and walked out to the waiting room.

There was Tina, her hands up to her cheeks, crying.

"Are you hurt, Tina?" asked Miles. "Has something happened?"

Miles had been in battlefields, scoured ground and dusty
expanses littered with burned trucks and strewn bandages,

smelling of diesel and desperate women under the hot sun. His job at home had different kinds of battlefields. People often came to his office to cry. Some came because of some recent pain, a pain that had taken them by surprise. Others came on a kind of schedule; it could be the moon, the weather, or some personal orbit that brought them back to an old injury that continued to overwhelm. There was plenty of old pain in Cold Storage.

In any northern village there is a darkness lurking: the differing terrors of childhood; the men who have victimized children and inoculated them with dread that will last for the rest of their lives; the refugees from family wars who are as shell-shocked as any soldier on the front. Some grow up swearing they'll never again end up in that situation, but most do. Some, from sexually battered families, know no other emotional territory and can't leave. In happy circumstances, they feel like foreigners whose papers have been revoked; they're always waiting for the knock from the secret police to take them back to their real lives. There are more than 700 villages in Alaska. No matter how much oil lay in the ground on the north slope and no matter how wisely it was allocated, it was at times hard for Miles to imagine how a twentieth century mind could navigate a Paleolithic world without a lot of chemical coaxing. Most of the people in Cold Storage drank, some of them lived alone and avoided human contact, but all of them periodically became unhinged and ended up in Miles's clinic.

Miles suspected Tina's pain was recent. "What's happened?"

She lifted her head up out of her hands, looked up at the ceiling, and held her breath.

"What happened?" she repeated. "Oh . . . I'm sorry, Miles, nothing happened . . . It's just . . . It's just . . ." and she started crying into her hands again.

He put his hand on her shoulder, led her gently to the examining room. "Come on in," he said softly. "No sense in you standing out here."

She sat on the edge of the table and talked; her shoulders heaved; her words came out in spasms. Miles sat on a low stool with his elbows on his knees and looked up at her, listened to her voice float around the small room.

"It's just the weather," she explained, blowing her nose. "You know we get more than two hundred inches of rain a year here?"

Miles shook his head.

"People in Seattle think they have a lot of rain, but they only get some thirty-seven inches. I mean, really . . ." Her tears kept flowing. "Thirty-seven. That's nothing . . . but the worst of it is, we only really get some fifteen really sunny days a year. Fifteen!" Again she started sobbing, for the fifteen clear days, Miles supposed.

"What else?" asked Miles.

They stared at each other for a while. Rain ticked down on the tin roof; they could hear kids rumbling by, pulling a wagon down the boardwalk.

"How's Ed?" Miles asked, and Tina's dam broke.

THERE ARE SO many people with broken hearts: there are parents and their children, husbands and wives, the hard-hearted and the sensitive. They do horrible things to each other with whatever weapons they can muster. These emotional battles in Cold Storage were like drunken broadsword fights: sloppy and inaccurate. But the blows, when struck, were often crippling. It wasn't the rain filling the fishing streams and creating the gamelan of their tin roofs that made people sad. It was the wrong turns their love had made. But the rain didn't help.

As a teenager, Miles had been unsympathetic to these people. People in books and films—people in the real world had survived worse. Whole orders of magnitude worse. And they still did, every day. Not that the teenage Miles knew how they did it.

But when Tina let words push past her tears, a recognizable story began to unfold: Ed did not love Tina, or that was her fear. Ed was pulling away from her. School was starting, and he was sullen and distant. He disappeared out on his own to gather specimens for their classrooms, and when he returned, he would hang up his slicker and say nothing. In bed he rolled away from her, feigning sleep. Tina stared at his back and her mind rewound where they had been and where they were going, and discovered she couldn't imagine a coherent future, or even a story of one.

It hadn't always been that way. Ed and Tina had shared a common story, or so it seemed to her, from the moment they met. This was the story of two young people who went on an adventure to Alaska to touch, walk, and study the wild country other people only imagined—two people who each needed the other to reach their destination: the driver and the navigator. But now it seemed that Ed had always been happy to both drive and navigate and was ready to go on ahead by himself.

Miles was growing impatient. A thought was building up pressure in the depths of his mind: *Why should I care about this woman's sadness?* he thought to himself, while at the exact same moment he knew that he did care. A world away, his friends still walked a battlefield where smoke roiled up from charred holes in the ground, and widows wailed for the missing. Brave men died while rescuing strangers, and here he was listening to this mildest form of suffering. But he listened for there was nothing else to do. Pain, no matter how slight, has a magical way of filling whatever container it finds—much like happiness but apparently more often.

Tina told Miles about the time she and Ed came up on the ferry. They had to back their rented moving van onto the ship in Bellingham. Tina stood in back and waved the directions. She waved and yelled and gestured, and all the while Ed was swerving back and forth in the lane. Finally, when the van pushed up against a parked car and broke off both vehicles' side mirrors, Ed got out yelling.

"I was giving you good directions," she countered.

"But you weren't standing where I could see you," he yelled.

"Now you tell me, Miles, whose fault was that?" Tina tried to pull herself up straight in her chair, but all she could muster was a defiant kind of slump.

Miles's shoulders jerked, and he stirred himself. "He could have adjusted the mirror," Miles said, "or he could have stopped and figured out a better way."

"Or maybe I was standing in the wrong place, at the wrong time, trying to talk to the wrong guy." She blew her nose again, smiled.

Miles smiled, too, and reached out and touched the top of her hand; she took her other hand and covered his; they said nothing. They stared down at their hands on her lap until Miles stood up, but she kept hold of him.

"Thanks, Miles, for letting me talk. It helps. It does. What about you, do you need anybody to talk to?"

"No," he said, "my life's not that interesting."

She squeezed his hand and said, "You look funny."

"I'm all right, I guess."

"What are you thinking?"

"I'm thinking that I'm a crappy salmon fisherman." His voice held more seriousness than he'd expected.

"That's pretty bad, Miles."

She cupped his face in her hands and kissed him on the mouth, hard enough and long enough that he had to put his hands around her waist to hold her there. The rain, which was neither tears nor music, continued to fall on the tin roof, making a fine rhythm in the room, and slowly smeared down the windows.

CHAPTER THIRTEEN

T HE CLINIC'S DOOR opened, and they heard Ed's voice out in the waiting room. "Miles, you with somebody?"

Miles had his arms around Tina; he brushed her cheek with the back of his hand, and she looked straight up into his eyes. She did not look startled, she did not look worried, and she did not look guilty. Miles felt almost inordinately happy.

"Just one second," he said to her and walked out to the waiting room.

"Tina came in; she's in the examining room; she'll be out in a minute."

"Is she okay? What's the problem, Miles?" Ed stood up on his toes to look over Miles's shoulder, as if Tina were standing there. "She just ran out of school. I had to finish up by myself."

"She was upset."

"Well, I mean, what's the problem? Is she going to be okay?"

"I think she's going to be okay. But she needs to tell you what the problem is."

"Does she need medication? Can you give her something?"

It occurred to Miles that Ed was asking him a lot of questions considering she was his own wife.

"No," he said, "I don't think she's going to need any medication. If this keeps up I think I could get her a telephone appointment with a counselor in Sitka. Maybe she just needs to talk things over with someone else."

"Someone else?" Ed let the words linger in the air.

"A counselor in Sitka," Miles said again to snip off the thread left floating. "I'll see how she's doing."

Miles walked back, and Tina grabbed him—forcefully—kissing him even harder this time.

He ran his hands over her shoulder blades and down the curve of her waist. He pulled her toward him, feeling her legs against his, her breasts against his chest, his hands shaking against her strong back. Then he pulled away.

"I don't know, Tina. You've got to talk to him. Tell him the story about backing the van onto the ferry."

"I want to sleep with you, Miles," she said. "I've just decided."

"Well, that's something to consider." Miles made it sound like they were talking about alternative therapies; quite possibly they were. "But I can't see you here in the clinic, and I really want you to talk to Ed."

"You are a good guy, Miles." She kissed him and pushed past him out of the room.

Miles stayed; he didn't want to be in a room with those two right now. He pulled the paper lining down from the table, checked the connections on all the telemetry machines, even looked down in the trash basket to see if there was anything there that needed his attention, before opening the door to the waiting room.

It was empty, so he went to his office and filled out his log, identified Tina's visit as a "wellness-consult, no treatment schedule."

He had a stomachache. Sleeping with Tina would definitely qualify as a change in his circumstances. It would be a happening in Cold Storage once word got out, as it surely would. Tina probably hadn't considered that yet; perhaps she was new enough to town that she thought that keeping something of a sexual nature secret was a possibility, which it certainly was not.

People would know. There were the obvious tip-offs, of course—being seen walking out of someone's door at an unexplainable time or being seen kissing through a partially closed curtain. These things were common risks in a small town but didn't explain people's near-miraculous ability to divine the sexual quality of any relationship. The people of Cold Storage had an uncanny sensitivity to the body language of lovers and their slight changes in habits.

Edna Whelaby, while sitting on the examining table, had once told Miles that she couldn't keep a boyfriend in town because of "everybody's damn sex radar." Edna was eighty-three years old at the time and between boyfriends. Miles had known her all his life so it was with some trepidation that he asked her to explain "sex radar" and to his discomfort she was happy to oblige:

"Ah, Christ Mary on a crutch, Miles. Everybody in the coffee shop, everybody at the post office or the library can tell if you've been sleeping with somebody. They just know. It's like radar. It's the least little thing. Lipstick on when it usually isn't. Teasing somebody when you usually don't, *not* teasing somebody when you should. These are all the signs, Miles, and the people around here just have a sense for it, I swear. One night in the sack, and there's hell to pay when you go for your next cup of coffee. There's not enough men around who can stand up to that kind of treatment," she complained. "I've been thinking of moving to Juneau."

Miles had been skeptical. He thought the old woman was just elaborating to show off her superior knowledge of life. But after, he had been alarmed when his own sex radar started to kick in. He saw a woman flush at the mention of someone's name. He noticed a fisherman, who had always slapped his money and the check down on the counter, was handing them to the waitress instead. It wasn't just that he handed it to her, either, for that could be just his attempt to flirt. It was the way her fingers curled up quickly around the money in a furtive attempt to touch the tips of his fingers; it was how she leaned forward on the dairy case and smiled as he came in and would sometimes walk around the counter when he left.

These were things that told Miles that the two of them were sleeping together. And he knew this because he hadn't been sleeping with anyone in the years since his return. He had become finely attuned to all aspects of desire, as if the loneliness he hadn't even admitted to himself had honed his senses. Lonely people recognize those in love like a parched tongue senses moisture. It may not be their own love, but it feels like a blessing to them.

Miles opened the door to the empty waiting room and stepped out into silence. Weasel waved from the boardwalk, and Miles had a sick feeling in his stomach. He had become accustomed to thin rations of affection, and these two kisses, as thrilling as they were, had given him a stomachache. It was as if he had eaten a rich meal much too quickly.

JAKE WAS LYING on a pad on the floor on the upper tier of Lester's studio/home. He had a phone cradled against his shoulder and was listening to Miss Peel speaking with a kind of urgency that reminded him of a typewriter key striking a roller on the end of the line. She was holding onto a subpoena to appear in front of a grand jury. Jake tried to soothe her, even though the pain in his arm was twisting up his torso and into his brain like an electric drill bit. He was making it clear that he was not advising her to avoid responding to the subpoena, then he paused and read an account number for a bank in Arizona plus two addresses in Tucson. "Yes, yes. Now read those back to me please." He paused. "Good. Thank you, Miss Peel. You, too, dear. You, too. Good luck and have a good trip. Yes, God bless."

He hung up, gritted his teeth until the pain subsided, stared up at the ceiling as Lester carved on a two-inch strip of silver that would become a bracelet.

The pain passed, and he eased back down onto his sleeping pad. "So, how come you live here then?" he asked. "I mean, why don't you live in one of those, you know, Indian villages?"

"I'm on a scouting mission." Lester peered through his jeweler's glasses down onto his design.

"You said you been here ten years. That's quite a scouting mission. When you going to make your move?"

"We're a patient people."

"That's bullshit." Jake tried to heft himself up onto his good arm so he could look at Lester. "My bet is you got thrown out of whatever life you had before. Just the little I've seen of this place, I can't believe anybody would live here if they weren't hiding out from someone."

"This place grows on you." Lester didn't look up from his work.

"Yeah, like toe fungus," agreed Jake.

"Exactly." Lester looked over at Jake sprawled out on the mat and started to add something. He was almost tempted to justify himself, to launch into an explanation, but he stopped and looked down at the bracelet he was making instead.

It was a bear design. Bear had been the clan crest of his mother's people; he thought of telling Jake about the different clans with their strict rules and the rivalries between them; he thought of telling him about the complex structure of proto-col, politics, and ancient grudges that a contemporary Tlingit person needed to understand in order to live peaceably in a village. He thought of telling him about how he had quit drinking only after it was too late, but he stopped himself. Lester was not in the mood to teach Indian 101 to another uninterested white man.

"So," Lester said, "tell me what you think of my story idea."

"It's got no arc."

"What do you mean, no arc?" Lester was a little irritated.

"Christ, man. Arc. You know, what connects the story from beginning to middle to end. Listen." Jake took a deep breath and broke into a professorial tone: "Movies are really about one thing happening to one person. That's it."

"That's not true," Lester threw down his carving knife. "*Jurassic Park*, what was it about?" Jake stared at the ceiling.

"It's about people's greed and arrogance toward natu-ral systems they don't understand," Lester explained, took another tool and started back to work.

"That's the message, but that's not what it's about. *Jurassic Park* is how a snotty scientist discovers that he really loves kids. That's the one thing that changes during the entire movie. In the opening, he hates kids, and by the end, he's cuddling with them in the friggin' helicopter. That's what's going on."

Lester gestured toward Jake. "The lawyer gets eaten."

"True, and that was a great moment. But it's a perk, an extra bit of action that happens while the snotty scientist is learning to bond with the kids. Your story is all perks. Little bits of action strung together with an implausible mission of this Indian cop, but the main character doesn't really change. He's a sarcastic shit heel in the beginning, and he's a sarcastic shit heel at the end. He's just eaten up a hundred and twenty minutes sleeping with sexy women and killing irritating white men. It's an interesting setup, but it's no story."

"You know, you don't have to sugarcoat your opinions for me. Just spit them out." Lester picked up a tiny fleck of silver and placed it carefully in a jar of similar flecks. "James Bond doesn't change," he added, almost petulantly.

"Fucking James Bond is a franchise. He's not a character. The problem with your guy is he just keeps killing the bad guys off, but he never rescues anybody. He doesn't learn anything, and nobody is going to give a shit about him by the end of the movie."

"So, you want him to change?" Lester looked up through his jeweler's glasses.

"Hell, man, I spent ten minutes with your snotty fucker, and I was begging for him to change."

"This is a white thing, isn't it? You're saying to make him dance and shuffle, make him some mystical holy man, make him 'sympathetic' to the mass audience, aren't you?" Lester's annoyance was obvious.

Jake continued to stare at the ceiling. He could hear the

rain falling on the roof. No rush of freeway, no car horns, no sirens. Just the rain, the fire in the stove, and the wind against the house. He lay there, examining the hand-hewn beams above his head.

"Hey, Lester," he said. "I think you should use your left hand to carve that bracelet. It would give it a rougher, more primitive effect."

Lester stopped carving. "You don't know shit about carving or about me or about anything, as far as I can tell."

Jake didn't look at Lester. He just spoke calmly. "You are two-thirds right. I know dick about silver carving and I know nothing about you, but I know about movies and your idea sucks, at least as it stands now."

Lester was standing now, ready to take a step toward the injured man lying on the floor.

"And don't give me that 'make him dance' crap. I don't care if your guy kills everybody in Washington, DC, and declares himself emperor. I don't care if he is a mystic or a Republican. I'm just here to tell you that if you don't know who he is, and if he doesn't meet some challenge that substantially changes him, if you don't get him to help some-body—even himself—you aren't going to get fucking Sitting Bull to watch your movie."

Lester took a step away from his workbench, a step back, and sat down. "I'll give it some thought," he said.

"You could give him a pet," Jake suggested. "That would make him sympathetic."

"I'll give him an ugly dog who eats white people."

"That could work," Jake agreed. "You could make it a buddy movie."

There were footsteps in the outer porch, a stamping of

boots, and Jake leaned up on his good arm to watch Miles walk into the room and hang his coat on a peg by the door. It wasn't wet enough to hang by the stove.

Lester lifted his head slightly. "Hey, Miles." He kept working.

"I've come to announce that Tina McCarty wants to have sex with me. She just told me. I know you guys will hear about this sooner or later so I wanted to tell you right off the bat."

The fire popped and sent a small spark soaring out through the grate down onto the scarred piece of tin beneath the stove.

"Christ, Miles, that's old news. Everybody knows she wants to have sex with you." Lester was nonplussed.

"I've only been here two days, and I knew it," chimed Jake.

Miles, deflated, sat down on the splitting stump. "I know you're lying," he said to Jake, "but Lester, come on, you didn't really know she wanted to have sex with me, did you?"

"Come on, Miles, there's a betting pool." Lester reached into his pocket and pulled out a small scrap of paper. "It was a twenty-dollar buy-in. I bought November sixteenth." He waved the stub at Miles.

"November sixteenth? So the person who buys the closest date to the actual date we . . ."

"Will be two hundred and forty dollars richer." Lester looked up through his jeweler's glasses. His eyeballs looked like wobbly saucers.

Jake reached into his pocket with his good arm. "Let me in on some of this." But Lester waved him off.

Miles lowered his head into his hands. "She's a school-teacher! She's married to a schoolteacher!"

"Oh yeah," he said, "that's why the pool sold out in two days." He put the slip of paper back into his pocket.

"Well, I'm going to disappoint you, Lester." Miles sat up and straightened his shoulders as if someone had just called his name. "I'm not going to have sex with her. I've just decided that."

"Yeah, we'll see. I still have three months. I'm thinking my November is looking good. It gets mighty cold and lonely around here in November. I say right around the election time. I'm cashing in on your sex life because I put my money on Gore, and I think he's tanking."

"Well, I'm not." Miles sounded shaky but resigned.

"What? You're betting on Bush?" Lester said with disgust in his voice.

"No. I'm not having sex with Tina."

"I'm glad that's cleared up," Lester said without taking his eyes off his work.

"What's the coverage in December?" asked Jake. "The holidays could be tough, you know. A little eggnog, a little mistletoe."

"You might buy in, but it's a waste of money because November is still a lock. I don't care what this mook says. Anytime a man announces that he's not going to have sex, either it means he already has or is just about to. This guy"—here Lester nodded to Miles—"is a little more earnest than most white people, so I'm giving him until November. You might as well give the money to me." Lester stood up and walked over to Miles, gave him a slap on the back, then went over to a desk in the corner and took out a spiral notebook.

"Don't worry about it, Miles. Nothing's really different," he said. "Everybody knew about it before, and everybody knows about it now. Nothing's changed." He took his notebook over to Jake. "Speaking of which . . . Jake here is going to help me out with the 'arc' of my story. You're just in time."

Lester pushed his jeweler's glasses up on his forehead and sat down on the floor beside Jake.

"Let's talk about change," he said to the crippled gangster.

CHAPTER FOURTEEN

I N T H E M A D E R A Canyon Sports Medicine Rehabilitation Center, just southwest of Green Valley, Arizona, the September sun was like a luscious orange in the sky. Oscar Laurentis sat with his leg unwrapped after his sixth surgery, soaking up the sun as he waited to go to rehab. It was the one thing that he had insisted upon when he worked for Jake: Oscar had the best healthcare plan that money could by.

But he had little else and that was why he had milked every ounce of his coverage to get his leg back into shape. He told the surgeons right from the start that he had been a top prospect for professional soccer clubs in Europe, that he had just been out of shape on a new training regimen. He was going to get a leg like Pele's, even though he barely knew who Pele was.

Oscar spent a lot of time reading crime novels in his various hospital beds. He began to seethe with the need for revenge. He also watched Bronson movies and Tarantino films. He loved how sexy damped-down rage could look. He thought that was what women must love: the man who could control his rage and release it in service of justice. This is what all the books and films seemed to teach. Chicks dug it. Oscar had a good cause. He was a victim. He was going to have a new kick-ass leg. All he needed was a big-ass gun. He

was going to get an insurance settlement. Ann Peel helped
him get policy limits from the insurance company as long as
he kept Jake's name out of the police reports. Fine. No big
deal. Chicks didn't like the whole courtroom bullshit. They
wanted the *mano a mano*, we-take-care-of-our-own approach.

Yes. He would definitely do it. Someday. He would stick
here a while. It was nice here. He didn't know where Jake was
anyway, and it was probably a long ways off.

It was some big deal visitation day. Some baseball player
was supposed to sign shirts and cards for the patients today,
to raise their spirits and everything. Oscar looked down the
veranda, shading his eyes, and saw a massive Hispanic man.

"Who's the meat?" Oscar asked the patient next to him,
who wore a full lower body cast.

"I dunno. Manny Something. Hit over three hundred last
year."

But there, standing next to Manny Something and waving
like a little girl on a Ferris wheel, was Miss Peel. In seconds
she was clicking down the marble tiles to his raised and
sutured leg.

"Oooscar! Oh my gosh, you look . . .well, you look . . .
good. You've gained weight, even! They must be taking care
of you! How *are* you?"

She bent over and gave him a makeup-preserving kiss, her
right hand spread over her chest to protect her gold jewelry
from hitting him or to prevent him from looking down her
silk blouse.

"I'm, uh, good, Ann . . . ah, Miss Peel."

"Oh, Ann. Please. So, have you heard from Jake in Alaska?"

As Manny spent the next two hours signing baseballs and
having his picture taken, Oscar and Miss Peel caught up on

the intricacies of life in the world of Jake Shoemaker and what the world might hold for the financial security for his former employees.

THE AUTUMN MOVED down from the north. Hunters ranged closer to town, afraid to be caught out in the storms. Kids stayed closer to home because there wasn't enough daylight to wander past the boardwalk and up into the river valleys. The plumage on the diving ducks began to change. The mergansers appeared whiter, and the old squaw ducks showed up in shimmering white rafts near the inner harbor.

The bears stopped coming into town for garbage, and the dead salmon carcasses washed out into the inlet with the heavy October rains. The water of the inlet itself appeared brown as tea for a few weeks during the heaviest of the rains, and sometimes the ghost fish floated near the surface with their hollow eye sockets and rotted flesh staring into the sky.

The bathhouse stayed busy even though people weren't covered in summer's grime. Men came during men's hours and women during women's hours. They came to warm their pale bodies as the chill of the turning year started gaining a foothold in their bones.

Mrs. Cera let Anthony go back to Juneau, and he turned out for the wrestling team. He'd eventually win State at 164 pounds, break a finger in the last match, and come back to Cold Storage.

Little Brother began eating from a bowl in plain view of people. He stopped wandering up the hillside and never ate another cat that anyone missed. Every evening after Clive locked up, the dog walked down the boardwalk and up the stairs to Annabelle's house. He waited for Clive to open the door and walked in ahead of him, settling himself onto a blanket beside the oil stove. He'd lift his jeweler anvil head and stare at Clive's ankles as they passed by his resting place. The two had grown more relaxed in each other's physical presence, but Little Brother had not spoken since he had tried to eat Jake's arm. Clive spoke to the big dog as he lay on the bed. He would make small talk, discuss the weather or his unimportant list of errands for the day. Little Brother would lift his head with effort and simply stare back at Clive as if to say, "Are you talking to me?" and then, "Why?" then plop his head back on his paws. Clive was getting the impression that his dog was not much of a conversationalist and would only speak if, and when, he had something important to say.

Every Sunday, Clive preached a sermon at the Love Nest. He stuck closely to his major theme of love and slowly circled around the whole issue of obedience. He read the story of Jonah, mostly for the character of the worm who God commanded to destroy the shade tree. He stayed away from the crushing tedium of Ecclesiastes.

It snowed on Halloween, but the flakes were fat and soggy so that as soon as they hit, they disappeared into a sloppy film on the boardwalk. But three hundred feet above town, the branches of the spruce and hemlock trees gathered white pillows of snow.

The contested election came, and people were pissed off for a few weeks. But no one in Cold Storage could really muster much enthusiasm for the race. Almost everyone agreed that there was certainly some sort of criminality involved, but no one could decide exactly the nature of the crime or the mastermind behind it, although theories abounded.

The movie clubs continued to meet, and eventually

Weasel brought a monitor and VCR into the Love Nest for one evening a week for the men's movie club. Clive made an exception to his no-pop-culture rule and offered the use of the bar to both the men's and women's movie groups, but the women politely declined—not because they didn't approve of the surroundings, but because they had a nice setting of their own along the water side of the back of the library. And because, as one man said, "They don't want to mix their pleasures, lest the whole thing go sour."

Some American sailors were killed in Yemen by a group of people unhappy with the US. Several people in Cold Storage hung yellow ribbons on their fences, but most of the people in town were not sure what the ribbons meant, other than a vague sense of patriotism.

Miles didn't have sex with Tina McCarty in November, for which Lester barely forgave him. Instead, Tina and Ed took a three-day weekend trip to Juneau after the second parent-teacher conferences of the school year and came back with gifts for the schoolchildren. Tina brought Miles a sweater from an Irish woolens shop, and he noticed that Ed had begun to drink beer at the Love Nest late into the evenings, even on school nights.

JAKE'S SHOULDER STAYED sore for weeks. He scratched under the cast with thin pieces of firewood and complained loud and long whenever he saw either Miles or Clive. Miles pleaded with him to go to Sitka for X-rays, but Jake refused. He tried calling Miss Peel on her cell phone, but there was never an answer; eventually, he was greeted with a recorded message that the phone had been disconnected. This seemed to satisfy him for some strange reason.

Jake spent his days sprawled out on the floor of Lester's shop, working on their story ideas. Jake had convinced Lester to put the novel aside and work out the story as a film script, and he sat on the floor, cast propped up on pillows, with a large board that Lester usually used for cutting up meat on his lap. Twenty large sheets of butcher paper were attached to the top of the board; each sheet was divided into six sections, and each section represented a page or approximately one minute of running time.

Jake and Lester argued over the relative merits of each plot point and every subtle change in the character's growth. Jake wrote in pencil, often rubbed out whole scenes with a fat pink eraser while holding the pencil in his teeth. Sometimes at night he lay on his pad listening to the wind in the trees; somehow they didn't sound as lonely as he'd once imagined they would.

As the days went by, Jake could see that he and Lester were shaping something original and unexpected, something that had the feel of the familiar but was, upon second look, completely new. And Jake forgot about the ranch above Santa Monica; he forgot about dot-com holdings and real estate. All he thought about was Lester's story and the strange transformation of the beautiful land mass now called North America.

Lester sometimes sketched out scenes or props that Jake couldn't visualize, and Jake would tape them onto his flopping butcher papers. The manuscript grew; he'd forgotten about his other script ideas and never even mentioned *Till Death Do Us Part*. Since that ugly dog had nearly torn his arm off, he'd learned something about himself: he was a natural critic. He was such a good critic, in fact, that he couldn't bear to work on his own ideas, and it finally became clear to him that he was the kind of writer who enjoyed talking about his stories but couldn't really bear to be in their company. A husband-and-wife hit team going in for marriage counseling was a good idea as long as it stayed an idea, but just the thought of trying to write it up started to make him sick because his first impulse always had been, and always would be, to rip ideas to shreds.

In Lester, he found the perfect partner. Lester was a fountain of ideas, most of which were terrible, Jake had to admit, but for some reason having a terrible idea didn't seem to bother Lester or impede his progress. He just kept on spinning out new ones.

Lester had a definite point of view. It was hard for Jake to understand this, but Lester *was* somebody, as opposed to most of the people he'd met in the movies who had only wanted to *be* somebody.

Even if Jake had been willing to risk the possibility that the police were still looking for him, he didn't have enough money to travel very far. As it was, Clive footed most of his expenses: food, coffee, and medical treatment. In the end, though, it was neither the lack of money nor the fear of the cops that kept him in town.

There was something amorphous about the place, about the smell of the wood stove and the clattering sound of the carts in which people carried their groceries up and down the boardwalk. As hard as this was for him to admit, Cold Storage was a place his father would have chosen for himself. Jake could imagine his old man sitting at the corner of the bar or wrestling a big fish up the dock to show his cronies, and when he thought of such things Jake's body became somehow more solid, as if there were something in his chest besides his bruises that made him feel like he didn't want to muster the energy to move on.

Jake liked the easy rituals of the days in Cold Storage: coffee, work, visiting with people who seemed to spend their afternoons wandering along the boardwalk. He looked forward to walking down to the Love Nest every evening at nine o'clock. Once in a great while, Lester would come along, too, would drink coffee and listen to old records with him. It was on such a night in the middle of November, that an event happened that would change everything in Cold Storage for years to come.

The first real snow of the year was falling on the boardwalk, and the only footprints to be seen were those of Lester and Jake. Inside the bar, Ed played pool with the young visiting Lutheran minister, and Clive listened to Charlie Parker records. Visibility had been down in all directions, and no planes had landed in the inlet for three days. Weasel had come into the bar earlier to say that a small boat had tied up to the dock. "Who'd be wandering around in weather as crappy as this?" he'd asked.

Lester was lifting his coffee cup to his lips and bouncing his head to the looping sax of *Ornithology* when the door of the Love Nest opened. In a perfect cinematographic moment, the falling snow on the boardwalk made a silhouette of two figures standing there in the doorway.

Little Brother looked up and growled.

Bonnie Sue Mellon and Billy Cox walked in with packs on their backs and pushing padded cases on pieces of plywood in front of them. They'd come in answer to the ad for a new house band.

Clive sounded stunned. "There's never been an ad," he said.

"Then there shouldn't be much competition for the job," said Bonnie and put her amplifier down next to the bar.

CHAPTER FIFTEEN

"YOU ARE GOING to have to play before I sign you on," Clive said to the group. "I'm mighty fond of this record machine."

The band didn't hear much; they were busy searching for electrical outlets and a place to set up. Nix was taking off her coat, looking for a hook on which to hang it. She had a gold stud through her lower lip and a golden rose through one nostril; her short golden brown hair shimmered with blue highlights, and to Clive, she looked like a fairy child sneaking into his bar to warm up before flying out of a window, back into the forest.

"Hey, puppy!" she squealed and leaned down beside the ugly dog.

"I really wouldn't . . ." Clive started, but she was already on the floor, Little Brother's head in her arms. She was hugging him as if he were a childhood toy. " . . . do that . . ." Clive's voice trailed off.

The dog's eyes drooped serenely. He was panting, and his tongue lolled out the side of his face.

"You are just a big lover, aren't you? Just a lover . . ." Nix was cooing and hugging him close.

Little Brother's spotted tongue licked her face, and she rocked back laughing, wiping her cheek on her sleeve.

"Yuck, sloppy kisses on our first date!" She stood up, still laughing, while Clive watched her in amazement. "I'm Nix," she said. "I'm the bass player. You're going to love the band." She held out her hand.

"Do you have this kind of effect on all animals?" Clive motioned to Little Brother, standing next to Nix now, looking up at her with adoration.

"Oh yeah," she said. "I'm an animal person. A big animal person." She took back her hand from Clive, who seemed to have taken temporary possession of it.

"Then you should go over well in this place." Clive kept staring at her.

She looked around the room and smiled winningly at the three patrons. "Oh yeah, I think we're going to be good for business. Definitely." She held out her hand again. "I'm Nix, by the way."

"We've already done this, you know, Nix." Clive held onto her hand again, though.

"That's right, we have." She held on and smiled. "We have."

Lester called, "Did you say your name was Nix?"

"That's right," she replied.

"That's really funny because I think Clive has your name tattooed on his ass." The Indian carver-turned-screenwriter eyed them over the lip of his coffee cup.

"Really?" Nix turned to Clive with an interested twinkle in her eyes, and for the first time since he could remember, he started to blush.

"No . . . not really . . . he's just fooling around." He picked up a clean glass, started wiping it down with a dirty bar rag. "Don't listen to him."

But she pointed her index finger at him and winked. "More about this later," she said, and picked up her bass, bringing it over to the corner of the room where her bandmates were setting up. Little Brother followed close on her heels.

"You are cut off," Clive hissed at Lester.

"That's fine by me," he said, and rapped his coffee cup down on the bar. "I'll never get to sleep as it is anyway."

THE ORCHESTRA FROM the *SS Universe* had been fired in Vancouver after a spectacular fight with the cruise director. They had been playing livelier and livelier music and been making continuous, subtle modifications to their costumes until Nix was wearing Billy's tuxedo and Billy was wearing a strapless evening gown. The two of them had been racing through a medley of songs by The Talking Heads. This was grounds to terminate their contract, proclaimed the director, but the union got them the rest of their season's salary and part of the next season's as a severance package. They decided to start a new dance band. This had been Billy's idea, and he'd been working out the details even as he'd zipped up the back of his gown.

So now they were a seven-piece band: bass, drums, guitar, saxophone, trombone, trumpet, and vocals. Bonnie, their manager, insisted they find a "wood shedding gig," that is to say, a place where they could work on their sound away from the public eye. This was important. They were looking at forming a band that crystallized the cross-influences of swing, The Squirrel Nut Zippers, and the Canadian folk tradition, with perhaps some spare kind of New York electronica reminiscent of Arthur Russell. Nix had been playing her bass with a bow. Bonnie said that the band was shooting for a kind of hep-cat hallucinatory maritime swing sound, and they already had a name: Blind Donkey.

They'd spent some of their severance money on a portable sound system, and in a matter of minutes they were set up in the corner behind the pool table and launching into their first number. They were a bit ragged at first. Because they wanted to impress the owner, they ripped into a swing version of "Sailor's Hornpipe," but their fingers were cold and the horn section slurred a little, so they bailed out of it after the second set of changes and pushed on into a ska version of "The Wreck of the Edmond Fitzgerald" that came off quite nicely. Billy sang to the enthusiastic applause of the audience and took a deep bow. He was happy to be home. He smiled at everyone; he even smiled at the pool table and the dog in the corner.

They played an original composition to close out the audition, an instrumental ballad that Billy introduced as "Love Is the Answer, But What Was the Question?" The horns started in together in kind of a minor key fanfare until the saxophone picked up the melody and played it through twice before coming back to the turnaround with the rest of the band. There was something lonely and ardent about the tune; it sounded like a foghorn at night or a train running past a slaughterhouse. It made you sad, but there wasn't an ounce of self-pity in it. It said that this life is just too goddamn short, and we're lucky to be here. This was the song Mouse Miller would have wanted to dance to, the melody he would have been humming while he pinned dollar bills on the rotten ceiling of the abandoned bar.

Miles walked in during the middle of the ballad and stopped short. He didn't even close the door. He was surprised to see a live band, surprised to see so many strangers, surprised to see Billy back from the sea. But mostly, he was surprised to hear a strange and affecting melody coming from the saxophone.

"How do you like the new house band?" asked Clive.

"They'll do." Miles didn't want to talk. "They'll do all right."

Bonnie was leaning against the door, watching the band, watching them make all the changes she'd heard them rehearse a hundred times, and she smiled. *Not everything is an accident*, she thought.

The song ended. Bonnie applauded along with everyone else as the band nodded, took their bows. Rick kissed his saxophone and walked to the bar.

Lester, Jake, and the minister stood around Billy; Lester made introductions, and the minister slapped Billy on the back. Ed talked with Nix as she wiped down her bass guitar and unplugged the cord. Clive looked at his ledger and tried to total up some numbers.

And Bonnie turned to Miles, since they were the only two people in the place who weren't engaged in something else. "I'm Bonnie Sue Mellon," she said, and Miles introduced himself.

"You know the guy who runs this place?" she asked.

"He's my brother. But don't take that as it sounds. I'm not really that familiar with him."

Bonnie squinted at Miles, tried to figure out if he was serious or not. "Think he'll give us a job?"

"He'll give you work," he said. Ed was laughing at something with Nix, and Clive appeared to notice.

"Will he be sneaky and try and screw us over?" Bonnie was conscious of how she sounded, but she was taking her managerial position seriously.

"No. If anything, he'll screw you right up front. Are you their manager?"

"It sounds lame, doesn't it? Manager." She shrugged and wrinkled her nose. "Did you know people in high school who were managers of things? Manager of the fencing team, manager of the chess club." She turned her head away in a sudden spasm of embarrassment.

"You know it's not the same thing, being the manager of a band. These guys are really good. How in the world did you get hooked up with Billy?"

"I pulled him out of the ocean." She didn't look at Miles.

"Now see? That's not lame. Those guys in high school didn't have answers like that."

"It's true, you know. He had fallen out of his kayak. I'm the one who pulled him out," she said. "I'm not kidding."

"I know you're not kidding." They walked over to the bar, and he rapped the bar for service. "And I for one would like to thank you for bringing him home. Now, what would you like?"

"I'd like to meet the owner." She watched Clive walk toward them, and she held out her hand.

Clive was the older brother and as such had always felt superior in the biological sense; that is, he never gave much thought to his younger brother as they were growing up. When Miles was toddling around the living room, Clive was playing in the woods up behind the house. When Miles played T-ball, Clive was in Little League. When Clive was a criminal, Miles was a student. It wasn't until now, as this young woman walked toward him, that Clive realized that he didn't want to be out ahead of Miles.

Bonnie and Clive bantered back and forth about what Clive would be willing to offer Blind Donkey in the way of remuneration. She tried to smile but kept nervously brushing her hair back; a poker player would've called it her "tell." Clive nodded and tried to look serious while tapping on the closed ledger book.

Miles knew that Clive was reaching the end of the money that he'd sewn into the lining of his coat. He knew that there had to be some new source of income soon.

Business in the autumn was lively but hardly profitable, even in a small town of alcoholics. And the truth was that Clive wasn't catering to the alcoholics. There was too much sunlight in the bar during the day and too much laughter at night. The hard drinkers stayed at home drinking in their caves where no one could see them, and they didn't have to deal with the world.

But it was December, and no one could pay for a seven-piece band in a town like this. Then again, it was December, and Miles hoped that they stayed.

He looked at Bonnie dickering with his brother, and he smiled. She had a nice way of being forceful, as if she really were looking out for your best interests even as she tried to put forward her own agenda.

"That's what I can offer. Does this look like the Copacabana?" said Clive.

Bonnie looked around. The band had more than doubled the population in the bar. Now that the music had stopped, Lester and Jake were putting their coats on and were getting ready to leave. Ed was deep in conversation with Nix, and the minister had already gone home. It was Saturday night.

"This bar looks like a place that really needs a band," she said.

"I couldn't agree more," said Clive, "and so here is my offer. You all can live with me up at the house. There's a small cabin out back we can turn into an extra room. I'll provide dinner every night and a five-dollar bar tab per player. You play a minimum of Thursdays through Mondays, and if we start turning a profit on a weekly basis, I'll give you a percentage of the bar. *If* we start turning a profit. Which we might have a shot at between Christmas and New Year's. That's all I can do."

Billy came up, whispered something in Bonnie's ear. She nodded and turned back to Clive. "The band can buy food and supplies in Juneau, and you will pay the shipping. And you'll let me look at the books so I can see for myself when you start turning a profit."

Clive smiled and shook his head. "She's tough, Billy. You're lucky she was there when you dumped your sorry butt into the ocean." He held out his hand but quickly added, "No special flights. I'll pay your freight as long as it's coming out with the supplies for the bar."

Bonnie glanced back; Billy shrugged, nodded. She shook Clive's hand, and it was done: Blind Donkey was the official house band for Mouse Miller's Love Nest.

Clive brought out a bottle of champagne someone had given him when the bar opened. He'd had it buried down in the ice machine, but now he started pouring it into beer glasses while the band members came surging toward the bar.

"And," said Clive as if proposing a toast, "I want you to play that last song, that instrumental, every night at closing."

Blind Donkey raised their beer steins of champagne to their great good fortune.

"Love is the answer," toasted Nix.

"Hear, hear!" came the answer from the bar.

They drank their champagne, and the band started to

unplug. Clive chatted with the horn section about creating a small riser on which they could play; they were pacing off distances in the bar and looking for a new place for the pool table. Nix came up to Bonnie and Miles, Little Brother still beside her. The ugly dog was apparently keeping Ed at a respectable distance.

"So we're good to go?" asked Nix.

"Looks like it," Bonnie said.

"Ed—I think he's the biology teacher or something—said he could show me where we're staying. He also said he'd take me out kayaking tomorrow, if that's cool with you." Her voice was tentative, as if she didn't really know if she needed to ask permission but wanted to all the same.

"Sounds good, just be careful, okay? Crazy things happen kayaking around here." Bonnie smiled.

"I'm nothing if not careful." Nix headed for the door, and Ed held it open for her. Just as she got to the threshold, though, she bent down and cupped the ugly dog's massive head in her arms, kissed him on the top of his coffin-shaped snout. "Good night, puppy," she cooed to him. She waved gaily to the room, winked at Little Brother, and walked out the door with Ed. She was gone, but something of her still lingered, like an echoing bell.

Little Brother stood flat-footed, contemplating the door for a full minute, then walked slowly over to his pad, let out a low groan, and flopped down, hitting his lower jaw on the floor. He let out another long breath, a sigh which sounded for all the world like a moan.

"Oh, just great!" groaned Clive.

"What?" Miles asked him.

"Just what I need now. A love-sick bouncer."

©

THE NEXT DAY Ed met Nix down near the floatplane dock. He'd carried the kayaks there so she would have an easier time getting in. It was still snowing, but there was not a breath of wind. The snowflakes fell silently into the milky green sea.

Nix, already bundled with a hat, a pair of mittens, and a fleece coat, put on the float vest Ed gave her. She listened to a few instructions on paddling and some reassurances: the water was very cold but they weren't going far, and there wouldn't be any need for sudden movements. She sat in the little slipper of a boat awkwardly but when she pushed away from the dock, she felt as if she were suspended in air. She moved as easily as a cloud gliding through the sky while snow gathered on her hat, on her mittens, on her kayak.

Ed got into his boat and paddled toward the wharf of the inner harbor. He loved showing people the world around Cold Storage. He especially wanted to show Nix everything there was to see; he wanted to talk his head off. He wanted to explain about the rain forest and the tidal environments, the rivers that flowed into the inlet. He wanted to tell her everything about the place, and as he dipped his paddle into the green, he started thinking of every story he knew: the stories about deer and bear and salmon, the stories about the black cod and the shorebirds and the diving ducks. He wanted to tell her everything all at once. But he had sense enough not to talk.

The tide was approaching the low water mark, so he was able to paddle under the wharf of the old cannery building into a forest of tarred pilings. Some were cocked at odd angles. Water dripped from a broken water pipe, and everything sounded cavernous. Alongside them, a few gulls paddled about, making a clucking sound as they swam, nodding back and forth, searching for the small fish darting beneath the surface. Further away, some gulls swam on the surface, riding the tide back up the poles to fresh feeding areas. Others stayed by the pilings, picked at encrusted mussels. Red starfish clung to the sides of the pilings and below them drooped flaccid sea anemones. Just under the surface, Nix could see anemones coming to life, billowing like silk flowers in the water.

Ed pointed toward the back of the wharf near the shoreline where the shadows were the darkest. She looked back at him and saw a heron that had been watching them let out a great yawp and lumber into flight. The bird seemed prehistoric as it flew over, its long neck stretching out, its nearly six-foot wingspan beating the air in half-stalled flight. The heron pulled itself awkwardly through the pilings, but once clear of the wharf, it lengthened out into a steady rhythm, flying through the falling snow. Nix laughed and pointed after it with a clumsy mittened hand.

They paddled for another hour, drifting slowly along the shoreline, watching river otters darting up the beach, coming upon a seal that watched them with curious human eyes. Nix loved everything she saw but she started to shiver, and Ed suggested they paddle hard to help warm up on the way back to the dock.

Ed was full of things he wanted to tell Nix. He wanted to tell her about his students and about the projects he'd planned for them; he wanted to tell her about the age of the short raker rockfish and about collecting smolts in the streams in spring. Nix held the aura of the exotic. Ed looked at her and felt a door opening. He didn't know where this door led or who might be on the other side, but it didn't seem like a problem. He just looked at her and felt opportunity, felt that if he passed it up now he might never get another chance. He hadn't expected this fullness in his heart and he knew it was both stupid and dangerous, but he hadn't been in love long enough with Tina to know that he should be taking the small feelings of restraint more seriously.

Nix was awed. She was grateful and flushed and looked for all the world as if she were in love, but she wasn't, not with Ed anyway.

It was this place, this forest in the sea, and it was the experience of paddling through the snow. She'd thought that Ed might have a crush on her, but that wasn't unexpected. Many men fell in love with the bass player; bass was a sexy instrument. And it was easy enough to shake men off in bars. There was always lots of space to fade into, and other people to fade away with. But this morning, as she paddled back to the dock and looked at the tiny village, at how much it looked like a little town inside one of those snow globes, she realized that her tactics had better change.

The bow of her boat bumped the dock, and Ed was already out of his own and ready to help her tie up.

"That was amazing," she said. "Thanks, Ed, I'll never forget it."

"Aw, don't worry about it." He was slapping his gloves together and shifting from foot to foot. "Listen, I have a sauna out in back of my place. I was thinking of getting it warmed up later. You all could come. You could bring the whole band by. We could eat something, take a sauna, you know, get warmed up."

"That might be great. I'll ask the guys. Would we get to meet your wife?" Nix beamed wholesomely. She didn't want her question to sound like a sleazy accusation; she wanted to sound casually friendly, but she saw Ed's expression change.

"Yeah . . . yeah . . . you could meet Tina, and we could take a sauna. That would be great. Maybe in an hour or so the sauna will be hot."

"You know, Ed, I think I'm going to pass this time. We're talking about getting the stage set up and getting our gear and set list together. Why don't you bring Tina to the club tonight? We'll meet her there. I tell you what, the drinks will be on me. We can talk about a sauna then."

"Sure . . . good." For a moment Ed started to despair in the way only desperate lovers do. But then it occurred to him that she was saying she wanted to see him again, and he was buoyed by blissful optimism in the way only desperate lovers can be.

"Yeah, great, I'll see you tonight then," and he waved as she walked up the ramp to the boardwalk.

The great blue heron had flown up to the top of one of the light poles in the harbor, had settled there to survey the vastness of the inlet. It watched Ed stuff the spray skirts into the boats and Nix walk up the ramp and the entire world fill up with snow.

Back at Clive's house, the rest of the band was just waking up. Bonnie was making scrambled eggs, and Rick was cutting up green onions; Clive was standing in front of the window drinking a cup of coffee; Earl the drummer was wrapped in his sleeping bag on the couch watching *It's a Wonderful Life* on television. He'd worked a week in a rhythm and blues band in Victoria and got tired of it; he'd turned down a salsa band in Winnipeg; he'd decided to follow the band to Alaska.

"Man, I *hate* that fucking Mr. Potter," he said. "I mean, the man *has* that fucking eight thousand dollars. It pisses me off every time I see this movie. I tell you he'd be missing something more than his legs if I worked at that bank. You can believe that!"

"They needed you in Bedford Falls, man," Rick called out from the kitchen.

"Damn," said Earl. He got up and ambled to the kitchen in his underwear. "I'd get Uncle Billy his eight grand *long* before they have to have that party and shit." He cocked his thumb and pointed his forefinger at the side of Rick's head. Rick laughed and scraped the green onions into the eggs.

Earl was showing off for Clive, and the other band members knew this. They knew Earl was always a lot more "black" around club owners, a sort of defense mechanism or something. They liked him both ways, but they knew he wasn't really "street." He came from a wealthy family in Toronto with a father who was an orthodontist and a mother who taught piano in their home. Before attending Oberlin, he'd studied at McGill. Before that he'd probably been a hockey player. He was a hell of a good drummer, and Rick wanted to hold onto him.

Billy was down on his boat checking his gear. Weasel had promised to look after things and he'd done the minimum, but the old boat felt cold and dank. Mildew had set in on the pads and the bedding; rainwater had started to leak in from the top of the house next to the radar pulpit. Nothing feels as cold as an old wooden vessel that's been left unattended; it's a bone-cold that goes all the way through you. Billy sat on the edge of his bunk and wondered what he was doing back in Cold Storage. As soon as he'd walked onto the boat, his old life had come up and hit him in the face. His old life felt like this boat. It was cold, cramped, and impractical. It took a force of will to enter the dream world of Cold Storage, and Billy didn't know if he had the strength to reclaim that life. He didn't know if he wanted to.

He rummaged around, trying to get the stove started so he could at least get the stink out of the bedding. He unpacked some of the gear he'd brought along from Vancouver, found *The Tibetan Book of the Dead*, and held it in his hands for a few moments before putting it back in his pack. He turned off the oil stove, plugged in an old heat lamp that worked off of the shore power, grabbed everything that wasn't mildewed, and trudged back to the boardwalk. He would live in the house with Bonnie and the band.

Billy's old life was gone; it had left him when he went into the water off the coast. It was yet to be seen what his new life would be or to whom it belonged, but one thing was certain. It didn't belong on this boat in the winter.

THE WINTER EASED along from one dark day to the next. Lester and Jake worked on their script, and Blind Donkey played at the Love Nest. Trooper Brown was apparently off chasing crooks in some other part of the state because no one in town reported any contacts.

For two weeks in January, the snow piled up along the boardwalk until a northern high pressure system stalled over the outside coast. The clear skies brought temperatures in the low teens, and the town was encrusted in a frosting of snow. The school children got out early to go skating up on the little lake behind the main water supply for the fish plant. Ed took the kids up there, but Tina stayed in school, preparing lessons.

A few fishermen came in with winter king salmon, and a local diver hauled king crab up from the inlet. After Christmas, the café started offering a "Feast of Kings" buffet on Sunday mornings. It featured crab, crab omelets, eggs any style, poached salmon, and bagels flown in from Juneau; it cost twenty-five dollars a head but was all you could eat, at least until something ran out.

The Sunday morning buffet became a regular event for the band after their Saturday night gigs. If they could make it to the café before eleven o'clock in the morning, they could count on having a meal that lasted them the rest of the day. They were under contract to play a full set on Sunday after the church service and usually rehearsed Sunday evenings while the regulars listened, playing records between sets.

Miles finished off his crab omelets and watched kids bundled in hats and gloves run along the boardwalk. Their toboggans slipped along behind them and through the windows—steamed up from the coffee urn, which had overflowed earlier in the morning—they looked like Christmas decorations. Miles was content.

He drank the last of his tea and was about to get up when Tina came in the door. She smiled at the waitress and waved at the two other people sitting on stools at the counter but walked directly to Miles's back booth and sat down.

"If I get a divorce, will you be my boyfriend?"

Only a few months ago, before Clive had returned to town and reopened the Love Nest, Miles might have answered differently, but now he thought for a moment and asked, "Would you be a Betty or a Veronica kind of girlfriend?"

"Betty or Veronica?"

"You know, like in the Archie comics." He got up, grabbed another pot of tea from the counter.

She opened the menu. "I'm a Betty. Definitely a Betty."

"Jeepers, I don't know. I've always been more of a Veronica kind of guy," said Miles.

"First of all," she said, leaning in with real urgency, "you are not a Veronica kind of guy. Every man thinks he's a Veronica kind of guy, and that's just crap. You want to have sex with Veronica, you might even marry Veronica for her money, but you'll divorce her and end up with Betty. But whatever. I can change. Betty . . . Veronica . . . I can change." She brushed her hair back from under her collar and sat back in the booth. Clearly irritated now, she went on, "What I want to know is will you be there for me if I got a divorce?" She closed the menu, turned her head, looked at him.

Miles stirred some milk and sugar into his tea and looked down into the muddy swirls. The kid washing dishes in the kitchen dropped a salad bowl, and someone was swearing at him.

"I don't think you can change that much," he said. "I think you just have to be either a Betty or a Veronica. It's like saying you could become a Reggie or a Moose if you were really a Jughead . . ."

He stopped mid-sentence, embarrassed now. She stared at him for a long moment. Someone in the kitchen cracked an egg on the hot grill.

"Are you making fun of me?" she said.

"Ah . . . I don't think so," he said through a painful grimace, wishing now he could turn back the conversation like a page of a book.

Clive came in, pulling off his mitts. He looked around, walked over to their booth.

"Which character from the Archie comics do you think I am?" Tina asked, her voice rising.

Clive pulled off his hat, slid in beside Tina, lifted up the lid on the teapot and peered in. "Oh man . . . Let me think . . ." He snapped down the lid and looked her up and down three times before speaking again. "She is secretly a Veronica, but she wants the world to think she's a Betty." He pulled off the scarf wrapped around his neck, looked at her again for a long moment, then shook his head in confirmation of his own judgment.

Tina was becoming upset. "Fine. I'm a Veronica. Fine. But will you be my boyfriend if I get a divorce?"

Now the cooks were out leaning their elbows on the counter waiting for the answer.

"Wow . . . This is a different conversation than I thought." Clive turned and waved to Meredith in the kitchen, got up and walked over to the buffet.

"And I suppose you guys think you're both Reggies?" Her voice was rising in pitch as if she were about to start screeching for her butler.

"That's a *very* Veronica thing to say," Clive called. He kept loading bagels, cream cheese, and prehistoric-looking crab legs on his plate.

"Yeah," Miles said, as if he were reappraising Tina in a new light.

"But . . ." Clive sat down and cracked one of the fifteen-inch crab legs against the corner of the table. ". . . to answer your question, I only *think* that I'm a Reggie. In fact, I am much more a Jughead but with some of Dilton Doily's intelligence."

"And your brother?" Tina leaned back and crossed her arms.

"My brother wants the world to think he's an Archie, when in *fact* he's really Mr. Weatherbee."

"Mr. Weatherbee?" Miles didn't have much fight in his voice.

"Oh, yeah," Clive insisted. "The B. Ever since he was a kid, he's had that frustrated authority thing going."

The door opened and Nix came in, looking like she'd been skiing or sledding. Her nose was running and her face was flushed and Little Brother was following close behind her. She stopped and said to him, "I'm sorry, sweetie. You wait outside, and I'll try and bring you something later."

He looked at her for a moment as if pretending not to understand. She pointed at the door and scowled at the dog. He slowly backed out, turned to jump onto a snow-covered table by the window. He circled twice and settled down, his head level with the bottom of the glass, his sad eyes scanning the inside of the café.

Nix walked through the steamy clatter, pulling off her stocking cap and unwinding the long scarf around her throat. Clive jumped up and waved Nix over.

"Whew, it smells good in here. I'm hungry." She sat down opposite Tina and slipped the parka off her shoulders but awkwardly kept her arms in the sleeves. Clive smiled, offered to buy her breakfast, and she was about to go over to the buffet when Tina reached over and grabbed her arm.

"Don't you think I'm a Betty?" she pleaded.

"You mean like Betty Rubble in the *Flintstones*?"

"Oh, Christ." Tina put her head in her hands and almost started sobbing. Outside, Little Brother lifted his head and squinted to see what was going on.

"That could be it," Clive exclaimed. "Betty Rubble."

"She's hot." Miles smiled as if remembering an old affair. "I always had a kind of secret thing for Betty Rubble."

"Me, too!" Nix put her hand on Miles's shoulder. "I'm so glad to hear you say that. I thought I was the only one. That nice little shape, the short skin dress. Rowww." Nix got up, ambled lazily over to the buffet table.

"Betty Rubble was married to a dope," Tina moaned.

"But she was sexy as all get out," Nix called over, "and besides, her husband was a lovable dope."

Meredith made Nix some scrambled eggs with crab and melted cheese on top and added some toasted English muffins to her plate. Nix poured a mug of black coffee, leaned back in the booth.

"My husband has a crush on you," said Tina after a while. Clive and Miles watched without moving. Meredith came running back out of the kitchen to listen.

"I know," Nix apologized. "I'm sorry. I haven't done anything to encourage it. Do you believe me when I say that?"

"I do . . . I think." Tina hesitated. "But are you maybe sending him signals that give him hope?"

Nix picked up her English muffin, bit into it, and melted cheese pulled away like a thread. Everyone in the restaurant, including the dog out front, waited while she swallowed.

"When I think about it now," she said, "Ed's a definite Barney Rubble. He's nice. He's nice to me. But I don't want to sleep with him, and I definitely wouldn't want to get between him and that gorgeous Betty." She rolled her eyes heavenward at the mention of Bedrock's siren.

Tina smiled. Meredith went back and got a bowl of oatmeal. Little cups on the side held yogurt, raisins, and brown sugar, and Tina looked down at it.

"I think I'll have the buffet," she said. "I'm a brand-new Betty." She sounded amazed, but Nix held the palm of her hand up and they high-fived.

THE REST OF the band came in one by one. They stamped the snow off their feet before opening the door and blew on their bare hands once they were inside. Earl walked over to the booth, greeted them with, "They're not out of the crab, are they?"

They weren't.

Miles took his pot of tea over to the counter where Bonnie was sitting on a stool, hunched over a menu.

"We really only look at the menu when we don't want to talk to folks, but since you are relatively new here, I could be misinterpreting the signals," Miles said to the side of her face.

"Huh?" Bonnie looked up. "I'm sorry, Miles, I was just thinking."

He sat down. Billy billowed through the door, nodded over to Bonnie, and then walked to the back of the café.

"Billy's got a whole new look now." Miles turned to watch the jeans and black tuxedo jacket, the unshaven face, and the new haircut stride over to the horn section. "It's that half-shaven, magazine model, 'Oops! I didn't realize I was so sexy' look."

"Tell me about it." Bonnie didn't look up.

"Let me buy you breakfast." His good mood was holding up rather well, probably would until the southerly weather blew up in a couple of days. The wind that would come and make a grey, sloppy mess of the whole town.

"No, that's okay, Miles." She smiled weakly at him. "I'm just going to have some toast and coffee. I'll save up your offer for the time I can really soak you."

"You look like you're thinking about heading out of here."

Bonnie kept her eyes on his. "No . . . not really . . . well, I don't know. I like this place, Miles." She looked at the plate of toast that Meredith set in front of her as if it held some answers. "You know, my life has been screwy for the last few months. I took some right turns when everyone expected me to go straight ahead."

"But now the glamorous rock and roll life has jaded you?"

"No, that's not it. I don't regret coming to Cold Storage, it's been great . . ." Her voice drifted off.

"But?"

Bonnie looked out the steamed up window, out past Little Brother waiting on the cold table. The snow was falling past the rigging on the boats in the harbor; the water was a flat slate-green, and the snow fell into it without a ripple. A crow was standing on the handrail of the boardwalk, snow gathering on its back.

"I don't know what I'm doing here." It sounded as though the thought had just occurred to her. "It's dumb, I know, but I'm still not sure if I'm in the right place, doing the right thing." She put down her mug and turned toward him; opened her mouth; stopped and looked down into the swirl of her coffee; didn't notice the sound of the door opening, one person coming in, another one leaving.

Miles spoke finally. "Heck, Bonnie, I don't think anybody ever really knows." He played with the damp string on the tea bag.

The crow on the handrail strutted back and forth for a moment, jabbing the air with his pointy beak until a kid with a sled came barreling down the boardwalk.

"You know what I thought your big question was?" asked Miles.

"No . . ." Bonnie drew the word out. She looked as if she were expecting a scolding.

"I thought you were wondering if you should have bothered rescuing Billy."

"Ah, no, that's not it." She looked at Miles. "That was a good thing. The weird part is, as incredibly romantic as this all sounds, pulling him out of the ocean and all, I just don't love him."

"That's the weird part?" His eyebrows arched.

"That's terrible, isn't it?"

"Heck, no. It's not terrible. Jumping in and grabbing him was a choice you made at the time. It wasn't a contract," said Miles clearly.

Bonnie shook her head. She looked him straight in the eye. "I know *that*, Miles, but . . . you know . . . sleeping with him for a few months could give him an impression that I was in love with him."

"People make that mistake all the time." Miles smiled at her.

"I don't."

"Well, do you want to stick this out with Billy because you rescued him?"

"No."

"So, where do you want to go? What do you want to do?" Miles picked up a triangle of her buttered toast.

"Maybe I just need to go some place warm for a while." She sighed, hunched up her shoulders.

Miles stood up and pulled on his gloves. "You want to come up with me to the tubs?"

Bonnie looked down again and slowly took a sip of her coffee. Outside on the rail, the crow lifted into the air and shook off the snow like a spray of water. Cold Storage, Alaska, was too small, she thought to herself, but then the crow flapped off into the same sky that covered the Pacific Ocean, the same sky that covered Hawaii and the Sea of Japan. The crow was either gone forever or just around the corner.

"Yes." She stood up, walked directly out the door without fanfare.

Clive turned and watched from his booth. "Come by the bar later?" he asked. "I need a signature on the last of the forms. I promised to mail them. Can you do that?"

"Uh . . . yeah . . ." Miles tried to look out the door and over at his brother all at the same time. "Yeah . . ."

"Well, don't worry about it now. You better get going."

"Uh . . . yeah . . ."

"Go!" said Clive, and Miles went.

IN ITS HEYDAY, Cold Storage had been the summer headquarters of the salmon fleet. There had been a well-stocked store with fishing and mechanical supplies, three shipwrights, a welder, a portable sawmill, and a fair selection of lumber. There had also been a snack bar on the docks and three fully professional whores who lived above the two bars. When one of the whorehouses featured a short wave radio and a tall antenna to pick up late night radio signals in distant towns, the old timers complained about the encroachment of civilization.

Use of the bathhouse had been divided into men's and women's hours, but in the summertime at the height of the season, it was generally acknowledged that any time after eleven o'clock at night the tubs might be used by both sexes. By eleven o'clock in late June, the sky was a purple bruise of twilight; if you were walking down the boardwalk on such an evening, you would likely see the impossibly white skin of Norsky fishermen's backsides as they stood naked and steaming by the railing outside the bathhouse. They would be drinking from a can of cheap beer and talking about fish prices. They would nod to you with their chins as you passed, without an ounce of shame at their startling white nakedness. It had not become so civilized that a man couldn't stand naked in the middle of town.

ON SUNDAY AFTERNOONS now, the bathhouse was closed for cleaning. Different volunteers signed up for duty but it was hit or miss if any of them ever showed up, so even though it was noon on the dot by the time Miles and Bonnie showed up with towels and cleaning brushes, the place was empty. Weasel, looking more than slightly hungover, had just arrived, but he wasn't overwhelmed with enthusiasm at the prospect of draining the tub, scouring the rock sides, and scrubbing the concrete decking. When Miles suggested that he and Bonnie take care of the cleaning, Weasel handed his buckets to them with a smile and walked away without saying a word.

Miles swung the sign on the door over to the CLOSED FOR CLEANING—DON'T BOTHER KNOCKING BECAUSE WE WON'T LET YOU IN side and locked the door.

"What do we have to do?" asked Bonnie.

"We warm up in the tub. Then we drain it, scrub it, mop around the sides with some cleanser, and then sweep out the dressing room on the way out." Miles started to unbutton his shirt. "There are some extra bathing suits in the lost and found, or you can work in your underwear. I usually just take my clothes off, if that's okay." He stopped and looked at her, trying to look completely impassive about working in the nude.

"That's fine. I'd rather not wear someone else's old suit anyway," she said, and slipped off her parka, sat down to untie her snow boots.

The oil stove didn't throw out enough heat to keep the air much above freezing; they took their clothes off, went into the next room and down the concrete steps to where the tub lay sunken into the floor. Miles filled one of the plastic dipper jugs. He carried it over to stand by one of the drains and poured the water over his head, and Bonnie followed suit. The sound of the water hitting the concrete clattered in Bonnie's ears like marbles. Then they walked back and eased themselves into the warm water.

The skylight above them was covered with snow that melted around the edges, and the only sound in the cavernous room was the fat plonking of drops falling into the hot water where they leaned back across from each other, their white skin flushed red, their heads resting on the upper lip, and their legs spread out. The tub was large enough that their legs overlapped but their toes didn't touch the sides.

"Are you in love with anyone here, Miles?" Bonnie's voice echoed.

"No." They listened to the drops hitting the water.

Bonnie turned away, rolled into the water, dunked her head, embarrassed. Sputtering, she came up next to Miles's outstretched legs. He noticed that her hair was very thick and more red than it had first appeared.

"I'm sorry. I didn't mean to pry," she said. "Just forget I asked that."

Miles sat in the hot water, felt the heat easing into his bones, and fanned the water with his hands, held up one red leg to let a fat drop of snowmelt land on it. He didn't say anything. He lowered his leg back into the water and watched drops falling through the gloom and plopping into the water near Bonnie's face.

"All right, tough guy. Enough out of you." She smiled. "I don't want to know anymore." She cupped his bare foot in her hand for a moment and sat up on the ledge. She had small breasts and broad shoulders, like a good swimmer, Miles thought, and his mind flashed on a picture of her pulling through the waves to snatch Billy out of the sea.

"You pretty warm?" he asked her.

"Yeah, I'm hot." She waved her hand in front of her face.

"Come on," he said, and walked over to the darkest corner of the concrete bunker, to a door of thick planking with mildewed canvas stuffed around the edges to keep out the cold air. He wrenched it open.

Outside at the base of the hillside was a small fenced yard, smooth as a blanket, with fifteen inches of undisturbed snow. Fence posts wore white caps, and trees were laden with pillows of snow. Wind blew near the ridge up on the mountain, and snow sizzled off the trees like goose down. The woods were a tangle of dark green, and Miles stepped out into the yard, lifted his feet like a crane and punched holes through the snow.

"This used to be where they stored coal for the dressing room furnace. They used up all the coal and switched to oil," Miles explained and turned toward her, spread his arms wide and looked straight up into the falling snow. Flakes clung to his hair, melting as they touched his flushed skin, and he fell backward, landing with outstretched arms to make a snow angel.

Bonnie jumped in, too, swung her arms and legs, shrieked as the cold crept back into her bones. She was ready to run and jump into the hot water until she looked over at Miles. Snow lay on his chest, around his groin, and his penis had retreated; she reached over and put her hand on his chest.

"Holy cow, Miles," she asked. "How much cold can you take?" She rubbed her cold hands up and down his chest.

"I don't know," Miles kept staring up into a maelstrom of flakes, "but I've just decided something."

"What's that?" She rolled over, her belly and breasts against his chest, and started to shiver, but he could feel her warm breath on his face.

"I've decided I don't want to find out." And he jumped up, rolled Bonnie off into the snow.

"Good," she said, "because I'm not up to saving another man."

Miles looked down at her pale heat-pink body curled into the outline of the snow angel, steam rising from every inch of her. He pulled her up with both hands, and as he did, he kissed her. He had meant it to be a quick kiss, a sort of introductory offer, but she held him hard and her slick mouth stayed against his mouth. Her skin was warm underneath the melting snow clinging to her back, and as they kissed, he moved his hands up and down her back, wiped the ice off her body. She wiped the ice off the back of his arms, then leaned away from his face, wiped the snow from his hair and put her cold fingers to his cheeks.

"Let's go get warm," she said, and put the flat of her cheek against his chest.

GETTING BACK INTO the hot water, their bodies ached at first; their hands and feet stung where the cold had taken hold. Miles sucked in his breath and eased into the water and felt as if his bones were bending out of place, but then the warmth came on like the blush of morphine and his body relaxed into the thermal water. Bonnie's eyes closed and she pushed the water with her hands, floated over to the ledge and put an arm around Miles's waist.

He got up to get the bucket and the stiff-bristled deck brushes from the dressing room and, as the water level went down, he showed her how to clean the sides of the pool. They spent an hour scrubbing the walls while hot water continued pouring in through cracks in the rocks, and if they began to cool, they poured water over their heads. Miles finished his side of the tub; he sat near a small stream of hot water at the bottom of the rocks, sluiced water over his head, and watched Bonnie.

She had her back to him, and against the sharp angles of grey-green rocks, her body seemed a miracle of smooth edges and pliable strength. She poured water over her head; Miles watched it slide down her throat to the groove along her spine, between her shoulders, up over the curve of her hips, then spread over her bottom, flowing to her legs. Miles had never looked at a woman like this before. Her arms were strong and, as she worked the rock with the brush, the wings of her shoulder blades widened and her muscles pushed against her reddening skin; she occasionally reached behind her back and scratched the skin above her waist or on her upper thigh, and in the heat-soaked atmosphere, her fingers left faint red tracks.

He felt almost dizzy watching her. He wanted to say something about how beautiful she was, but he didn't know if he could say anything clearly; he had become too thick-headed. But they talked about their lives, about the different wars they had fought and the journeys they had made. They talked about people they had lost and books they had read and music they loved. The talk was easy as they were working in the nude, and their minds were unhinged with the strangeness of it all.

They finished scouring the rocks, put the plug back in, and scrubbed the decking around the tub as it filled with fresh water, then sat in the clean water on the freshly scrubbed rocks and enjoyed the product of their labor for a few moments.

Miles swept the floor of the dressing room and Bonnie got dressed, then she folded some towels for the lost and found as Miles got dressed. The job was done, and they looked around. A silence overtook them as if the door to the dressing room opened up onto a busy city street, and they didn't want to walk out there just yet. Bonnie reached up on a shelf where someone had left some hair bands wrapped around a pair of reading glasses. She stretched the hair bands between Miles's fingers and plucked them with her thumb.

"Come by the club tonight. They are going to be working on some new material," she said. "It's good. Some really wild arrangements of Stan Rogers songs, kind of sea shanty swing." She nudged his shoulder with hers and smiled. "Don't be glum."

"I'm not glum," said Miles. "I'm just not ready to go outside, you know, to work and everything."

"What would you rather do?" she asked.

"I would rather watch you clean those rocks," he said seriously.

"You were watching me?" She laughed. "My God, Miles, I thought you were a professional."

Miles started to lean away from her, embarrassed, but she stepped forward and kissed him and he could feel the heat of the earth through her clothes as they held on to each other in a long kiss, until they heard footsteps coming toward the door. It was time to open the bathhouse for men's hours. There was a knock on the door, but Bonnie and Miles kept hugging each other in their damp clothes, each of them wanting just one more second.

The knocking came again, and Miles said, "I better get that, or they just might break it down." He went over and unlocked the door, and there was Lester, standing in sweatpants and slippers with a towel slung over his shoulder. He stared at them, and they picked up their towels, got ready to go. His eyes scanned them: Miles, then Bonnie, then back to Miles.

"I'm glad you two finally got together," he said. "Is it like official now, or do you want me to keep it on the QT?" Lester smiled. It might have been the most perfect smile of irony that Miles had ever seen.

THEY WALKED THE boardwalk down to the Love Nest through snowflakes floating like dust motes. Bonnie slipped her warm hand into Miles's, and he squeezed softly but let go.

The bar was dark, a CLOSED sign hanging in the door. Miles rapped against the glass, tried the handle and they walked in, flipped on the one set of lights behind the bar.

Little Brother raised his head from his bed and growled but only halfheartedly.

"I think this dog trusts women," Miles said. He looked around the bar. Where was Clive?

"I'm not saying a thing about this dog and who he trusts or does not trust." Bonnie eased around the other side of the bar away from the dog, but his eyes followed her and his chest heaved gently like a bellows with the fire banked down.

"Clive?" his brother said, and shined a beam of light around the room. He spoke to Bonnie. "He said he needed me to sign some papers." The beam of light landed on a missing ceiling panel with a ladder standing underneath. They stopped to listen.

No sound.

And then a bump in the attic. Little Brother was up off his pad, standing beside the ladder, and growling up into the mouth of the hole in the ceiling. Miles started to climb but he heard scuffling along the rafters; he held the flashlight high above his head and away from his body in case it attracted the wrong kind of attention . . . or he had to use it as a club. The ugly dog roared, and Miles jumped up the ladder, two rungs at a time, shining the light toward the rustling.

There was nothing to see at first, just a series of forms stacked along the rafters. Then he saw the top of Weasel's head, poking out from between a dozen or so bales of marijuana.

"Some fucking lookout you are!" yelled Weasel.

Little Brother barked and lay back dwn on his pad by the door.

CHAPTER SIXTEEN

T HE NEXT MORNING, Tina wrote a letter to the school board asking for an extended period of unpaid leave to last for an indefinite period of time. She walked up the boardwalk, dropped the letter on the counter of the city office, and asked Betty to give it to the school board. She walked down the ramp to the floatplane dock, swung her small daypack up to the pilot, climbed into the back seat, and flew away.

Ed was at the clinic within half an hour. Miles was there waiting for a kid who had phoned ahead to tell him, very loudly, that he had a peanut stuck in his ear.

"Jesus, Miles, you could at least have told me you were sleeping with my wife!"

Miles sat at his desk, stared out the window overlooking the harbor. The southerly weather had come in overnight and rain was falling on the snow, turning the ramps and floats of the harbor into rutted runways of slush.

"Ed, I've got someone coming to see me in five minutes. I don't have time to get into this with you."

"So you are not denying it?" His face was flushed, his leather boots were soaked, and he looked like he was hot and cold at the same time.

"I'm saying I can't get into this right now. Come back at five. We'll go have a cup of coffee and you can yell at me all you want, and I'll tell you everything I know about this situation."

"Shit!" Ed blurted. "You know that Trooper Brown? He called me. He's coming out here tomorrow. I'm going to fucking tell him everything. You know, I'm going to tell him everything about Weasel and the marijuana. " He stormed out and slammed the door.

Miles felt the echo as he watched rainwater streaming off the icicles hanging from the eaves. Maybe he should have told Ed that he had never slept with Tina, but it wouldn't have helped. Ed would have blustered and fought, and he would have still been arguing when Mark White walked through the door to have Miles take a look in his right ear.

When Mark was four years old, he'd had a raisin lodged up his nasal passage for "an unspecified number of weeks," according to his old medical records. Miles was curious to see what might be lodged down Mark's ear now and didn't want the kid scared off by the sight of an angry teacher screaming at the only health care provider in sixty miles.

Ed could wait. In fact, Miles thought it might be a good idea all round if Ed thought he had been sleeping with Tina. If word was out that Miles was sleeping with Tina, the local judgment against him would be harsh, but if it were followed by the rumor that he was actually sleeping with Bonnie, then he would be redeemed and brought back into the fold without ever having done a thing. This was the backfire theory of gossip, and Miles had seen it successfully applied on a number of occasions.

But the idea of Ray Brown coming back to Cold Storage was worrying him. There were bails of marijuana in the rafters of the bar, and it wouldn't take much of a drug dog to sniff it out; there were probably patrons of the Love Nest who were coming in there just for the contact high.

Fine, Miles thought, *let him come.* Search warrants and evidence teams, lawyers and plenty of gossip, his only brother being flown out of town in handcuffs—there was nothing Miles was going to try and do about it. He had to get a peanut out of a kid's head.

Mark claimed to have no idea how a cocktail peanut had wedged itself into his ear, and Miles didn't press him for a confession; he just flushed it out with baby oil and a soft plastic probe, got the papery peanut skin out with warm water, and sent Mark scrambling out the door to meet his sledding buddies. In Cold Storage, the snow season was so short that kids were willing to put up with the regional challenge of snowboarding through slush.

Miles was in his office when Jake arrived.

"Where's your receptionist, for God's sake?" he called down the hall.

"She's on vacation."

"Really?" His voice was headed for Miles's office. "How long has she been gone?"

"I don't know." Miles didn't look up from his desk. "I think she went to Disneyland sometime in the winter of 1979. No one has heard from her since."

"I can see why. They've added a lot of good stuff in Disneyland." Jake pulled up a chair and sat down, his blue sling visible under a wool coat of Lester's.

Miles finished up his report on Mark. "Are you getting tired of our idyllic little corner of the world?"

"I've lived in worse spots."

"You aren't interested in getting back to your old life?"

"Which old life you talking about?"

"Your glamorous life of crime."

"You know, Miles, I don't care how good Quentin Tarantino makes it look. Crime sucks." Jake had refused to go into Sitka for treatment. He'd cut his cast off months ago. He and Lester had fashioned a unique type of binding/sling arrangement that still bedeviled him with itching and periodic rashes. He flopped down in the clinic chair and started poking a knitting needle he had brought with him down into his binding.

"How so?" Miles set the notepad down and looked at Jake, watched him scratch his arm.

"Too much stress. And you have to deal with too many assholes." Jake closed his eyes and moaned slightly as he scratched under the calico fabric he had bought from Tina.

"Isn't the money good?"

"You know how much you can make on one of those friggin' spaceship movies?"

"Which spaceship movie?" asked Miles.

"Christ, pick one!" Jake kept scratching. "A ton of fucking money. Even a bad spaceship movie is better money than cocaine, and the best part is people love you. They point you out to their kids. Waiters are genuinely nice and ask for your autograph. That kind of shit doesn't happen to Pablo Escobar." Jake withdrew the knitting needle and inspected it as if expecting to find some strange organism stuck on the end of it. "At least not in America, and who the fuck wants to be famous in Columbia, no matter how much money you've got?"

Miles wheeled over on his chair and started inspecting Jake's arm and gently unwinding the packaging.

"That is true," Jake continued. "Trust me. Not many

people make it. But that's the same in crime. Shit, crime is a lot more competitive, and of course the competition is a lot rougher." Jake pantomimed a pistol to his head. "But this script. I can feel it, Miles. This script Lester and I have got going. It's bankable. I'm telling you it has what people are looking for: humor, social comment, great characters, and fresh action."

"You got an ending that is satisfying? That's my big problem with most movies." Miles watched Jake's face as he rotated his shoulder.

"Fucking endings. Ouch! Christ, that still hurts!" Jake tried to get his damaged limb back from the PA.

"That's because you have a torn rotator cuff. You are going to have to have that looked at when you get somewhere with a good hospital. You can tell them you did it playing softball."

"Yeah, softball . . . Let me ask you something: do you think Lester is stubborn?"

"Lester?" Miles looked amazed. "I don't know quite how to answer that. I've never heard of him apologizing or ever changing his mind, but I guess that doesn't necessarily mean he's stubborn. He may be the one person who is always right."

"This guy! He's a genius. He comes up with things that I couldn't in a million years, you know what I'm saying? He's like a pipeline directly into some deep fucking well or something. But he doesn't know how to piece the stuff together. I mean, if it were up to Lester this would be a six-hour picture. I'm begging him to cut, and then I go on and he forgets about what he wanted. But this ending, he won't cut it and he won't forget it. I'm telling you, this ending is just not going to work, and I can't get him to budge."

"What's the problem?" Miles started wiping down the

pale white and discolored yellow skin of Jake's arm with an antiseptic lotion and a disposable wipe.

"In the last shot he wants everybody, all the characters, every single one, to turn into animals." Jake stared straight into Miles's eyes.

"And there is a problem with that?"

"This is an action picture. Can you imagine the look on the face of some studio big shot when I try to pitch the ending? Christ, I mean, we do something like that, we might as well make a movie about trees or something. I don't know. I might have to go back into crime." Jake raised his good hand to his forehead.

"You say Lester is good at his script ideas?"

"He's the best I've ever come across. I mean it." Jake reached out and touched Miles's elbow as he made his point.

"Then do the ending his way, wait a bit, and read it back to him. If it's stupid, he'll know how to finish it. But my advice is not to try to fight him. It's a no-win proposition."

"I believe you are right." Jake stood up. "But I've got too much time invested here to come up empty. You know what I'm saying?"

"Yes, I do," Miles ushered Jake out the door. "There's a cop coming to town tomorrow. He's an Alaskan state trooper. I just thought I'd tell you in case you've got something you might be worried about."

In the waiting room, Jake stood by the window, looking at the boats in the harbor. "I'm not in on that action. Shit . . . all that pot, having it dumped in the ocean side and bringing it back here to dry out. What's he going to do with it now? He needs a better business model. But I ain't giving it to him."

"Why don't I ever hear about this important stuff? I hear

all the bullshit, but when a member of my own family is committing multiple felonies no one says a word. Didn't you ever think of telling me?"

"No," replied Jake.

"What do you think I should do? About Clive and all this pot?"

Jake still stared out the window. "I don't know. Maybe we'll smoke some and all just turn into animals," he said, and his breath made an ovoid circle of fog on the windowpane.

Miles gave him some ointment for the itching and started saying something about obstructing justice and the possibility of going to jail, but Jake was lost in thought. "Yeah," he said absently, "we just need a good ending."

GLORIA BALLISTER CAME to see Miles every other week because she felt terrible. She weighed 285 pounds, smoked two packs of cigarettes a day, and easily drank a fifth of vodka every two days. Her husband was a heavy drinker, and she had stopped trying to get him to cut back. They lived out past the end of the boardwalk in a damp cabin with broken fishing gear piled in front: nets with holes and rusty haulers moldering into the moss.

Gloria was sick. Miles had given her everything he could think of in the way of practical health advice. She had boxes of books and pamphlets on everything from weight loss to sobriety. She had an oxygen bottle to help her breathe even though it was not strictly necessary, and she had gotten this on her own; she said the oxygen made her feel better, and Miles didn't dispute it.

Gloria wouldn't get up on the scales anymore. She came to the clinic to talk about her aches and pains; she came to ask questions about getting her stomach stapled; but mostly, Miles was convinced, she came just to get out of her cabin, have some human contact.

"Your color looks better this week, Gloria," Miles said. "Have you tried to walk a little more each day, like we talked about?"

She overflowed the small chair in the exam room, her arms folded awkwardly high up on her chest as if her body was trying to pinch them off. Her red eyes sank back into the folds of her face. She slurred her words, she was drunk, and everything about her spoke of unhappiness.

Miles had tried to be stern with her. He threatened not to see her at the clinic unless she flew in to Sitka and had a full screening, started taking responsibility for her health. She missed a few scheduled visits after that, and Miles got a call from a neighbor up the trail that Gloria hadn't been seen outside. He went and found her, lying on a filthy pad on the floor, her ankle badly sprained, blood and vomit smeared across her face; her husband sprawled unconscious on the bed in the middle of the room, his white belly extended like a corpse. Miles got a wheelchair, stopped her nose from bleeding, and made sure her ankle was propped up. She'd cried as they bumped down the trail to the boardwalk and as they'd trundled along to the clinic; Miles had let her spend the night there.

"You've just got to be ready, Doc," she said to Miles. "You've got to be ready before any change will come."

"What can we do, Gloria?" He spoke in a soft voice and patted her on the shoulder. "What will it take to get you ready for that change?"

"I don't know, Doc." She wheezed, touched his fingers. "Maybe I am as ready as I'll ever be."

So Miles let her visit the clinic every other week, and he tried to say something to inspire her to fly to Sitka. Every week he talked about a new diet plan or told her stories of people who had turned their lives around. She picked apart every suggestion, waved them away as if they were flies.

But Miles knew she was ready for change, ready for the most substantial kind of change. Nothing was going to shake her off her course. She was not going to stop drinking or start exercising, no matter how possible or even easy Miles made it look, and one day he would get a call from a neighbor or her husband might be sober enough to make it down to the clinic. Miles would grab some volunteers and a stretcher and lug Gloria's empty and unhappy body to the plane for Sitka where they would do a postmortem examination and ship her to the mortuary to be cremated.

Both Miles and Gloria knew that the day was coming soon, and after acknowledging it with gestures and subtle shifts in the tone they used with each other, they both relaxed. Miles still pestered her, but gently, and she still came to see him; she'd been the first to tell Miles the joke about a patient with only a few minutes to live.

Now she heaved herself up and said, "Well, Doc, you boiled me up another couple of eggs. I'll see ya." And she put on her rain slicker, picked up the two bent ski poles she used as walking sticks, and lumbered out the door onto the slushy boardwalk.

"I'll see ya, Gloria," Miles called, but she was already poking her shoulder back into the clinic.

"Hey, I heard that cop is coming to town to arrest your brother," she said.

"I hadn't heard that. I don't think that's true. Clive's broken no law I know of," assured Miles.

"Oh yeah. Okay." Gloria smiled weakly. "We've been talking about it, Doc. That cop can shove it up his ass as far as we're concerned. We're no snitches."

"That's good to know, Gloria." Miles unenthusiastically patted her shoulder, and she was gone.

By four thirty, it seemed dark as midnight. The rain had let up, but the air that rode in through the door with Billy seemed as wet as seawater.

He walked straight into Miles's chest. "Whoa! I'm sorry there, Miles." He peered up at Miles's nose.

"You okay, Billy? Something you need?"

"Naw, not really. I just came by, you know, just came by to talk." He looked around the room as if expecting someone else to be there; followed Miles as he walked back to get the fat folder of notes on Gloria; stood in the doorway and watched him write in the file.

"What you need, Billy?"

"I don't know really, Miles. I just kind of wanted to talk to you about something . . ." Billy eyes roamed around the room, not stopping to rest anywhere.

"I've got some time," said Miles. "Is this about Trooper Brown's visit tomorrow?"

"Huh? Oh, no, that's under control. I wanted to talk to you about something else."

"Good, because I think Ed is going to come by in about half an hour to shoot me, but I've got some time before that."

Billy laughed nervously. "Well, you know, Miles. I was kind of wanting to talk to you about Bonnie." He scratched the knuckles of his right hand and made a strange kind of grimace.

"Just spit it out, Billy."

"I'm just kind of screwed up is all, Miles. You know she saved my life and you know we were really close on board the ship, but now I don't know. She's nice and everything, but I don't know. It's different here. It's not like it was on the ship."

"Why are you telling me this, Billy?"

"I don't know, man. I know she likes you. I thought maybe you had some advice for me. Or maybe . . ."

"You want me to talk with her?" Miles tried to dampen the incredulity in his voice.

"Yeah . . . that would be great. Maybe you could talk to her like my doctor. You could tell her I've been unbalanced all my life. I've got some personality disorder or something. It's kind of true, you know, it wouldn't be like . . . lying or anything."

Miles stared at him. "So you are telling me you'd rather have me tell her you are crazy than talk to her yourself about your own completely understandable feelings?"

"Well, yeah, I guess so." Billy looked like he, too, couldn't believe how dense he was. "Yeah, I do . . . I mean, it's not all that strange. She saved my life. How can I just dump her right here in this little dinky town with nowhere for her to go?"

"Shit, Billy, there is always somewhere to go."

Miles had been prepared to fend off an accusation, so this strange request came as kind of a letdown. He had been prepared to justify his own feelings for Bonnie, so this suggestion that she was helpless and not worth fighting for was making him grumpy.

"And you want to dump her because of what?" He frowned at Billy. "Because she saved your life? Because there are so many other gorgeous women for you to choose from around here? I don't get it."

"Listen, Miles, what if . . . say . . . Ed McMahon came to your door and gave you a million bucks? You'd be happy, right?"

"Ed McMahon? You mean the guy from Johnny Carson?"

"Yeah, him. So say he shows up at your house and tells you you won a million dollars. You'd be so happy you might even invite him in and have a drink. You'd feed him a meal and maybe go out and get drunk with him. But hell, you wouldn't want him to be your best friend, would you? I mean it would be hard. You'd be hanging out with your friends and you would be like, 'Oh yeah, this is Ed, he's my new friend because he gave me a million bucks,' and they'd all look at you and all they'd think about was how this guy had saved your ass and then pretty soon that would be the only thing you could think about and pretty soon you wouldn't know what the fuck to say to Ed McMahon and you'd kick his sorry drunken-sidekick ass out on the street. You know what I'm saying?"

"The scary thing is," nodded Miles, "I think I do."

"So you'll talk to her for me?"

"Sure. Sure, Billy," he agreed and smiled weakly. "I won't even bill you."

Billy said something else, but Miles didn't hear him. He listened to Billy's footsteps fade out past the door and disappear, looked at his notes and didn't read them; he wanted to go home.

He wanted to avoid Ed. Something about the combination of Gloria and Billy had put him in a bad mood. He looked at his watch; he could close up shop and be gone before Ed could show up if he hurried.

He had unplugged the coffee pot and turned out his office light when Liz came in with her cat.

"Miles, I don't mean to trouble you, but can you help me? I don't know who else to ask." Her voice was shaking, her face was pale.

"Come on in, Liz." He hid his irritation. "What's wrong?"

She held out Louise, a delicate tabby with a white chest, two white paws, and a three-inch cut on top of her head. There wasn't a lot of blood, but the cut gaped through the grey fur. The cat was calmer than Liz.

"Let me take a look," said Miles.

Everyone knew that he wasn't supposed to work on pets, but it was too expensive to fly to Sitka. Before he'd agreed to the "no complaints, no returns" policy, most sick animals had been slung into a sack and buried at sea; now they lived. And even though it was against his policy, Miles started allowing "follow-up" exams for which he generally got paid with food: fish, berries or venison. Since he had terrible luck with his hunter-gatherer skills, this was not a bad thing.

Liz held Louise while Miles gently stitched up the wound.

"Does this have anything to do with my brother's dog?"

"No, I don't think so. We'd be looking at something worse than this. No, I think she got tangled up with a tomcat down at the cold storage. I try to keep her in the house, but with Bob and Matt running in and out all day long, she slips out."

Miles gently put one of her fingers on the thread to maintain the tension while he reached for scissors. She kept her gaze elsewhere, and they talked about new books in the library and the decline in the number of kids in school and whether the school would be able to stay open much longer.

"I hear we might be having a decline in the number of teachers, too." Liz looked at him for the first time since he'd started patching up Louise.

"I heard Tina flew out this morning," he countered. "You know anything about that, Liz?"

"No . . . nothing." Her eyes swept through the office. "Just what I've heard . . ." Liz's words drifted out on the still silence between them.

"And we all know how reliable boardwalk gossip is," said Miles, sounding cheerful but carefully changing direction. He snipped the thread and said, "There! You can bring her back in a couple of days. Don't tell my bosses back in Sitka, though."

"I won't, Miles." She picked up the cat, held it in her arms and thanked him, but she looked sad, sheepish.

"Don't worry about it, Liz." Miles said it again. "Really, don't worry about it," and they understood each other.

Tears welled up in her eyes. "I don't know what we'd do without you, Miles."

He did not look directly at her. He was touched by her words particularly because he knew that she was sober. He tried to remember. Was she a drinker? He didn't think so.

"Take good care of Louise, and I'll see you both in a couple of days." Tears ran down her cheeks.

MILES WAS GRATEFUL that Ed was late. He rushed around, turning off all the lights and grabbing his coat off the rack in his office. But Billy tapped him on the back as he was locking the door, and Miles jumped back as if he'd been shot with a dart.

"Christ, you scared me." Miles put his hand over his chest, leaned against the door.

"Here she is, Miles."

Bonnie stood there, perplexed, as if waking up from a vivid dream into unfamiliar surroundings.

"Here she is," Billy said again. "I told her you wanted to talk with her." He scratched the top of his head, shifted from one foot to the other. "Okay, I'll see you back at the bar," he said, and hunched his shoulders, rushed away through the rain that gleamed like pins under the few houselights along the boardwalk.

Bonnie had thought about Miles ever since they'd cleaned the tubs. She'd wondered what he was doing at odd times during the day. She'd tried to remember the smallest thing they had talked about, and this irritated her because she didn't want to be in love, not with anyone. Miles was good looking; he appeared to know who he was and what he was doing with his life, and while he didn't want to talk about his service in the war, he didn't seemed damaged in any way. He just seemed sensitive, as if he recognized some great beauty in her that he was perfectly willing to let slip away, or perhaps possess forever. This made her want him all the more, and it was driving her crazy.

"Did you want to talk to me, Miles?" she asked.

"Well, not really. I don't know how I got into this really, but Billy wanted me to talk to you."

"About what?" She took a half step toward him, her forehead furrowed.

"Well," he said, "it's kind of hard to explain, but he wants to break up with you because you saved his life and you remind him of Ed McMahon."

"Ed McMahon . . . you mean Johnny Carson's announcer?"

"Yep."

"And that's why he wants to break up with me?"

"Yep."

"Well . . ." She drew out the syllable and followed Miles's

gaze down the boardwalk. "I'm relieved. I thought he was going to make some kind of lame excuse about commitment or something."

"Exactly." Miles took her arm, and they walked toward Lester's house. "I mean, reminding someone of Ed McMahon is pretty serious. It's something that I think would be hard to overcome. No matter how much therapy you put yourself through. I'd say it's one of those insurmountable differences."

Bonnie stopped walking. "Do I remind *you* of Ed McMahon?"

"No. Not a bit."

"Good." And she leaned forward to kiss him lightly on the lips.

"For the love of God, Miles, what is it with you?" Ed stood ten feet behind them, yelling loud enough that gulls in the harbor lifted away from the water and started hee-hawing, laughing into the dark. "Weren't you happy enough fucking my wife? Tina's gone a day, and you're on to your next woman!" Ed clenched his teeth.

Miles's voice came louder than he'd intended: "I HAVE NEVER HAD SEX WITH YOUR WIFE!"

The gulls whirled in a chorus above the town. Miles looked up, and in the darkness they looked like bits of white paper caught in an updraft. Stragglers rose up in the lights of the fish plant and glowed like miniature space ships.

"It's true, Ed," said Miles. "I have never had sexual relations with that woman. I'm sorry, I mean Tina, you know. I have never had romantic relations with your wife. I have never kissed her or seen her naked." His voice must have been louder than he thought, for he looked over Ed's shoulder and saw the women's movie club standing in front of the café. Clive and Nix stood beside them, and Nix was holding a magazine up to protect herself from the rain. Everyone's eyes were fixed on Miles.

"I didn't catch the first part of that, Miles," said Clive. "I got the part where you said you hadn't fucked Ed's wife, but what were you talking about before that?"

Rain made little splashes on either side of Ed's shoes.

"I was telling Bonnie that she didn't remind me anything of Ed McMahon." Miles's voice hung in the air like one of the gulls.

"Well, thank goodness for that," said Colleen Sheehan. "I thought you were talking about running for president," and everyone chuckled, then walked back into the café.

"Say goodbye to your brother, asshole," Ed said to Miles over his shoulder and stormed down the boardwalk.

CHAPTER SEVENTEEN

THE COMMUNITY CENTER'S barrel stove burned a lot of firewood during the coldest part of winter. So every year a work party went across the inlet to fell some dead spruce trees. They bucked them up into logs small enough to roll out on the beach, floated them off at high tide, towed them back across to town and cut them into stove wood. The job took two days, and there were two crews: the logging crew and the splitting crew. This year, Billy wasn't signed up for any job, but Ed was on the splitting crew.

Thinking to keep himself out of town for most of the day and his brother as far as possible from Mouse Miller's Love Nest, Miles decided to join the logging crew and take Clive along. He had slept a little later than he'd planned; by the time he called his brother's house and Nix answered the phone, she told him to meet Clive after church, which was both odd and irritating because the longer they stayed in town, the greater the opportunity for Trooper Brown to find them. Miles had an uneasy feeling that he'd been left out of the loop on something.

He was walking to the bar, striding through the slushy tracks left by the slick-soled, leather-heeled shoes of people going to church, when he heard the blare of a floatplane taking off. That meant the trooper had already landed, and Miles

doubled his pace, hurrying to get to the church service in the
bar with a ceiling full of marijuana bales.

BEFORE THE SECOND preacher had left town and Mouse
Miller's Love Nest had become a place of worship, the only
church building had been shared by three congregations.
Every Sunday the Catholics had mass, then the Lutherans
celebrated communion, and finally a small group of Unitarians gathered to eat and tell stories from their membership.
The Catholics were workmanlike in their devotions and
were in and out pretty quickly; the Lutherans lingered only
somewhat longer; the Unitarians, however, could soak up the
rest of the day if the spirit moved them, so they were always
scheduled last.

Miles didn't belong to any of the congregations. He occasionally made it in time to hear part of a sermon, but mostly
he enjoyed sitting outside on a bench under the eaves, leaning
his head against the wall, listening to the singing, and drinking the coffee he'd brought along with him.

The church building was uphill from the fish plant on a
little flat of muskeg surrounded by trees. It was high enough
that you could see out almost to the mouth of the inlet,
and fishermen often came up to check the weather out on
the fishing grounds. To get the best view, they'd sometimes
climb the stairs into the modest bell tower. On Sundays,
they'd come tiptoeing along the back wall and clamber up
the stairs while the ten or so people in the congregation kept
going at their meditations, hammer, and tongs.

But this Sunday, the biggest congregation was meeting in
a bar. From fifty feet away, Miles could recognize the voice
booming through walls and windows, and he winced at what

was awaiting him inside. He had never heard his brother, his convicted felon of a brother, deliver a sermon, and he couldn't imagine what the text would be. In this area of his brother's redemption, what little faith Miles ever had was squandered.

Dressed in his warmest coveralls, he stood outside the bar and listened to the sermon. The scent of the yellow cedar trees blended with the aroma rising from his cup of coffee and he should have felt optimistic, but he was impatient, every moment thinking he could hear the trooper's footsteps coming along the boardwalk.

The bar was surprisingly full. A board had been placed over the pool table and covered with a white cloth to serve as an altar, and on chairs lined up especially for the service sat the parishioners: Gloria in a flowered blouse with an oxygen tank beside her; Liz and her cat Louise a row behind; Bonnie in a broad-brimmed white hat over by the bar; Weasel and Billy in clean blue jeans and Hawaiian shirts; Jake in black jeans, a white shirt, and his sore arm still hanging to his side. On the far side of the pool table sat Rick and the rest of the band with their instruments. Clive stood in his dark suit and skinny black tie beside the makeshift altar.

Clive saw his brother enter the room, and he launched into the scripture reading for the day. Romans, chapter thirteen. His voice was a bit shaky but it built as he read and was without irony or sarcasm; it had the quaver of humility.

"Owe no one anything," Clive began, "except to love one another; for he who loves his neighbor has fulfilled the law. The commandments—'you shall not commit adultery, you shall not kill, you shall not steal, you shall not covet,' and all the other commandments—are summed up in this sentence: 'you shall love your neighbor as yourself.' Love does no wrong to a neighbor; therefore love is the fulfilling of the law.

"Besides this, you know what hour it is, how it is full time now for you to wake from sleep. For salvation is nearer to us now than when we first believed; the night is far gone, the day is at hand. Let us then cast off the works of darkness and put on the armor of light."

Out on the boardwalk, Miles felt a blue shadow fall across his face.

"I want to talk to you," mouthed Ray Brown. Miles heard his brother's voice hesitate, saw the parishioners turn to watch through the open door to the outside, but he followed the trooper down the boardwalk.

"I don't know what you think you are doing here," Brown sputtered, "but I've been talking to the school teacher, and he's got an interesting story to tell."

"Before you get started, Trooper Brown," Miles interrupted, "I want you to know that I'm to blame for all this trouble." He could hear the congregation inside singing "Many Rivers to Cross." "Did Ed tell you that Clive was involved in any criminal activities?"

"He said that your brother was importing marijuana. He said he was associating with his former drug lord connection. He said your brother assaulted that old associate."

Miles spoke politely. "Well, Trooper, first of all, if you have reason to believe that anyone has broken the law, then you should make an arrest. I think you'll find all the parties here." He held out his hands toward the congregation as if inviting Ray Brown into the church and continued in the same low voice. "But you have to understand the motives behind Ed's statements to you, Ray. You see, he is very, very angry with me." Miles spoke softly, as if not wanting to disturb the devotions going on inside.

"Does he have good reason to be angry with you?" Brown asked with some interest.

"Actually, yes." Miles lowered his voice further. "You see, I've been having sex with his wife for several months now," he lied.

The trooper nodded nervously. Inside the church, a chorus of cracked voices swooned up to the high notes. Brown looked over the top of Miles's head through the dirty front window into the church where Clive stood with his arms wide and his voice raised in song while the musicians of Blind Donkey churned out the rhythm. The trooper watched dumbfounded, until Rick took a step forward to take his saxophone solo; then he swung back to speak fiercely to Miles. "I don't know what you think you've got going here, but I'm going to keep an eye on all this," he said, and stalked down the boardwalk, out of his face, but certainly not gone for good.

A murder of crows rose in a chorus and whirled out over the boardwalk. Miles wondered where Bonnie had got the hat she was wearing; he wondered if he would be able to see her after he got back from cutting trees and, if he did see her, what her expression would be. He looked at the sunlight slanting down through the wet cedar boughs and smiled at the thought of donning the armor of light.

"The day is at hand," Miles said out loud. He stood up, poured cold coffee over the edge of the boardwalk, and walked toward the harbor. He could hear the floorboards of the bar creaking as people got to their feet; he could hear them chatting as Clive stood in the doorway shaking hands, thanking everyone for coming, while this new sunlight slanted all around him through the clouds. It was almost ridiculously serene.

MILES WAS THE first one down to the boat. He sat and sharpened an axe for a few minutes until he heard footsteps banging down the dock.

"Christ, it's cold in here." Jake jumped onto the boat, still wearing his church clothes but with a canvas jacket thrown over his shoulders. "Let's get this thing going. Don't we have some wood to cut?"

More boots clomped down the dock, and the boat tilted with the weight of the men getting on board. Clive thudded onto the deck and started putting coveralls on over his black suit. "Brother!" he shouted to Miles with a fine smile on his face. "Good to see you in church this morning."

For the rest of the morning and on into the early afternoon, the logging crew was busy in the woods on the other side of the inlet. It took them half an hour to fell two spruce snags just off the beach. Their tips just reached the beach and the six men limbed them, bucked them into manageable lengths, and rigged the hand winches to pull them to the tide line. Clive and Miles used a heavy axe; the others whined and rattled with the saws. Lester worked on the rigging to pull the logs down onto the beach, and Jake tended the fire and sharpened a couple more axes. For a man with a torn up arm, he looked remarkably happy.

They took a lunch break at one thirty. The silence as the saws stopped seemed to rise from the ground. They'd worked up a fair sweat, so they put on dry jackets and gathered around the fire, spread their life jackets against the hillside and leaned against them to eat sandwiches and drink coffee.

The day held clear and cold. The slush from the previous day's rains had frozen on this side of the inlet. The sun slanted through the canopy, created pools of light on the forest floor, and icy snow lay in patches beneath the bare bushes. Everything seemed frozen and brittle.

Jake came over and sat down next to Miles and Clive. He put his head back and raised his face to the sunlight; he took a deep breath, smelled the wood chips and the earth they'd disturbed on the forest floor, smelled the wood smoke and felt the heat from the fire warming his legs. "Hey, boys, chow!" he said, and bit into his sandwich. He swallowed and turned to Miles. "So," he asked, "is the trooper happy?"

"I don't think he'll ever be happy until one or the other of us are in jail."

"I'm a little disappointed that he didn't search the place."

Miles swallowed his hot coffee too quickly. "Why's that?" he choked.

"It would make Weasel feel a lot better about what he has to do."

"What are you talking about?"

Clive whistled into the woods and a forlorn Weasel came down the bank dragging a tarp behind him. The cutters had been building up the warming fire with slash and had split up rounds of an old hemlock which had long ago bleached silver on the beach. They were smiling broadly.

"Jesus, you're not really going to make me do this, are you?" Weasel pleaded as he used two hands to drag the bundle down the street.

"I paid you the money you fronted, and I'm giving you a job at the bar. That pot is my product, and I know what I want to do with it."

"But my God, Clive." Weasel was desolate.

"Come on now. I know you have some personal use put away. This is a good deal for you now, Weaz. You shouldn't have put that stuff in my place. You know that. It was a mean thing to do, and you are not cut out to be a mean guy."

"No . . . I suppose not." And with that Weasel pulled back the edges of the tarp and exposed three very chunky bricks of compressed marijuana, each one about the size of a five gallon can. Miles was surprised at how much bigger they had looked under the rafters of the Love Nest.

"Go on now," Clive said, and Miles noticed just the hint of threat in his voice. As soon as he recognized the tone, he noticed that Weasel had a rather prominent black eye. Clive shook his head as if he had been bitten by a wasp. "Go on now."

"Ah . . . I just can't, Clive. You do it." Weasel slumped down on one of the slick beach rocks.

With that, Clive got up and put the three chunky bricks of pot on the beach fire. All the cutters shifted around to stand downwind.

THE AFTERNOON PASSED at a fine, lugubrious pace. The men ate their peanut butter sandwiches slowly, chewing each morsel, and those lucky enough to have salmonberry jam licked it off their fingers.

The sweet smelling smoke shimmied around the cove like a belly dancer, and no one worried about the tide or the time but took simple pleasure in their work of rolling the firewood to the beach.

"Why in the hell did Weasel put his pot in your attic?" Miles finally asked.

"Who the hell knows?" Clive smiled. "He probably thought that if anyone found it he could always blame me. But I also suspect he had some half-assed idea of selling the stuff out of the bar. Like I wouldn't notice him going in and out of the attic all the time?"

They both laughed too long. Then stopped. Then laughed again, embarrassed. Then they let the silence fall around them like tropical rain.

"Seems like kind of a waste," Miles said finally.

"I suppose so." Clive sighed.

"Why are you doing this?" his younger brother said as if the rashness of the act had just occurred to him.

"I guess I didn't want Weasel going to jail," he said, and took a deep breath as the trees sighed softly with a damp breeze blowing down the inlet. "And I guess there has to be some obedience if you want the love."

The brothers sat in silence again, the words churning over in Miles's fogged and tingling mind.

"Do you think Ed is going to kill me?" Miles finally said.

Clive watched his brother chew his peanut butter sandwich. "No," he said. "I don't think so. I don't think he's as pissed at you as he used to be."

Miles stared down at the toe of his boot as he spoke. "He was fairly pissed at me last night. Lord knows what he's going to think after this morning." He stopped for a moment. "I'm sure the trooper will tell Ed I confessed to sleeping with his Tina."

"Yeah, but I'm pretty certain Ed's mad at me now."

"You? How come?"

Clive stood up; he turned his back to the fire and held his hands behind him, palms to the heat. The other men were already down on the beach re-anchoring the boat. "He's mad because he heard that I'm in love with Nix."

Miles rocked back and forth gently, unwittingly. "Whoa . . ." was all he managed.

"After that little drama he had with you on the boardwalk, Ed asked Nix if she would move in with him, and she told him that she was moved in with me."

"Is that true? I mean . . . is that true?" Jake squinted and moved his head to be more directly in the smoke.

"Which?" asked Clive. "That she told him, or that she's moved in with me?"

Miles wore a twisted grin. "Is it true that you are in love with her?"

Clive rocked his head up and down slowly as he watched the smoke from the burning weed curl into the sky. "Yes," he said finally. "The best part is she feels the same way about me."

"Has she really moved in with you?"

"Yeah." Clive blew on his hands, taking a new pleasure in everything about the gesture, the warmth of his breath, the smell of wood chips, even the look of the dirt under his fingernails. "Imagine a love that isn't unrequited," his voice drifted off. "But of course Ed didn't take it well."

"I don't imagine." Miles started putting on his work gloves.

"You know what her name is?"

"Who, Nix?"

"Yeah, her name is Maya. Really. It's Maya Kendricks. She's from Madison, Wisconsin." Clive said the name of the city as if it were one of the moons of Jupiter.

The brothers were silent. The fire popped, and Mayan dancers far off in Madison, Wisconsin, were dancing in the streets.

"No kidding," Clive said eventually. "Her father teaches anthropology, and her mother's a freelance photographer. Maya Kendricks, can you believe it?"

The fire crackled, the sparks swirling upward in twisty courses toward the green boughs above, and Jake shook his head. "Yes," he said. "I think I can believe it." He pushed himself upright, steadied his legs, and walked toward the mountain.

By two o'clock, the sun was behind the ridgeline, and the cold began to bite down through their work clothes. The fire had burned down, and Weasel kept standing over the ashes, stirring them with a stick.

The rest of the crew wrestled logs down to the beach and rolled them with Peaveys over the rocks and onto the beds of eel grass; they set an anchor in the mud and tied a line to staples they'd driven into the logs. Someone would come back after dark when the tide was higher and pull the anchor and tow the logs across the inlet. They would tie the logs to the pilings of the community center, and then the splitting crew would take over, would buck and split and carry the stove wood up the hill to the woodshed to be stacked for the winter. Those fat columns of spruce were as satisfying as rolls of coins waiting to be unwrapped.

The day darkened until there was only a violet glimmer on the water. Miles's muscles were sore. His contact high from sitting near the fire was wearing off, leaving him feeling a little prickly, but he was content sitting in the cabin of the boat as it ran across the water to town.

When they got back to the dock, it was four o'clock and stars were starting to blink in the lavender sky. Miles and Clive helped put away the tools and headed along the boardwalk

toward the Love Nest. Across the inlet, killer whales broke
the surface, headed back out to sea. They stood and watched
a moment and tried to count the animals. A mile to the north,
an unscheduled floatplane was easing down for a landing.

THAT EVENING THEY built a big fire in the community
hall and planned to watch Jake's movie. Weasel was still sulk-
ing, but he thought that watching a movie might make up for
the loss of his capital investment in marijuana.

Jake hadn't seen the final cut of *Stealing Candy*. He'd told
himself he wasn't going to see it at all, but when Weasel
showed him the tape box with the title of the film in some
secretary's handwritten lettering, an icicle of envy ran down
his back. He had to see it, after all. Call it pride, vanity, or
morbid curiosity, but he wanted to see what they had done
with his original story.

Weasel had carried over a big video monitor from the school
and propped it on a coffee table; had hooked up the cables,
plugged in the machine, and pushed PLAY. The film buffs
settled into their chairs; Jake felt nauseated. But as the
credits started to roll and the film began, he lost himself
in the dream of a man staring at a fire. Images flared and
flickered: a blonde woman with red lips holding a revolver
close to her face as she walked down a deserted hall with
no pictures on the wall, a man in a leather coat crawling
through the heating duct of a building. Then there was the
blur and rattle of gunfire, the squealing of car tires with fat
yellow California sunlight in the background of every exterior
shot. Jake watched the movie, felt the images pushing him
back further into his head, and he had the sinking feeling that
he was watching dated pictures from his old life, a life before

Cold Storage, a life of machines and concrete. He might have been watching jerky black-and-white images from a documentary about the French Crimean War.

He got up just as the blonde woman with big lips was putting her pistol in a holster strapped to her upper thigh. He walked out and stood on the porch and watched wet snow slice down to the ground. He could hear the wood stove rumbling and the characters' voices limping through their dialogue; their faces seemed like emissaries from another country, a nation of which Jake had once been a citizen. He didn't want to answer questions about *Stealing Candy*. He wanted to go for a walk, so he curled up his collar and stepped out into the sleet.

But there was a hand on his elbow.

"You wrote that?" asked Lester.

"Well, I wrote something like that. I'd like to tell you it was a lot better in my version . . ." Jake looked at Lester. " . . . but I'd be lying."

"It got made, though." Together they walked back toward the café and the clinic. "You've got a track record."

"I got nothing really. I didn't get a cent. I didn't get a credit."

"So, what you are trying to tell me is you are not really a Hollywood big shot?" Lester's voice was grave.

"No. I am not a big shot. I'm a small-time crook. Actually," he added to save a bit of face, "I'm a medium-size crook."

"That was never really a secret." Lester spoke more seriously to his friend than he ever had before.

"I guess I knew that too," Jake said. "I was just hoping we didn't have to deal with it."

"Well, from what you're telling me, there is nothing to

deal with. If we're talking about your reputation, that is."
Lester smiled. "It's no big deal. I don't care about any of
that. I never did. We got a movie. We play it in our minds.
It will be here." Lester tapped on his forehead with his
index finger. "And if we finish it, we can watch it anytime
we want."

"Great," Jake said, but he sounded like he was stepping
into a dentist's office.

The sleet was gradually turning to snow, the grey slashes
of ice floating, curling into balls, and rolling down the inlet
on the westerly wind. Jake started to shiver.

"You are going to have to go back and talk to those folks."
Lester nodded over his shoulder.

"I don't want to." Jake jammed his good hand into his
pocket and hunched his shoulders; he'd stretched a wool sock
over the end of his sleeve to keep his other hand warm. "Let's
talk about our movie. We need an ending."

"He can't die."

"Why not?"

"I'm sick of movies where the Indian dies. That's just no
fucking story at all." Lester was resolved.

"What?" Jake asked. "Indians are immortal? Would it be
better if he were white and then he could die?"

"Yes."

"I can't fucking believe this."

"Listen, I just don't want him to die. I don't want him to be
some kind of mystic or some kind of wild spiritual guru. He's
just as fucked up as anybody else alive in this century. Maybe
a little more."

"Now wait a minute." Jake stopped. "You don't want him
to be some kind of mystic, but you want him and everybody

else to turn into animals in the last scene of the movie. What in the fuck is that about anyway?"

"It would be cool," said Lester.

"Cool," Jake grunted. A young heron flapped through the curtain of snow and landed on the hand railing of the ramp to the dock; it sat and stared at the men walking along the slick boardwalk, rubbed its beak against the metal rail and looked up again as they drew nearer; stood perfectly still for several heartbeats, then unspooled its body back up into the air.

"So what do you want for an ending?"

"I think we've got him set up to become a martyr. He has done some terrible things in the movie, things that were understandable given the context, things that were heroic from a certain point of view, but hell, he's spent, he's alone, and besides we've got no sequel. Why not just kill him off?"

"Nope." Lester wasn't changing his mind.

Rinds of ice began to build along the toes of Jake's shoes. "So you are going to stick with your animal ending? Everybody simply transforms into wild creatures at the end of the movie?" Jake said, as if pleading.

"Unless you think of a better ending."

They walked in silence for a little ways until they reached the café. Lester decided to go in and have a cup of soup, said he'd meet Jake back at the community center later after the movie was over, and the question-and-answer session began. Jake grimaced.

"I'm going to get a warmer jacket and maybe a hat," he said, and pointed toward Lester's house. "I'll be back over there in a few minutes."

As Jake stepped inside and turned to switch on the light, someone grabbed his bad arm, spun him around, and crushed his face against the wall. His shoulder flared with pain so intense it numbed his face. He saw blue sparkles, as vivid as if someone had smashed him on the skull. Slowly the pain subsided, and he felt the barrel of a gun jutting into the base of his skull.

"Weren't expecting me?" asked a voice behind him. "That's perfect."

CHAPTER EIGHTEEN

OSCAR PRESSED ALL of his weight into the barrel of the gun. His good leg was planted firmly on the floor. His crippled leg hung between them.

"Hi, Jake," he spat. "You don't look so good. I'm kind of disappointed." And surprisingly, Oscar did feel disappointed. He had been thinking—almost obsessing—about the sweetness of this moment ever since Ann Peel had put the idea into his mind, after she had told him how they had both been hung out to dry by their ungrateful employer who had deserted them. But now here he was in Alaska, the moment had come and Jake looked a little shriveled, an old man with a busted-up arm. Not the object of Oscar's revenge fantasies.

"I got chewed up by that ugly dog you gave to Clive," said Jake as casually as he could, considering his nose was mashed against the wall.

"I see Clive's still around," Oscar grunted. "He looks good. Looks like he's been spending a lot of money. Why didn't you shoot *his* knee off? Or was that something you reserved just for me?" Oscar was painfully aware of sounding whinier than he should have for his big moment.

"Listen," Jake huffed, "if it would make you any happier, I'd be glad to go blow his knee off. Just give me the gun and

I'll go take care of it right now." He waved his good hand behind his back.

The old warehouseman tried to get back on script. "You have any hobbies where you use your head, Jake? I mean, it wouldn't inconvenience you too much if I blew out the back of your skull, would it?" Oscar leaned, and Jake could feel his bone twisting under the strain; his vision was beginning to go dim.

"Actually, I'm working on a writing project right now and maybe for a couple more months. I don't have much money left, unless of course we sign a development deal. But I'm sure we can work something out."

"Yeah." Oscar suddenly let go, stepped back. "Like how about giving me back my leg?"

Jake rubbed his shoulder. "That's better," he said, and smiled. "Listen, I know it's a bad deal about your leg. We can work something out."

He was still smiling as Oscar stepped backward, leveled the pistol at Jake's right knee, and fired one round, shattered his kneecap and the underlying musculature. Then Jake was rolling on the floor, holding his knee, and Oscar was pulling back the hammer for another shot.

"Bullshit." Jake started to cry. "Not the other one. I didn't take both."

Oscar watched the blood flowing down Jake's leg. He watched him roll back and forth in pain, watched him painting the floor red with his own blood, and he uncocked the revolver. The truth was he was getting sick to his stomach remembering his own pain, remembering the long months of boredom and surgery.

"Maybe you're right," he said, tucked the gun back into

the top of his pants, stepped over him, and strolled out the door.

MILES HAD NOT been at the screening of Jake's movie; he'd been wrapping a bandage around Mary Baker's ankle when the boom of the handgun rolled down the boardwalk. Mary hadn't heard the shot; she'd been talking about her sprain. So Miles finished up, lent her a pair of crutches, patted her on the back, and told her to come back in three days; he'd take another look at her ankle then.

Gunshots in the middle of the day weren't that unusual. There were celebratory shots; there were accidental misfires. What troubled Miles was that those shots were usually accompanied by other sounds: the laughing and whooping of celebrations, the loud apologies and urgent walks to the clinic after accidents. This shot was followed by silence.

He put on his coat and went to take a look. A heavyset man with hunched shoulders was limping along the boardwalk. Had he been shot? Was he looking for the clinic? Miles called after him but the stranger didn't respond, and there was no one else to be seen. So he went home, was putting his hand on the knob of his own door, when he heard a streak of curses coming from Lester's house and he ran toward it.

Jake was on the floor. Miles stopped the bleeding and treated him for shock; told him to lie still and ran back to the clinic to grab his medical kit. He didn't ask any questions. He tried to call the state troopers; the phones were dead. He tried the marine radio, but there was no response.

Miles might be able to connect with boats fishing at the front of the inlet, but the way the weather was now, most of the fleet would be tucked back inside and out of radio range.

He'd try again later. First he'd take care of Jake and then maybe look for the gimpy man who'd been running down the boardwalk.

Lester was home when Miles returned with his medical kit. He had Jake's leg elevated and had put a blanket over him. Lester's .30-.30 was leaning against his carving stool.

"You guys have some artistic differences?" Miles bent quickly, lifted the blanket, and started immobilizing Jake's knee and trimming away his pants.

"I wouldn't have shot him in the knee."

"Fuck, this hurts!" Jake kept saying it over and over. "This really, really hurts!"

"Of course it does, buddy," Lester said with more tenderness than Miles had heard in his voice before.

Weasel poked his head through the door to say, "Hey, Jake, it's done. Everybody wants to ask you . . . Whoa, shit!" He came into the house. "What happened to you?" he said in amazement.

"Go get Clive!" Jake's voice was tight. "Tell him Oscar is here, and he wants his dog back."

"He shot you because of that dog?"

"Listen," Miles interrupted, "could you just find Clive and ask him to come down here?"

Weasel kept standing there, blinking as if trying to focus. "I knew we shouldn't have burned all that pot," he said with conviction.

"Jesus Christ," said Lester, "can you go get Clive?"

"Yeah, sure," Weasel mumbled, then added, "Does this mean you won't be talking to the movie group?"

"Go!" All three men shouted at the same time.

The rest of the evening was a blur of crises and crazy

rumors. Meanwhile, snow was falling heavily, and there was no hope of getting a plane in. Miles talked to Billy. Would he take his boat out to the head of the inlet and radio the Coast Guard air base in Sitka? Tell them that they had an emergency patient who needed a transfer to the hospital? Tell the dispatcher that the patient was stable and could wait until better weather, that there was no need to risk their life for a patient in Jake's condition? Billy understood. He went to warm the engine of his boat.

Kids peeked in the clinic windows; the young Lutheran minister came to offer his services, and Jake told him he'd call if he needed the last rites. And down at the bar, at a table in the back, Lester saw Clive talking with a man no one recognized. The stranger was angry, rapping his beer glass down on the table and reaching out to jab Clive in the chest with a finger. Lester heard the words "money" and "bust," or maybe "Goddamn money" and "trust." He couldn't be sure but by the time the vigilante gang was rousted from their temporary headquarters in the café, both Clive and the strange man were no longer in the bar; sadly for the vigilantes, the bar was locked up tight.

The movie club members still wanted to ask Jake questions about *Stealing Candy*, but Miles refused admittance to the clinic. He said Jake was resting, couldn't be disturbed, but by four o'clock that afternoon people started sliding get well cards under the door; most of them had taken the opportunity to slip in questions along with the well wishes. *We hope you get well soon. P.S. Have you ever met Jack Nicholson? Just wondering.*

Jake just nodded, turned to Miles and asked for more painkillers.

Billy returned with news that the Coast Guard would send

a helicopter as soon as the weather cleared, and Bonnie came by in the evening with a basket of food: warm venison pie, coleslaw, baked potatoes. Slowly, the tracks of the day were smoothed away by the white curtain outside the clinic windows; all the wild rumors and frantic activities were erased by the snow. The boats in the harbor turned into frosted vanilla cakes, and everyone's tracks along the boardwalk were vanishing as if the snow could wipe out the past.

Lester came to offer food and stayed to share the meal Bonnie had brought. They sat around listening for Jake and watching the miraculous snow until Lester finally got up and went home, telling them not to wake him unless there was another shooting and the victim was somebody he really liked.

It was after midnight when Bonnie spread out camping pads on the floor of Miles's office. She unfolded some quilts and unzipped an old felt sleeping bag and spread it out, making a bed wide enough for two people; she took off her shoes and lay down in her clothes.

"I just want to be here with you," she said, and patted the pillow next to her head.

Miles took off his shoes, too. He lay down beside her and she draped her arm across his chest and he smelled the soap on her skin; he cupped her hand in his. He lay there, looked up at the bottom of his desk, and watched the shadows of snowflakes ripple down the walls; everything seemed strange to him from this angle.

He looked at her, and he wanted to love her more than he had ever wanted anything. He looked out the window and saw snow sloughing off the roof. He wanted to love her but wasn't sure exactly how to begin.

He fell asleep, and he dreamed of being out in the inlet. He was in his boat, and he was fishing. Bonnie was swimming behind his boat, and he was panicked that she might accidentally get snagged on his line. He took a hammer and beat on the side of his metal skiff, he was trying to scare her off, but of course he didn't want her to go. He kept hammering and waving, and Bonnie kept swimming closer, each stroke of her legs stronger than the last, her swimming easily able to outpace his boat.

The noise grew louder and louder until it was a banging, and Bonnie was shaking his shoulder and telling him that someone was at the door.

Billy stood outside. He was wearing a T-shirt and a pair of sweatpants; Miles could see his feet sunk down into the fresh snow. A strange, warm light played on the side of his face.

"The bar is on fire, Miles. I can't find Clive, Nix, or Bonnie." It was four o'clock in the morning.

"Bonnie?" Miles was confused. "Bonnie is here." She stood at his shoulder, and Billy reached out to hug her.

"Good. Good. Good," he said.

Orange light lashed up and down the snowy houses on the boardwalk as Miles pulled on his boots. People were yelling, and a low rumble traveled through the air.

Awake now, Miles barked, "Have you checked Clive's house?"

"Sure. He's not there." Billy's face contorted. "Miles . . ."

"What?"

"The doors to the bar are chained shut from the outside."

CHAPTER NINETEEN

A CREW FROM the cold storage tried to roll hoses from a
hydrant off the main water line, but all the junctions were
frozen. Moisture in the line had frozen in the unheated shed,
and now they sat like coiled springs. The hydrant itself was
buried in the snow, and men were running around in nothing
but their long underwear and rain gear, poking shovels into
the snow and trying to locate the main line.

Weasel walked back and forth, wringing his hands and
calling out for Clive. Miles ran along the boardwalk toward
the bar where great orange flames burst through the windows
and waved frantic arms in the air.

The heat blossomed out onto the night. Every surface
within fifty feet was either dry or shedding snow. The faces
of bystanders glowed orange and red as the fire reached
toward them; men in their bathrobes stepped back as if
being scolded; some called suggestions to each other on how
to get water to the site; others hugged their children close and
told them to stay put; others simply stared, dulled with worry.

Anthony Cera, his finger still in a splint from his wrestling
injury that cost him his spot on the championship team, had
a coat thrown over his shoulders and was chopping against
the front door of the bar with an axe. Flames howled through
the broken windows. The two front doors were held shut

by a length of shiny chain looped through the handles, and Anthony was chopping against the hinges. Between strokes Miles saw that someone was pushing hard from inside. Little Brother was standing next to Anthony and barking. He'd bark, charge to nip at the flames, retreat and bark some more.

"We can't find Clive or Nix." Lester came up beside Miles. "Someone said they were in the bar, cleaning up."

"What about the other guy? Oscar?"

"I have no idea. Someone said they saw a stranger stealing gas from the gas dock. He was filling up two five-gallon cans. But nobody has seen him since the fire started."

Miles put a scarf around his face and reached for Lester's coat, never taking his eyes off the door. The pounding from the inside had stopped.

"What about the back door on the mountain side?" he asked.

"It's chained shut. It might be easier to break down, but the fire is way worse back there. I'm betting he soaked his way out of the building, set the fire from the back door, and went up the hill in the snow. It won't be hard to find him."

"That can wait," Miles said. "We've got to get in there."

Anthony took a final stroke with the axe, and the fire pushed one side of the door away from the front wall; a smoky hole appeared and Little Brother squatted down; he jumped high into the air, straight through the opening. Lester and Anthony shielded their faces with the forearms and pulled the corner of the door to one side.

The bar was a pyre of burning timbers; a gas tank had exploded inside and broken glass spattered the snow up on the hill. "I don't know, Miles . . ." Lester said, but Miles had disappeared into the burning building.

Fire pumped through cracks in the walls; it seemed that

the flames were hysterical to exit the building. Anthony's hair, his coat, and his shirt caught fire. Lester pulled him back to the boardwalk, and his friends led him away. Then Lester ran back and rammed his shoulder against the burning door. From a distance, Billy could see that Lester's hair was burning and flames danced on his jacket. Billy took a step forward, and Lester turned away from the fire.

Lester had years to consider what had made him stop; what made him stand there and call out for help from the edge of the blaze. All he knew at the moment, standing in the fire, was that if he didn't pull his neighbors out he would bear the shame of it for the rest of his life.

And the fire concurred, for before Lester had any chance to reconsider, the floor gave and Mouse Miller's Love Nest collapsed in a shower of sparks, flames, and blackened mats of char-encrusted timbers.

EVERYONE IN TOWN was facing the fire as the building fell. They all put their hands up in front of them as if trying to hold the image upright in the air; if they had been able to turn around and look toward the inlet, they would have seen the light from the fire pushing out into the darkness, lighting the paddling gulls as if they were Christmas toys. The wind was calm, and the snow, which no one noticed now, was falling silently without a ripple into the black water. And if they had strained their eyes they might have seen Oscar getting into Miles's red skiff, starting the engine and moving slowly out into the darkness.

LESTER WALKED BACK toward the shadowy boardwalk where Bonnie put her arms around his neck. "Thank you for coming back," she said.

"I don't know where Miles went." Lester's tears trickled from ravaged eyes.

"He's in there," Bonnie said softly, holding Lester's head in her hands.

Crews got water flowing that night around the same time Nix showed up on the scene. She'd fallen asleep during Jake's movie and stayed asleep next to the stove in the community center for the entire evening. There were books on the shelves, and when she had woken up around eleven thirty, she lit a candle and started reading *Pilgrim's Progress* until she fell asleep again. What woke her the second time was the sound of the bar collapsing.

The tide was high at the moment it had collapsed, so there had been several feet of water underneath the front, but the back of the building nearest the hillside burned fiercely and a couple of volunteer fire fighters sprayed two feeble streams of water onto the flames. Meanwhile, tired men and women in sooty rain gear climbed under the boardwalk and waded into the frigid water, tried to pull pieces of the blackened wreckage away in their efforts to find the bodies. No one saw any sign of Clive, Miles, or the dog, but they called out their names. As the fire slowly quieted, their voices sounded thin, tired, like the bleating of goats.

Billy was down under the boardwalk when he saw the stainless steel ice machine that had been the cooler for beer bottles. The six-foot-long machine lay upside down, beneath several beams, on a piece of flooring that had broken away. It was rocking back and forth.

He heaved a shoulder against one of the timbers. The heat seared his shirt to flames, and he winced but pushed the beam off. Lester came, and they threw the next timber out into the inlet, and their hands were burned. But they rolled the chest over, and Miles fell out in a slurry of slushy ice cubes, beer, and broken glass.

He choked and Billy and Lester rolled him over, but he was clinging to something raw and red: a man whose clothes had burned away. Miles was holding his brother in his arms.

"Watch it!" someone yelled, and a section of wall plummeted onto the rocks below them; soot and sparks flew up.

"We have to go." Lester and Billy pulled the two brothers out from under the pier. Eight others were running down the beach with two stretchers from the clinic.

The next morning the snow stopped and the weather cleared; smoke drifted from the site of the bar and curled around town like a wandering cat. Trooper Brown and a crime scene team landed at first light, and the pilot flew Miles and Clive to the hospital in Sitka. Jake, whose injury had been forgotten in all the excitement, had accessed Miles's pharmacopoeia; he chomped down on painkillers in the privacy of Lester's home and said nothing. While out-of-town investigators scoured Cold Storage, the white gangster and the Indian artist quietly tended their wounds and stayed away from the police.

Nix had seen Clive before he'd been flown out unconscious. He hadn't looked human; his skin was too tight and blood frothed around the edges of his peeling flesh; burned meat, still breathing. She hadn't watched as they'd carried him away on a stretcher; she stayed in Clive's house and waited for news.

She couldn't read, couldn't concentrate, and there was no one to call so she found one of Annabelle's Peggy Lee records and played it over and over on the old portable record player. One by one, the other members of the band came by and someone made scrambled eggs and someone else made toast, but they left it on the stove too long and Nix started to cry.

Trooper Brown started looking for the stranger who'd purchased gas; he went door to door, asking questions, but he soon lost interest. He'd come to the conclusion that this had been a well-planned drug hit, and the perpetrator was already long gone and frankly, he wasn't concerned about drug people killing each other. "Saves on court costs," he'd told one of the lab technicians.

The real truth was that he didn't have the patience to wade through statements from the people of Cold Storage. He couldn't bear to memorialize the wild, almost mythic accounting of events: love triangles and drugs, mysterious boats waiting offshore to offload teams of assassins, Satanic cults, a dangerous dog who was probably responsible for the whole thing.

Very late in the day, someone discovered Miles's skiff was missing. Billy informed the trooper and a day later Brown requested that a helicopter fly the inlet, but no trace of the skiff was ever found. By the evening of the second day, troopers had secured the scene and an arson team had arrived to finish the investigation.

Smoke washed up and down the boardwalk, and all the houses were covered in a film of soot. People flung open their doors, fed the policemen at any time of the day or night, and drank whiskey from the bottle. They ate more sweets than usual, and their clothes carried the smell of fried food. They let their children stay up as late as they wanted, which wasn't that far from their usual routine, but now they felt good about it. Happy to be alive for one more day. No one had heard if Miles and Clive were going to live.

Bonnie tried to help. She talked to people at the clinic; sorted out the ones who genuinely needed attention from those who didn't; sent the former to the temporary EMT flown in from Sitka and listened to the others talk off their nervous energy; gave them simple chores to do: sweeping the already clean floors, sorting through the waiting room magazines, or checking the paper in the fax machine.

Lester came dressed in his sooty clothes, his hands wrapped in soft strips torn from someone's thrift store T-shirts, and Bonnie gently said, "You should see somebody about your burns."

"I got it covered. Got some stuff from my auntie. It's just what I need."

"All right," she said, and smiled up at her friend.

"Anybody heard from the hospital?" he asked.

"No . . ." Her voice barely cleared her lungs.

"Let's go to his house. I bet Nix is there. Maybe she's heard something." Lester's voice was beginning to crack, and that concerned her.

"Yes," she said, and stood up slowly. She let her hand rest on his arm for a moment, and he patted it. The adrenaline of the fire fading away into the soot and smoke, they walked out of the clinic. They walked down the boardwalk, past the café and the library, past the trail to the community hall, past the house with the parakeets in the window; they walked past the house with the tea kettle collection in the front yard and past the burning hole that had once been Mouse Miller's Love Nest.

The arson team was in a little shelter they'd made,

hooking up flood lamps and kerosene heaters so they could work through the night, photographing and sorting through evidence, trying to piece together the char pattern and the type of accelerant that had been used to feed the fire.

Lester and Bonnie looked over the edge. A charred storage cabinet sat at the tide line; melted records oozed out of blackened jackets; pool balls lodged like Easter eggs in the rocks; the broken neck of a bass guitar lay tangled in its own strings. Ravens were hopping in and out of the ashes, poking their beaks into soot near the blackened freezer. And even though Lester wasn't a drinker and was an outsider in his own land, his chest sank between his shoulders for he missed the bar already.

Ever since he'd been a kid, Lester had hated getting sick to his stomach. He'd choke back the urge to vomit with even the most violent stomach flu; he would gulp air and stand up straight and let the cramps rumble through his body. Now he looked at Bonnie and said nothing.

She rubbed her hands between his shoulder blades. "They will be okay. You did the right thing," she said, and reached over, put her arms around him.

Someone had left a frozen hose, still connected to a faucet, lying in snow that was melting away in the heat radiating from the scorched ground. The hose, thawing, started hissing and leaping like a fish as bits of ice chunked and rumbled down its length; broken cylinders of ice jumped out; clear water washed away; and the old canvas lay flat again.

Lester looked down at the wreckage of the bar. "I hope so," he said, and they made their way to Clive's house.

The members of the band were all there. Rick sat on a chair by the oil stove and played an acoustic guitar; the others drank beer and ate soda crackers they'd found in the cupboards. Nix lay on the couch, and Billy rubbed her feet; her hands were folded under her face like a sleeping child, her eyes red and her pale skin blotchy from crying; she said nothing and noticed no one in the somber crowd of friends.

Bonnie went over and kissed her face; Nix started to cry. Earl gave Lester a beer and clumsily hugged him; Lester tried to give the beer to someone else and wished Rick would stop strumming his guitar. The music sounded thin, like hearing a car horn from the top of a skyscraper.

They perched in their seats as if half expecting to be called away until Earl heard thumping on the porch and went outside. Lester heard his voice: "Oh my Lord." He was punctuating each word with an extra beat: "Oh . . . My . . . Lord."

Little Brother walked into the kitchen, past Lester and into the living room, dragging his right hind leg behind him. His brindled hide was smeared black, and his paws left smudges of blood on the floor. He smelled like a fire pit full of burning dog carcasses and looked even uglier than he had before.

But Nix sat up, let him up on the couch and onto her lap, rubbed her hands over his head and body, kissed his ears and jowls. Little Brother looked into space with his eyes half shut, savoring every caress.

"Well," said Nix, "there you are."

CLIVE WAS BEING prepared for a charter jet flight to a burn clinic in Seattle and down on the first floor, under the eaves of the emergency entrance, an ambulance sat idling.

Miles walked down the long hall toward the ICU pushing an IV pole. He should have been in a wheelchair; his chest ached from damaged lungs; his hands and legs were scoured by second degree burns. He turned the corner and stood in a doorway, watched his brother's chest rise and fall. Even though Clive was unconscious, he had a smile on his face and his breathing was steady and strong. Miles wasn't certain, but he could feel the promise of its continued rhythm like the coming of spring and summer.

AND THIS IS HOW THINGS WORKED OUT IN THE MONTHS AND YEARS AFTER

FOLLOWING THE FIRE, the smoke hung in the air for weeks on end. The future lay behind the membrane of each moment and remained hidden as Miles went on living and sitting by his brother's bed.

A few months after his return to Cold Storage, Miles put a note on his desk for the woman who was temporarily replacing him at the clinic. "Gone salmon fishing. Will monitor radio for emergencies." Perfectly acceptable to anyone who'd spent a winter in Cold Storage, but it kind of irritated the young woman since she was earnest about her duties and wanted to do a good job.

Miles felt old now. He had served his country, he'd served his community, and he was proud. Now he wanted to serve his family. And he wanted to catch a king salmon.

Miles bought a brand-new skiff and motor from a shop in Juneau. The first thing he'd done was read the engine's repair manual. He took the powerhead apart, down to its largest constituent pieces, for the newer engines seemed to be made of several bricks of electronic gear bolted onto a sleek-looking aluminum block; he used every ounce of his intellect to understand this engine; he invested in the best fuel filters and fuel additives; he gapped the plugs himself and checked the automatic oil injector by inspecting the plugs for dark spots. He was determined not to be bullied.

He gathered all his new gear together and walked resolutely to the boat, stowed the gear, went through a quick checklist on the engine, and pushed the electric starter button. The engine sputtered and hummed without entreaty.

He steered his new skiff standing up, holding onto a steering wheel, not like his old skiff where he'd had to sit, reaching back for the tiller arm. A VHF communication radio was mounted on the console, as well as a GPS unit, a depth sounder, and a compass for navigation; he had a separate, small engine that he'd lower once he arrived on the fishing grounds. Miles was better outfitted than he'd ever been on this, his first fishing trip of the new year.

The engine easily pushed the new skiff over the light chop in front of the town, and as he drove down the inlet, he noticed that for the first time in a long time he didn't smell smoke in the air. He pushed the throttle forward; his skiff lifted up onto a gliding plane, and the grey-green water turned silver in his wake and this silver matched the curve and color of the mountains mirrored on the surface of the inlet. Something rose up in Miles's chest. It was as if the speed of the boat pressed against the boundary that confined each moment, and he pushed the throttle forward as if there was a chance he could break through that membrane and into the happiness that must surely lie ahead.

Miles's injuries had healed well enough. He still wore protective gloves and his doctors didn't want him exposing his burns to fish bites, or to gasoline or dirt, or much of anything, but Miles wanted to catch a fish today. All he wanted at this point was to be open to good luck. He would prepare himself for any eventuality and try to be ready for whatever good fortune came. Clive would be weeks more in the burn unit; his good luck would come in smaller and slower increments. With not one feeling of disloyalty to his brother, Miles was ready for some good luck that very day.

He got to the grounds at the opening of the inlet and set his gear. He put on the brightest herring he could find from the one packet of bait he'd brought along. He threaded the line through the belly and set the hooks perfectly. He attached the leader behind a brand new flasher, snapped the line into the downrigger, and sent the line down to where his depth sounder was showing a ball of feed. His new engine ran perfectly, and he watched his GPS to judge his trolling speed.

The sun sparkled on the water, the distant horizon gleamed robin's egg blue, thin clouds blew like banners to the north, and an easy swell lifted the boat in a rhythm that loped along the seas.

Miles settled into his chair and steered the engine with a foot on the wheel, watched the end of his line.

"Let us cast off the works of darkness," said Miles and laughed at himself for remembering the scripture.

On the end of his downrigger not four feet from where he sat, a raven landed, cocked its head back and forth, watched him carefully.

"And put on the armor of light," he added, nodding to the bird.

"Miles!" said the raven.

Miles's feet turned cold, his hands turned cold, and he felt like puking. Had it said his name?

"Miles!" said the bird again, poking its head back and forth as if to indicate he should come closer.

He stood up, frightened, startled, and leaned closer to the glittering bird.

"Yes?"

The raven fluttered, jumped into the bait cooler, and grabbed the entire packet of herring. It lumbered into the air and flew down the inlet carrying the small cellophane packet, little silver fish spilling out into the sea.

Miles watched the fat black bird fly to the southern shore, drop the packet on the beach and land on top of it with a kind of open-winged victory jig; he watched it eat the remaining silvery fish; listened to it laugh; began to be angry but then started to laugh, too, at the absurdity of it all. And he cried.

He cried as if something in his chest had broken. His nose ran, his eyes were blinded, and he cried as if he'd become unfrozen, great heaving sobs so powerful he felt like everything inside was going to spill out of him into the water and into the air.

When he slowly hiccuped to a stop, he was light-headed. He looked back at the distant beach; the raven was gone. He looked toward Cold Storage; a great cloud of birds circled the town. He thought he saw large, brown, four-legged forms walking on the beach, and he thought he saw two deer walking into the fringe of the beach. And he thought that it might be possible that everyone in the village, maybe everyone in the world, had turned into animals.

He reached for his radio to call someone, to hear the comfort of a human voice, but just then the tip of his fishing rod jerked down and line screamed off the reel. Twenty yards behind the skiff, a massive salmon rose from the water, shaking itself against the hooks set deeply into its jaw.

@

OF COURSE THE world changed, and the past both was and remains a hallucination that intrudes into our day-to-day life. Buildings fall and rise again, elections are won and lost, armies parade into the field and then find their way home. In Cold Storage, Alaska, stories came into currency concerning the whereabouts—or even the existence of—the person who had shot Jake in the leg and burned down the bar. The safe money said it was the man with the limp who had flown into town that same afternoon. There were some who speculated that Ed had torched the bar in revenge for Clive sleeping with Nix, although this rumor never gained much purchase; for one thing Ed both denied it and had an alibi, and for another he didn't fit the gossip machine's requirements for an arsonist. Ed was too pale a personality to be a firebug.

Of course the man with the limp had disappeared, and most people speculated that he had taken the skiff on the outside coast in a snow squall, dumped it over, and died in the frigid waters. This story had a ring of poetic justice to it, but early that next spring a doctor from Juneau opened up his fishing cabin on the coast and found that it had been broken into sometime during the winter; all of his emergency food was gone, and Miles's old cranky skiff was hauled up into the trees near the beach fringe where it appeared someone had put a bullet through the engine's power head. The doctor also reported that the kayak he kept stored at the cabin was missing.

Jake finally went in to the hospital in Sitka for surgery on his leg. Each day when he woke up he thought it would be the day a police officer with a warrant from Seattle would come take him into custody, but it didn't happen. Miss Peel called from her rented house in Arizona. She was sounding a little sheepish and did not tell Jake how she got the hospital's number or knew how he was there but *asked* if Jake had gotten the news about the IPO that the kid in Seattle and a couple of his friends had gone ahead and held. He had never taken Jake off the corporate papers and now, instead of owning stock in a company that never produced anything, he owned fifteen million dollars' worth of stock in a company that never really produced anything. Miss Peel giggled when she told him this, and all Jake could do was shake his head and wonder at the strangeness of it all.

Miss Peel had stood up to the DA in Seattle, had gotten out of the grand jury proceedings without perjuring herself or snitching off Jake. As a result, the grand jury "no true billed" the proposed indictment against him, so that there would be no federal charges coming. When she asked so sweetly for the numbers to take care of the IPO account transfer money, of course Jake gave it to her, and when Jake asked if she had heard anything from Oscar, she answered in a very sing-song voice that she had and that he was safe and sound after his trip to Cold Storage this winter and that in fact he was renting a house right there in Sitka. This was the moment that Jake Shoemaker realized that he was not an independent business man but just the beard for Miss Peel's own business dealings. He had been working for her unwittingly all along.

He put down the phone, shivered once, then smiled broadly.

It was in this atmosphere of the miraculous that Lester wheeled Jake out of the hospital and into a cab for the airport where they picked up their tickets and flew to Seattle to meet the glorious Miss Peel and start discussing how to liquidate all of Jake's business holdings.

After he got his money together, Jake gave Miss Peel five hundred thousand dollars in cash and three quarters of all of his investment assets, and he moved to California. He and Lester spent a month at the ranch in the Santa Barbara hills where they finished the final draft of their script, and Jake made appointments to pitch the project to several studios. Jake never spoke to the police about Oscar, figuring that at best they were even and at worst, it would piss Oscar off; even so, Jake kept a nine millimeter under the seat of his car and in the drawer beside his bed in case Oscar ever wanted to come by for another chat.

Jake's injuries from his season in Alaska continued to nag him for the rest of his life. He would never throw a ball overhand and would always have a hard time swimming the crawl, which hurt his vanity more than having to carry a silver-tipped cane wherever he went. The cane became his trademark, made a nice stylish statement, but not being able to swim in the ranch's marble-lined infinity pool out on the bluff made him feel old.

Lester enjoyed Hollywood but came home by early summer saying that, while he liked the restaurants, he couldn't take the traffic. He came back just in time to help with the rebuilding that had started on the site of the old bar.

Clive spent months living near the burn center in Seattle. The troopers made noise about charging him with something, but Miss Peel's lawyers helped dissuade them. And sitting on a bench outside of a courtroom in Seattle one uncomfortable day, Clive came up with a new plan for the Love Nest.

Nix's parents flew to Cold Storage, presumably to bring their daughter home, but ended up staying the spring and summer. Once they arrived, Nix began going by her given

name, and after that she was called Maya by newcomers to the
village. Miles went back and forth with the names, but Bonnie
always called her Nix.

Nix's parents gave her the money they'd saved against the
day she'd want a formal wedding. That money combined with
the fire insurance Clive had purchased became the working capital for the new building. Nix, Bonnie, and Miles all
became partners in Clive's property. They built a new business: a bakery, a coffee shop, a bar with a dance floor, and up
on the hillside a fifty-seat theater that had a small stage, a
twenty by thirty screen, and a real sloping floor with theater
seats. The new place was called "Little Brother's," and the
ugly dog presided over every aspect of its financing and construction. The older citizens worried and fussed that it spelled
the end of the town and the final acceptance of decadent
urban life, but this was to be expected. Once the joint opened,
people defended it or complained, but gradually it worked its
way into the story of a town that kept bumping along from
one tragedy to the next.

Clive oversaw the project like a family patriarch. His
skin was too painful for him to move quickly, too prone to
infection to get dirty. He sat with a broad brimmed hat,
drinking lemonade and gin with Weasel as others swung
hammers. On the first day of framing up the walls, he hung
a sign on the center beam. It was hand painted on rough
plywood and read:

How can I curse whom God has not cursed?
How can I denounce whom the Lord has not denounced?
For from the top of the crags I see him,
From the hills I behold him;

Behold a people dwelling alone,
And not counting itself among the nations.

The framers didn't know why it was there, but they didn't mind. They liked the parts about the mountains.

BONNIE TOOK TO the construction with a vigor people had not seen in Cold Storage since the long-dead founders cribbed together the first storefront. She loved shoveling debris and setting pilings in that blackened spot on the boardwalk; she loved the wild country that came in and out of focus from the building site. When she wore her tool belt and worked framing in a wall, she knew exactly where she was and what she was doing. She loved measuring and making a clean cut; she loved setting up the wall and feeling the future of that interior space; and she loved to look through the studs to see the wind lifting snow off the mountains. Fashioning a new building on the site of the fire felt as good as saving lives.

It took three years for the partnership to complete the project, but the inaugural party was well worth any wait, for the first event was the premiere of *Circling the Wagons*. The movie became the hot center of gossip in the film industry for years to come, particularly because of its controversial ending.

Robbie Robertson had done the music, and he was there. Sherman Alexie was listed as a producer, and he came to the party. Harvey Keitel, even though he wasn't in the cast, had been invited, and everyone expected him to come solely on the strength of Weasel's five-page invitation. On the weekend of the party, Weasel met almost every plane that came to the dock and smiled at everyone who wandered up the boardwalk, but he finally had to make do with Gary Farmer, who was the star of the film, and Clint Eastwood, who was the executive producer along with Miss Peel. Jake had an associate producer and screenwriter credit and a berth on Eastwood's yacht. Clint had sailed his own boat from over the horizon to the docks of Cold Storage, Alaska, and had impressed the locals by helping his crew tie off the docking lines while keeping a cold beer in his pocket.

Members of the international press stayed in the newly refurbished cold storage bunkhouse. Mrs. Cera served smoked black cod collars at the pre-screening reception, and that season, smoked black cod started turning up in many of the more expensive restaurants in Los Angeles. Blind Donkey played at the post-screening party, and Robbie Robertson came on stage and did a set that ended in a terrific version of "Love Is the Answer, But What Was the Question?" Weasel became so drunk that he missed the set; he complained about it for years to come.

Jake appeared wearing a Spanish designer's suit that looked like it was made from a kind of weather balloon, but he was laughing, joking, calling everyone by their first names, and generally acting more local than any of the locals.

Lester wore his regular work clothes, held his own open house for his friends and family back at the studio, and refused to take a back seat at any of the proceedings. He'd been getting out more in the last few years, had spent time in Hoonah with his aunties and nephews, had fished with them, and gathered herring eggs in Sitka to take to them in spring. He was no longer a student of other people.

At the opening of his movie, Lester strolled through the crowd like the host of the evening. He kept mixing up the seating so that his friends and family could be together, and he would not be shunted to one side. He teased Jake every chance he got but let his collaborator enjoy the Hollywood spotlight and later admitted that he'd enjoyed the evening more than he'd expected. For several seasons, his jewelry became one of the required accessories for both men and women in Hollywood, but Lester never wrote another film script.

Bonnie, Miles, and Nix served the food and, together with Clive, tended the bar. Ed and Tina watched Miles and Bonnie's little girl, who was almost the same age as their son. Ed would come to the party and then go back and stay with the kids, while Tina came and listened to the music and to the celebrities. Neither of them watched the movie. They were afraid to spoil their hopes for it, but later when they were alone together, they watched it in the new little theater; they laughed and clapped until their hands were sore.

While the party raged on, Miles continued to serve food. As he came out of the kitchen with a plate of black cod, he watched his brother Clive gingerly holding an LP between the palms of his hands, a smile dazzling out from his broken face. He'd been turned inside out by the fire and spoke very little now; but he still had the soul of a great liar, a trickster, which reassured Miles. Clive turned toward him and the brothers looked at each other for perhaps one beat longer than usual, and in that one second acknowledged all of their good luck. And then Miles turned and quietly offered a black cod collar to Mr. Alexie, who was joking with Lester and Chris Eyre, the director; he smiled at all of them and offered the fish all around.

Clive motioned to the door, and the big dog hobbled into the room and with a surprising show of strength jumped up onto the bar. Clive cleared his throat, and the guests settled down. He thanked Lester and thanked Jake, who he called the "Angel of Cold Storage, Alaska," then he thanked all the assembled luminaries. He paused and turned to Little Brother and asked him to say a few words. The crowd tittered, expecting a parlor trick. A pretty woman in a silk skirt and dull gold jewelry laughed aloud and asked for another drink. None of the locals smiled but leaned forward. As some people shuffled their feet and waited for something to break the tension, Clive just looked at the battered dog, expectant—and, as always, patient.

AUTHOR'S NOTE

Cold Storage, Alaska was the first book in the Cold Storage series. That it is the second one to be published (after *The Big Both Ways*) is an accident. *Cold Storage* was written as a tribute to one of my favorite genres: the screwball comedy. I'm drawn to comedy because it reminds me that all chaos does not resolve in tragedy, but sometimes chaos produces delightful connection. I also believe this is what both the Bible and Dharma teach as a possibility. I have long recognized that I am an oddball in the crime writing world in that I do not recognize revenge as the lifeblood of a great plot. Instead, after almost thirty years as a criminal investigator as well as a writer, I still believe that love and compassion are what move through the hearts of *all* characters.

I am deeply indebted to a wonderful reader, Sophie Rosen, from Abbotsford, British Columbia, who gave me intelligent feedback and insight into this story early on. Also to my editor, Juliet Grames, from New York, New York, who showed courage and patience by taking me back into the fold. My heartfelt appreciation and thanks go to both women.